TORT LAW

Tort Law: A Modern Perspective is an advanced yet accessible introduction to tort law for lawyers, law students, and others. Reflecting the way tort law is taught today, it explains the cases and legal doctrines commonly found in casebooks using modern ideas about public policy, economics, and philosophy. With an emphasis on policy rationales, *Tort Law* encourages readers to think critically about the justifications for legal doctrines. Although the topic of torts is specific, the conceptual approach should pay dividends to those who are interested broadly in regulatory policy and the role of law. Incorporating three decades of advancements in tort scholarship, *Tort Law* is the textbook for modern torts classrooms.

Keith N. Hylton is William Fairfield Warren Distinguished Professor and a professor of law at Boston University specializing in tort law, antitrust law, intellectual property law, and labor law. His last book, a utilitarian defense of the intellectual property laws, is *Laws of Creation: Property Rights in the World of Ideas* (2013).

Tort Law

A MODERN PERSPECTIVE

KEITH N. HYLTON

Can tort law be regarded as the basis for or th umbrella that spans most areas of the law?

CAMBRIDGE
UNIVERSITY PRESS

CAMBRIDGE
UNIVERSITY PRESS

One Liberty Plaza, New York, NY 10006, USA

Cambridge University Press is part of the University of Cambridge.

It furthers the University's mission by disseminating knowledge in the pursuit of
education, learning, and research at the highest international levels of excellence.

www.cambridge.org
Information on this title: www.cambridge.org/9781107563421

© Keith N. Hylton 2016

First published 2016

Printed in the United States of America by Sheridan Books, Inc.

A catalogue record for this publication is available from the British Library.

Library of Congress Cataloging in Publication Data
Hylton, Keith N., author.
Tort law : a modern perspective / Keith N. Hylton.
New York : Cambridge University Press, 2016.
LCCN 2016008949 | ISBN 9781107125322
LCSH: Torts–United States.
LCC KF1250 .H95 2016 | DDC 346.7303–dc23 LC record available at
    http://lccn.loc.gov/2016008949

ISBN 978-1-107-12532-2 Hardback
ISBN 978-1-107-56342-1 Paperback

Contents

Contents

1

Introduction

The purpose of this book is to provide something that in my view has so far not been provided in the literature: a reasonably comprehensive, functionalist presentation of tort law that hews closely to doctrine. As I worked on the manuscript, I envisioned the final product serving as a textbook, mainly for law students. But I have also held onto the vision that it would provide a more thorough policy-grounded justification for the common law of torts than has been provided to date.

I use the word functional here as a less formal way of saying utilitarian. It conveys my immediate goals while helping me avoid being dragged into debates about the merits of utilitarianism as a theory of law. If you do not like utilitarianism, at least you should have some interest in understanding the functions of common law doctrines, or the effects these doctrines are likely to have on rational agents, or the manner in which they influence social interaction and its consequences. Another sense in which the word functional is useful to me is that it signals an interest in advancing a positive theory of the law rather than a normative theory. Positive theory seeks to understand, explain, and justify the legal doctrines that exist, rather than to design anew some area of the law, which is the aim of normative theory. Utilitarianism can provide a framework for redesigning the law, as Bentham demonstrated. But I have made few efforts toward this end in this book. I have criticized specific decisions, and specific portions of the case law, but on the whole the aim here is to explain and make sense of tort doctrine as it is. To that end, I offer a set of consistent policy perspectives that might enable one to better predict the outcomes of tort disputes.

Another way of describing this book is to compare it to paleontology. Studying individual cases is like studying parts of the skeleton of an animal buried in the ground for millennia. One can know the details of the skeleton's parts without having a sense of how the animal moved. The approach of this book is to study the parts of tort law with a goal of understanding how those parts, as well as the whole body, move. Discerning the policies that shape tort law is crucial to determining how the law should work, and often how it actually does work.

Functional, utilitarian explanations of tort law have their roots in Holmes's third and fourth chapters of *The Common Law*.[1] I have had the pleasure of recognizing substantial pieces of this book, such as its chapter on strict liability, anticipated in brief passages of Holmes. But Holmes did not try to provide a comprehensive discussion of tort law. There are vast parts of most torts casebooks that are not discussed, or mentioned only in passing, in Holmes's book.

The other major examination of tort law in this vein is that of Prosser.[2] Prosser's hornbook is on nearly the opposite end of the spectrum from Holmes: Whereas Holmes is light on case law and heavy on fundamental doctrines and policy, Prosser is heavy on doctrinal detail and comparatively light on policy. Still, if one makes an effort, the core functional explanations of tort law that are offered here can be gleaned from Prosser. Prosser addressed practical questions and held the work of judges in too high regard to scrape arguments from their opinions to advance purportedly novel theories of the law, but the basic utilitarian premises of Holmes are visible throughout his book.

This book aims to fill the gap between Holmes and Prosser. Although it presents policy arguments directly, theory is put to the service here of making sense of tort law. I explore tort law in greater detail than Holmes, though not as much as Prosser. I have integrated policy arguments with law to a much greater degree than Prosser. For the new student, this book offers an introduction to the law and to policy reasoning at a level of depth not typically found in law textbooks. For the expert, this book offers an integration of policy and law that offers new insights on the macrostructure of tort law – its divisions between categories of intent, negligence, and strict liability – as well as doctrinal details within each category. Functionalism as an approach to tort law has been around for a long time, but criticized for giving short shrift to the fine points of doctrine and therefore dismissed by some on this ground. I aim to show that the functionalist perspective not only is capable of accounting for the fine points of doctrine, but also often offers the account that fits best with doctrinal details, resolving some superficial inconsistencies and puzzles along the way.

Modern functional and utilitarian theories in the legal academy typically come in the form of "law and economics" analysis today. Because of this, the scholarship of Judge Guido Calabresi and of Judge Richard Posner deserves a special place in the literature on torts.[3] Calabresi and Posner pioneered the use of economics to understand tort doctrine, though with very different approaches, since Calabresi's work is mostly normative while Posner's is positive. I make use of arguments drawn from economics in this book; but, again, the arguments are put to work in understanding the law, and they appear where necessary to understand the policies that shape tort doctrine.

---

[1] OLIVER WENDELL HOLMES, JR., THE COMMON LAW (Little, Brown & Co. 1881).

[2] WILLIAM L. PROSSER, HANDBOOK OF THE LAW OF TORTS (West Pub. Co. 4th ed. 1971).

[3] GUIDO CALABRESI, THE COSTS OF ACCIDENTS: A LEGAL AND ECONOMIC ANALYSIS (Yale Univ. Press 1970); RICHARD A. POSNER, ECONOMIC ANALYSIS OF LAW (Aspen Pub. 8th ed. 2010).

I have also drawn heavily from established torts textbooks. The main reason is that the textbooks tend to present cases that have been used to teach the law for many years and are likely to be recognized by most students who have studied torts. These familiar cases – chestnuts such as *Palsgraf v. Long Island Railroad Co.*[4] – provide excellent templates for exploring policy in greater depth than the casebooks and hornbooks typically permit. I therefore mined the Prosser hornbook repeatedly for cases and for explanations of doctrine.[5] The Epstein and Sharkey casebook[6] – formerly Epstein,[7] and before then Gregory and Kalven[8] – has been a major source of cases and ideas for the organization of topics. The organization of topics in this book follows that of Prosser, with deviations based primarily on my desire to impose functional coherence on the order of topics, because I view function and utility as the ultimate organizing principles for this material. For example, I present defamation law immediately after the chapter on strict liability because of the doctrinal and functional similarities between the two areas. The Wigmore casebook,[9] published in 1912, a national treasure in my view, has been another major source of cases and topics for this book.

The preface of Wigmore's casebook includes a list of "Wishes" that he hoped his book would further, one of which is that tort law would be made more scientific over time.[10] I am pleased to report that the scientization of tort law has progressed dramatically since Wigmore's day. Tort law has become a topic of study not only for the philosophically oriented, but also for economists, psychologists, and statisticians. Economic analysis of law has introduced mathematical models that permit a more rigorous study of the incentives created by tort law than had been available before.[11] The move toward science has required a shift from theorizing about a priori duties to a focus on facts and consequences, to better understand the policies reflected in the law. This shift has been controversial at times within the legal academy, but it has made such deep inroads into the policy arguments of courts that it is simply too late in the day to ignore its importance in understanding tort law. Although this book emphasizes legal doctrine, it also provides the student with an introduction to the increasingly interdisciplinary study of law.

---

[4] 162 N.E. 99 (N.Y. 1928).

[5] PROSSER, *supra* note 2. Another hornbook I consulted is DAN B. DOBBS, PAUL T. HAYDEN, & ELLEN M. BUBLICK, THE LAW OF TORTS (2d ed. 2011).

[6] RICHARD A. EPSTEIN & CATHERINE M. SHARKEY, CASES AND MATERIALS ON TORTS (Aspen Pub. 10th ed. 2012).

[7] RICHARD A. EPSTEIN, CASES AND MATERIALS ON TORTS (Aspen Pub. 9th ed. 2008).

[8] CHARLES O. GREGORY & HARRY KALVEN, JR., CASES AND MATERIALS ON TORTS (Little, Brown & Co. 1959).

[9] JOHN HENRY WIGMORE, SELECT CASES ON THE LAW OF TORTS (Little, Brown & Co. 1912).

[10] *Id.* at vii–ix.

[11] *See* WILLIAM M. LANDES & RICHARD A. POSNER, THE ECONOMIC STRUCTURE OF TORT LAW (Harvard Univ. Press 1987); STEVEN SHAVELL, ECONOMIC ANALYSIS OF ACCIDENT LAW (Harvard Univ. Press 2007).

Of course, this leaves open the question: Why study tort law? This would have seemed an odd question to ask 100 years ago, but the popular view of law has changed so much in the recent past that it is a question that needs to be addressed today. There have always been two popular senses of the law. One is of law as a system of rules that constrain private actors roughly equally. Another is of law as a medium for sending orders from one person to another, or from one group to another.[12] In the first view, law puts us all on an equal footing and is indifferent to our identities. In the second, law is directed toward changing power relationships and is keenly aware of the identities of the affected parties. Society has increasingly embraced the second view, and law schools have followed the popular interest by replacing common law courses with "public law" courses on statutory subjects.

For law students, tort law remains a mandatory topic in the first year of school, so there is little pressure at the moment to answer the question "Why study tort law?" But the mandatory status of torts may change over time, given the increasing preference in law schools for public law statutory subjects. A defense for studying tort law will therefore need to go beyond simply pointing to the mandatory status of the course.

To justify studying tort law, one has to believe that the core common law subjects – tort law, contract law, criminal law, property law – are still important parts of a sound education in the law. I believe this is a defensible proposition. Almost all of the statutory subjects so popular today rely on fundamental doctrines developed in the common law. Antitrust law relies on notions of deterrence and causation developed in tort law. Labor law, another modern statutory subject, relies on theories developed in the common law of contracts. Intellectual property law relies heavily on theories from tort law, and large parts of intellectual property law (trademark law, trade secret law) developed as subfields of torts.[13] Lawyers and judges will be in much better shape to understand these areas of the law and to apply them wisely if they take advantage of the lessons embedded in the common law.

In addition to this, common law has developed through the public resolution of thousands of disputes. In each, a court has operated with discretion to consider the social consequences of its decision. As a result, the common law has developed into a fine-meshed system of regulation, with each pocket of the squares reflecting a balance struck with respect to the consequences for future parties, like the ones in the dispute, and for the system as a whole.

Tort law is not only a part of the common law; it is arguably the core of the common law. Wigmore referred to tort law as the study of "general rights."[14] One way of supporting this view is by comparing tort law to criminal law or to contract

---

[12] This distinction between views of the law is noted in LON L. FULLER, THE MORALITY OF LAW 63 (Yale Univ. Press rev. ed. 1969).

[13] RONALD A. CASS & KEITH N. HYLTON, LAWS OF CREATION: PROPERTY RIGHTS IN THE WORLD OF IDEAS (Harvard Univ. Press 2013).

[14] Wigmore, *supra* note 9, at vii.

law. Criminal law consists of prohibitory rules (e.g., "do not steal") that developed societies state prominently to everyone. Contract law consists of rules that facilitate the process of making and enforcing promises.

Tort law differs from criminal law in that the rules of torts are often discovered through the litigation process. Many tort defendants are not aware that they have committed a tort until a court finds them guilty of it. While criminal law rules are fixed in advance and broadcast loudly to the public, tort law rules are dynamic, changing with society's preferences and technological capabilities, and understood to reflect norms of reasonable behavior that parties should adopt in social interaction. If an individual has not adopted the appropriate norm, a court hearing a tort dispute will consider itself free to state the norm publicly as a rule of law for the first time and apply it retrospectively to hold the individual liable.

Such dynamism and flexibility on the part of courts would be undesirable in criminal law. If criminal laws were generally unstated and applied retrospectively, law enforcers would have virtually unlimited power over citizens. They could choose individuals to punish on the basis of whatever outcomes the enforcers desired.

Tort law differs fundamentally from contract law in that the rules of tort regulate the conduct of parties directly whereas the rules of contract law seek mainly to facilitate the contracting process without controlling the terms of those contracts. In other words, whereas tort law sets rules that regulate the interaction between two individuals, contract law enables those individuals to choose the rules that regulate their interaction and to enforce the rules in an efficient manner. One could go so far as to say that contract law is an oxymoron, because the substantive regulation done by contracts is determined by mutual consent. But that would be an exaggeration; contact law includes many instances of substantive regulation, such as unconscionability doctrine. Still, it strikes me as fair to say that contract law has a largely procedural aim whereas tort law is decidedly substantive in nature.

Given the differences between tort law, on one hand, and contract and criminal law, on the other, tort law has a strong claim to be the core of the common law process, provided that we understand that process as the generation by courts of rules that regulate social interaction. If this claim is valid, then endeavoring to understand the policies that shape tort law is equivalent to endeavoring to understand the policies that shape the common law generally. And given the importance of common law to so many statutory subjects, to constitutional law, and to sound regulation in general, the study of tort law should be viewed as an important priority.

As I have done in my classes, I have emphasized rules in this book. It is possible to study tort law and walk away with the impression that there are no rules, that it is all a matter of weighing burdens and benefits in consideration of the facts of a dispute. This viewpoint implies that if a decision for the plaintiff is more costly to society than is a decision for the defendant, then the decision should be for the plaintiff. However, tort law does consist of rules, and a large part of this book is devoted to identifying them and stating them clearly.

Identification and statement of rules should be of interest to students of the law because legal argumentation involves the articulation and application of legal rules. A person who plans to argue in front of a court will have to be prepared to use the rules – judges for the most part are not interested in hearing one person's reasonableness or cost-benefit analysis. Finally, the law itself advances through the statement of rules. Rules give the law predictability and stability, which would not be observed if courts were left completely free to apply an unguided reasonableness analysis to every dispute.

Chapter 2 provides a survey of utilitarian and deontological (duty-oriented) theories of tort law. I present basic ideas from economic analysis of tort law and contrast them with the moral reasoning approach. This chapter also introduces the concept of externalities and the role of tort law in internalizing losses (negative externalities) to responsible actors. The term externality remains largely confined to the economics literature, which is unfortunate given its obvious relevance to tort law. Much of tort law would be described by economists as the law governing externalities. By introducing the concept of externalities early, I hope to put the reader in a position to see its usefulness in many specific areas of tort law. Of course, it should be kept in mind that the externality concept is important in understanding policy, and by this path gaining a deeper understanding of the law. The courts do not use the term externality much at all, and a course in tort law must in the end teach students how to present arguments to courts. For the most part, Chapter 2 is background material that can be assigned to students without teaching it. Alternatively, a teacher who uses this book might refer back to segments of Chapter 2 as he or she moves through the later chapters.

The economics presented in Chapter 2 may seem overly technical at times to law students, but the technical parts are short and not entirely necessary for understanding the basic lessons and implications for law. The student who prefers not to delve into economics can focus on the lessons for the law rather than the details of the analysis. Similarly, Chapters 5, 11, 17, and 18 delve into somewhat technical matters in economics (e.g., supply-demand analysis in Chapter 17, basic concepts of game theory in Chapter 11, present value calculation in Chapter 18), and there too the student can learn the basic lessons for tort law without having to master the details of economic analysis. On the other hand, perhaps gaining familiarity with modern tools of policy analysis, such as game theory, is a suitable goal for law students. Law increasingly demands an acquaintance with the analytical methods taught in business schools and in public policy schools. Under this view of the matter, the law student should be encouraged to study the technical material closely to prepare him- or herself for future challenges.

Chapter 3 covers intentional torts, such as trespass, battery, assault, and false imprisonment. Intentional torts, as a subject matter, has become less popular among torts teachers in recent years. I have talked to some who do not teach the subject at all in the limited time given in law schools today for teaching torts. However, I view intentional torts as an important foundation for studying negligence, nuisance, and other torts topics. Tort law began with intentional torts before spreading its net wider to offer protection against negligent conduct. Studying intentional torts lays the groundwork for understanding the policies of negligence and nuisance law. Basic notions of intent, or mental state, are important in understanding the boundaries between nuisance, negligence, and trespass law. Such notions are also important for understanding the boundary between tort and criminal law and the function of punitive damages.

Chapter 4 is a review of ancient cases and the early development of tort law. A popular view holds that tort law has developed from a simple presumption of strict liability, in ancient times, to a more complicated set of doctrines relying on notions of fault. Under this popular view, the substantive regulatory nature of tort law changed between ancient and modern epochs. I suggest in Chapter 4 that the important differences between early and modern tort law are procedural rather than substantive.

Chapter 5 presents an introduction to the doctrine of strict liability and provides a functional, utilitarian view of the doctrine as established in *Rylands v. Fletcher* and related cases, drawing on concepts and analytical tools introduced in Chapter 2. The framework provides a policy-based explanation for the scope of strict liability, the boundary between negligence liability and strict liability, and notions of duty in tort law.

Chapters 6 and 7 introduce and explore negligence doctrine. Negligence is often described as a failure to act as a reasonable person. Moreover, the reasonable person standard is objective, in the sense that it does not take into consideration the idiosyncratic preferences or psychological features of the defendant. Chapter 6 examines common patterns in negligence theories and the extent to which the reasonable person standard varies according to individual traits and with respect to widely shared moral intuitions. Chapter 7 extends this examination to incorporate compliance with customs and statutes.

Chapter 8 addresses the problem of inferring negligence on the basis of circumstantial evidence and the doctrines and policies that courts have adopted to provide consistency in these cases. This requires an acknowledgment of the respective roles of judge and jury in the negligence determination. I also discuss the role of baseline probabilities and statistical reasoning in the law on inference.

Chapters 9 and 10 present the major defenses to negligence: contributory negligence, assumption of risk, and comparative negligence. In addition to explaining the law, I offer a framework for understanding the incentives created by these doctrines. Chapter 11 covers joint and several liability, and vicarious liability. These chapters all fit together because they deal with a similar problem: how to structure incentives under tort law to encourage care on the part of two or more actors who can affect the risk of injury to a victim. The doctrines in these areas have a surprisingly similar structure in spite of differences in labels, because they are designed to address similar incentive problems.

Chapters 12 and 13 present the tort law on causation, first factual causation and then proximate causation. In addition to presenting the law, my aim in these chapters is to simplify and identify a useful conceptual apparatus. Chapter 14 discusses the duty to rescue and other relationship-based duties, such as the duties of land occupiers to land visitors. These chapters strive toward a policy framework under which the cases can be organized. The treatment in many torts textbooks leaves the reader with the impression that the cases are scattered about with no unifying conceptual framework.

Chapter 15 explores the law on strict liability. This chapter uses the doctrine of *Rylands v. Fletcher*, examined in Chapter 5, to offer a general account of the ultrahazardous activities and nuisance cases and presents a common framework for the law governing ultrahazardous activities and nuisances.

Chapter 16 is on defamation and shows that the *Rylands* doctrine and policy both provide a framework for understanding defamation law. One puzzle I address is why expression, a socially beneficial activity, would fall under the same legal framework as ultrahazardous activities. However, defamation liability does not apply to expression in general, only to false and socially harmful expression. The general patterns of theories of liability, and of defenses, observed in strict liability and defamation law are very much alike. Defamation law is much easier to understand when its similarity to ultrahazardous activities doctrine is kept in view.

Chapter 17 discusses products liability law. Although often described as strict liability, that is a fair description of only a part of the law – that governing manufacturing defects. The rest of the law governs failures to warn and defective design litigation. These areas fall under negligence or negligence-like standards. The policy bases for these tests are examined closely. Supply and demand analysis is introduced to provide a foundation for understanding the effects of products liability rules.

Chapter 18, the final chapter, presents the law on damages, compensatory and punitive, and examines the influence of damages on the operation of the tort system. I provide an explanation of the functions of both compensatory and punitive damages. The chapter also includes a discussion of incentives to file suit, to settle, to waive tort claims, and to enter into subrogation agreements.

This book can be used as a text for a lecture-based course on tort law or to supplement a case book. I have tried to make the book "cross-platform" – that is, capable of being used along with any torts casebook, or without any torts casebook, by discussing mostly well-known cases. The heavy emphasis on policy makes this book especially suitable for courses that have a doctrinal and policy focus.[15] Readers of the more practice-oriented casebooks can also use this book to learn about the policies that have influenced tort law. In addition, this book may be appropriate

---

[15] Two casebooks that fit this description are the Epstein-Sharkey casebook, *supra* note 6, and ROBERT E. KEETON, LEWIS D. SARGENTICH, AND GREGORY C. KEATING, TORT AND ACCIDENT LAW (West Acad. Pub. 4th ed. 2004).

for undergraduate or non-law-school courses, where it may be more useful to get students to think about the broader rationales behind the law than to master specific legal rules. Indeed, one might create a course on modern tools for legal analysis,[16] using this book, by focusing largely on the more technical parts of the text (in Chapters 2, 5, 11, 17, and 18) and relevant applications to law.

This textbook is the culmination of many years of teaching and writing on tort law. My colleagues, speaking broadly of torts professors with whom I have interacted throughout my career, have contributed mostly by identifying puzzles in tort doctrine that, when examined closely, seem to reveal yet more difficult puzzles. And so many students have assisted my research on torts that it would be difficult to list all of them. Two, however, worked on the entire manuscript: Nina Prevot and Matt Saldana. I asked both of them to read the manuscript from the perspective of a new law student, and they identified numerous passages that had to be changed to make the argument clearer. With luck I will continue to find able and energetic students to work with me on this project.

---

[16] Some law schools now offer courses on tools for legal analysis. Two books in this area are WARD FARNSWORTH, THE LEGAL ANALYST: A TOOLKIT FOR THINKING ABOUT THE LAW (Univ. of Chicago Press 2007), and FREDERICK SCHAUER, THINKING LIKE A LAWYER: A NEW INTRODUCTION TO LEGAL REASONING (Harvard Univ. Press 2009). Unlike these books, this book incorporates modern analytical tools in a detailed examination of a specific area of law.

2

Policy and Tort Law

Tort law has been shaped by the policies, often unarticulated, that appear most attractive and persuasive to courts. The two main sources of policies embraced by courts are the fields of economic reasoning and moral reasoning. But there are other sources of policy in addition to these.

Policy rationales can provide either a positive or a normative theory of the law. A positive theory seeks to explain and understand the law as it is. A normative theory seeks to provide a description of an ideal legal system. Positive theories are presented in an effort to provide a deeper understanding of a body of case law. Normative theories, in contrast, are used to criticize existing law and to suggest alternatives, though they sometimes can provide a deeper understanding of the law too. Since this book aims primarily to describe and explain existing tort law, it draws on policy arguments as sources of positive theory for the most part. This chapter surveys the most prominent policies reflected in tort law.

I. ECONOMIC PRINCIPLES

Economics has increasingly become an important perspective and set of tools to use in analyzing tort law. The reason is easy to see when you examine the cases. Many tort cases involve an explicit tradeoff between costly precautionary effort and risk. The standard example in our lives is driving. A driver can take more precaution by reducing his speed and looking to both sides of the road more frequently. Each time he does so he reduces the likelihood of running into a pedestrian or another car. But each additional precautionary effort costs the driver something – perhaps he arrives to work late as a result.

The tradeoffs tort law grapples with can be classified into two types. One is the tradeoff between instantaneous care and risk. Again, the typical example is driving with more or less care. The other is the tradeoff between activity and risk – that is, doing more or less of an activity, irrespective of how careful you are. For example, even if you are the most careful driver in the world, you can still reduce the risk that you will harm someone by driving less frequently. The first type of tradeoff is described in the economics literature as the *care-level* decision. The second type of tradeoff is the *activity-level* decision.

The Care-Level Decision

One basic lesson from economics is that the level of care that is best for the individual, taking only his own interests into account, will tend to be less than the level that is best for society. To explain this point, I will employ what economists refer to as *marginal analysis*. This requires consideration of the incremental benefits and incremental costs associated with an action.

Consider the benefits from taking additional care in an activity, such as driving. As you take more care, for example, by driving more slowly, you reduce the likelihood of an accident in which you are injured. That is the clearest benefit to the driver from taking more care.

Suppose, for example, that the risk of an accident in which you are injured is 5 percent when you are driving at 90 miles per hour, and that you will suffer a loss of $10,000 if an accident occurs. *The expected value of the loss* from an accident is the probability that the accident will occur multiplied by the value of the loss if it does occur. Thus, the expected value of the loss from an accident when you are driving at 90 miles an hour is equal to the product of 5 percent and $10,000, which is $500.

The concept of *expected value* will appear many times in this book and is important in tort law and policy. The expected value of an event is equal to the probability that it will occur multiplied by the payoff (or loss) from the event (Expected Value = Probability × Value). Thus, if I purchase a lottery ticket with a prize of $100, and the probability of winning is 50 percent, the expected value of the ticket is the product of 50 percent and $100, which is $50.

Now suppose the risk of injury falls to 2.5 percent when you cut your speed from 90 miles per hour to 60 miles per hour. The expected loss to you from an accident at this lower speed is $0.025 \times \$10,000 = \$250$. It follows that the incremental (or marginal) benefit to you from reducing your speed from 90 to 60 is $250 (because $500 − $250 = $250).

The marginal benefit to an actor from taking additional care is the *marginal private benefit of care*. This is likely to fall as the actor takes more care. For example, when a driver cuts his speed from 90 to 60, there is likely to be a larger reduction in risk than when he cuts his speed from 40 to 30. The reason for diminishing returns in care is that the risk of an accident is smaller at lower speeds, and so the returns from cutting speed eventually taper off.

Returning to the driving illustration, assume that if the actor reduces speed from 60 to 40, the likelihood of an accident falls from 2.5 percent to 1 percent. This implies that the marginal private benefit when he cuts speed from 60 to 40

the implicit horizontal scale
increment should be the same.

Policy and Tort Law

TABLE 2.1. *Costs and benefits of care*

Care decision	Cost of care	Benefit of care to actor	Benefit of care to victim	Social benefit of care
90 to 60	$150	$250	$250	$500
60 to 40	$200	$150	$150	$300
40 to 30	$220	$50	$50	$100

is $150.[1] Finally, assume that if the actor reduces speed from 40 to 30, the likelihood of an accident falls from 1 percent to 0.5 percent, which implies that the marginal private benefit is $50.[2]

These assumptions generate a marginal private benefit schedule, which shows how the marginal benefit to the actor changes as he takes more care. This is illustrated in Table 2.1, third column.

The marginal private benefit schedule shows the incremental benefits to the actor as he takes more care. However, it fails to show the incremental benefits to society. The benefits to society are greater than the benefits to the actor, because when the actor takes more care he reduces the likelihood of harm to himself and he also reduces the likelihood of harm to someone else. For example, if you run into someone with your car, you may cause a $10,000 loss to yourself and a $10,000 loss to the other person. Given this, the marginal benefit to society from reducing your speed from 90 to 60 is $500 – twice the marginal private benefit.[3]

This suggests that there is another schedule of interest, the *marginal social benefit*, which consists of the sum of the benefits of care to the actor and to the potential victim. Thus, if the actor reduces his speed from 90 to 60, the marginal private benefit is $250 and the marginal social benefit is $500. The last column of Table 2.1 shows the marginal social benefit schedule.

Now let's consider the cost of taking care. Suppose the primary form of care while driving is moderation of speed. As the actor reduces his speed, he increases the likelihood that he will be late to appointments. This is costly to him, because he may miss out on business opportunities or arrive late to important meetings. We can illustrate a marginal cost schedule for care, following the same arguments used to illustrate the marginal benefit schedules. The assumed values for the marginal cost schedule appear in the second column of Table 2.1. The marginal cost schedule assumes that the incremental cost of taking more care is higher when the actor cuts his speed from 40 to 30 than when he cuts his speed from 90 to 60.

[1] The marginal private benefit of care is calculated as follows: $0.025 \times \$10,000 - 0.01 \times \$10,000 = \$250 - \$100 = \$150$.

[2] The marginal private benefit of care is $0.01 \times \$10,000 - 0.005 \times \$10,000 = \$100 - \$50 = \$50$.

[3] The marginal social benefit of care is calculated as follows: $0.05 \times \$20,000 - 0.025 \times \$20,000 = \$1,000 - \$500 = \$500$.

Now, if an actor considers only the losses to himself when driving, how much care would he take? He would choose the level of care that yields the greatest net benefit to him in light of the costs he would incur. As long as the marginal private benefit of care exceeds the marginal cost, he would take additional care, since the net benefit he perceives from additional care would be positive. For example, suppose he reduces his speed from 90 to 60 and thereby reduces the expected harm to himself by $250 while incurring an additional $150 in the cost of care (Table 2.1). Since the net incremental benefit would be $100, he would reduce his speed. Would he reduce his speed further, from 60 to 40? If he did so, the marginal private benefit would be $150 and the marginal cost would be $200. Since the net benefit would then be −$50, he likely would not reduce his speed to 40.

The level of care that an actor would take if he considered only the losses to himself is generally lower than the level of care that he would take if he considered the losses to everyone. In other words, the *privately optimal* level of care is generally less than the *socially optimal* level of care. To see this, return to Table 2.1.

If you considered the social benefit of care instead of only the private benefit, you would take additional care as long as the marginal social benefit is greater than the cost of additional care. Consider the decision to reduce speed from 60 to 40. If you consider only private benefits and costs, the net benefit of such a reduction would be −$50; consequently you would not reduce your speed from 60 to 40. However, if you consider the social benefits and costs, the net benefit of such a reduction would be $300 − $200 = $100, and since this is positive, you would reduce your speed.

Would you reduce your speed further, from 40 to 30, taking the social benefit into account? If you did so, you would incur a cost of $220 and the social benefit would be $100 (Table 2.1), leading to a net social benefit of −$120. Thus, you would not reduce your speed to 30 when taking the social benefit of risk reduction into account. It follows that 60 mph is the *privately optimal level of care* and 40 mph is the *socially optimal level of care*.

Now we can begin to see the impact of tort liability. Suppose the law holds the actor liable for the losses to others. For simplicity, suppose the law adopts *strict liability*, which requires the actor to pay damages when he runs into someone with his car, no matter how careful he was.

Under strict liability, the private benefit of care becomes, in effect, the same as the social benefit of care. The reason is that the actor will be held strictly liable for the losses to others. Every time he decides whether he should take more care, he will consider both the losses to himself and the losses to others.[4] *As a result, the level of care an actor will choose under strict liability will be socially optimal.*

This example illustrates how tort liability can improve society's welfare. Liability encourages actors to take the potential losses of others into account when they decide

---

[4] Using Table 2.1, imposing liability causes the private benefit of care to become equivalent to the social benefit of care, which means that Column 5 replaces Column 3.

how much care to take. In the absence of liability, they would not take the potential losses of others into account, and would therefore take too little care in light of society's interests.

I have so far considered the effects strict liability on the care decision. The other legal standard encountered in tort law is the *negligence* rule. Under the negligence rule, the actor is held liable only if he fails to take a certain (reasonable) level of care.

Suppose the negligence rule holds the actor liable any time his level of care is less than the socially optimal level. To see what this implies, return to Table 2.1. Recall that socially optimal care requires a speed of 40 mph. If the actor chooses 60, he will be held liable under the negligence rule. However, if the actor chooses 40, he will not be held liable. In this case, because of the negligence rule, the private benefit of care becomes equivalent to the social benefit of care up to the point at which the actor complies with the socially optimal level of care, 40.

This means that if the actor starts at 90 and reduces his speed to 60, he gains $500, by avoiding losses to himself and liability for losses to others, and loses $150 because of the cost of taking additional care. Since the net gain is $500 − $150 = $350, he would reduce his speed from 90 to 60. If he then reduces his speed from 60 to 40, he gains $300 and loses $200, for a net gain of $100. If he then considers reducing his speed from 40 to 30, he would see that he would gain $50 and suffer a cost of $220, for a net loss of −$170. Thus, the actor would adopt the socially optimal level of care, driving at 40, under the negligence rule.

Note that in this illustration the level of care adopted by the actor is the same under strict liability and under negligence. Of course, this is the result because the negligence standard was assumed to require the socially optimal level. However, it turns out that the claim that care levels are the same under negligence and under strict liability is valid whenever negligence is determined by comparing the burden of additional care to the social benefit of additional care. I will introduce this approach later, under the label *Hand Formula* (Chapter 8).

Using Diagrams to Make the Same Point

Instead of using a table to describe the schedule of marginal private and social benefits of care, we can use a diagram. Let the horizontal axis in Figure 2.1 measure the amount of care the actor takes. For example, care could measure the speed of the driver or the frequency with which he looks to both sides of the road. As we move to the right on the horizontal axis, the actor is taking more care (e.g., driving more slowly). The vertical axis measures the economic variable of interest, dollars per unit of care. Thus, if care is represented by the reduction in speed, the vertical axis would be measured in dollars per mph reduction in speed.

The downward sloping line *MPB* represents the marginal private benefit of care. It reflects the same assumptions used for Table 2.1 (third column). The key assumption

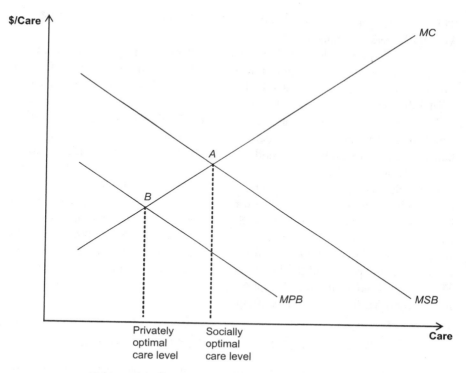

FIGURE 2.1. Privately and socially optimal care levels

is diminishing returns: The marginal benefit of care declines as the actor takes more care.

MSB represents the marginal social benefit of care. It is shown above the marginal private benefit schedule because the harm to society from failing to take care is greater than the harm to the individual actor. The harm to the actor consists of his own injuries, while the harm to society consists of the sum of the actor's injuries and the injuries inflicted on others.

MC shows the marginal cost of care to the actor. It is upward sloping on the assumption that the cost to the actor of taking care increases as he takes more care. For example, cutting your speed from 30 to 10 is probably more costly (e.g., missing more appointments) than cutting it from 90 to 60.

The actor will find his privately optimal care level by taking additional care until the personal gain is offset by the cost – that is, where the marginal private benefit is just equal to the marginal cost of care. For example, if taking care consists of reducing speed, the actor will continue to reduce his speed until the gain – in the form of a reduced risk of injury – is just offset by the cost of a reduction in speed.

This privately optimal care level is shown by the intersection of the lines MPB and MC in Figure 2.1 (labeled point B).

The socially optimal level of care is found at the point at which the social gain is offset by the cost at the margin, shown by the intersection of the lines MSB and MC in Figure 2.1 (point A). Just as in Table 2.1, the socially optimal level of care is greater than the privately optimal level of care.

Under strict liability, the actor is required to pay for the losses he causes to others, which means the actor's private benefit of care becomes the same as the social benefit of care. Put another way, under strict liability, the line MPB shifts up to the same position as the line MSB.

Under the negligence rule, the actor is required to pay for the losses he causes to others only when his care level is below the socially optimal level. Thus, the private benefit of care is, because of liability, the same as the social benefit of care for all care levels below the socially optimal (point A, Figure 2.1). Put another way, under negligence liability the MPB line shifts up to the same position as the MSB line, but only for the portion of the line between the origin and point A in Figure 2.1. For care levels above the socially optimal, the actor is responsible only for his own losses, so the MPB line does not shift up.

The Activity-Level Decision: Missing Markets Perspective

Even if you take a great deal of care when engaging in a risky activity, there is still the option to reduce the risk to others further by engaging in the activity less. If your activity increases the risk of loss to others, then it may be socially desirable for you to scale back the activity. What factors determine privately and socially optimal activity-level decisions?

Return to the driving example. Instead of applying marginal analysis to the decision to take care, now let's apply marginal analysis to the decision to drive more or less frequently. Suppose activity is measured by the frequency the actor drives his car.

First, consider the marginal benefit, to the driver, of increasing the frequency of driving. Driving provides a benefit to car owners because it permits them to be mobile over much larger areas than would be possible to cover on foot. However, the benefits from additional driving decline at some point. Increasing your frequency of driving from 0 miles per week to 30 miles per week probably would offer a significant benefit to you, say, by allowing you to live and work in different towns. If you increase your frequency of driving from 30 to 60 miles per week, there might still be a benefit, but it would probably be less than the benefit you derived from the first increment in frequency. Given this, the marginal private benefit schedule (MPB) is likely to slope down, as shown in Figure 2.2.

Second, consider the marginal cost of increasing the frequency of driving. If you increase the frequency of driving from 0 to 30 miles per week, you have certainly

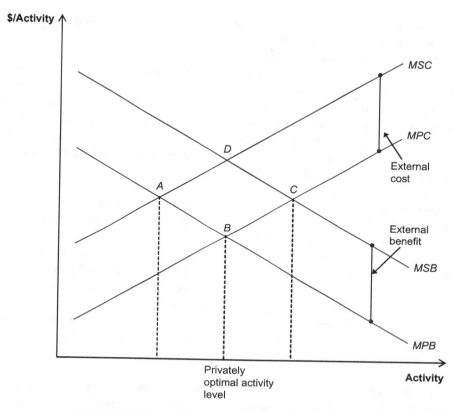

FIGURE 2.2. Privately and socially optimal activity levels

taken on some additional costs. One is maintenance of the car. Another is the risk of an accident. If you increase your frequency from 30 to 60 miles per week, you have probably taken on additional costs at least as great as the costs you took on with the initial increment in activity from 0 to 30. Thus, the marginal private cost schedule for the activity of driving (labeled *MPC*) probably increases, as shown in Figure 2.2.

Using the reasoning of the previous section, the *privately optimal activity level* is shown by the intersection of the marginal private benefit schedule and the marginal private cost schedule (point *B* in Figure 2.2). This is the point at which the net private benefit from additional driving is zero.

I included accident losses as one of the factors determining the marginal private cost of the activity, but I considered only the accident losses to the driver. Obviously, this leaves out the losses to the other parties involved in the accident. If we take those losses into account, we can generate a marginal social cost schedule for the activity of driving. This marginal social cost schedule (*MSC*) is shown in Figure 2.2.

Now we have a result similar to that of the preceding section: The actor, taking only his own interests into account, is likely to choose an activity level that is higher than the optimal level for society, because he ignores the accident losses he imposes others. The optimal level of activity for society is shown by point A in Figure 2.2. The actor, however, chooses point B.

But this conclusion is premature. Suppose the actor provides benefits to others as a result of his driving. Suppose, for example, he provides rides to coworkers, or suppose the mere presence of an additional driver makes the roads safer (e.g., someone to help if there is an emergency). If so, then the social benefit from the activity of driving is greater, at every level of activity, than the private benefit from driving. Put another way, there is a marginal social benefit schedule that lies above the marginal private benefit schedule, as shown in Figure 2.2.

The marginal social benefit schedule reflects the benefit provided to others when a driver increases his level of activity. If the benefit to others is substantial, it would no longer be clear that the driver's incentive is to choose an activity level that is too high from society's perspective. Return to Figure 2.2: if the driver provides no benefits to others, the socially optimal level of activity is shown by point A. However, if the driver provides benefits to others, the socially optimal level of activity is the level associated with point D, which happens to be the same (given the position of the lines in Figure 2.2) as the privately optimal level of activity.

How can we determine when the actor will choose an activity level that is too high, or too low, from society's perspective? This will be determined by the extent to which there are costs imposed on others or benefits provided to others by his activity.

The costs an actor's activity imposes on others are *external costs*. Similarly, the benefits provided to others are *external benefits*. We can see from Figure 2.2 that the driver's activity level will be too high from society's perspective if the external costs from his driving are greater than the external benefits. On the other hand, if the external benefits are greater than the external costs, he will tend to do too little driving relative to the level that is optimal for society.

This analysis of activity levels is important because, as we will see later, the law adopts liability rules that are designed to regulate activity levels. Strict liability, for example, affects activity levels because it forces actors to pay damages whether or not they are careful. In the presence of external costs in the form of injury risks, strict liability *internalizes* those costs by shifting them back to the actor who is responsible for the costs. Looking at Figure 2.2, strict liability, by internalizing external costs, shifts the marginal private cost schedule (*MPC*) up until it is equivalent to the marginal social cost schedule (*MSC*).

Strict liability raises the cost to an actor of engaging in an activity that generates injuries to others. This, in turn, causes the actor to reduce his level of the activity. If the activity inflicts more harm on others than is the norm among other activities, then society should reduce it – unless the activity also externalizes benefits to others. We will see later that strict liability performs this function in tort law (Chapter 5).

We will also see that tort law takes benefits into account. When an activity externalizes benefits, tort law tends to limit liability, in order not to impede the activity. For example, the provision of information, say, through speech (or writing), is an activity that externalizes benefits. A newspaper, for example, provides useful information to the purchaser, and also to others who benefit from the purchaser's acquisition of the newspaper. If the purchaser leaves the newspaper on a park bench, a passerby can read it and get the same benefit from the newspaper as the initial purchaser did. People who talk to the news purchaser can get the information from him. The initial purchaser's consumption of news does not exhaust or diminish its value to others who get the news through him. Thus, as in Figure 2.1, the marginal social benefit of news (which includes the benefit to the initial purchaser and to others who get the news from him) exceeds the marginal private benefit of news (the benefit to the purchaser alone). For activities that generate substantial external benefits, the best policy the law can adopt is to subsidize such activities – that is, a policy of using the law to shift the marginal cost schedule downward in Figure 2.1. Tort law, it turns out, adopts such a policy. Tort law responds to the existence of external benefits by limiting the risk of liability for speech and related activities, and for other activities that generate external benefits, such as rescue efforts.

The extreme case of a market activity that externalizes benefits is the *public* or *collective good*. A public good is a good or service that, like national security, is effectively provided to the entire community once it is provided to any one individual within the community. The standard lesson in the literature is that the market tends to provide less than the socially optimal quantity of public goods.[5] The reason is that no individual has an incentive to purchase the public good when he can wait for others to purchase it and reap the benefits in full. The law can respond by subsidizing provision or by imposing a duty to provide a minimal level of the public good.

In an ideal setting, markets would exist in which a person would pay for the costs he imposes on others or be compensated for the benefits he confers on them. Such markets obviously do not exist in the real world. When tort law imposes strict liability to internalize external costs, or limits the scope of liability in light of external benefits, it provides a substitute for missing markets.[6] The missing markets perspective suggests a policy framework for understanding the scope of strict liability and duty doctrines in tort law (Chapters 5 and 6).

The missing markets perspective also helps us understand the function of rules protecting property. When tort law permits a property owner to enjoin a threatened invasion, it encourages the invading party to bargain with the owner for access to the property. This encourages market transactions in settings where some actors might be inclined to bypass the market.

[5] Paul A. Samuelson, *The Pure Theory of Public Expenditure*, 36 Rev. Econ. & Stat. 387 (1954).
[6] Keith N. Hylton, *Duty in Tort Law: An Economic Approach*, 75 Fordham L. Rev. 1051, 1505 (2006).

II. MORAL JUSTIFICATIONS AND ANALYSES

The major alternative to the economic approach to understanding tort law is the moral reasoning approach. The moral reasoning approach differs from the economic approach in its emphasis on compliance with moral duties (*deontological ethics*) as opposed to weighing consequences (*consequentialism*). Still, the moral reasoning approach generally reaches conclusions that are consistent with the economic approach. Although the academic literature has long emphasized the differences – with one side rejecting the other as an appropriate theory of tort policy – it is easy to show that the moral and economic approaches have vast areas of agreement. The areas of disagreement are relatively minor.

We can use much of the foregoing economics to help explain the moral reasoning approach. The key starting point for the moral reasoning approach is the *Golden Rule*. The rule can be phrased in several ways to make it applicable to tort law. In the context of precaution, *the Golden Rule requires that a potential injurer always take as much care as he would take if he, instead of another person, were the potential victim. In other words, the actor should always envision himself as an integrated (or merged, or unitized) entity consisting of both injurer and victim.*

Care-Level Problem

Return to the driving example. Suppose now that if the actor speeds, he risks damaging his own car and another item of his property – or his wife's (or son's or daughter's) car. All of the expenses of an accident will come out of his own pocket. How will the actor decide how much care to take?

The actor will take both his precautionary burden as well as the loss he might impose on the victim into account. After all, the victim's loss will be his own loss. If the incremental loss avoided by taking more care exceeds the incremental burden of taking more care, he will take more care. Thus, the moral approach requires the actor to take the socially optimal level of care (point A in Figure 2.1).

I have so far suggested that the moral approach leads to the same recommendations for care as the economic approach. Do the approaches ever lead to different recommendations?

The answer is unclear. In many cases where someone asserts that the moral approach differs in its conclusion from the economic approach, the difference is really due to a different set of premises or assumptions rather than the aims of the approaches. Also, another broad area of uncertainty as to agreement between the approaches involves the evaluation of personal injury.

Return again to the driving example. Suppose, instead of injury to property (e.g., damage to a car), we consider personal injury. The actor has a choice to reduce or to maintain his speed, and the potential damage is a serious physical injury to the victim – e.g., shearing a leg off.

Superficially, it would seem that the economic and moral approaches imply starkly different conclusions. A superficial economic analysis would require the injurer to calculate the monetary value of the injury to the victim, and to take that value into account in deciding whether to moderate his speed. But this analysis immediately runs into problems. What is the value of the loss of a leg to the victim? One might answer by going to a valuation expert who can determine the wage losses that would be suffered by the victim as a result of losing his leg. The valuation expert might propose the wage loss estimate as the sum that the actor should take into account in calculating the level of care he should exercise.

It is at this point that we begin to see how the economic and moral approaches might lead to different answers, and why proponents of the moral approach sometimes reject the economic approach. Recall that under the moral approach, the injurer should behave as an integrated or unitized entity with the victim; that is, he should take care as if he were both injurer and victim in an accident. If you were at risk of causing an accident in which the only injury would be the loss of your leg, how would you calculate the level of care that would be optimal from your perspective? Whatever you choose to do, you probably would not base your decision entirely on the value of your expected wage losses.

How would you decide how much care to take when you are considering yourself as both injurer and victim in a serious accident? First, you probably would consider potential wage losses. However, in addition you would consider other losses as well. An injury that causes you to lose your leg would change your life drastically in many ways unconnected to your work compensation. Although you would have difficulty arriving at a sum, you would view the loss to yourself as far greater than the wage losses that the valuation expert had identified.

In contrast to personal injury, in cases of injury to property the decisions of the economic analyst, who focuses on costs and benefits, and the moral analyst, who follows the Golden Rule, are likely to be the same. In cases of personal injury they may differ, depending on what the economic analyst decides to count in his summation of losses.

Still, it is not absolutely clear that the moral and economic analysts will disagree on the level of care that should be taken in the personal injury scenario. The economic analyst may do such a thorough accounting of potential losses that he chooses a recommended level of care that is the same as that chosen by the moral analyst. But many of us would have a strong suspicion that the economic analyst might come up short in his accounting of losses.

One thing should not be doubted: *Neither the moral nor the economic analyst will treat the losses in the personal injury case as infinite.* Moral analysts often speak of categorical duties, as if the loss resulting from a failure to comply with such a duty (for example, to take care) were infinite. But if the moral analyst were to treat personal injury losses as infinite, he would quickly find himself unable to function in the real world. Treating losses from personal injury as infinite would require the highest feasible level of care in every setting. Drivers would have to set their speeds at extremely low levels, perhaps at walking speed, or maybe never drive at all. After all, the use of a dangerous machine, such as a car, puts lives at risk even when operated with the utmost care, so putting an infinite value on life would require the state to ban the use of such machines. Modern society could hardly function under such constraints. Recognizing this fact, the moral analyst will concede that people have to be allowed to get on with their lives.

Moral intuitions are often useful correctives to the economic approach. The economic approach might, if conducted hastily, lead to an overly stingy assessment of losses to the victim and would therefore suggest a level of care that is too low from society's perspective. The moral approach may point more readily to the right answer, simply by inquiring into common sense intuitions about the level of care that would be appropriate under the circumstances. These common sense intuitions are often obvious and easily derived without the assistance of a valuation expert. Rather than being seen as in perpetual tension, the moral and economic approaches should be seen as offering safeguards against the mistakes that might be made working exclusively within one of the approaches. The economic approach tends to undervalue personal injury, leading to recommended care levels that are too low. The Golden Rule approach, on the other hand, tends to overvalue personal injury, at least at first glance. The economic approach is a useful corrective to this tendency to overvalue because it demands that the analyst put a price on the losses suffered from an accident, a necessary first step to making rational tradeoffs between the risks and benefits associated with alternative courses of action.

To the extent that the moral approach has a philosophical basis, the Kantian ethical system appears to be the most attractive source.[7] At the core of Kant's system is a belief that moral norms should be *universalizable,* in the sense that they apply equally to all rational agents. The Kantian system prohibits a policy of arbitrarily preferring your own welfare to that of others. Other rational humans are to be treated as ends in themselves and not as a means to one's own ends; to respect the dignity and autonomy of others we cannot use them as instruments in our own schemes of self-advancement.[8] The Golden Rule is a natural implication of the Kantian system.

There are other sources for moral analysis of law, in addition to the Kantian ethical system. Some scholars draw on Aristotle's assertion that law should cancel unjust

---

[7] IMMANUEL KANT, GROUNDWORK OF THE METAPHYSICS OF MORALS (H. J. Paton trans., Hutchinson's University Library 1948) (1785). Tort scholars who have relied on Kantian arguments are Charles Fried and Ernest Weinrib. *See* CHARLES FRIED, AN ANATOMY OF VALUES: PROBLEMS OF PERSONAL AND SOCIAL CHOICE (Harvard Univ. Press 1970); ERNEST WEINRIB, THE IDEA OF PRIVATE LAW (Harvard Univ. Press 1995).

[8] KANT, *supra* note 7, at 95–100.

[handwritten annotation] Where is the Kantian thesis for moral justification in conflict w/ "Economic Principles"? Can we use Malthus, Ricardo, Smith to reconcile?

gains.[9] Aristotle has been applied by some scholars to argue that tort law's function is to *cancel unjust gains and losses.*

Negligence can be described as the combination of an unjust loss and an unjust gain. The gain accrues to the injurer who avoids the burden of taking care, B. The loss is imposed on the victim, who suffers the risk of injury as a result of the injurer's decision not to take care. If the probability of the loss occurring is P and the amount of the loss is L, the expected loss imposed on the victim by the injurer's refusal to take care is $P \times L$. Since negligence law internalizes the victim's loss to the injurer, it cancels the gain from avoiding the burden of care when the burden of care is less than the expected value of the losses avoided by taking care – that is, when $B < P \times L$.

John Rawls is another foundational source for the moral reasoning approach to tort law.[10] Rawlsian social contract theorists have argued that society, in an original position, behind a veil of ignorance in which actors do not know their own strengths and weaknesses, would choose a *rule of reciprocity* to govern risk-imposing conduct.[11] Under the rule of reciprocity, an individual would be permitted to impose risk on others only to the extent that it is consistent with an equal right of others to impose risk on the individual. This would imply a balancing of the benefits from imposing the risk against the severity of the risk.

There are other theoretically plausible moral approaches, but some of them would generate ethical guidelines that are not useful in understanding tort law, and not universally commendable as guidelines for behavior. A committed Marxian, for example, would argue that one's moral outlook is determined by the class to which he belongs. Instead of universalizable rules, the Marxian approach would lead to moral guidelines that are dependent upon the actor's class. A capitalist, under this view, should then demand tort rules that enhance the value of capital, and a worker should seek rules that enhance labor's claim to capital. Some historical analyses of tort law,[12] and particularly the Horwitz thesis that negligence law developed in the

---

[9] ARISTOTLE, NICOMACHEAN ETHICS 125–28 (Terence Irwin trans., Hackett Pub. Co. 1985) (discussing corrective justice). *See also* Jules L. Coleman, *Tort Law and the Demands of Corrective Justice*, 67 INDIANA L. J. 349 (1992) (suggesting an application of Aristotle's corrective justice theory to tort law); Richard A. Posner, *The Concept of Corrective Justice in Recent Theories of Tort Law*, 10 J. LEGAL STUD. 187 (1981) (explaining Aristotle and critiquing corrective justice theorists); Stephen R. Perry, *The Moral Foundations of Tort Law*, 77 IOWA L. REV. 449 (1992) (friendly critique of corrective justice theories).

[10] JOHN RAWLS, A THEORY OF JUSTICE (Harvard Univ. Press 1971). Tort scholars who have relied on Rawls's theory are George Fletcher and Charles Fried. *See* George P. Fletcher, *Fairness and Utility in Tort Theory*, 85 HARV. L. REV. 537 (1972); CHARLES FRIED, AN ANATOMY OF VALUES: PROBLEMS OF PERSONAL AND SOCIAL CHOICE (Harvard Univ. Press 1970).

[11] FRIED, *supra* note 7, at 183–193.

[12] MORTON J. HORWITZ, THE TRANSFORMATION OF AMERICAN LAW, 1780–1860 (Harvard Univ. Press 1977); LAWRENCE FRIEDMAN, A HISTORY OF AMERICAN LAW (3d ed. 2005).

middle of the 1800s to support emerging industry,[13] appear to be grounded in this sort of moral positivism.

III. PROPERTY RULES VERSUS LIABILITY RULES

To this point, I have considered how the law should attempt to control risks that society wishes to see undertaken. But not all risks fall in this category. There are some types of risk-generating conduct that society might wish to prohibit altogether.

Since I have used the automobile to illustrate the arguments of this chapter, I will continue with the same illustration. We can imagine two general approaches to regulating the activity of driving. One is to prohibit it altogether (or at certain times or places). Another is to permit driving, but to use the law to provide incentives for care, and for constraining the activity to a frequency at which its risks seem tolerable in light of its benefits.

In an article published in 1972, Guido Calabresi and A. Douglas Melamed referred to the two approaches just suggested as *property rules* and *liability rules*.[14] Property rules prohibit conduct, often with the support of criminal sanctions. In addition, such rules permit a potential victim to enjoin conduct and to seek damages for any violations of the law. Liability rules, on the other hand, do not attempt to prohibit conduct, but merely set "prices," in the form of damages, for violations of the law.

Returning to the driving example, property rules are like stop signs. To serve this function, property rules should clearly say "stop" to the potential transgressor and provide penalties that send the same prohibitory signal. It would be inconsistent to say "stop" to the transgressor and then fail to impose any punishment once the transgression occurs ("never mind").

Liability rules, in contrast, are like toll booths. They permit injurers to engage in their risky activities, but require injurers to pay a toll, in the form of compensation for injuries, for various types of transgressions – for example, for driving too fast at certain times or in certain areas.

The property rule approach is best exemplified by the law of trespass. Trespass law permits a property owner to enjoin a potential violation and to seek damages for any violations that occur. The liability rule approach is exemplified by the rules governing strict liability and negligence. Strict liability and negligence law do not, in general, permit a potential victim to enjoin a potential injurer's conduct.

---

[13] Horwitz, *supra* note 12.

[14] Guido Calabresi & A. Douglas Melamed, *Property Rules, Liability Rules, and Inalienability: One View of the Cathedral*, 85 Harv. L. Rev. 1089 (1972). For related articles, *see* Louis Kaplow & Steven Shavell, *Property Rules Versus Liability Rules: An Economic Analysis*, 109 Harv. L. Rev. 713 (1996); Henry E. Smith, *Property and Property Rules*, 79 N.Y.U. L. Rev. 1719 (2004); Keith N. Hylton, *Property Rules and Liability Rules, Once Again*, 2 Rev. Law & Econ. 137 (2006); Keith N. Hylton, *Property Rules and Defensive Conduct in Tort Law Theory*, 4 J. Tort L. 1 (2011).

Why do we see property rules applied in some areas of the law and liability rules in other areas? In other words, why not adhere to only one type of rule?

To answer this question, consider an example. Suppose Richard Roe announces that he plans to cut down the old oak tree on John Doe's property. With only liability rules, John Doe would not be able to enjoin Richard Roe. He would be forced by the law to wait for the transgression to occur, and then to sue for damages. If a property rule (e.g., trespass law) applied, however, John Doe could enjoin Richard Roe.

One could argue that it doesn't matter whether John Doe is protected by a property rule or a liability rule. Either way, John Doe will be able to collect compensation from Richard Roe for chopping down the oak tree. This suggests that John Doe should be indifferent as between the property rule and the liability rule. Is this valid?

No, this argument is not valid. The key difference between the two rules is that under the property rule, John Doe can set his own terms with Richard Roe, while under the liability rule, Doe is forced to accept the compensation terms determined by the court. While the court will provide an objective determination of the value of the tree under the liability rule, John Doe will be able to name the price that best suits him under the property rule.

The oak tree's value to John Doe consists of an objective component, the market value, and a subjective component – that is, the extra value to John Doe beyond the market price. The property rule permits John Doe to be compensated for both the objective and subjective losses he would suffer by Richard Roe's cutting down the tree. In other words, property rules differ from liability rules because they protect subjective valuations.

Given all of this, why don't we see only property rules in tort law? Why do we ever observe liability rules, if property rules provide better protection to potential victims? The answer provided by Calabresi and Melamed is *transaction costs*, the costs of bargaining and reaching an agreement to transfer some entitlement.

The transaction costs explanation for liability rules runs as follows. In some settings, it is virtually impossible for the parties to bargain before the transfer (or violation) of a legal entitlement occurs. Consider, for example, traffic on the roads. Generally there is no time for parties to bargain about compensation for risk imposition before they meet each other on the road in an accident. Because of this, transaction costs are high in the traffic setting. And, as we will see later, liability rules, rather than property rules, apply such settings.

Where, then, are transaction costs low? Consider again the case of the adjacent landowners, Richard Roe and John Doe. If Roe wants to cut down the old oak tree on Doe's property, it is fairly easy for him to knock on Doe's door and ask for permission. He can ask directly how much he would have to compensate Doe for chopping down his tree. This is an easy transaction to arrange, and for this reason transaction costs are low in this setting, involving one party who wishes to interfere with the property rights of another. As we will see later in Chapter 4, the trespass rule applies in this setting.

In addition to the low transaction cost scenario just described, the property rule approach is also adopted for certain types of conduct that can be described as unambiguously socially undesirable, because the benefits are trivial in relation to the harms imposed. For example, reckless conduct, such as speeding in the wrong direction on a single-lane road, is always socially undesirable. Far better to prohibit such conduct altogether, than to try to regulate it down to some theoretically ideal level.

The property rule approach consists of giving the potential victim the right to enjoin and an immediate claim to damages for injuries that result from a violation. In some cases, additional penalties (e.g., punitive damages) may be assessed against the injurer. Property rules are appropriate, according to the Calabresi-Melamed theory, in the context of intentional torts, such as trespass and battery, on the assumption that in most such instances it is easy for a potential injurer to seek the consent of the potential victim before taking an action that injures the victim.

IV. PROPERTY RULES, LIABILITY RULES, AND COASE THEOREM

The property and liability rules model of Calabresi and Melamed offers a simple explanation for tort law's treatment of actors who fall within some fundamental legal categories – such as trespassers, negligent actors, reckless actors, etc. Ronald Coase offered a more controversial proposition about the law's function in an article published in 1960.[15]

According to Coase, when the cost of transacting is low – let's say zero, to make things simpler – the assignment of a legal right will have no effect on the ultimate allocation of resources. This proposition is known as the Coase Theorem.

Return to the example of the old oak tree on John Doe's land. Recall that Richard Roe wants to cut down the old oak tree on Doe's property. Under trespass law, Doe can enjoin Roe. In the face of an injunction, backed by criminal sanctions, Roe will have to pay Doe for the right to remove the tree. Suppose Roe is willing to pay $5,000, and Doe is willing to have it cut down for as little as $1,000. Under these conditions, Roe will make a bargain with Doe to cut down the tree, for some price between $1,000 and $5,000.

Suppose the property right is reversed: The law says that Roe has the right to invade Doe's property and cut down the tree. Now Doe will have to pay Roe if he wants to keep the tree. But if Doe values the tree at only $1,000, and Roe is willing to pay $5,000 to remove the tree, there will be no agreement to save the tree. On the other hand, suppose Doe values the tree at $10,000. Then he will bargain with Roe and they will reach an agreement to save the tree, with Doe paying some price between $5,000 and $10,000 to Roe.

The bottom line is that when the cost of transacting is zero, the outcome of the tree dispute will be determined entirely by the respective valuations Doe and Roe

---

[15]　R. H. COASE, *The Problem of Social Cost*, 3 J. L. & ECON. 1 (1960).

put on the old oak tree, not by the assignment of the property right. This is the point of the Coase Theorem: The ultimate allocation of a resource is not dependent on the nature of the property right.

The Coase Theorem implies that the allocation of the property right is unimportant, and perhaps we do not need property rights at all![16] But this implication holds only for the very special case in which the cost of transacting is zero. As soon as we introduce some impediments to bargaining – such as delay, informational disparities, paying for lawyers, distrust, enmity[17] – the assignment of property rights begins to affect the ultimate allocation of resources.

The proper way to think about the Coase Theorem is that it establishes a theoretical benchmark against which to analyze the law's function. In the almost-never-observed case in which the cost of transacting is zero, the assignment of legal rights does not matter; the ultimate allocation of resources is the same regardless of the assignment. In the real world, in which the cost of transacting is not zero, the assignment of property rights does matter, and this is where the distinction between property rules and liability rules performs a service. In areas where the cost of transacting is relatively low, we tend to see property rules. In areas where the cost of transacting is relatively high, we tend to see liability rules.

There is one additional complication we should consider before leaving this topic. I have suggested that the zero transaction cost benchmark of the Coase Theorem is hardly ever observed. But suppose we find a setting that comes very close to zero cost. In such a setting, maybe it should not matter whether we have property rules or liability rules, because parties would bargain to an ideal outcome either way.[18] But even this claim is doubtful. The liability rule does not protect subjective valuations. Even if, under the liability rule, the parties managed always to bargain to an agreement to transfer a legal entitlement, the bargaining process under the liability rule would still be distorted by the fact that the rule provides only modest protection to entitlements. If the holder of an entitlement foresees that he will be pressured, in effect, to sell it at a low price because of the weakness of legal protection, he will hardly consider himself better off than if he had no legal protection at all.[19] Hence, the liability rule is likely to generate wasteful expenditures and misallocations of resources that could be avoided under the property rule.[20] For example, the party whose property is likely to be transferred under the liability rule will spend resources on securing or defending his property – resources that would not be wasted in such

---

[16] Kaplow & Shavell, *supra* note 14.
[17] *See, e.g.*, Ward Farnsworth, *Do Parties to Nuisance Cases Bargain after Judgment?: A Glimpse inside the Cathedral*, 66 U. Chi. L. Rev. 373 (1999).
[18] Kaplow & Shavell, *supra* note 14.
[19] Hylton, *Property Rules and Liability Rules, supra* note 14.
[20] *Id.* (surveying misallocations: socially wasteful expenditures on law enforcement and litigation to protect property, discouragement of investment in property).

a manner under the property rule.[21] Thus, even if we could find a setting where rational and informed bargaining is virtually free of any impediments, there would still be a strong case in that setting to prefer the property rule to the liability rule.

V. SOURCES OF TORT LAW

Up to this point I have offered a survey of theories of what forms the content of tort law. Whether tort law is shaped primarily by economic or by moral considerations, one question that remains is how those considerations work their way into the law. In other words, what are the sources of tort law?

Legal positivists argue that the law consists of rules provided through sources authorized by the state, such as legislative codes or judicial opinions. Whatever the underlying theory from which the law springs, that theory must find its way into the intentions of legislators, judges, and other officials with authority to state the law if that theory is to have any effect on the law's form. Law, in the positivist vision, has no necessary connection with morality,[22] or with economic optimality.[23] Law is imposed on a society, like a birdcage, and it need not respect the patterns or conventions that arose before or during the law's formation.

Natural law theorists,[24] in contrast, believe that law can consist of norms and conventions that are adopted by society, or even of religious injunctions. In the natural law theorist's view, moral norms that are accepted by society should be viewed as laws. Thus, if a society adhered to the Kantian system of ethics, that system would constitute a source of law. If law is comparable to a birdcage, it is one that must respect the pathways already cut by a society.

The natural law position was given its most influential exposition in 1765 by William Blackstone in his *Commentaries on the Laws of England*. According to Blackstone, the common law

is the perfection of reason, . . . it always intends to conform thereto, and . . . what is not reason is not law.[25]

---

[21] Hylton, *Property Rules and Defensive Conduct, supra* note 14; Smith, *supra* note 14.

[22] H. L. A. Hart, *Positivism and the Separation of Law and Morals*, 71 Harv. L. Rev. 593 (1957); Joseph Raz, The Authority of Law (Clarendon Press 1979). For a modern overview, *see* Anthony J. Sebok, *Misunderstanding Positivism*, 93 Mich. L. Rev. 2054 (1995).

[23] Modern positivists have drawn many subtle distinctions between the law versus morality divide. For example, one such distinction is that while the moral content of rules is largely irrelevant in determining legal validity, the rules themselves have moral value in serving to settle rights. *See* John Gardner, *Legal Positivism: 5 ½ Myths*, 46 Am. J. Juris. 199 (2001).

[24] John Finnis, Natural Law and Natural Rights (Clarendon Press 1980). On morality and law from a perspective generally favorable to natural law theorists, *see* Lon L. Fuller, The Morality of Law (Yale Univ. Press rev. ed. 1969); Ronald Dworkin, Taking Rights Seriously (Harvard Univ. Press 1978); Brian Bix, *On the Dividing Line between Natural Law Theory and Legal Positivism*, 75 Notre Dame L. Rev. 1613 (2001).

[25] 1 William Blackstone, Commentaries on the Laws of England *70.

In Blackstone's view, society develops rules of reason, through contracts, conventions, understandings, and implicit agreements. Courts adopt these reasonableness norms as law through their decisions in disputes. Thus, in the natural law theory presented by Blackstone, courts take a passive role in creating common law rules, because those rules are based on reasonableness norms that exist independently of the courts as guidelines for social interaction. Courts do not create common law as much as they discover it through adjudication.

The opposing positivist vision was soon offered, in a rebuke to Blackstone, by utilitarian philosopher (and former Blackstone student) Jeremy Bentham.[26] To Bentham, rules of reason were meaningless in an objective sense. The only way anyone could understand reasonableness, according to Bentham, was in the subjective sense of thinking that anything that he or she likes must be reasonable. The only alternative to the mystical notion of reasonableness was that of the state that declares and enforces legal rules. Governments do not consult society, religion, philosophy, or economics to create legal rules in Bentham's account. They impose those rules to meet the needs of whoever is in power. And far from being the perfection of reason, Bentham thought that the common law contained many rules designed to transfer wealth to lawyers and other advantaged classes.

Tort law, as will become clear in the chapters that follow, is full of rules of reason. Most tort law violations are described as violations of the reasonable man standard. This is a reflection of the common law basis of tort doctrine, and also due to the adherence of judges to the modes of explanation adopted hundreds of years ago.

Roughly a century after Bentham, Oliver Wendell Holmes, Jr., became the chief exponent of legal positivism in the United States. However, unlike Bentham, Holmes viewed the common law favorably and offered a comprehensive utilitarian justification for it.[27] Holmes is also credited as the chief exponent of legal realism, the notion that law does not evolve, as legal formalists believed, in strict logical adherence to existing rules.[28] Law reflects experience, and courts use it to solve practical problems. Because of this, the content and the application of law to new cases cannot be deduced, in a top-down fashion, from existing legal principles. The law cannot be traced back or reduced to a fundamental set of axioms, as Christopher Columbus Langdell, founder of the case method of law teaching, had instructed students of Holmes's era.

Holmes did not view the common law as inherently corruptible, as did Bentham, but he recognized that it is influenced by the demands of litigants and the preferences of judges. In any event, the floodgates of legal realism have since opened wide. The

---

[26] JEREMY BENTHAM, A FRAGMENT ON GOVERNMENT (F. C. Montague ed., Clarendon Press 1891) (1776); see also RICHARD A. POSNER, Bentham and Blackstone in THE ECONOMICS OF JUSTICE 13, 13–47 (Harvard Univ. Press 1983).

[27] OLIVER WENDELL HOLMES, JR., THE COMMON LAW (Little, Brown and Co. 1881).

[28] Following Holmes, Roscoe Pound developed a philosophically based defense of legal realism in his book AN INTRODUCTION TO THE PHILOSOPHY OF LAW (Yale Univ. Press 1922).

utilitarianism of Holmes has been modernized in the form of economic analysis of law. The class-based exploitation through law discussed by Bentham has given way to a variety of critical theories based on Marxism, sex, and race.

Although largely a matter of theoretical interest today, the contrast between positive and natural law views has some practical implications for tort law. Under the positivist vision, courts should strive to make the rules of tort law as clear and predictable as possible, so that individuals can learn them and conform to them.[29] Once a rule has been stated clearly, there is no need for a court to consult a jury other than to determine some contested issue of fact. On issues of law, the only time that a court should consult a jury is when it is not sure that it has enough information to decide a case correctly under its own legal standards.[30]

Holmes attempted to impose this positivist model onto the common law in two cases: first, as a Justice of the Massachusetts Supreme Judicial Court, in *Lorenzo v. Wirth*,[31] and later, as a U.S. Supreme Court Justice, in *Baltimore and Ohio R.R. v. Goodman*.[32] *Lorenzo* dealt with a coal hole – an unfamiliar feature today, but common when homes were heated by coal. A coal hole is an underground bunker, with an opening on the sidewalk, where a coal supplier deposits coal so that it can be used in the furnace of a home. The plaintiff had been injured by falling into a coal hole. Holmes held that the plaintiff was negligent as a matter of law, given that everyone was on notice about the existence of coal holes, and that courts should not permit juries to examine every such case in an effort to find a basis for awarding damages to the plaintiff. *Goodman* dealt with a plaintiff who had been run over by a train at a rail crossing, an unfortunately frequent occurrence in the late 1800s and early 1900s. Holmes held that it was negligence as a matter of law for a person to fail to stop, get out of his car, and look and listen at a rail crossing; again, there should be no need for juries to look for some basis to award damages to the plaintiff in such cases.

Under the anti-positivist or natural law view, tort law should consult the jury on a continuous basis to ensure that law remains consistent with norms of society,[33] because there is no separation between society's norms and legal standards. Moreover, the law can be mistaken because it departs from the reasonableness norms adopted by society.

No judge has articulated this anti-positivist vision clearly and consistently, but the closest that a judge has come to it is Supreme Court Justice Benjamin Cardozo's opinion in *Pokora v. Wabash Ry.*,[34] another case involving an accident at a rail crossing. *Pokora* overturned the presumptive negligence rule Holmes established

---

[29] *Id.* at 123–124.
[30] *Id.*
[31] 170 Mass. 596, 49 N.E. 1010 (1898).
[32] 275 U.S. 66 (1927).
[33] *See* Pokora v. Wabash Ry., 292 U.S. 98, 105–106 (1934) (Cardozo, J.).
[34] *Id.*

in *Goodman*, and Cardozo added a few extra lines rejecting the positivist theory of Holmes.

Some of the rules of tort law that will be examined in later chapters have more to do with the allocation of power between judge and jury than with substantive content. This is not to suggest that these rules are unimportant; whether a legal standard is applied by a jury or by a judge can have serious implications for the regulatory effect of the standard. When courts examine these rules, however, they are making decisions about the source of tort law – whether it will be drawn from social norms and conventions or whether it will be superimposed over those folkways by judges on the basis of their preferences, inclinations, and reading of prior case law. The policies that inform tort law are vitally important, and so are their sources.

3

Evolution of Tort Law

The previous chapter introduced the basic concepts of strict liability and negligence, and examined incentives under the two standards. But these tort standards have not always been available to plaintiffs. The tort system began with a very narrow scope of application, basically restricted to giving victims of crime a forum in which to seek compensation from their injurers. As time passed, tort law expanded to permit victims of less serious infringements, such as accidents on the roads, a means of seeking redress in the courts. This chapter examines how this change came about.

The short answer is that the change occurred through an evolutionary process. As the tort system expanded, the old rules that worked reasonably well under its early narrow scope began to generate unintended consequences and poor results. This led, in turn, to pressure to reform the tort system within the common law process, through modifications of tort doctrine, which is what occurred over the centuries. This chapter examines this process of evolution from the earliest to the modern tort cases.

Along the way this chapter explores one long-standing controversy in tort theory: whether the underlying norm of ancient tort law was strict liability or liability based on fault (negligence). This question was addressed by Holmes in his book on the common law.[1]

Holmes argued that the fault principle was evident in the earliest tort cases, and distinguished his position from two alternatives: that an individual always acts at his peril (strict liability) and that tort liability results from a failure to comply with moral norms (ethical liability).[2] The strict liability theory, a prominent account of tort liability at least since the mid–nineteenth century, has received additional support from the modern thesis that courts adopted the fault principle near the end

---

[1] OLIVER WENDELL HOLMES, JR., THE COMMON LAW (1881).
[2] *Id.* at 77–129.

. of the Industrial Revolution to subsidize emerging industries.[3] The ethical theory has also been a prominent account, but it has not featured much in the historical controversy over the nature of ancient tort liability. Hence, in this chapter I will explore the broader distinction between strict liability and fault as foundational principles in tort law – not the more fine-grained distinction between objectivist and ethical theories of fault.

I find that the evidence supports Holmes's view that the fault requirement has been a basic element of tort liability from early on, and that strict liability was not the default rule of ancient tort law. My goal in this chapter is to fill in additional pieces in this long-running argument: first, by showing the similarity between modern and early tort law, and, second, by explaining in functional terms how the law has changed between ancient and modern epochs.[4]

I. EARLY CASES

The writ system greatly impacted the development of early tort law. *A writ was a formal order giving the plaintiff access to the king's court, authorizing a designated court to try the case, and directing the sheriff to summon the defendant to court.*[5] A simple way to think of the writ is as a type of ticket that permitted the plaintiff to get into a common law court and argue his case. It also required the defendant to show up and defend himself. The early tort cases involved the *trespass writ*, which was formally restricted to cases involving a direct application of force.

The Thorns Case

Following the tradition of the textbooks, I offer the *Thorns Case*,[6] of 1466, as the principal illustration of ancient tort liability. The *Thorns Case* and other early cases appear in the Year Books, which were the law reports of Medieval England.[7]

---

[3] MORTON J. HORWITZ, THE TRANSFORMATION OF AMERICAN LAW, 1780–1860 85–89 (Harvard Univ. Press 1977).

[4] The order of cases and topics addressed in this chapter follows the discussion in Holmes's book and especially RICHARD A. EPSTEIN & CATHERINE M. SHARKEY, CASES AND MATERIALS ON TORTS (Aspen Pub. 10th ed. 2012). The Epstein & Sharkey casebook, in turn, follows Epstein's masterful treatment in CHARLES O. GREGORY, HARRY KALVEN, AND RICHARD A. EPSTEIN, CASES AND MATERIALS ON TORTS, 47–74 (Little, Brown and Company 3d ed. 1977). The chapter on the evolution of negligence in the third edition of the Gregory, Kalven, and Epstein casebook, the first edition to which Epstein contributed, is considerably more sophisticated and thorough than the presentations of the topic in other casebooks. The original presentation of Epstein, and in several revisions of his casebook, appear to reject Holmes's view of the centrality of the negligence principle in early tort law.

[5] *See, e.g.,* C. GORDON POST, AN INTRODUCTION TO THE LAW 30 (Prentice-Hall 1963).

[6] The Thorns Case (Hull v. Orange), Y.B. Mich. 6 Edw. 4, f. 7, pl. 18 (1466).

[7] The Year Books are the principle source of materials regarding the development of legal concepts, doctrine, and methods between 1290 and 1535, during which time the common law developed into the form we recognize today. For a searchable database of the Year Books compiled by

Containing summaries written in Law French and Latin, the Year Books are not a source that law students or lawyers today would regularly consult; indeed, only the most committed legal historians would attempt to read them. I will take advantage of Fifoot's magnificent presentation of the case:[8]

> A man brought a writ of Trespass quare vi et armis clausum fregit . . . and alleged the trespass in 5 acres and the defendant said, as to the coming, etc. and as to the trespass in the 5 acres, not guilty and, as to the trespass in the 5 acres, that the plaintiff ought not to have an action for he says that he has an acre of land on which a thorn hedge grows, adjoining the said 5 acres, and that he, at the time of the supposed trespass, came and cut the thorns, and that they, against his will, fell on the said acres of the plaintiff, and that he came freshly on to the said acres and took them, which is the same trespass for which he has conceived this action. And on this they demurred and it was well argued, and was adjourned.

The report continues with an account of the arguments presented by the lawyers (Catesby, Fairfax, Pigot, Yonge, and Brian) and closes with the conclusions of the judges, Littleton and Choke. Judge Littleton said:

> If a man suffers damage, it is right that he be recompensed; and to my intent the case which Catesby has put is not law; for if your cattle come on to my land and eat my grass, notwithstanding you come freshly and drive them out, it is proper for you to make amends for what your cattle have done, be it more or less. . . . And sir, if it were the law that he could enter and take the thorns by the same reasoning, if he cut a great tree, he could come with his carts and horses and carry off the tree, which is not reason, for peradventure he has corn or other crops growing, etc.[9]

Chief Judge Choke said:

> [W]hen he cut the thorns and they fell on to my land, this falling was not lawful, and then his coming to take them away was not lawful. As to what has been said that they fell ipso invito (without his intent), this is not a good plea; but he should have said that he could not do it in any other manner or that he did all that was in his power to keep them out; otherwise he shall pay damages. And, Sir, if the thorns or a great tree had fallen on his land by the blowing of the wind, in this case he might have come on to the land to take them, since the falling had then been not his act, but that of the wind.[10]

Professor David J. Seipp and additional information on the Year Books, *see Legal History: The Year Books*, Bos. Univ. Sch. of Law, *available at* http://www.bu.edu/law/seipp/.

[8] C. H. S. Fifoot, History and Sources of the Common Law: Tort and Contract 195–197 (Stevens 1949).

[9] *Id.*

[10] *Id.*

Some scholars have argued that the *Thorns Case* adopts a theory of strict liability.[11] Littleton's statements, coupled with the court's decision to hold the defendant liable, seem to support this view. On the other hand, the court's decision and the words used by both judges can be reconciled with modern negligence law. Notice that Judge Choke says that the defendant should have pleaded "that he did all that was in his power to keep them out," which suggests that he did not think that strict liability was the appropriate legal standard.

Consider what modern tort law would say about the facts in the *Thorns Case*. At its core, the case involves the privilege to enter another's land to recapture one's personal property. Suppose I'm cutting thorns off a tree, and for some reason I regard the thorns as valuable. The thorns land on my neighbor's property. Do I have a privilege to enter his property to retake the thorns? Will I have to pay damages for any harm that I do to his property?

To answer these questions, consider the ways in which the thorns might end up on my neighbor's property. One: The wind blows them over. Two: I throw them over myself. Three: I negligently drop them on his property.

Supposing the wind blows the thorns over with no negligence on my part, the doctrine of *necessity* (part of modern tort law discussed in Chapter 4) may provide a legal privilege for me to enter my neighbor's property to recapture the thorns. Necessity law excuses land invasions that would otherwise be trespasses when they result from an effort to recapture valuable property in danger of being lost or stolen, provided that the property being recaptured did not enter the other person's land through the fault of the recapturing party. In addition, given the absence of fault in connection with the thorns' landing, I would not be liable for any harm done to my neighbor's property by the thorns when they fell.[12]

Now consider what happens if I throw the thorns over, or if I negligently let them fall on my neighbor's property. In this case I am liable for whatever harm the thorns do to my neighbor's property. Moreover, I do not have a privilege to enter the neighbor's property to recapture the thorns. I am a trespasser the moment I enter his property.

Compare this summary of modern law to what the judges said in the *Thorns Case*. Littleton's comments aren't helpful because they do not suggest any defenses. Focus instead on Choke's remarks, which instruct the defendant's lawyers on what they should have said. He notes that the argument that the thorns fell without the

---

[11] *See, e.g.,* David J. Ibbetson, A Historical Introduction to the Law of Obligations 58 (Oxford Univ. Press 2001) (1999); and more generally, Morris S. Arnold, *Accident, Mistake, and Rules of Liability in the Fourteenth Century Law of Torts,* 128 U. Pa. L. Rev. 361, 374–376 (1979).

[12] Two additional implications follow from the more detailed examination of necessity doctrine in Chapter 4. First, since the privilege to recapture means that I am not a trespasser, the neighbor does not have the right to use force to expel me (Chapter 4, discussion of *Ploof v. Putnam*). Second, I will be held liable for whatever damage I do to the neighbor's property when I invade it to recapture my personal property (Chapter 3, discussion of *Vincent v. Lake Erie*).

defendant's intent was not a good plea; the defendant should have said that the thorns fell in spite of the fact that he did all that was in his power to keep them out. In other words, Choke explains that the defendant should have set out statements in his responsive plea that countered any notion of negligence as the reason the thorns fell on the plaintiff's land. Choke goes on to mention the wind blowing them over as another possible justification.

Choke's remarks are remarkably close to the modern law regarding the privilege to recapture. Still, differences are noticeable. First, the early pleading convention put the burden on the defendant to enter a plea countering any notion of intent or negligence. That is different from today's law, which requires the plaintiff to allege intent or negligence (*Brown v. Kendall*, later in this chapter). Second, Choke's comments say nothing about the duty to compensate even when one has a privilege (Chapter 3, *Vincent v. Lake Erie*). Perhaps the law, still at a relatively primitive stage, did not require compensation by the privileged party. Or perhaps the judges saw no need to address the compensation issue given the state of the pleadings. In any event, modern law recognizes a privilege on the part of the defendant under the right conditions (for example, no negligence), which would prevent a court from finding him guilty of trespass. The law at the time of the *Thorns Case* appears to have been the same.

All of this suggests that the *Thorns Case* tells us more about differences in procedure than about differences in substantive law. Under common law pleading, the defendant had to set forth his justifications in response to a writ of trespass. And once one of the parties had demurred, the judges had to make a decision based on the contentions in the pleadings. Blackstone defined the *demurrer* as a statement that "confesses the facts to be true, as stated by the opposite party; but denies that, by the law arising upon those facts, any injury is done to the plaintiff, or that the defendant has made out a legitimate excuse."[13]

The demurrer was a litigation gambit. It was equivalent to throwing your cards on the table, and saying to the judges, "Tell us who wins." The case would be decided on the basis of the pleadings and the evidence supporting them.[14] In light of this, it would be a dangerous thing for a litigant to make a mistake in the pleadings and forget to set out an important legal justification. And that is what we see in the *Thorns Case*; the plaintiff demurred, and the defendant had not, as Choke explained, set out a valid legal justification. The only justification offered by the defendant was *ipso invito* (without intent), which was legally insufficient.

Although the *Thorns Case* has been described as adopting a presumption of strict liability, a close look suggests that it does not. In fact, the law declared in the *Thorns Case* is quite close to the law that exists today.

---

[13] 3 BLACKSTONE, COMMENTARIES, *314.

[14] *Id.* at 314–324; THEODORE FRANK & THOMAS PLUCKNETT, A CONCISE HISTORY OF THE COMMON LAW 413 (Little, Brown and Co. 1956).

The Shooting Cases

A series of cases involving accidental shootings have been cited in support of the proposition that the default rule in early tort law was strict liability. The first is *Weaver v. Ward*,[15] followed by *Dickenson v. Watson*,[16] *Underwood v. Hewson*,[17] and *Castle v. Duryee*.[18] The shooting cases following *Weaver v. Ward* relied on the precedent in that case.

In *Weaver v. Ward*, two military men were practicing their exercises when one accidentally shot and wounded the other. The defendant pleaded that the shooting happened without his intent, that it was an accident. The plaintiff demurred, and the court awarded damages to the plaintiff.

As in the *Thorns Case*, the defendant's plea, that it happened without any intent to harm, was insufficient to avoid liability. The court noted that even if the defendant were a "lunatick" he still would have been held liable for the shooting. However, the court also suggested certain arguments the defendant could have made to avoid liability; specifically, the defendant should have set forth facts to show that there was no negligence on his part.

We see two things in *Weaver v. Ward*. First, the court's reference to the defendant's failure to plead lack of negligence indicates that it did not adopt a theory of strict liability. The court explained, for the benefit of other lawyers, that if the defendant's lawyers had pleaded lack of negligence he might have avoided liability.

Second, we see again the impact of common law procedure. Under common law pleading, the defendant had a duty to set out pleas justifying his conduct. If the defendant failed to do so, and the plaintiff demurred, the defendant lost his case. That is different from modern civil procedure, which as a general matter never puts the burden on the defendant to prove his innocence. Under modern procedure, the defendant can simply deny the plaintiff's allegations, leaving the burden on the plaintiff to prove his case.

The later shooting cases follow the same pattern as *Weaver v. Ward*. In *Dickenson v. Watson*, the defendant accidentally shot the plaintiff and argued that he should not be held liable for trespass *vi et armis* (by force and arms) because the shooting was not done with an intent to harm. The plaintiff demurred, and the court held the defendant liable, citing *Weaver v. Ward*. However, the *Dickenson* decision, unlike *Weaver v. Ward*, does not discuss the negligence issue, perhaps because the court thought that its citation to *Weaver v. Ward* would have made such a discussion unnecessary. Whatever the reason, this omission may be responsible for the impression that the shooting cases were applying strict liability. But given their

---

[15] 80 Eng. Rep. 284 (K.B. 1616).
[16] T. Jones 205, 84 Eng. Rep. 1218 (K.B. 1682).
[17] 93 Eng. Rep. 722 (K.B. 1723).
[18] 2 Keyes 169, 175 (N.Y. 1865). *See* Holmes, *supra* note 1, at 87.

reliance on *Weaver v. Ward*, the shooting cases do not support the strict liability theory.

II. THE EXPANDING TRESPASS WRIT

Any discussion of early tort cases will say a great deal about civil procedure. The previous cases have provided examples of the importance of pleading conventions under the trespass writ. As I noted earlier, the writ system – that is, ancient civil procedure – greatly impacted the development of tort law.

The early cases considered to this point involved the trespass writ. The trespass writ was formally restricted to cases involving a direct application of force. The *Thorns Case* begins with a statement that the plaintiff brought a writ of trespass *quare vi et armis clausum fregit* (by force and arms breaking the plaintiff's close). The phrase *vi et armis* was standard for trespass claims, because the assertion of a breach of peace was necessary to gain access to the king's courts, instead of the default option of the manorial courts. However, the *Thorns Case* did not involve anything approaching a breach of peace. That a nonviolent, mundane trespass claim of the sort in the *Thorns Case* would be brought under a writ titled "trespass by force and arms" suggests that the trespass writ, by 1466, had expanded in scope to encompass a much larger set of claims than initially intended.

The steady, creeping expansion of the trespass writ is an important part of the story of the development of tort law, and of the common law generally. The royal courts were originally part of a system of law enforcement designed to maintain peace in the entire kingdom. For that purpose they served to resolve disputes involving serious breaches of the peace: felonies, such as attempted murder, rape, and burglary, or land disputes falling outside of the jurisdiction of the manorial system. The manorial courts were inadequate for resolving disputes of this sort. Thus, under the original design, royal courts were essential in maintaining general security and stability throughout the country, while manorial courts focused on less significant disputes, such as petty thefts and accidents.

While the general security provided by a system that credibly promises to capture and punish murderers is obvious, the social stability benefit should not be discounted. Feudal lords had access to their own private militias. The royal courts, by providing a relatively neutral dispute resolution forum for the most serious harms, probably played a role in preventing the state from spiraling into a chaotic hell of warring factions.

As time passed, the jurisdiction of the royal courts expanded as they permitted a larger number of plaintiffs to gain access through the trespass writ. One of the ways in which more plaintiffs were given access is the simple process of reasoning by analogy. If a direct application of force is necessary to gain access to the king's courts, then, one could argue, any direct application of force, no matter how unimportant in its implications for general security, should be sufficient under the trespass writ.

Through this process of reasoning disputes such as the *Thorns Case* found their way into royal courts. Another way in which more plaintiffs gained access to royal courts was through the use of *legal fictions*, interpretive ruses in which courts assumed the presence (or absence) of a fact to permit a plaintiff to bring a lawsuit that did not really meet the requirements of the trespass writ. For example, disputes involving injuries done to horses by blacksmiths found their way into royal courts under the trespass writ because of these legal fictions,[19] as did lawsuits against carpenters for forcibly chopping up timber.[20]

The security and independence that made royal common law courts necessary for resolving disputes that involved serious breaches of the peace also made them attractive to plaintiffs with complaints of a less serious nature. Thus, if a person had a dispute with a manorial lord, or someone closely connected to such a lord, he would have a strong preference for the king's courts. The king's judges could be relied upon to decide a case according to the common law, rather than under the threat of force from a lesser lord. This preference for the greater security enveloping the king's courts would be just as strong whether the dispute involved a direct use of force or an accidental injury. If a manorial lord, or one of his relatives or friends, had injured a tenant through the careless management of his horse, the tenant would have every reason to prefer to be in the king's courts over such a dispute as when the injury was accomplished through an intentional trampling.

These developments occurred in an environment that was depressingly violent and chaotic. The murder rate in England in 1300 was roughly 100 times its present level,[21] and this estimate does not include war casualties. One estimate that presumably includes war casualties puts the percentage of deaths due to violence among elite English males at 26 percent in the year 1400 – a rate that implies that one out of four of the associates of such a male would be killed in a private dispute or in a war or warlike event.[22] The carrying of weapons was common: a knife, for example, was seen as a necessary implement given that eating utensils were not readily available. Almost every man owned a longbow or crossbow and practiced shooting at archery fields (butts) regularly, both for sport and for obligatory war preparation, which led to numerous accidental injuries of a very serious nature. Tools used for farming

---

[19] S. F. C. MILSOM, HISTORICAL FOUNDATIONS OF THE COMMON LAW 283–313 (Butterworths, 2d ed. 1981); Epstein & Sharkey, *supra* note 4, at 89–90. It is unlikely that any of the blacksmiths had committed a trespass in the traditional sense of the term. If a substantial percentage of blacksmiths forcefully took horses from their owners and deliberately injured them, the entire profession would have gone out of business. However, a negligent practice complaint could be made to fit within the trespass writ by describing only the strike and the injury that occurred, leaving out any reference to the fact that the horse had been entrusted to the blacksmith.

[20] J. H. Baker, AN INTRODUCTION TO ENGLISH LEGAL HISTORY 61 (4th ed. 2002).

[21] Manuel Eisner, *Modernization, Self-Control and Lethal Violence: The Long-Term Dynamics of European Homicide Rates in Theoretical Perspective*, 41 BRIT. J. CRIMINOL. 618 (2001).

[22] GREGORY CLARK, A FAREWELL TO ALMS: A BRIEF ECONOMIC HISTORY OF THE WORLD 122 (Princeton Univ. Press 2007).

or herding, such as the quarterstaff, were turned into weapons with ease. Indeed, the quarterstaff, or "stick," was so common that one of the lawyers arguing for the plaintiff in the *Thorns Case* offered a hypothetical to the court in which "a man makes an assault upon me," and "in my own defence I raise my stick to strike him, and a man is behind me and in raising my stick I wound him."[23]

The ever-present threat of violence, the oldest method of resolving disputes, cast a shadow over the courts. In a critique of ancient common law rules prohibiting third parties from funding and supporting litigation, Jeremy Bentham noted that the prohibitions arose in response to attempts to intimidate judges through threats of force.[24] Bentham described it as "a mischief, in those times but too common," that a feudal lord "would buy a weak claim, in hopes that power might convert it into a strong one, and that the sword of a baron, stalking into court with a rabble of retainers at his heels, might strike terror into the eyes of a judge upon the bench."[25] In such an environment, it is not surprising that plaintiffs would prefer the relative security of the royal courts, backed by the king's armies.

In addition to the attractiveness of common law courts to plaintiffs, jurisdictional expansion occurred because courts themselves had strong incentives to take in more cases under the trespass writ, through reasoning by analogy and the use of legal fictions. The courts were a source of revenue for the crown. Moreover, judges earned additional income from hearing more cases. As much as 30 percent of the judge's income came from the fees paid by litigants.[26]

Given the magnet effect of security and the private incentives of the king's judges, there was little to stand in the way of the expansion of the scope of the trespass writ. The only barrier to continuous expansion was the formal limitation of the writ to instances of direct and immediate applications of force.

That barrier began to give over the late 1300s,[27] as courts began to develop a new writ called *trespass on the case*. Blackstone described it as follows:

> There are wrongs or injuries unaccompanied by force, for which there is a remedy in damages by a special action of trespass, upon the case. This action, of trespass, or transgression, on the case, is an universal remedy, given for all personal wrongs and injuries without force; so called, because the plaintiff's whole case or cause of complaint is set forth at length in the original writ. For though in general there are methods prescribed and forms of action previously settled, for redressing those wrongs which most usually occur, and in which the very act itself is immediately prejudicial or injurious to the plaintiff's person or property, as battery, nonpayment of debts, detaining one's goods, or the like; yet where any special consequential

---

[23] The Thorns Case (Hull v. Orange), Y.B. Mich. 6 Edw. 4, f. 7, pl. 18 (1466).

[24] 3 THE WORKS OF JEREMY BENTHAM (DEFENSE OF USURY) 19–20 (Bowring ed. 1843).

[25] *Id.*

[26] Daniel Klerman, *Jurisdictional Competition and the Evolution of the Common Law*, 74 U. CHI. L. REV. 1179, 1189 (2007).

[27] Elizabeth Jean Dix, *The Origins of the Action of Trespass on the Case*, 46 YALE L. J. 1142, 1168 (1937).

damage arises which could not be foreseen and provided for in the ordinary course of justice, the party injured is allowed, . . . to bring a special action on his own case, by a writ formed according to the peculiar circumstances of his own particular grievance. For wherever the common law gives a right or prohibits an injury, it also gives a remedy by action; and therefore, wherever a new injury is done, a new method of remedy must be pursued. And it is a settled distinction, that where an act is done which is in itself an immediate injury to another's person or property, there the remedy is usually by an action of trespass vi et armis: but where there is no act done, but only a culpable omission; or where the act is not immediately injurious, but only by consequence and collaterally; there no action of trespass vi et armis will lie, but an action on the special case, for the damages consequent on such omission or act.[28]

In view of the history of the trespass writ, the development of the action on the case, the precursor to the modern negligence claim, was more a recognition of existing reality than a new development in the common law. The forces that led to the development of the action on the case had been at work for many years under the trespass writ. The jurisdictional expansion of the common law courts resulted primarily from their enhanced security: The king's judges could decide disputes relatively free of the threat of force from the lesser lords.[29] This, in turn, enabled common law judges to professionalize and the law to develop free of the biases that would have been induced by intimidation.

III. TRESPASS AND CASE

The development of the action on the case led to a regime in which plaintiffs had to choose between two writs: trespass and case (or trespass on the case). The distinction between the two was that trespass was appropriate for direct harms and case was appropriate for indirect harms. The standard examples used to illustrate this distinction were the following. If I throw a log and it hits you in the head, you have an action against me for trespass (for assault and battery) because the harm is "direct and immediate." On the other hand, if I throw a log, and it lands on the road, and later you are injured by tripping over the log in the road, you have an action against me for trespass on the case.[30]

The formal distinction between trespass and case was a source of trouble for some plaintiffs. As a general rule, distinctions in the law between direct injuries and indirect injuries typically lead to confusion. The reason is that the terms direct and indirect do not have obviously distinct applications that would allow someone

---

[28] 3 WILLIAM BLACKSTONE, COMMENTARIES ON THE LAWS OF ENGLAND 122–123 (University of Chicago Press 1979) (1765).

[29] On the role of security in the development of the common law, see Edward L. Glaeser & Andrei Shleifer, *Legal Origins*, 117 Q. J. ECON. 1193 (2002).

[30] Reynolds v. Clarke, 1 Str. 634, 92 Eng. Rep. 410 (1726).

to determine the appropriate term in every instance. Inevitably, some case arises in which it is difficult to determine whether an interference or invasion should be characterized as direct or indirect.

The most famous example of the uncertainty generated by the distinction between trespass and case is *Scott v. Shepherd*.[31] Shepherd, walking by a market-house (a covered structure supported by arches and open at the sides) on the day of a fair, threw a lighted squib into it. The squib landed near the table of Yates. Willis, nearby, picked it up and threw it across the house, and it landed near the table of Ryal. Ryal immediately picked it up and hurled it away from him. It hit Scott in the face and exploded, putting out his eye.

Scott brought a trespass action against Shepherd. The judges (Nares, Gould, Blackstone, and De Grey) were divided. Nares and Gould argued that the action was maintainable because the injury was a natural and probable consequence of the defendant's conduct. Blackstone (yes, of Blackstone's *Commentaries*) thought that the plaintiff's claim should be rejected. According to Blackstone, each intermediate decision to throw the squib was an independent trespass, severable from the initial act of Shepherd. It was as if Shepherd had thrown a rock into the market-house and the intermediaries proceeded to throw the rock around, and eventually hit Scott. Under this line of reasoning, the correct writ, to be brought by Scott against Shepherd, would be trespass on the case. Chief Judge De Grey agreed with Nares and said that he did not consider the intermediate actors to be "free agents." He thought that they acted out of a "compulsive necessity" for their own safety. The plaintiff, Scott, won.

The difference between the opposing positions of the judges in *Scott v. Shepherd* is based on whether the intermediate actors should be viewed as free agents. If they were free agents, then they acted rationally and purposively in deciding whether, and where, to throw the squib. It was a voluntary decision, though apparently not done with intent to harm anyone. Still, they acted in full awareness of what they were doing, capable of weighing the consequences. As we will see in the following chapter, this level of awareness – making a deliberate choice between alternative courses of action – is both necessary and sufficient for trespass liability.

If the intermediate actors were not free agents, then they were not acting rationally and purposively when they decided to throw the squib. To use De Grey's language, they may have acted out of compulsive necessity, unable under the circumstances to weigh the consequences of their actions. The only thought that may have been clear to them at the time was the intense desire to expel the squib as soon as possible. Their actions were reflexive and instinctive, rather than rational and deliberate.

Scott v. Shepherd has implications for our understanding of trespass law (see Chapter 4). It tells us that the intent required to be held liable for trespass assumes some level of rational choice or decision making connected to the actor's conduct. If the defendant's actions were as instinctive as putting up your arm to block your

---

[31] Scott v. Shepherd, 96 Eng. Rep. 525 (K.B. 1773).

face from a blow, that is insufficient to meet the intent (or mental state) required for trespass.

IV. PROBLEMS WITH THE WRIT SYSTEM AND THE INTRODUCTION OF MODERN TORT PLEADING

As *Scott v. Shepherd* illustrates, the availability of trespass and trespass on the case cast a cloud of uncertainty over some disputes, with the result that a plaintiff with a perfectly legitimate claim could lose his suit because he used the wrong writ. In many accidents it was difficult for the plaintiff to tell whether the injury was direct or indirect, or whether it was due to the carelessness of the defendant or to the intentional use of force.[32] In addition, the availability of two writs allowed defendants to game the system strategically.

For example, if my horse-drawn carriage runs yours off the road, was that due to carelessness in maintaining my carriage,[33] or did I intentionally veer over, knowing that the effect would be to run you off the road? If you sued in trespass, I could argue that this was all due to carelessness on my part in maintaining the carriage, leading to the conclusion that you had sued under the wrong writ and must therefore lose. If you sued in case, I could explain to the court that I intended to run you off the road, again pointing to the conclusion that you had sued under the wrong writ.

The formal distinctions between trespass and case provided almost limitless opportunities for strategic gamesmanship by defendants. To take one simple example, consider *Hopper v. Reeve*,[34] a fine illustration of the gamesmanship problem. The defendant ran his gig (a light, two-wheeled carriage drawn by one horse) into a carriage carrying the plaintiff's wife. The plaintiff brought an action for trespass to the wife. The defendant sought (unsuccessfully) to overturn the verdict for the plaintiff on the ground that the plaintiff had sued under the wrong writ. The defendant said that the plaintiff should have brought an action on the case rather than a trespass claim, because the plaintiff's complaint alleged only that the defendant had run his gig into a carriage carrying the wife, and since it could have been anyone's carriage, the injury to the wife was a consequential rather than immediate result of the defendant's action.

---

[32] Epstein & Sharkey, *supra* note 4, at 95; M. J. Prichard, *Trespass, Case and the Rule in Williams v. Holland*, 22 *Cambridge* L. J. 234 (1964); Thomas Atkins Street, The Foundations of Legal Liability: A Presentation of the Theory and Development of the Common Law 250–265 (Edward Thompson Co. 1906), available at http://books.google.com/books/id=AnQaAAAAYAAJ. For an example of the difficulty of distinguishing whether trespass or case is the right action, consider an accident on the seas. The defendant's ship may have been deliberately steered into the plaintiff's, or it may have been pushed by the wind. *See* Covell v. Laming, 1 Camp. 492 (1808) (finding trespass action valid).

[33] Day v. Edwards, 5 Term Rep. 648, 101 Eng. Rep. 361 (1794); Leame v. Bray, 3 East 593, 102 Eng. Rep. 724 (1803).

[34] 7 Taunt. 698 (1817).

TABLE 3.1. *Case characteristics and writ type*
under ancient law

	Intentional	Negligent
Direct	Trespass writ	Trespass writ
Indirect	Case writ	Case writ

[handwritten annotations: "battery trespass"; "road accidents"; "trip over dropped log"; "trip over thrown log"]

The solution to the strategic gaming problem came when *the courts held that a plaintiff could sue in case whether the harm was direct or indirect, as the long as the plaintiff could show that it resulted from the defendant's fault.*[35] Fault encompasses the notions of both negligence and intent, so that the defendant could not escape liability by saying that he intended to injure the plaintiff.

The history of the writ system can be summarized in a pair of diagrams. Recall that the key issues in determining the appropriate type of action were whether the defendant's conduct could be characterized as direct or indirect, and whether the thought process behind the defendant's conduct could be characterized as intentional or negligent. Under the traditional writ system, the relationship in Table 3.1 had developed.

In this table, the categories describing the defendant's mental state at the time of the injury are shown in the columns (intentional versus negligent), and the categories describing the connection between his conduct and the injury are shown in the rows (direct versus indirect). The category of intentional and direct torts includes the classic batteries and trespasses, such as deliberate strikes. The category of negligent and direct torts includes incidents that could be attributed to negligence, such as accidents on the roads. The category of intentional and indirect torts includes those where an intentional act leads indirectly to harm, such as the case where the plaintiff trips and falls over a log that was deliberately thrown into the street. Finally, the category of negligent and indirect torts includes obvious cases in which careless conduct leads to injury, such as the case where the plaintiff trips over a log that was accidentally dropped in the street. The assignment of writs to categories of tort, as shown in Table 3.1, led to the difficulties observed in *Scott v. Shepherd*, and to defendants strategically gaming the writ system to avoid liability.

Letting the plaintiff sue in case whether the harm was direct or indirect led to the relationship in Table 3.2 between writs and case characteristics.[36]

Although the more liberal construction of the case writ suggests that it could have been used in every tort category shown in the table, the set of cases in which

---

[35] Williams v. Holland, 131 Eng. Rep. 848 (C.P. 1833); Rogers v. Imbleton, 127 Eng. Rep. 568 (C.P. 1806); Ogle v. Barnes, 101 Eng. Rep. 1338 (K.B. 1799). For discussion of these cases and the development of the rule in *Williams v. Holland*, see Street, *supra* note 32, at 263–265; *see also* Epstein & Sharkey, *supra* note 4, at 95–96.

[36] Table 3.2 replicates, with minor changes, a similar diagram in Prichard, *supra* note 32, at 251.

TABLE 3.2. *Case characteristics and writ type under modern law*

	Intentional	Negligent
Direct	Trespass writ	Trespass writ, Case writ
Indirect	Case writ	Case writ

the writ's greater reach really mattered is that involving negligent and direct torts. A plaintiff who had been the victim of an intentional and direct tort would have a strong incentive to use the trespass writ because of the precedents established under it.

This new scheme gets us away from the regime in which defendants could strategically game the system by saying whatever they thought might work to avoid being found liable under the writ chosen by the plaintiff. In cases where the defendant's conduct could be characterized as either intentional or negligent, represented by the upper right cell of Table 3.2, the plaintiff could thwart the strategically gaming defendant by going to court with a case writ. In particular, cases where the defendant's conduct is both direct and potentially attributable to negligent omission rather than intention represent the set of scenarios in which the strategic gamesmanship problem arose. In those scenarios, the defendant could no longer avoid liability, if the plaintiff sued under the case writ, by asserting that the harm was intentional.

But the new scheme in Table 3.2 introduced a new problem: inconsistent legal rules applying to the same facts. Note that the plaintiff has a choice, in the event of a direct harm that could be attributed to negligence, to sue under trespass or under case. The law under these two writs had developed along different paths. *Case involved some allegation by the plaintiff of negligence on the defendant's part. Trespass proceeded on a theory of strict liability.* Although the defendant minimized the risk of strategic gaming by the defendant if he sued in case, he might still prefer the trespass writ because it came along with writ-specific law implying that liability was strict, and, most importantly, that the burden was the defendant's to show that he should not be held liable (*Weaver v. Ward*).

The functional overlap between the two writs, coupled with the tension between writ-specific legal rules, led to an important decision in *Brown v. Kendall*,[37] by Chief Justice Shaw, one of the most influential judges to serve on an American state court. *Brown v. Kendall* sets out the basic distinctions between the legal requirements of actions based on negligence and actions based on intent.

The facts of *Brown v. Kendall* are simple. The defendant was in the process of using a four-foot long stick to separate two fighting dogs, one of which belonged to the plaintiff and the other to the defendant, when he lifted the stick over his shoulder

---

[37] Brown v. Kendall, 60 Mass. 292 (1850).

and struck the plaintiff in the eye. The plaintiff brought a trespass action against the defendant.

Looking back at Table 3.2, the facts of *Brown v. Kendall* appear to fit neatly in the category of direct and negligent torts. The harm to the plaintiff resulted from a direct application of force. To the extent the defendant was legally culpable, it was because he may have been negligent. Given this, the plaintiff had a choice to plead trespass or case, and he chose to plead trespass. If the plaintiff had pled case instead of trespass, he would have avoided the risk of the defendant escaping liability on some theory that the harm was indirect or consequential, but that risk was extremely small given the facts. Given the precedents under the trespass writ discussed earlier in this chapter – *Weaver v. Ward*, *Hopper v. Reeve* – the plaintiff's trespass claim would have appeared at the time to be a strong one. The plaintiff won in the trial court, but Justice Shaw, on appeal, ordered a new trial.

The most important lesson of *Brown v. Kendall* is that *Weaver v. Ward* is no longer the law. Under *Weaver v. Ward*, a plaintiff who brings a trespass writ in response to some direct though accidental injury could assert that it is the defendant's responsibility to show that the accident was inevitable, and that in the absence of such a showing the defendant should be held strictly liable. Justice Shaw said that *it is the plaintiff's responsibility* to prove that the defendant's harmful conduct was either intentional or negligent. The defendant does not have a responsibility to prove that the accident was inevitable; he can defend himself simply by denying the plaintiff's charges. Put another way, *Brown v. Kendall* shifts the burden of proof to the plaintiff.

The other lessons of *Brown v. Kendall* concern the definition of negligence and the management of a negligence case. Negligence is defined in *Brown v. Kendall* as the failure to take *ordinary* care. In most cases, negligence is described as the failure to take *reasonable* care. However, it is clear from Shaw's description that ordinary care is the same as reasonable care. Shaw defined ordinary care as

> that kind and degree of care, which prudent and cautious men would use, such as is required by the exigency of the case, and such as is necessary to guard against probable danger. A man, who should have occasion to discharge a gun, on an open and extensive marsh, or in a forest, would be required to use less circumspection and care, than if he were to do the same thing in an inhabited town, village, or city.[38]

Shaw said that it is the plaintiff's responsibility to prove that the defendant was negligent. In addition, the defendant will be liable for negligence only if he was negligent and the plaintiff was not negligent. In every other scenario (neither negligent, both negligent, plaintiff negligent, and defendant nonnegligent), the defendant would not be liable.

---

[38] *Id.* at 296.

It should be clear from *Brown v. Kendall* that the law had traveled quite a distance from the *Thorns Case*. But the road traversed was a different path from that described by many commentators. There is a popular opinion that the law has moved from strict liability, as the background principle, to negligence.[39]

The cases reveal a more complicated picture of tort law's evolution. First, the background principle suggested in the early cases was not strict liability. It is clear in the *Thorns Case* that the court was interested in whether the thorns had fallen on the defendant's property as a result of the carelessness of the defendant. The defendant's failure to offer any evidence on that question led to a finding of liability. The *Thorns Case* illustrates the negligence principle in an early application, involving the privilege to recapture property.

The notion that the principle of strict liability is embodied in early tort law receives its strongest support from *Weaver v. Ward*. However, even there the court was interested in the defendant's precautionary effort. The striking feature of *Weaver v. Ward* is the court's statement that in response to a trespass writ, it is the *defendant's* duty to bring forth evidence of precautionary effort on his part. This procedural rule was also implicit in the *Thorns Case*.

Brown v. Kendall does not introduce negligence as a requirement of tort liability or give it a stature in the substantive law that it did not have before. The negligence principle had been at the core of tort actions from early on, certainly by the time of the *Thorns Case*. Rather, *Brown v. Kendall* overturns the ancient procedural framework of *Weaver v. Ward*. After *Brown v. Kendall*, the burden of proof would fall on the plaintiff, in all cases, to show that the defendant failed to take reasonable care.

In sum, the most important shift in tort law from the *Thorns Case* to *Brown v. Kendall* was procedural. The substance of the law has been remarkably stable. The key procedural change was a move from a convention requiring the defendant to bring forth evidence of reasonable care, in response to a trespass writ, to a new convention requiring the plaintiff to bring forth evidence of a failure on the part of the defendant to exercise reasonable care (which encompasses unlawful intent). Of course, to say that the key change has been procedural should not be understood as a trivialization. Shifting the burden from the defendant to the plaintiff had major consequences for litigation incentives and strategies. It not only increased the costs borne by plaintiffs in prosecuting their claims, but also forced plaintiffs to bear the risk of failing to meet the burden of proof. The burden shift probably led to some level of shielding from liability for defendants. However, it has not led to any degree of formal immunity from liability that had not existed from very early times.

[handwritten note: In light of "Economic Principles" and "moral justification" are we surprised by this evolution? Which drove the evolution?]

---

[39] For a critique of this view, *see* Holmes, *supra* note 1, at 103.

4

Intentional Torts

The law on intentional torts is a broad area of tort law, governing physical assaults, takings of property, and related direct invasions of rights. The question of how much care an individual should take to avoid an accidental injury to someone else, treated abstractly in the second chapter, will have less relevance in this chapter. Intentional torts result from conduct that clearly will impose a loss on someone. Tort law regulates intentional conduct by determining how those losses ultimately will be allocated.

I. THE INTERNALIZATION PRINCIPLE

When a man goes upon his neighbor's land, thinking it his own, he intends the very act or consequence complained of. He means to intermeddle with a certain thing in a certain way, and it is just that intended intermeddling for which he is sued. . . . One who diminishes the value of property by intentional damage knows it belongs to somebody. If he thinks it belongs to himself, he expects whatever harm he may do to come out of his own pocket. It would be odd if he were to get rid of the burden by discovering that it belonged to his neighbor.[1]

The foregoing passage from Holmes pretty well sums up the function of liability for intentional torts. Put simply, liability serves an *internalization* function, by shifting the losses an actor imposes on others through intentional conduct back to the actor.[2] For example, if A throws a rock through B's window, the internalization principle requires A to pay for the loss he imposed on B.

Why internalize losses caused by intentional conduct? Because, as Holmes suggested, if you take an action that directly imposes a loss, such as breaking a window,

---

[1] OLIVER WENDELL HOLMES, JR., THE COMMON LAW 97 (1881).
[2] Keith N. Hylton, *Intent in Tort Law* (Monsanto Lecture), 44 VAL. U. L. REV. 1217 (2010).

that loss will have to be borne by someone. Internalizing the loss compels the actor to take the loss into account in deciding which action to take. Thus, internalization induces the actor who handles someone else's property to follow the same decision process he would follow when handling his own property, to treat the losses he imposes on others as if they were his own.

What is desirable about making actors treat the losses they impose on others as their own? Return to the window-breaking example. Why would a person choose to break his own window? There are many reasons. Perhaps he needs to break the window in an emergency to retrieve something valuable or to get out of his house. If he needs to break the window to avoid a serious injury to himself, he will do so even though he is aware that he will bear the cost, for the simple reason that it is cheaper to fix a window than to suffer a serious bodily injury. Alternatively, perhaps he just enjoys breaking windows. If so, he will break his own window only when the psychic benefit he perceives from doing so is greater than the cost of repair (or of living with the broken window). Internalization is a desirable policy, then, because it induces actors to engage in intentional conduct that imposes a loss only when doing so avoids an even greater loss or is necessary to secure a greater benefit.

The internalization principle implies that the law should impose strict liability for intentional torts. Facing strict liability, an actor whose intentional conduct will impose losses on others will be motivated to anticipate those losses to the best of his ability. Moreover, someone who anticipates the losses his intentional conduct will impose on others is more likely to seek consent from the likely victims of his actions before taking actions that might harm them. The cases in the first half of this chapter show the extent to which the internalization principle has been adopted in the law of intentional torts.

The torts considered in this chapter are battery, trespass, false imprisonment, assault, and intentional infliction of emotional distress. This is by no means an exhaustive list of intentional torts, but it is sufficient as a sample to illustrate the fundamental policies and rules in effect in this area of tort law.

II. BATTERY: INTENT AND FORESIGHT

The standard reference on battery is *Vosburg v. Putney*.[3] Two schoolboys, fourteen-year-old Vosburg and eleven-year-old Putney, were sitting opposite each other in separate rows in a classroom. Putney, seeking Vosburg's attention, kicked him in the shin of his right leg. The kick was described as slight, a touch. A few seconds after the contact, Vosburg felt a sharp pain and cried out. Things went downhill from there. Vosburg fell ill and needed assistance to get to school the next day, and by the fourth day he was vomiting. The leg became infected and he never recovered full use of it. Vosburg sued Putney for battery.

---

[3] 50 N.W. 403 (Wis. 1891).

The core of the court's analysis consisted of the defenses it rejected. First was the argument that the defendant, Putney, *did not intend to harm* the plaintiff, Vosburg, and for that reason should not be held liable for battery. Let's take a close look at this argument.

To begin, Putney made a *contention*: that he did not intend to hurt Vosburg. Next, Putney proffered a *rule*: that to be held liable for battery the defendant must have intended to harm the plaintiff. Third, Putney *applied* the rule to his case: because he did not intend to harm the plaintiff, he could not be held liable for battery. Legal arguments follow this formula: *contention, rule, application*.

The court rejected Putney's argument on the ground that his proffered rule, requiring intent to harm to be held liable for battery, is inconsistent with the law. The correct rule, noted the court, is that to be held liable for a battery you do not have to intend to harm the plaintiff; it is enough to intend to do the unlawful act, because "if the intended act is unlawful, the intention to commit it must necessarily be unlawful."[4]

Notice that the court's rationale for its holding on intent is incomplete because it is circular: to be held liable you must intend to do something unlawful; and if you do an act that is unlawful, then the intention is unlawful. But the circularity of the court's rationale does not mean it is wrong. The problem with a circular argument is that it fails to provide a sound justification. We may pause briefly to marvel at the circularity, but we will have to continue to search for a justification.

The best justification for the court's holding on intent follows from the internalization principle introduced at the outset of this chapter. The principle implies that to be held liable for an intentional tort, it should be sufficient that the defendant made a choice between actions with clear (that is, easily foreseeable) immediate consequences. Further, the principle implies that there is no need for an additional requirement that the defendant intended to harm the plaintiff. As long as the defendant made a choice between actions with clear immediate consequences (to kick the plaintiff or not to kick the plaintiff), internalization requires him to bear the full costs of his chosen action (that is, the costs to himself *and* to others), so that he will compare the benefits he perceives (psychic, monetary, or whatever) to the full costs. At the same time, the internalization principle would support excusing a defendant from battery liability when he had no opportunity to make a choice between options, such as the case of a person who in an emergency acts instinctively to save himself, as did the intermediate actors who threw the lighted squib in *Scott v. Shepherd* (Chapter 3).

This justification is consistent with the law: Courts generally say that to be held liable for an intentional tort, the defendant only has to have intended to do the act that harmed the plaintiff. Put concisely, the rule on intent, to a first approximation, is that *to be held liable for an intentional tort, the intent required is to execute the*

---

[4] *Id.* at 403.

(margin handwritten note: should be tied to its econ. principle via social benefits)

<u>*act that caused harm*</u>. Applying this rule, it appears that the defendant Putney did intend to do the act that the court believed caused the injury – that is, Putney did intend to kick Vosburg – and that is all that is required for liability.

Was Putney too young to understand what he was doing? He was certainly too young to foresee the serious injury that transpired. But he was not too young to know that a kick is associated with unpleasant consequences, if only hurt feelings. As we get further into the cases, we will see that the intent requirement for battery essentially requires the defendant to be aware of potentially negative consequences to the plaintiff, or at least that the plaintiff may not have desired the contact.

Let's consider the second defense in *Vosburg v. Putney*, that of *implied license*. The rule is straightforward: <u>*Implied license means that the plaintiff consented to the defendant's act, and the defendant cannot be held liable for battery if the plaintiff consented*</u>.

License, or consent, can be <u>express or implied</u>. An express license will be found where the evidence shows that the plaintiff explicitly consented to the defendant's act, such as a written contract or verbal agreement. But even if there is no evidence of an express license, an implied license may still be found. For example, an implied license may result from a pattern of behavior that implies consent. If the boys always kicked each other to get each other's attention during class, then there may have been implicit consent. More generally, an <u>implied license</u> defense can be grounded on facts that indicate (a) that *the invasion that occurred is one that is routinely accepted within the community in which the plaintiff and defendant are members,*[5] or (b) that *the plaintiff's conduct was such that a reasonable person would perceive it as indicating consent to the invasion.*[6]

The court accepted the rule on implied license proffered by Putney, but rejected his application of it. The court said that if the kick had happened on the playground, Putney's implied license theory might be valid, but in the classroom, after class had been called to order, the kick was a "violation of the order and decorum of the school."[7] Hence, the facts failed to support the implied license theory.

The third defense in *Vosburg v. Putney* was based on the notion of *foreseeability*. Putney argued that he should not be held liable because he could not have foreseen the severe damage to Vosburg's leg.

The foreseeability argument's usefulness as a defense depends on the nature of the plaintiff's claim. If the plaintiff claims that the defendant breached an agreement between them – for example, an agreement to keep their kicks to the playground or

---

[5] For example, in the employment setting, implied license, or assumption of risk, is found on the basis of evidence that a risk is a recurrent, fixed feature of the workplace. *See, e.g.,* Lamson v. American Axe & Tool Co., 58 N.E. 585 (Mass. 1900) (discussed in Chapter 10).

[6] For example, a person who holds her arm up to a doctor who has asked if he can administer a vaccination would be viewed as having indicated consent by her conduct. *See* O'Brien v. Cunard S.S. Co., 28 N.E. 266 (Mass. 1891).

[7] Vosburg, 50 N.W. at 403.

to free time within school – then it is in essence a breach of contract claim, and the law limits damages to foreseeable harms.[8] On the other hand, if the claim is in tort, there is no such limit on damages.

The court decided that Vosburg's claim was in tort, not in contract. *In a tort claim, a defendant who is found guilty is liable for the victim's loss resulting directly from the tort, no matter how unforeseeable the loss.* The absence of a foreseeability limitation for losses resulting directly from a tort means that the tortfeasor takes his victim as he finds him. This is sometimes referred to as the *eggshell skull rule*, because of the saying that even if the plaintiff has an eggshell skull, the defendant still has to pay for the entire loss.[9]

General Rule on Intent

Another standard reference on battery is *Garratt v. Dailey*.[10] Brian Dailey, a five-year-old boy, snatched the seat from under Ms. Garratt as she was about to sit down. She fell and fractured her hip. The question was whether Brian intended to inflict a harmful contact on Ms. Garratt.

Because Brian did not touch Ms. Garratt, the intent issue is a bit more difficult than in *Vosburg v. Putney*. After all, when you kick someone, it is hard to argue persuasively that you did not intend the kick. But if you pull the chair out before someone sits down, you have some room to avoid the intent finding. You can say, for example, that you needed the chair yourself and you did not see the person trying to sit down. Or, you could say, as Brian did through his lawyers, that you were trying to help the plaintiff by placing the chair beneath her, but you couldn't get it there in time. Brian's age adds an additional layer of complexity. A little boy probably thinks that if he snatches the chair away before a person sits down, the victim of his prank will bounce back up, just as he would, without any injury.

There are no bright-line rules that tell a court how to determine intent. The facts are set out, and the court has to infer whether it was a mistake, as Brian claimed, or an intentional tort.

However, there is a rule emphasized in *Garratt v. Dailey* that is especially useful in cases of battery that do not involve a direct touch. The court said that a battery would be established if it was proved that when Brian moved the chair, he knew with *substantial certainty* that the plaintiff would attempt to sit down where the chair had been. Applying this rule, the court found that Brian had the requisite intent and held him liable for $11,000.

---

[8] Hadley v. Baxendale (1854) 156 Eng. Rep. 145, 147 (Ex.) ("The debtor is only liable for the damages foreseen, or which might have been foreseen, at the time of the execution of the contract").

[9] WILLIAM L. PROSSER, HANDBOOK OF THE LAW OF TORTS 261 (West Pub. Co. 4th ed. 1971). For a more comprehensive discussion of the eggshell skull rule, *see* Chapter 10.

[10] 279 P.2d 1091 (Wash. 1955) and 304 P.2d 681 (Wash. 1956).

Even at Brian's age, he knew with substantial certainty that Ms. Garratt would fall, and that her contact with the floor would not be pleasant. He was too young to foresee the precise injury to Ms. Garratt, but not too young to know that pulling the chair out would inflict a harmful contact. The internalization principle set out at the start of this chapter implies that Brian's knowledge was sufficient to hold him liable, because if courts required precise foresight of the victim's injury few intentional tortfeasors, whether children or adults, would ever be found liable.

We can apply the substantial certainty rule to other cases of battery in which the defendant never lays a hand on the plaintiff. Take the case of a person who leads another into an empty elevator shaft. A court would ask whether the defendant knew with substantial certainty that the plaintiff would step into the elevator shaft. In general, *a court will find the required level of intent for battery if the defendant knew with substantial certainty that his conduct would inflict a harmful bodily contact upon another person*. An alternative, though more cumbersome, wording is that the defendant *intended to execute an act knowing with substantial certainty* that it would inflict a harmful contact upon another.

Note that in the more general articulation of the intent standard I have included the phrase "harmful contact." This does not mean that the defendant must have intended or foreseen a physical injury or serious harm; *Vosburg* implies that it is enough if the contact is unpleasant or not desired. If the contact is deemed to have been pleasant or desired, or generally acceptable, courts do not treat it as a battery.[11] For example, suppose a senior partner in a law firm congratulates a junior associate by patting him on the shoulder and telling him that he has done excellent work, and the associate's shoulder collapses. Should the associate decide to sue the partner for battery – admittedly a risky move at the start of a legal career – he is likely to find the courts unreceptive to his battery claim. This is a topic I will return to shortly.

Transferred Intent

If the injurer throws a stone and hits the victim in the eye, though intending to hit someone else, the court will hold the injurer liable for battery. This follows from the doctrine of *transferred intent*: If the defendant intended to hit someone, and he hit another person instead, he will be liable for battery to the actual victim even though he did not intend to hit that particular person.[12] Put generally, *the level of intent required for battery liability is satisfied if the actor intended to inflict a harmful contact on someone*.

Transferred intent is implied by the internalization principle. Internalization means forcing the actor to consider the losses he imposes on others when he acts. If

---

[11] Cole v. Turner, 6 Modern Rep. 149, 90 Eng. Rep. 958 (1704); Wiffin v. Kincard, 2 Bos. & P.N.R. 471, 127 Eng. Rep. 713 (1807); Coward v Baddeley (1859) 4 H & N 478, 157 Eng. Rep. 927 (1859); Rawlings v. Till, 3 M & W 28, 150 Eng. Rep. 1042 (1837).

[12] Talmage v. Smith, 59 N.W. 656 (Mich. 1894); Carnes v. Thompson, 48 S.W.2d 903 (Mo. 1932).

he throws a rock aiming to hit Bill but hits Sam instead, Sam's injury is a loss that the injurer intentionally imposed on someone. If the injurer could avoid the loss by saying that he was aiming for Bill and not Sam, then the law would, perversely, treat people who commit batteries against groups more leniently than those who commit batteries against a single person. Someone who fires a gun into a crowd in an effort to hit one person is certainly no less dangerous than someone who fires at a person standing alone. But if the intent standard required a direct intentionality link between actor and actual victim, then the person who fires a gun into a crowd to hit Sam but instead hits Bill would be treated as a favorite of the law. The internalization goal requires the loss that results from a battery to be shifted to the injurer, and it does not matter whether he claims to have aimed for Sam or Bill as long as he intended to hit someone.

Prosser argued that the transferred intent doctrine applies whenever the defendant's conduct falls within the scope of the ancient trespass action: a battery, an assault, a false imprisonment, a trespass to land, or a trespass to personal property.[13] But Prosser's theory raises the puzzle why the transferred intent doctrine exists at all, even if limited in this fashion. The internalization principle easily incorporates the types of injury within the ancient trespass writ and provides a functional explanation of the transferred intent doctrine. Intent will be transferred whenever not doing so would imply legal immunity for an actor who harms someone through intentional conduct substantially certain to do so.

A recurring question arises where an employer anticipates that at least one person will be killed during the course of a project (for example, a construction project) or where there are potentially harmful products (cigarettes, alcohol) that a manufacturer anticipates will kill at least one consumer.[14] Are these intentional torts? There are important distinctions here that make battery liability doubtful. First, there is some degree of consent on the part of the victims. Second, the social utility of the underlying activity is not obviously negative (for example, the benefit the smoker perceives is greater than the cost of his cigarettes, which is why we observe consent).[15] Third, the injurer (employer or product seller) takes no discrete act that can be described as intending a harmful contact with substantial certainty. These cases do not meet two of the basic requirements of the battery standard. One is that the harmful activity is without the explicit or implicit consent of the victims. The other is that there was a *discrete act* done with intent to inflict a harmful bodily contact or knowledge that a harmful bodily contact was substantially certain to occur.

[13] William L. Prosser, *Transferred Intent*, 45 Tex. L. Rev. 650 (1967).

[14] Richard A. Epstein & Catherine M. Sharkey, Cases and Materials on Torts 10–11 (Aspen Pub. 10th ed. 2012); Kenneth W. Simons, *Statistical Knowledge Deconstructed*, 92 B.U. L. Rev. 1 (2012).

[15] Of course, social utility should take into account the losses imposed on third parties by smokers or drinkers. When those losses are taken into account, the social utility of the underlying activities may be negative.

III. TRESPASS

We now move from battery to trespass – that is from kicks and slaps, to trampling over gardens and taking personal property. Tort law divides the area of trespass into two parts: trespass to real property, and trespass to chattels (personal property).

Trespass to Real Property

Trespass is the *intentional interference with exclusive possession of real property*. Interference means ousting or physical displacing the possessor from some space on his land, as occurs when the actor physically occupies the space or sends some object, such as a rock, over to the possessor's land.

Under the *ad coelum* rule,[16] the owner of a parcel owns the land beneath and the space above it. So, if an adjoining property owner B builds a basement underground that cuts across the property line of A, B is guilty of trespass. Or if B builds a structure in such a way that part of the roof hangs over the property of A, B is guilty of trespass.

In *Herrin v. Sutherland*,[17] the defendant, standing on the land of another person, repeatedly fired his Winchester shotgun over the plaintiff's land as he hunted ducks and other game birds. This was held a trespass under the *ad coelum* rule, because the bullets interfered with the plaintiff's exclusive possession of the space above his land.

What about airplane overflights? Since tort law accommodates federal regulation of air travel, flights in accordance with federal air traffic rules do not violate the law. If someone brought a tort suit in such a case, the plaintiff's claim would be preempted by federal law.[18] However, airplane overflights within 500 feet of the ground, in violation of air traffic rules established by the federal government, are trespasses.[19]

The type of intent required for trespass is similar to that required for battery: intent to execute the act. In other words, the rule on intent in trespass is (to a first approximation): *To be held liable for trespass, the intent required is the intent*

---

[16] 2 BLACKSTONE, COMMENTARIES *18 ("Land hath also, in its legal signification, an indefinite extent, upwards as well as downwards. *Cujus est solum, ejus est usque ad coelum*, is the maxim of the law, upwards; therefore no man may erect any building, or the like, to overhang another's land: and downwards, whatever is in the direct line between the surface of any land, and the center of the earth, belongs to the owner of the surface; as is every day's experience in the mining countries.").

[17] 74 Mont. 587, 241 P. 328 (1925).

[18] For more on preemption and tort law, *see* Chapter 17 (Products Liability).

[19] Smith v. New England Aircraft Co., 170 N.E. 385 (Mass. 1930) (flight of altitude as low as 100 feet, trespass); Swetland v. Curtiss Airports Corp., 41 F.2d 929 (N.D. Ohio 1930) (flights of altitude less than 500 feet constitute trespasses or maintenance of nuisance); Neiswonger v. Goodyear Tire & Rubber Co., 35 F.2d 761 (N.D. Ohio 1929) (Goodyear Blimp passed over farmer's land at altitude less than 200 feet, causing farmer's horses to stampede, injuring farmer); *see also* AIR COMMERCE REGULATIONS § 74 (g).

to execute the act that causes the trespass. If a person walks onto someone else's property, he is liable for trespass even if he thought the property was his own. The internalization principle, captured in the Holmes quote at the outset of this chapter, explains this feature.

However, note that there is a subtle difference between the intent standard for trespass and that for battery. The intent standard for trespass does not include the "harmful contact" requirement of battery and in this sense is stricter that the battery standard. One judge said that the maxim *de minimis non curat lex* (the law doesn't cure trifles) never applies to "the positive and wrongful invasion of another's property."[20] Why? The most plausible explanation is that it is relatively easy to get the consent of a property owner before invading, while slight touches that occur on the street, in the hustle and bustle of ordinary life, will occur under conditions in which no one has time to gain consent. The burden of gaining consent is the factor that probably explains the relatively strict intent standard for trespass.

There is no requirement to prove damages to maintain an action for trespass.[21] If the plaintiff has no provable damages from a trespass, he will receive a *nominal award* – typically $1, given in cases in which the plaintiff's rights have been violated without any significant harm.

Why bother to sue at all if you can get only a nominal award of $1? First, you may want a public declaration by a court that the defendant trespassed. You may want the public record as a signal to the trespasser and to other potential trespassers that you will defend your rights. You may want to create a record that stands against that particular trespasser, which could be used against him in the future. Second, in the English courts where our trespass law developed, the winning party would be awarded his reasonable litigation expenses. This means that if someone trespassed on another person's property without causing any damage, the aggrieved person could bring a suit and collect his litigation expenses from the trespasser. Under the English convention on litigation costs, the victim of a trespass would happily sue in many cases even if he could not prove any compensable harm.

Trespass to Chattels

Trespass to chattels (personal property) is the intentional interference with exclusive possession of personal property. Here, interference means denying the lawful possessor exclusive possession or interfering with his possession.

Some courts have held that there is no need to prove damages to maintain an action for trespass to chattels, as is true of trespass to real property.[22] For example,

20 Seneca Road Co. v. Auburn & Rochester R. Co., 5 Hill, N.Y. 171, 175 (1843) (Cowan, J.).
21 Champion v. Vincent, 20 Tex. 811, 815–816 (1858); Dougherty v. Stepp, 18 N.C. 371, 371 (N.C. 1835); Brame v. Clark, 62 S.E. 418, 418 (N.C. 1908); 3 Blackstone, Commentaries *209–210.
22 Champion v. Vincent, 20 Tex. 811, 815–816 (1858); Bruch v. Carter, 32 N. J. L. 554 (1867); Blondell v. Consolidated Gas Co. 43 A. 817 (Md. 1908).

in <u>*Blondell v. Consolidated Gas Co.*</u>,[23] the defendants (gas company customers) had attached governors (regulating gas flow) to the plaintiff gas company's meters. The court held that the defendants had trespassed, irrespective of the amount of damage done to the meters.

Other courts have required the plaintiff to prove damages, based on actual injury to or dispossession of the chattel, with the proviso that dispossession subjects the trespasser to liability for nominal damages even in the absence of actual injury.[24] In <u>*Glidden v. Szybiak*</u>,[25] the plaintiff, four years old, sued for injuries from a dog bite. The dog bit the plaintiff after she climbed on its back and pulled its ears. The defendants argued that the plaintiff was engaged in a trespass, by climbing on the dog without permission, and that they were therefore exempted from a duty of care. The court held that given the absence of any proof of harm to the dog, the plaintiff had not committed a trespass.

What accounts for the different decisions in *Glidden* and *Blondell*? The difference between a dog and a gas meter is that one is in constant interaction with humans while the other is stationary and dumb. Children play with dogs without pausing to seek permission from owners. This implies that as a practical matter the burden of gaining consent to touch a dog is higher than the burden of gaining consent to attach a device to a gas meter. But this difference, although suggestive, cannot provide a complete explanation of the different outcomes in *Glidden* and *Blondell*, because it would require courts to decide trespass to chattels cases according to the degree of burden in gaining consent. Such an approach would offer little guidance to litigants. Instead, the courts have developed broader category-based distinctions.

Trespass doctrine, we will see in other applications, responds primarily to the degree to which it is burdensome to gain consent before physically interfering with exclusive possession of property. Because the burden of gaining consent is high in many instances involving chattels, the common law restricts the scope (i.e., the number of potential violations) of trespass to chattels. Unlike the case of land, not every instance of a physical interference with exclusive possession is deemed a trespass to a chattel. The Restatement (Second) of Torts, § 218, limits the scope of trespass to instances where "(a) [the trespasser] dispossesses the other of the chattel, or (b) the chattel is impaired as to its condition, quality, or value, or (c) the possessor is deprived of the use of the chattel for a substantial time, or (d) bodily harm is caused to the possessor, or harm is caused to some person or thing in which the possessor has a legally protected interest."[26] If a court finds that one of the first three conditions is satisfied, then a technical trespass will be found, even if the plaintiff cannot

---

[23] 43 A. 817 (Md. 1899).

[24] *See* RESTATEMENT (SECOND) OF TORTS § 218 (1965); *see also* Glidden v. Szybiak, 63 A.2d 233 (N.H. 1949); Morrow v. First Interstate Bank of Oregon, N.A., 847 P.2d 411 (Or. Ct. App. 1993).

[25] 63 A.2d 233, 235 (N.H. 1949).

[26] *See* RESTATEMENT (SECOND) OF TORTS § 218 (1965).

prove actual harm. A finding of trespass entitles the plaintiff to at least a nominal award.

In light of this understanding of the law, the varying decisions on trespass to chattels, such as *Glidden* and *Blondell*, can be reconciled. First, because the burden of gaining consent is higher in general with respect to personal property than with respect to real property, the scope of trespass to chattels is narrower than the scope of trespass to land. *Glidden* is an illustration of this narrower scope. In contrast, *Blondell* (the gas meters case) is an application of the dispossession rule (*Restatement Second* § 218(a)). The installation of governors on the gas meters was a permanent physical occupation of the gas company's personal property. Given the seriousness of the interference, the defendants in *Blondell* had committed a technical trespass, irrespective of whether the gas company could prove injury.

IV. CONSENT AS A DEFENSE VITIATING INTENT

One lesson of *Vosburg v. Putney* is that consent is a defense to battery. To be precise, consent annuls or vitiates the theory that the defendant acted with the intent required under battery law. Thus, if the plaintiff consented to the defendant's conduct, the defendant could not have intended to inflict a harmful or offensive bodily contact upon the plaintiff. Instead of being harmful or offensive, the contact was precisely what the plaintiff desired or accepted. Going back to the internalization principle mentioned at the start of this chapter, a consensual transaction typically is not one that imposes losses on either of the consenting parties, so there are no losses to be internalized.

As a general matter, the defenses to battery come in the form of (a) *arguments that vitiate the theory of unlawful intent, implying the absence of a battery*, or (b) *justifications or excuses for the battery that occurred*. One might think that it is improper to refer to arguments of the former type as defenses, because they are part of the plaintiff's *prima facie* case,[27] but this is a distinction with little practical effect.

Some interesting implications follow from the recognition that consent annuls the theory of unlawful intent. Suppose a frog promises to pay a beautiful princess $1,000 if she allows him to kiss her. After the kiss, the frog refuses to pay. The kiss was not a battery, because the princess consented to it.[28] The princess may have a valid claim for fraud or for contract breach, but she does not have a meritorious battery lawsuit. And while fraud may vitiate consent as a general matter, the common law

---

[27] A lawsuit consists of two parts: first, the plaintiff's prima facie case and second, the defendant's contradictory evidence, justifications, or excuses. The plaintiff's prima facie case is the set of arguments sufficient to establish a violation of the law if the evidence is not contested and there are no excuses or justifications.

[28] R. v. Clarence, [1888] 22 Q.B.D. 23.

traditionally has held that the only sort of fraud that annuls consent to a physical contact is fraud as to the nature of the act itself.[29]

It follows that consent as to the nature of the act generally operates as a valid assent in the context of battery. Of course, this proposition leaves several questions open when applied to real cases. What happens if consent appears to be partial, as where a patient agrees to one operation and the doctor performs a different, related operation?

Implied Consent and Medical Battery

Two medical battery cases confronting this question are *Mohr v. Williams*[30] and *Kennedy v. Parrott*.[31] In *Mohr*, the doctor operated on the left ear after obtaining the patient's consent to operate on the right ear. In *Kennedy*, the plaintiff was injured after the doctor, without the plaintiff's consent, punctured cysts on her left ovary during an authorized appendectomy.

During an operation authorized for the right ear, the doctor in *Mohr* looked at the patient's left ear, while she was under anesthesia, and decided on the basis of his examination, and after consulting another physician on hand, to operate on the left ear. The patient later complained of impaired hearing in the left ear and sued the physician for battery. The issues raised were whether the physician had obtained consent, whether consent should be implied under the circumstances, and whether, if the court found that there was no consent, the physician should be held liable for battery.

The court had no difficulty rejecting the consent defense. The patient had consented only to an operation on the right ear and had never complained to the physician about or sought treatment for her left ear. The patient's family physician attended the operation and was consulted by the operating physician in the course of it, but he was never authorized by the patient to consent to any change in the operation.

The court had little difficulty rejecting the implied consent defense too. Implied consent in the medical care setting is often based on the *emergency rule,* according

---

[29] *Id.* A more accurate description of the holding is that fraud as to the nature of the act or *the identity of the actor* annuls consent. However, the identity-of-actor exception seems to be implied by the nature-of-act exception – because if the actor is of a different identity than the one represented, the nature of act arguably changes too. The Second Restatement expands on the traditional nature-of-act exception by including fraud as to *the extent of the harm to be expected. See* RESTATEMENT (SECOND) OF TORTS § 892B(2) (1979) ("If the person consenting to the conduct of another is induced to consent by a substantial mistake concerning the nature of the invasion of his interests or the extent of the harm to be expected from it and the mistake is known to the other or is induced by the other's misrepresentation, the consent is not effective for the unexpected invasion or harm."). For a case applying the more expansive exception, with discussion of similar cases, *see* Hogan v. Tavzel, 660 So.2d 350 (Fla. Dist. Ct. App. 5th Dist. 1995), *rev. den.,* 666 So.2d 901 (Fla. 1996).

[30] 104 N.W. 12 (Minn. 1905).

[31] Kennedy v. Parrott, 90 S.E.2d 754 (N.C. 1956).

to which *medical treatment is lawful under the doctrine of implied consent when a medical emergency requires immediate action to preserve the health or life of the patient.*[32] The mere fact that in the physician's view the operation looked like it would improve the patient's hearing was not enough to support an implied consent defense.

The doctor argued that he should not be held liable for battery because he had no intention to harm the plaintiff. We know from *Vosburg v. Putney* that this is not a defense to battery, and the court rejected it, noting that "any unlawful or unauthorized touching of the person of another, except it be in the spirit of pleasantry, constitutes an assault and battery."[33]

The noted exception for contact "in the spirit of pleasantry" has a special meaning in battery doctrine. It provides some degree of immunity from liability for contact that occurs for benign purposes, typically during ordinary social intercourse. For example, suppose a senior law partner pats a junior associate on the back to signal that he is pleased by his work, and as a result the associate suffers an injury. The pleasantry exception excludes these instances from the scope of battery liability.

In light of the pleasantry exception, why should we not view the defendant's conduct in *Mohr* as an intended pleasantry and on this basis distinguish it from the kick in *Vosburg v. Putney*? Indeed, the operation was better than a pleasantry because the point of it was to improve the health of the patient. How could this be the basis of a battery claim? If a business associate pats you on the back or shakes your hand and your arm falls off, you probably would lose your battery lawsuit. But if a doctor, without your permission, performs an operation for the purpose of improving your health, without your consent, he is liable for battery. What explains the difference?

One distinguishing factor, which also provides a policy justification for *Mohr*, is the burden of transacting – that is, the difficulty of seeking and gaining consent before the operation takes place.[34] In settings where a contact that would be deemed a pleasantry might arise, people typically do not stop to ask permission, and often the circumstances indicate implied consent, as when two people extend their hands for a handshake. In the (non-emergency) surgery setting, however, seeking authorization is the norm, and there is a lot of time to seek permission before acting. In other words, the burden of gaining consent is low. The law, correspondingly, asks for more patience on the part of the potential tortfeasor. The physician is required to obtain consent.

The upshot is that in the context of medical battery, the law is pretty strict. Having a sincere desire to help the victim does not support a defense to battery based on lack of intent to harm.

---

[32] Mohr v. Williams, 104 N.W. 12 (Minn. 1905); Canterbury v. Spence, 464 F.2d 772, 788 (D.C. Cir.), *cert. denied*, 409 U.S. 1064 (1972); Schloendorff v. Society of N.Y. Hosp., 105 N.E. 92, 93 (N.Y. 1914); RESTATEMENT (SECOND) OF TORTS § 892D(a) (1979).

[33] Mohr v. Williams, 104 N.W. 12, 16 (Minn. 1905).

[34] Hylton, *supra* note 2, at 1231–1234 (consent requirement is enforced more strictly as burden of obtaining consent declines).

Another policy justification for tort law's stingy approach to the pleasantry exception in the medical care context invokes ethical concerns. The pleasantry exception, if allowed to defeat the consent requirement in medical battery cases, might encourage the doctor to perform any operation on an unconscious patient – for example, unauthorized cosmetic surgery – that the doctor thinks would improve the patient's quality of life after he awakes from anesthesia. The dangers of such medical experimentation are obvious.

Kennedy v. Parrott articulates a narrow expansion of the implied consent defense: *Consent will be implied when the surgeon extends the operation to remedy any diseased condition in the area of the original incision when the physician determines that correct surgical procedure requires such an extension of the operation.* In *Kennedy*, the physician, while performing an appendectomy, punctured cysts on the plaintiff's left ovary. The operation was underway and there was no way to obtain consent at the moment. The choice before the doctor was to puncture the cysts, working within the existing incision, or to close the patient up and return to do another surgery later. The physician already had consent for the invasion and, once there, merely extended the operation.

There are probably few cases such as *Kennedy* today. Modern technology allows the doctor to see inside the patient's body in more detail than in earlier days. This makes it easier for the doctor to gain consent, before an operation, for any extension of the initially planned procedure. Since the burden of gaining consent has declined, the leeway for unauthorized invasion should narrow along with it.

The Limits of Consent

Although consent is a defense to battery, the traditional rule limiting the defense to *consent as to the nature of the act* has implications for the competence of certain parties to give effective consent. A six-year-old child can consent to a wrestling match with another child of the same age, since he is quite likely to understand the nature of the act to which he has consented, but if the child agrees to a boxing match with an adult, his consent is unlikely to be considered valid.[35] A six year old is unlikely to understand the immediate consequences of agreeing to a boxing match with an adult, while the adult would understand completely. For the same reason, the consent of a mentally retarded adult to a boxing match, or to sexual relations, is unlikely to be effective.[36]

Consent given under duress is ineffective.[37] If a person consents at gunpoint to being touched, no court would recognize it as valid. The common law defined

---

[35] *See, e.g.,* Commonwealth v. Nickerson, 87 Mass. 518 (1862) (incapacity of nine-year-old child to consent to assault and battery).

[36] *See, e.g.,* Saucier ex rel. Mallory v. McDonald's Rests. of Mont., Inc., 179 P.3d 481 (Mont. 2008); 1 Dan B. Dobbs, Paul T. Hayden, & Ellen M. Bublick, The Law of Torts § 109 (2d ed. 2011).

[37] 1 Blackstone, Commentaries *126–127.

duress narrowly as the "fear of loss of life, or else fear of mayhem, or loss of limb."[38] Courts have taken a more expansive view of the theory of duress more recently.[39]

Medical operations present an entirely different set of issues. Under emergency conditions, an operation performed without consent may be necessary to save a person's life. On the other hand, a legal guardian may withhold consent to an operation to preserve the ward's life when the quality of that life is sufficiently low.

Children, for the most part, are incapable of providing effective consent to a medical operation such as a surgery – again, because they are unable to understand the nature of the proposed invasion. *Thus, as a general matter, the consent of the parent (or guardian) is necessary for an operation on a child.*[40] However, even this rule has its limits. In emergency settings where life or health is at risk, children have been rushed into the operating room, and operations performed on them, in spite of the parents' refusal to give consent.[41]

The general choice here is between autonomy and utility as guiding principles. Under an approach that respected autonomy above all, no operations could be performed without the consent of the decision maker (patient, parent, or guardian). Any such operation would be a battery. In contrast, under the utilitarian approach consent would be unimportant. Anything that would be best for all parties on an overall cost-benefit analysis should be permitted.

The law on consent to medical operations is not strictly in line with either approach. However, in most cases autonomy is respected. For example, in end-of-life situations, where the patient is near death (for example, in a vegetative state) and the guardian must decide whether to continue medical treatment, autonomy appears to prevail, in the sense that the substituted judgment of the guardian generally controls.[42] Of course, the end-of-life cases often involve individuals who seek to cut off life support for a comatose family member. The unsentimental utilitarian would seek the same outcome. In situations where the invasion is for the benefit of another, such as where a physician seeks to transplant a kidney from an incompetent to another party, the autonomy of the incompetent's guardian is respected,[43] often with results that the utilitarian would strongly oppose.

---

[38] *Id.* at 127.

[39] *See, e.g.,* Grager v. Schudar, 770 N.W.2d 692 (N.D. 2009) (questioning whether consent of prisoner to sexual contact with jailer is effective).

[40] *See, e.g.,* Bonner v. Moran, 126 F.2d 121 (App. D.C. 1941); Zoski v. Gaines, 260 N.W. 99 (Mich. 1935); Moss v. Rishworth, 191 S.W. 843 (Tex. Civ. App 1916); Rogers v. Sells, 61 P.2d 1018 (Okla. 1936); Browning v. Hoffman, 111 S.E. 492 (W.Va. 1922); Franklyn v. Peabody, 228 N.W. 681 (Mich. 1930).

[41] Jackovach v. Yocom, 237 N.W. 444, 450 (Iowa 1931) (implied consent found where doctors amputated arm without parental consent); Miller ex rel. Miller v. HCA, Inc., 118 S.W.3d 758 (Tex. 2003) (implied consent; operation without parental consent).

[42] *See, e.g., In re* Guardianship of McInnis, 584 N.E.2d 1389 (Ohio Prob. 1991); Foody v. Manchester Memorial Hosp., 40 Conn. Supp. 127 (Super. Ct. 1984); *In re* Guardianship of Barry, 445 So.2d 365 (Fla. Dist. Ct. App.2d Dist. 1984); Matter of Spring, 405 N.E.2d 115 (Mass. 1980).

[43] *In re* Guardianship of Pescinski, 226 N.W.2d 180 (Wis. 1975); Strunk v. Strunk, 445 S.W.2d 145 (Ky. 1969).

What about mother versus fetus conflict situations? In *In re Baby Boy Doe*,[44] the doctors wanted to perform a caesarean section, but the parents refused on religious grounds. The doctors had concluded that the fetus was not receiving sufficient oxygen and would be born dead or severely brain damaged unless the mother underwent an immediate cesarean section. Autonomy won: The court ruled in favor of the parents.

In re Baby Boy Doe is perhaps the clearest case of conflict between autonomy and utility. A utilitarian would have required the mother to be strapped down and the baby cut out. However, allowing utilitarians to decide cases like *In re Baby Boy Doe* would generate troubling questions. Where should we draw the line on invading one person for the benefit of society? If it is permissible to strap the mother down without her consent and cut the baby out, why is it not permissible to harvest transplantable organs from individuals without consent?

[handwritten margin note, left: "mother & harm is physical"]

[handwritten note below paragraph: "being forced to give up a kidney is a physical harm"]

Consent and Mutual Combat

We have already considered consent as a defense to battery, but the law becomes more complicated in the case of mutual combat, such as prizefights or impromptu agreements to fight. In the typical scenario in the torts cases, the victim and injurer have agreed to fight, and the victim, severely injured, sues for battery.

Consent is generally a defense to battery, but there is an exception for consensual violence. *The rule in the majority of states is that consent to mutual combat is not a defense to battery* – though consent is taken into account in mitigation of damages.[45] The rationale often provided is that if there is a breach of the peace, as there surely is in the case of a fistfight, the state is immediately a party, and no one can waive the state's right to intervene. In addition, this right on the part of the state to intervene is thought to be so broad that it permits the state to entertain a lawsuit for battery from the victim who consented to take part in the fight.

The rule in the minority of states is that consent to mutual combat is a defense to battery, unless the injuring party used excessive force or acted with intent to severely injure the other party.[46] The First Restatement of Torts adopted a version of this consent rule, without the excessive force proviso, and permitted an exception *when it is a crime to inflict a particular harm irrespective of consent and the policy of the law is to protect a class of persons from their inability to appreciate the consequences of their consent.*[47] The exception applies generally to young men and women who

[handwritten margin note, right: "mixed martial arts"]

---

[44] *In re* Baby Boy Doe, 632 N.E.2d 326 (Ill. App. Ct. 1994).

[45] *See* Littledike v. Wood, 255 P. 172, 174 (Utah 1927); Adams v. Waggoner, 5 Am. Rep. 230, 231 (Ind. 1870); Barholt v. Wright, 12 N.E. 185, 188 (Ohio St. 1887); Royer v. Belcher, 131 S.E. 556, 556–557 (W.Va. 1926).

[46] Hart v. Geysel, 294 P. 570 (Wash. 1930); White v. Whittall, 71 N.W. 1118 (Mich. 1897); Smith v. Simon, 37 N.W. 548 (Mich. 1888); Lykins v. Hamrick, 137 S.W. 852 (Ky. 1911).

[47] Restatement (First) of Torts §61 (1934).

might agree to some type of potentially harmful physical contact without being fully aware of the risks they may be confronting.

Which rule is the best – the majority or the minority rule? The minority rule seems most consistent with traditional notions of respecting autonomy. If someone agrees to take part in a prizefight, a law that respects autonomy presumably would hold the person to that agreement. If you've agreed to be punched, you shouldn't later complain about the consequences of your agreement.

However, the incentives created by the rules are complicated. The majority rule seems, at first, to reduce the likelihood of severe injuries in the boxing ring. The reason is that it discourages people from boxing, to the extent that they fear tort liability. And for those who choose to box, the majority rule seems to discourage overkill, that is, continuing to punch an opponent long after he is a spent force. On the other hand, the majority rule may encourage boxing to the extent that it gives the fighters a possible payoff if they are hurt. In short, there are conflicting incentive effects associated with the majority rule: the general activity of mutual combat is more costly under it, but for those who have chosen the activity, the cost of actually fighting rather than surrendering may be lower.

On the other hand, the minority rule creates its own special incentive and interpretation problems. One important difficulty presented by the minority rule is determining just what a prizefight combatant has consented to. Suppose his opponent uses excessive force (a weapon) or engages in overkill in the sense just defined. Has the combatant agreed to that? The combatant might argue that he agreed to fight in a match to a fixed number of rounds or the defeat of one participant. But how is defeat defined? Most people would not equate defeat with death; they would say that defeat means the point at which the losing party can no longer put up a decent fight. To use excessive force or to continue punching after the point at which the losing party can no longer fight would appear to be a breach of the underlying agreement. The majority rule rejecting consent as a defense has the virtue of recognizing the difficulty of determining the true scope of consent to battery.

Keep in mind that this is a special case of consensual battery: agreements to fight. In general, consent is a defense to battery. In the context of mutual combat, one observes in most jurisdictions an inversion of the general rule, rejecting consent as a defense.

The issues raised in the mutual combat cases appear to some degree in sports in which violent physical contact is common. Vicious "hits" in American football, in which one player runs full-speed, ramming his shoulder or helmet into another player, sometimes result in severe injuries. But they are part of the game, at least as it is now played. Can the victim bring a tort suit against the injurer?

Intentional blows in sports are actionable torts if they are inflicted with an intent to harm – that is, willful, wanton, or reckless – and outside of the rules of the sport.[48]

---

[48] *See, e.g.*, Hackbart v. Cincinnati Bengals, Inc., 601 F.2d 516 (10th Cir. 1979).

Torts that do not satisfy this standard (for example, negligent contact) are among the risks assumed by the participant. Because tort liability is limited to only those injuries committed with intent to harm, tort law gives participants in such sports a *qualified immunity* to tort actions. This is distinguishable from *absolute immunity* (or absolute privilege), which would give the participant immunity to all tort suits, whether based on negligence or intent. Judges, for example, enjoy absolute immunity with respect to lawsuits from disappointed litigants in their courts.

The qualified immunity observed in contact sports is a compromise designed to allow aggressive play and at the same time preserve some deterrent against violent criminal batteries. To hold participants subject to the general tort law would make it prohibitively expensive to play these sports – almost any victim of hard contact could sue on the theory that the injurer failed to take sufficient care to avoid causing the injury. For the same reasons, police officers enjoy qualified immunity from tort suits. Absolute immunity, on the other hand, eliminates the risk of tort liability entirely as a consideration in the actor's decision-making process. Judges are given absolute immunity because it is desirable that they make their decisions on the basis of the facts and law before them rather than concerns over personal liability.

V. INSANITY AS A DEFENSE VITIATING INTENT

The defenses to battery considered up to this point concern the intent of the defendant when he acted. Brian Dailey argued that he should not be held liable because he did not intend to cause Ms. Garratt to fall when he moved her chair. The doctor in *Mohr v. Williams* argued that the plaintiff had consented to the surgery – and consent implies that the defendant could not have had an intention to inflict harmful contact on the plaintiff. In this part, I consider the extent to which insanity annuls or vitiates intent in battery.

In <u>McGuire v. Almy</u>,[49] the plaintiff was a nurse employed to take care of the defendant. The plaintiff learned before she was hired that the defendant was insane and in good physical condition, a worrisome combination. During the period that the plaintiff cared for the defendant there had been violent incidents in which the plaintiff had to call for help to subdue the defendant.

One day the defendant went into a violent rage, breaking furniture and other objects in her room. The plaintiff called for help from the defendant's brother-in-law. Watching the defendant from outside her room, the plaintiff and the brother-in-law decided that they should remove the broken items from the room before the defendant injured herself. The defendant stood in the middle of the room holding a furniture leg above her head. The plaintiff walked in and the defendant struck her on the head.

---

[49] 8 N.E.2d 760 (Mass. 1937).

The key defense in the battery lawsuit was insanity. The defendant contended that she could not have had the intent required under battery law because she was insane.

The court held that *an insane person is liable for a tort under the same conditions in which a sane person would be held liable.* In the case of an intentional tort, this implies that *an insane person is liable for a battery as long as the person knows that his or her action will inflict a harmful bodily contact on another person.* Applying this rule, the court found that the defendant was liable because, although she was insane, she did know that her conduct would result in a harmful contact with the plaintiff.

The rule on insanity, as a defense to battery, implies that if the defendant had really thought that she was in a prizefight with a professional boxer, that explanation would still not provide a justification. As long as the defendant knew that she was striking someone, the intent requirement is satisfied.

Can an insane defendant ever escape liability under this rule? Suppose the insanity is of a type that prevents the defendant from knowing that he is touching a person. For example, suppose the defendant can prove that when he grabbed the plaintiff's arm, he thought he was grabbing the handle of a door. The defendant would escape liability because he would not meet the intent requirement of battery law. Although it would be difficult to prove this argument in court, it is not totally fanciful. Neurologist Oliver Sacks offered the following description of an encounter with a patient, Dr. P.:

> There was a hint of a smile on his face. He also appeared to have decided that the examination was over and started to look around for his hat. He reached out his hand and took hold of his wife's head, tried to lift it off, to put it on. He had apparently mistaken his wife for a hat! His wife looked as if she was used to such things.[50]

Had Dr. P.'s wife sued him for battery, his lawyer may have been able to present enough evidence, with the help of an expert in neurology, to avoid being held liable.

Another defense examined in *McGuire* is implied license or *assumption of risk*. The defendant argued that the plaintiff had impliedly consented to the battery because she chose to work as the nurse even though she was aware of the defendant's violent outbursts. The court's rejection of this argument reveals important limits on the assumption of risk defense.

The assumption of risk defense, in the employment setting, requires evidence that the risk that materialized was one that the plaintiff should be considered to have accepted as part of the working conditions. In most cases, the hazard is part of the fixed landscape of the workplace – for example, a sharp object dangling above the

---

[50] Oliver Sacks, The Man Who Mistook His Wife for a Hat and Other Clinical Tales 11 (Summit Books 1985).

plaintiff as he works.[51] *McGuire* is distinguishable from these cases. Although the defendant had erupted violently a few times, violent assaults were not a constant feature of the workplace. The court's rejection of the assumption of risk defense is consistent with the view that the defense is limited to risks associated with frequent, ordinary, and predictable features of the worksite.[52]

Another distinction between *McGuire* and the typical assumption of risk case is that it involves an intentional tort. The battery cases suggest that courts are reluctant to recognize an implied consent defense to offensive battery.[53] To do so would generate difficult questions about the scope of consent, considered earlier in this chapter in the discussion of mutual combat.

VI. JUSTIFICATIONS: SELF-DEFENSE, DEFENSE OF PROPERTY, AND RULES OF REASON

The defenses we have considered so far have been in the form of denials. A *denial* of the infringement or prima facie tort is a statement that the tort did not occur, or that if it did, it was not the act of the defendant. The argument that the defendant did not *intend* to execute the act that inflicted a harmful physical contact on the plaintiff is an example of a denial. The argument that the plaintiff *consented* to the defendant's contact is another type of denial. Similarly, the argument that insanity kept the defendant from meeting the intent requirement is yet another type of denial.

A justification is distinguishable from a denial. A justification concedes that the prima facie intentional tort occurred but holds that it was privileged under the law. In other words, a justification implies that ordinarily the defendant would be liable for battery, but under the circumstances of the case the actions of the defendant were justified.

In this part, we look at self-defense and defense of property as justifications. Both self-defense and defense of property have long been recognized as justifications for intentional torts. Along with this recognition have come rules governing the scope of justifiable defensive conduct.

Self-Defense

In *Keep v. Quallman*,[54] plaintiff and defendant, described as neighbors but not friends, met in a public highway. The defendant asked the plaintiff why he had been slandering him about town. The plaintiff, who had a reputation for being quarrelsome and for shooting people, suddenly put his hand in his pocket. The defendant, fearing the plaintiff would pull out a gun, struck the plaintiff on the head

---

[51] Lamson v. American Axe & Tool Co., 58 N.E. 585 (Mass. 1900).
[52] *See, e.g.,* Mullen v. Bruce, 335 P.2d 945 (Cal. App. 1959).
[53] Vosburg, 50 N.W. 403; *see also* the discussion of mutual combat in this chapter.
[54] Keep v. Quallman, 32 N.W. 233 (Wis. 1887).

with his cane twice, knocking him down. At trial, the jury was instructed that the defendant had offered no legal justification for the battery, since he was not being assaulted by the plaintiff when he used his cane as a weapon. The appellate court reversed and remanded for a new trial.

In *Courvoisier v. Raymond*,[55] the defendant (Courvoisier), owner of a jewelry store, was asleep in his bed on the second story of the building that housed the store when he was awakened in the middle of the night by men trying to shake open the store's doors. When Courvoisier asked them what they wanted, they demanded to be let in and responded to his refusal with abusive words. They then broke signs at the front and entered the building by another entrance, walked upstairs, and knocked on the bedroom door of Courvoisier's sister. Courvoisier grabbed his gun and put the men out, where they joined others on the street. Courvoisier fired a shot into the air to scare them away, but they did not run off. They walked around to the front of the store, throwing stones. Courvoisier fired more shots in the air. The noise attracted police officer Raymond and two deputy sheriffs. The deputy sheriffs stopped when they reached the men in the street and arrested them. Raymond proceeded alone toward Courvoisier calling out to him to stop shooting. Courvoisier took aim and shot Raymond.

At trial, Raymond said he was carrying out his duty as a police officer and that Courvoisier, knowing this, recklessly fired at him. Courvoisier claimed that Raymond was approaching him in a threatening manner, and that he thought his life was in danger. The jury was instructed that if they believed from the evidence that at the time the defendant shot the plaintiff, the plaintiff was not assaulting the defendant, they should give a verdict for the plaintiff. The appellate court found the instruction defective.

The instructions to the jury in both *Keep* and *Courvoisier* were erroneous because they left out a full consideration of the basis for the defendant's justification. In both cases, the defense required consideration of whether, under the circumstances, a reasonable person might have believed his life to be in danger, even if that belief later proved to be incorrect.

As for the rules on self-defense, *Keep* and *Courvoisier* deliver the lesson that the defendant is not liable for battery if he acted in self-defense, provided that (1) *his perception of the need to act in self-defense was reasonable,* and (2) *the force used in self-defense was also reasonable.* In short, *reasonable perception* and *reasonable force* are the key components of the self-defense argument. Both must be found for self-defense to justify a battery.

Reasonable force can be viewed as a proportionality requirement. Even though the court in *Courvoisier* suggested that the defendant may have had a reasonable perception of the need to act in self-defense, the question of reasonable force is conceptually independent. A trial court might find that Courvoisier reasonably

---

[55] Courvoisier v. Raymond, 47 P. 284 (Colo. 1896).

believed that his life was in danger when Raymond approached him, yet the court still could find that he acted with unreasonable (disproportionate) force given the nature of the threat. If, for example, Courvoisier used a machine gun to fire several rounds at the police officers, such a disproportionate response would likely fall outside of the scope of reasonable force.

One might ask whether the law on self-defense is consistent with the internalization principle invoked in several other parts of this chapter. It seems to be. Many cases of self-defense occur under emergency settings involving instinctive conduct and would not amount to intentional torts even if there had been no defensive motive. In the noninstinctive cases, self-defense, within its lawful scope, is clearly distinguishable from ordinary battery because it tends to advance the regulatory purposes of tort law: to persuade potential tortfeasors to consider and to respect the rights of others, and to seek consensual rather than predatory transactions. Take the case of an attacker who uses deadly force against his victims. If the victims were deprived of the legal right of self-defense, the attacker would kill his victims and their right to sue the attacker for damages would be of little value. Self-defense provides a ready deterrent threat against aggression and, under lawful use, imposes harms no greater than the harms avoided.

Defense of Property

What if the defendant is trying to protect his property rather than his life? Does the law limit his right of self-defense? Tort law permits the use of force to defend property, just as it permits the use of force in self-defense. The rule of reason in the self-defense setting carries over to the defense of real property. Thus, there must be a reasonable perception of the need to use force to defend the property, and the force used must be reasonable under the circumstances.

The reasonableness standard is quite general, as it must be to be applied in an infinite variety of settings. However, to say it is general does not mean that it fails to provide guidance of any sort. The reasonableness standard would lead most courts to the same conclusion in the vast majority of cases, because it involves making tradeoffs between types of property (for example, destroying a shed to prevent the destruction of a house), or between property and life, that most objective observers would accept. Moreover, courts have gone beyond the generality of the reasonableness standard and set out rules governing the propriety of specific actions in defense of property. This is sensible, given that some fact patterns involving defensive conduct are observed repeatedly.

In the most common fact pattern, the intruder enters property without the consent of the possessor, and the possessor uses force to expel the intruder. *Green v. Goddard*,[56] an English case of 1702, appears to be the earliest decision on record

---

[56] 2 Salk. 641 (K.B. 1702).

of this sort. A bull belonging to a stranger ran onto the defendant's property, and as the defendant tried to drive the bull out, the plaintiff came onto the defendant's property, to impede him and to rescue the bull. The defendant forcefully expelled the plaintiff.

In *M'Ilvoy v. Cockran*,[57] a Kentucky case, Cockran sued M'Ilvoy for injuring him as he was trying to break into M'Ilvoy's property. Cockran was in the process of tearing down a fence on M'Ilvoy's land when M'Ilvoy wounded him with a gun. M'Ilvoy argued that he was defending his property, and that he was permitted by law to use force to do so.

These cases deliver specific rules governing the use of force to protect property. *If the intruder enters peacefully, the possessor must first make a request that he leave the property. If the intruder refuses that request, or if the intruder enters with force at the start (e.g., breaking down a gate), the possessor is entitled to use force to expel the intruder. However, the force used must be reasonable under the circumstances.*

The notion of reasonable force implies that *the use of deadly force is justifiable only if the possessor reasonably perceives that he is being personally assaulted by the intruder*. Even then, the force used must be reasonable, in the interest of self-defense.

The level of force that is reasonable will be implied by its purpose. If a person is trying to protect his property, then reasonable force should be understood in light of that end. Killing an intruder to protect property will therefore often be unreasonable, because it goes well beyond what is necessary merely to eject or to stop the intruder.

In *Bird v. Holbrook*,[58] a young man jumped over the fence of the defendant's property to recapture a pea-hen that had gotten away from a young woman. Before jumping over, he called out to make sure no one was there and got no response. He did not know that the defendant had set a spring gun, no warning had been provided. The defendant had been the victim of thieves who had stolen valuable tulips from his land. The young man tripped the gun wire and was wounded in the leg. The court held the defendant liable.

There was evidence suggesting that the gun had been set with the deliberate aim of wounding an intruder. One witness reported that when he asked the defendant whether he would post a notice of the spring gun, the defendant said he would not, because he wanted to catch the thief.

The judges also referred to the inhumanity of using deadly force merely to catch a property thief, saying, in effect, that one should not trade life for property. Framed as a legal standard, the court held that as a general matter *it is unreasonable to use deadly force merely to protect property*. But this broad proposition is not easy to

[57] McIlvoy v. Cockran, 2 A.K. Marsh 271 (Ky. 1820).
[58] Bird v. Holbrook, 130 Eng. Rep. 911 (C.P. 1828).

apply to cases in which the use of deadly force translates, at most, to a probability of death.[59] In the vast majority of instances, life is not traded for property, but a risk of death is imposed to deter or prevent a theft from occurring. The inhumanity of such a tradeoff is less clear than one of life for property.[60]

More importantly, the court held that in the context of deadly force, *one cannot do indirectly what he is prohibited from doing directly*. Under *Green v. Goddard* and *M'Ilvoy v. Cockran* an owner or occupier can use deadly force to protect property only when he is threatened by an assault. Applying this doctrine to *Bird v. Holbrook*, the owner could not lawfully use a spring gun to protect his tulips because he was not personally under threat of serious harm at the time of the taking, and the situation was not one in which he would be personally at risk if he were on the property. If the owner had been on the property, he would not have been permitted to use deadly force to prevent someone from taking his tulips. It follows that the owner could not lawfully use deadly force indirectly.

What if a 400-pound man settles on your property? You ask him to go, and he doesn't. You try to forcefully remove him, but he doesn't budge. Although you do not owe the intruder a duty of care, you cannot use lethal force against him unless he assaults you. Not only can you not use lethal force, you might break the law by using nonlethal force that is likely to cause a serious injury. In *Palmer v. Gordon*,[61] a Holmes opinion, the trespassing plaintiff, a fifteen-year-old boy, sat with two other boys in the kitchen attached to the defendant's restaurant, with his feet near the oven to warm them. The defendant, after warning them to leave several times (the boys were not there to purchase food), went to the stove and moved a pan of scalding water back and forth, causing the hot water to spill onto the legs of the plaintiff. The court held the defendant liable for battery.

What if there are spikes on the top of a wall? *Bird v. Holbrook* distinguishes this case, because the intruder sees the spikes during the day, so they serve as a deterrent.

---

[59] Posner has argued that the amount of force that is reasonable has been viewed in many courts as proportional to the value of the property being defended, *see* Richard A. Posner, *Killing or Wounding to Protect a Property Interest*, 14 J. LAW ECON. 201, 219 (1971). One of the cases Posner cites in support of this proposition is Higgenbotham v. State, 116 So.2d 407 (Miss. 1959), where the defendant threw a heavy metal object at another person in an effort to prevent the destruction of a valuable store of frozen fish. It is possible, however, to read *Higgenbotham* as supporting a more limited proposition that the force used was reasonable in view of the low probability of harm. In any event, the proposition that greater force may be used to protect more valuable property is implied by the reasonableness rule.

[60] Consider the following hypothetical. Sam, after working all of his adult life to improve his ranch, sells it to someone else for cash. He puts the cash in an envelope in his jacket pocket. A thief, who observes the transaction, steals the envelope from Sam, and runs off. Sam draws his gun and shouts to the thief to stop. When the thief does not stop, he fires the gun in the thief's direction, hoping to stop but not to kill the thief. The bullet pierces the thief's heart and kills him instantly. Retrospectively, Sam has traded life for property. Prospectively, though, what should Sam have done?

[61] 53 N.E. 909 (Mass. 1899).

The law permits the use of a deterrent to protect property. The intruder gets hurt when he voluntarily confronts the danger. If he intrudes during the night, he assumes the risk.

Tort law distinguishes deterrents, which are visible, from traps. While a property possessor will not be held liable for battery when an intruder deliberately confronts a deterrent, he may be held liable for battery when an intruder is injured by a trap set by the possessor. Consider, for example, the use of a vicious dog to defend property. Generally, the intruder will see the dog, so it is a deterrent, like spikes on a wall. But if the possessor hides the dog, so that the intruder does not see or hear it, then the principle of *Bird v. Holbrook* may apply. In addition to being hidden, a dangerous agent sitting on the property is likely to be deemed a trap if it serves no other purpose than to injure the intruder. The intruder who climbs a fence and is gored by a bull will have difficulty arguing that it was a trap, because people do not keep bulls solely to injure intruders; they keep them for breeding purposes.

To sum up, a possessor can use a spring gun to protect his property under the same conditions that he can use any gun in defense of self or of property: when he is personally threatened by the intruder, or would have been personally threatened if he were present at the time of the intrusion. When an intruder breaks into a dwelling (a residence in which people live), the possessor can use a gun because it is assumed in the law that an intruder into a dwelling will harm the possessor. The early common law required the intrusion to occur in the night for deadly force to be used lawfully.[62] American common law, perhaps reflecting a more violent culture, relaxed this requirement.[63] Against an intruder who breaks into a dwelling, whether day or night, deadly force can be used.

The Restatement (Second) of Torts, Section 85, on the "use of mechanical device threatening death or serious bodily injury" says:

> The actor is so far privileged to use a device intended or likely to cause serious bodily harm or death for the purpose of protecting his land or chattels from intrusion that he is not liable for the serious bodily harm or death thereby caused to an intruder whose intrusion is, in fact, such that the actor, were he present, would be privileged to prevent or terminate it by the intentional infliction of such harm.[64]

Last, consider the issue of notice. Suppose the possessor sets up a spring gun in his house and provides notice. A burglar enters and gets shot. Does the notice make a difference in the outcome of a lawsuit by the burglar? Perhaps, but probably not a great difference. The possessor has a privilege to use deadly force in these circumstances. The notice merely bolsters the possessor's defense by making it clear that the plaintiff (burglar) did not act reasonably in view of the risk.

---

[62] 4 Blackstone, Commentaries *180.
[63] Scheuerman v. Scharfenberg, 50 So. 335 (Ala. 1909).
[64] Restatement (Second) of Torts §85 (1965).

Suppose the property possessor sets up the spring gun to protect old bottles housed in an empty shack (not a dwelling), as in *Katko v. Briney*.[65] A trespasser enters and gets shot. Does the notice make a difference? The notice clearly indicates that the trespasser did not take reasonable care for his own safety. However, the possessor used excessive force under the circumstances and will be held liable, as was the defendant in *Katko*. Although the possessor does not have a duty to take care for a trespasser's safety, he does have a duty to avoid intentionally harming him (Chapter 15).

Defense of Personal Property

Just as one can lawfully use force to defend real property, one can use force to defend personal property. The rule of reason applies here as well, with special contextual implications.

In *Kirby v. Foster*,[66] a warehouse manager, Foster, gave an employee, Kirby, some money with an instruction to pay the help. This provided the opportunity Kirby had been waiting for. Earlier, a sum of $50 had been lost, for which Kirby had been held responsible. The amount was deducted from his pay. Kirby, acting under the advice of a lawyer, took $50 out of the money entrusted to him, returned the extra, and said he had received his pay and was going to leave. Foster, with the help of others, grabbed Kirby and a struggle ensued during which Kirby was injured. Kirby sued for battery.

The issue was whether the defendants were privileged to use force to recover $50 from Kirby. The defendants argued that the money belonged to them when they handed it over to Kirby, and that Kirby held it as their agent strictly for the purpose of transferring according to their wishes. Kirby's subsequent appropriation of the money was therefore conversion (Chapter 16) according to the defendants. The court rejected this argument and held that there was no privilege to use force to recapture the money because the defendants had entrusted it to Kirby, in the absence of any wrong on his part. Given this, the defendants had to rely on their legal remedies to recover the money.

There is indeed a privilege to use force to retake property, but it is limited by the rule of reason. Our previous cases suggest that the reasonableness inquiry involves two questions: (1) *did the defendant have a reasonable perception of the need to use force* and (2) *did the defendant use reasonable force to retake his personal property?*

As to the first question, regarding the perception of the need to use force, courts have held that there is <u>no reasonable basis for using force when you give the property to someone else voluntarily, and in the absence of fraud</u>.[67] Contrariwise, *use of force*

---

[65] Katko v. Briney, 183 N.W.2d 657 (Iowa 1971).
[66] 22 A. 1111 (R.I. 1891).
[67] *Id.*

to retake personal property is reasonable if your possession was wrongly interrupted by force or fraud.[68]

On the second question, the reasonableness of force, courts have held that *the privilege to use force to retake personal property must be exercised within a reasonable period of time.*[69] If you wait too long, you may lose the right to respond with force to retake property and will have to go to court. Suppose someone takes your bicycle and you watch him ride around, treating it as if it is his own, for a substantial period – five years, a month, or even a week. During this time you never protest or attempt to take the bicycle back. All of a sudden, at the end of the period, you assault the thief to recapture the bicycle. You will be found liable for battery, because your conduct is not within the privilege to use force for recapturing property.

In the same sense, the right to oust someone who occupies your land phases out over time. If you "sit on your rights" by allowing a trespasser to stay on your land for a sufficiently long period, a court may find that the squatter has gained your consent and is no longer a trespasser, and has become a licensee (see Chapter 15 on categories of land visitors). You can convert his status back to a trespasser by revoking the consent. If he refuses to go, the rules examined earlier in this chapter in connection with the defense of real property apply.

If you allow the squatter to remain on your property for a very long time – say, twenty years – you may lose your right to evict him. Under the doctrine of *adverse possession*, a person who occupies property in an open and uninterrupted fashion for a sufficiently long period (depending on the law of the jurisdiction) gains ownership of the part that he has possessed. Courts hold that the adverse possession must be open, continuous, and hostile to the interests of the owner, in a manner that publicly indicates an assumed control and use of the premises.[70]

There are policies behind these rules. One is *consent*, both express and implied. *Kirby v. Foster* shows that if you voluntarily give your personal property to someone else, in the absence of fraud on the receiver's part, you will lose the privilege to use force to recapture the property. This follows because the new possessor has received your property with your express consent. If someone takes personal property from you by force and you wait several years to attempt to take it back, even though you could have easily done so earlier, you will lose the right to use force to recapture the property. The reason at the core is implied consent. By waiting so long, you have created the impression that you are content with the new arrangement. The party who took your personal property may have come to rely on your acceptance of the new arrangement. In other words, there is a *reliance interest* protected by the requirement that you act within a reasonable time period to retake personal property. The build-up of a reliance interest (e.g., investments based on possession) suggests

[68] *Id.*
[69] *Id.*
[70] *See, e.g.,* Monroe v. Rawlings, 49 N.W.2d 55 (Mich., 1951).

that a failure to act with force immediately will lead to more harmful consequences, and perhaps a more harmful confrontation, if you use force later. Thus, the reliance interest implies that force applied later will be more costly to society than force applied early. Finally, as in the case of adverse possession of real property, if you wait a very long time you will lose not only the legal privilege to use force to recapture, but the right to the property as well.

There is a connection here to the doctrine of *laches*, a defense that can be asserted against a plaintiff who waits a long time to file his lawsuit. The theory behind the defense is that the plaintiff has suggested consent, allowed for the build-up of reliance by the other party, and may be acting opportunistically by filing a lawsuit late when he could have filed much earlier. Laches is a general defense to any lawsuit, whether connected to the taking of property or to any other grievance.

VII. FALSE IMPRISONMENT AND RULES OF REASON

In addition to protecting bodily integrity, tort law also protects liberty, or the freedom to move about as one wishes. A person who confines another to a dungeon can be sued for the tort of false imprisonment. As the term "false" implies, it is possible to be justifiably or reasonably imprisoned. Just as one has a right to use physical force in self-defense, or to protect or recapture property, force can be used to detain or temporarily imprison someone for the same purposes.

Reasonableness principles similar to those introduced in the previous part apply to the action for false imprisonment. For the moment, I will focus on the plaintiff's claim, and consider the defendant's justifications later.

Reasonable Perception and Acquiescence

In *Whitaker v. Sandford*,[71] a woman held on the defendant's yacht was given freedom to roam about the yacht, but not the same freedom to roam on shore when the yacht docked. The court held that the plaintiff was falsely imprisoned on the yacht to the extent that she was not given reasonable access to shore when she desired.

In *C. N. Robinson & Co. v. Green*,[72] the plaintiff was held captive on an island for more than two years and forced to work for the defendant, essentially as a slave. He was part of a team of laborers who had been induced to go to the island with a promise that they would be paid to drive cattle from the island plantation to Decatur, Georgia. Once they arrived, they were forced to stay on the island under threat of violence.[73] The court held the defendant liable for false imprisonment.

---

[71] 85 A. 399 (Me. 1912).

[72] 43 So. 797 (Ala. 1906).

[73] On the size of the area of captivity, the Second Restatement of Torts offers the following: "A by an invalid process restrains B within prison limits which are coterminous with the boundaries of a considerable town. A has confined B." RESTATEMENT (SECOND) OF TORTS §36, comment b (1965).

A hypothetical example: A young man who can swim and is in good physical condition is left alone on a boat in a pond, anchored only a few yards from shore. Since he can easily jump out of the boat and swim to shore, a court would likely say that he does not have a valid claim of false imprisonment. If, however, he has a reasonable basis for believing that the pond is stocked with flesh-eating piranha, he has a valid claim of false imprisonment.

These examples suggest that a false imprisonment plaintiff must have a reasonable basis for believing that he is imprisoned. In other words, there must be *a reasonable perception of confinement on the part of the plaintiff.*[74] Although it may seem an obvious implication, we can add as a second requirement that there must be *reasonable acquiescence in the confinement.*

What is a reasonable perception of confinement? Courts have been unable to provide a bright line rule, and it would be impossible to do so. The question of reasonable perception of confinement seems to boil down to the degree to which the plaintiff is actually imprisoned or confined. A barrier that prevents the plaintiff from going in one direction but leaves him free to go in any other direction would not be considered an imprisonment in most cases.[75] Why? If the barrier only prevents the plaintiff from going in one direction, then the plaintiff would appear to have imprisoned himself, or to have consented to the defendant's request to stay put. In addition, a "prison" consisting of one wall raises the question whether the defendant intended to imprison – that is, intended to execute his actions while knowing with substantial certainty that his actions would imprison the plaintiff.

The perception of confinement is reasonable if to the ordinary person it would appear that there are substantial costs, in terms of physical or emotional injury, or loss of property,[76] that would result from leaving the space of confinement; and that the costs are sufficiently high that the average rational person, with the same physical abilities as the plaintiff, would choose not to leave the space of confinement under the given conditions. This is an inherently circular definition, but juries are asked to step into the plaintiff's shoes and make the determination anyway.

The question of reasonable acquiescence overlaps to a large degree with that of implied consent. A decision to remain in a confined space in response to a threat of death or of severe physical injury is not a valid assent because it is made under duress. Acquiescence in the face of such a threat would be reasonable, and hence no court would say that the plaintiff had not been imprisoned. A court may find reasonable acquiescence even if the threatened loss is not so severe. In *Griffin v. Clark,*[77] the plaintiff missed a train she needed to take to get to work on time because

---

[74] *See, e.g.,* Bird v. Jones, 115 Eng. Rep. 688 (K.B. 1845); Whittaker v. Sandford, 85 A. 399 (Me. 1912).

[75] Bird v. Jones, 115 Eng. Rep. 688 (K.B. 1845).

[76] *See, e.g.,* Fischer v. Famous-Barr Co., 646 S.W.2d 819 (Mo. App. 1982) (valid claim where plaintiff submitted to detention to keep a bag of purchased clothing); Griffin v. Clark, 42 P.2d 297 (Idaho 1935) (valid claim where plaintiff submitted to detention to remain with her luggage).

[77] 42 P.2d 297 (Idaho 1935).

the defendant removed her luggage from the train, put it in the back seat of his car, and insisted on driving her instead as the train left the station. She did not have enough money to take another train and was unfamiliar with the local bus system. During the drive, she was injured in a collision. The court found that she had not consented to the confinement.

More generally, one can distinguish several forces or conditions resulting in imprisonment. First, direct threats of severe physical harm would support a finding of imprisonment. Second, conditions of imprisonment that impose the same risk of physical harm, such as an elevated confinement space that would require the detained person to fall several hundred feet to escape, would support a finding of imprisonment. Third, conditions that make escape physically impossible, such as a cage with steel bars, would constitute imprisonment. Fourth, a threat of loss of property, if the resulting harm is sufficiently severe, may lead to a valid claim of imprisonment. Reasonable acquiescence is clear in the first three cases just mentioned, and a question for analysis in the fourth. For example, if the defendant in *Griffin v. Clark* had taken a candy bar belonging to the plaintiff rather than her luggage, the argument that she had reasonably acquiesced in the imprisonment would be much less persuasive.

Suppose a person is imprisoned and doesn't know it? The Second Restatement of Torts offers the following example: "A by an invalid process restrains B within prison limits which are coterminous with the boundaries of a considerable town. A has confined B."[78] The Restatement's example raises the question how the victim imprisoned in a "considerable town" could discover that he had been falsely imprisoned. Suppose the victim tries to leave the town but finds every exit blocked, with no explanation. Does he have a valid claim for false imprisonment? Even though the victim may not have been aware at the moment that he was *falsely* imprisoned, he was aware of the confinement. As long as his perception of confinement is reasonable, the plaintiff would appear to have a valid claim.

As a general matter, in any instance in which a reasonable person would perceive himself to be confined, even though unaware of its wrongful nature during the period of confinement, there should be a valid claim for false imprisonment.[79] Damages can be reduced to the extent that the victim did not suffer material harm.[80]

This answer is consistent with the law of other intentional torts, such as battery. Suppose a battery takes place and the victim is not aware of it when it happens. A woman is kissed by a stranger while she sleeps. She later discovers what happened.

---

[78] RESTATEMENT (SECOND) OF TORTS §36, comment b (1965). On the other hand, one court has held that being confined to Taiwan does not constitute imprisonment, *see* Shen v. Leo A. Daly Co., 222 F.3d 472 (8th Cir. 2000).

[79] *See, e.g.,* Herring v. Boyle, 149 Eng. Rep. 1126 (Ex. 1834) (court rejects false imprisonment claim because plaintiff unaware of confinement).

[80] Whitaker v. Sandford, 85 A. 399 (Me. 1912).

Does she have a valid battery claim against the stranger? Yes, all of the elements required to support an action for battery are present.[81]

Reasonable Cause and Reasonable Force

Some cases of imprisonment are justified because they are reasonable. The law· recognizes the right to confine to prevent a battery or damage to property. But when confinement is used in this defensive manner, it must satisfy reasonableness requirements similar to those discussed earlier in this chapter.

In *Coblyn v. Kennedy's, Inc.*,[82] the plaintiff, a short seventy-year-old man, was abruptly stopped by store employees as he left a department store. One employee, Goss, confronted the plaintiff and asked him where he had gotten the ascot he was wearing. He then grabbed the plaintiff by the arm and told him that he had to see the store manager. Other store customers stared as this was occurring. On the way to see the manager the plaintiff suffered chest pains and eventually was treated for a heart attack. The salesman who had helped the plaintiff told Goss that the ascot belonged to the plaintiff. The plaintiff won his lawsuit for false imprisonment.

Was the plaintiff's perception of imprisonment reasonable? The threat of force and the embarrassment were sufficient, in the court's opinion, to induce the plaintiff to do as directed by the store employees. Thus, the plaintiff's perception of confinement was reasonable, and it was reasonable for the plaintiff to acquiesce in the confinement.

Was the confinement itself reasonable? The defense to false imprisonment has two requirements: *There must be a reasonable perception of (or probable cause for) the need to confine, and there must be reasonable force used to confine*. The court found that there was neither a reasonable basis for the confinement nor reasonable force used in confining the plaintiff.

VIII. NECESSITY DEFENSE

The defenses considered so far have been in the form of denials or justifications. Recall that a denial of the infringement or prima facie tort is simply a statement the tort did not occur, or that if it did, it was not the act of the defendant. A justification, on the other hand, is an argument that the infringement did occur, but that it was legally justified. The self-defense and defense of property arguments we have considered are in the justification category. The reason is that self-defense justifies the defendant's intentional conduct (for example, battery or imprisonment)

---

[81] Wilson v. Bellamy, 414 S.E.2d 447 (N.C. App. 1992) (plaintiff intoxicated, raped while asleep; battery).

[82] Coblyn v. Kennedy's, Inc., 268 N.E.2d (Mass. 1971).

by proving that it was not a wrong under the law. Self-defense, within the constraints of the law, is reasonable conduct.

In this part, we consider a third type of defense, an excuse. An excuse is an argument that although the conduct of the defendant may not be viewed as reasonable under the law, it is also not a violation of the law under the circumstances of his case. The necessity defense is often put into the category of excuse, though in some cases, falling under the label "public necessity," it is better viewed as a justification.

Necessity and the Scope of Rights

In *Ploof v. Putnam*,[83] the defendant Putnam was the owner of an island in Lake Champlain with a dock attached to it. Ploof, his wife, and two minor children were sailing on the lake when a sudden violent storm arose. Ploof tied his sailboat to Putnam's dock. Putnam's servant untied the boat, and it was driven by the wind to the shore – its contents, including Ploof's wife and children, cast into the lake.

Ploof brought a trespass claim against Putnam for intentionally unmooring the ship and a negligence claim on the alternative theory that Putnam had carelessly unmoored the ship.

The court held that there is a *doctrine of necessity, which justifies unauthorized entries onto land and interferences with personal property resulting from the proper exercise of a right*.[84] Under this doctrine, Ploof was not a trespasser because he had a privilege to enter Putnam's land, to save his family from the danger of the sudden storm. And since Ploof was not a trespasser, Putnam did not have a privilege to use force to defend his property.

In explaining the necessity doctrine, the court offered several examples of intrusions that have been held not to be trespasses:

> In Millen v. Fandrye, . . . trespass was brought for chasing sheep, and the defendant pleaded that the sheep were trespassing upon his land, and that he with a little dog chased them out, and that as soon as the sheep were off his land he called in the dog. It was argued that, although the defendant might lawfully drive the sheep from his own ground with a dog, he had no right to pursue them into the next ground. But the court considered that the defendant might drive the sheep from his land with a dog, and that the nature of a dog is such that he cannot be withdrawn in an instant, and that as the defendant had done his best to recall the dog trespass would not lie. In trespass of cattle taken in A, defendant pleaded that he was seized of C, and found the cattle there damage feasant, and chased them toward the pound, and that they escaped from him and went into A, and he presently retook them; and this was held a good plea. . . . If one have a way over the land of another for his beasts to pass, and the beasts, being properly driven, feed the grass by morsels in

[83] 71 A. 188 (Vt. 1908).
[84] *Id.* at 189.

passing, or run out of the way and are promptly pursued and brought back, trespass will not lie. . . . A traveler on a highway, who finds it obstructed from a sudden and temporary cause, may pass upon the adjoining land without becoming a trespasser; because of the necessity.

An entry upon land to save goods which are in danger of being lost or destroyed by water or fire is not a trespass. . . . In Proctor v. Adams . . . the defendant went upon the plaintiff's beach for the purpose of saving and restoring to the lawful owner a boat which had been driven ashore and was in danger of being carried off by the sea; and it was held no trespass. This doctrine of necessity applies with special force to the preservation of human life. One assaulted and in peril of his life may run through the close of another to escape from his assailant.[85]

Pause and look again at these examples. They are all cases in which the defendant's conduct was deemed nontrespassory. But the reasons for not finding trespass differ; they are not all cases of necessity. The example of beasts feeding on the grass is not a trespass because it does not involve an intentional invasion. Similarly, in *Millen v. Fandrye*,[86] the defendant's conduct has a justification unrelated to necessity. The plaintiff's trespass claim was based on the injury to his sheep as a result of being chased by the defendant's dog. The court found that the defendant had a right to use his dog to chase the sheep off of his property – that is, the defendant's conduct was within his right to use limited force to eject an intruder from his property. The remaining examples involve intentional invasions not otherwise justified and therefore serve as illustrations of the necessity defense.[87]

The examples considered suggest that necessity can be described as involving, at a minimum, the exercise of a right on the part of the intruding party, such as the right to protect life, to protect personal property, or to move freely. The other important feature of the necessity cases is an emergency requiring immediate action and at the same time making it virtually impossible for the intruding party to seek permission before the intrusion. Put simply, the necessity defense requires the existence of a right and an emergency.

Ploof modifies the rules presented earlier in this chapter governing the defense of property. Suppose the intruder runs onto the possessor's land. Under the rules presented earlier, the possessor first has to ask the intruder to leave, provided that the intruder entered peacefully (*Green v. Goddard, M'Ilvoy v. Cockran*). After asking, the possessor can use force if the intruder refuses to leave. But if the intruder has a necessity defense, the possessor loses his privilege to use force to eject the intruder. As this example suggests, the necessity defense does more than simply remove the

---

[85] *Id.*

[86] Millen v. Fandrye, Popham 161, 79 Eng. Rep. 1259 (K.B. 1626).

[87] In the cattle trespass example, the defendant found the cattle causing damage ("damage feasant") to his property and drove them to the pound (a community holding pen used for stray cattle). The cattle got away from him and ran into the plaintiff's land, where he recaptured them to take them to the pound.

label "trespasser" from the intruding party: it readjusts the rights of possessor and intruder.

Loss of the privilege to use force in defending property has implications for the incentives of the party whose property is invaded. In the absence of the necessity rule, the possessor threatened with invasion would have no reason to consider the loss to the invading party. If untying a boat led to a loss of $1 million to the trespassing boat owner, that would not matter at all to the possessor because the loss would be suffered by a trespasser, to whom he owes no duty. The necessity rules changes the possessor's calculation. Now he has to compare the damage to his own property to the loss that would be suffered by the intruder as a result of being denied access to the property. If letting the boat stay on the property leads to a loss of $1 to the possessor, and untying the boat leads to a loss of $1 million to the intruding boat owner, the possessor would have an incentive to choose the less costly course of action (i.e., allow the intrusion) under the necessity rule.[88]

Necessity and Liability

In *Vincent v. Lake Erie*,[89] the steamship *Reynolds*, owned by the defendant, was tied to the plaintiff's dock when a violent storm developed. To prevent the ship from drifting away, the defendant's crew tied it to the dock and held it fast, replacing fraying lines when necessary. The ship was hurled by the wind against the dock repeatedly, resulting in damage to the dock. The plaintiff sued on the theory that it was negligent for the defendant's crew to moor the boat as they did. The court held that it was not negligent, and that the necessity doctrine excused the defendant's conduct. However, the court held that in spite of the necessity defense, the defendant still had a duty to compensate the dock owner for the damage.

Vincent v. Lake Erie establishes the proposition that *even though the doctrine of necessity excuses intrusions that would otherwise be trespasses, the defendant who intentionally intrudes on the property of the plaintiff, to protect himself or his own property, must still compensate the plaintiff for the damage done to the plaintiff's property.*

The court's rationale distinguishes three cases. One is that of an inevitable accident, as where a sudden violent wind picks up the ship and hurls it against the dock. There would be no basis here for holding the ship owner liable for damage to the dock, because he could not have foreseen the incident and did nothing to cause the damage beyond being present, which was lawful because of the consent of the owner.

---

[88] *See* Keith N. Hylton, *The Economics of Necessity*, 41 J. Legal Stud. 269 (2012). One might argue that the property owner should have no incentive to use force because he can always sue and be compensated under trespass doctrine. But it costs money and takes time to sue. Given this, the property owner will prefer to expel the intruder quickly if that can be done cheaply. In the absence of any fear of liability, the property owner has no incentive to consider the harm expulsion causes to the invading party.

[89] 124 N.W. 221 (Minn. 1910).

The second case is that in which "life or property was menaced by an object or thing belonging to the plaintiffs, the destruction of which became necessary to prevent the threatened disaster."[90] Suppose, for example, a portion of the dock holding a powerful explosive were about to break free and career among the ships, and destroying the portion holding the explosive would prevent or greatly lessen the imminent disaster. The defendant would not be held liable for the damage to the dock, for more than one reason. First, the defendant's conduct prevented greater losses to others, and for that reason would be deemed reasonable, or justifiable under the doctrine of *public necessity*. To hold the defendant liable would destroy his incentive to take steps to save a greater disaster to others. Suppose, for example, destroying the dock would lead to liability of $10,000, and the explosive would cause $20,000 in damages to others. If the defendant knew that he would be held liable for destroying the dock, he might choose not to do so, and let the others suffer a loss of $20,000. Second, if the explosive would have destroyed the dock anyway, there would be no basis on *causation* grounds for liability.[91]

The third case distinguished in *Vincent* was the one actually before the court, in which a defendant takes deliberate steps to preserve his property by invading or taking possession of the property of another. This is the case in which the intruding party has a duty to compensate for the injury caused by the intrusion. This rule provides the right incentives, from society's perspective, to an actor in the position of the defendant in *Vincent*. If an actor has to choose between losing his own property and destroying that of another, he should consider the loss his destruction would impose on the other property owner. If the actor has to pay for the destruction he causes, he will choose to preserve his own property when, and only when, it is more valuable than that of the other. Consider the difference between necessity and defense of property. Suppose building A is next door to building B, and B is on fire. The owners of A fear that the fire will communicate from B to A. Suppose, also, that there are no other properties threatened by the fire (i.e., no public necessity issue). If the owners of A destroy B, to contain the fire, will they have to pay damages under *Vincent*, or is this simply a case of exercising the right to protect one's own property from destruction? If building B is clearly at risk of falling over and destroying building A, invading the B property to destroy building B might be justifiable. As long as the perception of the risk to A is reasonable, and the force used is reasonable, the owner of A could rely on his right to protect his property. On the other hand, if the defendant's conduct fails to satisfy the reasonable defense test, then the necessity doctrine may apply and the owner of A would owe compensation to the owner of B.

The necessity doctrine appears in other settings in addition to the defense of property scenario. Criminal defendants plead necessity when the crime was the result of a choice between two evils. In *Holmes v. United States*,[92] the necessity

---

[90] *Id.* at 222.
[91] I refer to factual causation here, which is covered in Chapter 13.
[92] United States v. Holmes, 26 F. Cas. 360 (C.C.E.D. Pa. 1842) (No. 15,383).

defense was asserted by a ship crew charged with murder. After their ship had been destroyed in a storm, Holmes and his crew were adrift in a lifeboat with passengers. The lifeboat could not support all of the people on board. Holmes and crew decided to throw several male passengers overboard to save the lifeboat. When they reached shore, they were charged with murder. Their necessity argument was rejected on the ground that the crew should have first drawn lots among themselves to decide which of the excess crew members should be put off the lifeboat before ejecting passengers. There is a sensible policy basis for this decision: If a ship's crew could avoid criminal responsibility for sacrificing passengers to save themselves, they might care little about the dangers of storms and shipwrecks.

One of the most fascinating tort cases ever, *Laidlaw v. Sage*,[93] is not a necessity case, but can be analyzed from the perspective of necessity. Russell Sage, one of the wealthy robber-barons of the railroad industry in the early 1900s, was in his office when a man named Norcross came to visit him, with a demand for money. Norcross carried a satchel full of dynamite, which he threatened to explode unless given the money. As Sage pretended to think about the request, he walked behind his secretary, Laidlaw. Norcross dropped the satchel, causing it to explode, and Sage held tight to Laidlaw as he cowered behind him. Laidlaw was seriously injured. Sage suffered only minor injuries. Laidlaw sued Sage for compensation.

The necessity defense was not explicitly considered in the prolonged litigation that followed, but one can easily see the parallel between *Laidlaw* and *Vincent*. In both cases, the defendant, faced with a sudden violent outburst beyond his control, used another to avoid injury. It would appear, then, that the doctrine of *Vincent* should apply to *Laidlaw*. Thus, Sage, the defendant, should not be considered a trespasser with respect to Laidlaw, the secretary he held onto and cowered behind. However, *Vincent* implies that Sage had a duty to compensate Laidlaw.

However, at this point the causation issue arises – an issue considered, among others, by the appellate court in its reversal of the trial court's judgment for Laidlaw. Sage arguably had a duty to compensate Laidlaw under *Vincent*. But compensation would have been required only if the injury to Laidlaw could be attributed to Sage's act. This is where the case breaks down for Laidlaw. In *Laidlaw*, unlike in *Vincent*, the plaintiff likely would have been injured even if the defendant had not used him as a shield. Laidlaw was standing in the path of the dynamite blast, and that would have been true even if Sage had not cowered behind him. Laidlaw's claim for compensation was rejected in the end, and he never received a penny from Sage to compensate him for his injuries.

There are cases in which a building has been intentionally destroyed to prevent a fire from spreading to other buildings, and the owner of the destroyed building is denied compensation.[94] This reflects a public necessity doctrine that differs from the *Vincent* (private necessity) doctrine by not imposing a duty to compensate the

---

[93] Laidlaw v. Sage, 52 N.E. 679 (N.Y. 1899).

[94] *See, e.g.*, Bishop v. Mayor of Macon, 7 Ga. 200 (1849).

party whose property has been intentionally injured. As I noted earlier, there are two are two rationales for these decisions.

One is reasonableness: The destruction of a building to contain a fire capable of destroying many structures may be reasonable conduct. The other is causation: If the intentionally destroyed building would have been destroyed anyway by the fire, the damage caused by the intentional destruction is zero.

The Fifth Amendment of the U.S. Constitution requires compensation when the federal government takes private property for public use.[95] This constitutional provision suggests that government conduct based on the necessity principle should be reviewed with more care than similar conduct by private actors. However, there are additional principles that indicate when the constitutional compensation requirement applies. One can distinguish between taking property for *public use* and the prevention of a *public nuisance* or public injury generally. In the former, the government takes property to provide some benefit to the public, such as a new road. In the latter, the government takes property to prevent it from causing or being an instrument of harm to the public. Compensation to the property owner is required in the former, but not in the latter. This distinction is consistent with the reasonable conduct defense that applies when a private individual destroys property to prevent a greater harm to the public.

Let's return to the distinction between justification and excuse. As I noted before, some commentators have described self-defense as a *justification* and necessity as an *excuse*. This distinction is a bit simplistic. In both *Ploof* and *Vincent*, the rule of reason observed in the self-defense cases does not appear in the court's analysis. For this reason, one might be led to view necessity law, generally, as excusing conduct that is not justifiable on reasonableness grounds. But once one steps away from the private necessity settings in *Ploof* and *Vincent*, and considers the setting in which a person acts to save the public from a threatened injury, then the rule of reason does appear as part of the analysis of liability. The responsibility to compensate when an actor invades the plaintiff's property to save the property of others is governed by the rule of reason. It follows that courts will try to determine whether there was (1) a reasonable perception of the need to act to prevent harm to the public and (2) reasonable conduct on the part of the actor. In this setting, the necessity defense has a broader scope and rises to the level of justification.

IX. WILLFUL, WANTON, RECKLESS CONDUCT

The previous parts have considered conduct that is either intentional or unintentional. The dividing line between the two is based on the actor's perception of the immediate consequences of his act. If a person acts, knowing with substantial certainty that his actions will inflict a harmful physical contact on someone, then

---

[95] U.S. Const. amend. V.

he satisfies the mental state requirement for liability under the law of intentional torts.

In this part, we consider torts that require for liability a "higher" or more aggravated level of intent. The more aggravated level of intent is often described as willful, wanton, or reckless.

Willful, wanton, or reckless conduct refers to a course of action that evinces a deliberate intent to harm, or, if the action is not intentional in this precise sense, an utter indifference to the welfare of the potential victim or victims. Examples of intentional conduct within this category: A deliberately punches B in the nose, A deliberately spits in B's face. In both of these cases, A's conduct evinces an intent to harm B, which is more aggravated than, or a level beyond, the intent observed in cases such as *Vosburg v. Putney*, where the defendant's kick was for the purpose of getting the attention of the plaintiff, not to harm him. In the second example (spitting in the face), the injurer's conduct does not necessarily result in a physical injury to the victim, but the anticipated insult or embarrassment is sufficient to satisfy the willful and wanton standard. The intent associated with willful and wanton conduct goes beyond the minimal intent required for battery, which is just an intention to inflict physical contact that is unlikely to be desired or sought.

A willful battery may occur even without a direct touch. In *Fisher v. Carrousel Motor Hotel, Inc.*,[96] the plaintiff, a mathematician employed by NASA, attended a buffet lunch meeting at the Brass Ring Club located in the defendant hotel. As he was about to give his tray to a server, an employee of the hotel snatched the tray from his hand, and snarled that he, a Negro, could not be served in the club. The hotel was held liable for battery and a punitive judgment of $500 for malicious conduct.

Reckless conduct is typically not intentional but evinces indifference to the welfare of those put at risk by it. A person acts recklessly if he knows of the high risk of harm created by his conduct, and the precaution that would eliminate the risk is slight. Examples: playing with a loaded gun on a crowded subway car, or knowingly driving on the wrong side of the road against traffic. In *Aiken v. Holyoke Street Ry. Co.*,[97] the motorman could see that a six-year-old boy was clinging to the front steps crying to be let off the electric car; instead, he abruptly increased the power to speed the car up, throwing the boy off and injuring him. The railway was held liable for the reckless conduct of the motorman.

Courts tend to treat the conduct within the willful-wanton-reckless category as if it is all the same in terms of legal culpability. This is an understandable position. Reckless conduct, although not willful in the sense of targeting a specific individual, is arguably worse because it imposes harm indiscriminately. Someone who plays with a loaded gun on a crowded subway car is at least as dangerous as a person who

---

[96] 424 S.W.2d 626 (Tex. 1967).
[97] 61 N.E. 557 (Mass. 1903).

takes aim and fires the gun at a particular victim. It would be strange if he could avoid liability by claiming that he did not intend to shoot anyone.

Obviously, an actor who injures someone through willful, wanton, or reckless conduct will be held liable, since any actor who meets this level of intent necessarily meets the more basic, "intent to execute the act," level required for liability for intentional torts. In addition, an actor who satisfies the willful, wanton, or reckless standard is eligible to be held liable for punitive damages (Chapter 19).[98] Punitive damages are designed to punish and deter the injurer rather than to compensate the victim. Two examples of willful torts are assault and intentional infliction of emotional distress.

Assault

An assault is an attempt or threat to physically harm another person, even if physical contact never occurs. The assault is accomplished if the actor's conduct would lead a reasonable person to believe that a harmful or offensive physical contact is imminent. For example, if A throws a punch at B and misses, or if A raises his fist threatening to strike B, A has assaulted B.

To hold a defendant liable for assault, the evidence must indicate that he *intended to harm the victim*.[99] Of course, this includes conduct that creates an immediate fear of being harmed.[100] The intention-to-harm requirement for assault is higher than the intent level required for liability under battery doctrine. For battery, the plaintiff need only show that the defendant intended to execute the act that caused a harmful bodily contact – subject to the proviso that the defendant knew or should have known that the bodily contact would not be desired by the plaintiff.

Assault requires more than words. It requires threatening *conduct*. Threatening conduct can take many forms. There are many people who convey threatening signals in the course of argument; walking up face-to-face with their opponents, jabbing fingers toward them. While such conduct may violate norms of etiquette and collegiality, depending on the setting, it generally does not qualify as an assault. For example, in *Brower v. Ackerley*,[101] the defendant made a series of threatening phone calls to the plaintiff's home at night, saying that he would find where the plaintiff lives and beat him up. Still, the court found that the calls did not constitute an assault because there was no threat of imminent harm.

---

[98] *See, e.g.*, Day v. Woodworth, 54 U.S. 363 (1852).

[99] RESTATEMENT (SECOND) OF TORTS §21 (1965) ("An actor is subject to liability to another for assault if: (a) he acts intending to cause a harmful or offensive contact with the person of the other or a third person, or an imminent apprehension of such a contact, and (b) the other is thereby put in such imminent apprehension.").

[100] Allen v. Hannaford, 244 P. 700 (Wash. 1926) (pointing unloaded gun at plaintiff); Beach v. Hancock, 27 N.H. 223 (1853) (same).

[101] 943 P.2d 1141 (Wash. Ct. App. 1997).

The difficulty in drawing the line between heated argumentation and assault has forced courts to limit the definition of assault to <u>conduct that poses an immediate threat of physical harm to the victim</u>. This is necessary. Otherwise, many defendants would be held liable for assault on the basis of conduct they engage in during ordinary arguments. Courts must endeavor to set clear boundaries on the definition of assault to prevent the law from being used to constrain speech.

We can understand the law's reluctance to constrain speech in terms of the internalization goal set out at the start of this chapter and the activity level analysis of Chapter 2. The benefits from speech are widely disseminated. It is a "public good" in the sense that the benefits that flow from informative speech can extend to many people at the same time without any diminishment resulting from its mass dissemination. If A expresses information to B, that information can be passed on in full to C and to D, and so on. Speech, then, is a classic example of an activity with externalized or public benefits, and in view of these benefits, a policy of internalizing losses without also internalizing benefits would excessively dampen the activity.

Since there are external benefits associated with speech, and some related expressive conduct, society should prefer liability rules that encourage it to some degree, by providing a subsidy. That is, in effect, what the law on assault does by making it more difficult to successfully prosecute an assault claim than a battery claim. The law makes it more difficult to prevail in a civil action for assault by requiring proof of intent to harm rather than the more easily satisfied requirement under battery of proof of intent to execute the act.

Intentional Infliction of Emotional Distress

When the defendant has by <u>extreme and outrageous conduct intentionally or recklessly caused severe emotional distress to the plaintiff</u>, he can be found liable for the tort of <u>intentional infliction of emotional</u> distress. The tort was first recognized in an English case decided in 1897, *Wilkinson v. Downton*.[102] The defendant, playing a practical joke, told the plaintiff that he had been sent by her husband to inform her that he had been badly injured in an accident and was in the hospital with both legs broken, and that she must go at once in a taxicab to bring him home. This caused a "violent shock" to the plaintiff's nervous system, followed by nausea and weeks of suffering and incapacity.

The court gave the plaintiff her out-of-pocket expenses (for travel to the hospital) as compensation for the tort of deceit. It also awarded her £100 for intentional infliction of emotional distress, independent of (not parasitic to) the tort of deceit.

As this description of the facts suggests, the £100 probably could have been awarded by the court in connection to the tort of deceit. This is because the defendant is liable for all damages, foreseeable and unforeseeable, directly caused by an

[102] Wilkinson v. Downton, 2 Q.B. 57 (1897).

intentional tort (*Vosburg v. Putney*), and deceit is an intentional tort.[103] Put another way, a damages judgment can be awarded for mental distress that is parasitic to an intentional tort, such as battery or assault.

Why introduce a new tort for intentional infliction of emotional distress? If a court decides to award damages on the independent ground of intentional infliction of emotional distress, it does not have to find that the defendant is guilty of some other tort, such as deceit. For example, suppose the tortfeasor informs the wife that her husband has been severely injured in an accident, and the information is true. Suppose, in addition, the defendant does this in a manner calculated to maximize the emotional injury – say, by laughing as he shows her pictures of the accident scene. The defendant could be held liable for intentional infliction of emotional distress even though it is true that the plaintiff's husband had been severely injured. The tort of deceit would not be available to the plaintiff in this scenario.

When a court awards damages for intentional infliction of emotional distress, there is an issue of remoteness that should be considered, according to *Wilkinson*. Put another way, when the damages award is not parasitic to some intentional tort such as battery, there is a question of foreseeability that enters the analysis. If the plaintiff's injury appears to be due to his own conduct, or is totally out of proportion to the defendant's actions, then a court may hold that the plaintiff's asserted losses, or some portion thereof, are too remote to be recovered.[104]

The tort of intentional infliction of emotional distress requires conduct that is extreme and outrageous. In general, mere insults and indignities do not meet this standard. Why the search for outrageous conduct? For the same reason stressed earlier in the discussion of assaults: The common law is reluctant to hold people liable for speech. The law takes this position because speech is an activity that tends to be socially beneficial – because information is a free and inexhaustible resource, the speaker often conveys a benefit to third parties beyond the direct recipient of his message. Holding actors liable for speech discourages expression and obstructs the flow of information in society. Laws that discourage speech are likely to do more harm than good.

X. INTENT LEVELS AND LIABILITY

Taking a broader view of the landscape of intentional torts, we can describe several levels of intent and the tort rules connected with them. Start with the lowest level of intent, *involuntary conduct*. The category of involuntary conduct includes acts that are not directed by the thoughts of the actor. For example, if the actor is thrown off of his horse and lands on the victim, the victim's injury is due to the involuntary

---

[103] The issue is a bit more complicated than suggested here. While English law does not impose a foreseeability limitation, it prevents recovery in a deceit action for damages that could have been avoided by the plaintiff. Doyle v. Olby 2 Q.B. 158 (1969). Whether emotional distress would be considered an injury that could have been avoided by the plaintiff is an open question.

[104] Spackman v. Good, 245 Cal. App.2d 518 (Cal. Ct. App. 1966).

conduct of the actor. As additional examples, suppose the actor is blown by the wind, or carried by a band of ruffians, over to the plaintiff's property.

The second level of intent includes conduct that is *automatic, compulsive, reflex-ive, or instinctive*. This is voluntary in only the weakest sense – voluntary without direction. This category includes some acts of instinctual self-defense. Suppose the actor, to avoid a punch, jumps backward and lands on the victim, or to avoid a ferocious animal, runs onto someone else's property. Sleepwalking probably also falls in this category. In *Scott v. Shepherd* (Chapter 3), the defendant threw a lighted squib into a market stall, after which the squib was tossed away by two intermediate actors, frantically trying to evade the blast, before the squib exploded, putting out the eye of the plaintiff. The conduct of the intermediate actors was governed by this second level of intent.

The third level of intent is *volitional* – voluntary with direction. This category includes conduct that is directed by the actor at the most basic level (directing movement of limbs). It is the *intent to execute the act*. A trespasser who innocently walks on the property of the plaintiff has the level of intent associated with this category. The conduct of the defendant in *Vosburg v. Putney*, who kicked the plaintiff to get his attention, satisfies this level of intent.

The final level of intent is *intent to harm.* This category includes conduct that is directed by the actor not only at the most basic level (directing movement of limbs), but also at the level of intending some harmful effect on the victim. An actor who intentionally punches a victim in the nose would satisfy this level of intent.

Now we can consider some basic tort rules connected to these intent levels. In general, involuntary conduct is not subject to liability for trespass or battery. Such conduct may form the basis of a negligence lawsuit, as we will see later. But intentional torts require a minimal level of self-direction, which is not true of conduct in the involuntary category.

Conduct that falls in the voluntary-without-direction category is also exempt from trespass and battery liability. If the actor simply acts instinctively to avoid being injured, and thereby causes harm to the victim, the actor will not be liable for an intentional tort.

Liability for battery and trespass, the core intentional torts, begins at the level of volitional conduct. If the actor walks on the plaintiff's property and his actions are self-directed in the sense that he is aware of and in charge of the movements he is making, he will be found guilty of trespass. Similarly, the actor who touches another, in a setting in which he is in command of his movements, will be found guilty of battery.

The key feature of the volitional category is the element of rational choice. The actor in the volitional category is in a position to choose among courses of action. He can choose to walk on the plaintiff's property, or on another parcel of land, or to stay put. He can choose whether to touch the plaintiff or not. This element of rational choice is not present in the cases of involuntary conduct and voluntary-without-direction conduct.

The final category of conduct involves intent to harm. This is the most difficult burden for the plaintiff to satisfy, because he must offer evidence that is consistent with an intent to harm the victim, rather than merely to execute an act that inflicted a harmful physical contact.

There is a well-known distinction in the law between general and specific intent. *General intent* refers to the category of volitional conduct where one has an intention to do precisely what he is doing (walking on the plaintiff's property, touching the plaintiff). *Specific intent* refers to the intention to harm the victim.

Assault, in contrast to battery, requires specific intent. To hold the defendant liable for assault, there must be evidence that the defendant intended to harm the plaintiff, or put him in fear of immediate harm. This is a more demanding proof requirement for the plaintiff than observed in the battery context.

The same is true of the tort of intentional infliction of emotional distress. The outrageousness requirement puts the burden on the plaintiff to offer evidence that the defendant intended to harm him. Evidence that is consistent with the defendant being a nasty person is not enough to support liability for intentional infliction of emotional distress.

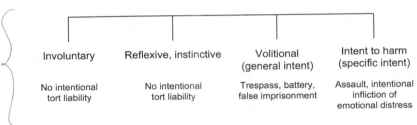

The intentional torts that require evidence of specific intent involve conduct that society is reluctant to discourage, because it tends to be beneficial. People engaged in a heated argument often behave in ways that might appear to threaten harm, but if these instances were treated as cases of assault, or intentional infliction of emotional distress, the law would punish, and consequently discourage, a great deal of expression. This risk of punishing expression is reduced by the intent-to-harm standard.[105] The internalization principle introduced at the start of this chapter is still at work here, though constrained to a narrower set of potentially harmful acts.

The end result is that some plaintiffs who have nonfrivolous claims for assault or for intentional infliction of emotional distress will lose in court. But tort law has accepted this as one by-product of a rational tradeoff of the costs of erroneous decisions on both sides of the question of liability. Such rational tradeoffs, reflecting the consequences of alternative approaches to regulating volitional conduct, are observed throughout the law of intentional torts.

---

[105] For discussion *see* Keith N. Hylton, *Intent in Tort Law*, 44 VAL. U. L. REV. 1217 (2010).

5

Theoretical Foundations of Strict Liability

The fundamental components of modern tort law are strict liability and negligence. The focus of this chapter is strict liability, as developed in *Rylands v. Fletcher*.[1] As in the previous chapter, I will continue to develop a functional account of tort doctrine. In particular, I will try to explain the purpose and limits of strict liability from an instrumentalist perspective. Of course, any theory that explains the scope of strict liability should also be capable of explaining the scope of negligence, or precisely when negligence liability ends and strict liability begins.

The first part of this chapter (sections I and II) presents the *Rylands* doctrine and an instrumentalist justification for it. The second part (section III) extends the theory of *Rylands* to provide a justification for the boundary between strict liability and negligence as well as the boundary between negligence and tort immunity.

I. *RYLANDS V. FLETCHER*

Ancient coal mine shafts ran beneath the surface of the adjacent properties of the defendant and the plaintiff. These shafts were filled with soil, so their paths would not have been immediately clear to anyone who found them while excavating. The defendant built a reservoir. The water from the reservoir burst through the shafts, flooding the plaintiff's property.

Engineers employed by the defendant became aware of the ancient shafts as they were constructing the reservoir. However, they did not know how far the shafts extended. Although there was evidence suggesting that the engineers did not use proper care, this was inconclusive.

One of the issues in the lawsuit was whether the defendant was guilty of a trespass. Trespass, recall, involves the intentional invasion of another's property. The kind of

[1] Rylands v. Fletcher, L.R. 1 Ex. 265 (1866), *aff'd*, L.R. 3 H.L. 330 (1868).

intent required for trespass is simply an intention to invade, not necessarily to do any harm to the plaintiff.

Was this a case of trespass? How would a plaintiff present a credible trespass theory? To do so, the plaintiff would have to argue that the defendant knowingly sent the water over to his property. That would imply the defendant was aware of the ancient shafts and filled them with water knowing with *substantial certainty* that the water would flood the plaintiff's land. Alternatively, the plaintiff could argue that the defendant knew enough to strongly suspect (or knew with substantial certainty) that the ancient shafts led underneath the plaintiff's land, but filled his reservoir anyway because he was indifferent to the suffering of the plaintiff.

The trespass theory was not successful, and it is easy to see why. The facts failed to show that the defendant had enough information to enable a court to find that he had acted with an intent to invade the plaintiff's property. It would be a trespass case, for example, if the defendant had shot water directly onto the plaintiff's property. But the defendant simply put water into a hole on his property, and the water came out in a place that the defendant could neither see, nor easily predict, under the circumstances.

The Court of Exchequer Chamber, reversing a verdict for the defendant in the intermediate appellate court, held the defendant strictly liable. The court analogized this case to one of keeping cattle on your property that stray and cause damage to someone else's property. Earlier cases had held the cattle owner strictly liable for the harm – that is, liable without regard to his level of care.

The court announced a new rule: "the person who for his own purpose brings on his lands and collects and keeps there anything likely to do mischief if it escapes, must keep it in at his peril, and, if he does not do so, is prima facie answerable for all the damage which is the natural consequence of its escape."[2] The court added, "he can excuse himself by showing that the escape was owing to the plaintiff's default; or perhaps that the escape was the consequence of the vis major, or the act of God."[3]

The court provided examples falling under the rule: escaping cattle that damage someone's crops, a bursting reservoir, a cellar invaded by the filth of a neighbor's privy, or air polluted by the fumes of a neighbor's alkali works. In each of these cases, the court noted, the law imposes strict liability, that is, liability without regard to fault. However, *damages are limited to the foreseeable consequences of an escape.* For example, in the case of escaping animals, "he will be answerable for the natural consequences of their escape . . . for our ancestors have settled that it is not the general nature of horses to kick, or bulls to gore; but that if the owner knows that the beast has a vicious propensity to attack man, he will be answerable for that too."[4]

---

[2] Fletcher v. Rylands, L.R. 1 Ex., at 279.

[3] *Id.*

[4] *Id.* at 280.

The court distinguished these cases from the standard scenario where the negligence rule applies: accidents on the highways. When a person drives on the road, reasoned the court, he imposes risk on others and accepts some risk in return. In other words, where there is *a reciprocal exchange of risk*, the negligence rule applies. The court also distinguished the case of an accident on the defendant's property (for example, the plaintiff, walking on the defendant's property, is hit on the head by a bale of cotton that the defendant's employees are lowering), on the ground that the plaintiff *implicitly assumes the risk*. It would seem appropriate to infer that the plaintiff assumes some risk when he voluntarily enters the defendant's property, and, more generally, when the benefits the plaintiff anticipates receiving from the defendant's activity make it worthwhile for him to accept the risks imposed on him, as a land visitor, by that activity.[5]

This description of the court's holding and rationale is taken mostly from Judge Blackburn's opinion in the Court of the Exchequer Chamber. It is a remarkable piece that synthesizes decisions from several areas of tort law under a general rule and provides a theoretical foundation, based on the reciprocal exchange of risk and assumption of risk.

Taking into account the theoretical arguments (and the minor descriptive changes in the Blackburn's opinion when it was appealed to the House of Lords), the doctrine of *Rylands* can be stated as follows:

> The person who for his own purpose brings on his land and keeps an unreasonable thing or activity that is likely to harm others if it escapes, is strictly liable for all the damage which is the foreseeable consequence of its escape. The defendant can excuse himself by showing that the escape was due to the plaintiff's fault or the result of an "act of God." The defendant's activity may be reasonable if the risk it imposes on neighbors is reciprocal to the risks of activities common to the community or if the activity benefits neighbors.

The *act of God defense* has not been defined with precision. Some courts have mused that if a defendant held a tiger on his property, he would be strictly liable even if a lightning bolt snapped the tiger's chain.[6] Such statements suggest that the act of God defense is extremely narrow.

To the extent that the act of God defense can be reconciled with other statements in the case law based on *Rylands*, it seems to shield the defendant from liability for escapes caused by natural disasters, such earthquakes, hurricanes,[7] or extremely unusual rainfalls.[8] But the defense also assumes that the potential destructiveness of

---

[5] For example, a customer who visits a grocery store accepts some risk that he will slip on spilled food in one of the aisles, provided that there is no negligence on the part of the store owner. But the customer is willing to accept this risk to get the benefit of shopping for groceries.

[6] *See, e.g.,* Baker v. Snell, [1908] 2 K. B. 352, at 354.

[7] Golden v. Amory, 109 N.E.2d 131 (Mass. 1952).

[8] Nichols v. Marsland, 2 Ex. D. 1 (1876).

the harmful agent on the defendant's land is modest under ordinary conditions, and only the act of God imparts a special destructiveness to the agent.[9] The implication of this defense is that the only way to have prevented the harm to the plaintiff resulting from the conjunction of the defendant's activity and the act of God would have been to prevent the defendant from engaging in ordinary and even socially beneficial uses of his property.

The other excuse recognized in *Rylands* arises where the escape of the hazardous agent is due to the plaintiff's unreasonable conduct. Thus, if the plaintiff unreasonably caused the defendant's tiger to escape – for example, the plaintiff breaks the tiger's chain – the defendant would have a strong contributory fault defense, where the plaintiff's fault amounts to gross negligence or recklessness.

II. *RYLANDS V. FLETCHER* IN FUNCTIONAL TERMS

The theoretical foundation of *Rylands* is the concept of *risk externalization*.[10] First, let's define the "residual risk" externalized by an activity as the risk of harm associated with an activity when it is conducted with reasonable care. *Rylands v. Fletcher* suggests that *the rule of strict liability does not apply when the residual risk externalized by the defendant's activity is roughly the same as risks reciprocally externalized by other activities, or the same as the benefit externalized by the defendant's activity*. Put another way, strict liability applies under *Rylands* when the risk externalized by the defendant is disproportionately large in comparison to the risk externalized by other actors, or disproportionate in light of the benefit externalized.

For example, consider the common activity of driving. The risk externalized by driver A is the risk of injury from a car accident that might occur even when driver A is taking reasonable care. However, other drivers (B, C, and D) externalize the same risk to driver A. Under the theory of *Rylands*, strict liability should not apply. Negligence is therefore the appropriate legal standard governing liability for road accidents.

Why does *reciprocal exchange of risk* imply that the negligence rather than the strict liability standard is appropriate? Because strict liability is designed to act as a tax that reduces the level of a harmful activity (see Chapter 2). That tax is appropriate when an activity externalizes far more risk than is reciprocated back to it or than the benefit it externalizes. However, when an activity generates roughly the same risk as other activities, there is no need to tax it to scale back its presence. Since there is no need to adopt strict liability, the rule of negligence should apply.

Consider a numerical example illustrating the reciprocal exchange of risk. Suppose there are two drivers, A and B. When A drives with reasonable care, there is

---

[9] Nichols v. Marsland, L.R. 10 Ex. 255 (1875) (distinguishing tiger hypothetical from defendant's artificial pools, which overflowed due to heavy rain).

[10] *See* Chapter 2; *see also* Keith N. Hylton, A *Missing Market Theory of Tort Law*, 90 Nw. U. L. Rev. 977 (1996); Keith N. Hylton, A *Positive Theory of Strict Liability*, 4 Rev. Law & Econ. 153 (2008).

still a risk that he will accidentally run his car into B's car. Suppose this accident risk imposes an expected cost (measured by the probability of an accident multiplied by the likely injury loss) of $10 per mile on B.[11] Assume also that when B drives with reasonable care he imposes an accident risk of $10 per mile on A.

Consider the activity level effects of strict liability and negligence when there is a reciprocal exchange of risk. If the law imposes strict liability on each driver, the expected accident costs faced by A when he takes to the road can be determined as follows. First, since liability is strict, he will not have to bear his own losses. Second, since liability is strict he will have to pay for the losses to B. Under strict liability, A's expected liability is $10 per mile, which consists entirely of his expected payments to B.

Now suppose the negligence rule applies, which holds A liable only when he fails to take care, and likewise for B. Assuming A and B take reasonable care, A's costs are as follows. First, he will have to bear his own injury loss because B is taking care, which amounts to $10 per mile. Second, he will not have to pay for A's injury losses in an accident that he causes, because his care is reasonable. Thus, under negligence, A's expected liability is $10 per mile, which consists entirely of his own losses.

Notice that in this example of reciprocal risk bearing, there is no reason, based on activity-level incentives, for switching from negligence to strict liability. Under negligence, the activity cost borne by A is $10 per mile. Under strict liability, the activity cost borne by A is the same, $10 per mile. Given this, no gain, in terms of activity level reduction, can be achieved by switching from negligence to strict liability. Strict liability is of no use, as a method of reducing the scale of accident-causing activity, in the context of reciprocal risk bearing.

Now consider the case in which there are benefits externalized in addition to risks. Suppose A imposes a risk of $50 per mile on B and also confers a benefit of $40 per mile on B. Suppose driver B imposes a risk of $10 per mile on A, while conferring no benefit.

Under strict liability, A's activity costs amount to $50 per mile. B's activity costs amount to $10. As a result, A will reduce his activity relative to B.

Under the negligence rule, A's activity costs will amount to $10, which is the cost imposed on him by B. B's activity costs will be $50 in accident losses less $40 in conferred benefit, which is a net cost of $10 per mile. Since the net activity costs are the same for both drivers, they will choose the same activity levels.

The outcome under negligence is the preferable outcome. The reason is that strict liability overtaxes A's activity. The net cost to society of A's activity is only $10, while strict liability taxes A as if the net cost to society of his activity were $50. The negligence rule reaches the best result in this case. This example illustrates the

---

[11] For example, if the probability of an accident is 0.10 and the loss imposed by the accident would be $100, then the expected cost of an accident is 0.10 × $100 = $10. On the concept of expected cost, *see* Chapter 2.

claim that when external risks are largely offset by external benefits, negligence is preferable to strict liability.

To link this with *Rylands*, note that the reciprocal risk exchange theory appears to fit the scenario of accidents on the roads. The negligence rule applies in this scenario because there is no gain to be had by switching from negligence, the default legal standard, to strict liability.[12]

The other case suggested by this theory in which the negligence standard should apply is where the externalized benefit is at least as great as the externalized risk. These are settings in which the implied assumption of risk theory would seem appropriate.

The best illustration of the role played by externalized benefits in the *Rylands* doctrine is *Rickards v. Lothian*.[13] The defendant leased a commercial building with a lavatory on the fourth floor. The plaintiff was a tenant whose business occupied part of the second floor. An unknown person snuck into the building late one night, stuffed the sink, turned the faucet on full blast, and left it running overnight. The next morning, the plaintiff found his stock-in-trade (largely schoolbooks) ruined, and brought a strict liability suit against the defendant on the theory that the introduction of the lavatory was equivalent to the reservoir in *Rylands*. The court rejected the plaintiff's claim. The court noted that "the provision of a proper supply of water to the various parts of a house is not only reasonable, but has become, in accordance with modern sanitary views, an almost necessary feature of town life."[14]

The difference between the outcome in *Rickards* (no strict liability) and that in *Rylands* (strict liability) can be explained by the presence of externalized benefits in *Rickards*. In *Rickards*, the provision of water supply to a building provides benefits to all who use the building – whether tenants or not. The benefits provided to nontenants are clearly externalized because they do not have to pay for the water. Even for tenants, some of the benefits may have been externalized because it is unlikely that their water use was metered with a charge that fully offset the value of the use. Since the externalized benefits in this scenario probably were substantial, there is no reason to believe that the introduction of a lavatory externalized more risk than benefit. By contrast, in *Rylands* the externalized risks created by the water reservoir seemed to exceed the benefits to neighbors.

Carstairs v. Taylor[15] is another case that illustrates the balancing of external risks and benefits under the *Rylands* strict liability doctrine. The plaintiff and defendant

---

[12] Another way of making the same argument exploits the missing markets perspective introduced in Chapter 2. Recall that if the benefits externalized by the driver are roughly the same as the costs externalized, the privately optimal level of activity is the same as the socially optimal level of activity. There is no justification, based on society's welfare, for the law to intervene in an effort to alter activity level choices.

[13] Rickards v. Lothian, [1913] A.C. 263 (P.C.).

[14] *Id.* at 281.

[15] Carstairs v. Taylor, L.R. 6 Ex. 217 (1871).

were occupants of the same building, the plaintiff in the lower floor and the defendant in the upper floor. A tank was constructed on the upper floor and connected to the gutters and the roof, so that rain falling on the building could be collected for use by both occupants. A rat ate a hole through the bottom of the tank, causing the water to flood the plaintiff's premises. The court refused to apply the *Rylands* strict liability rule on the ground that the water had been collected for the mutual benefit of both plaintiff and defendant.

Mutual benefit and reciprocity of risk are both concepts that have much to do with the expectations of actors who must interact with each other from a distance. The law of strict liability tries to incorporate those expectations. The moral or deontological basis for doing so is easy to state and runs along lines parallel to the instrumentalist argument set out here.

III. STRICT LIABILITY VERSUS NEGLIGENCE VERSUS LIMITED DUTY

The previous parts of this chapter introduced *Rylands v. Fletcher* and its theory for distinguishing scenarios in which liability should be strict from scenarios in which liability should be based on negligence. Under *Rylands*, strict liability should be applied when (1) the risks externalized to neighbors by the defendant's activity substantially exceed the risks externalized by the activities of neighbors, or (2) the risks externalized to neighbors by the defendant's activity substantially exceed the benefits externalized to neighbors by the defendant's activity.

Under this theory, strict liability was appropriate in *Rylands* because the risks externalized to neighbors by the defendant's water reservoir, in an area with abandoned underground mine shafts, exceeded the risks externalized by neighbors, and the defendant's activity did not benefit the neighbors to a degree that would make it reasonable for them to bear those risks. By contrast, the negligence rule is appropriate for accidents on the roads, because drivers impose reciprocal risks on one another.

This part has two aims: first, to summarize the instrumentalist theory of *Rylands* without using numerical examples, and, second, to show that the theory of *Rylands* can be expanded to provide a justification for tort doctrines limiting the duty to take care.

Rylands *and Incentives*

To discuss *Rylands* in terms of its implications for incentives, it helps to distinguish, as in Chapter 2, care levels and activity levels. The "care level" refers to how careful you are when engaged in an activity. For example, if the activity is driving, taking more care while driving means moderating your speed, or looking more frequently to both sides of the street to watch for pedestrians and other motorists. The "activity level" refers to the amount or degree of one's participation in an activity. In the case of driving, increasing the activity level means taking the car on the road more frequently.

The reason for imposing strict liability is to discourage the defendant's activity, to tax and thereby shrink the defendant's activity relative to other activities. To see the discouraging effect of strict liability, in comparison to negligence, consider an example. Suppose the defendant decides to keep a lion in his backyard in an urban residential area. Let's consider the differences in the defendant's incentives under strict liability and under negligence. Under negligence, a court will ask whether the defendant took reasonable care in penning the lion in. If the court finds that the defendant did take reasonable care, say, by using a titanium chain, it will not find the defendant liable for injuries caused by the lion. Under strict liability, the defendant will be held liable for injuries caused by the lion no matter how careful he was in penning the lion. The result is that strict liability taxes the defendant's activity, and the additional tax will encourage the defendant to reconsider his decision to keep a lion. He may decide to move the lion out to another home in a rural area where the risk to neighbors, and the risk of liability, will be lower.

The strict liability imposed under *Rylands* also acts as a form of insurance to the defendant's neighbors against the excessive risk created by the defendant. Thus, if the defendant moves into an urban residential area and keeps a lion in his backyard, the imposition of strict liability on the defendant discourages his activity and at the same time insures the neighbors of the defendant.

Whatever level of care the defendant finds worthwhile to take under the negligence rule he will take under strict liability. If the defendant found it preferable to spend an additional $100 in precaution to avoid a liability of $200 under negligence, he will certainly have the same incentive under strict liability. It follows, then, that moving from negligence to strict liability will not lead to less care on the defendant's part; it will lead to the same or perhaps greater care. But even after taking reasonable care along every imaginable dimension, the defendant will still have to pay liability bills under strict liability.

So the choice between strict liability and negligence boils down to a choice between encouraging the defendant to take reasonable care while also discouraging his activity, or encouraging the defendant to take reasonable care while continuing his activity. Strict liability does the former, negligence the latter.[16]

Discouraging, Leaving Alone, and Subsidizing

The choice is actually somewhat broader than one between discouraging versus not discouraging an activity. In some cases, we may want to *encourage* the defendant's

---

[16] On the general incentives created by strict liability and negligence, see Guido Calabresi, *Optimal Deterrence and Accidents*, 84 YALE L. J. 656 (1975); Steven Shavell, *Strict Liability Versus Negligence*, 9 J. LEGAL STUD. 1 (1980).

activity. That might lead us to reduce the defendant's liability to reduce the costs to him of engaging in the activity. Liability rules can be used to discourage (tax), leave alone, or encourage (subsidize) an activity. When should we choose one of these directions?

The *Rylands* framework can be used to answer this question.[17] *Rylands* implies that we should leave the activity alone – that is, neither tax nor subsidize it – when the externalized risks to neighbors from the activity are roughly the same as those of neighbors' activities in the same community (reciprocal risk exchange) or when the externalized risks to neighbors are no greater than externalized benefits to neighbors from the activity. When externalized risks are not reciprocated or when they far exceed externalized benefits, strict liability is appropriate. When externalized risks are substantially less than externalized benefits, we should encourage the activity by subsidization.

The easiest way for the common law to subsidize an activity is to relieve actors from a duty of care. Relieving the actor of a duty of care implies that the actor cannot be held liable for negligence. Thus relieved, the actor does not have to worry about liability to the same extent as under the negligence rule, nor does the actor have to bear the burden of taking care.

It turns out that the law does in fact subsidize some actors by relieving them of a duty of care, or shielding them from liability, in some settings. For example, the law encourages rescue efforts by relieving the rescuer of a duty to take reasonable care for his own safety (Chapter 8). The common law shields charitable institutions from tort liability under certain conditions (Chapter 12). In addition, the law relieves property owners of the duty to take care for trespassers (Chapter 15). In subsequent chapters of this book I will argue that the justification for the first two of these exceptions can be found in the reasoning of *Rylands*.

Rylands, *Duty, and Negligence*

Tort liability rules generally fall into one of four categories: (1) liability for intentional torts, (2) strict liability, (3) negligence liability, and (4) immunity under the concept of limited duty. *Rylands v. Fletcher* provides policies for distinguishing the strict liability and negligence categories. I have suggested that the risk-reciprocity comparison and the external benefit and external cost comparison at the core of *Rylands* are also important in distinguishing areas in which the negligence rule applies from areas in which injurers are shielded from liability – that is, where tort immunity applies.

Formally, tort law uses the concept of duty to distinguish instances in which negligence liability may adhere from instances in which the defendant's activity is

---

[17] *See* Keith N. Hylton, *Duty in Tort Law: An Economic Approach,* 75 FORDHAM L. REV. 1501 (2006).

shielded from the risk of negligence liability. Because of this, duty is a question in the background of every negligence case.[18]

Indeed, a negligence lawsuit consists of four elements: *duty, breach, causation*, and *damages*. The plaintiff has a responsibility to show, or the facts must indicate, that the defendant had a duty to take care to avoid injury to the plaintiff. If the defendant did not have a duty to take care, then he cannot be held liable for negligence.

If the court is satisfied that the defendant had a duty to take care, the plaintiff must present evidence that the defendant breached his duty. This is often what people refer to when they say that the defendant acted negligently or failed to act as a reasonable person – negligence is the specific conduct constituting a breach of the duty of care.

If the plaintiff shows that the defendant breached his duty of care, he must still show that the breach *caused* his injury. The causation prong of a negligence case consists of two parts: *proximate causation* and *factual causation*. If the plaintiff's case fails either causation test, he loses. In other words, the defendant's breach must have caused the plaintiff's injury under *both* the proximate causation test and the factual causation test to find the defendant liable.

Proximate causation analysis generally boils down to a simple question: *Was the plaintiff's injury a foreseeable consequence of the defendant's breach*? Put another way, if the defendant's actions leading to the plaintiff's injury were reenacted, would we predict that the injury to the plaintiff would occur? For example, in *Palsgraf v. Long Island Railroad Co.*,[19] the plaintiff claimed she suffered an injury when railroad employees negligently pushed a man, as he boarded a train, causing him to drop a package which exploded, knocking a scale over onto the plaintiff as she stood on the train platform. The court held that the injury was not a foreseeable consequence of the defendant's negligence.

Like proximate causation analysis, factual causation analysis reduces to a simple question: *Would the injury have happened even if the defendant had not breached the duty of care*? If the accident would have happened anyway, even if the defendant had taken care, then a court would say that the defendant's breach was not a factual cause of the plaintiff's injury. Some courts would say that the defendant's breach was not a *substantial factor* leading to the plaintiff's injury. Intuitively, the factual causation test asks us to view the sequence of events in reverse – from the injury to the defendant's act. If the injury appears to have been equally likely even if the defendant had taken the precaution urged by the plaintiff, then the defendant's failure to take that precaution is not a ground for liability. For example, in *Palsgraf*, the explosion probably would not have occurred if the railroad's employees had not

---

[18] For a discussion of the prevalence of duty doctrines in tort law, *see* John Goldberg & Benjamin Zipursky, *The Restatement (Third) and the Place of Duty in Negligence Law*, 54 VAND. L. REV. 657 (2001).

[19] 162 N.E. 99 (N.Y. 1928).

pushed the man carrying the package of explosives, so the factual causation test was satisfied.

The last step of a negligence lawsuit is proof of damages. If the plaintiff cannot prove damages, then he loses his negligence case. This is different from the law of trespass, which does not require proof of damages to prevail.

In the immediately following chapters I will explore negligence liability in detail. The policies of *Rylands* will remain useful in understanding the duty of care, as well as special applications of negligence law.

6

The Reasonable Person

Tort law relies heavily on the concept of reasonable care, and specifically the *reasonable person* standard. Negligence is typically described as a failure to act with the prudence of a reasonable person. The reasonable person standard, we will see in this chapter, is *objective*, in the sense that it does not depend on the particular preferences or idiosyncratic psychological features of the defendant before the court. And although it is objective, it is not easily summarized in the form of a simple cost-benefit test. The reasonable person standard incorporates the typical individual's ability to make long-term plans that might affect the risks he imposes on others and to make tradeoffs that affect those risks.

Recall that in *Brown v. Kendall* (Chapter 4), Chief Justice Shaw defined reasonable care as the care that a prudent and cautious man would take to guard against probable danger. In many of the early negligence cases, this is as specific as it gets in terms of a definition of reasonable care. However, even this thin formulation is sufficient to convey some important ideas. The reasonable person, it appears, will take probable losses to others into account and will modify his conduct to avoid causing harm to others.

Most of the early formulations of the reasonable person standard do not explain just how much weight the reasonable person would put on the danger to others. Would the reasonable person treat the danger to others with the same level of concern as he would treat danger to himself, or would he treat it with less concern? The difficulty in specifying precisely how much weight should be put on risks to others suggests that the reasonable person should treat them as equals and put just as much weight on probable harms to others, in his calculus of precaution, as he would put on probable harms to himself. Indeed, it would seem contradictory for the reasonable person to discount probable harms to others, because he values his own interests more than theirs, and at the same time demand that those others not discount the harms their conduct might impose on him.

TABLE 6.1. *Speed levels and care*

Care decision	Burden of care	Benefit of care to actor	Benefit of care to victim
60 to 50	$10	$25	$20
50 to 40	$20	$10	$15
40 to 30	$30	$8	$8

The reasonable person, then, should be an "impartial spectator"[1] who treats the burdens and probable harms of the potential injurer and potential victim as worthy of the same level of consideration. He does not arbitrarily give preference to the interests of one party over those of another.

Some courts have captured this reasoning by referring to the reasonable person as someone who treats the probable harms to others resulting from his conduct as if they were his own.[2] One can think of the reasonable person test as a *Golden Rule* in the sense that it treats the potential injurer and potential victim as a merged entity, sharing the burdens of precaution and the probable harms from precautionary failures.[3]

To get a sense of just what the reasonable person test means in a particular accident setting, I will consider two examples. The first involves risks connected to various levels of precaution while driving. The second involves risks to bystanders connected to a sport. In both examples I will attempt to determine what a merged entity – one who shares the interests of both injurer and victim – would do to balance precautionary burdens against risks.

I. AUTO ACCIDENT EXAMPLE

Suppose the actor is driving a car, and his primary means of taking care is reducing his speed. Each decision to reduce speed imposes a cost on the actor, say, by causing him to arrive later to business meetings. The benefit of care is the reduction in probable injury losses to himself and to others. Table 6.1 shows the assumptions. The actor can reduce his speed from 60 to 50, from 50 to 40, and from 40 to 30. If he reduces his speed from 60 to 50, the expected loss to himself declines by $25, and the expected loss to the potential victim declines by $20.

If the actor considers only the burdens and benefits to himself, how much care would he take? Return to Table 6.1. He would choose to reduce his speed from 60 to

---

[1] ADAM SMITH, THEORY OF MORAL SENTIMENTS 129–137 (D. D. Raphael & A. L. Macfie eds., Clarendon Press 1976) (1759).

[2] *See, e.g.*, Bolton v. Stone, [1951] A.C. 850 (Radcliffe opinion).

[3] For discussion of the universality (or unitization) standard, the Golden Rule, and sources in the ethics literature, *see* Chapter 2.

50, because he gains $25 in harm reduction and suffers an extra precaution burden of only $10. Would he reduce his speed from 50 to 40? No. If he reduces speed from 50 to 40, he would experience a personal benefit in risk reduction of only $10 and suffer a burden of $20. Thus, if the actor considers only the costs and benefits to himself, he would choose to drive at 50.

Suppose, conversely, that the actor considered only the risk reduction benefit to the victim and ignored his own burden. He would therefore treat the burden of care as if it were zero. Under this assumption, he would choose to take more care as long as the risk reduction benefit to the victim is positive. He would therefore cut his speed to 30.

Now suppose the actor takes into account the gains and losses to himself and to others. How much care would he take? He would choose to reduce his speed from 60 to 50 because the burden would be $10 and the benefit (to both actor and victim) in terms of risk reduction would be $45 (the sum of $25 and $20). Would he reduce his speed from 50 to 40? Yes. If he reduces his speed from 50 to 40 he would suffer a burden of $20 and generate a risk-reduction gain of $25 (the sum of $10 and $15). Would he reduce his speed from 40 to 30? No. If he reduces speed from 40 to 30 he would suffer a burden of $30, and the risk-reduction gain would be only $16 (the sum of $8 and $8). Thus, if the actor considers the potential losses to himself *and* to others, he would likely choose to drive at 40.

The reasonable person would give equal consideration to the risk-reduction benefits to others as well as to his own benefits and burdens. This implies that the reasonable actor would not choose the lowest possible level of care, because that could result only from discounting the benefit of care to the potential victim. It also implies that the reasonable person generally would not choose the highest feasible level of care, because that could result only from discounting his own burden. This suggests a general rule for determining the level of care that a reasonable actor would adopt: *The reasonable person will take more care as long as the burden of additional care is less than the foreseeable harm imposed on others if he failed to take the additional care.*

II. CRICKET FENCE EXAMPLE

This example is a bit more complicated than the previous one because it incorporates probability estimates directly into the actor's evaluation of alternative courses of conduct. However, the same principles illustrated earlier are illustrated here.

Suppose the actor is building a fence around a cricket field. He has to choose between setting the fence height at 12 feet, 20 feet, or 30 feet. If he goes without a fence, a lot of cricket balls will hit neighbors or their property. Assume that if the actor does not erect a fence, the likelihood of injury to a neighbor in a given year will be 100 percent. If he sets the fence at 12 feet, the likelihood of an injury to

TABLE 6.2. *Fence height and care*

Care decision	Burden of care	Benefit of care to victim
0 to 12	$200	$800
12 to 20	$200	$150
20 to 30	$300	$40

a neighbor in a given year will be 20 percent.[4] If he sets the fence at 20 feet, the likelihood of injury to a neighbor in a given year will be 5 percent. Finally, if he raises the fence to 30 feet, the likelihood of injury falls to 1 percent.

Suppose the harm done by a cricket ball in the average accident is $1,000. To remove concerns about trading life for property, let us assume that $1,000 represents the average damage to property surrounding the yard (e.g., smashed car windows), and that the risk is zero of any serious physical harm. The expected harm to victims (property owners near the yard) when the fence is at 12 feet is $0.20 \times \$1,000 = \$200$.

We can describe this example in a way similar to the previous description of the auto accident. The care decision is now focused on the height of the fence. Since the actor himself cannot be a victim in this example, there is no need to consider the risk-reduction benefit of care to the actor.

The numbers shown in Table 6.2 for the benefit of care to the victim are determined by the probability of an injury and the average harm value of $1,000. For example, if the fence is increased from 0 to 12 feet, the probability of an injury over a given year falls from 100 percent to 20 percent. That means that the risk-reduction benefit (to the victim) of raising the fence from 0 to 12 feet is found by taking the difference in the probabilities, $100\% - 20\% = 80\%$, and multiplying that difference by the average harm of $1,000, which yields $800. Raising the fence from 12 feet to 20 feet reduces the likelihood of harm to the neighbor from 20 percent to 5 percent. Thus, the risk-reduction benefit of raising the fence from 12 feet to 20 feet is $150 ($15\% \times \$1,000$). Finally, raising the fence from 20 feet to 30 feet reduces the likelihood of harm from 5 percent to 1 percent, yielding a risk-reduction benefit of $40 ($4\% \times \$1,000$).

Clearly, if the owner considered only his own burden, he would go without a fence, saving $200. Going fenceless leads to the greatest risk being imposed on neighbors, but if the owner considers only his own burden, that will not trouble him at all.

If the owner is a reasonable person and therefore takes into account the harms to others, he would choose a fence height of 12 feet. To see this, first notice that the

---

[4] Stone v. Bolton, [1950] 1 K.B. 201 (C.A.).

owner would not choose a fence height of zero, because it would be better to spend $200 to avoid a loss of $800. He would not raise the fence from 12 to 20 feet, because that would require spending an additional $200 to avoid an additional harm of $150. We would have the same result if the owner of the cricket ground also owned all of the property surrounding the ground.

As in the previous example, this one illustrates two basic principles guiding the conduct of the reasonable person. One is the equal weighting of his own interests and those of others. The other principle guides precaution: The reasonable person will take additional care whenever the burden of that additional care is less than the foreseeable additional harm.

So far we have considered only the case in which the cricket ball damages property outside of the cricket ground. Suppose there is a risk of harming people too. How would the reasonable person act in that case?

It should be clear that it will be difficult in such cases to lay out a table with numerical estimates of the risk-reduction benefit and the burden of care. To do so would require putting a value on life, or on health.

The reasonable person standard is attractive in this case because of its generality and flexibility. The standard tells the potential tortfeasor to set the fence height at a level that he would choose if he were also at risk of being injured by a cricket ball. To the extent that we are all alike in assigning a greater value to life than to property, the reasonable person standard encourages potential tortfeasors to act according to that common intuition. Because we value life more than we value property, if an activity has a risk of injuring or killing someone, a reasonable person would take more care than if it were just a risk to property.[5]

III. REASONABLE PERSON STANDARD

The preceding examples are useful introductions to the concept of reasonable care – the care taken by a reasonable person – and its implications. The examples show that the reasonable person examines both the burden to himself and the foreseeable harm, to himself and to others, in determining whether to take care and how much care to exercise.

In the course of developing a reasonable person test that can be used to resolve disputes, courts have had to settle many questions about the test. The most important is whether the reasonable person test takes into account individual idiosyncratic inabilities, and to what extent it does so. The following cases examine this branch of development in the negligence standard.

---

[5] *See* Chapter 2 for a discussion of the roles of moral intuition and cost-benefit analysis in the determination of reasonable care. For a discussion of moral defenses of cost-benefit analysis in negligence law, *see* Kenneth W. Simons, *Tort Negligence, Cost-Benefit Analysis, and Tradeoffs: A Closer Look at the Controversy*, 41 Loy. L.A. L. Rev. 1171 (2008).

Reasonable Care and Individual Capacity

In *Vaughan v. Menlove*,[6] the defendant had placed a hay stack just inside the boundary of his land near the plaintiff's two cottages, ignoring warnings from the plaintiff that the hay would ignite. As predicted, the hay stack did ignite and burned down the plaintiff's cottages. The plaintiff brought a negligence claim against the defendant. The defendant argued that he did not have a duty of care to the plaintiff, and that, even if he did have such a duty, he did not breach it.

The defendant tried to convince the court that there were limits on the scope of his duty of care in this setting. He claimed that he did not have a duty to look out for the risk of fire because he was not a common carrier or bailee. In addition, the defendant argued that he had a right to put a hay stack anywhere he wanted on his own land, without having to look out for risks to neighbors.

On the breach question, the defendant argued that, in view of his limited duty, he should be judged on a *good faith standard*. Under such a standard, the court would try to determine if the defendant did his best, given his own capacity for judgment. He should not be punished, urged the defendant, for failing to foresee risks that a more intelligent man might have foreseen. In other words, the standard for determining negligence should be *subjective*, in the sense that it takes into account a defendant's peculiar inabilities to assess risks. The alternative to a subjective test is an objective test, which determines negligence according to the abilities of the average person in the community.

The defendant claimed that a subjective standard would be more predictable for him. Under an objective standard, by contrast, he would have trouble figuring out what a reasonable person would do and, if unable to conform to that standard, would be effectively operating under a strict liability standard.

The court rejected both of the defendant's arguments – the limited duty argument and the good faith defense. The court said that the duty to take care is a general duty that is not in any sense limited because the defendant is not a bailee, or because he is acting on his own property. Even though the defendant was acting on his own property, he still had a duty to look out for risks imposed on neighbors.

On the good faith defense, the court held that an objective standard of negligence applies. One reason is administrative: It would be quite difficult to determine whether a defendant had complied with his own subjective standard. Indeed, if the defendant's compliance with good faith were determined entirely by his own reports, virtually no defendants would ever be found liable for negligence, because it would be the extremely rare defendant who would reveal to the court that he had failed to meet his own standard of care. Negligence law would be rendered useless by the good faith standard.

---

[6] 132 Eng. Rep. 490 (C.P. 1837).

Another reason the court rejected the good faith test is the *reliance interest*: Others need to be assured that you will be held liable if you fail to meet the expected level of care. They should not be put in the position of trying to figure out whether the potential injurer would be judged against a lower standard, and having to therefore compensate for the potential injurer's lack of care. Yet another reason offered by the court is that an objective standard is more predictable than a subjective standard, and therefore provides a more certain standard for the potential injurer to reach, and on which the potential victim can rely.

These arguments correspond to the rationales for tort liability discussed earlier in Chapter 4. Recall that *McGuire v. Almy* provided three policies for holding an individual liable for his torts: (1) deterrence, (2) risk spreading, and (3) administrative costs. The deterrence argument is elaborated here by noting that an objective standard provides a standard of care – prudent conduct for the average person of normal physical and mental capacity – that is predictable to most people. Of course, one might argue, as did the defendant in *Vaughan v. Menlove*, a subjective standard is more predictable for the potential injurer because he alone knows his own capacity to take care. But the subjective standard fails to give any notice to the potential injurer of what he should try to do to avoid being found negligent. And whether the injurer is psychologically incapable of taking care or not, it is clear that potential victims do not know the potential injurer's individual capacity for care. The objective standard serves a coordinating function that regulates the conduct of both potential injurers and potential victims – injurers directly, by giving them a certain standard; victims indirectly, by allowing them to rely on the injurer's compliance with the standard.

There is an additional version of the deterrence argument that can be distinguished from the coordination or reliance argument just stated. Strict liability is sometimes desirable because it acts as a tax on activity – that is, it discourages the activity to which it applies. In the case of a driver who is unable to meet the reasonable person standard of care, strict liability discourages that person from driving. This may be morally unjustifiable, as Holmes suggested,[7] because it fails to credit the actor for a good faith effort to take care. However, it has the benefit of keeping unsafe drivers off the roads. Drivers who externalize an unusually high degree of risk, because they are unable to meet the objective reasonable care standard, are in effect subject to strict liability, which is appropriate under the policy articulated in *Rylands v. Fletcher* (Chapter 5).

To sum up, there are several arguments for the objective reasonable person test adopted in *Vaughan v. Menlove*. *Compliance and deterrence*: An objective standard provides at least some guidance to potential tortfeasors. *Reliance and coordination*: Potential victims need to be able to determine in advance whether the potential injurer's conduct is permissible under the law to determine what is reasonable

---

[7] Oliver Wendell Holmes, Jr., The Common Law 108 (1881).

on their parts. *Taxing or discouraging hazardous activity:* The objective standard imposes strict liability on those who are unable to meet the average, which is desirable because those people externalize far greater risks to potential victims than the risks reciprocated by potential victims. *Administration:* The objective standard can be easily administered by courts and juries, whereas a subjective standard is extremely difficult to administer. The objective standard guards against strategic gaming by the defendant, who under a subjective standard can fraudulently argue that he did his best and is unable to take care as competently as the average person.

The rationale and policies behind *Vaughan v. Menlove,* in addition to supporting an objective negligence standard, apply more broadly to the *choice of law* problem.[8] Suppose X is standing in state A and throwing stones at Y, standing in state B. Y brings a tort suit against X. Which state's law applies?

The traditional rule in the law is *lex loci:* the law of the site of the injury. *Lex loci* can be defended on the same basis as the objective standard in *Vaughan v. Menlove. Lex loci* allows potential tort victims to rely on the law that applies where they stand. That relieves potential victims of the burden of trying to figure out whether the potential injurer falls under a completely different set of legal rules. In addition, to the extent that the site where the injury occurs has rules that are more protective of residents in light of particular or special vulnerabilities within the site of injury, the *lex loci* rule encourages injurers to become familiar with those rules if they can, and, if they cannot learn the rules, *lex loci* subjects them to a form of strict liability that discourages activities that generate cross-border torts.

Reasonable Care, Maturity, and Physical Disability

The reasonable person test has different implications for the very young and the very old. In determining the negligence of a child, for example, the courts seek to determine if the child *exercised the degree of care commonly exercised by the ordinary child of the defendant's age and maturity.* In the case of an old man, the reasonable person test is said to provide no special breaks based on age.[9]

The different treatments of old and young can be explained by thinking of the test in terms of foresight and burden. The very young are unable to foresee the dangers that the average adult would foresee. In addition, the burden on them of meeting the average adult care standard is much greater, because of size, lack of physical dexterity, and strength. Without an adjustment, the foresight and burden elements of the negligence inquiry would punish the young. Since it is difficult for children to meet the care level of the average adult, adults in their presence are required to compensate for the inability of children to exercise the level of care that would be considered reasonable for an adult.

---

[8] Keith N. Hylton, *Torts and Choice of Law: Searching for Principles,* 56 J. LEGAL EDUC. 551, 554 (2006).
[9] *See, e.g.,* Roberts v. Ring, 173 N.W. 437 (Minn. 1919).

For the old, the foresight and burden tests work in a less clear way. The burden of taking care is often greater for the old, because of loss in physical dexterity and strength. But the old are typically, except in cases of senility, no less able to foresee harms than is the average adult. Indeed, they are better at foreseeing risks, and they are well aware of their own infirmities. They are expected to take additional precautions to compensate for their own inabilities to react quickly to avoid danger. For example, if an old man is too slow in reacting to be able to safely drive down a crowded street, the negligence rule holds him liable on the ground that he should have foreseen the dangers associated with driving.[10] The negligence rule informs him to stay off the road, or take additional precautions, if he wishes to avoid liability.

On closer inspection, the reasonable person standard when applied to the old operates at two decision stages. The first is when the actor decides whether and where to drive. If the actor's age prevents him from meeting the reasonable person standard, then his decision to drive is negligent – unless the motivation for driving is extremely important (for example, saving a life). Once he is driving, his operation is subjected to the reasonable person standard for the reasons stressed in the previous discussion of *Vaughan v. Menlove*: It provides an objective standard for the actor to try to reach, it discourages the activity of those who cannot comply with the objective standard, and it permits others to coordinate their care levels on the assumption that the actor can meet the objective standard.

What if the child is engaged in an adult activity, such as driving a car? The child is then held to the adult standard.[11] Why? First, other adults cannot tell whether it is a child driving the car. They will not know that they should compensate for his inability to take care. Since they will not see a need to compensate, there is no argument for reducing the required care level, from the adult to the child standard, to encourage compensating care on the part of the adult. Second, applying the adult care standard to the child is equivalent to imposing a strict liability standard. This is desirable in terms of incentives, because the strict liability standard discourages the activity of children driving. Parents who let their children drive cars will be, in effect, taxed by strict liability, shrinking their particular activity choice (letting their children drive) relative to the alternative (parents driving their children).

What comes from this is that the reasonable care standard sometimes adopts a lower standard of care, in recognition of the actor's inability to meet the ordinary standard, when it is possible to compensate for it by requiring more of others who interact with the actor. We see this in the case of adults interacting with children, provided that the children are involved in age-appropriate activities. In cases where this shift of burden is infeasible or unlikely to be effective, as when children are driving cars, the reasonable care standard gives no break at all to the injuring party.

---

[10] *Id.*
[11] *See, e.g.,* Dellwo v. Pearson, 107 N.W.2d 859 (Minn. 1961).

If the actor is unable to meet the adult reasonable person standard, then it operates as a tax on his activity.

The same principles apply to obvious physical incapacities, such as blindness. Blindness is a physical characteristic that is generally observable to others. Just as an individual can take additional care to compensate for a child's inability to meet the ordinary care standard, so can he take care to compensate for a blind person's inability to meet the standard. Moreover, blindness is not something that can be faked in court easily. Consequently, the reasonable person test adopts a lower standard of care for the blind and requires compensating care on the part of those who can see.[12] On the other hand, if a blind person attempts to do an activity that is inappropriate given his condition, such as driving a car, he will be subjected to the objective standard.

The importance of policy in understanding these rules suggests that the rules may be altered depending on the circumstances. Return to the case of the child who drives a car and is subjected (generally) to the adult standard of care. Suppose the child is a passenger with his grandfather, and the grandfather suffers a heart attack, forcing the child to take over the steering wheel. Now, the policy of discouraging driving by children is no longer a desirable one; we would prefer that the child take over the car. It is true that other drivers cannot modify their care in response to the child, because they cannot tell it is a child driving the car, but that is only one policy justification for holding the child to the adult standard. In this example, we have a conflict in the policies that should be referenced to determine whether children should be subjected to the adult standard when driving. Facing such a conflict, a court might choose to apply the child standard rather than the adult standard.[13]

Reasonable Care and Sudden Incapacity (Including Insanity)

Is insanity a defense to negligence? Recall that for intentional torts, insanity is not, as a general rule, a defense. The same intent standard applies whether or not the defendant is insane.

Similarly, the law offers no special exemption, based on insanity, from liability for negligence. Insanity may or may not provide a defense to a negligence claim. For insanity to serve as a defense, it must be a sort that impairs the actor's ability to foresee the particular risk generated by his conduct, or impairs the actor's ability to take care to avoid the harm. In addition, it must be a type of insanity that comes unforeseen upon the actor, so that he has no forewarning. For if the actor has warning of the possibility of an attack of insanity, he must take care not to put himself in a position in which he imposes risk on others.

---

[12] Fletcher v. City of Aberdeen, 338 P.2d 743 (Wash. 1959).

[13] For example, even in the absence of an emergency, if there is no possibility of reliance on the part of other drivers, the policy basis for holding a child to the adult standard weakens. *See, e.g.,* Mahon v. Hein, 332 A.2d 69 (Conn. 1973) (accident on private road with no one else around; court refuses to apply the adult reasonable person standard).

Negligence law treats insanity as just a special type of sudden incapacity, like a heart attack or a seizure. There is a two-part test to determine negligence in a case in which the actor is subject to sudden incapacity. *The first part of the test asks whether the actor was aware of the risk of sudden incapacity.* If aware, the actor must take care to avoid putting himself in a position where it may arise and endanger others. If he chooses to put himself in a risky setting, such as driving, he will be held liable, unless the reason for driving is so important that it justifies the risk he imposes on others. *The second part of the test looks at the point at which the actor has put himself in a risky setting, such as driving, on the assumption that he did not foresee the risk. Having been unable to foresee the sudden incapacity, the test asks if the incapacity is such that it prevents the actor from meeting the reasonable care standard.* If so, the actor may avoid a finding of negligence.

Let's apply this test to the case of a heart attack. If the actor is unaware that he has heart disease, he will not foresee the risk of a sudden heart attack. His decision to drive, for example, may therefore be reasonable. Once he is on the road, if a heart attack of such severity develops that he is unable to manage his car, he will not be held negligent. On the other hand, if the heart attack is not so severe as to prevent him from managing his car, he may be held liable if he fails to take reasonable care under the conditions.

Now suppose that the actor is aware that there is a substantial risk of a heart attack coming on soon. Then, if the actor drives, and a heart attack occurs, he will be held negligent in most cases because he was aware of the risk of incapacity and chose to drive anyway. An exception might arise if the actor had to drive a short distance to save someone's life; a court might hold that it was reasonable to take the risk of sudden incapacity to prevent a greater and more certain harm.

IV. THEORIES OF NEGLIGENCE AND DETERMINING REASONABLE CARE

The previous section considered the extent to which the law of negligence takes into account idiosyncratic inabilities to comply with its requirements. This part examines the actual operation of the negligence standard.

In a negligence trial, the plaintiff usually alleges some specific failure of precaution on the part of the defendant. As Mark Grady noted,[14] plaintiffs do not sue defendants for failing to find the optimal level of care along a continuous spectrum of possible care levels. Instead, plaintiffs typically have one or more specific failures in precaution that form the basis of a negligence claim. The plaintiff's theory of negligence usually implies some specific precaution that the defendant should have taken to avoid being negligent.

Thus, the typical negligence case involves a choice between two courses of action, one negligent and the other nonnegligent. For example, if the plaintiff is suing

---

[14] Mark F. Grady, *Untaken Precautions*, 18 J. Legal Stud. 139 (1989).

because he was hit by a cricket ball that flew over a fence, the plaintiff might assert that the defendant was negligent because his fence was unreasonably low. This theory implies that to avoid being found negligent, the defendant should have raised his fence to a level that would have prevented the ball from flying over.

How do courts determine negligence in cases alleging a specific failure of precaution? The reasonable person standard articulated earlier in this chapter provides a general guideline. However, courts have developed a more detailed algorithm for determining negligence.

The most famous articulation of the algorithm was provided by Judge Learned Hand in *United States v. Carroll Towing Co.*[15] Discussing whether the owner of a barge could be found negligent for failing to prevent the barge from breaking away from its moorings, Learned Hand said:

> Since there are occasions when every vessel will break from her moorings, and since, if she does, she becomes a menace to those about her; the owner's duty, as in other similar situations, to provide against resulting injuries is a function of three variables: (1) The probability that she will break away; (2) the gravity of the resulting injury, if she does; (3) the burden of adequate precautions. Possibly it serves to bring this notion into relief to state it in algebraic terms: if the probability be called P; the injury, L; and the burden, B; liability depends upon whether B is less than L multiplied by P: i.e., whether $B < PL$.[16]

Learned Hand's statement of the negligence test is sometimes described as the *Hand Formula* (or BPL test, or Hand Test). The defendant should be held negligent when he fails to take a specific precaution when $B < PL$. The defendant should not be held negligent when fails to take the specific precaution and $B > PL$.

Although the Hand Formula provides a simple algorithm for determining negligence, it will not need to be applied rigorously in most cases, as Hand once noted.[17] The test tells us which factors to pay attention to in determining negligence: burden and foreseeable loss. However, in many cases it will be difficult to provide numerical values for either factor. Moreover, in some cases, even if you could get numerical values, the numbers would fail to incorporate all of the elements of interest in a negligence determination.

It is important to keep in mind that the Hand Formula is not the only way of conducting the reasonable person inquiry in negligence law. In some cases, courts have issued rules that appear to be inconsistent with the calculus recommended by the Hand Formula. For example, in *Bird v. Holbrook* (Chapter 4), the court suggested that it is *unreasonable per se* to trade off life for property in the defense of real property. Similarly, a court applying the reasonable person test might find a defendant's decision to protect his personal property while putting the lives of

---

[15] United States v. Carroll Towing Co., 159 F.2d 169 (2d Cir. 1947).
[16] *Id.* at 173.
[17] Moisan v. Loftus, 178 F.2d 148, 149 (2d Cir. 1949).

others at risk to be unreasonable per se, without making any attempt to compare the value of the property protected to the value of the lives put at risk. For example, suppose the defendant swerves his expensive car, a Rolls Royce, into a group of pedestrians on the sidewalk to avoid a collision with another car that threatened only minor damage to the exterior of the Rolls Royce. A court would hold the defendant's conduct unreasonable per se and reject any attempt to use the Hand Test to compare the value of the car to the value of the lives taken.

General Negligence Theories: Operation, Design, and Warning

In addition to negligence cases being about specific failures of precaution (for example, you should have raised the fence on the cricket ground by five feet), there are types of negligence claims that show up in some form in just about every case. We can distinguish three types: *negligence in operation, negligence in design,* and *negligence in warning.*

A negligence-in-operation theory asserts that the defendant was negligent in the day-to-day operation of some activity. For example, suppose that the owner of a cricket ground hired a monitor to sit by the fence and look for balls that sailed over. Each time the monitor saw a ball clear the fence, he would be obligated to catch the ball or to prevent it from harming a nearby resident. Suppose the ball flies over the fence and hits someone, and the monitor fails to see it. In this case, the plaintiff could argue that the defendant was negligent in conducting the monitoring and prevention function.

A negligence-in-design theory asserts that the defendant was negligent in the design of some product or facility. Return to the cricket example. A claim that the fence surrounding the cricket ground was unreasonably low would be a negligence-in-design theory.

A negligence-in-warning theory asserts that the defendant was negligent in informing or warning potential victims of a danger. In the cricket example, the theory could be that the owner of the cricket field failed to adequately warn the nearby residents of the high risk of being hit by a cricket ball.

Illustrations

In *Blyth v. Birmingham Water Works,*[18] a water pipe ruptured, sending water into the plaintiff's house. The court described the accident as follows:

> On the 24th of February [1855], a large quantity of water, escaping from the neck of the main, forced its way through the ground into the plaintiff's house. The apparatus had been laid down 25 years, and had worked well during that time. The

---

[18] Blyth v. Birmingham Water Works, 156 Eng. Rep. 1047 (Ex. 1856).

defendant's engineer stated, that the water might have forced its way through the brickwork round the neck of the main, and that accident might have been caused by the frost, inasmuch as the expansion of the water would force up the plug out of the neck, and the stopper being encrusted with ice would not suffer the plug to ascend.[19]

The plaintiff claimed that the waterworks company had been negligent in failing to remove the ice around the plug. The jury found for the plaintiff. The appellate court reversed after finding that the accident was so unlikely that no reasonable person would have taken the precaution urged by the plaintiff to avoid it.

This is a good case to examine the three types of negligence theory: negligence in operation, negligence in design, and negligence in warning or informing.

The negligence-in-operation claim holds that the defendant conducted his activity in a negligent manner. It looks to the defendant's routine and finds something the defendant should have done, or should not have done, in conducting his activity. For example, a negligence-in-operation claim against a driver would be an assertion that the driver was negligent in failing to reduce the speed of his car when crossing through a busy area with many pedestrians.

The plaintiff's theory in *Blyth v. Birmingham Water Works* was a negligent operation claim: specifically, that the defendant should have sent its agents out to monitor the ice build-up and to clear ice from around the necks of the water plugs in areas throughout the city. This theory entails an assertion that the danger associated with an ice build-up was foreseeable under the circumstances, and that the burden of removing the ice was reasonable in light of the threat it posed to residents near the iced-up water plugs.

A negligent design theory – which was not examined in *Blyth* – would assert that the water pipes should have been designed to withstand the severe frost that occurred in the winter of 1855. To show negligence, the plaintiff would have to bring forth evidence that a frost of the severity experienced in 1855 was a foreseeable event over the life span of the existing design. Such evidence would imply that the waterworks company had a duty to design pipes that would withstand the frost, if such a design were technically feasible. The plaintiff would have the burden of proving the availability of a superior and feasible design.

A negligent warning claim – again not examined in *Blyth* – would assert that the waterworks company was in a better position to know of the risk to residents than the residents themselves. Given this, the waterworks company should have sent a notice to city residents to clear the ice around the water pipe plugs to avoid pipes bursting. The negligent warning claim involves showing that the dangers to residents were foreseeable once the frost had set in. At that point, the cost of notifying residents was trivial in comparison to the potential expense of the danger they faced. Because

[19] *Id.*

the burden is so low, the level of foreseeability of danger required by the negligent warning claim is probably lower than that required by the negligent operation claim. If only five out of 20,000 water pipe plugs had become encrusted with ice, it might seem unreasonable to require the precaution of searching all of the plugs for evidence of excessive ice. But even in this scenario, a warning to city residents might be deemed a reasonable precaution.

Notice that the foreseeability and burden arguments change as we move from one negligence theory to another. The negligent operation theory requires foresight of the frost danger reaching a level that would justify a search-and-clear mission covering an entire city. The negligent design theory implies or requires foresight of the frost danger over the lifespan of the pipes, and a comparison of the burden of an alternative design to the aggregate injury that would be avoided by the alternative design. The negligent warning theory requires foresight of the frost danger reaching a level that would justify a warning only.

Blyth is a straightforward negligence-in-operation case, and I have considered the negligence-in-design and negligence-in-warning theories only as illustrations of alternative arguments that could have been examined in the case but were not. The following cases provide examples of negligence-in-design claims.

In *Adams v. Bullock*,[20] a twelve-year-old boy was injured by an electric shock when an eight-foot-long wire that he was swinging came into contact with the overhead wires for a trolley car system. The boy was walking across a bridge that ran over the trolley line. The sides of the bridge were protected by a parapet, and the trolley wires were positioned roughly four and a half feet beneath the top of the parapet. The court, overturning a trial verdict for the plaintiff, held that the accident was insufficiently foreseeable to impose a duty on the trolley line to change its design – say, by running the trolley wires underground rather than above ground. Moreover, the court noted, the accident was the sort that could have happened anywhere along the trolley line – for example, the boy could have hit the wires with a pole while standing on the ground. A finding that the trolley line was negligent for the injury to the boy would have required it to redesign its entire system.

In *Cooley v. Public Service Co.*,[21] the plaintiff complained about a traumatic neurosis that had resulted from a loud explosive noise in her telephone. The noise occurred when one of the defendant power company's cables snapped during a heavy storm, landed on a telephone cable running several feet beneath it, and burned through the telephone cable. The plaintiff argued that the power company was guilty of negligence because it failed to maintain devices, where its wires crossed over the telephone lines, that would have prevented the accident that injured her. She proposed a wire-mesh basket that would catch the power line before it landed on the telephone line. The court found, however, that while the plaintiff's proposed

[20] 125 N.E. 93 (N.Y. 1919) (Cardozo, J.).
[21] 10 A.2d 673 (N.H. 1940).

design reduced the risk of an accident of the sort that occurred, it increased the risk of electrocution to a person on the street. An accurate assessment of reasonable care would require comparison of the burden of the alternative design to the net change in aggregate harm resulting from the design. Since the electrocution danger involved a foreseeable harm of far greater severity than the traumatic neurosis suffered by the plaintiff, the proposed precaution would have increased the aggregate risk to society.

In addition to the standard foreseeable-risk and burden-of-precaution balancing, negligence-in-design theories, as *Cooley* illustrates, raise the question of unintended consequences. A design change can fix one problem and at the same time create new ones. This is especially so where the proposed design is not, and has never been, in use. Of course, one could argue that a warning also may have unintended consequences, but the consequences associated with a warning are likely to be easier to foresee than those associated with a design change. An existing design, or general custom, reflects the evolution of an industry – embodying, by its presence or absence, the methods that have been successful and the methods that have failed.

Because of the problem of unintended consequences, courts examining modern products liability lawsuits (Chapter 17), where negligence-in-design theories are commonly observed today, tend to require plaintiffs to prove the existence of an alternative feasible design – usually by showing that the alternative is or has been in use in the market.[22]

The final illustration is of a negligence-in-warning case. In *Rinaldo v. McGovern*,[23] the defendant's errant golf ball shattered the windshield of the plaintiff's car as she was driving on a public street next to the golf course. The plaintiff charged that the defendant was guilty of negligence in hitting the ball and in failing to warn her of the risk of an accident. The court viewed the errant golf ball as an inherent risk of the game and rejected the negligence-in-operation theory in the absence of any evidence that the golfer's shot was reckless. The negligence-in-warning theory was also rejected. The court held that a warning would have been ineffective. Even if the golfer had been able to yell loudly enough to be heard by drivers in the street, the drivers would have had virtually no chance to turn around or drive away to avoid the errant golf ball. It follows that a failure to warn, to be actionable negligence, must involve a warning that could have been effective. The other danger in warning, noted by the court in its discussion of an earlier golf case, is that warnings could be too frequent. If homeowners near the golf course had to be warned every time a golfer thought that his ball might veer off course, warnings would fly thick and fast. The homeowners would soon learn to ignore the constant warnings of impending

---

[22] *See* Aaron D. Twerski & James A. Henderson, Jr., *Manufacturer's Liability for Defective Product Designs: The Triumph of Risk Utility*, 74 BROOK. L. REV. 106, 1079–1094 (2009); *see, e.g.*, Disher v. Synthes (U.S.A.), 371 F. Supp.2d 764, 771 (D.S.C. 2005) (alternative feasible design is a required element of plaintiff's case).

[23] 587 N.E.2d 264 (N.Y. 1991).

injury. In this latter scenario, the warning is ineffective because it vastly overstates the risk to potential victims.

V. THE REASONABLE PERSON TEST VERSUS THE HAND FORMULA

The Hand Formula tells us the key factors that should be considered in a negligence determination and precisely how they should be considered. However, the formula is incomplete because it fails to incorporate elements that most of us would consider relevant in guiding the conduct of a reasonable person.

It is important, therefore, not to forget that the Hand Formula is an instructive algorithm used in applying the reasonable person test. The reasonable person test is a general approach, under which the Hand Formula is merely one method of reaching an answer. In addition, the answer generated by the Hand Formula may go against our intuitive sense of what a reasonable person would do. When this happens, we should try to determine whether the Hand Formula analysis is excluding some features of the problem that a reasonable person would take into account.

The cases that best illustrate this point involve companies that conduct a cost analysis of some design change that would reduce the risk of injury to consumers, and after the analysis conclude that the design change would be too costly in light of the company's estimates of the benefits to consumers. The most famous example is the "Ford Pinto case," *Grimshaw v. Ford Motor Company*.[24]

The fuel tank of the Ford Pinto automobile was positioned in a way that caused it to explode in flames under certain accident conditions. Ford had conducted an analysis of alternative designs that would have reduced the risk of injury and had rejected the safer designs because of cost concerns.

The lawsuit arose out of a rear-end collision that occurred on a freeway. The driver, Lilly Gray, accompanied by 13-year-old Richard Grimshaw, had just changed lanes when her Pinto stalled and coasted to a halt. A driver behind them crashed into the car, pushing the fuel tank forward and causing it to be punctured, which sprayed fuel into the passenger compartment. The fuel caught fire, severely burning both passengers, Gray fatally, and permanently disfiguring Grimshaw. The jury awarded compensatory damages to the plaintiffs and punitive damages of $125 million to Grimshaw. The punitive award was reduced by the trial court to $3.5 million.

Ford had been aware of the vulnerability of the Pinto fuel tank to such a fire. Ford had examined the per-car cost of alternative designs that would have reduced the risk of severe burns to passengers. The per-car costs of the various design changes examined ranged from $1.80 to $15.30. The cost of the Pinto (hatchback model) in 1972 was roughly $2,000. Ford decided to either forgo or delay the design changes

---

[24] Grimshaw v. Ford Motor Company, 174 Cal Rptr. 349 (Cal. Ct. App. 1981). For a study of the case, *see* Gary T. Schwartz, *The Myth of the Ford Pinto Case*, 43 RUTGERS L. REV. 1013 (1991).

to save money. In a study unrelated to the case, Ford examined the costs and benefits of redesigning its fuel tank in several models and concluded that the per-car liability to Ford from burn-related deaths and injuries was considerably less than the per-car cost of altering its fuel tank design.[25]

Ford was unsuccessful in its attempt to get the trial court verdict overturned on appeal. Ford's argument is rather easy to see, using the Hand Formula reasoning. The firm had compared the burden of additional care to the expected losses that would be avoided by it, just as the Hand Formula requires. What basis could there be for holding the firm liable, especially for punitive damages?

Before attempting to answer this question, consider another case that provides an even neater illustration of the problem: *Andrews v. United Airlines.*[26] A suitcase fell from an overhead luggage compartment in an airplane, injuring the plaintiff. The plaintiff sued United Airlines on the theory that United should have designed its overhead luggage compartments differently to reduce the risk of items falling out and injuring passengers. The trial court dismissed the suit. The appellate court reversed and remanded the lawsuit.

The case for dismissal in *Andrews* can be set out in very clear terms. At the time of the lawsuit, United Airlines ran roughly 175,000 flights each year. A United official who testified at the trial reported that in 1987 the airline had received 135 reports of items falling from overhead compartments. These were just reports of things falling out – and not necessarily leading to injuries. The number of serious injuries resulting from items falling out was presumably much lower than 135. Of course, it may be that there were incidents of items falling out that were not reported to the airline – perhaps a passenger, in a rush to get off the plane, decided he would rather not take the time to report.

To make the numbers easier to compare, suppose there were 175 incidents of items falling out and hitting passengers in 1987, which is probably an overestimate but a convenient number to consider. The per-flight risk of injury from items falling out would then be

$$175/175,000 = 1/1,000.$$

In other words, in each flight there is, at most, a one-out-of-a-thousand chance that a passenger would be hit by an item falling from an overhead bin.

Now, not every case of contact leads to an injury. Sometimes pillows or light briefcases fall out, leading to no injuries worth reporting. Suppose the average harm

---

[25] *See* Gary T. Schwartz, *The Myth of the Ford Pinto Case*, 43 RUTGERS L. REV. 1013 (1991). On the relationship between internal cost-benefit calculations and liability, *see* W. Kip Viscusi, *Corporate Risk Analysis: A Reckless Act?*, 52 STAN. L. REV. 547 (2000).

[26] Andrews v. United Airlines, Inc., 24 F.3d 39 (9th Cir. 1994).

from being hit by items falling from the overhead bin is $100. If so, the expected harm to passengers per flight is

$$1/1{,}000 \times \$100 = \$0.10.$$

Suppose the expense of redesigning and reconstructing the luggage bins amounted, on an amortized basis, to only $0.50 per flight. Even at such a small cost, it would not make sense on cost-benefit grounds for the airline to reconstruct the overhead bins.

We have a clear argument for dismissal: It would not be reasonable, on cost-benefit grounds, for United to reconstruct its overhead bins to reduce the risk of injury to passengers. The burden of reconstructing the overhead bins outweighs the risk to passengers. Using the Hand Formula, United would say that it was not negligent. It would be cheaper for the passengers to buy insurance to cover the risk of harm than for the airline to reconstruct the overhead bins.

Why, given these valid points, would the appellate court in *Andrews* overturn a trial court dismissal and permit the case to proceed to a jury? How could a lawyer convince a judge to overturn the trial court given these facts? Note that this is the same problem raised by *Grimshaw*, where the appeals court refused to overturn a trial court finding of liability even though a Hand Formula analysis appeared to fully justify the defendant's conduct. To answer this question I will focus on *Andrews*, because it is the simpler of the two cases.

Return to the reasonable person standard as set out earlier in this chapter: Negligence is falling below the standard that one would set for oneself and require of others – the Golden Rule interpretation of the negligence standard. Suppose, in *Andrews*, you owned the airline and you were also a passenger. Would you evaluate the reasonable care question on the same terms as the Hand Formula? Probably not. There is a good chance you would have required the airline to suffer an extra $0.50 in cost per flight to reduce the risk of an injury to you that could be serious. That is because people do not make the same tradeoffs between life and property as they make between property and property.

One reason for these different approaches to risk tradeoffs is *risk aversion*. Suppose people are more afraid of risk when confronting life versus property tradeoffs than in property versus property tradeoffs, a plausible conjecture. If so, the usual approach of the Hand Formula, comparing the monetary burden with the monetary value of the risk, would be inadequate to the task of assessing reasonable conduct. Some adjustment would have to be made to take into account the individual's aversion to risk.

To see this in the context of this case, suppose airline passengers are risk-averse. A risk-averse individual would not be willing to pay $1 to enter a gamble in which the expected payout is equal to $1; he would offer some amount less than $1 for such a gamble. Thus, if given a chance to buy a ticket for a lottery that has a 50 percent chance of paying out $2 and a 50 percent chance of paying out $0 (thus, having an expected payout of $1), a risk-averse person would pay less than $1 for such a lottery ticket. How much less than $1 the risk-averse person would pay depends on his degree of his risk aversion. Considering losses instead of gains, a risk-averse person would pay more than $1 to avoid a risk that imposes an expected loss of $1 – for example, a risk that has a 50 percent chance of leading to a $2 loss and a 50 percent chance of leading to a $0 loss.

Now return to the facts of *Andrews*. An airline passenger is faced with a gamble: With probability 1/1,000 he will be hit by an object from the overhead bin, losing $100 as a result. With probability 999/1,000 he will not suffer any loss. The average or expected loss is only ten cents. But since the passenger is risk-averse, he would be willing to pay more than ten cents to avoid the risk. The amount he would be willing to pay to avoid the risk depends on the severity of his risk aversion. If he is extremely risk averse, he might be willing to spend $1 or more to avoid the risk. Given the larger sums that risk-averse passengers would pay to avoid the risk of injury, it now seems plausible that the burden on United Airlines from reconstructing the overhead bins might be less than the amount passengers would be willing to pay to avoid the risk of harm.

What would a reasonable passenger do when confronted with this scenario? Would a reasonable passenger refuse to spend $1 more for a plane ticket and put up with the risk of a 1/1,000 chance of injury from an item falling from overhead? Since airline ticket prices run into the hundreds of dollars easily today, it seems unlikely that every passenger would refuse to pay the extra dollar or two. A reasonable (or ordinary or average) passenger, if offered the option to pay the small extra amount to avoid the risk, might choose to do so.

It follows that an attorney would make precisely this appeal to a judge and jury. And it also follows that a reasonable judge might uphold a jury's finding that United Airlines was negligent for failing to reconstruct the overhead bins, or to at least take some effective precaution to reduce the risk of injury.

As I noted before, *Andrews* is a less famous version of the problem examined in *Grimshaw v. Ford Motor Company*. The error in Ford's approach is that it discounted the desire of the typical consumer to avoid the risk of death by combustion. A reasonable person arguably would recognize the intensity of this desire. Given such risk aversion, the typical car purchaser probably would be willing to add $15.30 to the purchase price of a car, already in the thousands of dollars, to avoid the risk of being engulfed in flames. A jury might reasonably find that a car company's failure to recognize this likelihood is not merely negligent but grossly negligent, and therefore award punitive damages to the victim of a fuel tank fire.

7

Customs, Statutes, and the Reasonable Person

The previous chapter explored the individual characteristics taken into account in the reasonable person standard and the ways in which these characteristics are assessed under the standard. This chapter explores external factors, such as customs and statutes.

The reasonable person standard is largely an objective test, though sometimes it takes individual incapacities into account. Judge Learned Hand's *Carroll Towing* opinion (previous chapter) suggests that the reasonable person standard operates as a cost-benefit test at its core, though it often incorporates factors that cannot be quantified as part of such a test.

The reasonable person standard also takes into account rules that people follow as customs, norms, or laws. This takes the test even further away from the cost-benefit formulation suggested by Judge Hand.

This chapter looks at the extent to which customs and statutes affect the application of the reasonable person test. Compliance with custom would appear to be a natural way of determining whether an actor's conduct was reasonable. Similarly, the violation of a statute would appear to be a natural way of determining whether an actor's conduct was unreasonable. Of course, any student of history knows that there have been customs and statutes in the past that have been harmful to society overall but were imposed because the winners had greater political power than the losers. Because of this, not every custom or statute should be presumed to be reasonable. Still, the customs and statutes that have the broadest application, that burden and benefit almost everyone in the same way, such as rules of the road, are likely to be the sort that have a strong claim to being regarded as reasonable.

One question lying slightly beneath the surface throughout this chapter is the extent to which an external standard, such as a custom or a statute, supplants or displaces the reasonable person test. No court has argued that external standards entirely displace the reasonable person test. However, one court famously held that compliance with custom should be treated as negating any theory of negligence,[1] and another court said that violation of a safety statute is "negligence in itself."[2] The case law has not uniformly supported such strong statements, especially the claim regarding custom, but has indicated factual conditions under which custom is a defense, and has provided legal tests for determining the effects of statutes on the negligence assessment. This chapter describes those conditions and tests, and tries to justify them in functional terms.

I. CUSTOM AND THE REASONABLE PERSON TEST

When compliance with custom is accepted by a court as a defense to a negligence claim, it serves to negate the plaintiff's theory of negligence. In other words, a finding that the defendant complied with custom is equivalent to a finding that the defendant was not negligent. But not every court has accepted the custom defense. Indeed, the use of custom as a defense to negligence appears to be largely a thing of the past today – and it is not clear that the defense ever amounted to much even in its heyday.

There are two reasons for the decline of the custom defense. First, the setting in which the defense arose most frequently was that of employment, when an injured employee brought a negligence suit against his employer. These cases are now governed by workers' compensation statutes, which impose strict liability. Second, the law on custom has changed over time in a manner that has sapped the defense of much of its force outside of the medical malpractice area. In spite of this, the custom defense remains instructive because of what it reveals about the negligence standard.

In *Titus v. Bradford, B. & K. R. Co.*,[3] a railroad employee was killed when he was struck by a railroad car that tipped off of its base. The car tipped over because it had a round bottom, which caused it to sit precariously on its flat truck base. To secure round-bottom cars to flat truck bases, the employer had been using wood blocks and wire. In this instance, the fit was not secure. The plaintiff's suit asserted that the practice of rigging round-body cars to flat bases was negligent.

The key reason the court rejected the plaintiff's negligence claim was that the employer's practice was a custom of the industry. Under the custom rule, compliance with an industry custom is a defense to a negligence charge. In justifying the rule, the court said that "absolute safety is unattainable, and employers are not insurers."[4] Reasonable care, reflected by the "fair average" of the profession or trade, is all that

---

[1] Titus v. Bradford, B. & K. R. Co., 20 A. 517 (Pa. 1890).
[2] Martin v. Herzog, 126 N.E. 814, 815 (N.Y. 1920).
[3] Titus v. Bradford, B. & K. R. Co., 20 A. 517 (Pa. 1890).
[4] *Id.* at 518.

the law requires.[5] Moreover, juries should not be allowed to dictate the practices of an industry.[6]

Another justification the court offered was that the deceased employee had been with his employer working with the rigged cars for almost two years. This was sufficient time, in the court's view, for the employee to become fully aware of the risks of the business; and given this awareness, the employee assumed the risk.

Let's take a closer look at the custom defense as described in *Titus*. Why should such a defense be recognized in this case, or in any case? Although the custom defense has been harshly criticized, there is an argument in favor of it based largely on *informational asymmetry*. Industry customs are methods of doing business – producing goods or services, or selling – that are adopted because they are effective means of operating within existing resource constraints. The fact that they are referred to as customs, rather than as absolutely necessary methods, implies that there are alternatives. The customs are generally adopted over the alternatives because they are efficient in comparison to the alternatives. It follows that a custom probably reflects information about technologies, resources, and constraints that industry participants have which outsiders may not have. An industry outsider may think that he can design a better practice, but the outsider could easily be wrong. And customs sometimes reflect surviving practices, when many supposedly better ideas have failed.

The alternative basis for a custom defense is *assumption of risk*. Industry practices present especially appropriate conditions for an assumption of risk defense. An industry practice, in many cases, is something that the plaintiff employee has had to work with for a long period. An employee who has long worked in an industry has had time to observe the risk characteristics of the industry in comparison to alternative industries in which he could work. The employee may have decided to continue working in his chosen industry because the combination of compensation and risk seemed best to him in comparison to alternatives. If so, then the employee has received implicit compensation for accepting the inherent risks of his employment. To hold the employer liable for accidents that result from such inherent risks, rather than the negligence of the employer, would effectively impose strict liability on the employer.

Thus, there are two rationales for recognizing custom as a defense to negligence: *informational asymmetry* and *implied consent*. When both features are present, the defense is at its strongest, and this is observed in *Titus*. These features are matters of fact and therefore present in modern cases as well as in old cases.

The informational asymmetry justification implies that the custom defense is appropriate in instances where the industry practice is probably better than the feasible alternatives and probably reflects information not available to outsiders.

[5] *Id.*
[6] *Id.*

This seems true in *Titus*, where the plaintiff asked the court to reconsider the industry practice of rigging round-body cars to flat truck bases. It is unlikely that outsiders could have improved upon the industry's practice, working within the same constraints. However, in a case involving a practice that does not require special knowledge about the workings of an industry, the custom defense cannot be justified by this argument.

A case that illustrates the limits of the custom defense is *Mayhew v. Sullivan.*[7] The plaintiff, an independent contractor, was injured after he fell through a hole cut in a mining platform. The platform was 270 feet below the ground. The plaintiff claimed that the employer had cut a ladder hole in the platform without providing any warning, barrier, or light to prevent workers from falling into it.

The employer asserted the custom defense, and the court rejected it, noting that any jury would be as qualified as an industry expert to assess the negligence of the employer's conduct. The court added that even if such carelessness were universal in an industry, that fact would not necessarily serve as a defense to negligence.

It is easy to distinguish *Mayhew* from *Titus*. First, the plaintiff in *Mayhew*, as an independent contractor, had not been able to observe the practice of the employer over a long period of time. Second, and more important, the employer's conduct in *Mayhew* did not reflect constraints or technology peculiar to the industry. There is nothing special about cutting a hole in a platform. *Mayhew* is a different case from *Titus*, in terms of both the factual matter of informational asymmetry and the traditional assumption of risk inquiry. And even if the plaintiff in *Mayhew* had been a longtime employee, assumption of risk would be a doubtful defense. It would be quite difficult for an employee to assume (in the sense of understanding and foreseeing) the risk of an unpredictable decision by his employer to cut a hole in a platform on which he must work.

The informational asymmetry argument for the custom defense relies at bottom on wariness over "error costs" – that is, the likelihood of error and the costs of error. In a setting where special industry knowledge is important in judging the reasonableness of conduct, there is a high risk that an uninformed court will make a mistake in assessing reasonableness. That is, the court may find that the defendant's conduct was unreasonable when, if the court had access to all of the information in the defendant's possession, it would instead find the practice reasonable. In addition to the risk of error, the custom defense, under the theory presented here, should be sensitive to the cost of an erroneous decision. In *Titus*, the risk of error was great because of the informational asymmetry, and the cost was likely to be great too because the plaintiff was asking for an important industry practice to be declared negligent. In *Mayhew*, error costs were comparatively small because the jurors could assess negligence without any special knowledge, and the challenged practice was

---

[7] 76 Me. 100 (1884).

so trivial in importance to the industry that the cost of discontinuing it could not have been significant.

I have so far set out the factual grounds on which the custom defense can be justified. In spite of its justifiability, it appears that the doctrine was not applied by every court at the time of *Titus*. The custom rule has a relatively strong basis in the facts of *Titus*, but there are few cases of the period that articulate such a strong defense of the rule and offer similar factual support for it.[8] *Holland v. Tennessee Coal, Iron & R.R. Co.*,[9] an Alabama case, has an excellent discussion of the custom doctrine with references to other Alabama cases. However, the court refers to custom as evidence *tending* to negate a theory of negligence, not as dispositive proof of due care.[10]

Indeed, in *Texas & Pacific Railway Co. v. Behymer*,[11] a case from roughly the same time as *Titus*, the U.S. Supreme Court, without mentioning *Titus*, held the defendant railroad negligent even though the plaintiff had been injured in the course of a customary practice. The plaintiff, a brakeman for the railroad, was standing on top of a car covered with snow and ice when it was bumped by another car during the switching process, causing the plaintiff to fall to his injury. The court held that the railroad was negligent even though the evidence showed that the practice of brakemen standing on the tops of cars during the switching process, when cars often bumped against each other, was customary in the industry. Of course, *Behymer* is distinguishable from *Titus* because the presence of ice on the top of the car should have led the defendant to take additional precaution in the switching process. But this distinction suggests that the custom rule was never much of a general rule – a seemingly minor change in the facts could lead a court that had applied the rule in one case to reject it another.

The custom rule has now been relegated to the dustbin, at least as a general defense to negligence, as a result of Judge Learned Hand's forceful language in *The T. J. Hooper*.[12] The case involved a natural experiment. The tugboats *T. J. Hooper* and *Montrose* were lost along with the barges they were pulling during a storm off the coast of New Jersey. Four other tugboats that were on the same northbound

---

[8] For an argument that there were *no* cases of the period supporting the custom defense in the same manner as *Titus*, *see* Henry R. Miller, Jr., *The So-Called Unbending Test of Negligence*, 3 Va. L. Rev. 537 (1916). However, Miller's argument appears to be overstated. There were cases, such as Holland v. Tenn. Coal, Iron & R.R. Co., 8 So. 524 (Ala. 1890), that applied the custom doctrine to absolve defendants of negligence.

[9] 8 So. 524 (Ala. 1890).

[10] A stronger statement of the custom rule appears in some earlier Alabama cases, Louisville & N. R. Co. v. Hall, 6 So. 277, 282 (Ala. 1899); Propst v. Georgia Pac. Ry. Co., 3 So. 764, 766 (Ala. 1888) (railroad's duty of care satisfied if it conforms to industry custom). However, the custom rule appears to soften over time in the Alabama case law. In a later case, Louisville & Nashville R.R. v. Hall, 69 So. 106 (Ala. 1915), the Alabama Supreme Court applies a more fact-sensitive and conditional form of the custom rule.

[11] 189 U.S. 468 (1903).

[12] 60 F.2d 737 (2d Cir. 1932).

route as the *T. J. Hooper* survived the storm with no damage. The difference was that the four surviving tugboats were equipped with radios and stayed near the Delaware shore during the storm after hearing the weather reports.

The trial court found it was a custom for coastwise tugboats to be equipped with reliable radios. Learned Hand, on the appellate court, disagreed and held that the facts did not establish that equipping tugboats with radios was a custom, and that the tugboats that had radios did so only because their crews had brought them on board. More importantly, Hand said that

> a whole calling may have unduly lagged in adoption of new and available devices. It never may set is own tests, however persuasive be its usages. Courts must in the end say what is required; there are precautions so imperative that even their universal disregard will not excuse their omission.[13]

Since those words were written, the custom defense has never received the same level of deference from courts as it appeared to have been given in the days of the *Titus* decision. Custom remains a general defense in medical negligence (malpractice) litigation. However, outside of medical malpractice, courts now treat custom as relevant evidence to be assessed in a negligence case, but not as establishing a defense to a negligence charge. Perhaps this is just as well, and not really a big change in the status of the custom defense, given that the defense was not recognized uniformly by courts even before *The T. J. Hooper.* The early case law suggests that the custom defense is grounded in facts that would generate a concern for the competence of a jury to determine negligence. A plaintiff's claim that a technical design, process, or method of operation is negligent in and of itself, in the absence of any evidence that a safer alternative is in practice within the defendant's industry, would generate such a concern. Given this, it is easy to see why medical malpractice litigation continues to include the custom defense. Most ordinary juries are too ill-informed to determine the reasonableness of a doctor's conduct.

Even though the custom defense remains safely entrenched in medical malpractice litigation, there have been some important variations in this area. The most important is *Canterbury v. Spence,*[14] which establishes the doctor's duty to disclose material risks to the patient before undergoing some potentially dangerous procedure such as surgery. Compliance with the disclosure duty is determined by the reasonable person test, not by professional custom. Another interesting though short-lived variation famously occurred in *Helling v. Carey,*[15] where the court held that a doctor's decision whether to give a pressure test for glaucoma would be evaluated under the reasonable person test rather than professional custom. The professional custom at the time was not to routinely perform a pressure test for patients under

---

[13] *Id.* at 740.
[14] 464 F.2d 772 (D.C. Cir. 1972).
[15] 519 P.2d 981 (Wash. 1974).

the age of 40, since the incidence of glaucoma was rare for such patients (1 out of 25,000, or 0.00004). The *Helling* court posited that the pressure test was easy to apply and the loss from glaucoma severe; therefore it followed that a reasonable doctor would give such a test in response to the slightest suspicion, whatever the age of the patient. But the court failed to consider the costs of false positives. If the rate of false positives is sufficiently high, giving the test could lead to unnecessary medical costs or procedures, as well as unnecessary fears on the part of the patient. Given that the false positive rate was 95 percent, it is not difficult to conduct a Hand Formula analysis to show that a reasonable doctor would *not* generally give a glaucoma test to a patient under 40. To see this, suppose the loss to the patent (in unnecessary harms) from a false diagnosis is $200, and the loss from glaucoma is $50,000. The Hand Formula would require the test only if the losses that could be avoided by the test are greater than the burden of giving the test. For a person under 40, the expected loss from glaucoma is $2 (0.00004 multiplied by $50,000). The expected loss from a false positive is $189.99 (0.99996 multiplied by 0.95 multiplied by $200). The expected loss to be avoided by giving the test is therefore negative ($2 − $189.90). Thus, the Hand Formula suggests that a reasonable physician would not give the test.

It has been noted that customs may lag behind the most efficient practices because of third-party costs (externalities).[16] Suppose the parties injured as the result of some industry custom are bystanders who have no connection to the business. If courts treated custom as a defense to a tort claim in such a case, the injuries created by the custom would not affect the costs of firms in the industry (because the tort claims of victims would be dismissed). And, unlike industry customers, bystanders would have no opportunity to demand that the industry take their injuries into account, or to seek price reductions in exchange for bearing risk. Consequently, the industry would have no incentive to abandon a custom that injures only bystanders. This provides a justification for Learned Hand's conclusion in *The T. J. Hooper* because it suggests that the custom defense can generate unreasonably low levels of care when the potential victims are largely industry bystanders.[17]

II. STATUTES, REGULATIONS, AND THE REASONABLE PERSON

Statutes and regulations can be distinguished from customs on the ground that statutes tend to be imposed from above by governments, while customs are adopted

---

[16] Richard A. Posner, *A Theory of Negligence*, 1 J. LEGAL STUD. 39 (1972).

[17] However, if the case of bystander victims is not a common one, this defense of Hand's argument would be valid only for special cases. The broader question is whether bystander victims are common or relatively rare. In industries where bystander victims are rare, Hand's argument for rejecting the custom defense would be less persuasive. For a theory of the custom defense that relies largely on the capacity of the parties to contract, *see* Richard A. Epstein, *The Path to the* T. J. Hooper: *The Theory and History of Custom in the Law of Tort*, 21 J. LEGAL STUD. 1 (1992).

internally among participants in an activity. Because customs tend to be based on agreements, or implicit agreements, they are more likely to provide an accurate description of what a reasonable person would do, provided that the agreements reflect the interests of all of the members of the relevant community. A reasonable person would comply with norms and customs that have worked in his industry or community.

A statute, unlike a custom, may be imposed by a legislative majority in response to pressure from a concentrated interest group[18] and therefore may bear no relation whatsoever with reasonable norms within the industry or community in which the statute applies. Because of this, the reasonable person framework should be somewhat more skeptical of statutes than of customs as descriptions of reasonable conduct.

A statute becomes an issue in negligence litigation when a plaintiff asserts that the defendant should be found guilty of negligence because he has violated the statute, or when a defendant claims that he should not be found guilty of negligence because he complied with the statute. When a plaintiff uses a statute to argue that a defendant is guilty of negligence, he is attempting to take advantage of the *negligence per se* doctrine.

The negligence per se doctrine was set out in the clearest terms in *Osborne v. McMasters*,[19] where the court held that it is *negligence per se when a statute or municipal ordinance* (1) *imposes upon a person a specific duty for the protection or benefit of others and the person neglects to perform that duty,* (2) *the victim is from the class of those for whose protection or benefit the statute was imposed,* (3) *the injuries are of the character that the statute or ordinance was designed to prevent, and* (4) *the injuries were proximately caused by the neglect.*

The rule certainly applies to the facts of *Osborne*, where a store clerk sold to the victim a deadly poison without labeling it as such. The victim ingested the poison and died.

The failure to label the poison violated a state statute, and the purpose of the statute was to prevent drugstore customers from accidentally consuming poison. The victim, an ordinary consumer, was certainly within the class the statute aimed to protect. The injury was surely the type that the statute aimed to prevent. Last, we come to the proximate cause prong of the negligence per se test.

What does the proximate cause test require? First, we should read the test as requiring both *factual* and *proximate* causation. Factual causation is not satisfied if the injury would have happened even if the defendant had exercised reasonable care. Proximate causation is not satisfied if the victim's injury is not a foreseeable result

---

[18] *See generally* Mancur Olson, The Logic of Collective Action: Public Goods and the Theory of Groups (Harvard Univ. Press 1971).

[19] Osborne v. McMasters, 41 N.W. 543 (Minn. 1889). The court referred to an earlier Minnesota decision, Bott v. Pratt, 23 N.W. 237 (Minn. 1885), as precedent, but *Bott* does not provide a statement of the doctrine as clear as that in *Osborne*.

of the defendant's negligence (Chapter 5). It should be clear that a court would be reluctant to hold a defendant liable when the factual causation requirement is not satisfied – statutory violation or not. In such a case, the injury would have occurred even if the defendant had done precisely what the plaintiff says he should have done.

Applied to *Osborne*, the proximate cause inquiry seeks to determine whether the injury (death) was a foreseeable result of the defendant's failure to label the bottle as poison. Clearly, failing to label poison as poison will lead to some cases of accidental consumption followed by death, so the proximate cause requirement is satisfied in *Osborne*.

The plaintiff would have had an equally valid claim in *Osborne* even if there had been no statute governing the defendant's breach. If you go into a drugstore and purchase medicine, and it turns out to be poison, and the only reason you bought it was because it had been incorrectly labeled as "painkiller," you would have a good negligence claim against the drugstore. So what does the statute do for the plaintiff in *Osborne*?

The statute, in conjunction with the negligence per se doctrine, removes from the plaintiff the burden of having to prove negligence and the risk of failing to prove negligence. Indeed, many decisions, including *Osborne*, have said that the doctrine removes the inquiry into evidence of fault from the case altogether,[20] though not every court shares this view. In addition, the removal of the burden to prove negligence from the plaintiff affects only the negligence determination respecting the defendant. The label "negligence per se" implies that common law defenses such as contributory negligence remain, unless explicitly barred by statute.[21]

The core function of the negligence per se doctrine is to relieve the plaintiff of the burden of proving fault and the risk of failing to prove fault. At the least, the negligence per se doctrine shifts the burden to the defendant to escape the presumption of liability. It follows that one should expect the negligence per se doctrine to appear in cases involving relatively clear instances in which a person's failure to take care would endanger others – like failing to put an accurate label on a bottle of poison.

Shifting the burden of proving negligence is not a small matter, because along with the burden to prove a legal theory comes the risk of failing to prove it. In most instances of negligence, the injuring party will have considerably more information than the victim has on the facts that can be used to prove or disprove negligence. After all, it is the injuring party who knows best whether he complied with a fixed

---

[20] *Osborne* held that the statutory violation provided *conclusive* evidence of negligence. A strong statement of this view appears in Martin v. Herzog, 126 N.E. 814, 815 (N.Y. 1920).

[21] Curry v. Chicago & Northwestern Railway Co., 43 Wis. 665 (1878). A farmer's cow was killed by one of the defendant's trains, where the defendant railroad had failed to fence the track as required by statute. The court upheld the jury verdict for the farmer but noted that contributory negligence must be taken into consideration even in a case of a statutory violation. *See also* Spofford v. Harlow, 3 Allen 176.

standard of care, of the sort that would be set out in a statute (for example, drive no more than 55 miles per hour). The standard convention of allocating the burden of proof to the plaintiff puts him in a position where he has to prove negligence based on limited information, while the better informed defendant gets to withhold information and deny the plaintiff's charges. The negligence per se doctrine corrects this informational disadvantage by placing the burden of proof on the defendant.[22]

There is a converse proposition that follows from the function of the negligence per se doctrine: If a plaintiff does not have a valid common law negligence claim, then he should not be permitted to use the negligence per se doctrine to shift the burden to or to impose liability on the defendant unless the relevant statute explicitly grants such a right to the plaintiff. Suppose, for example, the plaintiff is injured by something the defendant does, but it turns out that the defendant had no duty of care to the plaintiff under the common law. The mere fact that the defendant violated a statute should not convert the plaintiff's nonexistent common law negligence claim into either a conclusive or rebuttable presumption of negligence.[23] This proposition helps to explain some difficult cases in this area.

Perhaps an easier way to understand the converse proposition – that absence of a valid common law negligence claim implies an inability to use the negligence per se doctrine – is to think of these cases as presenting pure statutory interpretation issues. The legislature enacts a statute and fails to specify whether the violation of the statute resulting in an injury gives the injured party a right to sue for damages. What should a court do? One convenient way to interpret the statute is to read it so that it is consistent with existing common law. That approach assumes that the legislature was aware of the common law, and that courts are aware of it too. The legislature would not find a need to repeat everything in the common law when writing a statute to fill in interpretive gaps. The only time the legislature would have a responsibility, under this view, to explicitly resolve any ambiguities in the interpretation of the statute is when the legislature intends an interpretation that goes against the common law.

There is a simple justification for this approach to interpreting statutes. If the legislature tried to write statutes in a way that left no interpretive ambiguity, the statute books would fill up thousands of libraries, and no one would have time to read them. It makes sense for the legislature to leave interpretive gaps in statutes with the understanding that those gaps will be filled by existing common law. Under this approach, legislating is economically feasible and the administrative burden of statutory interpretation relatively small.

---

[22] The ancient common law procedural system, discussed in Chapter 3, put the burden of proof on the defendant under the trespass writ. The burden was shifted to the plaintiff in *Brown v. Kendall*, also discussed in Chapter 3.

[23] Brattleboro v. Wait, 44 Vt. 459 (1872) (the only remedy available for the violation of a new duty created by statute is the remedy provided by the statute).

This reasoning leads to another principle, in addition to the test stated in *Osborne*, for determining whether breach of a statute leads to liability under the negligence per se doctrine. Because interpretive gaps in statutes should be filled in by the common law, one should reject attempts to use the breach of a statute to create a negligence per se claim in settings where the plaintiff would not have had a valid legal claim under the common law. I will refer to this below as the *harmonization principle*. It implies that if the defendant violates a statute that is silent as to the plaintiff's right to bring a suit for damages, and the violation causes an injury to the plaintiff, the plaintiff should not be able to recover under the negligence per se doctrine if the common law holds that the defendant owed no duty of care to the plaintiff under the circumstances leading to the injury.

Consider a few examples. The first is a straightforward application of the negligence per se doctrine. In *Gorris v. Scott*,[24] the defendant shipowner agreed to ship the plaintiff's sheep, but failed to pen them in as required by the Contagious Disease (Animals) Act of 1869. The animals were swept overboard during a storm. If the animals had been penned in as required by the statute, they probably would not have been lost. However, the court denied the plaintiff's effort to recover for breach of the statute because the statute was enacted to prevent sheep or cattle from being exposed to disease on their way to England, not to prevent them from being swept overboard.

Return to the negligence per se test. Was the statute in *Gorris* enacted to impose a duty on the defendant for the benefit of others? Yes. Did the defendant neglect to perform the duty? Yes. Was the defendant within the class of those protected by the statute? Yes. Was the injury suffered by the plaintiff within the class of injuries the statute was designed to prevent? No. The statute was directed toward preventing the spread of disease among animals, not to keep them from being swept off of ships during storms.

Of course, the fact the plaintiff in *Gorris* lost his negligence per se claim does not imply that he had absolutely no claim for recovery based on the negligence of the ship owner. The plaintiff could fall back on his common law negligence claim. That would require the plaintiff to offer some negligence theory – some specific breach of duty on the part of the defendant – with evidence tending to prove why the defendant's conduct was negligent.

Gorris is easy to explain on the basis of the negligence per se test articulated in *Osborne*. However, there are cases that are much harder to explain using the per se test. And *Gorris* itself raises questions about the stinginess of the test, since it is hard to see why the plaintiff shouldn't be allowed to exploit the burden-shifting advantage of the negligence per se doctrine just because the loss wasn't of the type contemplated by the statute. Both of these issues take us into the common law harmonization principle mentioned earlier.

---

[24] Gorris v. Scott, L.R. 9 Ex. 125 (1874).

Consider the second issue: If the plaintiff's loss occurred because of the violation of a statute, what difference should it make if the statute was designed to protect against the risk of a different type of loss? The justification for the stinginess reflected in *Gorris* is based on the likely result of not limiting the negligence per se claim to losses directly implicated by the statute. If courts did not impose such a limit, then plaintiffs would assert negligence per se claims for losses that were not within the contemplation of the statute. Some of these losses may be within the risks allocated by a contract, explicitly or implicitly. Some of the defendants targeted by such claims might have a tenuous causal connection to the plaintiff's harm.[25] Expanding the negligence per se test to encompass losses not within the scope of the statute would invite plaintiffs to attempt to extend the burden-shifting advantage of the per se rule to weak or baseless negligence theories, in the hope that pointing to a statutory violation would enable them to prevail without having to prove fault or causation, or even the existence of a duty to take care. This would be inconsistent with the function of the per se rule, which is to relieve the burden from the plaintiff of proving fault for a set of especially strong negligence claims. The instances where a legislature takes the time out of its schedule to enact a statute that prohibits a specific type of carelessness, to prevent a specific type of harm, will tend to be those where the type of carelessness prohibited has long been understood to be negligent or maybe grossly negligent.[26]

I mentioned that there are cases that are difficult to understand in terms of the negligence per se test articulated in *Osborne*. In these cases, the harmonization principle referred to before helps to explain the outcome. The best set of examples is a line of cases governing the duty of an abutting landowner to remove ice from a public sidewalk.[27] In *Fitzwater v. Sunset Empire, Inc.*,[28] the defendant was required by a municipal ordinance to remove ice and snow from the public sidewalk in front of his restaurant. The plaintiff slipped on the ice and brought suit against the restaurant owner. The court denied the plaintiff's attempt to recover under the negligence per se doctrine.

---

[25] *See, e.g.,* Wawanesa Mutual Insurance Co. v. Matlock, 70 Cal. Rptr. 2d 512 (Cal. Ct. App. 1997). The defendant violated a state statute by selling cigarettes to minors. The minors caused a fire with the cigarettes. The plaintiff attempted to take advantage of the negligence per se rule, but the court held that the purpose of the statute was not to prevent fires. The proximate causation requirement could have been applied to reach the same result in this case, as in many similar cases. However, the proximate causation test is sometimes more difficult to apply than the statutory purpose test. For example, in Brown v. Shyne, 131 N.E. 197 (N.Y. 1926), the court used the proximate cause test to reject the plaintiff's negligence per se claim against a chiropractor for practicing medicine without a license. The court held that practicing without a license would not lead foreseeably to an injury unless the practitioner failed to perform with reasonable care. The dissenting judge argued that injury to a patient is always foreseeable when someone practices medicine without a license.

[26] OLIVER WENDELL HOLMES, JR., THE COMMON LAW 112–114 (1881).

[27] Fitzwater v. Sunset Empire, Inc., 502 P.2d 214 (Or. 1972); Kirby v. Boylston Market Assn., 14 Gray 249 (Mass. 1859); Flynn v. Canton Co., 40 Md. 312 (1874).

[28] 502 P.2d 214 (Or. 1972).

Applying the negligence per se test directly to *Fitzwater*, it is a difficult case to explain. Was the ordinance enacted to impose a duty on the defendant for the benefit of others? Yes, clearly a duty to remove ice and snow could only have been imposed for the benefit of others. Did the defendant neglect to perform the duty? Yes. Was the defendant within the class of those protected by the statute? Yes. Was the injury suffered by the plaintiff within the class of injuries the statute was designed to prevent? The answer is obviously yes: Why would a government impose a duty to remove ice and snow if not to prevent the very injury suffered by the plaintiff in *Fitzwater*? Was the injury proximately caused by the defendant's neglect? Clearly, a slip-and-fall is the most foreseeable injury one could imagine in connection with failure to remove ice from the ground.

All of the factors of the negligence per se test are satisfied in *Fitzwater*, so how could the court have denied the plaintiff's negligence per se claim? Setting aside some technical distinctions noted in the court's opinion, the court stated one distinction consistent with the statutory interpretation view set out here: The common law did not impose a duty on the abutting landowner to remove ice and snow from the public sidewalk for the benefit of pedestrians.

Fitzwater, then, is a case in which the plaintiff asserted a negligence per se claim when he could not have asserted a valid claim under common law negligence principles. The interpretation norm directing courts to read statutes so that they are consistent with the common law implies that the court should have been reluctant to permit the plaintiff to use the negligence per se doctrine – unless the statute or ordinance said clearly that it was overturning the common law. Since there was no such expression in the ordinance in *Fitzwater*, the court's decision to reject the negligence per se claim was a sensible reconciliation of common and statutory law.

Another illustration of the importance of reading a statute in a manner that respects the common law is *Tedla v. Ellman*.[29] *Tedla* involved a contributory negligence claim against plaintiffs who had been walking on the right-hand side of the road, with their backs to the oncoming traffic, in violation of a statute that required them to be on the left-hand side, facing traffic. However, the court noted that the common law contained an exception to this rule, permitting pedestrians to walk with the traffic if the traffic coming from behind was much lighter than oncoming traffic. The court refused to apply the statute to hold the plaintiffs guilty of contributory negligence, because in its view the statute had to be read in a manner consistent with the common law.

Like *Fitzwater*, *Tedla* cannot be reconciled with the standard test (*Osborne*) for determining whether the negligence per se doctrine applies. But *Tedla* makes perfect sense in view the underlying function of negligence per se, which is to convert a valid common law negligence claim into a conclusive or presumptive finding of negligence. It is not the function of the doctrine to create a presumptive finding of

---

[29]   19 N.E.2d 987 (N.Y. 1939).

negligence where the charging party would not have had a valid negligence claim under the common law.

Now let's consider an example in which the statutory law explicitly modifies common law rights. In *Kernan v. American Dredging Co.*,[30] the plaintiff, a seaman, lost his life on a tugboat that caught fire when an open-flame kerosene lamp on the deck of a scow (a low, flat-bottomed boat) that it was towing ignited inflammable vapors that had collected on the surface of a river. The lamp had been mounted at a height less than three feet over the water surface, in violation of a Coast Guard regulation requiring such lamps to be mounted at a height no less than eight feet. However, the Coast Guard regulation was designed to prevent collisions, not fire. In spite of this the Supreme Court allowed the plaintiff to recover for the statutory violation, because the suit had been brought under the Jones Act, which incorporated the Federal Employers' Liability Act. The statutory framework deliberately sought to modify common law rights to expand the employer's liability. *Gorris* would suggest that the plaintiff did not have a valid negligence per se claim. But *Kernan* is distinguishable from *Gorris* because the statute under which the plaintiff sued in *Kernan* had been understood to expand the liability of employers.

The negligence per se test is not a straightjacket for courts. When the injury that occurs is not precisely what the statute was designed to prevent, but closely related, courts have given the statute a slightly broader interpretation, so that the plaintiff's claim satisfies the negligence per se test. For example, in *Stimpson v. Wellington Service Corp.*,[31] a 137-ton truck driven over a street without the statutorily required permit caused a break in an underground pipe in an adjacent building, which flooded the plaintiff's property. The court read the law requiring the permit, whose purpose was to protect the streets, to also protect adjacent property owners. This is consistent with an approach that puts function over form. The negligence per se test appears to be formulaic, but its function and systemic effects in a regime in which common and statutory law must be reconciled should always be kept in view.

---

[30] Kernan v. American Dredging Co., 355 U.S. 426 (1958).
[31] 246 N.E.2d 801 (Mass. 1969).

8

Inferring Negligence

As Justice Shaw made clear in *Brown v. Kendall* (Chapter 4), it is the plaintiff's burden to prove negligence. In some cases, however, only circumstantial evidence of negligence is available to the plaintiff. If courts demanded that plaintiffs prove negligence in every case, plaintiffs would lose most negligence suits based on circumstantial evidence. The defendant could prevail simply by asserting that the plaintiff had not proved his case.

To avoid this outcome, courts have developed a special doctrine of inference for negligence cases. The label for this doctrine, *res ipsa loquitur,* means "the thing speaks for itself." The doctrine of *res ipsa loquitur* consists of rules that guide courts in their disposition of negligence cases involving circumstantial evidence.

In general, courts dispose of negligence cases involving circumstantial evidence by dismissing the plaintiff's case, allowing the case to reach a jury, or issuing a directed verdict in favor of the plaintiff. The core issue in *res ipsa loquitur* cases is whether the evidence is sufficient to warrant submission of the plaintiff's case to a jury.

Given the importance of the jury to this topic I will start with a brief review of the respective roles of judge and jury in negligence cases before introducing *res ipsa loquitur* doctrine.

I. JUDGE AND JURY: A BRIEF OVERVIEW

Legal disputes present questions of law, questions of fact, and mixed questions of law and fact. In theory, these questions could be answered by a judge or by a jury.

A question of fact is one that can be answered without any reference to the law. Suppose the defendant says that he was on the corner of Main Street and Elm Street at 8:00 a.m. on Tuesday morning, and the plaintiff says that the defendant was not on that corner at that time. Since this is a disputed question of fact, some decision maker in the court, either judge or jury, has to determine which factual claim the court will accept as valid.

A pure question of law is one that can be answered without any reference to the facts in a dispute. Suppose the defendant argues that to be held liable for battery there must be evidence that he intended to harm the plaintiff (see *Vosburg v. Putney*, Chapter 4). The correct legal standard for intent under battery does not require intent to harm, but instead only the intent to execute an act that was highly likely to result in a harmful or offensive contact with the plaintiff. This is a question of law because a court could determine the correct legal standard without any reference to what actually happened in the case. Alternatively, consider a question of statutory interpretation. In many disputes in which the interpretation of a statute is relevant, courts attempt to determine the proper interpretation by discerning the intent of the legislature or by applying norms of statutory construction. To the extent that a court can decide a dispute over the interpretation of a statute without considering the facts of the dispute before it, the question can be viewed as strictly one of law. Of course, as we observed in the negligence per se cases (Chapter 7), some interpretation questions will inevitably involve consideration of the facts of the dispute.

A mixed question of law and fact is one that cannot be answered without regard to both the law and the facts of the dispute. The most common example is the negligence question. In a negligence case, a court must identify the appropriate legal test – whether it is the reasonable person standard or some more determinate standard such as negligence per se – and apply the standard to the facts before it to determine whether the defendant is guilty of negligence. The applicable legal test and the facts of the case may all be in dispute.

The resolution of disputed questions of fact is understood to be within the province of the jury. In the negligence setting, this allocation of responsibility seems defensible. The run-of-the-mill negligence case asks whether a defendant took reasonable care, which courts often describe as the ordinary care of a prudent person. In many settings, this would be a decision better made by a jury than a judge. For example, in a farming community, jurors drawn from the local population would be in a better position than a judge to determine whether a defendant farmer exercised the ordinary care of a prudent person in carrying out his work. Such a decision might require the jurors to know something about how farmers go about their work, a matter on which most judges are ignorant.

The determination of disputed questions of law is within the province of the judge. Again, this is an allocation of responsibility that is easy to defend. Judges state the law, and most of them have gained a chess master's knowledge of its intricacies.

Mixed questions of law and fact are to some extent within the provinces of both judge and jury. The issue of controversy is the degree to which the jury or the judge should determine the answer to these questions.

Holmes argued that with respect to mixed questions of law and fact, the judge should consult the jury from time to time, but otherwise make the determination on his own most of the time.[1] Holmes recognized that the judge should give disputed questions of fact to the jury. He also noted that the jury should be consulted on the negligence question when the judge does not have a firm sense of the policies that should govern, because the policies would themselves be influenced by information about local customs, which judges may not have. But on matters of negligence where the courts had been able to consider the particular issue in previous cases, the judge should view the standard and its application to have been fixed by the earlier cases.

Holmes's policy trades off case-specific accuracy – by disallowing juries in some cases in which their informational input would be desirable – to gain better predictability in the law. The policy implies that errors will be made in some cases, because the facts are not precisely the same as the facts considered in earlier decisions on which the legal standard is based. But some errors will be avoided under the policy – especially those associated with the variability of opinion, or the tendency to decide on the basis of sympathy, commonly associated with juries. In addition, the judge is more likely than a jury to ensure consistency and predictability in the law. Better predictability means that potential tortfeasors will have enhanced incentives to comply with the negligence standard and at the same time will not be induced by fear of liability to take excessive care.

The *res ipsa loquitur* rule goes in the opposite direction of Holmes's model, expanding the scope of the jury, but relying on similar policies. If potential tortfeasors know that they are effectively immune from liability in negligence disputes involving circumstantial evidence, they will have weak incentives to take care where such disputes may arise. *Res ipsa loquitur* doctrine provides a solution to this problem by setting out rules that both permit and regulate the submission of circumstantial evidence negligence cases to juries.

II. *RES IPSA LOQUITUR*

Inference doctrine in negligence law begins with *Byrne v. Boadle*.[2] The plaintiff was passing along the highway in front of the defendant's premises when he was struck and injured by a barrel of flour being lowered from a window. The defendant, a dealer in flour, argued that the plaintiff could not prove his case because he had no evidence of negligence for the jury to consider. The trial court agreed and nonsuited the plaintiff after the jury had awarded him damages. On appeal, the court overturned the trial judge's verdict and held that it should have been presumed that the defendant's servants were engaged in removing the defendant's flour. It also said that there are certain cases of which it may be said "*res ipsa loquitur*": The mere fact of the accident having occurred is evidence of negligence.

The *res ipsa loquitur* rule permits a plaintiff with only circumstantial evidence of negligence to (1) reach the jury, or (2) establish a presumption of negligence, or (3),

---

[1] Oliver Wendell Holmes, Jr., The Common Law 123–124 (1881).
[2] Byrne v. Boadle, 159 Eng. Rep. 299 (Ex. 1863).

in some cases, obtain a directed verdict. The rule shifts the burden of proof to the defendant.

Under the influence of Wigmore's evidence text,[3] courts have summarized *res ipsa loquitur* doctrine in three rules: (1) *The event must be of a kind that ordinarily does not occur in the absence of someone's negligence;* (2) *it must be caused by an agency or instrumentality within the exclusive control of the defendant; and* (3) *it must not have been due to any voluntary action or contribution on the part of the plaintiff.*

Let's apply these rules to *Byrne v. Boadle*. First, was the event of a kind that ordinarily does not occur in the absence of negligence? A flour barrel being lowered from a window hits the plaintiff in the head. How often does this happen in the absence of someone's negligence? Rarely, under ordinary conditions. Suppose, for example, the barrel rolled out of the window. Unless some external force (the wind) can be identified, the most likely explanation is that someone negligently left the barrel by the window in a position that would allow it to easily roll out.

The important function of the first rule is to fix *baseline probabilities* – that is, how frequently events happen in the absence of negligence, and how frequently in the presence of negligence. Once baseline probabilities are determined, a person can make rational inferences about the likelihood that an event was caused by negligence.

Res ipsa loquitur guides courts in a process similar to statistical inference. According to Bayes' Theorem, inferring the probability of an event *A*, based on the observation of another event *B*, requires knowledge of the general frequency, or baseline probability, of event *A* under the conditions observed.[4] For example, consider a medical test that is accurate 95 percent of the time – like the pressure test for glaucoma examined in *Helling v. Carey* (Chapter 7). If the test is positive for a disease, inferring the probability that the patient actually has the disease, given the positive test, requires knowledge of the baseline probability of the disease among people of the patient's type (say, people under 40). If the disease is extremely rare among people of the patient's type (as was true in *Helling*), then a positive test is very likely an error.[5] In a similar fashion, inferring negligence based on the occurrence of an

---

[3] *See* WILLIAM L. PROSSER, HANDBOOK OF THE LAW OF TORTS 214 (West Publishing Co. 4th ed. 1971).

[4] Specifically, Bayes' Theorem holds that the conditional probability of event *A* given event *B* is equal to product of the conditional probability of event *B* given event *A* and the ratio of the probability of *A* to the probability of *B*:

$$P(A|B) = \frac{P(B|A)P(A)}{P(B)}.$$

For a discussion of Bayes' Theorem and its application to *res ipsa loquitur*, see David H. Kaye, *Probability Theory Meets Res Ipsa Loquitor*, 77 MICH. L. REV. 1456 (1979).

[5] Suppose the disease is present in only 1 percent of the population from which the patient is drawn. Using Bayes' Theorem, the probability that the patient really has the disease, given a positive test, is $P(\text{disease} \mid \text{test positive}) = P(\text{test positive} \mid \text{disease})P(\text{disease}) \div P(\text{test positive})$. The probability of a positive test in the patient's population is $0.95 \times 0.01 + 0.05 \times 0.99 = 0.059$. Thus, $P(\text{disease} \mid \text{test}$

event (barrel falls out of window) requires knowledge of the baseline probability of negligence in events similar to the one before the court.

Thus, to responsibly infer negligence solely on the basis of an injurious event, one must first choose an event that is associated with negligence. It should not be an injurious event that can easily happen in the absence of negligence. For example, negligence cannot responsibly be inferred when a hurricane blows open the windows of a flour shop and sends a barrel on to someone's head. Although the event – a hurricane-force wind – does not happen often, the joint event of the wind and the barrel being forced out could happen without any negligence on anyone's part.

It is important to establish appropriate baseline probabilities to prevent the *res ipsa loquitur* doctrine from being used erroneously. If the doctrine were applied in cases where accidents easily happen in the absence of negligence, then it would be equivalent to a strict liability standard – especially if the jury were predisposed to favor an injured plaintiff. Recall that strict liability taxes and thereby discourages activities (Chapter 5). The common law applies strict liability to discourage activities that externalize an unusually high level of risk (Chapter 5). *Res ipsa loquitur* is not a doctrine designed to discourage activities, but rather to provide courts with a consistent procedure for inferring negligence from circumstantial evidence.

The second rule asks whether the event was caused by an instrumentality or agency within the exclusive control of the defendant. The defendant in *Byrne v. Boadle* argued that it might not have been, because he might not have had control over the flour barrel; it may have been under the control of the purchaser. Here the court adopted a presumption that an accident of this sort, occurring on the premises of the defendant, in an operation usually controlled by the defendant's agents, was in fact the result of the actions of the defendant's agents. The court left it to the defendant to prove the presumption false.

The second rule goes to an important feature of *res ipsa loquitur* cases: They generally involve settings of informational asymmetry. In other words, the cases involve settings in which the defendant knows, or should know, how the accident happened but the plaintiff does not know. The second *res ipsa* rule effectively shifts the burden to the defendant to explain what happened. This is desirable because it forces evidence out into court that would otherwise never reach the judges.

Baron Pollock, author of *Byrne v. Boadle*, noted during argument with the defendant's lawyer that the fact of the accident could be taken as evidence of negligence, "as, for instance, in the case of railway collisions."[6] Negligence law regarding common carriers and innkeepers imposes on them a *duty of utmost care*, holding them liable for the slightest evidence of negligence. In its early applications the utmost

---

positive) $= 0.95 \times 0.01 \div 0.059 = 0.16$, which means that the likelihood of an erroneous inference of disease is 84 percent.

[6] Byrne v. Boadle, 159 Eng. Rep. 299, 299 (Ex. 1863).

care standard shifted the burden to the railroad in settings where the victim was unlikely to be able to produce evidence of negligence on the railroad's part.[7] Courts have had difficulty explaining the purpose of the utmost care standard, but Pollock's comment provides an important insight. The fundamental reason for the utmost care standard applied to common carriers is probably the same as that for the second rule of *res ipsa loquitur* doctrine: to encourage the only party competent to bring evidence to court to do so.[8] In this sense, *res ipsa loquitur* should be viewed as a more general application of the standard that traditionally has been applied to common carriers and innkeepers.[9] However, unlike the utmost care rule, *res ipsa loquitur* imposes an additional filter on plaintiffs' claims by requiring the injuries to be of the sort that is unlikely to occur in the absence of negligence. This additional filter was not imposed under the utmost care standard, probably because it would have defeated the purpose of the standard and diluted incentives for railroads to take care.

In *Byrne v. Boadle* we see a special interpretation of the second rule, regarding exclusive control. As the second rule is stated, there is certainly room for a defendant to point out that he did not have exclusive control of the agency or instrumentality causing the accident. The defendant did this in *Byrne v. Boadle*, arguing that just because it was his shop and his agents working in the shop did not mean that the flour barrel was under his control. The court, unpersuaded by the defendant's argument, adopted a presumption that the defendant did control the relevant agencies and instrumentalities (workers and barrels of flour). The purpose of the presumption is to carry into effect the goal of the second rule, which is to force the defendant to disclose information to guide the court to an accurate judgment.

The third rule applied to *Byrne v. Boadle* leads to an obvious conclusion. The plaintiff did nothing to cause the barrel to fall on his head, beyond simply being there. He was also innocent of contributory negligence.

Although there are rules for the application of *res ipsa loquitur*, at the bottom of it all is a question of inference in the light of available facts. The standard of proof for a negligence case, and for civil trials generally, is *preponderance of the evidence*. Thus, if a court concludes that the circumstantial evidence would permit a jury to find,

---

[7] Kelley v. Manhattan Ry., 20 N.E. 383 (N.Y. 1889).

[8] In Farwell v. Boston & Worcester R.R. Corp, 45 Mass. 49 (1842), Chief Justice Shaw justified the utmost care standard on the basis of informational disparity between the customer and the common carrier. This is consistent with the doctrine of Kelley v. Manhattan Ry., 20 N.E. 383 (N.Y. 1889), reserving the utmost care standard for accidents resulting from defective conditions in cars or tracks in the exclusive possession of the railroad.

[9] If information-forcing were the sole reason for *res ipsa loquitur*, then the other prongs of Wigmore's test would be unnecessary. I think the key difference between the common carrier cases and the general setting of *res ipsa* is that the common carrier cases involve a contractual relationship in which railroads (or innkeepers) are the only ones with information bearing on the likelihood of negligence for certain accidents. Given this, in the absence of the negligence presumption, the market would fail to reward firms that consistently took every reasonable precaution. *See* Steven Shavell, *Strict Liability Versus Negligence*, 9 J. LEGAL STUD. 1 (1980).

with a probability of at least 51 percent, that the defendant is guilty of negligence, then it would be justified submitting the case to the jury.

If a court concludes that the circumstantial evidence would permit a jury to find guilt with a probability of at least 95 percent, then it obviously would be justified in submitting the case to the jury. Such a case would also satisfy the *reasonable doubt* standard (requiring proof of guilt beyond a reasonable doubt) used in criminal cases. In such cases some courts have held that the plaintiff was entitled to a judgment in his favor in the absence of rebuttal evidence from the defendant.[10]

Baseline Probabilities and the Duty of Care

Because the *res ipsa loquitur* doctrine guides courts in the process of inferring negligence, it necessarily operates with the reasonable person test in the background, as an aide to determining baseline probabilities. Thus, in settings where the defendant should foresee a high likelihood of harm, his expected level of precaution – or equivalently, his duty to take care – increases. The *res ipsa loquitur* doctrine implies a stronger presumption of negligence in these settings.

Consider two famous cases involving objects falling out of hotels. In *Larson v. St. Francis Hotel*,[11] the plaintiff was hit by a chair thrown out of the window by someone celebrating V-J Day (victory over Japan in World War II). The plaintiff tried to use *res ipsa loquitur,* but the court rejected his argument because the hotel did not have exclusive control over the chairs.

In *Connolly v. Nicollet Hotel* the defendant hosted a Junior Chamber of Commerce convention that became rowdy.[12] The defendant had ample notice of drinking and hooliganism on the premises. Plaintiff was hit by an object thrown from the hotel and tried to rely on the *res ipsa* rule. He succeeded, and the court distinguished *Larson* as a case involving a surprise celebration.

How should one reconcile these cases on the basis of *res ipsa loquitur* doctrine? The reasonable person test has different implications in the two cases. In the first, *Larson*, there was no reason for the hotel owner to foresee the danger, and thus, his required care is what would be typical for everyday events. The hotel owner is not expected to foresee chairs being thrown out of windows. No court would impose a duty to foresee such an accident on the owner. If a chair is thrown from a hotel window, one should not infer negligence on the part of the hotel from this event alone.

In the second case, *Connolly*, the required level of care was higher because the owner was aware, or should have been aware, of the heightened danger to hotel

---

[10] Farina v. Pan American World Airlines, Inc. 497 N.Y.S.2d 706 (App. Div. 1986) (plane went off runway; summary judgment for plaintiff); Newing v. Cheatham, 540 P.2d 33 (Cal. 1975) (plane crash, strong evidence of pilot intoxication, plane's fuel exhausted; directed verdict for plaintiff).

[11] 188 P.2d 513 (Cal. App. 1948).

[12] Connolly v. Nicollet Hotel, 95 N.W.2d 657 (Minn. 1959).

guests and pedestrians near the hotel. The scope of the owner's duty expands under these conditions. If a chair is thrown from a window, a suspicion of negligence arises because the hotel owner had reason to anticipate and guard against the accident.

What is really happening in the hotel cases is that the baseline probabilities are changing. The inference of negligence, given the occurrence of the accident, becomes more plausible as one moves from the facts of *Larson* to the facts of *Connolly*.[13]

Larson and *Connolly* are both cases in which there is no question as to whether the defendant has a duty of care to the plaintiff. If the defendant does not have a duty to the plaintiff, then satisfying the three factors of the *res ipsa loquitur* test (the event indicates negligence, the defendant has exclusive control, and there is no plaintiff causal contribution) would still not lay the basis for reaching the jury. For example, suppose the plaintiff is injured on the defendant's property. The facts satisfy the three-factor test, but the plaintiff is a trespasser. Since the defendant would not have a duty of care to the trespasser, circumstantial evidence of careless conduct could not lead to negligence liability on the part of the defendant.

Inference based on *res ipsa loquitur* doctrine must flow along causal pathways consistent with valid negligence theories. Thus, if the plaintiff uses the *res ipsa loquitur* doctrine in a case involving three negligence theories, each consistent with the circumstantial evidence, at least two of those theories must state valid negligence claims. If most of the causal theories are inconsistent with valid negligence theories, the plaintiff's circumstantial evidence cannot meet the preponderance standard. Although Prosser describes *Galbraith v. Busch*[14] as a discredited case, it serves as a good illustration. The plaintiff was a guest in a car owned by her daughter and driven by the defendant. The plaintiff was sitting in the front passenger seat next to Busch, while her daughter sat in the back seat giving directions to Busch. Without warning, the car swerved across the center line of the road, exposing the plaintiff to the impact in a collision. The defendant Busch offered no evidence, leaving it to the plaintiff to rely on *res ipsa loquitur* . There were two likely causes of the accident: negligent driving by Busch or some mechanical failure in the car. With respect to the first theory of negligence (driving) the defendants (Busch and the plaintiff's daughter) had a duty to take care for the benefit of the plaintiff. With respect to the second theory of negligence (mechanical failure), the defendants did not have a duty to take care for the benefit of the plaintiff. Under the law of the jurisdiction, the guest was deemed to have assumed the risk of latent mechanical defects unknown to the car owner (the reasoning for such a rule is explored in Chapter 10). Given this structure, only half of the plaintiff's plausible negligence theories could rest on the *res ipsa loquitur* doctrine. The court refused to apply the doctrine.

---

[13] For a general theory of the factors that determine baseline probabilities, *see* Mark F. Grady, *Res Ipsa Loquitur and Compliance Error*, 142 U. Pa. L. Rev. 887 (1994).
[14] 196 N.E. 36 (N.Y. 1935).

Inference and Common Knowledge

Since *res ipsa loquitur* requires the jury to infer negligence on the basis of circumstantial evidence, there is a presumption that the inference is one that juries are competent to make. Consider *Byrne v. Boadle* again. If a barrel of flour falls out of a window, most people have enough experience with such scenarios to make an intelligent inference about the probability of negligence. *Res ipsa loquitur* doctrine permits juries to use their common fund of experience to draw inferences of negligence on the basis of circumstantial evidence.

This suggests, however, that *res ipsa loquitur* may be inappropriate when the facts are such that an ordinary juror could not make a competent, experientially grounded inference as to whether the defendant had been negligent. For example, suppose a complicated piece of new technology fails. If jurors are not familiar with the technology, how can they competently infer negligence on the basis of the fact that the technology failed?

In *Wilson v. Colonial Air Transport*,[15] a case decided when airplanes were a relatively novel technology, the court rejected the application of *res ipsa loquitur* on the ground that

> There is at present no common knowledge of which courts can take cognizance concerning the customs or usual practice of air transport companies as to operation, inspection and repair of their airplanes. There must be evidence. We are not as yet, in respect to the operation, care and characteristics of aircraft, in a position where the doctrine of cases like Ware v. Gay, 11 Pick. 106, as to a stagecoach; O'Neil v. Toomey, 218 Mass. 242, 105 N.E. 974, as to the qualities of ice; or Gilchrist v. Boston Elevated Railway Co., 272 Mass. 346, 172 N.E. 349, as to trolley cars or steam railroad trains, can be applied. The decision of cases of that nature rests upon facts constituting a part of a widespread fund of information. No ruling of that character could be made upon the meager facts here shown.[16]

Wilson suggests that *res ipsa loquitur* is a doctrine whose scope changes (expanding or contracting) with the community's level of familiarity with a particular technology. If the technology is new and unfamiliar, this reasoning implies that the plaintiff should have the burden of introducing expert testimony to bridge the gap between technical knowledge and jury's experience.

While this view is consistent with the inference-guiding function of *res ipsa loquitur*, it is in tension with another purpose of the doctrine: to compel an informationally advantaged defendant to disclose evidence bearing on the negligence question. Because of this, courts have not consistently adopted the view that the

---

[15] 180 N.E. 212 (Mass. 1932).
[16] *Id.* at 214–215.

plaintiff cannot take advantage of *res ipsa loquitur* unless he introduces expert testimony to inform jurors about the technology at issue.[17]

If there is a resolution to this dilemma, it is likely to be found in the reasonable person standard, as described by Judge Hand, which compares the burden of precaution to the harm avoided by additional precaution. As the harm that can be avoided by additional care increases, the social interest in deterrence increases too. The tradeoff here is between accuracy in adjudication and maintaining incentives for taking care. In settings where the need to maintain incentives for care is dominant, because of the great frequency or great severity of accidental injuries, the deterrence interest should trump the accuracy interest. This explains why the information-forcing function was so important in *res ipsa loquitur*'s ancestor, the "utmost-care standard" applied to common carriers. Outside of such settings, the inference-guiding function of *res ipsa loquitur* should be given the greater weight, which implies that the plaintiff should be required to lay the factual groundwork for the jury to infer negligence.

Res Ipsa Loquitur *and "Information Forcing"*

I have so far examined *res ipsa loquitur* as a doctrine that guides and formalizes the process of inference in cases where there is circumstantial evidence of negligence. *Ybarra v. Spangard*[18] emphasized a more aggressive role for *res ipsa loquitur*: to force defendants to provide evidence and information bearing on the negligence question to the court when the evidence is entirely within defendants' hands. As I noted earlier, this function encourages an expansive approach to *res ipsa loquitur* doctrine and could be used to justify applications of the doctrine in cases in which its formal requirements are not obviously satisfied. The information-forcing theory of *res ipsa loquitur* would lead a court to stretch the meaning of the requirements to find them satisfied.

In *Ybarra* the plaintiff was anesthetized for surgery and woke up with a sharp pain in his right shoulder, which later spread down to his arm, eventually resulting in paralysis and atrophy of the muscles around the shoulder. The defendants noted that there were several doctors and assistants who had worked on the plaintiff and any one of them could have done something that caused the injury. It followed, according to the defendants, that *res ipsa loquitur* could not be applied on behalf of the plaintiff, because the plaintiff could not show that the injury was caused by an agency or instrumentality under the exclusive control of any of the defendants. The court held that at all times the defendants either controlled or were at least

---

[17] *See, e.g.,* Rose v. New York Port Authority, 293 A.2d 371 (N.J. 1972) (automatic door malfunction); Colmenares Vivas v. Sun Alliance Insurance Co., 807 F.2d 1102 (1st Cir. 1986) (escalator malfunction).

[18] Ybarra v. Spangard, 154 P.2d 687 (Cal. 1944).

charged with controlling the agencies or instrumentalities that could have harmed the plaintiff, and that this was sufficient to shift the burden under *res ipsa loquitur*. The court defended its decision on the ground that shifting the burden would break a _conspiracy of silence_ among the doctors and force them to disclose relevant information to the court.

The application of *res ipsa loquitur* in *Ybarra* is consistent in most respects with its application in *Byrne v. Boadle*. The court's decision to treat the surgeon in charge of the operation as responsible for the conduct of the assisting doctors and nurses, and the instruments within their control, is similar to the presumption of control over operations adopted in *Byrne v. Boadle*. The differences are observed in the jury's competence to infer negligence and the motivating rationale for the doctrine. But these differences are not significant. As long as expert testimony, common in malpractice cases today, can enable a jury to competently infer negligence on the basis of the evidence presented, then *Ybarra* can be viewed as within the traditional inference framework of *res ipsa loquitur*.

9

Contributory Negligence and Assumption of Risk

adverse selection
moral hazard useful here

Recall from Chapter 4 the three-part structure of arguments available to defendants: denials, justifications, and excuses. This chapter examines two powerful justifications in negligence law: contributory negligence and assumption of risk. Contributory negligence is a defense based on the plaintiff's failure to take reasonable care. Assumption of risk is a defense based on the notion that the plaintiff consented to the defendant's conduct, which annuls the plaintiff's theory of negligence.

I. CONTRIBUTORY NEGLIGENCE

The law of contributory negligence repeats much of what has been said in previous chapters about negligence. Since damages are asserted in the plaintiff's negligence claim against the defendant, the defendant's contributory negligence charge involves only three elements: duty, breach, and causation. Since it is the defendant who is asserting the contributory negligence claim, he has the burden of proving its elements. If the defendant is successful in proving contributory negligence, the plaintiff's claim for damages is rejected – that is, the plaintiff gets nothing.

There are many ways in which a plaintiff can fail to take reasonable care. In the cases where the plaintiff is injured and the defendant has suffered no injury, the question of relevance is whether the plaintiff exercised reasonable care for his own safety. However, the determination of reasonable care may require a broader outlook than just the plaintiff's own safety. The plaintiff may have failed to take reasonable care not only for his own safety but for the safety of others, including the defendant, as well.

Not every failure to take reasonable care for one's own safety constitutes contributory negligence. In general, only those failures that contribute, with the defendant's negligence, in bringing about the plaintiff's harm constitute contributory negligence. This has been the common law rule at least since *Greenland v. Chaplin*,[1] an English case decided in 1850. The defendant's steamboat negligently collided with the steamboat in which the plaintiff was a passenger. The collision caused the anchor of the steamboat carrying the plaintiff to fall on the plaintiff's leg, breaking it. The court rejected the defendant's argument that the plaintiff should not be allowed to recover for negligently placing himself so close to the anchor, holding that only negligence of the plaintiff that contributes to the cause of the accident can bar the plaintiff from recovery.

Put another way, *courts have generally held that only failures of care on the plaintiff's part that, in conjunction with the defendant's failure to take care, increase the probability of an accident occurring can be found contributorily negligent.* A failure by the plaintiff to take measures that would reduce the severity of an accidental injury – say, by wearing protective gear – without affecting the probability of the accident, would not be considered contributory negligence.

To illustrate, let's reexamine the facts in *Vosburg v. Putney* (Chapter 4). Recall that Putney intentionally kicked Vosburg, after which Vosburg suffered a severe injury to his leg. The injury was due most likely to a preexisting infection in the area where Vosburg kicked Putney. Suppose the kick had been accidental. Should Vosburg have been found guilty of contributory negligence for coming to school, with his leg unprotected, knowing that he might be kicked by one of his classmates? If a court were to reach this conclusion, it would contradict the principle that a tortfeasor takes his victim as he finds him (Chapter 4).

The rule that a tortfeasor is responsible for the damages directly caused by his tort (foreseeable or not) implies that contributory negligence should be limited to failures on the plaintiff's part to take reasonable care that also combine with the defendant's negligence to increase the probability of the accident. The two doctrines are complementary. The tort victim who suffers a severe injury only because he has a preexisting condition that makes him especially vulnerable to injury, or because he has failed to sufficiently harden himself against injury, cannot be charged with contributory negligence on that basis alone.

Although the formal law of contributory negligence is similar to that for primary negligence, there are differences in application of the duty, breach, and causation elements. Under each of these elements special rules have developed for contributory negligence.

Duty

In the vast majority of cases, an individual has a duty to take care to avoid injury to himself or to his property. However, there are exceptions. One is observed in rescue scenarios. Courts have said that *when an individual exposes himself to danger in attempting to rescue another, he can be held responsible for contributory negligence*

---

[1]   155 Eng. Rep. 104 (Exch. Div. 1850).

only if his conduct is rash or reckless.[2] This means that the rescuer does not have a duty to take reasonable care for his own safety.

Why do courts relieve the rescuer of the duty of care for his own safety? The reason is that rescue is conduct that benefits others. When an actor's conduct externalizes benefits to others, it may be socially preferable for the law to provide a subsidy to the actor's conduct (see Chapter 2 or Chapter 5). Relieving the rescuer of the duty to care for his own safety makes rescue a less costly activity to the rescuer and therefore enhances the incentive to rescue.

Of course, relieving rescuers of the duty to take care for their own safety will not lead them to be totally unconcerned for their own safety. The survival extinct provides sufficient motivation for self-care. Given this, relieving rescuers of the legal duty to care for their own safety is unlikely to dilute self-care incentives greatly, but may encourage rescue by reducing the risk of uncompensated harm to the rescuer.

Another exception to the duty of self-care arises in the case of property. If a train negligently spits sparks onto a farmer's property, the farmer cannot be held guilty of contributory negligence because he failed to anticipate the sparks and move his crops out of the way. This was the conclusion of the Supreme Court in *LeRoy Fiber.*[3] Put in more general terms, *the property owner has no duty to take steps to avoid harms to his own property caused by the invasions (intentional or negligent) of others.*

For the law to hold otherwise would allow strangers to impose a type of servitude or easement on a person's property, weakening the protection of trespass law. The property owner would have to anticipate the harms resulting from the negligent (or intentional) conduct of his neighbors and take steps to minimize them, or otherwise suffer the loss. This would reduce the value of property generally and encourage activities that burden property owners.

By relieving the property owner of a duty to take steps to avoid tortious harms to his property caused by the invasions of others, the law discourages activities that tend to burden and thereby expropriate value from property. The law encourages would-be invaders or infringers to bargain with owners to gain rights to property, which in turn encourages the development and maintenance of markets for the rights associated with property and discourages attempts to bypass those markets.

Breach

In contributory negligence cases, courts determine whether the plaintiff has breached his duty of self-care by applying the reasonable person test, just as in the primary negligence setting. However, there is a difference in application. Courts

---

[2] Eckert v. Long Island R.R., 43 N.Y. 502 (1871).
[3] LeRoy Fiber Co. v. Chicago, Milwaukee & St. Paul Ry., 232 U.S. 340 (1914).

seem to be more forgiving in applying the contributory negligence test than in applying the negligence test.[4]

The likely reason for the relatively lenient approach under contributory negligence is that there are important differences between extralegal incentives to take care in the primary and contributory negligence settings. In the primary negligence setting, the rational, self-interested actor does not have a great incentive apart from the law to take care, assuming it is a stranger who will be the victim of an accident that he causes. In the contributory negligence setting, the opposite is the case: A self-interested actor would look out for his own safety regardless of the law.

This fundamental asymmetry implies that negligence law should exhibit a bias in its application. Since most people are relatively careful about their own safety and less careful about the safety of others, lapses of care in the primary negligence setting should be treated differently from lapses of care in the contributory negligence setting. Lapses of care in the primary negligence setting are more likely to have resulted from a failure to take into account the safety of others. Lapses of care in the contributory negligence setting are more likely to reflect momentary inadvertence.

This justification for the observed asymmetry in the application of the negligence standard in self-care and care-for-others situations is, at bottom, the same as the justification for *res ipsa loquitur* doctrine discussed in the previous chapter. Recall that in the *res ipsa* setting, it is important to first establish the baseline probability of negligence given the events leading to the accident. However, if we view negligence as a state of mind – a failure in one's thoughts to take into account the losses that might result from carelessness – then cases of real negligence will be far more frequent in care-for-others scenarios than in self-care scenarios. It therefore makes sense to apply the negligence test more leniently in the self-care scenario.

In his classic study of nineteenth-century negligence decisions in California and New Hampshire, Gary Schwartz found that there were several maxims stated by the courts that highlighted the relatively lenient application of the contributory negligence standard.[5] Courts said that plaintiffs are not required to exercise "great care" or to behave in "a timid and cautious way," and should not be held responsible for an "indiscretion" or mere "error of judgment." Courts excused plaintiffs for lapses and inadvertence. However, they were not so lenient with defendants. Schwartz's findings are consistent with what one would predict based on the differences in incentives to take care for others and to take care for one's own safety.

Many of the contributory negligence cases arise in the employment setting, which introduces another set of factors that courts take into account in determining whether a breach of the self-care duty occurred. Courts have recognized that realities of the

---

[4] Gary T. Schwartz, *Tort Law and the Economy in Nineteenth-Century America: A Reinterpretation*, 90 Yale L. J. 1717, 1761–1762 (1981).

[5] *Id.*

workplace should be incorporated into the reasonable person assessment.[6] In theory, it would appear that every worker should take reasonable care for his own safety. In practice, norms of sloppiness and corner cutting often develop in the workplace. Workers are encouraged by managers and coworkers to solve problems directly and quickly; they are criticized for showing timidity and indecision. A worker who observes a dangerous condition might feel pressured to work with the condition as it is, rather than wait for someone else to fix it. Given this, the contributory negligence test, in application, has tended to take into account the existence of social pressure to accept risks that a reasonable person might not accept in the absence of such pressure.[7]

Causation

Recall that contributory negligence cases can be separated into the distinct components of duty, breach, and causation. Duty, for the most part, is treated in the same manner in the contributory negligence setting as in the primary negligence setting: everyone has a duty of self-care (save for a few special cases, such as the rescue scenario considered earlier). Breach, as the foregoing discussion makes clear, is also treated formally in the same manner as in the primary negligence setting, though in practice it appears to have been determined under a relatively forgiving test. The remaining component to consider is causation.

1. Proximate Causation and Factual Causation

Negligence law distinguishes proximate and factual causation. Proximate causation is generally a matter of *foreseeability*. In the primary negligence setting, proximate causation is assessed by determining whether the plaintiff's injury is a foreseeable consequence of the defendant's negligence. Factual causation is often assessed by asking whether the plaintiff's injury would have occurred even if the defendant had not breached the standard of care. In more complicated cases – that is, where the counterfactual path of events is not easy to determine – courts have assessed factual causation by determining whether the defendant's breach was a *substantial factor* leading to the plaintiff's injury.[8] In the contributory negligence setting, the causation questions are whether the plaintiff's injury was a foreseeable consequence of his own negligence, and whether the plaintiff's injury would have happened even if he had taken care.

---

[6] *See, e.g.,* Gyerman v. U.S. Lines Co., 498 P.2d 1043, 1051 (Cal. 1972); Austin v. Riverside Portland Cement Co., 282 P.2d 69, 77 (Cal. 1955); Barboza v. Pacific Portland Cement Co., 120 P. 767, 769 (Cal. 1912).

[7] Gyerman v. U.S. Lines Co., 498 P.2d 1043, 1051 (Cal. 1972).

[8] The substantial factor version of the factual causation test is explored in more detail in Chapter 12.

Consider, first, a contributory negligence example in which proximate and factual causation inquiries lead to conflicting answers. In *Smithwick v. Hall & Upson Co.*,[9] the plaintiff was working on the defendant's icehouse while standing on a platform fifteen feet above the ground. He had been instructed to work on the west side of the platform because there was a railing there that would prevent him from falling to the ground if he slipped on the ice. There was no railing on the east side of the platform. The plaintiff, ignoring the instruction, worked on the east side of the platform. While he was on the east side, the wall on that side of the icehouse buckled, knocking him to the ground. The plaintiff sued on the theory that the defendant had negligently maintained the icehouse. The defendant argued that the plaintiff was contributorily negligent, because he chose to work on the east side of the platform where there was no railing.

The defendant's contributory negligence claim was rejected on proximate causation grounds. The plaintiff's negligence was his decision to work on the east side of the platform, where the slippery conditions and lack of railing could easily result in an injury from slipping off the platform. The foreseeable result of the plaintiff's negligence was slipping off the platform. The event of the icehouse wall buckling, however, was not within the set of foreseeable events associated with the plaintiff's negligence.

Now consider factual causation in *Smithwick*. Under the factual causation inquiry associated with the defendant's contributory negligence theory, a court would determine whether the accident would have happened even if the plaintiff had worked on the west side of the platform, where the railing was located. If the plaintiff had worked on the west side, the buckling of the east side of the icehouse wall probably would not have knocked him off the platform, and at least he would have been able to hang on to the railing. In other words, the accident probably would not have happened if the plaintiff had taken care. It follows that the defendant's contributory negligence theory does not fail the factual causation requirement. Nevertheless, because the theory fails on proximate causation grounds, the court held that the plaintiff was not contributorily negligent.

Now let's consider a hypothetical in which the defendant's contributory negligence claim passes the proximate cause test but fails the factual causation test. Suppose the plaintiff drives his car into the defendant's mechanical car wash and is injured by the excessive force of one of the pressurized water jets.[10] The force of the jet was excessive because of the defendant's negligence in maintaining the equipment. Suppose, in addition, that the plaintiff rolled his driver-side window down before entering the car wash, and failed to roll it back up as he entered, even

---

9 Smithwick v. Hall & Upson Co., 21 A. 924 (Conn. 1890).
10 In Wise v. Ford Motor Co., 943 P.2d 1310 (Mont. 1997), the plaintiff drove his daughter's 1987 Ford Escort automobile through a mechanical car wash. As one of the pressurized water jets was spraying water at the driver's side window, the window suddenly imploded into the car, injuring the plaintiff.

though the defendant had posted a sign warning drivers to roll their windows up before entering the car wash. Finally, assume that the force of the water jet was so great that it would have shattered and passed through the plaintiff's car window if he had rolled it up.

The plaintiff brings a negligence claim against the defendant for failing to maintain the pressurized water jet at the appropriate level of force. The defendant, predictably, asserts a <u>contributory negligence claim against the plaintiff for failing to roll up his window</u>. How would the defendant's contributory negligence claim fare on proximate and factual causation grounds?

In the *Car Wash Hypothetical* just described, the defendant's contributory negligence claim <u>passes the proximate causation</u> test. Ordinarily, you should predict the possibility of injury, and at least an unpleasant physical contact, if you fail to roll up your window as you enter a mechanical car wash. The plaintiff's injury is a foreseeable and direct result of his negligence.

The defendant's contributory negligence claim <u>fails the factual causation test.</u> Given that the force of the jet was so great that it would have shattered and passed through the driver's side window, the plaintiff's failure to roll his window up would not have prevented his injury. The accident would have happened even if the plaintiff had taken care.

So far I have considered two examples in which the factual and proximate causation analyses associated with the defendant's contributory negligence claim lead to conflicting answers. In *Smithwick*, the contributory negligence charge passes the factual causation test and fails the proximate causation test. In the *Car Wash Hypothetical*, the contributory negligence charge fails the factual causation test and passes the proximate causation test.

There are cases in which the factual and proximate causation tests associated with the defendant's contributory negligence claim appear to lead to the same answer. <u>Both tests essentially collapse into the question whether the plaintiff's contributory negligence was a substantial factor leading to his own injury.</u>

One example is <u>*Gyerman v. United States Lines Co.*</u>[11] The plaintiff was injured when he attempted to unload heavy fishmeal sacks that had been improperly stacked. The negligent stacking greatly increased the risk of injury to the plaintiff, a risk that materialized. However, the plaintiff failed to notify his supervisor of the danger before attempting to unload the sacks.

The defendant claimed that the plaintiff was guilty of contributory negligence for his failure to notify the supervisor, so that the improper stacking problem could be resolved. The appellate court, agreeing with the trial court, found that the plaintiff was contributorily negligent. However, the <u>court concluded that the evidence</u> did <u>not show that the plaintiff's contributory negligence was a</u> "<u>proximate cause</u>" of the injury, because even if the plaintiff had notified the correct official, there was no

---

[11] 498 P.2d 1043 (Cal. 1972).

evidence that any action would have been taken to resolve the negligent stacking problem before the plaintiff attempted to unload the sacks. In other words, the accident probably would have happened even if the plaintiff had taken care.

Interestingly, the *Gyerman* court used the term "proximate cause" even though the difficult matter is really one of factual causation. *Gyerman* is much easier to understand as a factual causation determination than as a proximate causation determination.[12]

I discuss causation from a general vantage point in Chapter 12. Still, a few words can be said here about the policy justifications for *Smithwick*, the *Car Wash Hypothetical*, and *Gyerman*.

In *Smithwick*, the plaintiff's failure to take care results in an accident that is analogous to being hit by lightning. The refusal of courts to hold victims of such unfortunate and rare events responsible for their injuries is a sensible result. One ordinarily does not plan ahead of time to take care in some activity on the off chance that you will be hit by lightning, or swallowed by an earthquake, if you do not take care.

In the *Car Wash Hypothetical*, the plaintiff's care is overwhelmed by the force of the defendant's negligence. Holding the plaintiff guilty of contributory negligence would reward the defendant who is really responsible for the injury.

Finally, *Gyerman* is a case in which care on the part of the plaintiff might help avoid the accident under ideal conditions, but those ideal conditions are not observed in the facts. Under the observed conditions, the plaintiff's care would not necessarily help avoid the accident, because the effect of the plaintiff's care depends entirely on the intervention of a third party. There is no way to determine, in this sort of case, absent information on the likelihood of the third party intervening, whether the plaintiff's failure to take care was negligent. These issues are addressed in more detail in Chapter 12.

2. Proximate Causation and Damages

In some cases where the plaintiff's conduct has contributed to the severity of his loss, courts have adopted proximate causation reasoning to apportion responsibility for the loss. In *Mahoney v. Beatman*,[13] the defendant negligently veered across the

---

[12] The factual and proximate causation analyses can lead, depending on how the proximate causation test is framed, to the same answer in *Gyerman*. Specifically, if one frames the proximate causation inquiry to take as given the low likelihood that any action would be taken by a supervisor to correct the improper-stacking problem, then it follows that the plaintiff's injury was not a foreseeable result of his failure to report. Of course, under this framing, the plaintiff would not have been negligent too. The key source of ambiguity over the proper causation language is the inherent uncertainty in the facts. No one knows precisely what would have happened if the plaintiff had notified his supervisor. The causation finding hinges entirely on an undetermined probability. This provides some justification to the court's use of proximate causation language, even though the assessment of counterfactuals ordinarily should be left to the factual causation test.

[13] 147 A. 762 (Conn. 1929).

line into oncoming traffic. The plaintiff was driving faster than the speed limit, but otherwise with ordinary care. The defendant's car hit the plaintiff's car. Because of the plaintiff's speed, his car careened off the road after the impact and hit a large rock. The initial collision with the defendant caused $200 in damages to the plaintiff's car, and the second collision caused an additional $5,650 in damages. The trial court did not find that the plaintiff was contributorily negligent. Still, it allowed the plaintiff to collect only $200, noting the causal contribution of the plaintiff's conduct. The appellate court, rejecting the trial court's apportionment, permitted the plaintiff to collect the whole $5,850.

The trial court's approach in *Mahoney* is an example of the application of proximate cause reasoning to the calculation of damages.[14] The trial court assigned damages according to relative contributions, in the absence of any finding of contributory negligence.

Would it be desirable, in general, to discount the damages given to the plaintiff under the proximate cause theory – that is, in a manner that takes the plaintiff's causal contribution into account? If the concept of proximate cause is applied to damages, it could serve as a substitute to the contributory negligence defense. Thus, even if the plaintiff's conduct was not contributorily negligent, a court might reduce the plaintiff's award to take into account his contribution to his own harm.

There are several reasons why such an approach may not be desirable. At the level of legal doctrine, it creates an asymmetry between the defendant and the plaintiff. The defendant will have to be found negligent to be held liable. The plaintiff, on the other hand, will be held liable, in effect, without a finding of negligence. This creates a bias that favors defendants, reducing their incentives to take care. A trucking company, for example, aware that it would be the defendant in several road accidents each year, would assume that it could whittle plaintiffs' damages down toward zero, in most cases, by pointing to the many ways in which the plaintiff's conduct contributed to the severity of his loss. And once expected damages are whittled down to a sufficiently low level, the pressure to take care, due to the threat of tort liability, may disappear.

To maintain formal symmetry, a proximate cause–based damages regime would have to abandon the requirement of first finding negligence on the part of the defendant. It would adopt a rule of strict liability and parcel out damages according to relative contributions. Of course, the problem with strict liability based on causation, as Holmes noted, is that a nearly infinite number of potential defendants could be held responsible for some share of an injury. A rider whose horse ran over the victim can be held liable, and so can the seller of the horse to the rider, and so on. However, to avoid suppressing much socially beneficial activity, strict liability has

---

[14] The court's approach attracted a great deal of attention from torts scholars because of the interesting legal issues that it generated. *See* Leon Green, Mahoney v. Beatman: *A Study in Proximate Cause*, 39 YALE L. J. 532 (1930).

been reserved, under the policy of *Rylands v. Fletcher* (Chapter 5), for activities that externalize unusually great risks.

As a practical matter, proximate cause–based damages could open the courthouse door to a large number of causation experts, multiplying the administrative costs of trials. Every car accident would require experts to assess the amount of harm attributable to the plaintiff's failure to wear a seatbelt, to drive at the optimal speed, or to have his seat in the optimal position.

The issue lurking beneath this discussion is how one should distinguish contributory negligence and proximate causation theory as applied to damages. Return to the Hand Formula analysis of Chapter 6, where Judge Learned Hand described negligence as a case of failing to take care when the burden of care (B) is less than the loss (L) multiplied by the probability of its realization (P). In other words, negligence is failing to take care when $B < PL$. In the contributory negligence setting, P is determined by the care of both the plaintiff and the defendant. The severity of the loss, L, is also determined by the conduct of both parties.

In general, contributory negligence refers to actions of the plaintiff that increase the probability of an accident.[15] This is an implication, recall, of the proposition that the tortfeasor takes his victims as he finds him. Proximate causation theory, *when applied to damages*, is concerned with actions of the plaintiff, or the defendant, that increase the loss without having any effect on the probability of an accident.

Consider a few examples in which the plaintiff's contribution affects the severity of loss but not the probability of loss. In *Mahoney v. Beatman*, discussed above, the plaintiff's conduct (driving fast) contributed to the severity of his loss but did not alter the probability of an accident occurring. In the so-called *seat belt defense* cases,[16] the plaintiff's failure to wear a seat belt contributes to the severity of his loss from a car accident, but does not increase the probability of the accident occurring. In the *sprinkler defense* cases,[17] the plaintiff's failure to install a sprinkler system in a building increases the severity of the loss from fire, but does not increase the probability of the fire occurring.

When the plaintiff's pre-accident conduct contributes to the severity of the loss but not the probability of the loss, tort law generally holds the defendant responsible for the entire loss on the theory that the tortfeasor takes his victim as he finds him – sometimes referred to as the eggshell skull rule.[18] But as the plaintiff's pre-accident

---

[15] Greenland v. Chaplin, 155 Eng. Rep. 104 (Exch. Div. 1850); Derheim v. N. Fiorio Co., 492 P.2d 1030 (Wash. 1972).

[16] Derheim v. N. Fiorito Co., 492 P.2d 1030 (Wash. 1972); Clarkson v. Wright, 483 N.E.2d 268 (Ill. 1985); Mott v. Sun Country Garden Products, Inc., 901 P.2d 192 (N.M. 1995); Dunn v. Durso, 530 A.2d 387 (N.J. Super. Ct. 1986).

[17] Brookings Lumber & Box Co. v. Manufacturers' Automatic Sprinkler Co., 161 P. 266, 282 (Cal. 1916); Waddey v. Davis, 254 S.E.2d 465, 466 (Ga. Ct. App. 1979); Gonzalez v. Tounjian, 2003 N.W.2d 705, 711 (N.D. 2003).

[18] WILLIAM L. PROSSER, HANDBOOK OF THE LAW OF TORTS 261 (West Publishing Co. 4th ed. 1971).

conduct comes closer to being simultaneous with the accident, the application of the eggshell skull rule becomes more doubtful.

In settings where the plaintiff's pre-accident conduct increases the severity of the loss but not the probability of the loss occurring, defendants have pressed courts to find plaintiffs guilty of contributory negligence for failing to take reasonable steps to reduce their losses.[19] Some courts have been persuaded, especially under comparative fault regimes.[20] In spite of this, the general approach to contributory negligence requires evidence that the plaintiff's conduct contributed to the probability of the accident occurring.

As states have adopted comparative negligence, the distinction between actions that increase the likelihood of an accident and actions that increase the amount of the loss has been blurred. Comparative negligence regimes encourage courts to take all of the plaintiff's actions into account under the concept of negligence. The common justification for comparative negligence is that it avoids outcomes in which the plaintiff gets nothing for damages. However, the blurring of the distinction between actions that increase the *probability* of harm and actions that increase the *severity* of harm tends to tilt the comparative negligence system in favor of defendants. Defendants are held liable only on a finding of negligence, while plaintiffs are potentially liable for all conduct contributing to the severity of the harm. Such a bias could reduce incentives for potential injurers to take care, relative to the traditional contributory negligence regime.

As a formal matter, tort law rejects substituting contributory negligence theory with proximate causation theory as applied to damages, because the law requires the defendant to take the plaintiff as he finds him. The likely reasons for this are the aforementioned administrative burdens implied by the proximate causation approach to damages and the worrisome deterrence implications of allowing defendants to reduce damages through the application of causal contribution theories.

II. LAST CLEAR CHANCE

One special feature of the law of contributory negligence falls under the heading *last clear chance*. The last clear chance doctrine applies in instances where both injurer and victim have been negligent, and the injurer has such a clear opportunity to avoid harming the victim that the injurer's failure to avoid the accident can be

---

[19] Derheim, 492 P.2d at 1030.

[20] Many courts in comparative negligence states have adopted the seat belt defense, allowing plaintiff's failure to wear a seat belt to constitute evidence of plaintiff's comparative negligence. *See, e.g.,* Hutchins v. Swartz, 724 P.2d 1194 (Alaska 1986); Law v. Superior Court in & for Maricopa County, 755 P.2d 1135 (Ariz. 1988); Ridley v. Safety Kleen Corp., 693 So.2d 934 (Fla. 1996); Spier v. Barker, 42 A.D.2d 428 (N.Y. App. Div. 1973). *But see* Swajian v. Gen. Motors Corp., 559 A.2d 1041 (R.I. 1989) (declining to adopt the seat belt defense and finding that evidence relating to seat belt use is irrelevant on the issues of comparative fault).

$Law = f (f (P(Harm), Severity (Harm)) = P(D) \cdot P(F)$

attributed to either recklessness, intent to harm, or gross negligence. For example, suppose the victim, through his own negligence, is stuck on the tracks of the injurer's railroad, as a train is approaching. Suppose the train is traveling at a negligently high speed. Suppose, in addition, that the train has time to stop, but it does not, running over the victim.[21]

The railroad (defendant) would argue that the victim (plaintiff) should not be awarded damages because of his contributory negligence. Under the last clear chance doctrine, the defendant still has to pay damages to the plaintiff because the defendant could have avoided the injury.

Although I initially described the last clear chance doctrine as a special feature of contributory negligence law, it is more than that. The doctrine is a special case of a more general "fault grading" rule: *If the defendant is guilty of intent, or recklessness, the contributory negligence of the plaintiff is not a bar to the plaintiff's recovery.*[22] Viewed as a special case of this fault grading rule, last clear chance applies when the defendant has been negligent in exposing the plaintiff to risk (first phase) and then has intentionally or recklessly failed to avoid injuring the plaintiff (second phase).

Return to the example of the train. If the engineer had time to see the victim on the tracks, why did he not stop? There are several possible explanations: He did not care if he ran over the victim; he realized that because of the contributory negligence defense, there would be no cost in running the victim over, so decided to keep going; he was distracted, perhaps playing a card game while operating the train. Each of these explanations suggests, because they indicate either recklessness or intent to harm, that the railroad should be held liable (since it is vicariously liable for the fault of the engineer).[23]

What is the reason for the general rule that the contributory negligence of the plaintiff is not a bar to his recovery when the defendant is guilty of intent to harm? The reason is that intentional (or reckless) harmful conduct is a higher order of bad conduct, which the law aims to suppress entirely. To reduce the defendant's damages when he has acted with an intent to harm would be to subsidize his conduct to some degree and thereby encourage it. The consequences of encouraging intentionally harmful (or reckless) conduct are far worse than excusing the occasional failure of the victim to look out for his own safety.

III. ASSUMPTION OF RISK

Assumption of risk is a special type of implied consent theory. Specifically, it is a strong form that finds agreement on the basis of a presumed awareness of the risks inherent in the conditions or circumstances leading to the plaintiff's injury, and in the plaintiff's presumed acceptance of those risks. It can be distinguished from

21   Fuller v. Illinois Central R.R., 65 So. 783 (Miss. 1911).
22   *See, e.g.,* Ruter v. Foy, 46 Iowa 132 (1877); Steinmetz v. Kelly, 72 Ind. 442 (1880).
23   On vicarious liability, *see* Chapter 11.

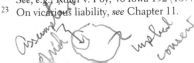

consent implied *by the conduct of the plaintiff* – as in the case of a patient who silently offers her arm to a doctor to facilitate vaccination.[24]

Given the theory underlying assumption of risk doctrine, it should not be a surprise to find that it has been applied most often in the employment setting. Specifically, it has been used to deny employee-plaintiffs damages in lawsuits against employers. There are two reasons for this. First, employees who have been at work for a long period have had time to become fully aware of the inherent risks of their worksites. This time-to-learn evidence weighs in favor of a finding that the employee was intimately aware of the risks of his employment. Second, employees are understood in most instances to work voluntarily. They do not have to return to a job that pays too little to compensate for the danger.

These points suggest that courts that are careful in applying assumption of risk doctrine limit it to cases in which *(a) the injury results from inherent and predictable risks of the defendant's activity, (b) the plaintiff's participation in the activity is voluntary, and (c) the plaintiff had time to become fully aware of the inherent and predictable risks of the activity.*

These three conditions were satisfied in *Lamson v. American Axe & Tool Co.*[25] The plaintiff sued his employer after being injured by a hatchet that fell from a rack stationed above the plaintiff's work area. About a year before the injury, the employer installed new racks at the plaintiff's workstation. The plaintiff complained that the hatchets were more likely to fall off of the new racks than the old ones. The employer responded that the employee could leave if he found the work too hazardous.

The judge, Oliver Wendell Holmes, Jr., noted that the plaintiff had been working for the employer for many years, and that he had more than a year to become familiar with the new racks:

> The plaintiff, on his own evidence, appreciated the danger more than any one else. He perfectly understood what was likely to happen. That likelihood did not depend upon the doing of some negligent act by people in another branch of employment, but solely on the permanent conditions of the racks and their surroundings and the plaintiff's continuing to work where he did.[26]

This quote from Holmes says clearly that the three conditions favoring application of the assumption of risk doctrine were satisfied: an accident resulting from inherent risks, voluntary work, and a plaintiff fully aware of those risks.

Given the theory of assumption of risk, *Lamson* should have come out differently if the employer had executed some negligent act that immediately caused injury to

---

[24] *See* O'Brien v. Cunard S.S. Co., 28 N.E. 266 (Mass. 1891) ("[I]f the plaintiff's behavior was such as to indicate consent on her part, he was justified in his act, whatever her unexpressed feelings may have been.").

[25] 58 N.E. 585 (Mass. 1900).

[26] *Id.* at 585.

[handwritten note: Would the ruling have been different if the injury happened right away?]

the employee. Suppose, for example, the employer, without telling the employee, widened the slots in the rack, so that the hatchets were more likely to fall, and the employee was injured immediately after. In this case there would be no reason to believe that the employee had become familiar with the heightened risk. The assumption of risk doctrine appears to be limited to inherent risks – risks that the employee faces on a daily basis and expects as part of the routine of work.

Lamson and similar cases implicitly assume that the employee's decision to stay with a dangerous job was entirely voluntary. However, the voluntariness of the decision to accept the risk is a factor that some courts have explicitly considered. Another Holmes opinion, *Pomeroy v. Westfield*,[27] illustrates this point.

In *Pomeroy*, the plaintiffs were injured when their horse-drawn carriage tipped over, spilling them to the ground. The carriage tipped as the result of a defect in the highway, which the defendant town (Westfield, Massachusetts) was under a duty to maintain. Holmes noted that the strongest argument for the defendant would be that the plaintiffs had assumed the risk by traveling at their chosen speed, in the dark, on a road that the driver (one of the plaintiffs) knew to be in poor condition. Rejecting this defense, Holmes said that

> there are two elements to be considered; first, how far [the plaintiff] is chargeable with knowledge of the danger which he incurred, and then under what exigency he acted.... Especially is this true in cases like the present, where the parties are not in an equal position. The plaintiffs were away from home, and had to get back. They depended on the defendant for safety in doing so, and it was the defendant's power and duty to keep the way free from defects. In such a case, even if it were found that the plaintiffs knew that they were attempting a dangerous drive, it could not be said, as a matter of law, that they were not warranted in doing so.[28]

Is it possible for the defendant to be negligent and the plaintiff to have assumed the risk? To be consistent with implied consent theory, the answer to this question must be no. Assumption of risk means that the plaintiff has accepted the inherent risks of the defendant's activity, perhaps in exchange for some compensation, or because he sought the risks. If the plaintiff has accepted the conditions of the defendant's activity, risks and benefits all, those conditions are no longer negligent with respect to the plaintiff. The standard of care is no longer an external one, it is the standard that has been agreed upon by plaintiff and defendant. Objective evidence can be used to infer the terms of that implicit agreement. But the role of the court is limited, under the doctrine, to inferring the terms of the agreement rather than supplanting it with an external standard of care.

An especially controversial version of assumption of risk in the employment setting is the *fellow servant rule*. Articulated by Chief Justice Shaw in *Farwell v. Boston &*

---

[27] 28 N. E. 899 (Mass. 1891).
[28] *Id.*

Worcestor R.R. Corp.,[29] the fellow servant rule holds that the employer is not liable, as a general matter, to an employee for the negligence of a fellow employee. For example, suppose A and B work for the employer's railroad. B negligently gives the wrong signal, or hits the wrong switch, causing a train to run over A's leg. Under the fellow servant rule, the employer is not liable to A.

There are exceptions to the fellow servant rule. First, if the employer negligently hired the fellow servant – for example, negligently hired an unqualified employee – the injured employee could maintain his suit against the employer.[30] Second, if the employer had a duty to monitor or control the fellow servant – say, because the employer had been notified of the risks created by the servant's incompetence – and failed to monitor or control him, the injured employee could sue the employer for negligence.[31] Third, the fellow servant rule does not immunize the employer from liability when the injured employee sues the employer because of the negligence of a supervisor in supplying safe equipment and structures in the worksite (sometimes called the "vice-principal exception").[32]

Reading the fellow servant rule in conjunction with the exceptions, it says the following: *If the employer was not negligent in hiring or monitoring employee B, employee A cannot sue the employer for injuries caused by the negligence of employee B.*

Although the fellow servant doctrine was controversial from the start, it does not appear unusual when viewed in its totality. Return to the example in which employee A is injured by the negligence of employee B. If the employer was not negligent in hiring employee B, or in monitoring him, then the employer was not negligent in any way relevant to employee A's injury. Under the common law, a non-negligent individual could not be held liable for the injuries negligently caused by someone else.

Assumption of risk is only marginally relevant to the fellow servant negligence cases. The key to the fellow servant defense is that the employer is not negligent in any manner relevant to the employee-plaintiff's claim. However, an employee-plaintiff might argue that the employer could have taken steps to minimize the likely harm from a particular employee's negligence. For example, the employer could have furnished a safer workplace. For any negligence theory of this sort, the assumption of risk argument would be relevant and would return us to the points

---

[29] Farwell v. Boston & W.R. Corp., 45 Mass. 49 (1842). *Farwell* is the clearest statement of the fellow servant doctrine and its policy, though not the first case to announce the doctrine. On its history, *see* Michael Ashley Stein, *Priestley v. Fowler (1837) and the Emerging Tort of Negligence*, 44 B. C. L. Rev. 689 (2002).

[30] For a thorough and concise discussion, *see* Wabash Railway Company v. McDaniels, 107 U.S. 454 (1883).

[31] *Id.*

[32] *Id.* For a more detailed discussion of the vice-principal exception and its functional basis, *see* Chapter 11.

made in *Lamson*. The validity of the assumption of risk defense would depend on whether the risk characteristics of the workplace were observable and fixed features.[33]

This justification for the fellow servant rule appears at first glance to be insufficient when compared to the law of *vicarious liability*. Under vicarious liability, an employer is liable for the negligence of a servant when that negligence results in the harm to someone outside of the enterprise – for example, a bystander or a customer. In other words, the law of vicarious liability holds nonnegligent employers liable for the harms of negligent employees.

What explains the different treatments of the employer under the fellow servant rule and under the vicarious liability rule? This question is probably best answered after taking a good look at vicarious liability law (Chapter 11). Still, a short answer can be offered here.

One justification is found in the theory expressed in the law. In vicarious liability, the law assumes that the employer and the employee are acting jointly. When an employee harms a bystander, it is understood to be the same as the employer acting on his own; the employee is, in the eyes of the law, the employer's right hand. The fellow servant situation is different; it is similar by analogy to the employer's left hand injuring the right hand.

Another argument for the fellow servant rule is based on incentives. If an employee injures a bystander, holding the employer liable improves the employer's incentives to train, monitor, and discipline his employees. The reason is that the injuries to bystanders or customers caused by the negligence of an employee are often attributable to the employer's inadequate training of his employee. If the employer is not held liable for injuries to bystanders or customers caused by the negligence of his employees, he will have little incentive to train them to avoid causing those injuries. The situation is different in the fellow servant context. If one employee negligently injures another employee, that will impose an immediate loss on the employer – again, as if the employer's left hand had injured his right hand. Because of this immediate internal loss, the employer has a strong incentive even in the absence of liability to train his employees to avoid causing these types of injuries. It is not clear that those incentives would be improved by liability – in fact, the employer might be induced by the threat of liability to avoid hiring, or to overinvest in safety for some employees (for example, the highly compensated) while underinvesting in safety for others. In addition, while holding the employer liable for intra-enterprise injuries may or may not enhance the employer's incentives to train, monitor, and discipline, it would weaken the employees' incentives to train, monitor, and discipline each other.[34] An employee who assumes that he would be

---

[33] For the vice-principal exception to be consistent with the theory of assumption of risk, a supervisor would have had to change the working conditions or provide unsafe equipment on the first day of work.

[34] *See* Richard A. Posner, *A Theory of Negligence*, 1 J. LEGAL STUD. 29, 44–48 (1972); Priestly v. Fowler, 150 Eng. Rep. 1030, 1032–1033, 3 M. & W. 1 at 5 (Ex. 1837); Farwell, 45 Mass. at 54, 57.

fully compensated for any accident due to the negligence of a fellow employee might be less energetic about correcting his fellow employees, especially if he thinks the risk of injury is small. Since the employer in most cases is an entity not physically present on the worksite, this incentive-dampening among employees may be the most powerful effect, resulting in more worksite injuries due to negligence.

In any event, the fellow servant rule and assumption of risk in general have been eliminated in the employment setting by workers' compensation statutes passed in American states during the 1920s. However, the fellow servant rule is not entirely dead as a legal doctrine. The workers' compensation statutes bar the use of assumption of risk, contributory negligence, and fellow servant defenses when an employee sues his employer. But if the employee sues someone else – say, the manufacturer of a machine used in the workplace or the owner of the worksite (if different from the employer) – then the fellow servant rule can be asserted by the nonemployer defendant.

Assumption of Risk and Imputed Contributory Negligence

Although largely a thing of the past now, there was at one time a version of assumption of risk, called *imputed contributory negligence*, in which the negligence of one actor could be imputed to another. The imputed contributory negligence doctrine was originally developed in *Thorogood v. Bryan*.[35]

In *Thorogood*, the driver of an omnibus (a large horse-drawn carriage that transported passengers) let a passenger (plaintiff's decedent) off in the middle of the street rather than pulling up to the curb. Another omnibus ran over the passenger and killed him. In response to the negligence lawsuit against the owner of the omnibus that ran over the passenger, the court held that the contributory negligence of the passenger's omnibus would be imputed to the passenger, barring his claim for damages. The court reasoned that the passenger had, by choosing the particular omnibus he had taken, identified himself with the chosen service in a manner that made it appropriate to impute the negligence of the omnibus to the passenger.

The doctrine of *Thorogood* was briefly accepted by American courts. But the U.S. Supreme Court rejected the doctrine in 1886, in *Little v. Hackett*.[36] Two years later, the English courts rejected the imputed contributory negligence rule of *Thorogood* in *Mills v. Armstrong* (the *Bernina*).[37]

The justification offered by the court in *Thorogood* can be understood as an assumption of risk theory. The doctrine has been roundly criticized, generally for

---

[35] Thorogood v. Bryan, 137 Eng. Rep. 452 (C.P. 1849), *overruled by* Mills v. Armstrong (*The Bernina*), 13 App. Cas. 1 (1888).

[36] Little v. Hackett, 116 U.S. 366 (1886).

[37] *See* Mills v. Armstrong, 13 App. Cas. 1 (1888). The case involved a collision between the two ships *Bernina* and *Bushire*, due to the negligence of both. Employees of the *Bushire* sued the *Bernina*.

good reason. However, to get a better sense of its function and its limitations, we should consider it in light of the justifications for the assumption of risk defense.

Assumption of risk is a defensible theory when it involves inherent and predictable risks confronted by the plaintiff. Many of the cases where the defense appears plausible arise in the employment setting. For worksite risks that are inherent and predictable, one can argue that the plaintiff would accept those risks only if he received compensation for them, and further that holding the employer liable for such inherent risks would effectively impose strict liability on the employer.

Could such an argument ever apply to the passenger of a bus? Yes, but only if the passenger is exposed to an inherent and predictable risk of the enterprise. If a bus service routinely let passengers off in the middle of the street, one might argue that the passengers assumed the risk. Even then a court might still bar the assumption of risk defense on the ground that the risk is simply too serious and likely to be imposed on the naïve. But in the admittedly unlikely scenario where the practice that exposes the passenger to risk is a fixed pattern of the business with which the passenger was entirely familiar, assumption of risk is a plausible defense.

If the conditions are such that assumption of risk is a plausible defense in the bus passenger case, then the doctrine would bar a lawsuit by the passenger against his chosen bus service. If the risk that causes the injury is predictable and routine, it would make sense to also bar the passenger's lawsuit against the other bus company involved in the accident, since the lawsuit would be based on the very same risk he assumed in his contract with his chosen bus service. This is the function of the imputed contributory negligence doctrine.

This argument suggests a general form for the imputed contributory negligence defense. *When the plaintiff has chosen to enter into a contract with service A, which he knows to be carelessly operated, and he is injured in an accident involving the careless conduct of both services A and B, which is so clearly within the class of risks foreseeably associated with A's carelessness that his negligence lawsuit against A would be barred by assumption of risk, his negligence lawsuit against B will be barred by the imputed contributory negligence defense.*

Of course, as soon as we identify the circumstances in which the imputed contributory negligence doctrine seems plausible as a defense, we also see its flaws. The conditions under which the imputed contributory negligence defense seems plausible do not appear to have been present in *Thorogood*. There were no facts recounted in *Thorogood* that would support the inference that the passenger's bus service had adopted a regular practice of letting passengers off in the middle of the road, or that if it had, the passengers were fully aware of the practice and its associated risks.

The imputed contributory negligence rule, as a special type of assumption of risk doctrine, may be plausible in some settings, but *Thorogood* is an unlikely one. The rule could survive as a viable doctrine in tort law, so long as it is limited to instances in which the plaintiff is exposed to a predictable and recurrent risk. In any event, the doctrine of *Thorogood* has been abandoned by common law courts, and this is probably best in light of the risk, which had materialized, that courts would fail to limit the doctrine to the rare settings in which it has plausibility as a special type of assumption of risk defense.[38]

There is, however, a version of imputed contributory negligence that continues to exist. *Thorogood* introduced imputed contributory negligence as a special assumption of risk theory, which courts have rejected. Another version of the defense is based on the *principal-agent* relationship (or joint agency). Suppose B actually directs A in conducting his activity. Then the negligence of A can be imputed to B. For example, suppose the passenger in car C is directing the driver, telling the driver where and how to drive, even directing the negligent acts. The driver gets into a collision with another negligent driver, of car D. The collision is the result of the negligence of both the drivers of C and D. In the passenger's suit against the driver of D, the negligence of his agent, driver of C, will be imputed to the passenger.

Assumption of Risk in the Consumption Setting

Although the assumption of risk defense typically arises in the employment setting, it is by no means restricted to that setting. Assumption of risk arguments are made in the consumption setting too.

One important set of cases involves risky activities that people pay to participate in or to observe – baseball games, hockey games, amusement parks. In *Murphy v. Steeplechase Amusement Co.*,[39] a Cardozo opinion, the plaintiff had gone on a ride called "The Flopper" at Coney Island amusement park. The ride, consisting of a rapidly moving belt on which participants stood, caused participants to fall. The plaintiff was injured on the ride and brought a negligence claim against the amusement park, on the theory that the moving belt operated at a fast and dangerous speed.

Cardozo held that the plaintiff had assumed the risk because the whole point of the ride was for the belt to move at a high speed, causing participants to fall. Cardozo noted that the name provided a warning and that the plaintiff had stood outside and observed the ride before entering. In addition, the plaintiff had voluntarily sought the experience promised by the ride.

Cardozo noted two exceptions that might apply: (1) *when the inherent risks of the activity are not observable* and (2) *when the injuries caused by the activity are frequent and serious.* Neither exception applied in this case.

---

[38] There is another imputed contributory negligence doctrine that has also been abandoned by the courts. Hartfield v. Roper, 21 Wend. 615 (N.Y. 1839), imputed the negligence of the parents to an infant who had been struck by a horse-drawn sleigh. Unlike *Thorogood*, *Hartfield* cannot be understood in terms of assumption of risk theory. The doctrine of *Hartfield* has been repudiated in every jurisdiction. For a critique of *Hartfield*, *see* Berry v. Erie & Western R.R. Co., 70 F. 679 (Ind. 1895).

[39] Murphy v. Steeplechase Amusement Co., 166 N.E. 173 (N.Y. 1929).

Unlike the employment setting, the plaintiff in a case like *Murphy* does not have the time to become intimately familiar with the inherent risks of the activity. Why, given this, have courts still applied the assumption of risk doctrine to these cases? The key factor is that the plaintiff in *Murphy* approached and paid for the ride precisely because of the risk that led to his injury.

In other words, there is a distinction between the employment and consumption settings that justifies application of the assumption of risk doctrine in the consumption setting even though plaintiffs often do not have long experience with the specific risks confronted in that setting. The distinction is that the plaintiff seeks the risk – the very risk, or some combination of experiences including the risk, that leads to injury – in the consumption setting. In the employment setting, the plaintiff typically does not seek the risk; in most cases he would be happy being paid for his work without bearing any risk at all. This factor of openly seeking and embracing risk as an element of consumption provides a basis for applying the assumption of risk doctrine to the consumption cases.

Another consumption setting in which implied consent is a relevant question is the scenario where a consumer purchases a product that turns out to be defective in a dangerous way. In some instances, courts apply the implied consent theory – specifically when the risk characteristics of the product are "open and obvious" (such as the open top of a convertible car). I will examine this in the chapter on products liability (Chapter 17).

Express Assumption of Risk, or Waiving Tort Liability

One can assume risk expressly by contract. A contractual assumption of risk is equivalent to a waiver of tort liability with respect to the risks assumed. The common law restricts the enforceability of such agreements, but it starts from a presumption that ordinary contract principles apply. Thus, if none of the restrictions on contractual liability waivers apply, and if the conditions for a valid offer and acceptance are found, a court will enforce a contractual assumption of risk.

A contractual assumption of risk might be effected by a provision similar to the following, from *Winterstein v. Wilcom*:[40]

> I, the undersigned, hereby request permission to enter the premises . . . and participate in auto timing and acceleration runs, tests, contests and exhibitions to be held this day. I have inspected the premises and I know the risks and dangers involved in the said activities, and that unanticipated and unexpected dangers may arise during such activities and I assume all risks of injury to my person and property that may be sustained in connection with the stated and associated activities, in and about the premises. In consideration of the permission granted . . . I do hereby . . . release,

---

[40] 293 A.2d 821 (Md. App. 1972).

remise, and discharge the owners . . . from all claims, demands, actions, and causes of action of any sort . . . due to negligence or any other fault.

The plaintiff in *Winterstein* was injured when his racecar ran into a hundred-pound cylinder head on the racetrack. The defendant's employees had negligently failed to remove the hazard from the track. After finding that none of the common law restrictions on waivers applied, and that the conditions for a valid contract existed, the court upheld the waiver.

The common law restrictions on the enforcement of waivers are several and capable of elastic interpretation. In addition, ordinary contract law principles give courts wide discretion over enforcement of waiver agreements. Given all of this, a fair summary of the law on waiver enforcement might say simply that hard bargains are unlikely to be enforced.

One class of common law restrictions on waiver enforcement falls under the label *public policy*. The public policy exception comes mostly from *Tunkl v. Regents of Univ. of Cal.*,[41] which involved a broad waiver of tort liability at a charitable hospital. *Tunkl* sets out a list of six factors that a court should examine in deciding whether to enforce a contractual waiver. The *Tunkl* factors stress whether the defendant provides a service of great importance to the public (a public necessity), whether the plaintiff suffered a bargaining power disadvantage, and whether the waiver was part of a standardized (adhesion) contract.[42] In *Winterstein*, the court found that the defendant's racetrack was not a public necessity. However, in *Dalury v. S-K-I Ltd.*,[43] a Vermont court held that a ski resort was a public necessity and refused, on public policy grounds, to enforce a contractual waiver. More specifically, *Dalury* held that in light of the public interest in safety at ski resorts, it would not enforce a contractual waiver as applied to the negligent placement of a ski lift maze pole. The court's argument implicitly distinguishes risks inherent to skiing (such as falling), as to which both skier and ski resort are equally informed, and risks created by the negligent design or operation of equipment and structures, which are likely to be much better known by the ski resort than by the skier.

---

[41] 383 P.2d 441 (Cal. 1963).

[42] These factors include whether (1) the transaction "concerns a business of a type generally thought suitable for public regulation"; (2) "[t]he party seeking exculpation is engaged in performing a service of great importance to the public, which is often a matter of practical necessity for some members of the public"; (3) "[t]he party holds himself out as willing to perform this service for any member of the public who seeks it, or at least for any member coming within certain established standards"; (4) "[a]s a result of the essential nature of the service, in the economic setting of the transaction, the party invoking exculpation possesses a decisive advantage of bargaining strength against any member of the public who seeks his services"; (5) "[i]n exercising a superior bargaining power the party confronts the public with a standardized adhesion contract of exculpation, and makes no provision whereby a purchaser may pay additional reasonable fees and obtain protection against negligence"; and (6) "[a]s a result of the transaction, the person or property of the purchaser is placed under the control of the seller, subject to the risk of carelessness by the seller or his agents." *Id.* at 445–446.

[43] 670 A.2d 795 (Vt. 1995).

Another class of common law restrictions on the enforceability of waivers consists of special contract law doctrines. Some courts have special rules on the enforcement of *adhesion contracts*. An adhesion contract is a standardized contract offered to the consumer on a "take it or leave it" basis. Courts that have adopted this doctrine refuse to enforce waivers in such contracts if they are outside of the reasonable expectations of the consumer, unless there is a clear and unambiguous notification of terms, and consent based on understanding.[44]

Special contract law rules also include *unconscionability doctrine*. An unconscionable contract is one whose terms are excessively unfair to one side. Although the term unconscionability is modern, the notion of an inherently unfair contract has been in the common law for a long time. Blackstone, in his discussion of slavery, said that it would be unenforceable as a contract because it was inherently unfair.[45]

Unconscionability doctrine has been divided into substantive and procedural forms. *Substantive unconscionability* refers to the inherent unfairness of the terms of the contract. *Procedural unconscionability* refers to the inherent unfairness of the procedure by which the contract was created. For example, requiring a person who needs emergency care to sign a waiver to get access to the hospital emergency room might be deemed procedurally unconscionable.[46]

A closely related doctrine of exculpatory overbreadth has led some courts to refuse to enforce contractual liability waivers. Thus, some courts refuse to enforce waiver provisions that claim to cover all injuries "from any sources," or "no matter how caused," or using similar language.[47]

A third set of common law restrictions on the enforceability of contractual liability waivers consists of ordinary contract law principles. Fraud or misrepresentation may provide a basis for refusing to enforce. Whether the specific act of negligence that the plaintiff complains of is within the set of risks contemplated by the waiver provision is also a matter of contractual interpretation. Most activities involve risks that can be categorized as either inherent to the activity,[48] such as falling while attempting to ski, or noninherent to the activity, such as colliding with a negligently placed ski lift pole.[49] This is ordinarily a fact-intensive inquiry, and general notions of offer

---

[44] *See, e.g.*, Bering Straight Sch. Dist. v. RLI Ins. Co. 873 P.2d 1292, 1294–1295 (Alaska 1994); Graham v. Scissor-Tail, Inc., 171 Cal. Rptr. 604, 612 (Cal. 1981); Nw. Fin. Miss. Inc. v. McDonald, 905 So.2d 1187, 1194 (Miss. 2005); Woodruff v. Bretz, Inc., 218 P.3d 486, 491 (Mont. 2009); Obstetrics & Gynecologists Ltd. v. Pepper, 693 P.2d 1259, 1260 (Nev. 1985); Spears v. Shelter Mut. Ins. Co., 73 P.3d 865, 868–869 (Okla. 2003).

[45] 1 WILLIAM BLACKSTONE, COMMENTARIES *411–412.

[46] Sosa v. Paulos, 924 P.2d 357 (Utah 1996) (holding arbitration agreement presented to patient less than one hour before surgery procedurally unconscionable).

[47] Fisher v. Stevens, 584 S.E.2d 149, 152 (Ct. App. 2003); Richards v. Richards, 513 N.W.2d 118 (Wis. 1994); Jesse v. Lindsley, 233 P.3d 1 (Idaho 2008).

[48] *See, e.g.*, Hughes v. Seven Springs, 762 A.2d 339, 334 (Pa. 2000) (waiver enforced because court concluded that the risk of colliding with another skier at the base of a ski slope is an inherent risk of skiing).

[49] Dalury v. S-K-I Ltd., 670 A.2d 795 (Vt. 1995) (waiver not enforced).

and acceptance do not provide clear guidelines that would enable one to determine precisely how a court will decide a case.

For example, in *Russo v. The Range, Inc.*,[50] the plaintiff was injured on a giant slide when its undulated slope caused him to fly up in a way that he did not anticipate. The court reversed a summary judgment for the defendant and suggested that the contractual waiver, printed on the back of the amusement park ticket, might be unenforceable because the risk the plaintiff experienced was outside of the risks he had reasonably expected. Such applications of simple offer and acceptance notions, though resistant to precise definition, are probably capable of accounting for the vast majority of decisions on the enforceability of contractual waivers.

---

[50] 395 N.E.2d 10 (Ill. App. 1979).

10

Contributory Negligence, Comparative Negligence, and Incentives for Care

The contributory negligence rule developed early in the common law.[1] It has been criticized for its harshness to plaintiffs and its seeming generosity to well-funded defendants, such as the railroads. Many legislatures, in response to these sentiments, enacted comparative fault statutes over the 1900s – though comparative fault developed within the common law of Georgia in the 1800s.[2] Under comparative fault, the plaintiff is permitted to collect some percentage of his damages against a negligent defendant, even though the plaintiff is guilty of negligence too. This is different from contributory negligence, which sets the plaintiff's damages at zero whenever he is guilty of any substantial degree of negligence.

I. COMPARATIVE FAULT BASICS

The percentage of damages that the plaintiff is permitted to collect under comparative fault is based on an assessment of the relative fault levels of plaintiff and defendant. A court, under comparative fault, might award a plaintiff 50 percent of his damages, based on its conclusion that the plaintiff and defendant were "equally at fault" or "guilty of equal degrees of fault."

Assessments of relative fault are not made with scientific precision. It is not clear how one would explain, in algorithmic form, the process by which a court determines the allocation of fault percentages. Some scholars have suggested mathematical algorithms.[3] But it is unlikely that a judge, after passing the question to the jury,

---

[1] Ward v. Ayre, Cro. Jac. 366 (1615). The plaintiff put his money into the defendant's heap of money, and the defendant kept it all. The plaintiff's action for trespass was rejected on the ground that his loss was his own fault.

[2] *See, e.g.*, Macon & Western R.R. Co. v. Winn, 26 Ga. 250 (1858).

[3] Mario Rizzo & Frank S. Arnold, *Causal Apportionment in the Law of Torts: An Economic Theory*, 80 Colum. L. Rev. 1399 (1980); Paul H. Edelman, *What Are We Comparing in Comparative Negligence?*, 85 Wash. U. L. Rev. 73 (2007).

could determine whether the jury correctly applied a particular algorithm to assign fault percentages. It appears that courts fix fault percentages by trying to determine, after finding that both plaintiff and defendant were negligent, the degree to which each party's negligence contributed to the cause of the injury.[4] To be sure, one could be more precise and much more rigorous in setting out a process for determining fault percentages but that would be pointless. Fault percentages are not determined by computers employing algorithms; they are determined by juries interpreting facts.

Suppose, then, that a plaintiff suffers an injury equal to $100 in an accident in which both he and the defendant were negligent. Suppose the jury determines that the plaintiff's negligence is 30 percent of the cause of the injury, and the defendant's negligence is 70 percent of the cause of the injury. Under comparative fault, the court will award the plaintiff $70 – that is, 70 percent of his damages.

Comparative fault regimes can be subdivided into *pure comparative fault* and *modified comparative fault* states.[5] In a modified comparative fault state, the plaintiff's damage award is set at zero whenever his fault level exceeds 49 percent. Thus, suppose the plaintiff suffers an injury of $100, and the plaintiff's fault level is 70 percent, while the defendant's fault level is 30 percent. Under a pure comparative negligence regime, the plaintiff would be awarded $30; under a modified comparative negligence regime, the plaintiff would be awarded $0.

What happens to the law on assumption of risk in comparative fault regimes? Assumption of risk has been divided, in many jurisdictions, into *primary assumption of risk* and *secondary assumption of risk*. Primary assumption of risk is based on consent. If a plaintiff is found to have assumed the risk, in the primary sense, then his damages award is set at zero. The reason for this is that assumption of risk in the primary sense implies that the defendant has met his duty of care to the plaintiff and therefore is not guilty of negligence. It follows, then, that a finding of assumption of risk implies that the plaintiff will not be awarded damages, whether he is in a contributory or a comparative fault jurisdiction.

Secondary assumption of risk holds where the plaintiff has voluntarily and unreasonably confronted a known risk created by the defendant's negligence. Because of this, secondary assumption of risk is viewed as equivalent to contributory negligence.

---

[4] *See, e.g.*, Moffitt v. Carroll, 640 A.2d 169, 175 (Del. 1994) ("[T]he Delaware comparative negligence statute apportions liability on the basis of the extent of each actor's contribution to the injurious result, i.e. proximate causation."); Rittenhouse v. Erhart, 380 N.W.2d 440, 463 (Mich. 1985) ("The jury is to determine the plaintiff's fault in bringing about the injuries, expressed as a percent of damages. The remainder is attributed to the universe of factors that caused damages, as to which the defendant at trial is responsible if the defendant's action was 'a' proximate cause of the injury."); Winge v. Minnesota Transfer Ry. Co., 201 N.W.2d 259, 263 (Minn. 1972) ("Our comparative negligence statute . . . requires a comparison of relative fault. While the statute speaks of a comparison of negligence, in application what is really compared, upon a consideration of all relevant facts and circumstances, is the relative contribution of each party's negligence to the damage in a causal sense.").

[5] *See* Meistrich v. Casino Arena Attractions, Inc., 155 A.2d 90 (N.J. 1959).

To distinguish it from primary assumption of risk, secondary assumption of risk necessarily applies in settings where the <u>factual conditions</u> that would <u>justify a finding of implied consent are not present.</u>

For example, suppose the defendant employer, in a bonding exercise, lays out a bed of hot coals for newly hired employees to walk through. Negligently, the defendant makes the coals so hot as to cause second-degree and third-degree burns. Some of the new employees, aware of the dangerous level of heat, and free to turn down the offer to walk across the coals, choose to walk across the coals anyway. Others choose not to. Although the issue of social compulsion should perhaps be taken into account, the conduct of the employees who walked across the coals might be deemed secondary assumption of risk. The employees were not intimately familiar with the risk, nor did they actively seek to experience the danger. It follows that their assumption of risk was not primary. The fault in their conduct, if any, is a failure to take reasonable care for their own safety.

Because secondary assumption of risk is equivalent to contributory negligence, it is merged into the comparative fault system. It is treated the same as contributory negligence and requires the assignment of a fault percentage to the plaintiff.

What happens if the defendant has acted recklessly or with intent to harm? The common law assigns grades of a sort to fault levels (Chapters 4 and 9), viewing intentional and reckless conduct as higher orders of fault. If a plaintiff is guilty of contributory negligence, and the defendant has acted recklessly or with intent to harm, the plaintiff will not lose his suit on the basis of contributory negligence. Similarly, the plaintiff will not have his damages claim reduced under comparative negligence if the defendant is guilty of willful or reckless conduct.

II. INCENTIVES FOR CARE

One question raised by the comparative fault rule is whether it dilutes the incentive to take care.[6] At first glance, it appears that it would do so. The Hand Formula indicates that a reasonable person would take care whenever the burden of taking care is less than the expected loss avoided by taking care (Chapter 6). But if the defendant under comparative fault will have to pay only some percentage of the victim's loss, his incentive to take care would appear to be diminished to a level below that of a reasonable person.

However, the comparative fault rule does not dilute the incentive to take care to a level below that of a reasonable person. The incentives of actors under comparative fault are equivalent to those under the contributory negligence rule. This is an important finding from the literature examining the incentive effects of tort law. I will explain the result here, because it is key to understanding the incentives created by contributory negligence, comparative negligence, and joint and several liability.

---

[6] On dilution effects in settings with multiplier injurers, *see* J. Shahar Dillbary, *Tortfest*, 80 U. Chi. L. Rev. 953 (2013).

$P(Acc|A \cap B) = .25$

$P(Acc|A \cap \bar{B}) = .65$

$P(Acc|\bar{A} \cap B) = .75$

II. Incentives for Care

	B	B̄
Care A	.25	.65	.90
Ā		.75

Negligence: Incentive for Care

To lay the groundwork for the examples I consider in this part, I start with a simple analysis of negligence without the complicating factor of contributory negligence.

Suppose the burden, or cost of care, for an actor is $20. The loss that would result to the victim in an accident is $100. If the actor does not take care, the likelihood of an accident is 75 percent. If the actor does take care, the likelihood of an accident is 25 percent. Under these assumptions, the expected loss that would be avoided by taking care is $(0.75 - 0.25) \times \$100 = \$50$.

What would a reasonable actor do? Since the burden of taking care, $20, is less than the expected loss avoided by taking care, $50, the reasonable actor would take care.

What are the actor's incentives under negligence? Under the negligence rule, the actor will be held liable anytime he fails to take care and the burden of care is less than $50. Given this, the actor would choose to take care under negligence.

Contributory Negligence: Incentives for Care

Now let's consider the incentives of actors under contributory negligence. Suppose there are two actors, A and B.

The loss each party suffers from an accident is $100, and the cost of taking care for each party is $20. When both actors take care, the likelihood of an accident is 25 percent. When both actors fail to take care, the likelihood of an accident is 75 percent. When A takes care and B does not take care, the likelihood of an accident is 65 percent.

What would a reasonable actor do? A reasonable actor would take care if the other actor takes care. The reason is that if B is taking care, the expected loss that would be avoided by A taking care is equal to the difference between the expected accident loss when only B is taking and the expected accident loss when both A and B take care. Given this, the expected loss avoided by A taking care, given that B is already taking care, is $(0.65 - 0.25) \times \$200 = \$80$. Since the expected loss that would be avoided by taking care, $80, is greater than the cost of taking care, $20, it is reasonable for A to take care, given that B is taking care. Hence, it would be negligent for A to fail to take care when B is taking care.

What are the actor's incentives under contributory negligence? The interesting question is whether A will actually choose to take care if B is taking care. To see if this is true, we have to look at the payoffs to both actors under their alternative courses of intended conduct (or strategies).

Figure 10.1 shows the payoffs that A and B receive under different strategy choices. The upper part of each cell (upper triangle) shows the payoff to A, and the lower part of each cell shows the payoff to B.

If A and B both take care (upper left cell of Figure 10.1), they each suffer an expected cost of $45. Why? The cost of taking care is $20. In addition, each faces a

Costs incurred

A's payoff / B's payoff		B's choices: Care	B's choices: No care
A's choices	Care	A: $20 + (0.25)($100) = $45 B: $20 + (0.25)($100) = $45	A: $20 B: (0.65)($100) + (0.65)($100) = $130
	No care	A: (0.65)($100) + (0.65)($100) = $130 B: $20	A: (0.75)($100) = $75 B: (0.75)($100) = $75

FIGURE 10.1. Analyzing incentives for precaution under contributory negligence.

25 percent risk that he will be in an accident, suffering a loss of $100, and will not be compensated since the other actor was taking care. The expected cost of the injury (the probability of the accident multiplied by the loss) amounts to an additional $25 for each actor.

Suppose A takes care and *B* does not take care (upper right cell). Now A will bear the cost of taking care, $20, but will be compensated (because *B* is negligent) if injured in an accident. In addition, since A has taken care (and therefore cannot be found negligent) he will not be held liable for any loss suffered by *B*. Hence, the overall cost to A when he takes care and *B* does not is $20. In the same scenario, *B* avoids the cost of taking care, but will have to pay damages if he injures A in an accident, and will have to bear the cost of the injury if he is injured by A in an accident. The expected award to A is (0.65) × ($100) = $65, and the expected cost of being injured by A is also (0.65) × ($100) = $65. Hence, the overall cost to *B*, when A takes care and *B* does not, is $130.

Finally, suppose both A and *B* do not take care. Each will avoid the cost of taking care but will have to bear the expected cost of injury, without compensation. The expected cost of the injury that each would bear is $(0.75) \times (\$100) = \$75$. Neither party will be held liable under the contributory negligence rule because both failed to take care.

Returning to the question of interest, *will A choose to take care if B chooses to take care?* One can answer this by checking to see if *A* would prefer to switch from taking care to not taking care when both *A* and *B* are taking care. If *B* is taking care, and *A* switches from taking care to not taking care, his expected cost rises from $45 to $130. It follows that *A* will prefer to continue taking care if *B* is taking care. In other words, *A* has no incentive to deviate from his decision to take care, when *B* is also taking care.

Suppose both *A* and *B* are not taking care, as in the bottom right cell of Figure 10.1. Would *A* choose to take care instead, rather than continue not taking care? The answer is yes, because if *A* switches from not taking care to taking care, he reduces his expected cost from $75 to $20.

The outcome in which both *A* and *B* take care (upper left cell of Figure 10.1) is the only stable outcome in the actors' strategies. It is the only outcome in which neither *A* nor *B* has an incentive to change his strategy. Because of this property, the upper left cell is a special type of equilibrium in strategies known as a "Nash equilibrium," named after the mathematician and Nobel Prize (in economics) winner John Nash.[7]

Thus, the contributory negligence rule generates an equilibrium (Nash equilibrium) in which both actors choose to take care.[8] Obviously, this is a desirable property for the rule to have.

I have used a simple numerical example, but the analysis here can be demonstrated in a more general framework. The article that first established this result is by John Prather Brown.[9]

Comparative Negligence: Incentives for Care

Here I examine incentives for care under comparative negligence. The first step in evaluating incentives to take care under comparative negligence is to identify the key differences between the comparative and contributory negligence rules.

I will continue with the assumptions of the preceding analysis of contributory negligence. Given this, the information in Figure 10.1 can be used with only minor modifications to analyze the incentive to take care under comparative negligence.

---

[7] John Nash, *Non-Cooperative Games*, 54 Ann. Math. 286 (1951).
[8] If the reader were to substitute different value for the loss, he or she would discover that if the loss is set at $26 (instead of $100), there would be two Nash equilibria – one in which both parties take care and another in which neither party takes care. Indeed, for any loss level between $25 and $26.6, these two Nash equilibria are observed. For losses below $25, the negligence test is not satisfied, so those losses can be ignored.
[9] John Prather Brown, *Toward an Economic Theory of Liability*, 2 J. Legal Stud. 373 (1973).

The important feature to notice is that the contributory and comparative negligence regimes differ only with respect to the incentives of the actors when they both fail to take care. In terms of Figure 10.1, only the last cell in the bottom right needs to be changed to reflect the different incentives created by comparative negligence.

Let's focus, then, on the case where both actors fail to take care. In this situation, the comparative negligence rule implies that the actors will share in the payment of damages.

Consider A's incentives. Under contributory negligence, A would predict that he is 75 percent likely to have to suffer an injury of $100, without receiving any compensation. Under comparative negligence, A would realize that, with probability 75 percent, he will share in the total losses suffered by both A and B, $200, the precise allocation depending on a jury's assessment of relative fault levels. If A thinks that the juries' assessments of his relative causal contribution are likely to be the same as their assessments of B's relative causal contribution, he will assume a 50 percent share of the damages in both cases. But this means that he will predict that his ultimate cost will be the same, $100, under comparative negligence as they would be under contributory negligence. Hence, under the assumption of equal fault levels, the incentives for A and B to take care are the same under comparative negligence as under contributory negligence.

Suppose, instead of assuming equal fault levels, A believes the court will assign a lower fault level to him than to B. Suppose the court assigns 10 percent to A and 90 percent to B. In this case, A will not have an incentive to switch to taking care when both A and B are not taking care, because doing so would increase his cost from $15 to $20.[10] B, on the other hand, would still have an incentive to do so, since it would reduce his cost from $135 to $20.[11] The incentives in this case differ slightly from the previous case examined, but the final message is the same. The scenario in which both A and B take care is the only equilibrium – that is, the only outcome in which *neither* party has an incentive to change his strategy.

The upshot of this analysis is that incentives to take care under comparative negligence are the same as under contributory negligence.[12] The key feature of

---

[10] If A pays only 10 percent of the loss, and such accidents happens with 75 percent likelihood, his expected cost will be 75 percent of $20, or $15.

[11] If B always bears 90 percent of the loss, then his expected cost will be 90 percent of $200 (taking into consideration the cases where he is the injurer and he is the victim), discounted further by the 75 percent chance of an accident.

[12] Here I must return to the technical point of footnote 8: for a narrow range of low accident losses, the outcome in which both parties take care and the outcome in which neither party takes care may be Nash equilibria, both under contributory negligence and under comparative negligence. However, it happens that within this narrow range of losses, the comparative negligence rule provides stronger incentives for care because it reduces the set of cases where the outcome in which neither party takes care can be a Nash equilibrium.

both regimes is that the cost to an actor rises dramatically if he chooses to be the only one that does not take care. Given this, actors are no more likely to fail to take care under the comparative negligence rule than they are under the contributory negligence rule. The article that first established this result is by David Haddock and Christopher Curran.[13]

Same Example, One Victim

The preceding discussion assumed that both actors, A and B, could be injured in an accident. However, as we have observed in many torts cases, there is often only one party who can be a victim of the accident. For example, in the railroad accident cases, which make up a large share of cases from the nineteenth and twentieth centuries, the railroad is almost never the victim of an accident.

The arguments of the preceding section continue to hold in the scenario where there is only one victim. Figure 10.2 adheres to most of the assumptions of Figure 10.1, but incorporates the new assumption that only A can be the victim of the accident. Still, one observes that the only outcome where neither party has an incentive to deviate from its chosen strategy is when both parties take care. The key reason is that the expected costs of each actor rise dramatically as soon as he switches from taking care to not taking care, while the other actor is taking care. The comparative negligence analysis of the preceding part also applies here.

A policy of reducing damages according to proximate cause–based contributions would disrupt the ingenious method by which the contributory (or comparative) negligence rule induces actors to comply with the negligence standard. Suppose, for example, that the court examined the victim's (A's) efforts to protect himself from harm and found those efforts lacking in some respects, though not qualifying as contributory negligence. If the court reduced A's damages to reflect his failure to take actions that would have reduced his own harm, then the inducement to B, the injuring party, to take care would diminish. A policy of applying proximate causation theory to the allocation of damages would obstruct the desirable incentive effects of the contributory negligence rule.

As an illustration, consider *Mahoney v. Beatman*,[14] discussed in Chapter 9. The plaintiff was driving his Rolls Royce at a fast rate. The defendant drove his Nash in the opposite direction of a two-lane highway. The defendant, engaged in conversation

---

[13] *See* David Haddock & Christopher Curran, *An Economic Theory of Comparative Negligence*, 14 J. Legal Stud. 49 (1985). *See also* Robert D. Cooter & Thomas S. Ulen, *An Economic Case for Comparative Negligence*, 61 N.Y.U. L. Rev. 1067 (1986); Samuel A. Rea, *The Economics of Comparative Negligence*, 7 Int'l Rev. L. & Econ. 147 (1987). For a discussion of limits of on the optimality result, *see* Oren Bar-Gill & Omri Ben-Shahar, *The Uneasy Case for Comparative Negligence*, 5 Am. Law & Econ. Rev. 433 (2003).

[14] 147 A. 762 (Conn. 1929).

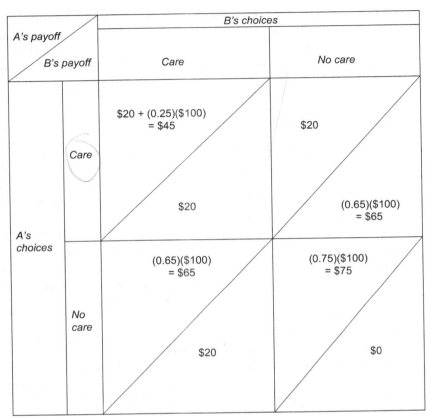

FIGURE 10.2. Analyzing incentives for precaution under contributory negligence, one-victim case.

with someone in the back seat, did not watch the road and veered into the oncoming lane. The plaintiff tried to avoid the head-on collision by pulling his Rolls Royce over to the shoulder of the road, but the Nash still hit the left front portion of the Rolls Royce, causing $200 worth of damage. The plaintiff could not stop his car quickly after the impact, and it careened into a stone wall, causing an additional $5,650 in damages.

The trial court held that the plaintiff's speed, although high, did not constitute contributory negligence. The court then divided the damages based on an assessment of causal contributions. The defendant was assessed a judgment of $200 and the plaintiff left to bear the remaining $5,650 of damages. The appellate court held the defendant liable for the entire $5,850.

The foregoing analysis of contributory negligence provides a justification, based on society's interest in maintaining incentives for precaution, for the appellate court's rejection of the trial court's apportionment in *Mahoney*. If courts were to regularly

allocate damages based on proximate causal contributions, t̶
generated by the contributory negligence rule would weaken su̶

The question examined here arises frequently in connection t̶
defense," or the "sprinkler defense" (see Chapter 9). In the seat belt d̶
defendants have argued that the plaintiff's failure to wear a seat belt s̶
deemed contributory negligence, and the plaintiff's damages accordingly set a̶
or reduced if the comparative negligence rule applies. The sprinkler defense ca̶
raise a similar question: Whether plaintiff's damages from a fire should be reduced
because of his failure to install a sprinkler system. The argument runs against the long-
standing proposition that the tortfeasor takes his victim as he finds him (Chapter 4).

The failure to wear a seat belt has the property that it increases the plaintiff's
harm if an accident occurs, but does not increase the probability of an accident
occurring. Recognizing a seat belt defense, and therefore reducing damages based
on the defense, might enhance incentives to wear seat belts, but at the same time
it would weaken incentives for care on the roads. This is unlikely to be a desirable
tradeoff.

---

[15] To see this using Figure 10.2, suppose the damages award is reduced from \$100 to \$10, based on a
court's assessment of the causal contributions – for example, the plaintiff could have worn a seat belt,
or adjusted his seat to a better position to withstand the accident impact, etc. If B has to pay only \$10,
he will choose not to take care, and it will be rational for A not to take care as well.

Joint and several liability governs the allocation of damages when there is more than one tortfeasor. Under joint and several liability, any one of the tortfeasors may be held liable for the entire damage award if the other tortfeasors are not parties in the lawsuit (say, because they have disappeared and cannot be found) or are unable to pay the judgment. Under *several liability*, tortfeasors are presumptively liable in equal shares, unless the court allocates the damages according to some other criterion such as relative fault. The inability to pay or the absence of some of the tortfeasors does not alter the court's allocation of responsibility for damages under several liability.

For example, suppose there are two tortfeasors, each equally responsible for the plaintiff's loss, and joint and several liability applies. If the plaintiff sues only one of the tortfeasors, that one tortfeasor may be held liable for the entire damages award. Alternatively, if the plaintiff sues both tortfeasors, and one of them does not have enough money to pay the damages award, the other can be held responsible for the entire award. Suppose, on the other hand, the several liability rule applies, and the plaintiff sues both tortfeasors (again, each equally responsible for the harm). Under several liability, each tortfeasor will be held liable for only 50 percent of the plaintiff's loss. If one of the tortfeasors cannot pay his share, the other tortfeasor's share of the damages (50 percent) remains the same.

Joint and several liability applies to cases involving *conspiracy, concert of action*, and *concurrent tortfeasors*. Conspiracy, familiar to students of criminal law, is an offense committed pursuant to an agreement among two or more actors, with intent to harm the plaintiff. If two offenders join to beat up the plaintiff, the court will apply the rule of joint and several liability in the plaintiff's battery lawsuit against the offenders.

Concert of action exists when two or more tortfeasors act according to a common plan or arrangement. The common plan could be an intentional tort, or it could be a course of conduct in which their negligence causes an injury to the plaintiff.

For example, suppose two actors together detain the plaintiff without his consent, according to a common plan, and their conduct harms the plaintiff. The plaintiff can sue for false imprisonment, and perhaps battery, and joint and several liability will apply to the allocation of damages. Or, suppose two actors, engaged in a common activity such as automobile racing, injure the plaintiff through their negligence.[1] The plaintiff can sue both actors for negligence, and joint and several liability will apply.

Concurrent tortfeasors refers to the case in which two actors commit torts concurrently, whether part of a common plan or not; the two actors may have acted independently of one another. Suppose, for example, two individuals camping in different parts of a forest negligently maintain their campfires, leading to two separate forest fires that join and destroy the plaintiff's property. Joint and several liability will apply to the allocation of damages in the plaintiff's lawsuit against one or both of the tortfeasors.[2]

Several liability applies in the settings that do not fall into one of the three categories described above – that is, to cases involving nonconcurrent and independent torts. Suppose, for example, a victim is injured by the negligent driving of one tortfeasor. Months later, he is injured by the negligent conduct of another tortfeasor.[3] These torts are independent and clearly sequential. If a court can separate the individual contributions, the liability of each tortfeasor will be capped by the amount of the injury for which he is responsible.

I. THE NO CONTRIBUTION RULE AND THE EQUITABLE INDEMNITY DOCTRINE

As a general matter, *the law prohibits contribution among joint tortfeasors*. If there are two tortfeasors, A and B, and A is held liable for the entire loss under joint and several liability, tortfeasor A cannot receive indemnity or contribution from tortfeasor B.

There is an exception to the *no-contribution rule* called the *equitable indemnity doctrine*. The best description appears in *Gray v. Boston Gas Light Co.*:[4]

When two parties, acting together, commit an illegal or wrongful act the party who is held responsible for the act cannot have indemnity or contribution from the other, because both are equally culpable or *participes criminis*, and the damage results from their joint offense. This rule does not apply when one does the act or creates the nuisance, and the other does not join therein, but is thereby exposed to liability and suffers damage. He may recover from the party whose wrongful act has thus exposed him.

---

[1] Lemons v. Kelly 397 P.2d 784 (Or. 1964).
[2] Kingston v. Chicago & N.W. Ry., 211 N.W. 913 (Wis. 1927).
[3] Bruckman v. Pena, 487 P.2d 566 (Colo. Ct. App. 1971).
[4] 114 Mass 149 (1873).

In other words, when one tortfeasor is active and the other is passive, but remains liable for the plaintiff's injury, the passive tortfeasor can obtain indemnity or contribution from the active tortfeasor.

In *Gray*, the Boston Gas Light Company attached a telegraph wire to the plaintiff's chimney without his consent. The weight of the wire pulled the chimney down, injuring a passerby on the street. The passerby brought suit against the property owner, Gray. After Gray settled the lawsuit, he sued Boston Gas Light, and recovered the settlement payment under the equitable indemnity doctrine.

The doctrine applies to the case of a property owner who hires an independent contractor, such as a landscaper, and the independent contractor creates a nonobvious dangerous condition on the property, such as a difficult-to-see hole in the ground, that causes injury to an invitee. The property owner would be liable to the invitee (see Chapter 14, on landowner duties). However, the property owner can seek indemnity from the contractor, under the equitable indemnity doctrine, for the damages he has paid to the invitee.

Consider the case of a property owner who stores a large quantity of water, as in *Rylands v. Fletcher*. An independent contractor on the property negligently punctures a hole in the water container, flooding the property of a neighbor, and the neighbor sues under the *Rylands* strict liability theory. Can the property owner, under the equitable indemnity doctrine, seek contribution from the independent contractor? Probably not, because the owner is strictly liable under *Rylands* for bringing the water onto his land with knowledge of the risks to neighbors. That is a sufficient basis for liability under *Rylands*; the negligence of the contractor has no bearing on the property owner's strict liability.

The active-versus-passive distinction suggested in *Gray* may be inadequate as a description of the instances in which the equitable indemnity rule applies. An alternative and perhaps better view is that the rule applies to *vertically related tortfeasors* – that is, to a relationship in which the risk created by the active party's conduct depends on the failure of the other actor to mitigate the risk. The property owner in *Gray* did not string up the telegraph wire, but could have taken steps before the wires were put up, or after, to minimize the risk to passersby. However, his failure to do so made him liable to any injured passerby, on the ground that he had violated an absolute duty to protect the safety of such travelers.[5] In this view, the telegraph company's negligence was dependent, to some extent, on the failure of the property owner to take steps to guard against its effects.

II. JOINT AND SEVERAL LIABILITY: INCENTIVES FOR CARE

It might seem at first glance that joint and several liability should distort incentives for care. The reason is that one tortfeasor may end up paying the entire damages award

---

[5] Gray v. Boston Gas Light Co., 114 Mass 149, 153 (1873). Under the duty, travelers by the property are put in the same category as invitees (*see* Chapter 14), which means that the owner has a duty to inspect for, and fix, defective conditions that could harm them.

while the other tortfeasor pays nothing. If the potential tortfeasors could predict the position in which they are likely to be at the end of a lawsuit (paying for the entire loss, or paying nothing), the tortfeasor who is likely to pay nothing would have little incentive to take care.

However, joint and several liability operates on incentives for care in a manner similar to the contributory negligence rule examined the preceding chapter.[6] Recall that it was shown that contributory negligence provides incentives for both parties to an accident to take reasonable care. The same is true of joint and several liability: It provides incentives for multiple tortfeasors to take reasonable care.

To see this, suppose there are two actors, A and B, who may cause an injury of $100 to a victim. The cost of taking care is $20 for A and $20 for B. If both take care, the probability of an injury occurring to the victim is 25 percent. If only one of them takes care, the probability of an injury is 65 percent. If neither of them takes care, the probability of an injury is 75 percent.

Under these assumptions, the failure of one actor to take care would be deemed negligent. The reason is that the loss that would be avoided by taking care, $(0.65 - 0.25) \times \$100 = \$40$, is greater than the cost of taking care, $20.

Figure 11.1 shows the incentives A and B face under joint and several liability. The cost borne by A is shown in the upper triangle, and the cost borne by B is in the lower triangle of each cell. In the first cell, in the upper left corner, both A and B take care and spend $20 each. Since neither of them would be held liable for accidently injuring the victim, the $20 cost is all that each bears. In the upper right cell, A takes care while B does not take care. In this scenario, A bears the cost of $20 for taking care, and B bears $65 in expected liability to the victim.

Recall that in the last chapter, to find the outcome most consistent with the incentives of two actors under a legal rule, we looked for an outcome in which neither actor would prefer to change his strategy (to take care or not to take care) under the rule, given the strategy choice of the other actor. Such an outcome, a Nash equilibrium, is the anticipated result of the rule. I will conduct the same exercise here.

It should be clear that in the first cell, the upper left corner, neither party has an incentive to change his strategy if the other keeps his strategy. If both A and B are taking care, neither would be better off by choosing not to take care while the other one takes care – because such a change would increase his cost to $65 from $20. Thus, the outcome in which both parties take care is a Nash equilibrium. It should also be clear that at least one of the parties would change his strategy in the off-diagonal cells.

In the last cell in the bottom right corner, both A and B fail to take care. This is the only scenario in which joint and several liability affects the damages judgment. The

[6] On the incentives created by joint and several liability, see William M. Landes and Richard A. Posner, *Joint and Multiple Tortfeasors: An Economic Analysis*, 9 J. LEGAL STUD. 517 (1980); Lewis A. Kornhauser & Richard L. Revesz, *Multidefendant Settlements: The Impact of Joint and Several Liability*, 23 J. LEGAL STUD. 41 (1994); Kathryn E. Spier, *A Note on Joint and Several Liability: Insolvency, Settlement, and Incentives*, 23 J. LEGAL STUD. 559 (1994).

cell shows some of the different allocations of the damages that might be observed. If A is the only tortfeasor in court, then A will pay the full award of $100, and his expected cost is therefore $75 (that is, $(0.75) \times (\$100) = \$75$); B's corresponding expected cost is $0. Under this allocation, A would prefer to spend $20 taking care rather than $75 in expected liability, so A would prefer to switch from not taking care to taking care. In the other extreme, where B is the only defendant in court, B's expected cost would be $75 and A's expected cost would be $0. B would switch to taking care, preferring to pay $20 rather than $75. The dots between $65 and $10 hold places for alternative allocations of the $75 expected cost – for example, $20 and $55, and so on. In these alternative allocations, the judge allocates some portion of damages judgment to one tortfeasor and the remainder to the other one. As long as the share of the expected cost for either tortfeasor is greater than the cost of taking care, $20, at least one tortfeasor would prefer to take care than not to take care. Since this will always be true, the outcome in which both tortfeasors fail to take care is not a stable outcome – not a Nash equilibrium, as described in Chapter 10.

The only outcome in which the tortfeasors' preferred strategies are stable, in the sense that neither tortfeasor would choose to deviate from his chosen strategy given the strategy choice of the other tortfeasor, is when both tortfeasors take care. Thus, the joint and several liability rule induces joint tortfeasors (more precisely, potential joint tortfeasors) to take reasonable care. Moreover, Figure 11.1 implies that a fault-based allocation of damages among the tortfeasors would not reduce the incentives for joint tortfeasors to take care, provided that all of the tortfeasors are joined in the litigation. Thus, a rule that allocates damages among negligent actors according to causal contribution would not weaken deterrence.

A rule of several liability that effectively caps damages for each tortfeasor according to some estimate of his causal contribution could weaken deterrence, in comparison to the joint and several liability rule, if the cap applies even when some tortfeasors are absent from the litigation. If damages are capped below $100 for each of the tortfeasors, then it is possible that one tortfeasor might prefer not to take care even when the other tortfeasor chooses to take care. For example, suppose damages for tortfeasor A are capped at $20. If tortfeasor A chooses not to take care (when tortfeasor B takes care), A's expected cost would be $13, which is less than the cost of taking care. In this case, several liability would lead to weaker incentives for care than under joint and several liability.

III. VICARIOUS LIABILITY

Vicarious liability is a label that encompasses relationships in which one party is legally responsible for the torts of another party. It is observed mainly in the employment relationship.[7] *Employers are vicariously liable for the torts of their employees*

---

[7] The topic is briefly discussed in Chapter 9, in connection with assumption of risk doctrine.

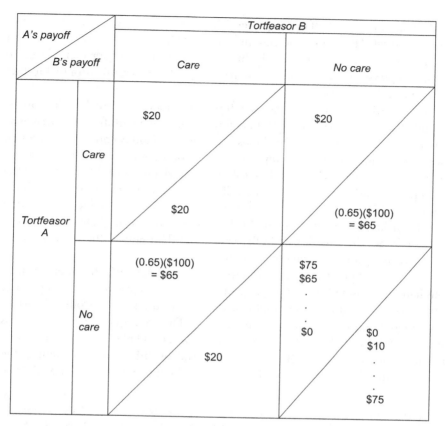

FIGURE 11.1. Analyzing incentives for precaution under joint and several liability.

committed within the scope of employment. For a tort to be *within the scope of employment*, it must be committed by the employee while engaged in the sort of work he is employed to do, *to further the interests of the employer*, and largely within the authorized time and space of employment.

The typical application of vicarious liability occurs when an employee negligently harms someone in the course of carrying out his work. For example, a railroad employee who carelessly throws the wrong switch, causing a train to jump the tracks and destroy neighboring property, would burden his employer with the resulting damages under vicarious liability.

Although the majority of applications of the rule involve negligent conduct of employees, the rule also applies to intentional torts, where those torts advance the interests of the employer. Suppose a driver for Blue Bus Company runs a bus owned by Red Bus Company off the road. One might argue that such an intentional tort could not be within the scope of employment. After all, most bus companies do not direct or train their drivers to run competing buses off the road. However, since the tort furthers the interests of the employer (Blue Bus Company would prefer to see its competitors off of the roads), most courts would hold the employer responsible under the doctrine of vicarious liability. Failing to do so would encourage employers to reward employees who commit intentional torts on their own initiative that further the employer's interests.

One recurring question in the literature is whether vicarious liability can be defended on utilitarian grounds. Holmes found it difficult to justify.[8] Modern writers have offered several theories. One holds that vicarious liability corrects the distorted incentives of judgment-proof employees.[9] A second theory is that it corrects for the distorted incentives that would result from the victim's inability to identify the injurer.[10] A third theory is that it permits optimal sharing of the risk of liability between employers and employees.[11] A fourth theory is that it reduces transaction costs by making the jointly preferred risk-sharing arrangement (between employer and employee) the default rule in the law, rather than putting the burden on the parties to create the arrangement by contract.[12]

The judgment-proof problem provides one obvious potential justification for vicarious liability. Most railroad employees could not afford to pay for the damages from train wrecks. Given this, the employee's incentive to take care would be biased toward too little care, from society's perspective. The employee would consider his own wealth to be the limit of what he might lose as a result of his negligent conduct, and take care accordingly. But if his own wealth is only a small fraction of the entire potential loss generated by his carelessness, his incentive to take care might be

---

[8] *See* O. W. Holmes, Jr., *Agency*, 4 HARV. L. REV. 345, 345 (1891) ("[T]he series of anomalies or departures from general rule which are seen wherever agency makes its appearance must be explained by some cause not manifest to common sense alone; that this cause is, in fact, the survival from ancient times of doctrines which in their earlier form embodied certain rights and liabilities of heads of families based on substantive grounds which have disappeared long since, and that in modern days these doctrines have been generalized into a fiction. . . . That fiction is, of course, that, within the scope of the agency, principal and agent are one.").

[9] Richard A. Posner, *A Theory of Negligence*, 1 J. LEGAL STUD. 29, 43 (1972). On judgment proof status and the incentive effects of liability, *see* Steven Shavell, *The Judgment Proof Problem*, 6 INT'L REV. LAW & ECON. 45 (1986). A more nuanced discussion of the judgment proof problem in the employment context is offered in Lewis A. Kornhauser, *An Economic Analysis of the Choice between Enterprise and Personal Liability for Accidents*, 70 CAL. L. REV. 1345 (1982).

[10] Richard A. Epstein & Alan O. Sykes, *The Assault on Managed Care: Vicarious Liability, ERISA Preemption, and Class Actions*, 30 J. LEGAL STUD. 625, 636–637 (2001); Alan O. Sykes, *The Economics of Vicarious Liability*, 93 YALE L. J. 1231, 1244–1256 (1984).

[11] Sykes, *supra* note 10, at 1244–1256. I do not mean to suggest that there are only four incentive-based theories of vicarious liability. For other analyses of the impact of vicarious liability on incentives for care, *see, e.g.*, Jennifer Arlen & Bentley Macleod, *Torts, Expertise, and Authority: Liability for Physicians and Managed Care Organizations*, RAND J. ECON. 494 (2005); Juan Carlos Bisso & Albert H. Choi, *Optimal Agency Contracts: The Effects of Vicarious Liability and Judicial Error*, 28 INT'L REV. LAW & ECON. 166 (2008); Giuseppe Dari Mattiaci & Francesco Parisi, *The Cost of Delegated Control: Vicarious Liability, Secondary Liability, and Mandatory Insurance*, 23 INT'L REV. LAW & ECON. 453 (2003).

[12] *Id.*

inadequate. For example, if the entire loss is $1 million and the employee's wealth is only $100, he will know that his personal liability cannot go beyond $100. If the perceived burden of taking care is $101, the employee will have weak incentives to take care, even though the loss to society far exceeds his burden of care.

Vicarious liability provides a corrective force in the judgment-proof employee scenario. Given that the risk of personal liability cannot provide appropriate incentives for care to the railroad engineer, the courts can induce additional care, on the part of engineer, by shifting the damages to the employer. The employer, facing the risk of an enormous damage judgment, would have a strong incentive to train and monitor the engineer to reduce the risk of liability.

Although the judgment-proof problem suggests a justification for vicarious liability, it leaves some questions unanswered. If vicarious liability exists largely because of the judgment-proof problem, why don't courts limit its application to the instances where employees are judgment-proof? In addition, why don't courts at least require employees to pay up to the levels of their wealth, before shifting damages over to the employer? These questions suggest that the judgment-proof problem may not be the sole or even the major reason that we observe vicarious liability.

Similar questions are raised by the risk-aversion theory, that is, the notion that the doctrine functions as a risk-sharing arrangement between the employer and the employee. If this is the explanation for it, why don't courts shift the damages to the employee when the employee is at least as capable as the employer to bear the financial risk of liability?

The other theories mentioned above – difficulty of identifying the wrongdoing employee, reducing transaction costs – lead to similar unanswered questions. If the commonly offered theories were all that could be found to justify vicarious liability, then we would have to conclude, with Holmes, that it is a policy in search of a sound justification.

However, there is a simple theory that justifies and explains the function of vicarious liability, and at the same time avoids the shortcomings of the other theories just surveyed: *vicarious liability is a special version of joint and several liability*. The reason is that the employer and employee are joint tortfeasors of a sort – specifically, *vertically related tortfeasors*, where the one actor's conduct creates conditions that make the other actor's negligence especially harmful.

The employer and employee can be considered joint tortfeasors because the probability that an employee negligently injures someone is a function of the employer's training and monitoring of the employee. An employee who has not been trained adequately in his line of work – say, an improperly trained railroad engineer – could be a danger to innocent bystanders. Similarly, the employer should have a duty to monitor employees who pose a high risk of danger to others. Managers and foremen often train and monitor employees in dangerous worksites.

Vertically related tortfeasors in the employment setting play upstream and downstream roles. The employee stands downstream, where his negligent commission or omission causes injury. The employer, in contrast, stands upstream in addition to standing downstream. Upstream, the employer can reduce the likelihood of employee negligence through training and the provision of proper equipment. Downstream, the employer can reduce the likelihood of harm from employee negligence through monitoring and supervision.

The vertical tortfeasors theory implies that vicarious liability is, for the most part, an application of joint and several liability to the employment relationship. Given this, the analysis of incentives created by joint and several liability in the joint tortfeasors setting, examined in Figure 11.1, can be applied directly to the incentives for care on the part of the employer and of the employee. Just as joint and several liability provides incentives for joint tortfeasors to take reasonable care, vicarious liability provides incentives for employers and employees to take reasonable care.

Let's consider the incentive effects of joint and several liability using the upstream-versus-downstream metaphor. In the downstream setting, both employer and employee have a contemporaneous duty of care to prevent an injury to a third party. The employer could be negligent in carrying out his duty to monitor or supervise – for example, the employer is on notice that a particular employee is a danger to others, yet fails to take steps to regulate the employee. Here, joint and several liability has the same effect on incentives as in the traditional joint tortfeasors scenario studied previously in this chapter. However, joint and several liability is not necessary in this scenario because the plaintiff can sue the employer directly for negligence, a point I will elaborate shortly.

In the upstream setting, the employer can take steps to reduce the likelihood that an employee will negligently injure someone in a later period (downstream). The employer can reduce the probability of negligent conduct on the part of the employee by training the employee, and by furnishing the employee the equipment necessary to carry out his work with reasonable care. But the employer's failure to train would be difficult to prove in a negligence lawsuit. Courts do not establish standards for reasonable levels of employee training or education. If the employer were subject to liability only for negligence, few bystander-victims injured by the negligent employee would be able to present a direct theory of negligence against the employer for failing to adequately train the employee. Hence, there would be little incentive on the part of the employer, apart from market reputation, to train the employee to minimize risks to strangers. Vicarious liability, by holding the employer liable for the employee's negligence, pushes the incentive to take care to the upstream level of decision making.

This explanation of vicarious liability suggests that in "borrowed servant" settings, where one employer hires the employee of another employer (general employer) because of special skills that the borrowing employer (special employer) does not have among its workers, the general employer, rather than the special employer, generally should be held vicariously liable for the torts of the borrowed employee. The reason is straightforward. The general employer is the one responsible for the borrowed employee's training. The special employer, on the other hand, is probably unable to adequately monitor the borrowed employee's work, given that the borrowed employee is there to provide services that are not within the special employer's workforce. The traditional common law rule, consistent with this policy, held the general employer vicariously liable for the torts of the borrowed employee.[13]

Viewing vicarious liability as a version of joint and several liability, several features of its application that seem puzzling at first begin to make sense. *First, the employee remains potentially liable under vicarious liability*. The rule does not relieve the negligent employee of the risk of liability. An injured victim could choose to sue the employee alone, even though the employee may be unable to pay the damages, and the law does not give the employee the right to gain contribution or indemnity from the employer. This feature of the law is consistent with the joint-tortfeasors theory. The law governing joint tortfeasors does not permit one tortfeasor to seek indemnity or contribution from the other tortfeasor, unless the equitable indemnity rule applies.

The observation that the employee cannot shift damages to the employer is inconsistent with other theories of vicarious liability, such as the judgment-proof theory, or the risk-sharing theory. If the rule of vicarious liability exists primarily because it permits employers to control employees who are judgment-proof, it would not give the plaintiff the option to sue the employee alone without also giving the employee the right to indemnification by the employer. Similarly, if the vicarious liability rule exists primarily to permit the employer and the employee to share the risk of liability between them in an optimal fashion, the rule would not give the plaintiff the right to sue the employee alone, canceling the benefits of the rule.

The second feature of vicarious liability that the joint-tortfeasors theory explains is that the law permits the employer to seek indemnity from the employee. Under the law of joint tortfeasors, the equitable indemnity doctrine permits the upstream (passive) tortfeasor to seek indemnity from the downstream (active) tortfeasor. In the employment setting, the employer who is forced to pay damages for the negligence of his employee is the upstream tortfeasor. He is permitted under vicarious liability law to seek indemnity from the downstream tortfeasor, the employee.

The right of the employer to seek indemnity from the employee is inconsistent with the alternative theories of vicarious liability. Consider, for example, the risk-aversion theory. If the purpose of the vicarious liability is to provide, through the law, a risk-sharing arrangement for the employer and employee pair, then it would seem strange that the law would give the employer the power to shift the risk back to the employee.

---

[13] Charles v. Barrett, 135 N.E. 199 (N.Y. 1922); Bartolomeo v. Charles Bennett Contracting Co., 156 N.E. 98 (N.Y. 1927). Where the borrowed employee brought no special skills with him and worked under the detailed supervision and direction of the special employer, liability shifted to the special employer, *see* Grunenthal v. Long Island R.R. Co., 292 F. Supp. 813 (S.D.N.Y. 1967).

Independent Contractors

As a general rule, vicarious liability does not apply to the independent contractor relationship. Since the employer is vicariously liable for the negligence of employees only, the employer has an incentive to have all of his work done by independent contractors, to minimize liability.

If an employer could easily evade vicarious liability by working only with independent contractors, he could just as easily fire all of his employees and rehire them the same day as independent contractors. Vicarious liability would eventually disappear, in its real world application, as employers converted employees to independent contractor status.

The law does not allow the employer to evade liability by simply relabeling his employees. If an agent is unquestionably an employee, the vicarious liability rule applies, provided its conditions are met. If an agent is an independent contractor, the courts will examine the nature of the relationship to determine if the vicarious liability rule should apply.

The test courts apply to determine if an employer should be held liable for the negligence of an independent contractor is the *manner, means, and details test*. Under this test, a person who employs an independent contractor will be held liable for the contractor's negligence if the person directs the manner, means, and details of the work of the contractor.

The manner, means, and details test is consistent with the theory that vicarious liability is a version of joint and several liability. The test targets, for purposes of employer liability, the instances where the employer has some degree of controlling influence on the level of risk created by the conduct of the independent contractor. If the employer exerts such an influence, then joint and several liability can provide the employer with incentives to make reasonable investments in training, provision of supplies, and supervision. If the employer does not direct or control the manner, means, and details of the independent contractor's work, then it is unlikely that he could influence the level of risk associated with the contractor's conduct. Liability applied to the employer would do little to affect the risks created by the contractor.

In addition to the manner, means, and details test, there is another exception that enables courts to hold employers liable for the work of independent contractors. If the employer hires an independent contractor to do work on his premises that he knows to be abnormally dangerous, then the employer will be held liable for the negligence of the independent contractor.[14] The reason for this follows, more or less, from the strict liability policy of *Rylands v. Fletcher* (Chapter 5). Activities that externalize extraordinary risks to others (such as blasting) are required to pay for those risks, by compensating victims, to encourage those responsible for such activities to

---

[14] Law v. Phillips, 68 S.E.2d 452, 459 (W.Va. 1952); Humble Oil & Refining Co. v. Bell, 180 S.W.2d 970, 973 (Tex. Civ. App. 1943); Hagberg v. City of Sioux Falls, 281 F.Supp. 460, 466 (D.S.D. 1968).

seek locations where they are unlikely to harm others. Holding employers liable for the negligence of independent contractors performing abnormally dangerous work is an implication of this policy.

Direct Negligence of Employer

The victim of a tort committed by an employee can sue the employer directly on a theory of negligence, rather than relying on vicarious liability. To be successful in his lawsuit, the victim will have to prove negligence on the part of the employer. The employer may have been negligent in hiring an employee who was clearly incompetent. Alternatively, the employer may have been negligent in failing to monitor or control an employee who presents a foreseeable risk to others. For example, if the injury-causing employee is known to be a constant source of danger to fellow employees, or to customers, the employer may have breached his duty to correct or constrain the employee.

Another direct theory of negligence posits that the employer failed to adequately supply the employee with materials necessary for the reasonably safe execution of his work. Just as it is understood to be the duty of the employer to train the employee, so it is also the duty of the employer to provide reasonably safe equipment. Under certain conditions, a court might find that the employee assumed the risk of working with unreasonably safe equipment (Chapter 9), but the same conditions would not necessarily imply that a bystander or customer had assumed the risk.

Interestingly, the failure-to-equip theory of negligence was recognized early on as an exception ("vice-principal exception") to the *fellow servant rule* (rejecting employer liability to employee for the negligence of a fellow servant; see Chapter 9) for the setting in which a supervisor had failed to adequately supply the employee with proper equipment.[15] Under the exception, an injured employee could sue the employer directly even though it was the negligence of the supervisor (a fellow employee) in failing to supply proper equipment that led to the employee's injury. The exception to the fellow servant rule here makes sense. The provision of

---

[15] *See, e.g.,* Moore v. Dublin Cotton Mills, 56 S.E. 839, 841 (Ga. 1907) ("Employees charged with the duty of providing machinery and appliances . . . have all been held to occupy the position of vice principals to the master, so as to render him liable to any servant for a dereliction of duty on their part."); Kelley v. Ryus, 29 P. 144, 145 (Kan. 1892) ("It is the duty of an employer in all cases to furnish his employees . . . with reasonably safe instruments or tools with which to work; and if he delegates these duties to another, such other becomes a vice-principal, for whose acts the principal is responsible."); Ross v. Walker, 48, 21 A. 157 (Pa. 1891) ("It is the duty of an employer to provide his laborers . . . with suitable tools and machinery to use, with suitable materials. . . . The person who is thus put in the place of the principal, to perform for him the duties which the law imposes, is a vice-principal, and quod hoc represents the principal so that his act is the act of the principal."); Hough v. Railway Co., 100 U.S. 213 (1880). On the history of employer defenses, *see* John F. Witt, *The Transformation of Work and the Law of Workplace Accidents, 1842–1910,* 107 YALE L. J. 1467 (1998).

reasonably safe equipment is not an activity that employees, including supervisors, have an incentive to do for each other or for anyone.[16] If, contrary to the law, provision of equipment were viewed as a responsibility of the supervisor alone, and not of the employer, then it follows that the provision of training should also be a responsibility of the supervisor alone, and the duty to take care in hiring a responsibility of the supervisor alone. This would be inconsistent with common expectations and settled negligence law.

As in most settings, negligence claims can be based on a potentially limitless set of theories grounded in the facts of a case. The only real limits on the potential negligence claims against the employer are placed by the availability of evidence and the range of duties that courts consider reasonable to impose on employers. Suppose, for example, the injured plaintiff wants to prove that the employer was negligent in failing to properly train the employee who caused his injury. This is a plausible direct negligence theory because it is within the set of duties expected of employers. But it is unlikely that the plaintiff could ever find proof to support it, or that a court would know how to determine whether the employer had been negligent in training his employee. The employer would have to voluntarily disclose evidence of inadequate training to the plaintiff, which he is unlikely to do. Vicarious liability of the employer relieves the plaintiff of the burden of procuring evidence to support a theory of negligence in training.

The only clear limitation on the employer's *duty*, under vicarious liability, is the "within scope of employment" requirement. Just because the employer hired the employee does not imply that the employer is liable for all of the torts the employee may commit – for example, torts the employee commits while at home on the weekend. The torts must be committed within the scope of employment. This requirement has generated questions when a case is at the boundary, where the employee is apparently at work, but not carrying out assigned tasks in an efficient manner.

The courts have said that the employer is not responsible when the negligence occurs while the employee is on a *frolic and detour*. There is no bright-line definition of a frolic; it is up to the discretion of courts. Slight deviations from the appointed task are still within the scope of employment, but a sufficiently large deviation may constitute a frolic. Consider two truck drivers, both of whom negligently run over a pedestrian. One commits the tort while driving one block away from his assigned route, to get a cup of coffee. The other commits the tort while driving to a city several miles away from his assigned route to spend time with a friend. The first case is probably within the scope of employment, while the second is almost surely

---

[16] If one employee pays for safety equipment, he provides a benefit for other employees. Given this, every employee would have an incentive to wait for some other employee to furnish the equipment first. Safety is sometimes referred to as a "workplace public good." *See* Richard B. Freeman & James L. Medoff, *The Two Faces of Unionism*, 57 THE PUBLIC INTEREST 69 (1979).

a frolic. Where to draw the line as the facts associated with these extremes come closer to each other is a question often left to juries.

Charitable Immunity

Charitable immunity is typically covered in the part of a torts textbook devoted to the various immunities provided by tort law. But charitable immunity bears a closer resemblance to the doctrine of vicarious liability than to other immunity doctrines and should be understood on the basis of the functional theories discussed here.

Under common law charitable immunity, a charitable institution is deemed immune from liability for the torts of agents committed in the course of providing services to beneficiaries.[17] In other words, charitable immunity is immunity from vicarious liability, limited to charitable institutions.

Like vicarious liability, the charitable immunity doctrine does not apply in a case of direct negligence; that is, where the charitable institution itself, through the actions of principal officers rather than agents, is negligent.[18] For example, if the charitable institution was negligent in the selection of its agent, then the charitable institution may be held liable, in a lawsuit by a beneficiary of the institution's services, for its negligence.[19] Similarly, if the charitable institution is on notice that its agent is a danger to beneficiaries, and the institution takes no steps to monitor or exert control over the agent, the institution may be held liable to the beneficiary who is negligently injured by the agent. In addition, the charitable immunity rule does not apply if a stranger (not a beneficiary) sues because of a negligent act done by an agent of the institution, or because of a nuisance created by the institution.[20]

When properly viewed as an exemption from vicarious liability, which is itself a type of strict liability, the charitable immunity doctrine's fundamental justification becomes clear. Since the charitable institution provides a benefit at no charge to the beneficiary, the immunity from vicarious liability provides, in effect, a subsidy to the institution's activity. Using the externality framework introduced in the discussion of *Rylands v. Fletcher* (Chapter 5), charitable immunity, by exempting charitable institutions from strict liability for the negligence of agents causing injury to beneficiaries, encourages the activities of such institutions. This is reconcilable with cases such as *Rickards v. Lothian,*[21] where courts have refused to impose strict liability on activities that externalize benefits to neighbors (e.g., water supply, natural gas supply).

---

[17] McDonald v. Mass. Gen. Hosp., 120 Mass. 432 (1876); Perry v. House of Refuge, 63 Md. 20 (1885).
[18] WILLIAM L. PROSSER, HANDBOOK OF THE LAW OF TORTS 214 (West Publishing Co. 4th ed. 1971).
[19] McDonald, 120 Mass. at 436.
[20] *See, e.g.,* Powers v. Massachusetts Homeopathic Hospital, 109 F. 294 (1st Cir. 1901); Bougon v. Volunteers of Am., 151 So. 797 (La. 1934); Case Comment, *Charitable Immunity: A Diminishing Doctrine,* 23 WASH. & LEE L. REV. 109, 109 n.3 (1966).
[21] [1913] A.C. 263.

Vicarious liability provides the employer with incentives to train and to monitor employees. In view of this, charitable immunity, one might argue, must rob charitable institutions of incentives to monitor and train their agents. However, this argument misses important distinctions between profit-seeking employers and charitable institutions. Vicarious liability solves a problem: In its absence a profit-seeking employer might skimp on investments in training, and on monitoring, to make more money. Indeed, competition with other profit-seeking employers might lead the employer to do so, even if he were not keenly devoted to maximizing profits. The charitable institution is different. If the charitable institution wants to increase its profits, it can do so most efficiently by getting out of the charity business. By providing a charitable service, the institution has already set itself on a course of incurring expenses with no guarantee of profit. It is by no means clear that a charitable institution's incentives to train and monitor will be weakened by exempting it from the vicarious liability that applies to profit-seeking employers. Indeed, holding charitable institutions strictly liable under the doctrine of vicarious liability, which is the trend of the law today, and thereby depleting their resources, might reduce the degree to which such institutions train and monitor their agents.

Whatever the ultimate incentive effect of abolishing charitable immunity, its function in the common law should be kept in view. It operates an exception to vicarious liability, which itself is a special form of joint and several liability. Hence the utilitarian case for or against charitable immunity is inextricably linked to that for joint and several liability.

12

Factual Causation

A negligence action can be broken down into four components: duty, breach, causation, and damages. The causation prong subdivides further into factual and proximate causation. We looked closely, in Chapter 9, at some factual and proximate causation issues in contributory negligence cases. This chapter examines factual causation doctrine in isolation and derives some rules for navigating this most intractable part of tort law.

The hornbooks and casebooks offer abstract causation rules that sometimes fall short of explaining the outcomes of particular cases. There are many decisions in which judges seem to make special exceptions to the abstract rules. The student feels pressure, at some point, to either stick to the rules, in the hope of finding reasonable guidance, or try to understand the decisions on a case-by-case basis. Focusing on individual cases, however, could cause one to lose sight of the rules and, more importantly, the policies in this area. In an effort to resolve this dilemma, I have articulated rules in this chapter at a high level of detail, with an emphasis on functional justifications.

I. CAUSE IN FACT

The traditional approach to factual causation seeks to determine whether the injury would have happened even if the defendant had taken care. This is known as the *but-for test:* Causation can be established if the injury would *not* have happened *but for* the defendant's negligence. The but-for test is satisfied only if the defendant's negligence is a necessary condition for the injury.

Basics

As a preliminary matter, there is one strikingly prominent source of confusion in the but-for analysis of causation. Take the case of death: My negligent conduct leads to your death; for example, by driving negligently I run you over with my car, killing you. One thing certain in life is death. Hence, it would appear that I have a pretty good factual causation defense against the negligence lawsuit brought by your survivors: You would have died at some point anyway. Doesn't it follow, then, that any tort suit brought in response to a negligent killing must be rejected on factual causation grounds?

Unsurprisingly, the courts do not accept this reasoning. A sufficient policy rationale is that if such a defense were accepted, tort law would unravel. If no lawsuit for a death could prevail on factual causation grounds, then it would seem illogical to let lesser torts prevail. To do so would treat tortfeasors who kill their victims more leniently than those who merely maim their victims.

As for the law, the immediate implication of this argument is a specificity principle in causation law: But-for causation requires reference to the discrete injury that occurred, identified by its place and time. Specifically, factual causation analysis in my driving hypothetical would seek to determine whether the injury causing the death that occurred, at the time and place that it occurred, would have happened even if I had been driving carefully. The test has to refer to a specific injury fixed by its time and place; otherwise every tortfeasor would have a plausible causation defense based on the fact that his victim would eventually die.

When I say that the claim that the victim's death would occur eventually is not accepted as a defense, I am speaking only of the test for factual causation. In contrast, the eventuality of death and the date of its likely occurrence in the future are, and should be, taken into account in the analysis of damages, the final component of the four-part negligence inquiry. If the defendant can prove that the victim would have lived for only one additional week had the defendant not been negligent, any award based on the expected life of the victim, such as lost support to the plaintiff, could be reduced accordingly.

Case Types

Factual causation cases can be separated into two types: simple and complicated. In the simple cases, the defendant's negligence played essentially no role in the plaintiff's injury. For these cases, it is straightforward to see that the injury would have happened even if the defendant had taken care – that is, the plaintiff's suit fails the but-for causation test.

In the complicated factual causation cases, it is not clear that the injury would have happened even if the defendant had taken care. The complicated cases involve one or more intervening causal factors in addition to the defendant's negligence. The question of interest is whether the defendant's negligence was too trivial to have played a role on its own, or other factors overwhelmed (or superseded) the defendant's negligence.

As one would expect, much of the law on factual causation is built around the complicated cases involving several causal factors. The law and its policy rationales are examined below. However, first I will discuss some examples of simple causation cases as illustrations of basic doctrine.

Simple Factual Causation Cases

One type of simple factual causation case is where the defendant's negligence was *an irrelevant factor* given the circumstances of the accident. Consider the case of a cricket ball hit over the fence, hurting a bystander.[1] The bystander brings a negligence suit against the owner of the cricket ground asserting that the fence surrounding the ground was unreasonably low. The fence is 12 feet high, and the plaintiff's theory is that a reasonable fence height would be 20 feet. The court accepts the plaintiff's theory of negligence. However, the facts also show that the cricket ball sailed over the fence at a height of 30 feet.

In this *Cricket Hypothetical*, the defendant's negligence is not just a negligible factor in the plaintiff's injury, it is an irrelevant factor. The defendant's failure to set the fence at a reasonable height did not affect the likelihood of the plaintiff's injury under the circumstances.

Now consider a real case in the simple category. In *Perkins v. Texas and New Orleans Railway Co.*,[2] the plaintiff was a passenger in a car that was driven onto a railroad track in the path of an oncoming train. The train was moving at 37 miles per hour at the time of the accident, 12 miles per hour in excess of the speed limit. It was conceded that the train was negligent in exceeding the speed limit. The issue was whether the accident would have happened even if the train had been moving at the required 25 miles per hour. The evidence indicated that the train would not have been able to stop in time to avoid the accident even if it had been moving at 25 miles per hour.[3] Moreover, there was no evidence that the victims would have been able to avoid the accident if the train had been moving at 25. All of the evidence pointed to the conclusion that the train's negligently excessive speed was an irrelevant factor on causation grounds.

---

[1] For similar facts, *see* Stone v. Bolton, [1950] 1 K.B. 201 (C.A.). The factual causation problem discussed in the text here was not an issue in the case.

[2] 147 So.2d 646 (La. 1962).

[3] There is an alternative way of thinking about *Perkins*, not a part of the actual case but interesting still. Suppose the plaintiff had argued that he was injured because the train's negligence – exceeding the proper speed – caused the train to arrive at the intersection in which the plaintiff was injured at the time the plaintiff was there. This theory depends on evidence that the train maintained its excessive speed throughout its journey. The bigger problem the theory runs into is that it is not foreseeable that maintaining an excessive speed throughout the journey would result in an injury at a railroad crossing.

In another type of simple factual causation case the defendant's negligence is superseded or clearly overwhelmed by other factors. Consider again the Car Wash Hypothetical from Chapter 9. In that example, the plaintiff is injured in a mechanical car wash when an excessively pressurized water jet shoots through his open car window. The excessive pressure is due to the defendant's negligence. The plaintiff is contributorily negligent in leaving his window rolled down. However, in the hypothetical, it is also assumed that the pressure of the jet is so strong that the jet would have shattered and passed through the plaintiff's window if it had been closed. Because the accident would have happened even if the plaintiff had taken care, the plaintiff's contributory negligence is not a cause-in-fact of his injury. Although the plaintiff's contributory negligence ordinarily plays a role in the likelihood of an injury occurring, it does not in this hypothetical because it is overwhelmed by the defendant's negligence.

Complicated Factual Causation Cases

The complicated factual causation cases are those in which the defendant's negligence is a relevant factor and is not clearly superseded or overwhelmed by other factors. Unsurprisingly, the common law of factual causation is largely based on such cases. If all of the cases were of the simple sort, there would be little need for litigation over causation questions.

The complicated cases are not easily resolved by the simple but-for test. As a result, these cases have generated the *substantial factor test* as an alternative: Was the defendant's negligence a substantial factor contributing to the plaintiff's injury?

II. FACTUAL CAUSATION: TESTS AND DEFINITIONS

Of the two approaches to determining factual causation – the *but-for* test (would the accident have happened even if the defendant had taken care?) and the *substantial factor test* (was the defendant's negligence a substantial factor leading to the plaintiff's injury?) – the substantial factor test sounds at first to be the most precise. But it is in fact the least precise approach. What does it mean to say that something is a substantial factor? More than trivial? The courts have not provided a precise definition. When should one use the substantial factor test instead of the but-for test?

The but-for test is the standard (i.e., default) approach to determining factual causation. The substantial factor test has been developed as an alternative specifically for cases in which there are intervening factors (including, for example, other negligent actors) that could easily account for the plaintiff's injury.

For example, suppose two actors negligently start fires in a forest, and the fires join to form a large fire that consumes the plaintiff's house. Under the but-for test, either actor, if sued alone, could argue that the plaintiff's injury would have occurred even if he had not negligently started a fire – because the other actor's fire would have

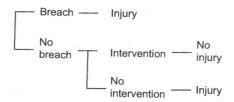

FIGURE 12.1. Causation tree diagram for uncertain injury avoidance cases.

caused the harm. The but-for test is unhelpful in this setting. Courts adopted the substantial factor test as a substitute to the but-for test in this type of case.

Since its development as a solution to the problem of concurrent tortfeasors, the substantial factor test has grown to take on a more general application. This expansion of the test has not altered the law because, as noted in Chapter 9, there are many cases in which the fundamental causation question is whether the defendant's negligence really mattered in light of intervening factors. In these cases almost any causation inquiry (proximate or factual) is going to lead to something like a substantial factor analysis.

The general application of the substantial factor approach in complicated causation cases can be illustrated with the help of a tree diagram, shown in Figure 12.1. The causation tree assumes that if the potential injurer breaches the legal standard, an injury to the victim is likely to follow. On the other hand, if the potential injurer does not breach the legal standard (that is, he takes care), then the likelihood that no injury occurs depends on the occurrence of an intervening factor. In other words, taking care is not enough, because the injury will still happen, if the injurer takes care, unless the intervention occurs. I will refer to this type of case as one of *uncertain injury avoidance*.

For example, the tree diagram in Figure 12.1 could represent the facts of *Gyerman* (Chapter 9). The plaintiff was charged with contributory negligence because he failed to notify his supervisor that heavy fish meal sacks had been stacked improperly, which increased the risk of injury to anyone who attempted to unload the sacks. He was injured when he attempted to unload the sacks. If he had not breached his duty to take care – that is, if he had informed his supervisor of the improper stacking – he could have avoided the injury, but only if other workers intervened to fix the improper stacking. Here the plaintiff's negligence is not an irrelevant factor, nor is it superseded by other factors. Since there was no evidence that other workers would have intervened if the plaintiff had notified his supervisor, the court concluded that the plaintiff's negligence was not a substantial factor in causing his injury. An injury to the plaintiff probably would have occurred regardless of whether the plaintiff had taken care (which implies that the bottom branch probabilistically outweighs the middle branch in Figure 12.1); thus the plaintiff's breach was not a substantial factor.

This example suggests that the substantial factor test can be a useful approach to complicated factual causation cases, because it invites a probabilistic assessment of the facts. The substantial factor test is equivalent to assigning probability weights, based on the evidence, to different branches of the causation tree, and then assessing whether the branches leading to the end state "Injury" are heavier than the branches leading to "No Injury." If so, the substantial factor approach implies that the case fails the causation requirement. In the remainder of this part, I will use the substantial factor approach to examine some well-known causation cases.

One highly cited case is *New York Central Railroad Co. v. Grimstad*.[4] The plaintiff's husband, captain of a barge, fell overboard when the barge was bumped by another ship. The plaintiff came out of the cabin and found her husband, who could not swim, calling for help in the water. She ran back into the cabin for a rope, and returned to find that he had disappeared. She brought a negligence claim against the defendant, owner of the barge, on the theory that the barge should have been equipped with lifebuoys.

The court rejected the plaintiff's negligence theory, on factual causation grounds. The plaintiff's theory was speculative, the court held, because there were many other factors that might have prevented the wife from saving the husband even if the barge had been equipped with lifebuoys. For example, the wife may not have been able to find a lifebuoy in time and, if she had, may not have been able to throw it in time, or may have thrown it too far from her husband to help.

Grimstad lacks the clarity in evidence observed in simple cases such as *Perkins*. While the evidence indicated that the train's excessive speed was an irrelevant factor in *Perkins*, the absence of a lifebuoy does not seem to be causally irrelevant in *Grimstad*. In spite of this, other causal factors appear to overwhelm the causal contribution of the absence of lifebuoys – and clearly the absence was not *sufficient* to deliver the unfortunate result. Although *Grimstad* was analyzed by the court under but-for reasoning, one could reach the court's conclusion just as easily through the substantial factor inquiry.

To elaborate, in *Grimstad* there are intervening causation nodes – that is, points at which causal pathways bifurcate – between the defendant's precaution of equipping the barge with lifebuoys and the desired end state in which the plaintiff avoids injury. One intervening node involves finding a lifebuoy in time, another involves grabbing the lifebuoy and getting near to the captain's location in time, another throwing the lifebuoy within the captain's reach, and yet another the captain actually grabbing the lifebuoy before drowning. These intervening nodes can be treated as competing causal factors, each sufficient in isolation to deliver the bad outcome (drowning) even when the defendant has taken reasonable care. Proving causation in the face of so many competing causal factors is a difficult burden. Returning to the causation tree in Figure 12.1, *Grimstad* is a case in which the causal pathways leading to injury

---

[4] 264 F. 334 (2d Cir. 1920).

appear to greatly outweigh, in probability mass, the pathways leading to rescue. Since the facts did not suggest that the intervening factors necessary to prevent the accident, working in conjunction with the defendant's taking care, were likely to have occurred, the defendant's failure to take care was not a substantial factor in the plaintiff's injury.

Grimstad is representative of a class of cases in which the substantial factor and but-for causation tests point to the same conclusion. The causation issue in these cases requires a comparison of competing factors and resolves into a weighing of evidence and probabilities. The causation question, in this context, could be framed generally as whether the evidence indicates that the defendant's negligence was, more likely than not, a but-for cause of the plaintiff's injury.

Consider another complicated causation case. In *Reynolds v. Texas & Pacific Ry. Co.*[5] the plaintiff fell down the stairs leading to a train platform. She had just rushed out of a lighted waiting room and onto an unlighted stairway. She claimed that the defendant was negligent in failing to light the stairway. The defendant challenged on factual causation grounds, arguing that she could have slipped and fell even if the stairway had been fully illuminated. The plaintiff prevailed.

Reynolds is quite comparable to *Grimstad*, though different in outcome for the plaintiff. The stairway lighting was obviously not an irrelevant factor in the plaintiff's injury in *Reynolds*. Also like *Grimstad*, there were competing causal factors that could have led to the plaintiff's injury even if the defendant had taken care. Even if the steps had been illuminated, the plaintiff might have misplaced her foot, or she might have gotten distracted. Similar to *Grimstad*, there were many other events that would have to happen, in addition to the defendant taking care, for the injury to be avoided, and these other events were all speculative. The difference is that in *Reynolds* the speculative nature of the proposed intervening causal factors made the defendant's causation defense weak, whereas in *Grimstad* the speculative nature of the proposed intervening causal factors made the plaintiff's causation argument weak. We all know from experience the visual difficulty in transitioning from a well-lit room to a dark area, and that the difficulty of such a transition could be *a sufficient cause* of the plaintiff's fall in *Reynolds*. There would have to be powerful evidence in favor of some intervening causal factor to lead us to reverse that inference. However, experience also tells us that merely having a lifebuoy on board is not sufficient to guarantee a rescue in a boating accident. When, as in *Reynolds*, the intervening factors that could have caused the accident appear to be potentially overwhelmed by the defendant's negligence, because of their comparatively speculative or conjectural nature, the plaintiff has met his burden of proof on causation.

Notice that *Reynolds* has a similar structure to the causation tree in Figure 12.1, though with the "Intervention" and "No Intervention" branches switched, as shown in Figure 12.2. In the class of cases to which *Reynolds* belongs, the injurer's decision

---

[5] 37 La. Ann. 694 (1885).

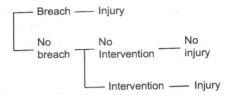

FIGURE 12.2. Causation tree diagram for uncertain injury cases.

to take care (illuminate the stairway) implies that no injury will occur, but an intervention may still cause the injury (something distracts the victim, causing him to trip). The evidence in *Reynolds* suggested that the middle branch of Figure 12.2 (injurer takes care and no intervention) could probabilistically dominate the bottom branch (injurer takes care plus intervention). *Reynolds* is representative of a class I will describe as *uncertain injury causation* cases, because there are other factors that could have caused the injury even if the defendant had taken care.

Factual Causation, Inference, and Proof

To say that the intervening factors appear to be potentially overwhelmed by the defendant's negligence as a causal factor is at bottom a statement about inference. The intervening factors would appear to be overwhelmed when, to a reasonable person, the accident is the type that is more readily associated with the negligence charged to the defendant than with the intervening factors. For example, in *Reynolds*, it is easy to see how shutting off the lights over the stairs would greatly increase the risk of falling down the stairs, especially for a person who has just exited a brightly lit room. There are, of course, many other reasons that a person might fall down stairs, such as inadvertence or distraction. But it is unlikely that these other factors would have as powerful an influence on the likelihood of falling as the absence of lighting. For this reason, most people would think, in the absence of unambiguous evidence pointing to some other cause, that the defendant's negligence in *Reynolds* probably overwhelms the other possible factors as causal agents.

Since the decision in *Reynolds* is essentially a conclusion on a question of inference, we are dealing at bottom with the same issues confronted under *res ipsa loquitur* doctrine (Chapter 8). It follows that where the inference of causation is strong, courts may choose to shift the burden to the defendant to disprove causation.

Reynolds is an illustration of a class of factual causation cases in which the inference problem is inescapable. I consider these cases in more detail below.

Uncertain Injury Causation Cases

In uncertain injury causation cases we observe an injury to the plaintiff and multiple potential causes. The inference of causation depends on evidence suggesting that the intervening factors that <u>could have caused the injury</u> were either <u>relatively unlikely</u> to occur (in comparison to the defendant's negligence) or <u>relatively less likely</u> (again in comparison to the defendant's negligence) <u>to lead to the observed injury if they did occur.</u>

Some courts have adopted rules that permit plaintiffs to submit their cases to the jury even though the evidence falls short of proving that the intervening factors were either causally irrelevant or superseded by the defendant's negligence. The underlying reasoning is the same as in the *res ipsa loquitur* cases: to <u>permit a plaintiff</u> to reach the jury when the <u>circumstantial evidence of negligence is significant</u>, and to <u>force the informationally advantaged defendant to produce eviden</u>ce negating causation.

Consider, for example, *Stubbs v. City of Rochester.*[6] The plaintiff, Stubbs, contracted typhoid fever and claimed that it was due to the city's negligence in allowing its drinking water to become contaminated. The evidence indicated that the city had negligently permitted its drinking water system to become contaminated. In addition, the plaintiff introduced expert testimony as well as several witnesses who had contracted typhoid fever from the same city water source. However, the defendant pointed to many other paths through which typhoid fever could have been communicated to the plaintiff: impure raw fruits and vegetables, infected milk, flies, contact with an infected person, infected ice, and fruits and vegetables washed in infected water. The defendant maintained that the plaintiff could not present his case to a jury until he had proved that the illness could not have been contracted from one of the other possible sources.

The court rejected the defendant's proposed rule as inflexible and concluded that a plaintiff has established causation to a level sufficient to reach the jury *if two or more possible causes exist, for only one of which a defendant may be held liable, and the plaintiff establishes facts from which it can be said with reasonable certainty that the direct cause of the injury was the one for which the defendant was liable.*

In <u>*Zuchowicz v. United States,*</u>[7] the plaintiff claimed to have contracted primary pulmonary hypertension, a <u>fatal lung condition</u>, as a result of the Naval Hospital <u>doctors' negligence</u> in prescribing an overdose of the drug Danocrine. The plaintiff's evidence of causation consisted of two main parts: (1) timing, as the plaintiff was healthy before taking the drug and was sick afterward; and (2) elimination of many other causes, specifically the elimination of other causes of secondary pulmonary hypertension and all previously known drug-related causes of primary pulmonary hypertension. However, the <u>plaintiff did not have direct evidence of causation</u>, such as studies showing, at a statistically acceptable level of proof, that a high dose of Danocrine would cause primary pulmonary hypertension. In spite of the gap in evidence, the <u>appellate court upheld the trial judge's verdict for the plaintiff</u>. Judge

---

[6] Stubbs v. City of Rochester, 124 N.E. 137 (N.Y. 1919).
[7] Zuchowicz v. United States, 140 F.3d 381 (2d Cir. 1998).

Calabresi offered the following rule for deciding uncertain injury causation cases: *if (1) a negligent act was deemed wrongful because that act increased the chances that a particular type of accident would occur, and (2) a mishap of that very sort did happen, this was enough to support a finding by the trier of fact that the negligent behavior caused the harm.*

Judge Calabresi attributed his rule to opinions by Judge Cardozo, in New York, and Judge Traynor, in California, but something like it appears to have been adopted at various times in other courts.[8] As stated, it is far too liberal in favor of plaintiffs. In application, the rule articulated in *Zuchowicz*, which formally appears to shift the burden on causation, is more conservative. The court noted that the plaintiff had introduced considerable evidence tending to prove causation.

The rule from *Stubbs* is probably too favorable to defendants, while the rule from *Zuchowicz* is probably too favorable to plaintiffs. Using a compromise formulation based on these cases, it appears that courts have adopted a rule permitting plaintiffs to reach the jury in uncertain injury causation cases when *two or more possible causes exist, only one of which the defendant may be held liable for, and the plaintiff establishes facts from which a reasonable jury could conclude that it is more likely than not that the cause of the injury was the one for which the defendant would be liable.*

Since the burden-shifting rule suggested by *Stubbs* and *Zuchowicz* has the same function as *res ipsa loquitur* doctrine, one should expect to find causation cases that reflect the more aggressive information-forcing approach introduced in *Ybarra v. Spangard* (Chapter 8). Such cases exist: In *Haft v. Lone Palm Hotel*,[9] the plaintiffs brought suit (for wrongful death) after a father and son drowned in the pool of the defendant's hotel. A statute required either lifeguard service or a sign indicating that no lifeguard would be provided. The hotel provided neither. There was no evidence explaining how the drowning occurred, and the plaintiff offered no evidence that would permit the court to infer causation. The court shifted the burden on causation to the defendants on the theory that their failure to provide a lifeguard made it impossible for the plaintiff to prove causation.

---

[8] *See, e.g.,* Lama v. Borras 16 F.3d 473, 479–480 (1st Cir. 1994) (referring to a Puerto Rico Supreme Court rule on causation in medical negligence that "when a physician negligently exposes a patient to risk-prone surgery, the physician is liable for the harm associated with a foreseeable risk"); Hicks v. United States, 386 F.2d 626, 632 (1966) ("If there was any substantial possibility of survival and the defendant has destroyed it, he is answerable. Rarely is it possible to demonstrate to an absolute certainty what would have happened in circumstances that the wrongdoer did not allow to come to pass. The law does not in the existing circumstances require the plaintiff to show to a *certainty* that the patient would have lived had she been hospitalized and operated on promptly." (emphasis in original)); Mitzelfelt v. Kamrin, 584 A.2d 888, 892 (Pa. 1990) ("[O]nce there is testimony that there was a failure to detect the cancer in a timely fashion, and such failure increased the risk that the woman would have either a shortened life expectancy or suffered harm, then it is a question for the jury whether they believe . . . that the acts or omissions of the physician were a substantial factor in bringing about the harm.").

[9] Haft v. Lone Palm Hotel, 478 P.2d 465 (Cal. 1970).

The most important area of uncertain injury causation litigation today consists of toxic tort cases, with asbestos exposure being by far the most significant. In these cases, a plaintiff comes to court with a disease – for example, asbestosis – and seeks compensation from a defendant who exposed him to an agent that causes the disease – for example, asbestos. Because of the large number of toxic tort cases, courts have recently begun to impose specific proof requirements on plaintiffs.[10]

In *Bostic v. Georgia Pacific*,[11] the plaintiff's decedent (Timothy Bostic) died from mesothelioma, a rare cancer of the lining of the body's internal organs. Asbestos is a cause of mesothelioma. The decedent's relatives sued Georgia Pacific, alleging that the defendant's products exposed Bostic to asbestos and caused his disease. After winning in the trial court, and losing in the appellate court, the plaintiff appealed to Texas's Supreme Court, which undertook an examination of the appropriate causation standard for toxic tort cases. The court held that the plaintiff must (a) *meet the preponderance of the evidence standard,* (b) *establish that the defendant's product was a substantial factor in causing the plaintiff's disease,* and (c) *prove that the defendant's product more than doubled the plaintiff's risk of contracting the disease to satisfy the substantial factor causation test* (in the absence of direct evidence of causation). Moreover, in the presence of evidence of exposure from other sources, proof of more than doubling of the risk may not be sufficient to establish substantial factor causation. If, for example, the evidence showed that another source of the toxin increased the risk of contracting the disease by a greater factor (for example, a factor of 10,000), the plaintiff cannot prevail under the substantial factor requirement. Several other state courts have adopted similar causation proof standards for toxic torts.[12]

The "more than doubling" requirement (relative risk factor of at least 2), as a component of the substantial factor test, plays a burden-shifting role. The requirement is not easy to meet, since it requires evidence that satisfies rigorous scientific standards. But if the requirement is met, the burden largely shifts to the defendant.

The more general question raised by *Bostic* is precisely what relative risk factor should be required in toxic tort cases, or other uncertain injury causation cases in which scientific evidence of causation can be produced. In justifying the more than doubling requirement, one Texas court said:

Assume that a condition naturally occurs in six out of 1,000 people even when they are not exposed to a certain drug. If studies of people who *did* take the drug show that nine out of 1,000 contracted the disease, it is still more likely than not that causes other than the drug were responsible for any given occurrence of the disease. . . . However, if more than twelve out of 1,000 who take the drug contract

---

[10] David Bernstein, *Getting to Causation in Toxic Tort Cases*, 74 BROOK. L. REV. 51, 52 (2008).
[11] Bostic v. Georgia Pacific Corp., 439 S.W.3d 332 (Tex. 2014).
[12] *See generally* Bernstein, *supra* note 10.

the disease, then it may be *statistically* more likely than not that a given individual's disease was caused by the drug.[13]

The concept of Bayesian statistical inference, introduced in Chapter 8, is useful here. The question the court is concerned with is whether knowing that the plaintiff has the disease makes it more likely that he was exposed to the defendant's agent than to other background factors. In other words, is the probability that a plaintiff has been exposed to the defendant's agent greater, given that he has the disease, than the probability that he has been exposed to background factors (again given that he has the disease)? As a general matter, if the relative risk factor is greater than the ratio of unexposed to exposed (to the defendant's agent) people in the population, the answer to this question is yes. In other words, the substantial factor requirement in toxic tort cases should require, as a general matter, that the relative risk factor be greater than the ratio of unexposed to exposed people.[14] Under this general standard, the requirement of a relative risk factor of 2 is still lenient to plaintiffs in many cases. If the ratio of unexposed to exposed is 6, for example, then the substantial factor test should require a relative risk factor greater than 6.

It is possible to go a bit further and see the similarity of the causation proof standards that have come out of the uncertain injury causation cases. The causation proof standards discussed so far are the traditional preponderance requirement and the relative risk factor test of *Bostic*. Note that the cases in this area either prove or implicitly assume that the exposure to the injury-causing agent was negligent. Such proof is often not difficult in these cases because the injury (a fatal disease) is typically severe and the burden of preventing exposure to the agent is low (e.g., just prescribe the correct dosage of medicine). The preponderance requirement means that the plaintiff must present evidence that shows that it is more likely than not that the injured plaintiff was exposed to the defendant's agent.[15] However, Bayes' Theorem implies that the preponderance test is equivalent to requiring that the probability that a diseased person was exposed to the defendant's agent be greater than the probability that a diseased person was not exposed to the defendant's agent.[16]

[13] E. I. du Pont de Nemours and Co. v. Robinson, 923 S.W.2d 549, 717 (Tex. 1995).

[14] Let E represent exposure to the disease causing agent, NE represent exposure only to background factors, and D represent disease. From Bayes' Theorem, $P(E|D) = P(D|E)P(E)/[P(D|E)P(E)+ P(D|NE)P(NE)]$ and $P(NE|D) = P(D|NE)P(NE)/[P(D|E)P(E)+P(D|NE)P(NE)]$. The plaintiff should be permitted to meet the substantial factor test only if $P(E|D) > P(NE|D)$, that is, that the probability that a diseased person was exposed to the defendant's agent is greater than the probability that a diseased person was not exposed to the defendant's agent. This holds only if the relative risk factor, $P(D|E)$ divided by $P(D|NE)$, is greater than the nonexposure odds ratio, $P(NE)$ divided by $P(E)$.

[15] Using the notation of footnote 14, this means $P(E|D) > \frac{1}{2}$.

[16] $P(E|D) > \frac{1}{2}$ implies $2P(D|E)P(E) > P(D)$, which is equivalent to $2P(D|E)P(E) > P(D|E)P(E)+ P(D|NE)P(NE)$, which is equivalent to $P(D|E)P(E) > P(D|NE)P(NE)$, which is equivalent to $P(E|D) > P(NE|D)$.

Moreover, using the same reasoning, this is equivalent to requiring that the relative risk factor be greater than the ratio of unexposed to exposed people.[17]

III. FUNCTION OF FACTUAL CAUSATION REQUIREMENT

This has all been introductory material so far. I have made no attempt in the preceding parts of this chapter to determine the purpose or function of the factual causation requirement. Here I will briefly discuss theories of the function of the causation requirement and will return to the substantial factor test.

There are two theories of the function of the factual causation test. One is that it provides a justification for not imposing liability in settings where the court does not have enough information to accurately determine negligence, while at the same time ensuring an actuarially fair allocation of liability over the long run. The other is that it prevents outcomes in which potential tortfeasors take excessive precaution, because of the fear that an erroneous finding of negligence could generate a dramatic increase in expected liability.

Information, Evidence, and the Causation Requirement

It seems obvious at first glance that a defendant should not be held liable if his negligence did not cause the plaintiff's injury. But this is not so obvious on later reflection. For example, consider *Grimstad*. The trial court, whose decision was overturned, found the defendant negligent for failing to install lifebuoys on the barge. Presumably, the negligence finding reflected the court's belief that there were substantial harms that could be avoided by having lifebuoys on the barge. If that is correct, why should it matter that in a particular instance no one may have been in a position to grab a lifebuoy in time to prevent a drowning? Holding the defendant liable would punish him for failing to equip his barge with lifebuoys, which would enhance the defendant's incentive to so equip his barges in the future.

While this reasoning seems right in terms of incentives, the fact that courts have rejected it suggests that the purpose of the negligence standard may not be to create incentives to adopt every potentially valuable precaution. Lifebuoys are valuable in general as a precaution, but they may not reduce the likelihood of a drowning in some settings. The factual causation test limits the liability of the defendant to those fact settings where the precaution at issue would have made a sufficient difference in the outcome.

This is obvious in cases where the untaken precaution is an irrelevant factor in the plaintiff's injury. Return to the *Cricket Hypothetical*. If the cricket ball sails over the fence at 30 feet, and the reasonable fence height is 15 feet, then the defendant's

---

[17] *See supra* note 14.

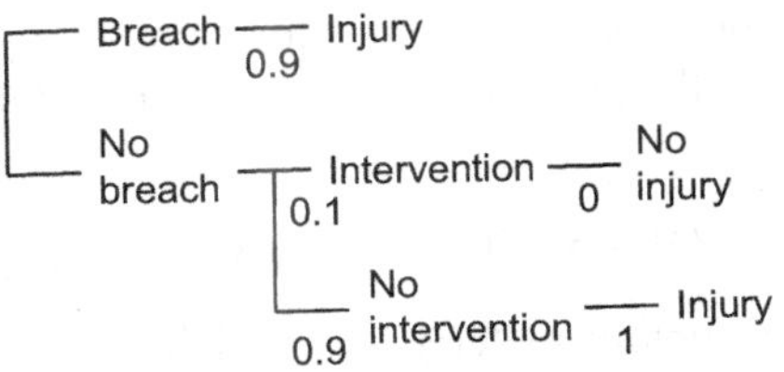

FIGURE 12.3. Causation tree with probabilities.

decision to erect a fence of only 12 feet had no effect on the likelihood of the injury occurring.

The same reasoning applies to the complicated causation cases. Suppose, in *Grimstad*, the probabilities associated with each branch along the causation tree are as shown in Figure 12.3. If the defendant breaches the legal standard (fails to equip the barge with lifebuoys), then the probability of a drowning is 0.9. If the defendant does not breach the legal standard (equips the barge with lifebuoys), then the probability of a drowning depends on the probability of an intervention – for example, whether someone present on the barge can get to a lifebuoy in time. Suppose the likelihood of the intervention is only 0.1. If the intervention occurs, the likelihood of a drowning is zero. If the intervention does not occur, the likelihood of a drowning is 1.

Consider the assessment of negligence here using the Hand Formula (Chapter 6). Suppose the injury loss has a monetary value of $1 million, and the burden of installing lifebuoys is $1,000. If the defendant equips the barge with lifebuoys, the expected injury loss is $0.1 \times 0 + 0.9 \times \$1$ million $= \$900,000$. If the defendant fails to equip the barge with lifebuoys, the expected injury loss is $0.9 \times \$1$ million $= \$900,000$. Thus, the benefit of taking care, which is the expected loss *avoided* by equipping the barge with lifebuoys, is equal to zero. Since this is smaller than the burden of taking care, the Hand Formula indicates that the failure to install lifebuoys is not negligent under the assumed conditions. This example shows that *in a case in which the defendant's breach is not a cause in fact of the plaintiff's injury, the defendant is not negligent under the facts of the case.*[18] Indeed, if courts have perfect information on the probabilities of an accident under the various intervention scenarios in a negligence case, then the negligence determination will already incorporate the causation analysis, and there will *never* be a need to conduct an independent causation analysis in addition to the negligence analysis.

But don't courts that excuse a defendant on causation grounds typically find that he is negligent first, and then find that the defendant's negligence is not a cause in fact of the plaintiff's injury? Yes, they do. These negligence findings are

---

[18] Steven Shavell, *An Analysis of Causation and the Scope of Liability in the Law of Torts*, 9 J. Legal Stud. 463 (1980); William M. Landes & Richard A. Posner, *Causation in Tort Law: An Economic Approach*, 12 J. Legal Stud. 109 (1983).

typically based on a preliminary assessment of the burden and benefit of taking the precaution demanded by the plaintiff. In cases of this sort, a court finds the defendant negligent when the preliminary assessment suggests that the burden of precaution is slight and the benefit in terms of injury avoidance is likely to be substantial – for example, as when a court determines that installing lifebuoys on a boat is relatively inexpensive and potentially of great value in saving lives. The factual causation inquiry, in contrast, requires courts to consider the benefit of taking care in light of facts revealed by the accident.

Another way to think of the factual causation inquiry is to view it as an ex post negligence evaluation – that is, an evaluation of negligence using information available only *after* the accident has occurred.[19] An ex ante negligence evaluation, in contrast, is a forward-looking assessment of the burden of precaution and the injuries that could be avoided by taking care. An ex post negligence assessment uses information revealed by the accident – such as, for example, whether an experienced sailor was present to grab the lifebuoy and throw it to the drowning captain, or whether the only person present was the captain's wife. An ex ante assessment would attempt to estimate the average likelihood of rescue given the different scenarios that might unfold. The factual causation cases suggest that it is possible for a defendant to be negligent ex ante, and at the same time nonnegligent ex post.

Which is the appropriate negligence concept, ex ante or ex post? The ex ante concept is appropriate because it relies on information available to the tortfeasor at the time he had to decide whether to take care. The information revealed by the accident is often not available to the tortfeasor before the accident occurs. Negligence means failing to take care when a reasonable person would have done so. A reasonable person, however, can act only on information available at the time that he chooses to act. Hence, an accurate assessment of negligence should be based on the ex ante perspective.

The core problem in the factual causation cases is that courts often have no way of knowing whether the defendant was negligent ex ante. In the typical case, the defendant has a choice to take care, and the benefit of doing so depends on contingencies that the court cannot competently assess. The defendant may have enough information to make a competent assessment of negligence ex ante, but he is unlikely to have an incentive to present an honest assessment of his own negligence to a court.

For example, in *Grimstad,* the barge owner may have known that there was a high likelihood lifebuoys would be ineffective, because of the general absence of capable intervening actors. The court, however, would not have had such information and could only speculate as it to its content. The court, constrained by evidence rules

[19] This point appears to have been made first in Guido Calabresi, *Concerning Cause and the Law of Torts,* 43 U. Chi. L. Rev. 69 (1975). Calabresi is also the first to have argued that the causation test leads to an actuarially fair allocation of liability over the long run.

and lack of information, could assess negligence only by examining the facts of the case before it. Indeed, when the court in *Grimstad* concluded that the likelihood of a successful deployment of lifebuoys was low, because only the captain's wife was on board when the accident happened, its conclusion was based on observing only one of many possible accident scenarios that could have unfolded. An ex post assessment of negligence based on the observed scenario is unlikely to yield the same answer as the appropriate, ex ante assessment would yield. Yet, the court is forced to conduct the ex post assessment because it does not have enough information to perform an ex ante assessment.

Although courts sometimes conclude, as in *Grimstad*, that the defendant was negligent before excusing him on causation grounds, the better view of these cases is that the court simply lacks sufficient information to determine whether the defendant was negligent, from the correct, forward-looking perspective. The factual causation test serves to justify a court's refusal to issue a finding of negligence when the evidence is too incomplete or ambiguous to enable a court to competently determine negligence in this manner.[20] In such cases, factual causation analysis turns out to be a second-best approach to determining negligence. In the long run, this approach has the virtue of assigning liability to the cases where taking care would have been reasonable.

Precaution and the Causation Requirement

Another functional justification for the factual causation test, provided by Mark Grady, holds that the causation test removes a "discontinuity" in the relationship between the level of care and liability.[21] As a result, the causation test generates better incentives for actors to take reasonable care. Unlike the previous information-based justification, which treats the causation test as equivalent to a retrospective application of the negligence test, Grady's justification assumes courts have sufficient information to apply the negligence test in a prospective manner, but may do so with error.

Grady's incentive-based justification for the causation test is best explained using the *Cricket Hypothetical*.[22] Recall that the ball sails over the fence at a height that would have still led to the same accident (injury from being hit by a cricket ball) even if the fence had been set at the reasonable height. Since the accident would

---

[20] Keith N. Hylton & Haizhen Lin, *Negligence, Causation, and Incentives for Care*, 35 Int. Rev. Law Econ. 80 (2013).

[21] Mark F. Grady, *A New Positive Economic Theory of Negligence*, 92 Yale L. J. 799 (1983).

[22] Marcel Kahan's mathematical treatment of Grady's theory discussed the cricket fence hypothetical; *see* Marcel Kahan, *Causation and Incentives to Take Care under the Negligence Rule*, 18 J. Legal Stud. 427 (1989); *see also* Thomas J. Miceli, *Cause in Fact, Proximate Cause, and the Hand Rule: Extending Grady's Positive Economic Theory of Negligence*, 16 Int. Rev. Law Econ. 473 (1996); Stephen Marks, *Discontinuities, Causation, and Grady's Uncertainty Theorem*, 12 J. Legal Stud. 287 (1994).

have happened even if the fence had been set at the reasonable height, the factual causation requirement would not be satisfied by the plaintiff's claim.

Grady's argument runs as follows. Suppose factual causation is not taken into account. Let the reasonable fence height be 10 feet, and consider the cricket ground owner's liability when the fence is set at 10 feet. In this case, the owner would not be held liable, because the fence is at the reasonable height. Now suppose the owner lowers the fence to 9 feet and 9 inches, which is less than the reasonable height. If factual causation is not taken into account, the owner becomes liable for all cricket balls that fly over the fence, irrespective of the height at which the ball clears. If factual causation is taken into account, the owner becomes liable only for cricket balls that pass between 10 feet and 9 feet 9 inches (the approximately 3-inch width of a cricket ball). So, when the factual causation test is taken into account, the owner's liability increases slowly and nearly continuously from zero as he lowers the fence from the 10-foot level. When the factual causation test is not taken into account, the owner's liability jumps discontinuously as soon as he lowers the fence below the 10-foot level.

If the court applies the negligence standard with perfect accuracy, and everyone knows this, the discontinuity should not affect incentives to take care. The reason is the same as that noted in the previous part, examining the *Grimstad* scenario. The negligence test already incorporates a factual causation inquiry, and a perfectly accurate application of the test would leave nothing for a distinct causation analysis.

The factual causation requirement can impact the incentive to take care if there is uncertainty surrounding the application of the negligence test. In particular, suppose the court makes mistakes in assessing negligence, and the mistakes are more likely as one gets closer to the reasonable fence height. Realizing this, an owner would consider the likelihood of liability if his fence is mistakenly found to be above or below the reasonable height. If the owner's fence is mistakenly found to be slightly above the reasonable height, his liability is zero. If his fence is erroneously found to be slightly below the reasonable height, his liability jumps dramatically – because he is responsible for harms caused by all of the balls that clear the fence, no matter how high. If, in contrast, the court takes the factual causation test into account, then a finding that the owner's fence is slightly below the reasonable height leads to a very small increase in liability above the zero level – because he is responsible only for the harms caused by balls that pass within the gap between the actual fence height and the reasonable fence height.

Given the asymmetrical effect of judicial errors in assessing liability, the potential injurer will err on the side of excessive care. In contrast, the tendency to overcomply with the negligence standard will be weaker when the factual causation test is applied. Thus, the factual causation test improves incentives for actors to take reasonable care.

Grady's assumption that the court can conduct an ex ante assessment of negligence means that the court has information on the various intervention scenarios and their respective probabilities. For example, a court in a case such as *Grimstad* would have information, under Grady's theory, on the frequencies with which the barge captain would be on his boat alone or accompanied by other sailors. However, if, contrary to Grady's premise, the court does not have such information, then it cannot competently conduct an ex ante assessment of negligence.[23] Since, under traditional evidence rules, a court is not permitted to base its findings on conjectures about possible intervention scenarios and their probabilities, the court would be in the same position of uncertainty discussed in the previous part, and forced by the circumstances to rely on causation doctrine as a justification for sometimes refusing to punish defendants where the evidence of unreasonable conduct is ambiguous.[24]

IV. ORIGIN OF SUBSTANTIAL FACTOR TEST: TWO FIRES JOINING AND THE MEANING OF SUBSTANTIAL FACTOR

In much of the preceding discussion, I have treated the substantial factor test as an alternative to the but-for causation inquiry that leads to the same answer, in a clearer form in some cases. However, I also noted that the substantial factor test has the potential to alter the law's application in other cases. In the concurrent tortfeasors setting, the substantial factor test avoids the outcome in which no tortfeasor will be held liable under the but-for causation test.

Two important cases in the development of causation doctrine for concurrent tortfeasors involved fires that joined and burned down the plaintiff's property. The leading case is *Anderson v. Minneapolis, St. Paul & Sault St. Marie Railway Co.*[25] Another important case, involving essentially the same facts, is *Kingston v. Chicago & Northwest Railway Co.*[26] I will refer to the law from these cases as the *Anderson-Kingston* doctrine.

The facts of *Anderson-Kingston* are as follows. Two fires join and destroy the plaintiff's property. One fire was set by sparks thrown off by the defendant's train. The other fire was of unknown human origin. Both fires were proximate (i.e., foreseeable) causes of the plaintiff's harm. Either fire alone would have been sufficient to destroy the plaintiff's property.

---

[23] This suggests that the causation cases fall into three categories in terms of the level of uncertainty. One, involving no uncertainty, consists of cases like *Perkins*, where a court can easily determine whether the train could have stopped in time to prevent the accident if it had been going at a reasonable speed. The negligence standard can be applied with little risk of error. The second category consists of cases like the *Cricket Hypothetical*, where there may be a great deal of uncertainty surrounding the application of the negligence test. The third category includes case like *Grimstad*, in which the court simply lacks sufficient information to competently estimate, from a forward-looking perspective, the correct reasonable care standard.

[24] Does the ex post assessment of negligence affect precaution levels? Yes, but the effects are complicated and depend on the variety of intervention scenarios and their associated frequencies. For details, *see* Keith N. Hylton & Haizhen Lin, *Negligence, Causation, and Incentives for Care*, 35 INT. REV. LAW ECON. 80 (2013).

[25] 179 N.W. 45 (Minn. 1920).

[26] 211 N.W. 913 (Wis. 1927).

The question examined in *Anderson-Kingston* is what the rule of liability should be in this type of case. Can the defendant argue that he is not liable because the property destruction would have occurred in spite of his conduct, and therefore his negligence was not a cause in fact of the plaintiff's harm? In answering this question, the cases deliver several important rules applicable to this scenario.

First, on *joint and several liability* (see Chapter 11): *Any one of two or more joint tortfeasors, or one of two or more wrongdoers whose concurrent acts of negligence result in injury, is each individually responsible for the entire damage resulting from their joint or concurrent acts of negligence.*[27] This rule also applies *where two causes, each attributable to the negligence of a responsible person, concur in producing an injury to another, either of which causes would produce it regardless of the other.*[28]

In other words, where there are two parties guilty of concurring acts of negligence, each of which in isolation would have produced the plaintiff's injury, both parties are jointly and severally liable, and both lose their but-for causation defense. Neither party can prevail on the defense that the accident would have happened anyway as a result of the other party's negligence.

The *Kingston* opinion, which is admirably clear on policy, offers two justifications. First, if the responsible parties retain the but-for defense, each would be able to avoid liability by pointing to the other's conduct as a sufficient cause of the plaintiff's injury. As the court noted, such an outcome would make the wrongdoer a favorite of the law at the expense of the innocent victim, weakening deterrence. Second, a presumption that the defendant could limit its damages to his own contribution would immerse the court in a difficult apportionment problem. The burden of apportioning the loss would effectively bar some victims from recovery, again weakening deterrence and multiplying the administrative costs of litigation.

Chapter 11 offers a more detailed examination of the incentive-based rationale for joint and several liability. In the concurrent tortfeasors setting, the joint and several liability rule deters tortious conduct by generating incentives for each tortfeasor to take reasonable care.

As a general matter, where there are two concurring events that cause harm to the plaintiff, the defendant will not necessarily lose his but-for causation defense. Suppose one fire is caused by the defendant and the other fire is caused by nature. Here the defendant retains his but-for causation defense, because this is not a case of concurrent tortfeasors. The traditional causation rule applies. If the fire caused by nature was sufficient to destroy the plaintiff's property, the defendant will avoid liability for negligence because the plaintiff's claim fails the factual causation test.

The second important part of the *Anderson-Kingston* doctrine concerns the *substantial factor test*. In the event that the plaintiff's injury is caused by two (or more) responsible parties, the defendant can assert a causation defense based on the

---

[27] *Id.* at 914.
[28] *Id.*

substantial factor test. Specifically, *the defendant can avoid liability for the plaintiff's injury if he can prove that his negligence was not a substantial factor*.

Recall that the first rule of *Anderson-Kingston* holds that the negligent defendant loses his but-for causation defense when there are two responsible parties – again to avoid making the defendant a favorite of the law. However, under the second *Anderson-Kingston* rule, the defendant retains a causation defense based on the substantial factor test. Moreover, the doctrine of *Anderson-Kingston* implies that for the defendant's negligence to be a substantial factor, it must at minimum be a sufficient cause in isolation.

Suppose A and B both negligently start fires that consume the plaintiff's property. B's fire is so large that it would have destroyed the plaintiff's property even if A had not set a fire. A's fire is therefore not a but-for cause of the plaintiff's loss. However, it is still possible that A's fire is sufficiently large that it would have destroyed the plaintiff's property on its own. If so, A's fire is a sufficient cause. On the other hand, if A's fire is so small that it probably would not have reached the plaintiff's property, then it cannot be a sufficient cause.

The other scenario noted in *Anderson-Kingston* in which A escapes liability under the substantial factor test is where A's fire may have been a sufficient cause and yet overwhelmed by a much greater fire. For example, if B's fire is ten times as large as A's, then A's fire is an insignificant contribution to the plaintiff's loss, even though it might be a sufficient cause in isolation. Summing up, this discussion implies that a *causal factor is substantial if it is a sufficient cause that is not superseded (overwhelmed) by other causal factors*.

Under the *Anderson-Kingston* doctrine, the substantial factor test provides the most important defense available when there are concurrent acts of negligence. The burden of proof is on the defendant to show that his negligence is not a substantial factor.[29] This is a difficult burden to meet in the merging fires scenario.

---

[29] An alternative to the substantial factor test is the NESS test (necessary element of a sufficient set). Under the NESS test, a factor is a cause if it is *a necessary element of a set of conditions sufficient to bring about the event*. The NESS test is based on the work of philosopher John Mackie, who developed a logical framework for determining causation in John L. Mackie, *Causes and Conditions*, 2 Am. Phil. Q. 261 (1965). The framework's influence was reflected in H. L. A. Hart & Tony Honoré, Causation in the Law (Oxford Univ. Press 2d ed. 1985), and later developed in Richard W. Wright, *Causation in Tort Law*, 73 Cal. L. Rev. 1735 (1985). Wright's article has helped clarify causation arguments in tort law. However, these efforts to ground causal inference in logical propositions devoid of any mathematical structure suffer from flaws patiently explained in Judea Pearl, Causality: Models, Reasoning, and Inference 314 (Cambridge Univ. Press 2d ed. 2009). Pearl presents an alternative, rigorous account of factual causal inference. Another treasure trove of insights for the development of a rigorous framework for causal inference in legal reasoning is provided in John Maynard Keynes, A Treatise on Probability (Macmillan and Co. 1921). I have adhered to the substantial factor formulation in this chapter because (a) it is the traditional framework of the causation cases, (b) it is relatively simple and consistent in application, and (c) it is associated with clear policy rationales. I doubt that it is possible to reconcile the various results in the causation case law without taking policies into account. In addition, the one instance where the NESS test seems to provide an explanatory

The substantial factor framework of *Anderson-Kingston* was developed in cases involving two concurrent and independent tortfeasors. What if there are three or more tortfeasors? If there are many concurrent tortfeasors the doctrine of *Anderson-Kingston* may need to be modified to remain consistent with its policy.

To see this, suppose there are ten negligently set fires. Each tortfeasor's negligence is a sufficient cause of the plaintiff's harm. However, for each tortfeasor it may also be true that his negligence was overwhelmed by the combined contributions of the other nine tortfeasors. This would return us to the very problem the substantial factor test aims to avoid: each tortfeasor evading liability by pointing to the negligence of other tortfeasors.

This suggests that when there are considerably more than two sufficient causes, the substantial factor test should be modified to prevent tortfeasors from escaping liability. The only recognized defense in large numbers cases should be proof that the defendant's negligence was not a sufficient cause.

V. SEQUENTIAL TORTS AND FACTUAL CAUSATION

I suggested earlier that the substantial factor test is applicable to sequential torts as well as to concurrent tortfeasors. Indeed, the causation and apportionment arguments that defendants would assert in the concurrent tortfeasors setting are equally applicable to sequential torts.

Consider the following *Rooftop Hypothetical*: A negligently pushes the victim from the roof of a twenty-story building, and while the victim is falling to certain death, *B*, located on the tenth floor, negligently shoots the victim in the heart. If we view this as a case of concurrent tortfeasors, the *Anderson-Kingston* doctrine applies, which means that both *A* and *B* lose their but-for causation defenses. However, this example can also be viewed as sequential, since *A* acts first and then *B* acts. If viewed as sequential torts, there is no reason to treat the case differently; the *Anderson-Kingston* doctrine can still be applied.[30]

---

advantage in comparison to the substantial factor test – where there are multiple insufficient causes – is easily analyzed under the policies of *Kingston* and the "alternative liability policy" discussed later in this chapter. For further discussion of the NESS test, and other philosophically oriented approaches to determining causation, *see* Jane Stapleton, *Choosing What We Mean by "Causation" in the Law*, 73 MISSOURI L. REV. 433 (2008).

[30] There is a variation on the *Rooftop Hypothetical* that is worthwhile to consider here because of what it shows about the bases for tort liability. Suppose the push and the shooting are both intentional. The law would not allow but-for causation defenses to be used, for the reasons provided in *Anderson-Kingston*. However, there is an additional basis for holding both defendants liable. If the torts are intentional, then each act is an independent battery, and therefore a basis for liability. The negligence test requires causation to be satisfied to hold the defendant liable. In the case of intentional torts – such as the push and the later shooting – causation principles would apply only to the question of damages, not to the question of liability. The defendant is liable for battery on the basis of intentionally causing an offensive physical contact (*Vosburg v. Putney*, Chapter 4). The defendant is liable even if the ultimate injury is not foreseeable. Hence, the mere fact that an actor intentionally *pushed* the

As one might expect, there are real cases similar to the *Rooftop Hypothetical*. In *Dillon v. Twin State Gas & Elec. Co.*,[31] a boy fell off a bridge upon which he had trespassed. As he plunged to his death he touched a high-voltage wire and was electrocuted. The defendant was held liable for negligently exposing the boy to the wire.

Now let's return to the two fires scenario, this time in sequence. Suppose A negligently starts a fire, which burns down the plaintiff's property. One day later, a fire of natural origin burns through the same area. A would like to assert a but-for causation defense: if his fire did not burn down the plaintiff's property, it would have been burned down the next day by the other fire. But the specificity principle referred to at the start of this chapter applies here: A's fire did burn down the plaintiff's property first. A may be able to reduce the amount he has to pay in damages on the basis of the limited life remaining for the plaintiff's property, but he cannot avoid liability altogether.[32]

To bring in the substantial factor doctrine of *Anderson-Kingston*, where there are two sequential fires, we have to consider a case of two fires of human origin. Suppose A negligently starts a fire, and after that, B negligently starts a separate fire. A's fire burns down the plaintiff's property. Minutes later, B's fire arrives at the same location. Although this is sequential, A would like to assert a but-for causation defense, since even if he did not negligently cause the first fire, the plaintiff's property would have been destroyed by B's later-arriving fire.

It should be clear that the *Anderson-Kingston* doctrine is applicable to *sequential and independent torts* in addition to concurrent torts. The policy justifications that support the doctrine are equally relevant to sequential torts as to concurrent torts.

In the case of two fires set *sequentially and independently* by negligent actors, the first tortfeasor would argue that the plaintiff's harm would have happened anyway, so his negligence is not a but-for cause of the plaintiff's harm. Under the *Anderson-Kingston* doctrine, the first tortfeasor loses his but-for causation defense but retains his substantial factor defense. However, the substantial factor defense does not help the first tortfeasor in this case, because it is clear that the first tortfeasor's negligent fire is a sufficient cause in isolation (it burned down the plaintiff's property) and was not overwhelmed by other factors – that is, the first fire is a substantial factor in the plaintiff's harm.

The lawsuit against the second tortfeasor is more complicated. If all of the damage is done by the first actor's negligence, then the second actor's negligence is not a cause in fact of the plaintiff's harm. The case is no different from that of one fire passing through one day, and another passing through a week later. The second tortfeasor cannot be held liable for the damage done by the first. More generally, if the harms

victim, or *shot* the victim, is a basis for battery liability. Causation analysis plays a secondary role limited to the damages calculation in cases of concurrent intentional torts.

[31] 163 A. 111 (N.H. 1932).

[32] Suppose the natural fire gets to the plaintiff first? A is not liable for the harm, because his negligence did not cause the plaintiff's injury.

are *divisible*, the second tortfeasor cannot be held liable for the damage done by the first. On the other hand, if the amount of harm done by the two independent tortfeasors is both distinct and difficult to separate (distinct yet indivisible harms), then the second tortfeasor has the burden of proving that his negligence was not a substantial factor, and if he fails to meet the burden can be held liable for the entire loss.

Another class of sequential cases involves *conditional torts*, cases where the injury caused by the second tortfeasor is made possible or facilitated by the negligence of the first tortfeasor. The torts are sequential with the latter tort being conditional on the first tort. In *Maddux v. Donaldson*,[33] the first tortfeasor's car negligently crashed into the plaintiff. Immediately after that, the second tortfeasor's car negligently crashed into the plaintiff. The court, applying joint and several liability, held the second tortfeasor liable for the entire harm.

In a conditional torts case, like *Maddux*, the first tortfeasor might argue that his negligence was not a but-for cause of the plaintiff's loss – that is, that the injury would have happened anyway or that he should not be held responsible for injuries caused by the second tortfeasor. But the second accident would not have happened anyway; it happened only because the first tortfeasor negligently harmed the plaintiff. In cases of this sort, the first tortfeasor's liability is based on the principle that he is responsible for foreseeable risks that he has imposed on the plaintiff by his negligence.[34]

The substantial factor test becomes relevant only for the second tortfeasor in the conditional torts setting. Here the analogy with the case of two independent fires is useful. If the harms are divisible, then the second tortfeasor is responsible only for the harm that he has caused. If the harms are indivisible, then the second tortfeasor has the burden of showing that his negligence was not a substantial factor in the plaintiff's injury; if he cannot meet this burden, he is liable for the entire loss. This reasoning justifies the court's decision in *Maddux* to hold the second tortfeasor liable for the entire harm.

The final class of sequential torts to consider involves *cumulative torts*. The plaintiff is injured by the negligent acts of *A*, *B*, *C*, and so on. Assume that the plaintiff is injured by the negligence of *A* in period 1, *B* in period 2, and *C* in period 3. For example, *A* negligently administers a poison, which injures the plaintiff, in period 1; *B* negligently does the same in period 2, inflicting additional injury on the plaintiff; and *C* does the same in period 3, killing the plaintiff.

Consider two lawsuit options. In the first, the plaintiff (i.e., his survivor) sues *C* after period 3. In the second, the plaintiff sues *A* after period 3. In each suit, the plaintiff is claiming damages for his ultimate injury, which reflects the cumulative effect of the torts of *A*, *B*, and *C*.

---

[33] 108 N.W.2d 33 (Mich. 1961).
[34] Marshall v. Nugent, 222 F.2d 604 (1st Cir. 1955); Hall v. Coble Diaries, 67 S.E.2d 63, 66 (N.C. 1951); Matthews v. Porter, 124 S.E.2d 321 (S.C. 1962); *see also* Chapter 13 on proximate cause.

In the first lawsuit, it is easy to see how *C* would attempt to use the substantial factor test as a defense. *C* would argue that his negligence was not a substantial factor, because most of the plaintiff's injury could be attributed to the torts of *A* and *B*. If each actor contributed equally to the plaintiff's harm, then *C* would have contributed at most 33 percent of the injury.

Expand the number of actors in the sequence, and eventually the contribution of the last actor becomes infinitesimally small. At this point the defendant's causation argument starts to have an intuitive appeal. The boxer Mohammed Ali danced around the ring peppering his opponent with jabs until finally, after many rounds, he threw a jab that appeared to be as light as a feather. On contact, his opponent's knees would buckle, and the fight was over. The final jab pushed Ali's opponent over the cliff, but at the same time its causal contribution was minimal.

In the second lawsuit, where the plaintiff sues *A* (the first tortfeasor), it is also easy to see how *A* would use the substantial factor test as a defense – making the same argument that his conduct was not a substantial factor. *A* contributed no more than 33 percent of the plaintiff's injury.

The cumulative torts case is different from the concurrent tortfeasors scenario. In the concurrent torts scenario, the but-for test fails because it leads to the conclusion that no tortfeasor can be held liable. In the case of sequential and cumulative torts, the but-for test does not fail. The last tortfeasor cannot avoid liability by arguing that the injury would have happened anyway, because that argument would be false. Rather, what the last tortfeasor seeks in the cumulative torts case is to avoid being held liable for the injuries due to previous tortfeasors – that is, he seeks to apportion the loss.

For cumulative torts, there are two special cases to consider. One is where the previous torts leave the plaintiff with *identifiable preexisting injuries* by the time he meets the last tortfeasor. The other is where the previous torts do not leave the plaintiff with identifiable preexisting injuries, but with an *enhanced susceptibility* to injury.[35]

In the case of identifiable preexisting injuries, the last tortfeasor has the burden, under the rationale of *Anderson-Kingston*, of proving that his negligence was not a substantial factor. This implies that the last tortfeasor must show that the harms are divisible, or that his negligence could not be a sufficient cause of the plaintiff's injury or is clearly overwhelmed, in causal contribution, by the previous torts.[36] If

---

[35] Smith v. Leech Brain & Co. Ltd., [1962] 2 Q.B. 405 (burned lip, in 1950, developed into cancer as a result of prior exposures to carcinogen from 1926 to 1935).

[36] To avoid the large numbers problem discussed in the previous part, the overwhelming defense should be limited to the small numbers cases. Suppose, for example, the tortfeasors have all negligently collided with the victim's car. Under the suggested application of the substantial factor test, the last tortfeasor would have to show that the injury to the plaintiff could not foreseeably result from his negligence, or, if the injury could have resulted, the last tortfeasor's negligence was overwhelmed in contribution by that of the other tortfeasors.

he fails to meet this burden, he is responsible for the plaintiff's entire loss; but if he is able to show that the harms are divisible, he is responsible only for the portion of the injury attributable to him.[37]

In the case of enhanced susceptibility, it will be impossible generally for the last tortfeasor to separate his contribution from the others, or to show that he was not a substantial factor. The rationale of *Anderson-Kingston* implies that he is liable for the entire loss. This is consistent with the basic rule that a tort defendant takes his victim as he finds him (*Vosburg v. Putney*, Chapter 4). If the victim is unusually sensitive, perhaps because of the previous torts of others, that does not provide a defense; the last tortfeasor is still liable for the full extent of the injury.[38]

What about the first tortfeasor in the cumulative torts scenario? In the preexisting injuries case, the answer depends on whether the injuries are divisible. If divisible, the first tortfeasor is responsible for only the injury that he caused. If not divisible, then the burden of apportioning the loss remains *with the plaintiff*. In this scenario, it is the plaintiff's burden to prove that the damages he seeks were proximately caused by the defendant's negligence.[39] If the plaintiff is unable to meet this standard, he

---

[37] David v. DeLeon, 547 N.W.2d 726, 730 (Neb. 1996) ("Once the plaintiff presents evidence from which a jury reasonably can find that damages were proximately caused by the tortious act, the burden of apportioning damages resulting from the tort rests squarely on the defendant."); Tingey v. Christensen, 987 P.2d 588, 592 (Utah 1999) ("[I]f the jury can find a reasonable basis for apportioning damages between a preexisting condition and a subsequent tort, it should do so; however, if the jury finds it impossible to apportion damages, it should find that the tortfeasor is liable for the entire amount of damages."); Bigley v. Craven, 769 P.2d 892, 898 (Wyo. 1999) ("[Jury] instructions must include the charge that if the jury is unable to apportion the plaintiff's disability between preexisting and accident-caused conditions, then the defendant is liable for the entire disability.").

[38] Newbury v. Vogel, 379 P.2d 811, 813 (Colo. 1963) ("[P]laintiff was entitled to an instruction advising the jury that if they could not apportion the disability between the pre-existing arthritis and the trauma then the defendant was liable for the entire damage resulting from the disability."); Blaine v. Byers, 429 P.2d 397, 405 (Idaho 1967) ("It is firmly established principle of the law that one injured by the tortious act of another may recover damages for the aggravation of a pre-existing disability."); Alexander v. White, 488 P.2d 1120, 1123 (Colo. App. 1971) (motor vehicle accident involving one defendant followed by slip and fall involving other defendant); Smith v. Leech Brain & Co. Ltd., [1962] 2 Q.B. 405 (burned lip developed into cancer as a result of prior exposures to carcinogen).

[39] Bruckman v. Pena, 487 P.2d 566 (Colo. Ct. App. 1971) (plaintiff injured in two separate car accidents one year apart; sued first injurer); McGuire v. Oliver, 227 So.2d 149 (La. App. 1969); Bolin v. Hartford Acc. & Indem. Co., 204 So.2d 49, 51 (La. App. 1967); Watkins v. Hand, 253 N.W.2d 287, 289 (Neb. 1977); Hashimoto v. Marathon Pipe Line Co., 767 P.2d 158 (Wyo. 1989); Goodman v. Fairlawn Garden Associates, Inc., 601 A.2d 766, 769 (N.J. Super. Ct. App. Div. 1992); Brake v. Speed, 605 So.2d 28, 33 (Miss. 1992); Wallach v. Allstate Ins. Co., 180 P.3d 19, 23 (Or. 2008); *see also* Gross v. Lyons, 721 So.2d 304, 311 (Fla. Dist. Ct. App. 1998) (Warner, J., concurring in part and dissenting in part, refers to *Bruckman* as the majority rule among jurisdictions). Rejecting *Bruckman* are the following cases: Gross v. Lyons, 721 So.2d 304, 308 (Fla. Dist. Ct. App. 1998), *approved by* 763 So.2d 276 (Fla. 2000) ("The instruction in this case failed to inform the jury that if the injuries could not be apportioned between the two accidents, the tortfeasor causing the first accident could be held responsible for the entire condition if plaintiff has made all reasonable efforts to apportion the injuries."); Montalvo v. Lapez, 884 P.2d 345 (Haw. 1994) (requiring equal division of damages when it is impossible to apportion loss). Hawaii appears to be unique in applying an equal division rule in cases of successive torts where the injuries cannot be apportioned by the jury.

loses his case against the first tortfeasor. This is consistent with *Anderson-Kingston* because the first tortfeasor is generally not a substantial factor in the cumulative injury scenario.

In the enhanced susceptibility case, the first tortfeasor is, again, unlikely to be a substantial factor. If all the first tortfeasor does is enhance the plaintiff's susceptibility to loss, then the first tortfeasor is not a sufficient cause and therefore fails to meet the minimal requirement of the substantial factor test.[40] To hold the first tortfeasor liable for the entire harm, the plaintiff will therefore have to prove that the entire harm was a foreseeable result of the first tortfeasor's negligence. The plaintiff generally cannot shift the burden of apportionment to the first tortfeasor.

This is consistent with the doctrine of *Anderson-Kingston*, but not entirely consistent with its underlying policy. Even in the case of the first tortfeasor, courts have reason to be wary of the substantial factor argument when used as a defense, because of its implication that every tortfeasor can escape liability and the apportionment problems that the defense generates. However, only a minority of courts appear to have been influenced by this concern.[41]

VI. ALTERNATIVE LIABILITY AND FUNCTIONALLY SIMILAR RULES

One lesson of the preceding section is that the but-for test of factual causation, which is the traditional test, fails to deliver sensible results in some cases of concurrent or sequential torts. In the concurrent tortfeasors case, the but-for test might result in an outcome in which no tortfeasor can be held liable. This section looks at another circumstance in which the traditional causation inquiry leads to undesirable results: the *alternative liability* scenario.

The alternative liability doctrine was established in *Summers v. Tice*.[42] Three hunters went out to shoot quail. At one point during the expedition, they were arranged in a triangle, the plaintiff at one vertex. A quail flew between the plaintiff and the other hunters. The others fired at the quail, with the result that birdshot (tiny pellets released by a single cartridge) lodged in the plaintiff's eye. There was no evidence indicating which of the two other hunters, defendants in the lawsuit, had fired the shot that injured the plaintiff.

Both of the defendants were negligent. The only issue was factual causation. Each defendant said that the accident could have happened even if he had not fired

---

[40] Under the NESS test, liability would follow in this instance because even though the first tortfeasor is clearly not a sufficient cause in isolation, he is a necessary element of a sufficient set of factors. In the case of cumulative successive injuries, the NESS test would appear to contradict the rule of *Bruckman*. That a significant line of cases is inconsistent with the NESS test suggests that policy considerations, rather than the logic implied by the NESS test, drive the decisions on successive torts.

[41] Gross v. Lyons, 721 So.2d 304 (Fla. Dist. Ct. App. 1998), *approved by* 763 So.2d 276 (Fla. 2000); Montalvo v. Lapez, 884 P.2d 345 (Haw. 1994).

[42] 199 P.2d 1 (Cal. 1948).

his gun because the other defendant's shot may have done the harm. There was insufficient evidence to prove which defendant injured the plaintiff. The court held both defendants liable, shifting the burden of proof on causation.

The policy justifications offered in *Summers* are similar to those mentioned in *Anderson-Kingston* (merged fires cases). One is *deterrence*: Letting each defendant use the but-for test to escape liability would lead to both defendants getting away scot-free. At the same time, requiring the plaintiff to determine portions of liability might also permit the defendants to get away scot-free. Another policy is *evidence production*: Requiring the defendants, who are likely to have better information than the plaintiff on the cause of harm, to work out the apportionment on their own is the best way of forcing information out in court.

This case differs from *Kingston* in the sense that only one person was responsible for the harm in *Summers*, while in *Kingston* both parties were responsible. That is clear in retrospect. Looking forward, however, the cases are the same. In both, the defendants simultaneously engage in the same negligent act that with some positive probability will harm the plaintiff, and the specific harm threatened by their actions materializes. Each defendant's shot in *Summers* is a substantial factor in the sense of *Anderson-Kingston* – that is, a sufficient cause not overwhelmed by the negligent act of the other defendant. If one defendant can prove that his shot was not a sufficient cause (for example, he fired in the wrong direction) or was overwhelmed by the acts of the other defendant, then he has met his burden of proof on causation and should escape liability.

Courts have treated *Summers* as shifting the burden on causation to the defendants where all of the tortfeasors are joined as defendants in the litigation, the negligence of the defendants is simultaneous and identical, and each defendant's negligence is a sufficient cause of the plaintiff's harm. The similarity of *Summers* to the *Anderson-Kingston* scenario suggests that the requirement of joining all potential defendants is overly protective of tortfeasors. *Summers*, from the forward-looking perspective, is sufficiently similar to *Anderson-Kingston* that shifting the burden on causation to the defendant would appear to be appropriate when the plaintiff, for reasons beyond his control, can bring only one of the potential defendants into court.

Exploring the Policies of Summers

Suppose that instead of two injurers and one victim, there are three injurers and one victim. If the victim is injured by one bullet, then the problem is the same as that in *Summers* and points to the same solution. Each injurer's shot is a substantial factor, because it is a sufficient cause in isolation and is not overwhelmed by the negligent acts of the other injurers. If all three injurers are joined as defendants, *Summers* implies that they can be held jointly and severally liable for the victim's injury.

Suppose that the victim is injured by two bullets, and each of the three injurers shoots only once. Now we have a slightly different problem. If we consider only one of the wounds, each defendant's conduct is a substantial factor. However, with respect to the total harm (both wounds), each defendant's conduct is not a substantial factor because it is not a sufficient cause of the harm.

Should the defendants be able to prevail on the ground that each of their actions was not a substantial factor in the total harm? This would be equivalent, in effect, to excusing both of the shooters in *Summers*, which violates the burden-shifting policies of *Summers* and *Anderson-Kingston*.

If all of the injurers are joined as defendants, the policies of *Summers* (avoiding exoneration of guilty defendants, encouraging evidence disclosure from defendants) imply that they should be held liable. The most plausible apportionment of harm would treat each of the three defendants responsible for one-third of the total harm.

Suppose some injurers shoot more than once. For example, half of the injurers shoot twice, and the other half shoot only once – and assume the two types of injurer can be distinguished. Now the allocation of liability to each injurer should be based on an assessment of each injurer's share of the total harm. The single-shot injurers should be held responsible for one-third of the total harm, and the double-shot injurers should be held responsible for two-thirds of the total harm.

Finally, suppose it is impossible to distinguish the injurers who fired once at the victim from the injurers who fired twice. Should the plaintiff's lawsuit be dismissed because he is unable to present an allocation of liability that reflects actual responsibility for the total harm? After all, if the total harm were allocated on a per capita basis among the defendants, some defendants would be forced to pay for harm that they could not have caused. On the other hand, a dismissal of the lawsuit would provide a windfall to the wrongdoers.

Summers offers policy guidelines for this scenario. First, dismissing the plaintiff's lawsuit is not a recommended solution under *Summers* because it removes tort law as a disincentive to harmful conduct. In addition, the burden-shifting policy of *Summers* would hold the defendants liable on a per capita basis for the total harm, for the purpose of providing the defendants with an incentive to come forward with evidence distinguishing injurers who fired once from those who fired twice.

I have assumed that all of the responsible parties are in court as defendants. If only a subset of the responsible parties are actual defendants, application of the policies of *Summers* becomes more difficult.

Start with the easiest case: two injurers, and only one is in court as a defendant. The key policies of *Summers* – avoiding exoneration of the guilty, encouraging production of evidence – would suggest that the one injurer present in court as a defendant should be held liable for the victim's harm. Refusing to hold the one defendant liable would make him a favorite of the law relative to the victim. Moreover, the likelihood of the one defendant being responsible for the harm, which is 50 percent, is the same as the likelihood of any one of the two injurers being responsible. Thus, *with respect to the one defendant*, extending the *Summers* doctrine to hold him liable, when he is the only one present in court as a defendant, does not involve any greater risk of error than is already implied by the application of the *Summers* doctrine when both of the responsible parties are in court. Moreover, the negligent act committed by the one defendant in court satisfies the substantial factor requirement.

The hypothetical in which only one of two shooters is present in court as a defendant points to two core requirements implied by the *Summers* alternative liability policy. One is that each defendant's negligence must be a *substantial factor* with respect to the plaintiff's injury, or some identifiably distinct and significant portion of it. The second is that the probability that the defendants who are held liable under the policy actually were responsible for the plaintiff's injury (or some divisible portion of it) must be greater than or equal to 50 percent. The second requirement can be labeled *weak preponderance*.[43]

Treating the substantial factor and weak preponderance requirements as the essential elements implied by the alternative liability policy permits one to apply the policy to new settings. Specifically, the alternative liability policy can be applied to settings where the defendants constitute only a subset of the responsible parties and, alternatively, where the responsible parties constitute only a subset of the defendants.

For example, suppose there are three injurers, each fired once, and the victim suffers from two gunshot wounds. All three injurers are joined as defendants. Weak preponderance is satisfied – indeed, the probability that the responsible parties are joined as defendants is 100 percent. The substantial factor test is more complicated because while any two of the defendants would satisfy the substantial factor test with respect to the two wounds, each defendant is a substantial factor only with respect to one of the wounds. To be consistent with the substantial factor requirement, the court should hold them each liable for no more than one-third of the total harm.[44]

Sticking with the same example, suppose only two of the three injurers are in court as defendants. Should the two defendants be held liable for the entire harm? The substantial factor requirement is satisfied. However, the weak preponderance requirement is not satisfied, because the probability that both are responsible for the two gunshot wounds is only one out of three.[45] Thus, the alternative liability policy implies that the two should not be held liable for the total harm.[46]

---

[43] The weak preponderance requirement implied by *Summers* was noted in Sindell v. Abbott Laboratories, 607 P.2d 924 (Cal. 1980), as a reason for refusing to apply the *Summers* doctrine to a case involving multiple potential tortfeasors, not all of them joined in the litigation, and lacking evidence linking any particular one of the joined defendants to the plaintiff's injury.

[44] The result suggested here is not inconsistent with the NESS causation test, since this is a case of overdetermined causation. However, the probabilistic basis for allocating damages is clearer under the policy of *Summers* than under the NESS (necessary element of a sufficient set) approach discussed previously in the notes of this chapter accompanying the analysis of the *Anderson-Kingston* doctrine.

[45] For the shooters example, the preponderance question is equivalent to asking for the probability that of the *n* candidates who appear in court as defendants (drawn from a population of N shooters, of which *m* actually fired the shots that hit the plaintiff), *k* of them are guilty.

[46] A different answer may be reached, in the case of divisible injuries, if the question is whether the two shooters can be held liable for the injury associated with only one of the gunshot wounds. The probability that any one of the defendants is responsible for one gunshot wound is two out of three,

Market Share Liability and Class Actions

Under market share liability, a defendant who produces a product that injures a consumer is held liable on the basis of his share of the market during the time period in which the consumer consumed the product.[47]

The foregoing discussion of the substantial factor test provides a partial justification for market share liability. However, it also suggests that the conditions under which the approach is justifiable under existing causation doctrine are narrow. To justify its application, the market share of each defendant must be a reasonably good approximation of its share of the harm suffered by the plaintiff (or plaintiffs).

This requires, at a minimum, that all of the defendants actually sold their products to consumers, in the same geographic market where the plaintiff purchased the product, and during the time period in which the plaintiff purchased the product. It also requires that all of the defendants are guilty of the same type of fault. In addition, it implies that the fault of each defendant is equally likely to harm the plaintiff.

In the merging fires scenario of *Anderson-Kingston*, the plaintiff's failure to join all of the potential defendants did not require the dismissal of his suit. However, the market share liability scenario is distinguishable from that of *Anderson-Kingston*.

If one defendant had only 2 percent of the market in the defective product within the relevant time period and relevant geographic area, then the probability that that defendant was responsible for the plaintiff's injury is no more than 2 percent. A 2 percent market share, in the absence of any other evidence connecting the defendant to the plaintiff, falls far short of indicating that the defendant was a sufficient cause. Moreover, unlike the shooting hypotheticals discussed previously, the plaintiff's harm cannot be divided, in the market share liability setting, into components of which some piece may be attributable to the conduct of a particular defendant.

Thus, one fundamental requirement of the substantial factor framework of *Anderson-Kingston* and *Summers* is not satisfied in the market share liability setting – that each defendant's conduct be a sufficient cause of the plaintiff's harm, or some substantial and identifiable component of the harm. Since the substantial factor requirement is not satisfied under market share liability, the other requirement of the substantial factor framework, weak preponderance, should be replaced by a stronger requirement. A market share liability lawsuit should not be allowed to proceed, under the policies of *Anderson-Kingston* and *Summers*, where the plaintiff has failed to join virtually all of the potentially responsible parties based on market shares.[48]

---

which satisfies the preponderance requirement. The policy suggested here would permit a court to hold both shooters jointly and severally liable, given divisible injuries, for only one of the gunshot wounds.

[47] Sindell v. Abbott Laboratories, 607 P.2d 924 (Cal. 1980).

[48] Ideally, the substantial percentage requirement should be translated into a specific probability threshold (e.g., 95 percent) required to say that the probability of the defendants (as a group) containing the responsible party or parties is above the threshold.

Sindell v. Abbott Laboratories,[49] the case that originated market share liability theory, holds that a *substantial percentage of the market* must be represented by the parties joined in the plaintiff's lawsuit. The percentage of the market joined by the plaintiff in *Sindell* was at least 90 percent.

If the market shares are not good approximations of each defendant's share of the total harm (e.g., because some defendants' products are less dangerous than others),[50] then it may be possible to adjust the allocation of liability based on market shares to arrive at a better approximation. This would be analogous to a case like *Summers* in which some subset of the injurers shoots twice while the other subset shoots only once, so that a simple per capita allocation of liability would be inappropriate. Such an adjustment, in a market share liability case, would require a great deal of information on each defendant's contribution to the total harm.

In a class action, in which a large pool of victims sues as a group, market shares could provide a reasonable approximation of each defendant's contribution to the aggregate harm. In the case of a single plaintiff, this is much less plausible, since the plaintiff could have obtained all of his total consumption of the product from a single defendant. The class action takes advantage of the law of large numbers to resolve attribution and apportionment issues with minimal error.

Still, there is an important sense in which the class action enhances the risk of error. In many cases, the most important issue is whether the defendant's negligence caused the plaintiff's harm. Put another way, even if there was only one injurer and one victim, sometimes there is no strong evidence linking the injurer's negligence with the plaintiff's harm. This issue is unrelated to the number of potential defendants. I have referred to these cases previously as cases of uncertain injury causation.

If injury causation is uncertain, the class action might maximize risk by failing to take advantage of the law of large numbers. The reason is that a trial is similar to one draw from an urn in which a slip of paper says either "liability" or "no liability." If ninety-nine of 100 slips of paper in the urn say "no liability," it is still possible for the class action trial to draw the one slip that says "liability," and once that occurs the process comes to an end. The way to minimize error in determining injury causation is to allow for several slips of paper to be drawn out of the urn and to read the paper trail. This suggests that where injury causation is contestable, as is true of many drug liability cases, class actions should be permitted only after courts have had experience with a sample of individual trials – bellwether trials – of a representative nature.

Another reason that the class action device can maximize risk in the uncertain injury causation scenario is that trials are a learning processes. Courts learn from

---

[49] 607 P.2d 924 (Cal. 1980).

[50] *See, e.g.,* Skipworth v. Lead Indus. Ass'n, 690 A.2d 169, 173 (Pa. 1997) (bioavailability of lead differs among different brands and vintages of lead paint); Daniel J. Grimm, *Accounting for Risk Disparity: An Alternative to Market Share Liability*, COLUM. BUS. L. REV. 549, 567–576 (2006).

preceding judgments. Sometimes new evidence is developed, or old evidence better understood. A class action conducted early in the process of litigation connected to a particular product prevents courts from taking advantage of lessons from earlier trials.

Of course, it is also possible, given these issues, to first certify a class, and then to conduct a random set of trials to gain an experience-based estimate of the defendant's liability.[51] But this alternative imposes an enormous threat to the defendant at the moment of certification. While it is true that the defendant's expected liability, after a set of sample trials, may turn out to be a fraction of the initial claim on behalf of the class, the initial certification can have damaging consequences. For example, if a court certifies a class seeking a trillion dollars in damages, a defendant corporation might come under enormous pressure from creditors to settle the class action immediately to remove the threat of financial catastrophe.[52] Such a settlement under duress would shed no light on the underlying causation question.

[51] *See* Robert J. Jackson, Jr., & David Rosenberg, *A New Model of Administrative Enforcement*, 93 Va. L. Rev. 1983 (2007) (arguing that class should be certified first, and then have random sampling of cases); Bruce Hay & David Rosenberg, *"Sweetheart" and "Blackmail" Settlements in Class Actions: Reality and Remedy*, 75 Notre Dame L. Rev. 1377, 1404–1407 (2000) (same).

[52] *See In re* Rhone-Poulenc Rorer Inc., 51 F.3d 1293, 1299 (7th Cir. 1995). Judge Posner focused on the risk aversion of the firm, and the consequent pressure to settle, as reasons to deny class certification.

13

Proximate Cause

While cause-in-fact doctrine addresses the question whether the accident would have happened even if the defendant had not breached his duty to take care, proximate cause doctrine fundamentally addresses the issue of foreseeability. In both areas, factual causation and proximate causation, the analysis begins with the plaintiff's identification of a specific breach theory – that is, some precaution that the defendant failed to take. After the breach theory is specified, factual causation analysis asks whether the accident would have happened even if the breach identified by the plaintiff had not occurred. In this sense, factual causation analysis works backward from the accident to the moment of the breach. In contrast, proximate causation analysis starts with identification of a specific breach and looks forward to determine whether the accident that occurred was foreseeable given the breach.

The language of foreseeability appears frequently in proximate causation cases, but the key concerns of the doctrine can be put into several categories. First, proximate cause doctrine is concerned with the predictability of the victim's injury, conditional on a particular instance of negligence. Second, proximate cause doctrine is concerned with the precision with which damages align with or target the most important source of the accident risk. Third, proximate cause doctrine attempts to avoid or reduce undesirable consequences of expansive and unpredictable tort liability. In short, proximate cause doctrine attempts to make tort liability operate on incentives a bit less like a mallet and more like a scalpel.

In carrying out this function, proximate cause doctrine appears to be shaped more by the general utilitarian policy reflected in the analysis of breach than by an effort to limit liability to the set of statistically predictable harms resulting from a given failure to take care. However, proximate cause analysis takes into consideration a broader set of consequences connected to holding the defendant liable than are considered in the breach phase of the negligence inquiry.

I. PROXIMATE CAUSE AS A LIMITATION ON THE SCOPE OF LIABILITY

Let's start with a comparison of factual and proximate causation doctrine in the context of the following *Lightning Strike Hypothetical*. Suppose an actor commits a negligent act that causes the victim to divert his path or delays the victim in his travel. For example, the actor, through his negligence, blocks the road, forcing the victim to wait for the path to clear. Five minutes after the victim returns to his journey, he is struck by a bolt of lightning. Under the factual causation test, the actor's negligence in blocking the road would be deemed a but-for cause of the victim's injury.

Every negligent act reshuffles life's deck of cards. Every injury that can be attributed to that reshuffling is caused, in the but-for sense, by the defendant's negligence. Given this, the but-for test implies a limitless set of potential claims for damages against the negligent actor.

The proximate causation requirement imposes a limit on this potentially unlimited set of claims. Under proximate causation analysis, any recovery for injury would have to result from an accident that was foreseeable given the defendant's negligence. Thus, in the *Lightning Strike Hypothetical*, the damages claim brought by the victim most likely would fail on proximate cause grounds because a negligently caused delay in travel would not lead one to predict that the delayed traveler would be the victim of a lightning strike.

On the other hand, there are other accidents that are easily foreseeable in light of the roadblock. For example, if the roadblock occurs behind a blind turn, a second traveler coming behind the delayed traveler might run into the delayed traveler because he discovered the roadblock too late to avoid a collision.[1] Indeed, one could say that the reason that the act causing the roadblock is negligent is because it creates the risk of just such an accident occurring.

Rational Estimation, Foreseeability, and Proximate Cause

The *Lightning Strike Hypothetical* – where the actor's negligence delays the victim in travel, resulting in the victim being struck by lightning – illustrates an important set of proximate cause cases. The key feature of the hypothetical is that the actor's negligence, although a but-for cause of the victim's injury, does not increase the rational estimate of the probability of the injury occurring.

The rational estimate of the probability of the injury occurring is the estimate that a reasonable person would offer after being provided with the information available to the actor charged with negligence. I use the term "rational estimate" because I assume that the objective, reasonable person will use the information available to him in a rational manner to estimate the likelihood of the injury occurring. In the

---

[1] *See, e.g.,* Marshall v. Nugent, 222 F.2d 604 (1st Cir. 1955).

Lightning Strike Hypothetical, the reasonable person would probably estimate the likelihood that a traveler would be hit by lightning (in the absence of any evidence of a brewing storm) as roughly zero. If told that the traveler would be delayed five minutes because of the negligence of another traveler, he would not update his estimate of the likelihood of a lightning strike to a number significantly greater than his original estimate of zero.

One famous case within this class of scenarios – that is, where knowledge of the actor's negligence does not increase the rational estimate of the probability of the injury – is *Berry v. The Borough of Sugar Notch*.[2] The Borough was negligent in its failure to maintain a large chestnut tree on public property. The plaintiff had been negligently speeding when the tree fell on his traction car (an electric trolleybus), injuring the plaintiff. The plaintiff sued the Borough for negligence, and the Borough argued that the plaintiff was guilty of contributory negligence in driving at an excessive speed. However, the plaintiff's negligence, although a but-for cause of his injury, did not increase the rational estimate of the probability of a tree falling on him. The court rejected the Borough's contributory negligence argument because it did not satisfy the proximate causation requirement.

Another case within this class is *Smithwick v. Hall & Upson Co.*,[3] previously discussed in Chapter 9. The plaintiff was working on a narrow platform attached to the defendant's icehouse when the injury occurred. Icehouses (which, as the name implies, store ice) were a mainstay of the business of supplying ice, an important industry before the wide dissemination of electric refrigerators. Blocks of ice were cut from the tops of frozen ponds and lakes and transported to be stored in icehouses.

The plaintiff had been warned to work on the west side of the platform, which had a railing along it. The east side did not have a railing; hence it would have been easy, given the nature of the business, for the plaintiff to slip and fall. The plaintiff, going against the warning, worked on the east side. Instead of slipping off, he was knocked off the platform when the icehouse wall buckled outward.

The defendant argued that the plaintiff was contributorily negligent because he worked on the east side of the platform, in spite of being warned not to do so. Although the plaintiff's contributory negligence was a but-for cause of his injury, it did not increase the rationally estimated likelihood of the accident. The court rejected the defendant's contributory negligence argument on proximate causation grounds.

These examples suggest the following proposition: *A necessary condition for finding proximate causation is that the actor's negligence increases the rationally estimated probability of the events leading to injury.*

Though seldom adverted to by courts, the policy supporting this proposition is easy to see. Courts have to impose some limits on hindsight-based attempts to

---

[2] 43 A. 240 (Pa. 1899).
[3] 21 A. 924 (Conn. 1890).

link a negligent act with a later injury, otherwise liability would be spread widely and indiscriminately, and sometimes opportunistically based on ability to pay the judgment. For example, in *Berry*, failure to apply the proximate cause test would have led to the plaintiff losing a valid negligence claim because of a spurious causal theory proposed by the defendant. Thus, the rational estimation requirement implicit in proximate cause analysis helps ensure that damages are allocated according to responsibility for harm.

Structure of Proximate Cause

The examples provided so far lay the foundation for a framework of proximate cause analysis, the primary components of which are as follows. First, a negligent act occurs. Second, between the negligent act and the injury, there are *intervening causal factors* that generate the injury. The third component is the injury itself:

Negligence → Intervening Causal Factors → Injury

Take the *Lightning Strike Hypothetical* as an illustration. The defendant's negligence causes the plaintiff to be delayed. The second stage involves the intervening causal factor – the lightning strike. The third stage of the causation chain is the injury itself. The plaintiff's negligence theory fails the proximate cause test because the delay does not increase the rational estimate of the likelihood of a lightning strike.

Obviously, an intervening causal factor may or may not satisfy the proximate causation requirement. In order for an intervening factor to satisfy the requirement, the defendant's negligence must increase the rationally estimated likelihood of the intervening factor occurring. However, as we will see, this is just a necessary condition, not a sufficient condition. In some cases courts find that the proximate causation requirement is not satisfied even though the defendant's negligence did increase the rationally estimated likelihood of the intervening factor contributing to the plaintiff's injury.

The proximate causation inquiry, as I noted at the start, is often described as a foreseeability analysis, and the term proximate cause is sometimes treated synonymously with foreseeability. A more precise statement of the foreseeability requirement, taking intervening factors into account, is that *a necessary condition for intervening factors to satisfy the proximate causation requirement is that they be foreseeable given the actor's negligence*. For the intervening factors to be foreseeable, the actor's negligence must increase their rationally estimated likelihood to a level that a court would consider significant. *Berry*, *Smithwick*, and the *Lightning Strike Hypothetical* fail the proximate cause requirement given this definition.

My approach so far has been to build up a framework for proximate cause analysis by discussing examples. My next example shows that *foreseeability of intervening factors is a necessary, but not a sufficient, condition for a court to find proximate causation.*

Foreseeability Necessary but Not Sufficient for Proximate Cause

Perhaps the best illustration of the disjunction between foreseeability and proximate cause analysis is a rule adopted at one time in several jurisdictions governing liability for a fire that communicates from one building to another. The source of the rule is <u>*Ryan v. New York Central Railroad Co.*</u>[4] The defendant negligently caused a fire in its woodshed. Sparks from the fire traveled more than 100 feet to light fire to the plaintiff's house, and the fire then spread to other houses. The court denied the plaintiff's claim for damages and adopted a rule that if a negligently caused fire burns a building, and the flames from the fire communicate to another building, the communication of the fire is *not* proximately caused by the defendant's negligence.

The *Ryan* rule should strike one as strange, if proximate causation has anything to do with foreseeability. If several houses are near each other, then nothing is more foreseeable than a fire in one house communicating to another. Put another way, informed that a house is on fire within a densely packed neighborhood of residences, one would rationally predict that the fire may communicate to an adjacent house. The *Ryan* rule on proximate cause defies common sense if viewed as a statement about foreseeability.

The court's rationale consisted of two parts: a legal argument employing proximate causation language, and a policy argument. The policy argument provides the strongest defense for the *Ryan* rule.

The <u>policy argument for limiting the liability</u> of the tortfeasor is that in the absence of such a limitation, the potential liability for negligently causing a fire in a crowded city would be nearly infinite. Facing a nearly infinite liability for negligently caused fires, city dwellers would be compelled to live elsewhere to cut insurance expenses and potential liability. Moreover, the incentive to purchase property insurance on the part of the more careful residents would be weak, given the high prices that insurance policies would have to charge, and this would drive the price of insurance even higher through the process of adverse selection (see Chapter 18).

A better arrangement would involve each city resident purchasing his own insurance policy – that is, an individual coverage mandate. By limiting the liability of the individual to his own loss, through shielding him from liability for fires communicated to other houses, the law would give individuals an incentive to purchase insurance and insurance companies an incentive to provide coverage at a reasonable price.

The *Ryan* court's legal argument on proximate causation runs as follows. The fire's communication from the initial structure to the second structure depends on several factors: The wind conditions have to be right, low humidity, the material of the receiving structure sufficiently quick to catch fire, the distance between the houses sufficiently short relative to the trajectory of the sparks. These factors

---

[4] 35 N.Y. 210 (1866).

were treated by the court as intervening causal influences. The court held that these intervening causal factors were too remote, as a matter of law, to satisfy the proximate cause requirement.

Ryan is an example of a court refusing to find proximate causation satisfied even though the intervening causal factors were very much foreseeable. Again, communication of a fire from one structure to another in an area of densely packed buildings is a highly foreseeable event. But *Ryan* holds that such communication does not satisfy the proximate cause test because it depends on intervening factors that are too remote as a matter of law.

Since the intervening factors at issue in *Ryan* are often obvious and foreseeable even to a child, the only conclusion that seems warranted is that the policy argument supporting *Ryan* is sensible even though the formal legal argument is questionable. The fundamental message is that a regime of liability for infinite losses would be inferior to a regime in which liability is limited.

Liability for virtually unlimited losses due to fire could have undesirable effects. First, because individuals would be judgment-proof with respect to the damages, it is not clear that unlimited liability would enhance the level of care beyond what would be exercised if liability were capped at the individual's loss. Second, unlimited liability would raise the cost of living in crowded cities to a prohibitive level, depressing economic activity.

The *Ryan* rule is not uniformly accepted today, and was not uniformly accepted even at the time when it was applied by many courts.[5] Still, it illustrates one important strand of proximate cause analysis in the common law. The lesson is that even though the intervening factors in a case may be foreseeable to the reasonable person, a court may nonetheless find that the proximate causation test is not satisfied because of the undesirable consequences of finding liability.

II. HUMAN INTERVENTION AND PROXIMATE CAUSE

The intervening factors that should be considered in proximate cause analysis fall under three main headings: *natural, structural, and human intervention*. The

---

[5] Smith v. London & S. W. R. Co., L.R. 6 C.P. 14 (1870) (a train caused a fire that damaged a building 200 yards away; one of the judges said "when it has been once determined that there is evidence of negligence, the person guilty of it is equally liable for its consequences whether he could have foreseen them or not"); Phillips v. Durham & Co. R. Co., 138 N.C. 12, 50 S.E. 462 (1905) (defendant railroad company liable for negligently caused fire that spread across the lands of several persons and reached the property of plaintiff; the court said that "the fact that the plaintiff's land did not adjoin the right of way does not per se absolve the defendant from liability, if in fact the defendant's negligence was the proximate cause of the damage to the plaintiff's property"). *Ryan* was followed in Pennsylvania R. Co. v. Kerr, 62 Pa. 353 (1870) (a fire spark emitted from a locomotive engine was transmitted to a house near the track and extended to another at a distance; the company was not liable for the loss, notwithstanding its negligence in allowing the sparks to escape) but was repudiated in Pennsylvania R. Co. v. Hope, 80 Pa. 373 (1876) (sparks from train engine fired a railroad tie, igniting grass adjoining and reaching plaintiff's fence and woodland about 600 feet from the railroad.).

intervening factors in these categories must be foreseeable for proximate causation to be found. The cases I will take up now involve human intervention.

The human intervention cases involve a simple pattern, consistent with the cases of natural intervening factors. The defendant commits a negligent act or omission. Between the defendant's negligence and the plaintiff's injury comes the intervening act of some person, either a third party or the plaintiff himself. The question before the court is whether the intervening act was foreseeable given the defendant's negligence. For example, the defendant might negligently leave a dangerous object, such as a knife, in the presence of children. Instead of a child getting hold of the knife and hurting himself, a deranged adult gets the knife and attacks other adults. A court would ask whether the deranged adult's intervention was foreseeable given the defendant's negligence.

In comparison to the natural intervention cases, foreseeability is a more difficult question in human intervention cases. Unlike intervention from natural forces, humans don't follow physical laws. If you drive a car full force into the side of a garage, physical laws might allow an observer to predict that the garage will collapse, injuring property or persons inside of it. But if you drive a car full force toward a person, the targeted person may evade the car and injure a passerby who would otherwise not have been at risk of injury given the direction and speed of the car.

Reflexive and Reasonable Conduct as Intervention

Because human intervention does not follow physical laws, some have argued it is never foreseeable.[6] Courts have not taken such an extreme position; they have treated human intervention that is reflexive, compulsive, or reasonable under the circumstances as a natural consequence of the actor's negligence. Recall that in *Scott v. Shepherd* (Chapter 3), a lighted squib tossed into a market stall by Shepherd was thrown across the stall by intervening actors, each trying to avoid the danger, before it exploded and put out Scott's eye. The actions of the intervening actors were not deemed to be independent trespasses by the court, because they were viewed as reflexive. The court did not use the language of proximate cause, but its decision, finding Shepherd liable for Scott's injury, implicitly holds that the conduct of the intervening actors was sufficiently foreseeable to satisfy the proximate cause requirement.

No physical laws could predict the sequence of events in *Scott v. Shepherd*. Still, the conduct of each intervening actor is predictable because it involved unthinking, instinctual, self-preserving action. It could be said to be part of the risk inherent in the defendant's initial trespass. Informed that a person threw a lighted squib into a crowded room, you could easily predict that it would explode and injure someone.

---

[6] City of Lincoln, 15 P. D. 15, 18 (1889) (Lindley, L.J.) ("[W]e have then to consider what is the meaning of the 'ordinary course of things.' Sir Walter Phillimore has asked us to exclude from it all human conduct.").

If you were then told that two intermediate actors tried to evade the danger by throwing the squib across the room, that additional information would not change your initial prediction that someone would be injured. The intervention observed in *Scott v. Shepherd* is well within the set of plausible causal pathways one would envision leading to the ultimate injury.

As a general rule, courts have held that the reflexive conduct, of the victim or of a third party, or conduct that is reasonable under emergency circumstances, does not sever the chain of proximate causation. The reason is that if a particular negligent or intentional act (throwing a lighted squib into a crowded room) leads to a prediction of a certain type of injury (loss of an eye), the intervention of reflexive conduct by a third party or by the victim generally will not change one's prediction with regard to the injury.

There are many examples where courts have held that the reflexive conduct of intervening third parties, or of the victim himself, satisfies the proximate cause requirement. Many of them involve leaping, ducking, diving, or swerving to avoid an injury.[7] For example, in *Tuttle v. Atlantic City Railroad Co.*,[8] one of the defendant's railroad cars flew off of the tracks during a flying drill and barreled across the street toward the plaintiff, Mrs. Tuttle. Afraid for her life, she ran and tripped, injuring her knee. The defendant argued that Mrs. Tuttle was guilty of contributory negligence because she would not have been injured if she had stayed in the spot where she had been when she first saw the runaway train. The court found that Mrs. Tuttle's effort to flee was a reasonable response to an imminent danger and therefore satisfied the proximate cause requirement.

The rule that intervening conduct viewed as reasonable under emergency circumstances does not sever the chain of causation also extends to rescue attempts. In *Wagner v. International Railway Co.*,[9] a Cardozo opinion, the plaintiff was injured in the course of trying to find the body of his cousin, who had fallen from the open doors of a crowded train as it began to pass over a bridge. The court held that the intervention of the plaintiff in conducting a reasonable, as opposed to reckless (see Chapter 9's discussion of rescue and contributory negligence), attempt to rescue did not sever the causal connection between the defendant's negligence (leaving the train door open) and the plaintiff's injury. In short, *Wagner* stands for the proposition that injury suffered by an individual in the course of a reasonable attempt to rescue a victim injured or threatened with injury as a result of the defendant's negligence will generally be regarded as a foreseeable result of, and therefore proximately caused by, the defendant's negligence.

That the plaintiff in *Wagner* had time to think about the rescue, and walked more than 400 feet before his injury, was rejected as a basis for refusing to find proximate

---

[7] Jones v. Boyce, 171 Eng. Rep. 540 (K.B. 1816); Stokes v. Saltonstall, 38 U.S. 181 (1839).

[8] 49 A. 450 (N.J. 1901).

[9] 133 N.E. 437 (N.Y. 1921).

causation. This feature seems to remove *Wagner* from the set of emergency cases, such as *Tuttle*, where courts have typically found that reasonable human intervention does not sever proximate causation. This reflects the general policy favoring rescuers, announced in *Eckert v. Long Island R.R.*,[10] which holds that rescuers may be found guilty of contributory negligence only if their conduct is reckless (Chapter 9). The policy of encouraging rescue leads in this case to a sheltering of the rescuer from the harsh result of a finding that his intervention severed the proximate causation nexus.

Inadvertent or Potentially Negligent Intervening Conduct

Outside of cases of intervening conduct that is reflexive or reasonable under emergency conditions, we can group intervening conduct into two other categories: (1) inadvertent or slightly negligent, and (2) negligent or intentional. In other words, the cases appear to divide along lines based on whether the intervening conduct was probably without fault (inadvertence or slight negligence) or whether it was culpable (intentional or clearly negligent).

The cases involving inadvertence or slight negligence follow the same pattern as the cases of reflexive intervention. Courts generally hold that *inadvertently careless intervention does not sever the causal connection.*[11] After all, if you dig a hole in the ground, in a place where people are likely to walk, you should foresee that a person

---

[10]   43 N.Y. 502 (1871).

[11]   Asher v. City of Independence, 163 S.W. 574 (Mo. App. 1913) (defendant strung electric wires along an alley and negligently failed to remove the danger caused by subsequent construction of a fire escape within a few inches of the wires; plaintiff burned by electric shock); Davidson v. Otter Tail Power Co., 185 N.W. 644 (Minn. 1921) (defendant, an electric power company, held liable when plaintiff came into contact with a live wire near the stairway of a switchhouse); Magay v. Claflin-Sumner Coal Co., 153 N.E. 534 (Mass. 1926) (unguarded coal hole in sidewalk); Hastings v. F. W. Woolworth Co., 250 N.W. 362 (Minn. 1933) (defendant store held liable when plaintiff fell after catching her heel in a hole while passing in an aisle); Eggen v. Hickman, 119 S.W.2d 633 (Ky. 1938) (prospective tenant injured when she stepped into hole in floor of building); Duteny v. Pennichuck Water Co., 146 A. 161 (N.H. 1929) (defendant water company liable for defective cover of hole containing meter, into which plaintiff fell); Landy v. Olson & Serley Sash & Donor Co., 214 N.W. 659 (Minn. 1927) (plaintiff fell into an unguarded elevator shaft suffering fatal injuries); Nelson v. William H. Ziegler Co., 251 N.W. 534 (Minn. 1933) (defendant liable for failing to guard electric coal conveyor); O'Neill v. City of Port Jervis, 171 N.E. 694 (N.Y. 1930) (defendant dug up sidewalk, forcing pedestrian into street); Mawson v. Eagle Harbor Transp. Co., 268 P. 595 (Wash. 1928) (transportation company furnished steep, unguarded gangplank descending from dock to ship, in which passengers were required to stoop; passenger lost balance and fell); Ryan v. Gordon L. Hayes, Inc., 22 A.D.2d 985 (N.Y. App. Div. 1964) (plaintiffs fell and suffered injuries when they were forced to go a defective portion of sidewalk to avoid ladder used in attaching sign to defendant's building); Judy v. Belk, 181 So.2d 694 (Fla. Dist. Ct. App. 1966) (defendant liable for not providing reasonably safe means of disembarking, plaintiff suffered injuries from falling into water while attempting to disembark, in the middle of the night, from defendant's houseboat, which had no gangplank and moved as far as two feet away from dock); McIntyre v. Holtman, 258 N.W. 832 (Minn. 1935) (defendant store failed to remove slippery substances remaining from oiling of floor the night before).

may inadvertently fall into the hole. Indeed, the main reason a court would find it negligent to leave a hole in the ground is the high risk that even a careful person will fall in. The same can be said of leaving dangerous objects, such as guns or knives, in the presence of children, who may inadvertently hurt themselves or others, or of leaving explosive material in a place where it can easily come into contact with something (a lit cigarette) that sets it off.

One paradox of proximate cause analysis – really, a paradox of safety – is that injury due to inadvertently careless intervention is more likely to occur, and therefore more foreseeable, in settings where the threat of danger is smallest. Take the case of a store with a hole in the floor large enough to catch the heel of a lady's shoe.[12] If all stores had such holes in their floors, people would stay constantly on the lookout for holes in the floor when they shopped. Any instance in which a heel was caught by a hole would lead immediately to an inference of negligence on the part of the victim, and a possible defense for the store based on contributory negligence or on proximate cause. But in settings where almost no stores have holes in their floors, no one expects to find a hole, and so it becomes highly foreseeable that any hole in the floor will result in an injury due to inadvertence.

Negligent and Intentional Intervening Conduct

The default position of courts has been that negligent or intentional human inter-vention severs the chain of causation between the defendant's negligence and the plaintiff's injury.[13] I will refer to this as the *human intervention principle*. There are recurring fact patterns in which courts have relied on the principle. One involves leaving keys in the ignition of a car. If you leave your keys in the ignition, it is foreseeable, one could argue, that a thief will jump in the car and driving hastily to get away will injure some innocent victim. But courts have for the most part rejected this view and adhered to the rule that the intervening conduct of the thief severs the chain of proximate causation between the defendant's negligence and the plaintiff's injury.[14]

---

[12] Hastings v. F. W. Woolworth Co., 250 N.W. 362 (Minn. 1933).

[13] For perhaps the clearest statement of this view, *see* Stone v. Boston & Albany R.R., 51 N.E. 1, 2 (Mass. 1898) (Allen, J.) ("The rule is very often stated that in law the proximate and not the remote cause is to be regarded; and in applying this rule it is sometimes said that the law will not look back from the injurious consequence beyond the last sufficient cause, and especially that where an intelligent and responsible human being has intervened between the original cause and the resulting damage, the law will not look beyond him."). For an account that suggests abstract principles, *see* H. L. A. HART & TONY HONORÉ, CAUSATION IN THE LAW 136–162 (Oxford Univ. Press 2d ed. 1985).

[14] Meihost v. Meihost, 139 N.W.2d 116 (Wis. 1966) (ordinance made it unlawful to leave a motor vehicle unattended on a public street without removing the ignition key, defendant not liable for damages caused by third party thief); Galbraith v. Levin, 81 N.E.2d 560 (Mass. 1948) (defendant not liable for injuries to pedestrian who was struck by car driven by thief, even if he violated law by allowing unregistered automobile to remain on public way with keys over sun visor); Richards v. Stanley, 271 P.2d 23 (Cal. 1954) (plaintiff struck by thief; defendant not liable for leaving automobile

If you dig a large hole in the ground, isn't it obvious that a wrongdoer may push someone into it? Yes, but many courts have held that the intervening conduct of the wrongdoer severs the chain of causation.[15] If you leave a window or door unlocked or open, isn't it obvious that a thief will break in? Yes, but the intervening conduct of the thief is, as a general matter, insufficiently foreseeable to satisfy the proximate cause requirement.[16]

Perhaps the most famous application of the human intervention principle is *Watson v. Kentucky & Indiana Bridge & Railroad Co.*[17] A tank car containing gasoline derailed as a result of the defendant railroad's negligence, causing gasoline to spill all over the streets in a heavily populated section of Louisville. A man named Duerr threw a lit match onto the gasoline, causing an explosion that severely injured the plaintiff and destroyed the plaintiff's house. The plaintiff sued the railroad for negligence. Duerr had been employed as a telegraph operator by the defendant railroad and had been discharged on the day of the accident. Witnesses provided testimony that Duerr intentionally set the gasoline on fire in retaliation for his discharge and that he had been indicted previously for arson. The court, remanding the case, held that if Duerr had intentionally thrown the match, then his intervening conduct severed the causal connection between the railroad's negligence and the plaintiff's injury; but if Duerr had inadvertently or negligently tossed the match, the causal connection was not severed.

Assuming Duerr's conduct was intentional, the foreseeability argument would appear to be strained. Would a rational person blow up a section of a city, putting himself and perhaps others close to him at risk, in retaliation for being fired from a job? Setting aside the human intervention principle used as a justification for the court's analysis, there is a good argument, based on inferring rational conduct,

---

unlocked and unattended with keys in ignition); Liberty Mut. Ins. Co. v. Kronenberg, 359 N.W.2d 180 (Wis. 1984) (defendant, cab driver, not liable for injuries to plaintiff in car accident with cab driven by thief); Lichter v. Fritsch, 252 N.W.2d 360 (Wis. 1977) (defendant not liable under Illinois statute for leaving motor vehicle unattended with keys in ignition, when a mental patient stole vehicle and caused accident).

[15] Milostan v. City of Chicago, 148 Ill. App. 540 (1909) (plaintiff could not recover from city for injuries when a boy willfully pushed him into an unguarded opening in cement sidewalk); Alexander v. Town of New Castle, 115 Ind. 51, 17 N.E. 200 (1888) (town not liable to plaintiff who fell into an unguarded excavation because someone seized plaintiff and threw him into the pit); Miller v. Bahmmuller, 108 N.Y.S. 924 (1908) (defendant not liable for keeping a cellarway open, since third person kicked plaintiff while he was sitting near the opening); Loftus v. Dehail, 65 P. 379 (Cal. 1901) (defendant not liable when plaintiff's brother pushed him into cellar); Camp v. Peel, 92 P.2d 428 (Cal. Ct. App. 1939) (defendant not liable when plaintiff, an eight-year-old girl, was struck in face and eyes by lime putty while playing with other children in construction site).

[16] Strong v. Granite Furniture Co., 77 Utah 292, 294 P. 303 (1930) (defendant not liable for leaving the window unfastened when removing furniture from plaintiff's house, which was subsequently damaged by burglar); Meihost v. Meihost, 139 N.W.2d 116 (Wis. 1966); Galbraith v. Levin, 81 N.E.2d 560 (Mass. 1948); Richards v. Stanley, 271 P.2d 23 (Cal. 1954); Liberty Mut. Ins. Co. v. Kronenberg, 359 N.W.2d 180 (Wis. 1984); Lichter v. Fritsch, 252 N.W.2d 360 (Wis. 1977).

[17] 126 S.W. 146 (Ky. 1910).

that Duerr's actions should not have been deemed foreseeable. Specifically, self-destructive conduct – that is, cutting off one's nose to spite the face – should not be regarded as foreseeable intervention. Unlike *Scott v. Shepherd*, where the intervention involved rational, self-protective conduct, the potentially self-destructive intervening conduct in *Watson* is not of the sort one would put within the set of plausible pathways leading to the plaintiff's injury.

The foregoing examples involve intentional torts by intervening third parties. The principle that human intervention severs the chain of causation has also been applied in cases involving intervening parties' negligent conduct.

In *Pittsburgh Reduction Co. v. Horton,*[18] the defendant, the predecessor corporation of Alcoa, negligently discarded a dynamite cap on its unenclosed grounds near a school. The cap was discovered by Charlie Copple, ten years old, who kept it and played with it for several days at home. His mother, married to a miner and presumably familiar with blasting caps, regularly picked up the cap for Charlie when he finished playing with it. After a week had passed, Charlie traded the cap to Jack Horton, thirteen years old. While Jack was picking dirt out of the cap with a match, the cap exploded, mangling Jack's hand. The court held that in spite of the mining company's negligence, the intervention of Charlie Copple's parents severed the causal connection between the mining company's negligence and the injury to Jack Horton.

In *McLaughlin v. Mine Safety Appliances Co.,*[19] a fire truck came to rescue a six-year-old girl who had almost drowned. A nurse who volunteered to help at the scene was given heat blocks by one of the firemen, with no instruction on how to use them safely. The nurse applied the heat blocks directly to the child's body, without wrapping them in a blanket or cloth as instructed on the containers for the blocks. The child suffered third degree burns from the blocks. The defendant, manufacturer of the blocks, was found negligent by the trial court for failing to provide a warning on each block, rather than only on the container. The fireman, who had been instructed in the proper use of the heat blocks by a representative of the manufacturer, was also negligent in handing activated blocks to the nurse without first wrapping them or instructing the nurse on how to use them. The appellate court overturned the trial court's finding of liability against the manufacturer, pointing to the intervening negligence of the fireman.

---

[18] 113 S.W. 647 (Ark. 1908). For a similar case, *see* Carter v. Towne, 103 Mass. 507, 507 (1807) ("A boy bought some gunpowder, and, in the absence of his parents, put it in a cupboard in his father's house with the knowledge of his aunt, who had charge of him and of the house while his parents were away; a week afterwards his mother gave him some of the powder and he fired it off with her knowledge; and some days later he took, with her knowledge, more of the powder out of the cupboard, fired it off and was injured by the explosion. Held, that the injury was not the direct or proximate, natural or probable, result of the sale of the powder, and the seller was therefore not liable to the child for the injury.").

[19] 181 N.E.2d 430 (N.Y. 1962).

The foregoing cases in which courts have held that <u>human intervention</u> severs <u>the causal connection</u> reveal a pattern in which the <u>defendant's negligence creates</u> <u>a risk of injury to someone</u>, and <u>human intervention brings about the injury.</u> The Pittsburgh Reduction Company negligently discarded blasting caps, exposing children to precisely the injury that befell Jack Horton.[20] The driver who leaves his keys in the car ignition exposes others to the risk of injury from a thief who speeds away to avoid capture.[21]

An alternative fact pattern in which courts have sometimes referred to the proposition that <u>human intervention severs causation</u> is where the <u>defendant's negligence</u> <u>does not expose the plaintiff to foreseeable</u> risk. Rather than looking to the human intervention proposition, these decisions can easily be explained by the fact that the defendant's negligence did not expose the plaintiff to any significant danger. Foreseeability of harm is a necessary condition for finding proximate causation. Thus, in any case in which harm to the plaintiff is not foreseeable given the defendant's negligence, a finding of proximate cause would be inappropriate, whether or not human intervention leads to the injury. One example within this set of "no foreseeability" cases is *Central of Georgia Railway Co. v. Price*.[22] The railroad negligently passed the plaintiff's desired stop. The railroad's conductor escorted her to a nearby hotel, where she stayed for the night. While in the hotel, the kerosene lamp in her room exploded and caught the mosquito netting over her bed on fire. The plaintiff burned her hands trying to put out the fire. The court referred to the intervention of the hotel staff in excusing the railroad's negligence, but the more persuasive justification for the court's decision (in favor of the defendant) is that the <u>defendant's negligence</u> <u>did not leave the plaintiff in a position of danger.</u>

It follows, then, that the best cases to examine for evidence that the human intervention principle really has influenced courts are those in which the defendant's negligence creates a substantial risk for someone, and the intervention brings the risk to fruition. That such cases exist (as discussed above), and that the decisions for defendants in such cases are often justified by pointing to human intervention, shows that the intervention principle has been accepted to some degree in the courts.

However, within the class of cases in which the defendant's negligence creates a risk brought to fruition through negligent or intentional intervention one can find many in which courts hold that human intervention does not sever the causal chain.

---

[20] Although *Horton* serves as one illustration of the human intervention proposition, it is a controversial one. Blasting could be treated as an abnormally dangerous activity, which would cast the risk of injury entirely on the actor responsible for the blasting. The mining cases in general present a muddled picture with respect to the human intervention proposition. *See* William L. Prosser, Handbook of the Law of Torts 288 (West Publishing Co. 4th ed. 1971).

[21] Meihost v. Meihost, 139 N.W.2d 116 (Wis. 1966); Galbraith v. Levin, 81 N.E.2d 560 (Mass. 1948); Richards v. Stanley, 271 P.2d 23 (Cal. 1954); Liberty Mut. Ins. Co. v. Kronenberg, 359 N.W.2d 180 (Wis. 1984); Lichter v. Fritsch, 252 N.W.2d 360 (Wis. 1977).

[22] 32 S.E. 77 (Ga. 1898).

A good number of these decisions rely on the simple notion of foreseeability: that the particular negligent or intentional intervention that occurred *should have been foreseen* by the defendant. For example, in *Lane v. Atlantic Works*,[23] the defendants left a truck with a heavy bar of iron in the back of it sitting open on the street. A twelve-year-old boy called the plaintiff and his friends over, from across the street, so that they could see him move the iron bar. They came close to the back of the truck, and as the boy moved the bar, it rolled out and onto the plaintiff's leg, severely injuring him. The court held the defendants liable on the ground that the intervention should have been foreseen.

However, the concept of foreseeability is inadequate to fully explain the cases that appear to reject the human intervention principle. Foreseeability, recall, is a necessary but not a sufficient condition for finding proximate causation. Put another way, there are cases in which the foreseeability requirement is satisfied, but courts still do not find proximate causation. The cases that eschew the human intervention proposition, finding proximate causation in spite of human intervention, suggest that foreseeability is required and additional factors are required too. The doctrine that has emerged from these cases can be described as *foreseeability plus*.

The cases rejecting the intervention principle appear to fall within a small number of fact patterns, depending on the nature of the intervention. *Specifically, courts find that negligent or intentional intervention does not sever the proximate cause nexus between the defendant's negligence and the plaintiff's harm when, in addition to the defendant's negligence exposing the plaintiff to a foreseeable risk of injury, (1) the intervention disables the plaintiff from protecting himself from injury, (2) the intervention enables the injurer to harm the plaintiff, (3) the plaintiff has relied on the defendant's care, or (4) the defendant has (or should have) knowledge of the high risk of injury facing the plaintiff and is in a position to control the risk.*

Let's start with the first category: *disabling the plaintiff from avoiding injury*. In *Brower v. New York Central & Hudson River Railroad Co.*,[24] the defendant railroad negligently ran into the plaintiff's horse-drawn wagon, killing the horse and destroying the wagon. The plaintiff survived but was unable, in a state of nervous shock, to prevent thieves from running off with the items in his wagon. The question was whether the railroad would be held liable for the value of the stolen property, in addition to the property destroyed by the collision. The evidence showed that the railroad had its own security employees present, guarding its own property, but the guards did nothing to protect the property of the plaintiff. The court held the railroad liable for the loss of the stolen property even though the loss was due to third-party intervention.

What distinguishes *Brower* from the previously discussed cases – where courts have adhered to the human intervention proposition – is that the defendant's negligence left the plaintiff in a position in which he was obviously vulnerable to thieves and

---

[23] 111 Mass. 136 (1872).
[24] 103 A. 166 (N.J. 1918).

at the same time disabled from protecting himself. The court justified its decision by saying that human intervention ordinarily severs the causal chain, but not when the intervention is foreseeable. This verbal formulation is both correct and at the same time inadequate to reconcile the outcomes in the cases. However, the factor of disablement does permit us to reconcile *Brower* with other cases of intervention and foreseeable risk in which courts have denied recovery.[25]

Hines v. Garrett[26] is another case suggesting that when the defendant's negligence puts the plaintiff in a position of foreseeable danger, and effectively disables the plaintiff from protecting herself, courts refuse to find the causal connection severed by human intervention. Because of negligence, the railroad dropped the nineteen-year-old plaintiff a mile past her stop at dusk, forcing her to walk home through an unsettled area. She was raped twice before making it home. The court held the defendant Hines (United States Director General of Railroads) liable in spite of criminal intervention. As in *Brower*, the railroad's negligence put the plaintiff in a position of foreseeable danger in which she was unable to protect herself.

Now, let's consider the second category of cases, in which *the defendant's negligence enables the injurer to harm his victims*. In *Lundgren v. Fultz*,[27] the police confiscated guns belonging to Fultz, who had been diagnosed a paranoid schizophrenic. Fultz, a doctoral student in theoretical physics, had talked to his psychiatrist about his desires to kill others. The psychiatrist later intervened on Fultz's behalf to get the guns returned to him, after which Fultz went into a restaurant and shot and killed a random victim, Ruth Lundgren. The court suggested that the killing was a foreseeable result of the psychiatrist's negligence and reversed a summary judgment in his favor. Most significantly, the psychiatrist's conduct amplified Fultz's danger to others.

Another case in the second category is *Kendall v. Gore Properties*.[28] The plaintiff's decedent was strangled to death with a towel by a man who had been hired to paint the interior of the decedent's apartment. The landlord, who knew that the decedent was a single young woman living alone, assigned the murderer to paint the apartment without investigating him or obtaining any references, and without any previous experience with him. The landlord gave the murderer a key and unrestricted access to the decedent's apartment, with freedom to go in and out without supervision. This is an obvious case in which the defendant's negligence enabled the intervening actor to harm the victim.

These two cases suggest the following proposition. *When the defendant by his negligence enables a third party to present a foreseeable risk of injury to others, the intentional intervening conduct of that third party will not sever the causal connection*

---

[25] One could also read *Brower* as a case where the court permitted recovery because the evidence suggested the defendant railroad did foresee the risk to the plaintiff, because the defendant had security guards present to protect its own property from thieves.

[26] 108 S.E. 690 (Va. 1921).

[27] 354 N.W.2d 25 (Minn. 1984).

[28] 236 F.2d 673 (D.C. Cir. 1956).

between the defendant's negligence and the injury to another inflicted by the third party.

The third category involves cases where the plaintiff has *relied on caretaking on the part of the defendant and therefore has disabled himself from taking care*. This is really equivalent to the first category (disabling); the only difference is that reliance causes the victim to disable himself instead of the defendant's negligence disabling him. One illustrative case is *Janof v. Newsom*.[29] The defendant employment agency had placed a maid to work in the plaintiff's home without checking whether the employee had a criminal record. The employee stole roughly $1,000 worth of jewelry. It was later discovered that the employee had a criminal record, one that involved working precisely this scam on unsuspecting housewives. The court reversed a lower court decision in favor of the employment agency. The proximate cause issue was not addressed directly in the court's opinion (largely because it involved a statutory breach for which the law on proximate cause was settled), but the decision implies that the court did not view the thief's intervention as severing the causal chain. The plaintiff's reliance on the employment agent led her to forgo any effort to check the employee's background. The employment agency's negligence effectively disabled the plaintiff, because of her own reliance, from avoiding the injury. Thus, *where the plaintiff relies on the defendant to take care to prevent an injury to the plaintiff that might be inflicted by a third party, and the plaintiff therefore fails to take care for her own safety, courts tend to find that proximate causation is satisfied in spite of the intentional intervention of the third party*.[30]

The fourth category of cases in which courts reject the human intervention proposition consists of settings where *the defendant has specific or superior knowledge of the high risk of injury facing the plaintiff and is in a position to control the risk*. In *Quigley v. Wilson Line of Massachusetts*,[31] the plaintiff was assaulted by two ruffians who had entered the defendant's cruise ship. Security guards (off-duty police officers) who had been hired by the defendant to maintain order grabbed the ruffians before the plaintiff was injured, took them to another location on the boat, and left them sitting unguarded on a bench. When the plaintiff walked into the same area, one of the ruffians punched him. Although the security guards probably could not have foreseen the initial assault, the second was highly predictable under the circumstances. The defendant was held liable.

In *Morse v. Homer's, Inc.*,[32] the plaintiff brought a diamond ring appraised at $2,000 to a store and requested that the store sell it for at least its appraised value, with the store taking as profit any excess above that value. The storekeepers displayed

---

[29] 53 F.2d 149 (D.C. Cir. 1931).

[30] A similar case to *Janof* is Wallinga v. Johnson, 131 N.W.2d 216 (Minn. 1964), where the plaintiff left jewelry to be kept in a hotel safe, but the safe was never locked. Thieves robbed the hotel and took the jewelry.

[31] 338 Mass. 125, 154 N.E.2d 77 (1958).

[32] 295 Mass. 606, 4 N.E.2d 625 (1936).

the ring in the store window on a shelf that could easily be reached from an opening behind it. Anyone walking by the window could see how to reach the ring. Moreover, the store had suffered previous instances of theft. Thieves walked in one day and took the ring. The court held that the theft was a foreseeable event.

In *Bullock v. Tamiami Trail Tours, Inc.*,[33] a married Jamaican couple that appeared to be interracial, though they were not, sat in the front seat of a bus as it passed through Florida, still under de facto racial segregation. A white passenger, assuming the couple to be interracial, violently assaulted them. The husband and wife were unaware of the severe racial discrimination in the southern United States in 1959. The bus driver was aware. Immediately before the incident the driver complained to a police officer, within earshot of the assailant, of the couple's presence in the front of his bus. The bus company was held liable for the assault.

In *Richards v. Stanley*,[34] the court held that the mere fact that the defendant left his keys in the car ignition did not provide a justification for holding him liable for injuries to an innocent victim caused by a carelessly driving car thief. In other words, the court adhered to the human intervention proposition. However, the court said that if the defendant had specific knowledge of the likelihood of a car theft in the location he parked, it might have concluded differently.

Lane v. Atlantic Works, a case I previously described as an illustration of the foreseeability language often used by courts, probably fits best within the category of cases in which the defendant has superior knowledge of a risk, relative to the plaintiff, and control over it. The defendants in *Lane* were in a considerably better position to foresee the risk, to anyone who meddled with the iron bar in their truck, than the boy who moved the bar and caused it to roll out onto the plaintiff's leg.

The lesson from these human intervention cases is that the proximate causation findings of courts are shaped by some consistent policies. The term foreseeability, standing alone, is inadequate to do all of the work in explaining the court decisions. A close look at the cases suggests that the human intervention principle is a default rule that courts discard when they observe negligence that greatly increases the risk of injury to someone in a setting in which the defendant should have been aware of the likely impact. The four exceptions examined here appear to cover most if not all of the circumstances in which these conditions are satisfied.

III. DIRECT CAUSATION

The previous parts of this chapter have dealt with cases in which some causal factor that can be characterized as human, natural, or structural intervenes between the defendant's negligence and the plaintiff's injury. Suppose, however, nothing

---

[33] 266 F. 326 (2nd Cir. 1959).
[34] 271 P.2d 23 (Cal. 1954).

intervenes. In other words, suppose the link between the defendant's negligence and the plaintiff injury looks like this:

Negligence → Injury.

Courts refer to cases in which nothing intervenes between the defendant's negligence and the plaintiff's injury as *direct causation* cases.

To mention this topic is to open a can of worms. One could argue that there is no such thing as direct causation. It would appear to be possible always to find some intervening causal factor.

Return, for example, to *Scott v. Shepherd*. There were intervening actors who threw the lighted squib around before it exploded and put out Scott's eye. Suppose, however, no actors intervened; the lighted squib left Shepherd's hand and exploded near Scott's eye in one unbroken chain of events. This would be a case of direct causation, but even here one could still argue that there were intervening causal factors. Once the lighted squib leaves Shepherd's hand, gravity begins to pull it to the ground. To overcome the gravitational pull, Shepherd would have to throw the lighted squib with sufficient force that its initial velocity allows it to overpower gravity, and at a launch angle that would permit it to travel a sufficient distance horizontally. There must also be sufficient oxygen in the environment for the fuse to burn. A powerful wind might blow the squib off its intended course. A wall or post or some other structure might be between Shepherd and Scott. Why should we not consider these factors (launch velocity, launch angle, wind, oxygen, structural barriers) as variables that may or may not meet the levels required to accomplish the injury to Scott? If we choose to view these factors in this way, then they become intervening causal factors, just as they were deemed in *Ryan* (burning buildings case). This view would imply that there is no such thing as a direct causation case.

Courts have not adopted such a broad view of intervening causation (and correspondingly narrow view of direct causation). There is a pattern in the cases, which runs roughly as follows. If the initial force or impact of the defendant's negligence is not deflected or modified by some intervening factor, then causation is direct. If, on the other hand, the initial force or impact of the defendant's negligence is deflected or modified by some intervening factor (natural, structural, or human), then it is not a direct causation case.

To illustrate, consider again the previous variation on *Scott v. Shepherd*, where the lighted squib goes directly from Shepherd's hand to Scott's eye. No actors intervene in this variation of the facts, so the causation is direct, and a court would therefore not treat such issues as launch angle and wind as variables to be examined in a foreseeability analysis. Now suppose there is human intervention, as in the real case, so that causation is not direct. Since causation is not direct, the launch angle, wind, and similar factors are relevant to a foreseeability analysis. Returning to the comparison with *Ryan*, recall that the connection between the defendant railroad's negligent fire and the burning of its own shed was direct, while the connection to the home burned by the sparks was indirect, because it resulted from a repercussion or deflection of the initial impact of the defendant's negligence (from the defendant's shed to the plaintiff's home). In examining the indirect or deflection phase, the doctrine on proximate cause authorizes courts to consider all of the relevant variables affecting the transmission of the injurious force.

Having said all this, the important question is whether it makes any difference to causation analysis if we label a case as direct, or if we treat it as indirect with potentially intervening factors. It does make a difference, and that is the lesson of *In re Polemis & Furness, Withy & Co.*[35]

In *Polemis*, the defendants chartered the plaintiff's ship. The charter contract said in clause 21 that the charterers were not liable to the ship owners for "[t]he act of God, the King's enemies, loss or damage from fires on board in hulk or craft, or on shore, arrest and/or restraint of princes, rulers, and people, collision, an act, neglect, or default whatsoever of pilot, master, or crew in the management or navigation of the ship."

The charterers used the ship to carry a cargo to Casablanca. The cargo contained benzene, a highly flammable liquid. While unloading the cargo at Casablanca, a heavy plank fell into the hold where the benzene was stored, causing an explosion that destroyed the ship.

The defendants argued that they should not be held liable because clause 21 operated as a waiver on the part of the owners, and, second, that the loss was too remote to be recovered in a negligence action. The court held that clause 21 did not operate as a waiver of the right to sue under the circumstances.

The interesting part of the case is the court's treatment of the remoteness issue. Saying that the loss is remote is equivalent to saying that the defendant's negligence is not a proximate cause of the plaintiff's loss.

The court discussed two approaches to determining proximate causation for unexpectedly large losses. One would hold the defendant liable for all losses resulting from the defendant's negligence, whether or not those losses were foreseeable. The other would deny the plaintiff's claim for damages, even when the defendant had acted negligently, when the loss was not considered foreseeable.

The court concluded that no foreseeability limitation should apply. More specifically, the court held that *whenever the plaintiff's loss is directly traceable to the defendant's negligence, proximate cause doctrine does not operate as a bar to or limitation on the plaintiff's claim for damages*.

The rule of *Polemis* holds the defendant liable for damages that are the *direct consequence* of the defendant's negligence, which means that there were no intervening causal factors contributing to the loss. If the loss follows directly in this sense, then the defendant must pay for it, even if it is orders of magnitude greater than the defendant would have expected.

[35] [1921] 3 K.B. 560.

The facts of the case fit within the rule. Dropping a plank into a ship will lead to some foreseeable loss, but one would expect only minor damage. For example, a wall may be dented, or paint knocked off. One does not foresee a plank falling into a ship causing an explosion that consumes the whole ship.

The *Polemis* doctrine can be viewed as a generalization of the rule that the injurer takes his victim as he finds him (Chapter 4). Recall that in *Vosburg v. Putney*,[36] the court said that there is no foreseeability limitation on damages caused by an intentional tort. If you slap someone in the face, and his skull fractures as a result, you will be held liable for the full amount of the harm ("eggshell skull" rule). *Polemis* shows that the rule generalizes to injuries caused by negligence. If you negligently injure a person, and the injury is much greater than would reasonably have been anticipated, you are liable for the full amount of the loss provided that it is directly traceable to your negligence.

Another perspective on *Polemis* can be gained by looking at its implications on intervention. The decision of the charterers to carry benzene could be characterized as an intervening act, though it occurred before their later act of negligence. But the intervention of carrying benzene merely affected the severity of the loss rather than the probability that a loss would occur. Thus, *Polemis* implies that intervention that increases the severity but not the probability of the plaintiff's loss will not justify a limitation of damages on proximate cause grounds. This is consistent with the rule that plaintiff conduct increasing the severity but not the probability of an accident does not constitute contributory negligence (Chapter 9).

One interesting feature of *Polemis* that appears not to have been discussed by commentators is that the charterers may have known from the start, before signing the charter contract, that they would carry benzene, while the owners may not have known. If so, the court's decision may have been based in part on the failure of the charterers to disclose that they would carry explosive material. If this is correct, then *Polemis* can be viewed as a close relative of *Hadley v. Baxendale*,[37] which limits contract damages to foreseeable losses. When a party contracting for access to the plaintiff's property (or person) is aware of an especially dangerous use that he intends, and refuses to disclose, courts following *Polemis* recognize a tort action for the entire loss when the evidence shows negligence and direct causation.

Polemis was overruled in England in a case known as *Wagon Mound No. 1*,[38] but then resuscitated partially in another case known as *Wagon Mound No. 2*.[39] The distinction between direct and indirect causation might suffice to distinguish *Polemis* from *Wagon Mound No. 1*, allowing the two cases to be reconciled under then-existing doctrine. In any event, Judge Henry Friendly, in *Petition of Kinsman*

---

[36] 50 N.W. 403 (Wis. 1891).
[37] 9 Exch. 341, 156 Eng. Rep. 145 (1854).
[38] Overseas Tankship (U.K.) Ltd. v. Morts Dock & Engineering Co., Ltd., [1961] A.C. 388.
[39] Overseas Tankship (U.K.) Ltd. v. The Miller Steamship Co., [1967] 1 A.C. 617.

Transit Co.,[40] a case decided after *Wagon Mound No. 1*, held that American law adheres to the distinction between direct and indirect causation.

IV. PROXIMATE CAUSE VERSUS DUTY ANALYSIS: POWER OF JUDGE RELATIVE TO JURY

Proximate cause is generally a question for the jury. The reason is that it is heavily bound up with questions of fact, which if disputed must be determined by the jury. Cardozo argued in an important case, *Palsgraf v. Long Island Railroad Co.*,[41] that a certain class of proximate cause problems should be analyzed as a matter of duty and is therefore within the remit of the judge.

In *Palsgraf*, a man carrying a package ran to catch a train. A railroad guard on the platform gave him a push to help him into the open doors of the train. When he was pushed, he dropped the package he was carrying and it fell onto the tracks. The package contained fireworks, though no one could tell from its appearance. It exploded, sending shockwaves through the station. The shockwaves caused a scale several feet away from the epicenter of the blast to tip over and fall on the plaintiff, Mrs. Palsgraf. She brought suit against the railroad on the theory that the guard was negligent in pushing the man carrying the explosives.

The case raises an obvious proximate cause issue. Should the railroad guard have foreseen the possibility of harm to Mrs. Palsgraf? Cardozo concluded that the railroad could not be held liable for the harm to Mrs. Palsgraf because she was an unforeseeable victim. More importantly, Cardozo held that *an individual does not have a duty to take care to avoid injuring an unforeseeable victim.*

Let's look at *Palsgraf* as a case of intervening causal factors. First, the railroad guard pushes the man carrying the package. The next step in the causation chain is the deflection phase where the man drops the package. The drop can be viewed as the first intervening factor – not unlike the first intervening actor to toss the lighted squib in *Scott v. Shepherd*. The next step in the causation chain is where the package explodes. The explosion may be considered the second intervening factor. The next step is the tipping of the scale caused by the shock waves from the explosion, the third intervening factor. The final step is the injury to Mrs. Palsgraf.

Ambiguities in laying out the causation chain are unavoidable and illustrate the difficulty in distinguishing direct causation cases from intervening causation cases. If the guard pushed the man who was running for the train, and the man fell from the train onto the tracks, suffering an injury worse than reasonably expected, it would be a case of direct causation, like *Polemis*. But if the guard pushed the man, and he dropped the package onto another passenger, then the case is no longer direct under this reasoning.

---

[40] 388 F.2d 308 (2d Cir. 1964).
[41] 162 N.E. 99 (N.Y. 1928).

In any event, however one chooses to identify intervening causes, it seems clear that *Palsgraf* has at least two or three intervening causal nodes. Given this, traditional proximate causation analysis requires consideration of the foreseeability of harm to Mrs. Palsgraf. A finding of foreseeability, recall, is a necessary condition for liability. The foreseeability question is often a judgment call based on the facts.

Given facts such as in *Palsgraf*, a judge might choose to give the case to the jury to make the call. Indeed, saying that proximate causation is a judgment call, because foreseeability is not entirely obvious given the facts, typically implies that it is a question for the jury (see Chapter 8). Still, the default position of submitting proximate cause questions to the jury is not necessarily followed in every instance, especially where courts have developed rules governing specific causation questions. A judge, given the facts of *Palsgraf*, could hold that the intervening conduct of the man who carried the explosives – intervening by carrying explosives onto the train – severs the chain of causation between the defendant's negligence and the plaintiff's harm. That is an established principle that the New York courts could have used to find that proximate causation was not satisfied in *Palsgraf*.[42]

Instead of relying on the human intervention principle, Cardozo held that the jury in *Palsgraf* should not have been given a chance to make the judgment call because the *victim* was not foreseeable. If the victim is not foreseeable, Cardozo reasoned, the defendant does not have a duty of care with respect to the victim. The question of proximate cause then is no longer a factual issue that presumptively goes to the jury, but a matter of law to be decided by the judge.[43]

In the end, *Palsgraf* does not amount to a significant change in the law on proximate cause. The outcome in the case could have been reached through a straightforward analysis under traditional causation doctrine. However, the decision does alter the balance of power between judge and jury; specifically it enhances the power of judges relative to juries. The "unforeseeable victim rule" of *Palsgraf* empowers the judge to decide the question of proximate cause without having to even consider submitting it to the jury.

The allocation of power between judge and jury has important practical implications, even when the substance of the law is unaffected. If a judge can decide the proximate cause question as a matter of law, then he can dismiss a case on the basis of the pleadings and spare defendants months or years of litigation before a case goes

---

[42] Indeed, one appellate judge did rely on the human intervention principle. *See* Palsgraf v. Long Island R.R., 222 A.D. 166, 168 (N.Y. App. Div. 1927) (Lazansky, P.J., dissenting) ("In my opinion, the negligence of defendant was not a proximate cause of the injuries to plaintiff. Between the negligence of defendant and the injuries there intervened the negligence of the passenger carrying the package containing an explosive. This was an independent, and not a concurring, act of negligence. The explosion was not reasonably probable as a result of defendant's act of negligence.").

[43] *See, e.g.,* Farwell v. Keaton, 240 N.W.2d 217 (Mich. 1976) (existence of a duty is ordinarily a question of law; however, where there are factual circumstances that give rise to a duty, the finder of fact must determine the existence or nonexistence of those circumstances).

to the jury. Cases should settle more readily since the outcome – in effect, the real law that applies on the ground – would be more predictable. But the negative side of this change is that juries would have less influence over the development of the law (see Chapter 2, discussion of *Lorenzo v. Wirth*), which means that the resulting negligence law may fail to reflect the customs and norms of ordinary people.

One modern illustration of the implications of *Palsgraf* is *Zokhrabov v. Jeung-Hee Park*.[44] The plaintiff Zokhrabov stood waiting for a train at a Chicago station. Hiroyuki Joho attempted to cross the train tracks, negligently failing to look out for the 70-mile-per-hour train barreling down on him. He was struck and instantly killed. His torso was catapulted forward and hit the plaintiff, 100 feet away from the collision, knocking her down, breaking her leg and wrist, and injuring her shoulder.

Zokhrabov sued Joho's estate on the theory that Joho was negligent in crossing before the train without looking, and that her injury was a foreseeable result of his negligence. The trial court, awarding summary judgment to the defendant, held that Zokhrabov was an unforeseeable victim, from the perspective of Joho, and thus Joho owed no duty of care to her. The appellate court, reversing the trial court and remanding the case, held that Zokhrabov was not an unforeseeable victim. The court explained that under the conditions of the accident, Joho could have foreseen that his body would be propelled by the collision into the crowd waiting for the train on the platform. The court did not say that Joho actually did foresee or should have foreseen the outcome. It held that under the conditions of the accident, one could not rule out that Zokhrabov (or someone else on the train platform) was a foreseeable victim from the perspective of Joho. Given this, Joho had a duty to take care for the safety of persons in the crowd on the platform. The court noted that the trial court, on remand, might find that although Joho had a duty to take care for the safety of persons such as Zokhrabov, his negligence was not a proximate cause of Zokhrabov's injuries because a reasonable person in Joho's position would not have foreseen the particular injury that occurred.

Zokhrabov shows that the issue in *Palsgraf* is very much alive, and still a matter of controversy in courts nearly a century after the decision. The trial court had taken advantage of the license given to it under *Palsgraf* to grant summary judgment for the defendant. The appellate court carved *Palsgraf* down to a narrow slice: If the defendant reasonably *could not* have foreseen that Zokhrabov *could be* a victim, then and only then did he not owe her a duty of care.

The appellate court's approach distinguishes *Zokhrabov* from *Palsgraf*, and indeed they appear to be different cases. It is highly unlikely that the railroad guard could have foreseen Mrs. Palsgraf as a victim of his negligence, no matter how carefully he thought through the possible outcomes of his actions. Joho, and most negligent victims of train collisions, probably do not actually foresee others who are struck by

[44] 963 N.E.2d 1035 (Ill. App. Ct. 2011).

their body parts as victims of their negligence, but that is simply because most who are negligent in this way don't think about such things. But someone who does think through the grisly implications of being hit by a fast-moving train near a crowded platform could easily foresee the danger to others in the *Zokhrabov* scenario.

V. EMOTIONAL INJURY: DAMAGES, DUTY, AND PROXIMATE CAUSE

In *Tuttle v. Atlantic City Railroad Co.*,[45] discussed previously in this chapter, the plaintiff was injured when she ran and fell while trying to avoid the defendant's run-away train. The sequence of events in *Tuttle* involved fright, followed by evasive action, followed by injury. The court held that the injury suffered by Mrs. Tuttle was foreseeable, and therefore proximately caused by the defendant's negligence, because her reaction to the run-away train was reasonable and entirely ordinary.

Suppose Mrs. Tuttle experienced fright and ran, but did not fall, and as a consequence of the emotional trauma later experienced a physical injury – for example, a miscarriage. Would she have been able to recover for the injuries associated with the emotional trauma? Courts at the time of *Tuttle* would have denied recovery based on the absence of any physical contact upon the plaintiff resulting from the defendant's negligence. The early position of courts, the *physical impact rule*, held that *the plaintiff could recover damages for injuries, both physical and emotional, resulting from negligently induced emotional trauma only if there had been some immediate physical impact.*[46] The impact could be slight, such as a dead mouse's hair touching the roof of the plaintiff's mouth,[47] but there had to be some impact for the plaintiff to recover.

The rule prohibiting damages for injuries resulting from negligently induced emotional trauma was often stated as a blanket limitation on recoverable damages and therefore could be viewed as a special rule in the law on damages, or in the law on duty, or in the law on proximate cause. However, the most persuasive legal argument given for the physical impact requirement pointed to the proximate causation rule.[48] Courts held that injury caused by emotional trauma, in the absence of any physical impact, was too remote as a matter of law to be recoverable in a negligence action.[49] The reason such injuries were deemed too remote was that permitting recovery would open the courts to frivolous and fraudulent claims.[50]

---

[45]　49 A. 450 (N. J. 1901).

[46]　Mitchell v. Rochester Railway, 45 N.E. 354 (N.Y. 1896); Spade v. Lynn & Boston RR, 47 N.E. 88 (Mass. 1897).

[47]　Kenney v. Wong Len, 128 A. 343 (N.H. 1925) (plaintiff discovered dead mouse in her mouth as she ate at the defendant's restaurant).

[48]　Mitchell v. Rochester Railway, 45 N.E. 354 (N.Y. 1896).

[49]　*Id.* at 355.

[50]　*Id.*

There is perhaps no clearer example of courts adopting a tort law rule because it avoids the administrative burdens associated with the alternatives. But administrative burden is not the only policy justification for the early common law rule severely limiting damages for negligently inflicted emotional harm. Compensating injuries caused by emotional harms introduces a risk of error that could distort incentives for precaution. If courts awarded such damages erroneously – that is, awarding damages in cases of feigned emotional trauma – then potential tortfeasors would find it difficult to compare the expected liability associated with alternative levels of precaution.[51] A high level of precaution might generate an unpredictable emotional injury just as easily as would a low level of precaution. The tort system's ability to provide incentives for reasonable care would be weakened.

The physical impact rule soon gave way to a *zone of danger* test.[52] Under the zone of danger rule, the plaintiff could recover if he was at risk of suffering an immediate physical injury as a result of the defendant's negligence.[53] Thus, if a run-away train hurtling toward the victim stopped just a few feet in front of him, he could recover for the physical and (depending on the jurisdiction) emotional injuries caused by his fright, even though there was no immediate physical impact. Most jurisdictions, however, require some physical manifestation of injury to recover under the zone of danger test.[54]

The final step in the evolution of negligence claims for injuries associated with emotional trauma is the bystander recovery rule of *Dillon v. Legg*.[55] Under the *bystander recovery rule* (or foreseeability rule), a person who suffers physical injury resulting from emotional trauma may be allowed to recover damages, depending on whether (1) the plaintiff was near the scene of the accident as contrasted with one who was a distance away from it, (2) the shock resulted from a direct emotional impact upon the plaintiff from the observance of the accident, as contrasted with

---

[51] Spade v. Lynn & Boston R.R., 168 Mass. 285, 47 N.E. 88 (1897).

[52] Dulieu v. White & Sons, [1901] 2 K.B. 669.

[53] As the Supreme Court noted in Metro-North Commuter R.R. Co. v. Buckley, 521 U.S. 424, 430–431 (1997), every case permitting recovery under the zone of danger rule has involved a risk of immediate physical harm to the plaintiff who sought recovery. The *Buckley* opinion cites the following: Keck v. Jackson, 593 P.2d 668 (Ariz. 1979) (car accident); Towns v. Anderson, 579 P.2d 1163 (Colo. 1978) (gas explosion); Robb v. Pa. R.R. Co., 210 A.2d 709 (Del. 1965) (train struck car); Rickey v. Chi. Transit Auth., 457 N.E.2d 1 (Ill. 1983) (clothing caught in escalator choked victim); Shuamber v. Henderson, 579 N. E.2d 452 (Ind. 1991) (car accident); Watson v. Dilts, 89 N.W. 1068 (Iowa 1902) (intruder assaulted plaintiff's husband); Stewart v. Ark. S. R.R. Co., 36 So. 676 (La. 1904) (train accident); Purcell v. St. Paul City Ry. Co., 50 N.W. 1034 (Minn. 1892) (near streetcar collision); Bovsun v. Sanperi, 461 N. E.2d 843 (N.Y. 1984) (car accident); Kimberly v. Howland, 55 S. E. 778 (N.C. 1906) (rock from blasting crashed through plaintiffs' residence); Simone v. Rhode Island Co., 66 A. 202 (R.I. 1907) (streetcar collision); Mack v. S. Bound R.R., 29 S.E. 905 (S.C. 1898) (train narrowly missed plaintiff); Gulf, Colo. & Santa Fe R.R. Co. v. Hayter, 54 S. W. 944 (Tex. 1900) (train collision); Pankopf v. Hinkley, 123 N.W. 625 (Wis. 1909) (automobile struck carriage); Garrett v. New Berlin, 362 N.W.2d 137 (Wis. 1985) (car accident).

[54] Consolidated Rail Corp. v. Gottshall, 512 U.S. 532, 544–545, 549 n.11 (1994).

[55] 441 P.2d 912 (Cal. 1968).

learning of the accident from others after its occurrence, and (3) plaintiff and victim were closely related.[56] Announcing and applying this rule for the first time in *Dillon*, the California Supreme Court permitted a mother to recover for the physical and emotional injuries resulting from the emotional trauma she suffered when her child was struck and killed by a negligent driver in her presence. The bystander recovery doctrine is now accepted in the majority of states.

It is important to distinguish between cases involving a mixture of physical and emotional injuries and cases involving only emotional injuries without any physical manifestation. Although courts have made it easier today, in comparison to the nineteenth century, for victims to recover damages for negligent infliction of emotional distress, most courts still do not permit victims to recover for emotional injuries in the absence of any physical impact resulting from the defendant's negligence, or physical injury resulting from the negligently induced emotional trauma.[57]

VI. ENHANCED RISK OF FUTURE INJURY

Close to the recovery of damages for negligently induced emotional trauma is the question whether a plaintiff who has been negligently exposed to some toxic substance can recover for the enhanced risk of future injury. Consider, for example, an individual who has been exposed to radioactive particles, or who has been pricked by a disease-infected needle. The victim might try to recover for the loss he anticipates from the future injury or for the costs of medical monitoring. As in the case of negligently induced emotional trauma, courts have been concerned with sorting genuine from frivolous complaints. Consequently, courts generally have held that plaintiffs cannot recover for the risk of future disease or injury, or for the costs of medical monitoring, in the absence of physical symptoms of the anticipated disease or injury.[58]

The policies that have kept courts from being generous to plaintiffs with claims of enhanced risk or of negligently induced emotional trauma are grounded in administrative concerns rather than the actual foreseeability of the plaintiffs' harms. In spite of this, proximate cause doctrine remains the primary vehicle through which courts justify refusals to award damages in these areas. This is nothing new, of course, because proximate cause doctrine has long provided a home for policies,

---

[56] *Id.* at 920.

[57] Jones v. CSX Transp., 287 F.3d 1341, 1347–1349 (2002); Consolidated Rail Corp. v. Gottshall, 512 U.S. 532, 549 n.11 (1994); John J. Kirchner, *The Four Faces of Tort Law: Liability for Emotional Harm*, 90 Marquette L. Rev. 789, 812 (2007).

[58] Metro-North Commuter R.R. Co. v. Buckley, 521 U.S. 424, 432–433 (1997). One case that may appear to be an exception to the symptom-manifestation requirement is Jackson v. Johns-Manville Sales Corp., 781 F.2d 394 (5th Cir. 1986), where the court upheld an award for the future risk of cancer to a plaintiff who had already contracted asbestosis, noting that the likelihood of contracting cancer was 50 percent. However, *Jackson* is arguably consistent with the symptom-manifestation rule, given the plaintiff's asbestosis diagnosis.

mostly sensible, that would otherwise be difficult to house within any other part of negligence law.

The courts have often used the language of foreseeability in the proximate cause cases, but policy plays by far the biggest role in reconciling these cases. The policies reflected in the court decisions are sometimes peculiar and case-specific, but more durable policies, based on recurrent fact patterns, tend to dominate proximate cause doctrine.

14

Duty to Rescue and Special Relationships

I. NO DUTY TO RESCUE RULE

An oft-repeated rule of tort law states that there is *no duty to rescue*. However, like many such rules, this one raises more questions than it answers. For example, what does it mean to rescue? Does the absence of a rescue duty imply that you never have a duty to take care to minimize the harm to someone that might be caused by a third person? If so, how can the rule be reconciled with the proximate cause cases of the previous chapter? The *no duty to rescue* rule begs the question of what it means to have a duty to rescue. The case law offers some answers to these questions and at the same time reveals policy-based exceptions to the no-duty rule.

Another way of looking at the rule was described in one American case as follows:

> There is a wide difference – a broad gulf – both in reason and in law, between causing and preventing an injury . . . The duty to do no wrong is a legal duty. The duty to protect against wrong is, generally speaking and excepting certain intimate relations in the nature of a trust, a moral obligation only, not recognized or enforced by law.[1]

The distinction between a duty not to do wrong and a duty to protect against wrong resembles the famous distinction between positive and negative liberties.[2] Negative liberty is freedom to take, or not to take, action that may harm others. Positive liberty is freedom to act, or not to act, in a way that enhances your own welfare or that of others. Tort law restrains negative liberty by holding you liable if you take actions that harm others. However, the rescue doctrine says, in effect, that tort law puts no restraints on positive liberty, because it does not compel you to act to enhance someone else's welfare.

---

[1] Buch v. Amory Mfg. Co., 44 A. 809, 811 (N.H. 1898).

[2] ISAIAH BERLIN, *Two Concepts of Liberty*, in FOUR ESSAYS ON LIBERTY 166–217 (Oxford Univ. Press 2d ed. 2002) (1969).

All of this sounds intuitive and reassuring, but these propositions do not take you far in the case law. To make sense of the rescue cases, we will have to look at examples and build up toward a general sense of the doctrine, examining one case after another.

Take the most straightforward example to start. The *no duty to rescue* rule applies to a potential rescuer who chances upon someone drowning in a lake. The potential rescuer is a great swimmer and capable of saving the victim without much effort. However, he chooses to watch the victim drown. Under the rule, the potential rescuer cannot be held liable for the victim's death.

The tale of the beachgoer who stands by and watches someone drown when he could easily carry out a rescue is a classic fictional illustration of the no-duty rule. It happens that there is at least one case of life imitating art, *Osterlind v. Hill.*[3] The defendant rented a canoe to the victim (plaintiff's decedent) and his friend, both recognizably intoxicated, who unsurprisingly tipped the canoe over once they had rowed out from shore. The victim held onto the canoe for a half-hour screaming for help. The defendant ignored the screams. The victim lost his grasp and drowned. The court held that the defendant was not liable because he did not have a duty of care to the victim.

II. NO DUTY RULE AND POLICY

Why is the *no duty to rescue* rule troubling? Setting aside the obvious moral issue, the rule is inconsistent with the theory of negligence, which requires a comparison of the foreseeable loss and the burden of avoiding it. An actor is negligent if he fails to take care when the foreseeable loss avoided by taking care is greater than the burden of taking care. The foreseeable loss from drowning is the value of the victim's life. The burden of avoiding that loss is the cost to the potential rescuer of going into the water to rescue the victim. If the potential rescuer is a capable swimmer, the cost of rescue is slight relative to the foreseeable loss to the victim. It follows that the reasonable person test (Hand Formula, Chapter 6) would imply that the potential rescuer is negligent if he fails to rescue.

Why don't courts hold potential rescuers liable when they fail to rescue? Because before a court can hold an actor liable for failing to rescue a victim, the court must first find that the actor had a duty to the victim. In the absence of such a duty, a court would not have a legal basis for engaging in the balancing exercise required by the reasonable person test.

Since it is obvious that a refusal to rescue is undesirable on utilitarian grounds in the scenario under consideration, why don't courts just impose a duty to rescue? Is there a policy justification for the *no duty to rescue* rule?

[3] 160 N.E. 301 (Mass. 1928).

The policy justifications for tort law rules fall into two general categories: moral and utilitarian. So far as I am aware, no one has offered a moral justification for the no-duty rule. Indeed, morality-centered theorists have long criticized the rule.[4]

The utilitarian school has offered justifications for the no-duty rule. The best known justification was offered by William Landes and Richard Posner.[5] According to Landes and Posner, imposing a duty to rescue would have adverse incentive effects, because it would discourage potential rescuers from putting themselves in positions where they may have to carry out a rescue.

Recall, from Chapter 2, that tort law's impact on behavior can be examined in terms of *care effects* and *activity effects*. Tort law affects how much care we take when we engage in an activity, like driving. Tort law also affects our decision to engage in the activity at all, or how much to engage in the activity. Thus, tort law gives actors incentives to drive with care as well as incentives to drive less frequently.

Landes and Posner argue that imposing a duty to rescue would increase the incentive for a potential rescuer to save someone. In this sense, a duty to rescue would lead potential rescuers to take greater care, of a sort, by giving them a financial incentive to rescue. On the other hand, a duty to rescue would make it more burdensome to be in a position where you might be called on to carry out a rescue, because a failure to rescue could result in liability. Potential rescuers might decide, therefore, not to go to the beach; or if they go to the beach, they might choose to sit far from where they may be implored to carry out a rescue, or with headphones turned up too loud to hear anyone calling for help. Thus, a duty to rescue would enhance the incentive to conduct a rescue (care effect), but might reduce the incentive to be in a place where a rescue could be conducted (activity effect). Since the two effects are offsetting, it is impossible to say a priori whether the imposition of a legal duty to rescue would enhance society's welfare.

An alternative utilitarian defense for the no-duty rule draws on the policies justifying the strict liability doctrine of *Rylands v. Fletcher* (Chapter 5).[6] In *Rylands*, the court explained that the negligence rule applies to accidents resulting from activities that impose reciprocal risks on one another, while strict liability applies to accidents resulting from activities that externalize to neighbors a disproportionate risk in comparison to other activities. Interestingly, the framework of *Rylands* implies that there

---

4   *See, e.g.*, James Barr Ames, Law and Morals, 22 HARV. L. REV. 97 (1908); Ernest J. Weinrib, *The Case for a Duty to Rescue*, 90 YALE L. J. 247 (1980).

5   William M. Landes & Richard A. Posner, *Salvors, Finders, Good Samaritans, and Other Rescuers: An Economic Study of Law and Altruism*, 7 J. LEGAL STUD. 83 (1978). *See also* Saul Levmore, *Waiting for Rescue: An Essay on the Evolution and Incentive Structure of the Law of Affirmative Obligations*, 72 VA. L. REV. 879 (1986); Paul H. Rubin, *Costs and Benefits of a Duty to Rescue*, 6 INT'L REV. L. & ECON. 273 (1986); Donald Wittman, *Liability for Harm or Restitution for Benefit?*, 13 J. LEGAL STUD. 57 (1984). On empirical evidence, *see* David A. Hyman, *Rescue without Law: An Empirical Perspective on the Duty to Rescue*, 84 TEX. L. REV. 653 (2006).

6   Keith N. Hylton, *Duty in Tort Law: An Economic Approach*, 75 FORDHAM L. REV. 1501 (2006).

should be immunity from liability when a person's activity imposes virtually no risk on anyone or is not the source of the risk facing the victim.

In general, human activity is desirable, as Holmes noted in his critique of absolute liability.[7] Put another way, activity tends to have beneficial externalities. For example, people who start businesses provide employment for others, which has a multiplier effect on economic activity. The same can be said of purely social endeavors. It follows that the law has no interest in suppressing activity as a general matter, and in fact, the law should seek to encourage activity beneficial to society.

Starting from this premise, a duty to take care should be imposed only when one engages in an activity that imposes risks on others. Even if an activity is beneficial to society overall, such as providing railroad service, it may still impose risks of injury on some members of society. A duty to take care provides incentives for actors who engage in socially beneficial activities that nevertheless impose risks on members of society to do so with reasonable care.

If, however, a person engages in an activity that imposes no risk on anyone, then it would seem consistent with the policy of *Rylands* for the law to relieve that person of a general duty of care. For example, the activity of walking through a park imposes no risk on anyone, in most cases, while it may provide a benefit, perhaps in the modest sense of making the park an attractive place for people to visit to see others whom they know or would hope to meet. Given this, the law should encourage, or at least not discourage, the park walker's activity. One way for the law to encourage the park walker is to relieve him of a general duty of care to rescue others in the park. In this way, the law avoids hanging a sword of Damocles, in the form of liability for failing to rescue, over the head of the park walker. Under this reasoning if A is at risk of injury because of the actions of B, or because of A's own actions, then C, who imposes no risk on anyone, should not have a legal duty to rescue A.

I have so far considered the simplest scenarios – the park walker or the beachgoer implored to rescue someone – in which the *no duty to rescue* rule applies. The rule also applies, clearly, to any case in which you do not owe a duty to protect a potential victim from harm. For example, the land occupier has no duty to warn or protect a trespasser against a hazard on the land of which the land occupier is aware. The absence of a duty of care toward the trespasser implies the absence of a duty to rescue the trespasser, since in many cases a duty of care and a duty to rescue will mean the same thing practically. Suppose, for example, there is a patch of quicksand on the property, and the land occupier sees the trespasser heading directly for it. The occupier does not have a duty to shout a warning to the trespasser.

The no-duty rule also applies in the scenario where a doctor is summoned by a sick person, in the absence of a preexisting contract or physician-patient relationship, to

---

[7] OLIVER WENDELL HOLMES, JR., THE COMMON LAW 95 (Little, Brown & Co. 1881) ("A man need not, it is true, do this or that act, – the term act implies a choice, – but he must act somehow. Furthermore, the public generally profits by individual activity.").

render medical care.[8] The doctor has a duty to act with reasonable care if he chooses to provide medical care to a person.[9] However, the doctor has no general common law duty to provide medical care.[10]

III. NO DUTY TO RESCUE EXCEPTIONS

Although there is no general duty to rescue, there are exceptions. In each of the exceptions, the factual conditions differ substantially from the classical no-duty scenario exemplified by the park walker and the beachgoer hypotheticals discussed above.

The exceptions to the no-duty rule are often presented in a case-by-case fashion, making it difficult to see patterns. Presenting case-by-case exceptions is a sensible approach to teaching law, because the common law is always evolving. Still, it is helpful to try to identify patterns in the case law, when they appear, to extract new lessons and to better predict outcomes of future disputes.

There is a pattern in the exceptions to the *no duty to rescue* rule. It follows the pattern of exceptions to the rule treating human intervention as a superseding cause, studied in the previous chapter ("foreseeability plus" doctrine). The four categories in which exceptions to the no-duty rule appear are (1) when the defendant's conduct introduced a substantial and foreseeable risk of harm to the plaintiff (enabling harm); (2) when the defendant's conduct disabled the plaintiff from avoiding a foreseeable danger or others from helping the plaintiff (disabling avoidance of harm); (3) when the plaintiff relied on the defendant's care to avoid harm (reliance); and (4) when the defendant knew (or should have known) of the specific danger facing the plaintiff, of which the plaintiff did not know, and was at the same time involved in the management or control of that danger (superior information and control).

Enabling Harm

Let's start with the first exception: *enabling harm*. In these cases, the defendant is held liable for failing to safeguard or to rescue a foreseeable victim after the defendant's conduct, whether tortious or innocent, creates a dangerous condition. For example, in *Montgomery v. National Convoy & Trucking Co.*,[11] the defendants' trucks stalled, without negligence on their part, on an icy highway, blocking the road. The trucks were sitting at the bottom of a hill, so that other drivers coming over the hill could

---

[8] *See, e.g.*, Hurley v. Eddingfield, 59 N.E. 1058 (Ind. 1901) (doctor not liable for refusal to aid sick person, even if he knew that he was the only doctor available and the condition of the person was serious).

[9] Owl Drug Co. v. Crandall, 80 P.2d 952, 953 (Ariz. 1938); Russell v. City of Columbia, 406 S.E.2d 338, 339 (S.C. 1991); Robinson v. Mount Logan Clinic LLC., 182 P.3d 333, 336 (Utah 2008).

[10] Gammill v. U.S., 727 F.2d 950, 954 (10th Cir. 1984); Hurley v. Eddingfield, 59 N.E. 1058 (Ind. 1901); Robinson v. Mount Logan Clinic LLC., 182 P.3d 333, 336 (Utah 2008).

[11] 195 S.E. 247 (S.C. 1937).

not see the trucks until they had started to descend over the ice. The plaintiffs saw the trucks too late to stop and collided with them. The court found the defendants negligent because they had ample time to set up a warning signal at the top of the hill, where it could be observed by drivers in time to avoid a collision.

There are other cases falling under the enabling-harm exception. In *Chandler v. Forsyth Royal Crown Bottling Co.*,[12] the plaintiff's automobile ran off the road after running into broken bottles and debris accidentally littered by the defendant. In *Newton v. Ellis*,[13] the defendant dug a hole at night and left it uncovered and without any warning. In *Hardy v. Brooks*,[14] the first defendant accidentally struck and killed a 900-pound cow while approaching the crest of a hill in his car. The cow's body remained in the road. The second defendant passed in the opposite direction at an excessive speed with bright headlights on. The plaintiff, blinded by the headlights, struck the cow's body, which lifted his car up and into the second defendant's car. In each of these cases, the court held that *the defendant's creation of a dangerous condition generated a duty to take reasonable care to safeguard potential victims from foreseeable harm resulting from the condition.*[15]

The dangerous condition might be created by the injurer's impact with the victim. Suppose, for example, the injurer runs into the victim with his car and leaves him in a state in which he is obviously vulnerable to additional harm. Some courts have imposed a duty in such cases for the injurer to take reasonable measures to aid the victim. In *Summers v. Dominguez*,[16] the plaintiff, walking along the highway, was struck and severely injured by a truck driven by the defendant. The defendant called out to the victim, but drove away after hearing no response. The court held that an additional basis for holding the defendant liable, in addition to negligence, was his failure to take reasonable steps to aid and protect the plaintiff after becoming aware that the plaintiff was in a helpless condition as a result of the defendant's misconduct.

Disabling Avoidance of Harm

The second category of exceptions to the *no duty to rescue* rule consists of conduct *disabling avoidance of harm*. In these cases, the injurer's conduct prevents the victim from avoiding harm or prevents others from coming to the victim's aid. For example,

---

[12] 125 S.E.2d 584 (N.C. 1962).
[13] 119 Eng. Rep. 424 (K.B. 1855).
[14] 118 S.E.2d 492 (Ga. Ct. App. 1961).
[15] The reader may wonder how the first defendant in *Hardy* could have removed a 900-pound cow from the road. However, the *Hardy* opinion is restricted to the duty question and notes that it is a question for the jury whether the first defendant breached his duty of care to the plaintiff. In other words, the court recognized that a jury could find that the first defendant was not negligent in failing to remove the cow or to set up a warning.
[16] 84 P.2d 237 (Cal. App. 1938).

in *Zelenko v. Gimbel Bros.*,[17] the plaintiff's decedent became ill in the defendant's department store. The defendant sequestered the plaintiff's decedent in an infirmary within the store, but instead of providing medical care left her alone without medical attention for six hours. The court noted that the defendant could have left the victim alone in the store rather than sequestering her, without violating any legal duty to provide care. But the defendant's intervention harmed the victim by removing her from the possible aid of others and at the same time not providing aid to the victim.

A special subcategory within the *disabling avoidance of harm* category consists of cases where a person attempts to help another in need of aid but terminates his efforts at a time, or in a place, where the other is at even greater risk of harm than he would have been if the person had never intervened. In these cases, the defendant did not create a dangerous condition, but made the plaintiff's position worse by terminating efforts to aid or performing such efforts in a grossly negligent manner.

For example, in *Black v. New York, New Haven & Hartford Railroad Co.*,[18] the plaintiff was an intoxicated passenger on the defendant's train. Two railroad employees helped the plaintiff off of the train, walked him halfway up a flight of stairs, and left him there, tottering. The plaintiff fell backward down the stairs, rolling head over feet to the platform.

If there was a dangerous condition in *Black*, it was created by the plaintiff's intoxicated state, which was not the railroad's fault. But the railroad employees' negligent termination of their efforts to aid the plaintiff before bringing him to a position of safety made it impossible for the plaintiff to avoid injury – say, by just sitting on a bench until he had become sober enough to walk on his own – or for others to help him.

The difference between "enabling harm" and "disabling avoidance of harm" is not great. Indeed, one could lump all of the disabling cases under the enabling category. One could argue, for example, that *Black* is a case in which the defendant created a dangerous condition by taking the plaintiff halfway up a flight of stairs when he was too intoxicated to walk. But the crucial distinction between these sets of cases is that the disabling cases involve conduct by the defendant that did not create a dangerous condition, but rendered the plaintiff more vulnerable to some dangerous condition that already existed when the defendant arrived on the scene. In other words, the disabling cases involve defendants who took the plaintiff away from a position of relative safety.[19] In contrast, the enabling cases involve defendants who introduced a serious risk of harm to the plaintiff.

---

[17] 287 N.Y.S. 134 (N.Y. Sup. Ct. 1935).

[18] 79 N.E. 797 (Mass. 1907).

[19] In *Black* and in *Zelenko*, the rescuer discontinues aid a point at which the victim is in foreseeable danger – hence, the duty to continue giving aid to the victim. An alternative scenario involves the rescuer negligently injuring the victim during the rescue attempt. In this scenario, the basis for liability would be a failure to take reasonable care that leads to a foreseeable injury. If injuring the victim is necessary to carry out the rescue, the rescuer has defenses based on reasonableness and causation.

Reliance

The third category of exceptions to the *no duty to rescue* rule consists of *reliance* cases, where the victim has relied on the injurer to take care to avoid some foreseeable injury to the victim. In *Erie Railroad Co. v. Stewart*,[20] the plaintiff was struck by a train at a crossing where the defendant had typically posted a watchman to warn travelers of oncoming trains. On the occasion of the accident, the defendant's watchman was either in his shanty or just outside of it, but not in a position to signal a warning to drivers. The plaintiffs, accustomed to the watchman's signal, thought it safe to proceed across the tracks. The court noted that the defendant railroad did not have a duty to employ the watchman in the first place. But after employing the watchman at the crossing, and thereby training drivers to rely on the watchman's signal, it was unreasonable for the railroad not to provide the watchman without notice to drivers.

The plaintiff's reliance in *Erie* was induced by the defendant's practice. Reliance can also be induced by a promise to take care for the plaintiff's safety. In *Marsalis v. LaSalle*,[21] the defendants promised to keep their cat indoors under observation for two weeks, to determine whether the cat was rabid, after it had scratched the plaintiff while she was shopping in the defendants' grocery store. Four or five days after the incident, the defendants allowed the cat to escape, and its whereabouts were unknown until it returned in good health a month later. In the meantime, the plaintiff underwent a costly and painful vaccination for rabies, for which the defendants were held liable. Since the cat had shown no vicious tendency before, the defendants would not have been held liable for the scratch alone, if that were all that had happened. After the scratch, the defendants may or may not have had a duty to keep the cat under observation, depending on their own awareness of the risk of rabies transmission. But having promised to keep the cat under observation to determine whether it was rabid, a duty arose to take reasonable care to follow through on the promise in light of the plaintiff's reliance on it.

The reliance-based duty requires reliance that is reasonable under the circumstances.[22] In *Heard v. City of New York*,[23] the plaintiff was severely injured when he dove off a jetty into shallow water. He had been ordered by a lifeguard to leave the jetty, but refused, pleading for one more dive. The lifeguard repeated his order, but relented after the plaintiff's continued pleading. The court rejected the

---

[20] 40 F.2d 855 (1930).

[21] 94 So.2d 120 (La. App. 1957).

[22] Light v. NIPSCO Indus., Inc., 747 N.E.2d 73, 76 (Ind. Ct. App. 2001) ("[W]hile a gratuitous promise without more will not impose a duty upon which tort liability may be predicated, when that promise is accompanied by reliance on the part of the promisee, and the reliance was reasonable under the circumstances, a legal duty may be found."); Martin v. Twin Falls School District #411, 59 P.3d 317 (Idaho 2002) (providing crossing guards at some crossings does not imply a duty to provide them at other crossings).

[23] 623 N.E.2d 541 (N.Y. 1993).

argument that the lifeguard's reluctant assent made it reasonable for the plaintiff to view the assent as an implicit assurance of safety.

Some courts have held that *the reliance-based duty will not extend to an indefinite number of potential victims who might claim a reliance interest based on a promise made by the defendant to a third party* – such as the promise of a waterworks utility to a municipal corporation, or an electric power utility to the owner of an apartment building. Cardozo limited the reliance-based duty in this manner in <u>Moch Co. v. Rensselaer Water Co.</u>[24] The plaintiff sued the waterworks company, which had a contract to supply water to the city of Rensselaer, for negligently failing to provide sufficient water to put out a fire that destroyed the plaintiff's warehouse. Cardozo held that the city residents, who were third-party beneficiaries of the contract between the waterworks company and the city, were not within the zone of duty created by the company's contract with the city. This is essentially <u>a proximate cause limitation</u> on the scope of liability, similar to that in *Ryan v. New York Central Railroad Co.* (burning buildings case, Chapter 13).[25] As in *Ryan*, the court in *Moch* was concerned that liability to the plaintiff (and similar third-party beneficiaries) would generate a disproportionate burden on the defendant.[26]

Superior Knowledge and Control of Risk, and Special Relationships

The fourth category of exceptions to the *no duty to rescue* rule involves potential injurers who have specific knowledge of the risk facing the potential victim, when the potential victim does not, and who are also involved in the management of that risk. The mere <u>fact that the injurer</u> knows (or should know) about a specific risk facing the victim is <u>insufficient</u> to impose a duty to rescue. If you are aware that a stranger who walks by you is heading in the direction of a tiger, you do not have a duty under the common law to warn the stranger. But the courts have taken a different view when you play a role in the management or control of the risk.

The principle of duty based on superior knowledge and control of risk appears to have been developed first in the common carrier cases. Common carriers and innkeepers traditionally have been held to a standard of utmost care.[27]

Chief Justice Shaw, in his *Farwell* opinion (Chapter 8), justified the utmost care standard on the basis of the trust that the customer necessarily places in the common

---

[24] 159 N.E. 896 (N.Y. 1928).

[25] 35 N.Y. 210 (1866).

[26] One of the functions of proximate cause doctrine is to limit the scope of responsibility to target or channel accident losses toward the actors who can most efficiently control the risk of harm. The expansive liability asserted by the plaintiff in *Moch* would have undercut incentives for city residents to purchase fire insurance and take steps to minimize the risk of fire damage; at the same time it would have made the cost of water supply to the city, passed on to residents through taxes or fees, prohibitively expensive for many residents. The likely result would have been an adverse selection spiral in which only the residents most likely to experience fires would find it advantageous to pay for the hydrant service. On adverse selection, *see* Chapter 18.

[27] *See, e.g.,* WILLIAM L. PROSSER, HANDBOOK OF THE LAW OF TORTS 180–181 (4th ed. 1971).

carrier (or the innkeeper),[28] because of the great informational disparity between them. The customer typically cannot predict the various hazards that might await him on a journey by rail, while to the railroad such hazards are well known. Many are hazards that the railroad effectively controls, and that the passenger cannot observe. And once an accident occurs, there are many settings in which the passenger has no way to determine how it occurred. Unless the railroad voluntarily reveals information on its lack of care, the injured passenger would be unable to prove negligence. In such settings, the common law, under the utmost care standard, adopts a presumption of liability, requiring the railroad to come forth with evidence disproving negligence rather than requiring the plaintiff to prove negligence.

In *Yu v. New York, New Haven & Hartford Railroad Co.*,[29] the plaintiff, a short woman who walked with a noticeable limp due to an injured hip, boarded a train carrying several packages. At her exit in New Haven, the concrete platform was fourteen inches below the last step of the stairway leading from the train car. It was dark. Her foot did not reach the platform when she tried to step off, and she fell forward, sustaining injuries. The court held that the railroad breached its duty of care toward the plaintiff by not aiding her as she disembarked.

In *Kambour v. Boston & Maine Railroad Co.*,[30] the railroad was held liable for injuries sustained by a fourteen-year-old boy who jumped from the train before it reached a stop at the station. The boy had jumped from the train several times before, in the presence of railroad employees, who made no attempt to stop him on previous occasions.

In *McMahon v. New York, New Haven & Hartford Railroad Co.*,[31] the court held that the railroad had a duty to take reasonable measures to prevent a drunken passenger from falling off the train. A railroad employee who was aware of the plaintiff's drunken condition left an exit door open in the back of the car, through which the drunken passenger walked and fell to his death. The court confirmed a principle in the Connecticut case law that *a common carrier, having upon its train a passenger who is so intoxicated as not to be able to take care for his own safety, when it knows or in the exercise of reasonable care should know his condition, must exercise a degree of care for his protection commensurate with his inability to guard himself from danger.*[32]

Since developing this information-and-control based duty to rescue in the common carrier setting, the principle that an actor has a duty to rescue when he is aware of the risk facing the plaintiff and exerts some degree of control over the risk has extended to other relationships – so called "special relationships."

---

[28] Farwell v. Boston & Worcester R.R. Corp, 45 Mass. 49, 58–59 (1842).
[29] 144 A.2d 56 (Conn. 1958).
[30] 86 A. 624 (N.H. 1913).
[31] 71 A.2d 557 (Conn. 1950).
[32] *Id.* at 558.

The Second Restatement says that a person has a duty to protect a foreseeable victim from an injury caused by a third party if the person has a *special relationship* with the victim or with the third party that would justify imposing such a duty.[33] The term "special relationship" is meaningless by itself and appears to do nothing more than create a new and undefined category of exceptions to the *no duty to rescue* rule. The case law that has developed after the common carrier cases provides examples that give meaning and content to the special relationship category. The special relationship cases impose liability on the basis of the defendant's control and superior information regarding the danger to the plaintiff.

One early special relationship (information and control) case established a duty to rescue in the context of landowner and invitee.[34] In *L. S. Ayres & Co. v. Hicks*,[35] the plaintiff, a six-year-old boy, fell at the bottom of an escalator and got his fingers caught in the space between the floor and the moving steps. The boy remained trapped in this position for almost five minutes because store employees had not been taught, and therefore did not know, how to shut the escalator off, a simple procedure that could have been carried out within a few seconds. The plaintiff's injuries were aggravated by the long period in which his fingers were trapped by the mechanism. The court did not find the store negligent in its choice or maintenance of the escalator. However, the court found the store negligent in failing to take reasonable measures, in light of the foreseeable danger, to avoid injury to the plaintiff.

Hicks falls within the principle developed in the common carrier cases. The store was aware (or should have been aware) of the risk to customers and of the mechanism for reducing the risk by stopping the escalator. Thus, the store was both aware of the risk to potential victims and exercised control over it, as in the common carrier cases imposing a duty to rescue.

In *Tarasoff v. Regents of University of California*,[36] Prosenjit Poddar revealed his intention to kill Tatiana Tarasoff to psychologists employed by the university. The psychologists had him confined by campus police, but he was released when the police concluded that he seemed to be rational. The psychologists directed that no further action be taken to detain Poddar. Poddar then carefully planned and carried out his murder of Tarasoff. The court held that the university had a duty to warn Tarasoff of the danger she faced.

Although *Tarasoff* is a controversial decision – because of its imposition on psychologists of a duty to warn the intended victims of their patients – it is well within

---

[33] THE RESTATEMENT (SECOND) OF TORTS §315 (1977) ("There is no duty so to control the conduct of a third person as to prevent him from causing physical harm to another unless (a) a special relation exists between the actor and the third person which imposes a duty upon the actor to control the third person's conduct, or (b) a special relation exists between the actor and the other which gives the other a right to protection.").

[34] Landowner duties are discussed later in this chapter.

[35] 40 N.E.2d 334 (Ind. 1942).

[36] 551 P.2d 334 (Cal. 1976).

the principal adopted in the earlier case law on common carriers. The psychologists were in the process of managing a risk, attempting to influence Poddar's behavior, and became aware of a specific danger directed at Tarasoff, of which Tarasoff was ignorant.

Probably the most controversial application of the principle that a duty to protect a potential victim from harm (i.e., to rescue) exists when the actor both manages a risk and is aware of the danger to the victim is to the special relationship between a landlord and a tenant. In *Kline v. 1800 Massachusetts Avenue Apartment Corp.*,[37] the court held that a landlord has a duty to adopt measures to protect tenants from foreseeable criminal acts committed by third parties in common areas of the apartment building.

The plaintiff, Sarah Kline, was assaulted and robbed by an intruder in the common hallway of her apartment building on the evening of November 17, 1966. She had moved into the apartment in 1959. When she moved in, a doorman was on duty at the main entrance twenty-four hours a day, and at least one employee manned a desk in the lobby, also twenty-four hours a day, from which the elevators could be observed. There was another door close to the entrance of a parking garage, and that door also had an attendant at all times. By mid-1966, all of these guards had disappeared. Around the same time reports of assaults and robberies were increasing, and the landlord had been informed of several incidents.

The difficult issues in *Kline* involve assumption of risk doctrine and the duty of a landowner to persons on his property. The common law held the landlord liable to tenants for defective conditions in common areas under his control that could be cured at reasonable expense. If a tenant fell through a weak spot in a common stairway, and that spot could have been discovered at reasonable expense by the landlord, the landlord would be liable. Thus, tenants are treated under the common law as *invitees* (discussed later, this chapter) in the common areas of apartment buildings. On the other hand, the landlord was not liable to the tenant for defective conditions in the tenant's unit of which the landlord was unaware. In other words, the tenant was treated by the common law as a *licensee* within his own unit. The law assumed that the tenant accepted some degree of risk in his own dwelling.

Given the relatively strict duty owed to tenants in common areas, one could ask why legal responsibility to tenants for criminal acts by third parties was not already a part of the landlord's common law duty before *Kline*. One answer is that crime is an obvious condition, like a tree standing in the landowner's front yard. *The landowner's duty to an invitee does not extend to obvious conditions, of the sort easily observed and avoided by the visitor.*[38] Another answer is that crime is different because it involves

[37] Kline v. 1500 Massachusetts Ave. Apartment Corp., 439 F.2d 477 (D.C. Cir. 1970).

[38] Ward v. Kmart Corporation, 554 N.E.2d 223 (Ill. 1990), Robert E. McKee, General Contractor v. Patterson, 271 S.W.2d 391 (Tex. 1954), Hemphill v. Johnson, 497 S.E.2d 16 (Ga. App. 1998).

the intervention of a third party, but we know from the previous chapter that human intervention is not always a defense to liability.

Kline strips away the "obvious conditions" defense that a landlord could have asserted against a tenant harmed by a criminal act committed by a third party on the landlord's property. The tenant is not presumed under *Kline* to assume the risk with respect to such crime, even though the tenant is capable of moving away from the property to escape it. The landlord is required to take steps to protect tenants from the risk of foreseeable crime on his premises.

Kline appears to be inconsistent with assumption of risk doctrine. On traditional assumption of risk grounds, the position that crime is an obvious risk assumed by the tenant seems at first to be obviously correct. If the tenant is afraid of crime on the landlord's property, he can move to another location. The tenant has the option to pay a higher rent at an apartment that provides security. Since the market for apartments is capable of providing the levels of security demanded by various tenants, why should the law impose a requirement of reasonable security?

The answer to this question, and one that reconciles *Kline* with assumption of risk theory, is that the market may fail to provide incentives for reasonable security in apartment buildings. There are two reasons for this: (1) the risk of crime is so variable that tenants may be unable to competently assume it, and (2) security is a public or collective good, in the sense that once it is provided for one member of a community it is provided for all members.

The assumption of risk argument takes as given that tenants can observe the level of danger and therefore assume the risk of criminal assaults. But this premise is questionable. Crime is not as stable and obvious as a low-hanging door or a tree in the yard. Criminals monitor their targets and react to changes in the vulnerability of a site. It may be virtually impossible for tenants to adjust their expectations to the actual level of risk of crime at any given moment. Rejecting the assumption of risk argument in this context would be no different from rejecting it in the context of a workplace where a dangerous feature changes from day to day. For example, in *McGuire v. Almy* (Chapter 4),[39] the court rejected the assumption of risk argument when the insane defendant became violent in a manner not observed before. In *Mayhew v. Sullivan* (Chapter 7),[40] the court rejected the assumption of risk defense when the dangerous feature was a hole cut in a mining platform 270 feet below ground, without any warning to the plaintiff independent contractor.

Now consider the public good argument. A public good is something that, like national security, is effectively provided to all consumers once it is provided to any one consumer.[41] The standard lesson in the literature is that the market tends to

---

[39]　8 N.E.2d 760 (Mass. 1937).
[40]　76 Me. 100 (1884).
[41]　For a brief discussion, *see* Chapter 2.

provide less than the socially ideal quantity of public goods.[42] The reason is that there are always incentives for some user or consumer of the public good to understate his intensity of preference, in the hope that he can unload the cost of providing the good onto others. For example, if I know that my neighbors are willing to pay for general security, I may have an incentive to avoid contributing to the costs myself, since my neighbors will cover the costs anyway and I can still enjoy the benefits.

Security in an apartment building is a public good, like national security. A landlord who passively waits for the market to signal the appropriate level of security may fail to provide security that is reasonable in light of the real (rather than expressed) preferences of tenants.

Since the purpose of assumption of risk theory is to leave certain risks to be allocated by the market, the fact that safety in common areas is a public good undercuts the basis for the assumption of risk defense. From this perspective, the decision in *Kline* can be fully reconciled with the theory of assumption of risk.

The public good nature of security suggests that the law should require some degree of precaution on the part of the landlord to prevent criminal assaults by third parties on the landlord's premises. The strong likelihood that individual tenants will be unwilling voluntarily to provide or fund the generally desired level of safety, or even to reveal their own valuations of security, implies that both the tenant and the landlord could be made better off by the imposition of a duty on the landlord to provide a minimal level of safety.

IV. LANDOWNER DUTIES

As I noted in the previous part, the relationships between landowners (or possessors) and visitors have long formed a basis for special tort duties. Visitors to land fall into three categories: *invitees*, *licensees*, and *trespassers*. An invitee is someone who is on the landowner's property for an exchange of some sort, typically a business deal in which both landowner and invitee have a joint interest. A licensee is someone who is on the land by the permission of the landowner, but not for an economic exchange mutually beneficial to both. A trespasser is someone who has not been invited and is on the landowner's property without his consent.

The duties of landowners (or possessors) have varied according to the category of the visitor.[43] To the invitee, the landowner owes a duty of taking reasonable care that the premises are safe. With respect to the licensee, the landowner does not have a duty to ensure that the premises are safe, but cannot create a trap or allow a concealed

---

[42] Paul A. Samuelson, The Pure Theory of Public Expenditure, 36 Rev. Econ. & Stat. 387 (1954).

[43] For cases setting out the law on the duties of owners and occupiers, *see* Robert Addie & Sons (Collieries), Ltd. v. Dumbreck, [1929] A.C. 358; Indermaur v. Dames, (1866) L.R. 1 C.P. 274. The policy arguments here are drawn from Keith N. Hylton, *Tort Duties of Landowners: A Positive Theory*, 44 Wake Forest L. Rev. 1049 (2009).

danger that is not apparent to the visitor but that is known to the landowner. To the trespasser the landowner owes no duty of care, but is liable if he injures the trespasser willfully or through reckless disregard for the trespasser's welfare.

Three policy arguments justify the legal distinctions among land visitor categories. First, the theory underlying the doctrine of assumption of risk provides a partial explanation for the assignment of varying landowner duties to visitor categories. Second, the theory of *Rylands v. Fletcher*, which holds that the negligence rule applies when there is a reciprocal exchange of risk among actors, and that strict liability applies when one actor exposes the other actor to a disproportionate risk, provides another partial explanation of the distinctions among land visitors. Third, the legal distinctions reflect a tendency to assign the burden of care to the party who can most effectively and efficiently take care to avoid the accident.

Consider first the distinction between invitees and licensees, viewed under the theory of assumption of risk. Invitees are typically people who visit a landowner's property for business reasons – such as a repairman. Repairmen have to travel to the residences of different customers. They do not have the time to become familiar with the properties and the personal habits of their customers. A requirement on the part of the landowner to treat the invitee with reasonable care is equivalent to saying that the invitee will not be deemed to have assumed the risk of a defective condition existing on the landowner's property.

The duty of the landowner toward the invitee is entirely consistent with the theory assumption of risk. Assumption of risk has been accepted as a defense when the plaintiff has had ample opportunity to become familiar with, and to voluntarily accept, the risks of his environment (Chapter 9). The invitee does not have such an opportunity.

The licensee, in contrast to the invitee, is typically a social guest. Social guests often are familiar with the properties and personal habits of their landowning friends. Given this, courts have adopted a presumption that the licensee assumes the risk with respect to defective conditions of which the landowner is unaware.

The second policy argument for the land visitor distinctions is based on the reciprocal risk-exchange arguments of *Rylands v. Fletcher*. As between the landowner and social guest, there are likely to be many reciprocated risks. If a social guest visits the landowner's property one day, the landowner may visit the guest's property another day. Since the risks associated with latent defective conditions, of which the landowner is unaware, are likely to be experienced on both sides, the negligence rule is sufficient to regulate incentives to take reasonable care (see Chapter 6). The law regarding the landowner's duty to the licensee is closer to a negligence rule, while the duty to the invitee is somewhat broader – similar to the utmost care duty imposed on common carriers and innkeepers.

In the relationship between the invitee and the landowner, it is far less likely that there will be a reciprocal exchange of risk. The risks, at least with respect to defective conditions on land, run one way: The invitee is the only party at risk. The broader duty imposed on the landowner enables the invitee to go about his business without having to bear the risk of, and without having to purchase insurance for, the presence of latent defective conditions on the properties of his customers. The risk is borne by the individual landowners based on the condition of their properties, of which they are likely to be informed, rather than passed on in the form of insurance charges to all of the invitee's customers irrespective of the condition of their properties. Putting the risk of latent defective conditions on the individual landowner enables the market to expand, while putting it on the invitee would cause the market to contract as a result of adverse selection.[44]

The third justification for the law's treatment of the licensee is that the social guest often roams unattended on the landowner's property and therefore necessarily assumes the risk from hazards that he chooses to confront. Such risks can be avoided with greater ease and more efficiently through the licensee's precaution than by imposing a duty on the landowner.

So far I have considered only the distinction between invitees and licensees. The absence of a duty of care with respect to the trespasser is the easiest rule to justify in light of established tort doctrine and policy. A person who invades another's property without consent both assumes the risks associated with his decision to invade and at the same time is guilty of failing to take reasonable care for his own safety. In addition to this, any duty imposed on a landowner to take care to make the premises safe for trespassers would drastically reduce the ownership rights protected by trespass law. A right to exclusive possession, which trespass law protects, implies the absence of a duty to take care to protect the person who would interfere with the right.

These policy arguments justify the land visitor categories as default categories, based on statistical regularities. The legal categories become more difficult to defend when the policy arguments conflict with the legal classifications. One example is *Burrell v. Meads*.[45] The homeowner invited a friend to help him install a ceiling in the homeowner's garage. The homeowner and friend had helped each other before with various tasks. The friend climbed up to the rafters and walked across a surface that looked like plywood but was not. The surface gave way and the friend fell to the garage floor, sustaining severe injuries. The court rejected the traditional category-based law, which would have classified the friend as a licensee, and held that the friend was an invitee.

The policy justifications for having a lesser duty to licensees than to invitees do not seem to apply to *Burrell*. Unlike the typical licensee, the friend did not climb up the rafters of the garage out of his own interest. The element of a decision to voluntarily confront a hazard because of curiosity or interest, rather than based on a contractual

---

[44] On adverse selection, *see* Chapter 18. If the invitee must charge every landowner who contracts for his services for the risk of defective conditions on the landowner's property, only the landowners who present the greatest degree of risk would find it advantageous to purchase the invitee's services. As a result, the market for the invitee's services would contract.

[45] 569 N.E.2d 637 (Ind. 1991).

obligation, is missing in the case. Moreover, whatever information the friend had on the homeowner was probably not enough to permit the friend to anticipate the risk that materialized. Finally, the risk that materialized in *Burrell* is not the sort that normally would be reciprocated among neighbors. For these reasons, the friend in *Burrell* was in many respects indistinguishable from the type of actor traditionally given invitee status.

Some courts, beginning with *Rowland v. Christian*,[46] have abolished the legal duty distinctions among land visitor categories. In place of duties associated with visitor categories, *Rowland* holds that the landowner owes a duty of reasonable care under the circumstances to the land visitor. To the extent the reasonable person standard of *Rowland* incorporates defenses based on assumption of risk and contributory negligence, it may replicate the results under traditional land visitor categories. The duty to a licensee and to an invitee would appear to be the same to the average person, given that they are both invited onto the property. However, a licensee is more likely to be found to have assumed the risk than an invitee, given that licensees often consider themselves free to roam the property. In general, the duty owed to a trespasser, under *Rowland*, will be less than that owed to an invited guest, because the burden of taking care for a trespasser typically will be greater. In addition, assumption of risk and contributory negligence defenses apply easily to the trespasser. Still, *Rowland* allows for the possibility of circumstances in which the reasonable person standard implies a duty to take care even for the trespasser.[47]

Rowland has generated some uncertainty, but it may have been useful for courts to reconsider the justifications for creating category-based distinctions in landowner duties. Tradition alone has never been a strong argument for maintaining legal rules. However, the duties formalized in tort law generally have not been based solely on tradition. They have reflected the same policies that shape most other tort doctrines.

---

[46] 443 P.2d 561 (Cal. 1968).
[47] Beard v. Atchison, Topeka & Santa Fe Ry. Co., 4 Cal. App.3d 129, 136 (Cal.Ct. App. 1970); Mark v. Pacific Gas & Electric Co., 7 Cal.3d 170, 183 (Cal. 1972); Mile High Fence Co. v. Radovich, 489 P.2d 308, 314–315 (Colo. 1971).

15

Strict Liability

Conversion, Abnormally Dangerous Activities, and Nuisance

Two sources of strict liability evolved early in the common law: trespass and *Rylands v. Fletcher*. Liability under trespass law is strict in the sense that the plaintiff does not have to prove fault on the part of the defendant. In a trespass action, the facts need only show that the defendant was aware of what he was doing when he interfered with the plaintiff's exclusive right of possession.

Similarly, the *Rylands* strict liability doctrine does not require the plaintiff to prove fault on the part of the defendant. The defendant will be held liable under *Rylands* if he keeps something on his property that escapes without the plaintiff's fault and causes harm, provided that certain conditions determining the unreasonableness of the defendant's activity are satisfied. Those conditions were examined in Chapter 5 and are reexamined in much greater detail here.

While Chapters 4 and 5 developed functionalist accounts of trespass and *Rylands* liability, this chapter will extend those perspectives to the doctrines of conversion, abnormally dangerous activities, and nuisance. Conversion is an offshoot of trespass, whereas abnormally dangerous activities and nuisance are offshoots of *Rylands*.

I. TRESPASS-BASED STRICT LIABILITY

The major categories of trespass-based strict liability are *trespass to real property*, *trespass to chattels* (personal property), and *conversion*. The law across these categories is consistent.

Trespass is the *intentional interference with exclusive possession of real property*. A trespass claim can be brought against the interfering party by the owner of the property or by someone who has a right to possess the property. Interference means ousting or physically displacing the plaintiff from some space on his land, as occurs when the defendant physically occupies the space or sends some object, such as a rock, over to the plaintiff's land (Chapter 4). The law defines this interference on the basis of visual cues, not science. One could argue that on a sufficiently small scale of measurement, at the molecular or atomic level, the plaintiff's exclusive possession has been invaded when the defendant's cigarette smoke wafts across the property boundary to the plaintiff's land. But this type of invasion generally has not been recognized as a trespass.[1] The invasions recognized in trespass law are those that occupy space, involving solids or liquids. While this may not be defensible as a matter of science, it is defensible as an operational legal standard. Invasions that obviously and exclusively occupy space are the types over which parties can identify parameters useful for bargaining.

Recall that in a trespass lawsuit, the plaintiff does not need to show that the defendant intended to cause harm (Chapter 4). The plaintiff need only show that the defendant interfered with exclusive possession of land, fully aware of his actions. The evidence does not have to suggest that the defendant knew he was trespassing on the plaintiff's property. It is enough that the defendant was aware of his actions at the time – aware that he was walking on land, anyone's land. The best justification for this minimal intent requirement was offered by Holmes and is the starting point for the policy discussion of Chapter 4. Holmes noted that if the defendant is engaged in conduct that has a physical impact on his own land he will bear the cost, and asked rhetorically why he should be allowed to evade the cost if he is engaged in the same conduct on someone else's land. Trespass law has an intent requirement that is easy to satisfy because the law aims to internalize harms associated with volitional conduct – that is, it aims to make the actor bear the losses resulting from his chosen course of action.

Trespass to personal property (or chattels, or personalty) is the intentional interference with exclusive possession of personal property. Intentional interference means nothing more than that the defendant intended to execute his actions. The plaintiff does not have to prove that the defendant knew it was not his own property. A defendant could be held liable for trespass to personal property even though he thought the property was his own. The internalization argument offered as a justification for the intent standard in trespass to land serves equally well to justify the intent standard for trespass to chattels.

Conversion is the wrongful assertion of a right associated with ownership, such as using, destroying, retaining possession, or selling an item of personal property. The conversion claim, like the trespass claim, can be brought by the owner or by someone who has a right to possess the property at the time of the conversion. Also as in trespass law, there is no requirement of evidence that the defendant knew that he did not in fact own the property. In this sense, liability for conversion is strict, in the same sense as in trespass. However, conversion may be asserted against a defendant who is not guilty of trespass. To be guilty of trespass to personal property, the injuring party must oust the victim from possession. A defendant may be guilty of conversion without

---

[1] One exception to this rule is Martin v. Reynolds Metals Co., 342 P.2d 790 (Or. 1959), which found that the settling of invisible fluoride particulates constituted trespass.

ever having ousted the plaintiff from possession. Of course, where the defendant has dispossessed the plaintiff, he may still be guilty of conversion in addition to trespass.

Though many trespasses are conversions too, not every trespass is a conversion. *The asportation (movement) of a chattel without any intention to make further use of it is generally insufficient to establish a conversion, even though it may be sufficient to establish a trespass.* Thus, if the defendant moves the plaintiff's property without intending to keep or use it, the plaintiff will have only the trespass claim.[2] Another important issue here is *abandonment*, which requires facts indicating indifference as to disposition of the property.

Consider the following examples. Suppose A owns a book. A lends the book to B. Later, C takes the book from B and sells it. A has a conversion claim against C. A does not have a trespass claim against C. B has a trespass claim against C.

A owns a book. B steals the book from A. Later, C steals the book from B and sells it. A has a trespass claim (as well as a conversion claim) against B. A has a conversion claim against C. B has no claim against C because he is neither an owner nor someone with an immediate right to possess.

A owns a book and lends the book to B; B lends the book to C, and D steals the book from C and sells it. A has a conversion claim against D. Interestingly, B has a conversion claim against D too, assuming he has a right to immediate possession. This shows that the plaintiff need not be the owner to bring a conversion claim. C has a trespass claim against D.

One modern illustration of the conversion theory in action is *FMC Corp. v. Capital/ABC Inc.*[3] The ABC television network, in connection with a news broadcast, obtained the only copies of FMC's internal pricing and business documents. The documents were stolen from FMC by a third party unaided in any way by ABC. The court held ABC liable for conversion, though only with respect to the documents for which FMC did not have copies, and required ABC to return those documents to FMC. However, ABC was permitted to keep copies of the documents and to report information contained in them in accordance with its rights under the First Amendment. Copies of documents do not interfere with the owner's exclusive possession and therefore cannot serve as the basis for a trespass or a conversion claim. Conversion doctrine protected FMC's interest in possession of the documents and the information contained in the documents, but did not prevent ABC, given its First Amendment defense and the fact that it obtained the documents through an independent third party, from reporting the information obtained from the documents.

Conversion and trespass to chattels protect different sets of legal interests, and for this reason the damages a plaintiff may receive differ under the two theories.

[2] *See* Fouldes v. Willoughby, 151 Eng. Rep. 1153 (Ex. 1841); Wilson v. McLaughlin, 107 Mass. 587 (1871).
[3] 915 F.2d 300 (7th Cir. 1990).

In an action for trespass, the plaintiff receives compensation for injuries caused by the defendant's interference with his exclusive possession. In an action for conversion, the plaintiff receives compensation not only for injuries received from the interference, but also for the market value of the converted property.[4]

Suppose, for example, the plaintiff parks his car in a parking lot. The defendant (a third party or a lot attendant), acting without the implied or express permission of the plaintiff, moves the plaintiff's car from one parking spot to another parking spot, within the same lot, and in the course of doing so damages the plaintiff's car. Assume that a court would find this interference insufficient under the circumstances to amount to a conversion.[5] Assume also that parking in the lot is not a transfer of possession of the car to the lot owner, as would be the case if the car owner had left his car with a valet. (If the car owner had left his car with a valet, he would have established a *bailment relationship* in which possession is transferred to the valet.) Since the act of moving the car without permission is a trespass, the plaintiff can seek damages for the injury to the car, and any other physical, economic, or emotional harm the plaintiff suffers as a result of the trespass. Now suppose, instead, that the defendant drives off with the plaintiff's car and refuses to return it. This is a conversion, in addition to a trespass. The plaintiff can seek damages for any physical, economic, or emotional harms resulting from the interference, and in addition damages for the market value of the car at the time of the conversion (forced sale remedy). Lastly, suppose that the defendant drives off with the plaintiff's car and returns it the next week. This is a conversion, in addition to a trespass. Conversion doctrine gives the plaintiff the right to choose whether to accept the returned car.[6] If the plaintiff chooses to accept, he can still sue for conversion and seek damages for injury to the car; for the physical, economic, and emotional harms resulting from the interference; and any other special damages resulting from the conversion, such as a loss in the car's market value.[7] If the plaintiff chooses not to accept the returned car, he can seek the same damages he would have sought if the defendant had refused to return the car (including, again, the forced sale remedy).

What if the defendant invests money in maintaining the car during the week that he uses it? Can the defendant deduct his maintenance costs from the damages he must pay the plaintiff in a conversion action? If the conversion was in good faith – for example, the defendant reasonably believed the car was his own – and the plaintiff accepts the returned car, then the defendant may deduct his maintenance

---

[4] In practical terms, the distinction between the legal entitlements protected under the two theories may not be significant, given the absence of a foreseeability limitation for harms directly caused by a trespass. On the absence of foreseeability limitation, *see* the discussion of *Vosburg v. Putney* in Chapter 4.

[5] Fouldes v. Willoughby, 151 Eng. Rep. 1153 (Ex. 1841).

[6] Renzo D. Bowers, A Treatise on the Law of Conversion 455 (1917).

[7] *Id.* at 456.

expenses from damages. However, if the conversion was in bad faith, the defendant will not be allowed to deduct maintenance expenses.[8] Under the same principle, if the defendant in bad faith harvests and sells timber from the plaintiff's land, the defendant will not be permitted to deduct his harvesting costs from the damages award. The case of harvesting timber provides an example of the different interests protected by trespass and by conversion. The trespass alone implies liability for all harms directly caused by the trespass, foreseeable or not (Chapter 4). The proceeds from the sale of the timber, however, are not obviously within the set of harms directly caused by the trespass.

II. *RYLANDS* STRICT LIABILITY

Outside of trespass law, the other major source of strict liability in the common law is *Rylands v. Fletcher* (Chapter 5). *Rylands* held that *"the person who for his own purpose brings on his lands and collects and keeps there anything likely to do mischief if it escapes, must keep it in at his peril, and, if he does not do so, is prima facie answerable for all the damage which is the natural consequence of its escape."*[9] The court added that the defendant could avoid liability by showing that the escape was due to the fault of the plaintiff.

The *Rylands* doctrine has been expanded from water reservoirs to many other activities that throw extraordinary risk onto others. This is not surprising, since the *Rylands* opinion (specifically, Judge Blackburn's opinion) noted other earlier applications of the strict liability doctrine – to fumes, odors, straying cattle – that were consistent with the theory articulated in the opinion.

One important offshoot of *Rylands* is the law on abnormally dangerous activities. The classic abnormally dangerous activity is blasting. Courts impose strict liability when the defendant's blasting causes harm to the plaintiff or to his property. Strict liability has also been applied to the storage of explosives[10] and to crop dusting.[11]

Consistent with the theory of *Rylands* examined in Chapter 5, blasting is an activity that externalizes a great deal of risk to neighbors even when conducted with reasonable care. Moreover, the risk is not reciprocated by the risk of neighboring activities: The blaster imposes an unusual risk on his neighbors, but his neighbors do not impose an equivalent risk on the blaster. This feature distinguishes the activity of blasting from driving on the road, where each driver imposes a reciprocal risk on other drivers. In addition, the blaster typically does not confer benefits on others in the course of his activity. Hence, the blaster's neighbors generally would have no reason to accept or tolerate the risk.

---

[8] *See, e.g.,* Maye v. Yappan, 23 Cal. 306 (1863).
[9] Rylands v. Fletcher, L.R. 1 Ex. 265, 279 (1866), *aff'd,* L.R. 3 H.L. 330 (1868).
[10] Yukon Equipment v. Fireman's Fund Insurance Co., 585 P.2d 1206 (Alaska 1978).
[11] Langan v. Valicopters, Inc., 567 P.2d 218 (Wash. 1977).

In Chapter 5, I offered a functional perspective on *Rylands*, looking closely at the entire rationale of the decision. However, *Rylands* has been usefully captured in a special part of the Restatement (Second) of Torts that applies to abnormally dangerous activities. In this part I will explore the Second Restatement's codified version of *Rylands*, because it is thorough and easier to apply to a new set of facts than the original opinion.

The Restatement (Second) of Torts sets out the *Rylands* doctrine in the form of a set of rules, under sections 519 and 520. Section 519 of the Restatement (Second) provides the "general principle" that "one who carries on an abnormally dangerous activity" is subject to strict liability, and that the strict liability is "limited to the kind of harm, the possibility of which makes the activity abnormally dangerous."[12] Thus, according to section 519, strict liability applies only when the harm that results is within the set of foreseeable injuries that one associates with the abnormally dangerous activity of the defendant. This principle, a proximate causation requirement, was originally stated in *Rylands*, which noted that liability should be limited to the foreseeable consequences of the escape.

Thus, if the defendant holds a tiger in his backyard and the tiger escapes and mauls someone, the mauling will be seen as within the set of foreseeable consequences of the tiger's escape. One would consider it an abnormally dangerous activity for someone to hold a tiger in his backyard precisely because of the risk that the tiger will escape and maul someone. On the other hand, if the tiger escapes and frightens the neighbor's horse, which then runs away and kicks down a fence in another town, the final outcome probably would not be considered within the set of foreseeable consequences related to the dangerousness of holding a tiger.

To illustrate, in *Madsen v. East Jordan Irrigation Co.*,[13] the defendant's blasting caused the mother mink at the plaintiff's mink farm to kill their kittens. The court distinguished the conduct of the mother mink from instinctive acts of self-preservation among humans (a topic discussed in Chapter 3) and treated the result as a "peculiarity of disposition which was not within the realm of matters to be anticipated."[14]

Provided the plaintiff's harm is within the set of foreseeable consequences of the escape, thus satisfying the proximate causation requirement, the intervention of a third party or force of nature that causes the escape will not excuse the defendant from liability. One judge remarked that if a bolt of lightning snapped the chain holding a tiger in the defendant's yard, the defendant would still be strictly liable for the harm done by the tiger.[15] In *Yukon Equipment v. Fireman's Fund Insurance*

---

[12] Restatement (Second) of Torts §519 (1977).

[13] Madsen v. East Jordan Irrigation Co., 125 P.2d 794 (Utah 1942).

[14] *Ibid.* at 795. For a similar case and decision, *see* Foster v. Preston Mill Co., 268 P.2d 645 (Wash. 1954).

[15] Nichols v. Marsland, L.R. 10 Ex. 255, 260 (1875) (Baron Bramwell).

Co.,[16] thieves broke into Yukon's explosives storage warehouse and set off some of the explosives to conceal evidence of their crime. The court held Yukon strictly liable under *Rylands*.

The foreseeability requirement has implications for the type of plaintiff who can recover, or type of harm that is compensable, under strict liability. Specifically, plaintiffs who are deemed *unusually sensitive*, for having suffered a harm that could not be foreseen given the nature of the escape, cannot recover (Second Restatement section 524A). Suppose the defendant is engaged in blasting. As a result of the concussions, paintings hanging on the wall of the plaintiff's home fall and are damaged. The plaintiff used nails that were so small that any slight tremor would cause the nails to fall out. Other neighbors, using sturdier nails, did not suffer damage to their paintings. The plaintiff would lose his claim under *Rylands* because he is unusually sensitive. Contrast this with an alternative scenario: Instead of small nails, the plaintiff's nails are sturdy, but his art collection includes a Rembrandt worth $50 million. If the same injury occurs, the plaintiff has a valid claim, even though the harm is unexpectedly large. The plaintiff in this second scenario is not unusually sensitive; his paintings fell because the concussions were strong enough to knock down anyone's paintings. Once the plaintiff has a valid claim for damages under *Rylands*, it does not matter that the injury exceeds the amount anyone would expect; the injurer takes the victim as he finds him.

A more basic implication of the foreseeability requirement is that liability should be limited to harms that are foreseeable given the nature of the defendant's activity – that is, that the activity itself put the defendant on notice about the potential harms to others. That is certainly true of holding a tiger in your yard. In *Cambridge Water Co. v. Eastern Counties Leather PLC*,[17] the defendant's tannery released toxic chemicals that seeped into an aquifer and then to the plaintiff's well more than one mile away. The court refused to find liability under *Rylands* and held that a reasonable person would not have foreseen the harm to the plaintiff.

Section 520 of the Restatement (Second) of Torts provides the following factors for determining whether an activity is abnormally dangerous:

(a) Existence of a high degree of risk of some harm to the person, land, or chattels of others
(b) Likelihood that the harm that results from it will be great
(c) Inability to eliminate the risk by the exercise of reasonable care
(d) Extent to which the activity is not a matter of common usage
(e) Inappropriateness of the activity to the place where it is carried on and
(f) Extent to which its value to the community is outweighed by its dangerous attributes.[18]

---

[16] 585 P.2d 1206 (Alaska 1978).
[17] [1994] 2 A.C. 264 (H.L.).
[18] RESTATEMENT (SECOND) OF TORTS §520 (1977).

The first three parts of section 520 can be collapsed into one question: Is the residual risk created by the defendant's activity high even when it is conducted with reasonable care? If so, then parts (a), (b), and (c) of section 520 are satisfied, which indicates that the activity may be abnormally dangerous, and therefore an appropriate candidate for strict liability.

The second half of the section 520 tests consists of rules (d), (e), and (f), which may be described as the "*Rylands* reasonableness factors" because they capture the theory of *Rylands*. Part (d), which asks whether the activity is a matter of common usage, suggests an inquiry into whether the defendant's risk is reciprocal to the risks thrown off by other activities in the community. Take the case of driving. No matter how careful you are, you will always impose the risk of an accident on other drivers, but they also impose the same risk on you. The activity of driving is therefore inappropriate as a candidate for strict liability because the risks externalized by one actor are reciprocal to the risks externalized by others. When this is true, strict liability and negligence are equivalent in the incentives they provide to an actor to reduce the scale of his activity (see Chapter 5).

Part (e) of section 520 asks whether the activity is inappropriate for the place where it is carried out. This factor is best viewed as an assumption of risk test based on locality. One way to determine the appropriateness of an activity is to ask whether actors in the community commonly engage in that activity, as in factor (d). Obviously, the example of driving meets this test. Services that form an infrastructure also fit under this category, such as the local provision of water, electricity, or natural gas. In addition to considering commonality, appropriateness can be determined by asking whether the plaintiff moved next to the defendant's activity after it had been established. If so, that would suggest that the defendant's activity was accepted, or viewed as appropriate, by the plaintiff; otherwise why would he move next door to it? Yet another way to determine appropriateness is to ask whether the benefits to neighbors from the defendant's activity are greater than the risks. If so, it would be reasonable to infer that the plaintiff would have accepted those risks as part of a bargain for being located near the defendant's activity.[19]

The final part, (f), of section 520 asks whether the value of the activity to the community outweighs its risks. This is closely related to the appropriateness question asked in part (e). However, inquiring into the risk-benefit exchange is not the same as inquiring into appropriateness. Appropriateness examines the problem from the perspective of a hypothetical (reasonable) plaintiff and may take the plaintiff's own conduct as evidence of appropriateness (did he move to the site of hazardous activity?). The risk-benefit test asks whether the risks externalized by the defendant's

---

[19] A fireworks exhibition raises questions of assumption of risk of the sort presented here. *See* Scanlon v. Wedger, 156 Mass. 462, 31 N.E. 642 (1892) (plaintiffs, by attending fireworks show, assumed risk of injury due to nonnegligent conduct); Cadena v. Chicago Fireworks Mfg. Co., 697 N.E.2d 802 (Ill. App. 1998) (fireworks not abnormally dangerous, given risk-benefit test); Klein v. Pyrodyne Corp., 810 P.2d 917 (Wash. 1991) (fireworks abnormally dangerous, since not a matter common usage).

activity exceed the benefits externalized. In many instances, the appropriateness and risk-benefit analyses will be repetitive, but that doesn't imply that risk-benefit analysis is useless. Risk-benefit analysis is a potentially useful safeguard against an excessively narrow approach to answering the appropriateness question.

One could argue that both the commonality and appropriateness factors are redundant in light of the risk-benefit test. In most cases, an activity that externalizes more benefit than risk will have some feature that makes it seem common, or that it at least should be treated as common. But it is not at all obvious that a person would reach the same conclusions with respect to the commonality, appropriateness, and risk-benefit questions in every case. Just because an activity is common does not imply that its benefits outweigh its risks to the community.

The Second Restatement, in section 524, provides that the "plaintiff's contributory negligence in knowingly and unreasonably subjecting himself to the risk of harm from the activity is a defense to the strict liability."[20] This is consistent with *Rylands*, which recognizes an *excuse, for the defendant*, if the dangerous agent kept on the defendant's property escapes through the "default" of the plaintiff. Thus, *Rylands* and the Second Restatement require an unreasonable, informed release of the dangerous agent by the plaintiff for the defendant to escape liability on the basis of the plaintiff's conduct. And *Rylands* refers to the plaintiff's default as providing an excuse, not a defense, which implies that the court did not view it as negating the defendant's culpability.[21]

The knowing and unreasonable requirement of section 524 seems closer to a gross negligence or recklessness standard than a contributory negligence standard. Suppose the defendant has a tiger in his backyard. If the plaintiff merely trespasses and thereby causes the tiger to escape and attack him, one might consider this an example of contributory negligence, on the ground that the trespasser failed to take reasonable care for his own safety (after all, who knows what the trespasser might find?). But *Rylands* and section 524 require a more extreme type of unreasonable conduct than this.

To see the functions of the *Rylands* tests of commonality, appropriateness, and risk-benefit, consider *Rickards v. Lothian*.[22] The defendant provided water supply to the building he owned. A third party snuck into the building at night, stuffed the sink, and turned the faucet on full blast. The water flooded the bathroom and leaked to the floor below, damaging the plaintiff's personal property. The court held that the strict liability rule of *Rylands* did not apply to the defendant's activity (supplying water to the building).

---

[20] RESTATEMENT (SECOND) OF TORTS §524 (1977).

[21] Given that both parties are guilty of unreasonable conduct, the Third Restatement's adoption of a comparative responsibility standard for strict liability cases – that is, apportioning liability based on comparative responsibility – is also consistent with *Rylands*. See RESTATEMENT (THIRD) OF TORTS, §25.

[22] Rickards v. Lothian, [1913] A.C. 263 (P.C.) (also discussed in Chapter 5).

Since the defendant introduced an activity that greatly enhanced the risk of harm to the plaintiff, even when conducted with reasonable care, one could say that the first half of the section 520 test – the residual risk factors (a), (b), and (c) – was satisfied in *Rickards*. Thus, the last three factors provide the only basis for distinguishing the activity in *Rickards* from that in *Rylands*.

The commonality factor (d) asks whether the activity was a matter of common usage. If the common usage test is interpreted as asking whether there is a reciprocal exchange of risk, the answer is no in *Rickards*: The defendant, by supplying water to the building, throws much more risk onto the plaintiff than the plaintiff reciprocates.

However, the appropriateness (e) and risk-benefit (f) factors of section 520 suggest that strict liability would be undesirable in *Rickards*. The benefits conferred to the community (including the plaintiff) by the defendant's activity were greater than the risks. It would therefore be reasonable for the plaintiff to accept the slight risk of water damage in light of the sanitation benefits from having water supply; and, thus, the defendant's activity was appropriate. These factors point to the conclusion that the defendant should not be strictly liable, which is what the court decided.

Suppose, instead of treating the common usage test as a prompt to examine reciprocity in risk bearing, we approach it literally and ask if the activity is one that has come to be viewed as a common and useful service. This is the approach taken by the section 20 of the Third Restatement of Torts.[23] Such an approach might lead a court to conclude that water supply should be subjected to strict liability if at the time of the plaintiff's suit it was not a common service. At the least, the commonality test of the Third Restatement would lead a court to engage in an empirical exercise of determining whether water supply in buildings was common, rather than attempting to examine the function of strict liability.

The Third Restatement takes the distinct doctrinal approaches developed in *Rylands* and collapses them into one test focusing on commonality. The theory of *Rylands* is put at risk of being lost in this approach. One could easily reach the conclusion that just because something is common, it must be reasonable; and if it is not common, it must be unreasonable. But nothing in *Rylands* equates commonality with reasonableness.

An activity may be common and at the same time unreasonable because the external risks exceed the external benefits. The storage of water in large reservoirs for manufacturing purposes may have been common at the time of *Rylands*, but the court held that it was not a reasonable activity. Driving under the influence of alcohol used to be common, but American states prohibit it today. Sometimes a new technology may spread before its adverse effects are fully understood. The spraying of the pesticide DDT was once common, but now we believe that it may be an unreasonable activity because the risks outweigh the benefits in some areas.

---

[23] RESTATEMENT (THIRD) OF TORTS §20 (2010). Comments to the section suggest that the other factors of RESTATEMENT (SECOND) section 520 (e.g., appropriateness, mutual benefit) may be considered in answering the common usage question.

As another illustration of risk-benefit balancing in the law of abnormally dangerous activities, consider *Strawbridge v. City of Philadelphia*.[24] Natural gas escaped from pipes constructed by the city to provide light. The resulting explosion destroyed the plaintiff's property. The plaintiffs, dry goods merchants (fabric, thread, clothing), had extended the basement of their store out beyond the curb, to store a vault. The underground vault was located close to a gas main, which had been exposed by some earlier sewer construction work. The gas main was ruptured near the vault, permitting gas to seep in to the area of the vault and into the basement. Employees of the plaintiff and a plumber went into the basement with a lighted candle to fix a water leak. The gas exploded, destroying part of the basement as well as the plaintiff's merchandise. There was no evidence indicating how the gas main was ruptured, and no evidence suggesting that it was due to anyone's negligence.

As in *Rickards v. Lothian*, the plaintiffs in *Strawbridge* attempted to exploit the principle of *Rylands*. Rejecting the plaintiff's theory, the court said:

> Even if the doctrine of *Fletcher v. Rylands* were accepted as the rule of law in Pennsylvania in analogous cases, there are such manifest and essential differences between the facts of that case and of the one now under consideration as to render it extremely doubtful as to whether it is applicable to a case like the present one.
>
> In that case the defendants built a large reservoir for the convenience of a mill which they were operating. For their sole advantage they collected in it an unusually large quantity of water, which would probably, if not necessarily, do harm to their neighbor's property in the event of its escaping...
>
> But in the present case the city is carrying on a business which, while for certain purposes it must be treated as a private business, cannot but be considered as a great public improvement, of inestimable benefit to all its citizens, by which property is made more valuable, and life and person more secure. And in all these benefits the plaintiffs directly shared. They were thereby greatly facilitated in carrying on their large business in safety and with profit. It was in no sense a business conducted by the city for its sole advantage. And may not the [plaintiffs]... sharing in the benefits and advantages of the business thus conducted, and especially in view of the fact that these pipes were laid in the streets by virtue of an ordinance of the councils of the city legally passed and approved, be presumed to have consented to such a use of the streets for their individual, as well as for the general, good? And to have waived their right to compensation for injury accidentally resulting to them therefrom, where neither fault nor negligence on the part of the city could be established?[25]

Strawbridge provides a good statement of risk-benefit balancing as a limitation on strict liability and suggests precisely how the appropriateness (e) and risk-benefit (f) factors of section 520 should be applied. *Rylands* is distinguished in *Strawbridge* on the basis of the appropriateness and risk-benefit factors. The provision of natural gas

---

[24] 2 Pennyp. 419 (Pa. 1882).
[25] *Id.* at 425–426.

for lighting provided substantial benefits to the community. In light of this, the court thought it was reasonable for the plaintiff to accept the small risk of harm that might occur in the absence of negligence.[26] The same principle was adopted in an English decision (from India) involving the storage of a large quantity of water. In *Madras Railway Company v. The Zemindar of Carvatenagaram*,[27] the court distinguished *Rylands* on the ground that water storage in India was necessary for agriculture and benefited the entire community.[28]

A much discussed modern illustration of the limits of *Rylands* is Judge Richard Posner's opinion in *Indiana Harbor Belt Railroad Co. v. American Cyanamid Co.*[29] American Cyanamid loaded 20,000 gallons of liquid acrylonitrile into a railroad tank car at its plant in Louisiana, bound for New Jersey. On the way, the tank car entered into a switching line in Illinois. While there, 5,000 gallons of the chemical spilled out of the tank car through an open valve. The plaintiff switching line (Indiana Harbor Belt R.R.) was required to clean up and decontaminate by the state's environmental protection agency, at a cost of almost one million dollars. The switching line sued the defendant on the theory that strict liability should apply to the transportation of acrylonitrile.

Judge Posner, applying the six factors of Restatement Section 520, concluded that shipping liquid acrylonitrile is not an abnormally dangerous activity. The opinion includes many arguments, but the most persuasive is that the residual risk of shipping the chemical, when conducted with reasonable care, is not unusually high. In other words, the court concluded that the shipping of acrylonitrile should be distinguished from blasting on the basis of the first three factors of the section 520 test (residual risk factors). Although there are other rationales provided in Posner's opinion, this is a sufficient ground for the decision. Indeed, to hold a defendant strictly liable on the basis of the section 520 test, both the residual risk factors (a, b, and c) and the *Rylands* reasonableness factors (d, e, and f) must point to strict liability. If the residual risk factors do not suggest a justification for strict liability, then the plaintiff's strict liability case is dead.

Another justification for the decision in *Indiana Harbor* can be found in the appropriateness factor (e) of section 520, which should be viewed as prompting an assumption of risk inquiry. The plaintiff in this case is the switching line, and

---

[26] For other cases rejecting the application of strict liability to natural gas suppliers, *see* Foster v. City of Keyser, 501S.E.2d 165 (W. Va. 1997); Mahowald v. Minnesota Gas Co., 344 N.W.2d 856 (Minn. 1984); New Meadows Holding Co. v. Washington Water Power Co., 659 P.2d 1113 (Wash. App. 1983); Brown v. Kansas Natural Gas Co., 299 F. 463 (8th Cir. 1924); Westfield Gas Corp. v. Hill, 169 N.E.2d 726 (Ind. App. 1960); Musolino Lo Conte Co. v. Boston Consolidated Gas Co., 112 N.E.2d 250 (Mass. 1953).

[27] Madras Railway Company v. The Zemindar of Carvatenagaram, 1 L. R. Ind. App. 364 (1874).

[28] *Rylands* was rejected in an American case, Turner v. Big Lake Oil Co., 96 S.W.2d 221 (Tex. 1936), on the same basis. Unlike *Madras*, *Turner* rejects rather than distinguishes *Rylands*. However, *Turner* can easily be reconciled with *Rylands* in the same manner as the court did in *Madras*.

[29] 916 F.2d 1174 (7th Cir. 1990).

it is the job of the switching line to move railroad cars from one line to another under contractual agreements. The risk associated with the temporary housing and transportation of railroad cars is a recurrent feature of the day-to-day work of the switching line. If the switching line finds that its expected cost of liability increases, it can pass on the cost through contracts with shippers.

Finally, one can also defend *Indiana Harbor* on the basis of section 519(2) of the Second Restatement, which limits strict liability to the foreseeable harms associated with the dangerous character of the activity.[30] Acrylonitrile is highly flammable at a temperature of 30 degrees Fahrenheit or greater, toxic, and possibly carcinogenic. However, no explosion or poisoning occurred in the case. The plaintiff's injury consisted of being forced to do a clean-up by a state environmental protection agency. This appears to be outside of the set of injuries contemplated by section 519(2) and the theory of *Rylands*. Holding the defendant liable would require the defendant to pay for an injury that is in large part the result of the intervention of a third party (the environmental agency) and in this sense conflicts with traditional notions of proximate cause. A decision for the plaintiff would have introduced the risk that the sometimes overly sensitive demands of environmental agencies will be fed into the strict liability doctrine of *Rylands*, which implies an ever-expanding scope for strict liability, increasingly distanced from its rationale in *Rylands*.

Using the foreseeability limitation of *Rylands* (or, equivalently, section 519(2)) provides a neat way to reconcile *Indiana Harbor* with *Siegler v. Kuhlman*.[31] In *Siegler*, the defendant's gasoline truck exploded, incinerating the plaintiff's decedent. The court applied *Rylands*, holding the defendant strictly liable. The court compared the transportation of large quantities of gasoline on public highways to the storage of a potentially dangerous element. As an alternative justification the court noted that the explosion of the gasoline truck wiped out evidence that could be used to determine negligence; thus *res ipsa loquitur* provided another justification for imposing liability.

Judge Posner seized on the *res ipsa loquitur* discussion in *Siegler* as a basis for distinguishing *Indiana Harbor*. However, a more obvious distinction is that the roadway fireball in *Siegler* was well within the set of foreseeable catastrophes associated with transporting large quantities of gasoline, and therefore within the foreseeability limitation of *Rylands*. *Indiana Harbor* is distinguishable because the clean-up requirement imposed by the state environmental agency is arguably not within the foreseeable catastrophe scenarios associated with abnormally dangerous activities.

III. NUISANCE

Nuisance law, like abnormally dangerous activities law, is an offshoot of *Rylands*. With this in mind, I will use the rules set out previously to explain nuisance law.

---

[30] RESTATEMENT (SECOND) OF TORTS §519(2) (1977).
[31] Siegler v. Kuhlman, 502 P.2d 1181 (Wash. 1972).

The classic nuisance is the smoke-belching factory. It is a nuisance to neighbors because the smoke invades their land and makes it difficult for them to enjoy the use of their property. Also, nuisances tend to be continuing disturbances, unlike the one-shot explosions in the abnormally dangerous activities cases. The following is a useful definition:

A *nuisance is as an intentional, unreasonable, nontrespassory invasion of the plaintiff's quiet use and enjoyment of property.* Almost each word in this definition has an important meaning.

Intentional, in nuisance law, means that the defendant either intended to cause the invasion or knew with *substantial certainty* that it was occurring and did not attempt to stop it. Thus, if the defendant's factory is blowing black smoke over into the plaintiff's house, and the defendant is aware that this interference is occurring, then his conduct is intentional in the law. The effect of the intent requirement is to charge a price, through the liability system, to the defendant for his decision to locate in a certain area and to release a nuisance, whenever the defendant is aware of the resulting interferences to neighbors. This is consistent with the function of the intent standard, which is to internalize harms so that actors will be incentivized to take those harms into account in making the decision that the law seeks to regulate (Chapter 4).

Nontrespassory means that the invasion is not one that interferes with the plaintiff's exclusive possession. A nontrespassory invasion does not physically displace the plaintiff from some portion of his land. Obviously, this limitation on the scope of nuisance law serves to distinguish it from trespass. On a deeper level, the function of the nontrespassory limitation was probably best explained by Thomas Merrill,[32] relying on Calabresi and Melamed's theory of common law rules.[33] According to Merrill, trespass law, by giving the plaintiff ample power to enjoin the defendant, encourages potential trespassers to bargain for access to the plaintiff's property. Such bargaining is likely to occur only when it is feasible and relatively easy to do – that is, when the transaction (or bargaining) costs are low. Transactions regarding physical invasions are likely to be relatively cheap – anyone can point to a boundary and negotiate over its crossing. In contrast, transactions regarding nontrespassory invasions (such as noise or smoke) are likely to be time-consuming and difficult. Since the end point of zero noise is impossible to attain, the parties would have to determine how much noise is permissible, and how to determine if the agreement has been violated. Because an injunction against a nontrespassory invasion could be unclear both in meaning and scope, and therefore unlikely to facilitate bargaining, nuisance law adopts a different legal framework than trespass law – specifically, one

---

[32] Thomas W. Merrill, *Trespass, Nuisance, and the Costs of Determining Property Rights,* 14 J. Legal Stud. 13 (1985).

[33] Guido Calabresi & A. Douglas Melamed, *Property Rules, Liability Rules, and Inalienability: One View of the Cathedral,* 85 Harv. L. Rev. 1089 (1972).

in which the right to enjoin a threatened invasion is not as secure as under trespass law.

Invasion implies that the interference is not consensual. The vast majority of nuisances involve activities that externalize harms to neighbors without their consent, such as the smoke-belching factory. However, courts may find an invasion in the context of a consensual relationship if the nature of the interference is unobservable to the plaintiff, at least initially. In *Vogel v. Grant-Lafayette Electric Cooperative*,[34] the plaintiff farmer had entered into a contract with the defendant electricity supplier, and the distribution setup led to excessive stray voltage injuring his cows. The court found that the mere fact that the plaintiff had contracted with the defendant for electricity supply did not preclude him from maintaining a nuisance action for stray voltage against the supplier.

Lastly, consider the term *unreasonable*. The courts have been reluctant to provide a clear definition of an unreasonable invasion. Since nuisance law has its roots in *Rylands* (though some nuisance cases predate *Rylands*), the *Rylands* doctrine can be used to explain the concept of an unreasonable invasion. Section 520 of Second Restatement codifies the theory of *Rylands*. Translating section 520 to the nuisance setting, the following rules determine whether an interference is unreasonable:

(a) Existence of a high degree of risk of some *interference with the quiet use and enjoyment of land*
(b) Likelihood that *the interference* will be substantial
(c) Inability to eliminate *the interference* by the exercise of reasonable care
(d) Extent to which the activity is not a matter of common usage
(e) Inappropriateness of the activity to the place where it is carried on and
(f) Extent to which its value to the community is outweighed by its obnoxious attributes.

The reasoning behind the application of these factors is the same as that for the abnormally dangerous activities doctrine. The first three factors (a, b, c) capture the existence of a high residual risk of interference, even when the defendant takes care. In other words, the interference is a by-product of the defendant's activity, rather than the result of some discrete failure to take a particular precaution. The last three factors go to the questions of reciprocity in burdens and the balancing of harms and benefits.

Nuisances have sometimes been classified as nuisances per se or at law and nuisances *per accidens* or in fact.[35] Nuisances per se are described as nuisances at all times and in all places, while nuisances in fact depend on the circumstances. More specifically, a nuisance per se is an activity that is unlawful, such as a junkyard that violates a state public health code. An activity that is lawful and that interferes with

---

[34] Vogel v. Grant-LaFayette Elec. Coop., 548 N.W.2d 829 (Wis. 1996).
[35] *See, e.g.,* Morgan v. High Penn Oil Co., 77 S.E.2d 682 (N.C. 1953).

quiet use and enjoyment of neighboring property would belong under the nuisance *per accidens* label. The framework developed here applies equally to both types of nuisance, but it is obviously more relevant to the *per accidens* category. A finding of nuisance per se, like a finding of negligence per se, lifts the burden of proof from the plaintiff and generates the questions of statutory scope examined in Chapter 7.

Harm-Benefit Balancing

As an illustration of harm-benefit balancing in nuisance law, consider a fire station. A person who lives close to the station may suffer from the noise of the alarm bells, or from the fire trucks moving in and out of the station. But he also benefits from the presence of the fire station, and the benefits probably outweigh the harms. The harm-benefit test of factor (f) would therefore suggest that the fire station is not a nuisance.

In *Malhame v. Borough of Demarest*,[36] the plaintiffs brought a nuisance lawsuit against the municipality because its fire alarm system was too loud. They sought to enjoin the use of the alarm system. The evidence indicated that the alarm was more than an annoyance; the sound level was close to the threshold at which the average listener would experience pain. However, the court found that in light of public safety benefits, in which the fire alarm system played an essential role, the noise from the alarm was not an unreasonable invasion. In addition, the court found that in the absence of evidence that the nuisance could be abated without simply transferring it from one group of residents to another (by moving the sirens), the alarm system constituted a reasonable activity.

One of the early examples of harm-benefit balancing in nuisance law is provided by *Baines v. Baker*.[37] The defendants proposed to erect a hospital for treating smallpox patients in Coldbath Fields, London. The plaintiff, an owner of rental property in the area, sued to enjoin the building as a nuisance. Denying the injunction, the court held that the plaintiff's property-value losses due to fears, even though rational, were not recoverable through a nuisance action, and that the public benefits of the hospital would justify the burdens on neighbors. Lord Hardwicke added, "I am of opinion that it is a charity likely to prove of great advantage to mankind. Such an hospital must not be far from town, because those that are attacked with that disorder in a natural way may not be carried far."[38]

The Joyce and Joyce treatise on nuisance, published in 1906, concedes that there are many harm-benefit balancing cases but suggests that these are largely limited

---

[36] Malhame v. Borough of Demarest, 392 A.2d 652 (Law Div. 1978).

[37] Baines v. Baker, 1 Ambl. 158 (1752). For a summary, *see* NATHANIEL CLEVELAND MOAK & JOHN THOMAS COOK, REPORTS OF CASES DECIDED BY THE ENGLISH COURTS: WITH NOTES AND REFERENCES TO KINDRED CASES AND AUTHORITIES 368–369 (1884), *available at* http://books.google.com/books?id=i3UyAAAAIAAJ.

[38] Baines, 1 Ambl. at 159.

to where the plaintiff seeks an injunction.[39] Whether this claim is empirically valid or not, it does not diminish the importance of harm-benefit balancing in nuisance doctrine. Nuisance plaintiffs have typically sought injunctions, so one should expect that much of nuisance law would have developed within the framework of equity jurisprudence. It was obvious to courts that it would make little sense, as a general policy, to deny an injunction and then issue a sequence of separate damages awards to compensate plaintiffs for the injuries caused by a continuing interference.[40] Damages have been issued mainly in cases involving relatively small or discrete (one-shot) interferences,[41] or where the balance of the equities disfavored an injunction.[42] But even when damages are awarded, and an injunction denied, courts must still find that the *interference* caused by the defendant's activity was unreasonable, and this requires balancing harms against benefits. Given that the damages award is less costly to society than the injunction, the balancing that occurs in a nuisance action for damages is limited to a comparison of the harms and benefits directly linked to the defendant's interference, and does not need to take into account the equitable concern that the remedy itself, by shuttering the defendant's activity, could be more harmful than the interference.

---

[39] Joseph Asbury Joyce & Howard Clifford Joyce, A Treatise on the Law Governing Nuisances 696–699 (1906).

[40] Campbell v. Seaman, 63 N.Y. 568, 583 (1876) (Earl, J.) ("Here the injunction also prevents a multiplicity of suits. The injury is a recurring one, and every time the poisonous breath from defendant's brick-kiln sweeps over plaintiffs' land they have a cause of action. Unless the nuisance be restrained the litigation would be interminable. The policy of the law favors, and the peace and good order of society are best promoted by the termination of such litigations by a single suit. . . . The nuisance has occurred often enough within two years to do the plaintiffs large damage."). Aside from an injunction, the alternative to a sequence of awards is a lump sum award for the entire future damage. But this would have required a level of sophisticated financial analysis not available to courts over the period of nuisance law's development.

[41] Lillywhite v. Trimmer, 16 L.T. 318, 36 LJ. Ch. 525 (1867). The plaintiff sought to enjoin the Board of Health from discharging sewage into the river, claiming that his health had been injured, and that the water from the river was no longer fit for agricultural and domestic purposes. However, reports from a water inspector described the water as tolerably pure. Dismissing the plaintiff's action, the court held: "It is a settled rule of law that where a work of great public importance cannot be effected without interfering with private rights, the private rights must prevail, and the public work must be carried out as best it can without such interference. But where a great public object is to be attained, as, for example, the drainage of a town, the court should put no difficulty unnecessarily in the way of carrying such object into effect. In considering questions of nuisance, the court must have regard to the extent of the nuisance, and to the balance of inconvenience, and if the extent of inconvenience sustained is trifling, and such as may readily be compensated by money, the right of parties creating the nuisance must not be interfered with where the objects which they seek to attain are of considerable importance." 16 L.T. at 318. *See also Campbell*, 63 N.Y. at 581–582 (on the availability of damages as an alternative to an injunction).

[42] *See, e.g.*, Clifton Iron Co. v. Dye, 6. So. 192, 193 (1889) (Company owned valuable iron ore land, and in the course of washing iron ores caused particles of earth and other materials to flow down the creek to plaintiff's land, polluting a stream. The court of equity, noting the company's substantial investment and the public convenience of its works, reversed the injunction based on the comparatively immaterial injury sustained by the plaintiff.).

One characteristically forceful statement of the balancing principle appears in an opinion by Oliver Wendell Holmes, Jr., *Middlesex Co. v. McCue.*[43] The defendant owned land on a slope that descended into a mill pond created by the plaintiff (Middlesex Company). In the course of working on his garden, applying fertilizers and tilling the land, soil eroded and slid in the plaintiff's pond, causing it to fill up partially. The plaintiff asked for an injunction. Holmes began his opinion with a discussion of the utilitarian basis of nuisance law and suggested that the outcomes ranging from zero damages to an injunction can be explained by the balance between the benefit of the defendant's activity (to the defendant and to society) and the harm to the plaintiff. He concluded that the defendant's activity, ordinary cultivation of land, using common and reasonable methods, was not a nuisance. If the defendant had employed a particularly offensive type of fertilizer, Holmes noted, he might have concluded otherwise.

In *Waschak v. Moffat*,[44] a mound of waste from the defendant's coal processing operation emitted hydrogen sulfide gas, which turned the color of the plaintiff's home from white to black. The court found in favor of the defendant on the grounds that the interference was not intentional, because the coal company did not know that the gas was being emitted or that it would have the effect that it had on plaintiff's home, and that the interference was not unreasonable, because the coal industry had long served as the main source of economic development in the region of Pennsylvania where the plaintiff lived. The court cited earlier Pennsylvania case law in support of its decision to count the economic development due to coal mining as a benefit that offset the harm from the defendant's activity.

The most important of the earlier Pennsylvania cases cited by the court in *Waschak* is *Pennsylvania Coal Co. v. Sanderson.*[45] In *Sanderson*, the defendants operated a coal mine and in the process brought up underground water. The waste water flowed into and polluted a surface stream used by the plaintiff, three miles away, as a source of drinking water. The court described the case as a purely private nuisance not affecting general access to usable water, because the plaintiff's community had "abundant pure water from other sources."[46] The court held that "private personal inconveniences" had to give way to the "necessities of a great community" and the development of natural resources.[47] In an explicit reference balancing harms and

---

[43] 21 N.E. 230 (Mass. 1889).

[44] 109 A.2d 310 (Pa. 1954).

[45] 6 Atl. 453 (Pa. 1886), *overruled by* Commonwealth v. Barnes & Tucker Co., 319 A.2d 871 (Pa. 1974). For an insightful discussion, *see* Todd J. Zywicki, *A Unanimity-Reinforcing Model of Efficiency in the Common Law: An Institutional Comparison of Common Law and Legislative Solutions to the Large-Number Externality Problems*, 46 CASE W. RES. L. REV. 961, 1017–1020 (1996); *see also* Robert G. Bone, *Normative Theory and Legal Doctrine in American Nuisance Law: 1850 to 1920*, 59 S. CAL. L. REV. 1101, 1160–65 (1986); Jed Handelsman Shugerman, *The Floodgates of Strict Liability: Bursting Reservoirs and the Adoption of Fletcher v. Rylands in the Gilded Age*, 110 YALE L. J. 333, 364–68 (2000).

[46] *Sanderson, supra* note 45, at 459.

[47] *Id.*

benefits, the court quoted approvingly from a dissent in an earlier decision in the same case:

> The population, wealth, and improvements are the result of mining, and of that alone. The plaintiffs knew, when they purchased their property, that they were in a mining region. They were in a city born of mining operations, and which had become rich and populous as a result thereof. They knew that all mountain streams in that section were affected by mine water, or were liable to be. Having enjoyed the advantages which coal mining confers, I see no great hardship, nor any violence to equity, in their also accepting the inconveniences necessarily resulting from the business.[48]

Sanderson was limited to its facts and essentially overruled, in 1974, in *Commonwealth v. Barnes & Tucker Co.*[49] The court did not say what remains of the doctrine that economic development could be counted as a benefit that offsets the harms, in a balancing of harms and benefits from a nuisance defendant's activity. However, both *Sanderson* and *Barnes & Tucker* are reconcilable with the harm-benefit balancing principle. At the time of *Sanderson*, economic development due to coal mining altered living standards dramatically. By the time of *Barnes & Tucker*, coal mining had a far lesser impact on living standards in Pennsylvania. A consistent application of harm-benefit balancing could justify both decisions.

The nuisance cases recognizing benefits sufficient to offset the harm from the defendant's activity involve, in one set of cases, safety, security, or infrastructure, such as the provision of a fire alarm system (*Malhame*), a hospital (*Baines*), or the supply of natural gas, and, in another set of cases, economic development, such as in *Sanderson* and *Waschak*. The decline of cases such as *Waschak* and *Sanderson* is to be expected as the result of economic growth; the benefits of additional mining of natural resources eventually taper off relative to its harmful environmental effects. But economic growth does not diminish the import of cases such as *Malhame*.

Some courts have explicitly rejected the harm-benefit balancing principle in actions for damages, the most famous of which is the Wisconsin Supreme Court's decision in *Jost v. Dairyland Power Cooperative*.[50] This must be taken as a minority view in light of entire body of nuisance law going back to cases referenced in *Rylands v. Fletcher*.

Many courts have noted that damages should be awarded instead of an injunction where the harm to society from the injunction would greatly exceed the social gain from the injunction.[51] The claim that harm-benefit balancing is restricted to nuisance cases in which plaintiffs have sought injunctions is based on the view, likely mistaken, that since the majority of nuisance plaintiffs seek injunctions, the law that

---

[48] *Id.* at 465.
[49] 319 A.2d 871 (Pa. 1974).
[50] 172 N.W.2d 647 (Wis. 1970).
[51] *Supra* note 40; Comment, *Injunction – Nuisance – Balance of Convenience*, 37 YALE L. J. 96 (1927).

has developed must be specific to the remedy sought by the plaintiff. The view that appears to be more consistent with the case law is that harm-benefit balancing is part of the process of determining whether the interference from an activity is unreasonable. The only difference connected to the choice of remedy is that the injunction requires a fuller consideration of the social costs imposed by the remedy. I will return to this issue later in this chapter.

Location

Cases exploring the limits of nuisance liability often discuss the importance of location. Many of them make the point that the decision to live in an industrialized area means putting up with some degree of interference from noise, smoke, and similar disturbances. The rationale for this doctrine can be found in the assumption of risk theory reflected in factor (e) or the reciprocity of harm notion reflected in factor (d).

Both theories, assumption of risk and reciprocity, were part of the court's rationale in *Bamford v. Turnley*.[52] The defendant had erected brick kilns on his property and proceeded to emit fumes and smoke that disturbed the plaintiff. Baron Pollock favored upholding the verdict for the defendant on the ground that some locations are appropriate for certain offensive activities, such as burning bricks, because of long usage. The theory of assumption of risk provides support for this position. Baron Bramwell's opinion, siding with the majority finding the defendant liable,[53] first presents the reciprocity concept as a limiting factor on nuisance liability, and then holds that the harms from the defendant's brick-making activity were too great to be reciprocated by the activities of neighbors. Bramwell said that nuisance liability should not extend to acts "necessary for the common and ordinary occupation of land,"[54] because the harms from such acts are reciprocally imposed among members of a community. But Bramwell concluded that the defendant's brick kiln was not an activity necessary for ordinary occupation.

Probably the finest discussion of the locality theory appears in *Campbell v. Seaman*,[55] another case involving brick kilns and fumes. The court said that

> [p]ersons living in organized communities must suffer some damage, annoyance and inconvenience from each other. For these they are compensated by all the advantages of civilized society. If one lives in the city he must expect to suffer the dirt, smoke, noisome odors, noise and confusion incident to city life.[56]

This passage highlights the utilitarian basis of the locality theory, as well as its basis in assumption of risk theory. If one chooses to live in a city, and thereby to enjoy the

---

[52] Bamford v. Turnley, 122 Eng. Rep. 27 (Ex. Ch. 1862).
[53] *Ibid.* at 32–33.
[54] *Id.*
[55] 63 N.Y. 568 (1876).
[56] *Id.* at 577.

benefits of the location (specifically, the infrastructure and agglomeration benefits that support productive activity), one should also bear some of the costs. Otherwise, the benefits would be curtailed by the burden of liability.[57]

Gilbert v. Showerman[58] and *Robinson v. Baugh*,[59] two cases from Detroit, Michigan, during the infancy of its formation into an industrial powerhouse, contain excellent discussions of the locality theory. In *Gilbert v. Showerman*, the plaintiff attempted to enjoin a factory next door to him. Denying the injunction, the court said:

> In a crowded city some annoyance to others is inseparable from almost any employment, and while the proximity of the stables of the dealers in horses, or of the shops of workers in iron or tin, seems an intolerable nuisance to one, another is annoyed and incommoded, though in less degree, by the bundles and boxes of the dealer in dry goods, and the noise and jar of the wagons which deliver and remove them . . .
>
> In the case before us we find that the defendants are carrying on a business not calculated to be specially annoying, except to the occupants of dwellings. They chose for its establishment a locality where all the buildings had been constructed for purposes other than for residence. Families, to some extent, occupied these buildings, but their occupation was secondary to the main object of their construction, and we must suppose that it was generally for reasons which preclude the choice of a more desirable neighborhood. The number of these families, moreover, was decreasing, and in view of the size of the block, was really insignificant at the time this machinery as put in. . . . We cannot shut our eyes to the obvious truth that if the running of this mill can be enjoined, almost any manufactory in any of our cities can be enjoined upon similar reasons. Some resident must be incommoded or annoyed by almost any of them. In the heaviest business quarters among the most offensive trades of every city, will be found persons, who, for motives of convenience, economy or necessity, have taken up their abode; but in the administration of equitable policy, the greater and more general interests must be regarded rather than the inferior and special. The welfare of the community cannot be otherwise subserved and its necessities provided for.[60]

Unusual Sensitivity

The locality and balancing theories are based, at bottom, on a single underlying test. That test, introduced in Chapter 5, examines two factors: whether the harms externalized to neighbors by the injurer are reciprocal to those externalized by others in the locality, and whether the benefits externalized to neighbors by the defendant's activity are greater than the harms. In the first scenario, that of reciprocal harms, it was demonstrated in Chapter 5 that strict liability and negligence have the same

---

[57] *See* Chapter 5, examining the foundations of *Rylands* doctrine.
[58] 23 Mich. 448 (1871).
[59] 31 Mich. 290 (1875).
[60] Gilbert v. Showerman, 23 Mich. 448, 452–456 (1871).

implications for incentives; hence, there is no reason to prefer strict liability over negligence. In the second scenario, where externalized benefits may exceed harms, strict liability would be undesirable because it excessively discourages the defendant's activity.

Locality, as a factor in the nuisance inquiry, can be defended on the basis of reciprocity in harms, or harm-benefit balancing. Some localities are appropriate for certain types of interference, such as the noise of a shop, because other activities within the same locality produce similar interferences. In other instances, the interference is appropriate for the location because the benefits the activity confers on the community clearly outweigh the costs. One of the reasons people choose to move to the location of the interference is because the activity generating the interference also benefits the locality.

In conducting the reciprocity and balancing tests, one has to look at the average burden suffered as a result of the interference. A nuisance does not generate a substantial interference unless it does so to the average member of the community. If the average member of the community does not perceive a substantial interference, then there really is no harm that needs to be considered for an inquiry into reciprocity or balancing.

The legal rule that reflects this policy denies a remedy in nuisance law for the unusually sensitive plaintiff. In *Rogers v. Elliott*,[61] the court rejected a nuisance suit from a plaintiff who claimed that the ringing of a church bell constituted a nuisance. The plaintiff claimed that he suffered convulsions as a result of the ringing. But the ringing of the bell was not a significant interference to the average member of the community.

Looking to law instead of policy, the rule denying a remedy for the unusually sensitive plaintiff is an implication of the special proximate causation test under nuisance law and under *Rylands v. Fletcher*. Strict liability is limited to those injuries that are foreseeable or natural consequences of the escape from the defendant's property. Foreseeable injuries will be those that would be experienced by the average member of the community. Someone who has a special sensitivity to the defendant's activity – so that the individual would suffer an injury from an invasion that would not cause an injury to anyone else – cannot gain protection for that special sensitivity under nuisance law.

Aesthetic Interferences: Blocking Light or Views

The locality and balancing factors are no longer relevant, it seems, when it comes to blocking light or blocking a view. The general rule is that nuisance law does not protect an individual's access to sunlight or a view (of the water, mountains, etc.) connected to a parcel of property. One exception recognized relatively early

---

[61] Rogers v. Elliott, 15 N.E. 768 (Mass. 1888).

in American nuisance law involves the case in which a person puts up a screen or fence to block another's sunlight, purely out of malice.[62] Where the obstruction serves no useful purpose at all, and is put up for the sole purpose of causing injury to the plaintiff, courts will enjoin the obstruction.

What explains the rule against easements for light? One formal doctrinal explanation is that the blocking of sunlight is not an invasion. Nuisances involve sending something over to the plaintiff's property – noise, smoke, bad odors. When sunlight or a view is blocked, that is simply denying the victim a type of easement over the property of another person. Ownership of land implies an entitlement to build up above the surface or below it (within whatever regulations apply). The rule against easements for light implies that an owner of land will have the rights that are typically associated with that status. In other words, the rule against easements for light is a complement of the *ad coelum* rule of trespass (Chapter 4).

While this provides a formal legal answer, it does not quite provide an answer based on any utilitarian rationale. It leads to the question: Why not give a person an easement to a view across someone else's property?

The basis for denying nuisance claims for blocking access to light has to be found in the practical problems that arise if such a claim were recognized, and, secondly, in the underlying structure of nuisance and trespass law. If courts permitted plaintiffs to enjoin property owners from blocking sunlight, then the enjoined owners would have to purchase the right to build up from the plaintiffs. But suppose there are five plaintiffs, each holding a different right to enjoin? How can the owner negotiate with all of them to "buy out" their injunctions? How can the owner be sure that each plaintiff has a legitimate claim of injury?

It follows that the transaction costs associated with a nuisance regime that respects claims of access to light would be enormous. And one of the reasons that the power to enjoin is narrower under nuisance law than under trespass law is that the transaction costs of transferring rights is lower in the trespass setting. It is far easier to transfer the right to a boundary than to transfer a right to "clean air."

The law on access to light, by denying nuisance protection to such an entitlement, forces those who claim that they want access to buy out the property owner who is blocking access. This should not be difficult. Indeed, the transaction costs associated with purchasing an easement to sunlight are likely to be low. The person who wants a sunlight easement over a tract of property need only contact the owner and seek a price at which the owner would be willing to forgo his build-up option. Moreover, if complainants are forced to pay for access to light, they are likely to do so in those cases in which it is really important to them. No one has to worry about the authenticity of their claims, since no complainant would offer to buy out a property owner unless he feels that the injury to him from having his access to light blocked is substantial.

---

[62] Flaherty v. Moran, 45 N.W. 381 (Mich. 1890).

The rule denying nuisance protection for access to sunlight does nothing more than recognize a clear assignment of property rights in a setting where the cost of transacting around the assignment is low. Each owner of land has a right to build up on his parcel, and there is an equally clear complementary rule that the neighbor must purchase an easement to sunlight from the property owner.

Some commentators have suggested that this rule is designed to foster economic development.[63] It may serve that purpose sometimes, but encouraging development may not necessarily be its aim. Under the law rejecting a common easement to light, property rules are clear, and transactions with respect to such easements can take place easily. Under a rule granting common law easements to light, property rights would not be clear, as owners would not know what they could do with their parcels, and transactions would be time-consuming, potentially endless, and pro-hibitively expensive. It follows that the existing law is good for economic development largely because the alternative would devolve into an economic and administrative quagmire.

Coming to the Nuisance

Another special topic under nuisance law is the matter of "coming to the nuisance." It would appear to be an obvious defense to a nuisance lawsuit. If the defendant set up his activity first, and then the plaintiff moved next door, it would seem obvious that the plaintiff has assumed the risk and should therefore be denied the power to enjoin the defendant's activity. However, the law does not consistently take this view.

Courts have said that the "coming to the nuisance" argument does not always serve as a defense to a nuisance claim. In other words, getting there first does not immunize you from nuisance liability.

This position is not hard to justify on utilitarian grounds. The defendant may have arrived first, but the character of the locality may have changed so much since his arrival that it would be better for the welfare of the community, even taking into account the demoralization of actors in the defendant's position, to enjoin the defendant's activity. That is the simple and short defense for the rule on coming to the nuisance.

The welfare balancing that justifies the rule often depends on the mix of uses in a locality, as suggested in the passage from *Gilbert v. Showerman* excerpted above. If the plaintiff moves into an industrial area, it would make sense for the coming to the nuisance defense to apply. The plaintiff may have, as the court suggested of households in the business locality in *Showerman*, moved to the industrial area for the convenience of the location. That does not give him a right to shut local

---

[63] Richard O. Zerbe, Jr., *Justice and the Evolution of the Common Law*, 3 J. L. Econ. & Pol'y 81, 118 (2006).

industries down. The plaintiff's decision to move to an area may indicate an assumption of the risk of interferences from activities common to the area. On the other hand, over time the locality may change. The businesses may move out, leaving a largely residential area. The one factory remaining will generate interferences to the residents – interferences that are not reciprocated by the activities of residents nor outweighed by benefits. It may be socially desirable, then, to enjoin the one remaining factory.

Damages versus Injunctions

Nuisances have generated three remedial outcomes: (1) no damages at all, (2) damages only, and (3) injunctions sometimes coupled with damages. Holmes suggested, in *Middlesex v. McCue*,[64] that this range of remedial outcomes could be explained by comparing the social value of the defendant's activity to the gravity of harm suffered by the plaintiff.

Although there appears to be a utilitarian balancing test at the core of nuisance law, we have also seen that, with respect to some types of interference, nuisance law immunizes the defendant from liability. For example, the defendant can block the plaintiff's sunlight, and unless the evidence shows that the blocking was motivated solely by malice, the plaintiff's nuisance claim will be rejected. For this type of interference, there is no balancing at all; rights are clear. When we move outside of this set of interferences, we encounter those that fall under the balancing framework. In some cases, courts will find that the balance weighs in favor of the defendant, resulting in no liability; in others, it will find in favor of the plaintiff, resulting in liability or an injunction, or both.

The structure of remedial outcomes implies that nuisance law, cleared of confusing terminology, distinguishes *unreasonable invasions* and *unreasonable activities*. A reasonable activity could give rise to an unreasonable invasion. When the activity is reasonable and the invasion is unreasonable, a court will award damages only. The damages awarded in such a case will seek to compensate victims for the permanent imposition of the defendant's interference – sometimes in the form of an award for permanent damages. When both the activity and the invasion are unreasonable, both an injunction and damages, for harms suffered that are not curable by the injunction, are appropriate. As the social value of the defendant's activity declines relative to the gravity of the plaintiff's harm, the appropriate remedy moves along the spectrum from no damages, to damages, to injunction (plus damages).

Another possible remedy, though rarely observed, is the *compensated injunction* order in *Spur Industries v. Del E. Webb Development Co.*[65] The court enjoined the defendant's cattle feedlot and required the developer, Webb, to compensate

---

[64] 149 Mass. 103, 21 N.E. 230 (1889).
[65] 494 P.2d 700 (Ariz. 1972).

the defendant. One can easily see how such a remedy might be preferred by the nuisance source, given the alternatives of being enjoined or paying damages to nuisance victims. The most efficient solution might be an arrangement where the plaintiffs compensate the nuisance generator to move his activity. Indeed, Calabresi and Melamed, in their article on the theory of remedies,[66] proposed the compensated injunction as a hypothetical ("Rule 4") almost at the same time the court was handing down its decision in *Spur*. If the nuisance source can continue to hire the same workforce, the cost of moving is just the one-time cost of a new facility, which may be relatively small in comparison to the gain the plaintiffs receive as a result of the injunction. For the same reason, one might observe a "reverse payment settlement" in which the nuisance source agrees to move his activity and the plaintiffs agree to pay money to the nuisance source (see Chapter 18).

Since injunctions have been a common remedy in nuisance cases, it is easiest to begin with a case in which the court has found a nuisance, adopted the injunction as the presumptive remedy, and then examined whether it should award damages rather than impose the injunction. Such a case would provide insights on how courts choose between damages and injunctions.

Boomer v. Atlantic Cement Co.[67] is the most famous modern case of this sort, though there have been others.[68] *Boomer* suggests that courts apply principles of equity,[69] which means balancing the costs and benefits of the injunction. Under principles of equity, a plaintiff seeking a permanent injunction must demonstrate (1) that he has suffered an irreparable injury; (2) that remedies available at law, such as monetary damages, are inadequate to compensate for that injury; (3) that, considering the balance of hardships between the plaintiff and defendant, a remedy in equity is warranted; and (4) that the public interest would not be disserved by a permanent injunction.[70] It follows that if it is more harmful to the welfare of the community to award the injunction, rather than deny the injunction and award damages, courts will not award the injunction. In other words, when courts consider the injunction question, they are encouraged by law take into consideration the benefits to the community from the defendant's activity.

The equity balancing test is cast in such general terms that it is difficult to see how it should be applied in a particular case. I will offer an accounting framework for equity balancing in the nuisance cases here.

---

[66] Calabresi & Melamed, *supra* note 33.

[67] Boomer v. Atlantic Cement Co., 257 N.E.2d 870 (N.Y. 1970) (refusing to enjoin a private nuisance justified by the adequacy of compensation in damages relief and significant discrepancy between the injury suffered and the cost in granting injunction).

[68] Comment, *Injunction – Nuisance – Balance of Convenience, supra* note 51.

[69] A more extensive discussion of the injunction question appears in Chapter 18. In that chapter, I note that when the nuisance amounts to a dispossession, the justification for an injunction is just as strong as in the case where a defendant builds a structure over the plaintiff's dwelling. One should expect courts to routinely issue injunctions in such nuisance cases. Such a case, of course, would probably lead the court to issue an injunction under the equity-balancing test too.

[70] *See, e.g.,* eBay Inc. v. MercExchange, 547 U.S. 388, 391 (2006).

A simple accounting framework can be applied to the injunction question in *Boomer*, where the court had to decide whether to enjoin the operation of a cement plant that emitted smoke, dirt, and vibrations. The plant was also a major employer of community residents. The total benefits and total costs of the defendant's activity can be itemized as follows:

$$Total\ benefits = Internal\ benefits + External\ benefits$$
$$Total\ costs = Internal\ costs + External\ costs.$$

Total benefits are decomposed into internal or private benefits and external or public benefits. The internal benefits are conveyed through the market – goods and services. They are measured primarily by the value of the goods provided by the defendant's activity. The external benefits are transferred outside of the market exchange mechanism – to people who are not consumers or employees of the defendant's activity. For example, a business may benefit people who are neither consumers nor employees by inducing other businesses (e.g., suppliers) to move in to the same community. The external costs or harms in the accounting above are the injuries generated by the defendant's activity – the smoke, dirt, and vibrations. The internal costs are simply the costs of carrying on the activity – for example, the costs of producing the plant's product.

A market activity, such as the production of cement in *Boomer*, will not exist if the internal benefit from the activity (value of goods) is less than the internal cost (cost of production), for then the activity would be unable to pay its own way. The internal benefit is determined by the market demand for the activity's output, and the internal cost is determined by the market supply of the activity's inputs.[71] The excess of internal benefit over internal cost is equal to the sum of consumer surplus and producer (or labor) surplus.[72]

This accounting framework suggests that the cement plant in *Boomer* should have been enjoined as an unreasonable activity if its total costs to the community exceeded its total benefits. If, on the other hand, the total benefits exceeded the total costs, the activity should not have been enjoined.

This framework further suggests that the injunction and damages questions are separable, which means that a court could find that an activity is reasonable but its resulting interference is not. In *Boomer*, the interference was deemed unreasonable – the harm to residents from the defendant's plant was not offset by any finding of a significant external benefit to them – and yet not sufficiently harmful to justify enjoining the defendant's activity. Instead of granting an injunction, the court required the defendant to pay for the *permanent damages* suffered by the plaintiffs – that is, an amount that would compensate for future harms. The court determined that the total of permanent damages to all of the plaintiffs was $185,000.

---

[71] On market supply, *see* Chapter 16.
[72] On the definitions of consumer surplus and producer surplus, *see* Chapter 16.

The total of permanent damages is equal to the *present value* of the harms imposed over the long run. The concept of present value is examined in detail in Chapter 18. For now, you can think about the present value of nuisance damages as follows. Suppose a nuisance imposes an injury of a fixed dollar amount every year on a victim (annual damages), and the nuisance, if unabated, will continue forever. The present value (permanent damages) is the amount that you would have to put in the bank today to be able to compensate the victim's annual damages every year. It follows, then, that the amount that you put in the bank today (permanent damages) would have to be a sum large enough that when multiplied by the interest rate on the bank account would generate the annual damages sum. Thus, the relationship between permanent damages and annual damages is

$$(Interest\ rate) \times (Permanent\ Damages) = Annual\ Damages.$$

It follows that if we know the interest rate and the annual damages, we can determine the permanent damages. Conversely, if we know the interest rate and the permanent damages, we can determine the annual damages. For example, if the annual damages amount to $20 and the interest rate is 5 percent, the permanent damages would be $400.

Assuming an interest rate of 5 percent, the total permanent damages of $185,000 in *Boomer* would imply annual damages of $9,250 per year.[73] For an injunction to be appropriate on equitable grounds, the excess, each year, of the internal benefit over the internal cost – which is the total consumer and labor surplus from the defendant's operation – would have to have been less than $9,250. Given that the defendant's plant employed over 300 people in the affected community, the total surplus probably far exceeded $9,250 per year. Thus, an injunction against the cement plant probably would have violated principles of equity.

IV. ANIMALS

Another offshoot of *Rylands v. Fletcher* is strict liability for dangerous animals. Liability for vicious animals has been described as strict, though the doctrine appears to be more complicated on closer inspection.

Strict liability applies to the holding of wild animals such as tigers and bears. For these cases, the law follows *Rylands*. The defendant gathers something on his land that is dangerous if it escapes, and is held strictly liable for the consequences of its escape. The reason is that the holding of a ferocious animal imposes considerably more risk on neighbors than they reciprocate, and the benefit to them is trivial.

---

[73] With an interest rate of 5 percent, an account with $185,000 would generate $9,250 each year. Thus, if the interest rate is 5 percent, a stream of income paying $9,250 per year would be worth $185,000 in present value. For more on present value, *see* Chapter 18.

Rylands recognized narrow contributory negligence and assumption of risk defenses. The only type of contributory negligence defense recognized in *Rylands* governs the case where the plaintiff is responsible for the release or for the attack. Assumption of risk is not explicitly mentioned as a defense in *Rylands*, but it is implied under the risk-benefit balancing rationale of the opinion.

The risk versus benefit tradeoff factor suggests an exception to the rule of strict liability for injuries caused by wild animals. Consider zoos. Unlike the case of a private person who holds wild animals for his own amusement, zoos provide recreational and educational benefits to the public, and the benefits are widely disseminated. The risk-benefit test of *Rylands* implies that the negligence rule, rather than strict liability, may be preferable in the case of zoos. The law is consistent with this: The negligence rule applies to cases of attacks within zoos.[74] Similarly, the negligence rule has been applied in the case of an attack in a wildlife park.[75] To some extent, assumption of risk plays a role here: if a person enters a zoo, he does so because he perceives the benefits to be greater than the infinitesimal risk that one of the animals will escape and injure him. However, the utilitarian basis for applying the negligence rule rather than strict liability continues to hold to some degree even in the case where the attack takes place outside of the zoo.[76]

For domesticated animals, the law is a bit more complicated. The negligence rule applies to injuries caused by domesticated animals (e.g., dogs, cats) that are known as a class to be tame.[77] Thus, if a dog attacks a person, the owner may be held liable, but only under negligence principles. That means that if the owner should have foreseen the attack under the circumstances and yet failed to take reasonable care to prevent it, he will be held liable for negligence.

If the dog has shown a vicious tendency, some courts and commentators have said that the owner is strictly liable for foreseeable injuries that it causes.[78] On closer inspection, the law of *Rylands* applies straightforwardly here. Courts have referred to liability as strict, but it is strict liability in the sense of *Rylands*. Thus, there are potential defenses based on contributory negligence and assumption of risk, though these defenses are extremely narrow. The contributory negligence defense applies

---

[74] Thomas M. Cooley, A Treatise on the Law of Torts or the Wrongs Which Arise Independently of Contract 350 (John Lewis ed., Student ed. 1907) ("The keeper of a zoological park was held not liable for injury by an escaped animal, unless he was negligent."); Spring Co. v. Edgar, 99 U.S. 645, 649 (1878); Jackson v. Baker, 24 App. Cas. D.C. 100 (1904); Marquet v. La Duke, 55 N.W. 1006 (Mich. 1893); City and County of Denver v. Kennedy, 476 P.2d (Colo. App. 1970).

[75] Spring Co. v. Edgar, 99 U.S. 645 (1878).

[76] Smith v. City of Birmingham, 270 Ala. 681, 121 So.2d 867 (1960). In *Smith*, a wild deer escaped while being transported to the zoo and attacked the plaintiff outside of the zoo grounds. The court held that negligence applied because the zoo was carrying out a governmental rather than ministerial function. However, the underlying rationale for the court's immunity finding was the defendant's provision of a public benefit.

[77] *See, e.g.*, Drake v. Dean, 19 Cal. Rptr.2d 325, 335 (Cal. App. 3d Dist. 1993).

[78] Van Etten v. Noyes, 128 App. Div. 406, 112 N.Y.S. 888 (1908); Russell v. Rivera, 780 N.Y.S.2d 699, 700 (N.Y. App. Div. 1st Dept. 2004).

in the case in which the victim is responsible for the escape or release of the vicious dog, or if the victim provokes the dog in a manner that makes the attack a response that any reasonable person would expect – for example, the victim, not acting in self-defense, beats the dog with a stick.

The assumption of risk defense is limited to the setting where there is a risk-benefit balancing argument that supports the defendant's decision to subject the victim to the risk of an attack by the animal. Suppose, to take a concrete example, the owner releases a dog that he knows to be vicious in the presence of people to drive away other animals, such as wolves. Once released, the dog drives away the wolves and then bites one of the humans it has protected. A court might hold, under *Rylands*, that the strict liability rule does not apply, and the owner will be held liable if at all only on the theory that he failed to take reasonable steps to control the dog in the presence of other people.[79]

Overall, the framework of *Rylands*, as helpfully codified by the Second Restatement, applies straightforwardly to animals as to any other potentially harmful escaping agent. Although liability is said to be strict, the law incorporates some rather complicated defenses to draw a line between activities that should and activities that should not be discouraged.[80]

---

[79] In ranching communities where "predator control dogs" have long been in use, states have been reluctant to apply strict liability to cases of injuries caused by such dogs. *See, e.g.,* Legro v. Robinson, 2012 Co. App. 182 (Colo. App. 2012) (Colorado statute excludes predator control dogs from strict liability).

[80] For more discussion of the policies reflected in the law, *see* Keith N. Hylton, *A Missing Markets Theory of Tort Law*, 90 Nw. U. L. Rev. 977 (1996); Hylton, *A Positive Theory of Strict Liability*, 4 Rev. Law & Econ. 153 (2008); Peter M. Gerhart, *The Death of Strict Liability*, 56 Buff. L. Rev. 245 (2008). For a view opposing utilitarian policy arguments, *see* Gregory C. Keating, *Nuisance as a Strict Liability Wrong*, 4 J. Tort Law 1 (2012).

16

Defamation

Defamation law governs liability for the dissemination of words that tend to disgrace, injure the reputation, or diminish the esteem others hold for a person. The words that can have this effect are uncountable, but a few common ones are easy to state: liar, cheat, thief.

This simple definition of defamation veils many complicated questions explored in this chapter. And even before we encounter any complicated questions, there are some obvious ones raised immediately by this straightforward definition.

First, a tort based on an injury to esteem is subject to the varying norms that govern social opinions on merit and value. Esteem, unlike a direct injury to person or to property, is a "social construct." A punch in the nose is a breach of reasonable conduct norms at all times and wherever you go. But esteem varies over time and across communities. Over the years, views have changed within many societies on what is considered disgraceful or repugnant.[1] Similarly, across communities within any given time period, views differ on the nature of disgrace.[2] Should society

---

[1] Matherson v. Marchello, 100 A.D.2d 233, 242 (N.Y. App. Div.2d Dep't 1984) (imputation of homosexuality is actionable defamation without proof of special damages); Yonaty v. Mincolla, 97 A.D.3d 141, 144 (N.Y. App. Div. 3d Dep't 2012) (statements that a person is gay or homosexual are no longer per se defamatory in New York); MacIntyre v. Fruchter, 148 N.Y.S. 786 (N.Y. Sup. 1914) (suggesting racial misidentification defamatory); Johnson v. Staten Island Advance Newspaper Inc., 824 N.Y.S.2d 755 (N.Y. Civ. Ct. 2004) (rejecting theory of defamation based on racial misidentification). *See* Samuel Brenner, *Negro Blood in His Veins: The Development and Disappearance of the Doctrine of Defamation Per Se by Racial Misidentification in the American South*, 50 SANTA CLARA L. REV. 333 (2010); 1 ROBERT D. SACK, SACK ON DEFAMATION § 2:4.4 (4th ed. 2010).

[2] Even during the period when many courts held that to falsely describe a person generally perceived to be white as black was defamatory, there was variation among the state courts on this matter. Compare Flood v. News & Courier Co., 50 S.E. 637, 639–641 (S.C. 1905) (holding a newspaper liable for defamation when they referenced a white man as a "negro"), with Deese v. Collins, 133 S.E. 92, 92–93 (N.C. 1926) (when the defendant called plaintiff "a free negro," "the words do not impute a crime or a misdemeanor punishable by an infamous penalty; they do not impute a contagious disease

continue to recognize a tort based on such an ephemeral and parochial notion as social esteem?

Second, the compensatory function of defamation law generates the question whether liability is strict, based on negligence, or based on intent to harm. Is defamation a strict liability tort, as Prosser teaches,[3] or is it a specific intent tort (requiring proof of intent to harm), as suggested by Holmes?[4] The evidence favors Prosser's characterization, but there is a basis for Holmes's view too.

Third, how does defamation differ in general from other torts? Obviously, a defamatory publication is distinguishable from the typical battery or nuisance. But if we try to look at tort standards in their most general characterizations, as recommended in previous chapters, is defamation really different? Prosser suggests that defamation is just a type of strict liability, like the *Rylands* doctrine for abnormally dangerous activities (Chapter 5). I contend that defamation law is, in many particulars, similar in form to the *Rylands* doctrine, and that drawing analogies to *Rylands* can provide a deeper understanding of defamation doctrine and policy. The analogy is not perfect, but it is good enough to account for the salient features of the law. However, defamation law is more accurately described as an amalgam of strict liability, negligence, and per se legality theories. The functional account offered in this chapter provides an explanation for the somewhat confusing and varying approaches reflected in defamation law.

The functional account also offers an explanation for the apparent strangeness of *Rylands* serving as a broad template for defamation law. *Rylands* applies to dangerous activities, like blasting. Defamation law, by contrast, applies to expression, which generally benefits society. Why would the law treat publishing in the same way as blasting?

This chapter begins with an examination of defamation as it has evolved under the common law, and later reviews the changes in American defamation law due to Supreme Court decisions beginning with *New York Times Co. v. Sullivan*.[5] The reason for this approach is first to capture in condensed form the work of the common law, so that it can be compared to the other subjects of tort law presented in previous chapters. Justifications for various rules of defamation law are easier to see when general patterns in tort law are observed. Second, the changes attributable to the Supreme Court's constitutionalization of defamation law are easier to understand,

---

by which plaintiff will be excluded from society; nor are they derogatory to plaintiff in respect to his trade or profession"). A statement that might be harmful to reputation in one community would not necessarily be harmful to reputation in another community, or in the general community. *See* Saunders v. Board of Directors, WHYY-TV, 382 A.2d 257, 259 (Del. Super. Ct. 1978) (statement that might be defamatory within a prison, such as that the plaintiff is an informant, may not be defamatory within the general community).

[3] WILLIAM L. PROSSER, HANDBOOK OF THE LAW OF TORTS 772 (West Pub. Co. 4th ed. 1971).

[4] OLIVER WENDELL HOLMES, JR., THE COMMON LAW 130–163 (1881).

[5] 376 U.S. 254 (1964).

and to justify or criticize, when the contours of and justifications for common law defamation are compared.

I. COMPARISON TO OTHER STRICT LIABILITY TORTS

The strict liability torts examined in previous chapters are liability for abnormally dangerous activities (*Rylands*), its cousin nuisance, and intentional torts generally. The classic examples of abnormally dangerous activities are blasting and holding a dangerous animal on your land, such as a tiger. If the tiger escapes, the owner will be held strictly liable for the foreseeable harm.

As both *Rylands* and Section 520 of the Second Restatement make clear, liability for an abnormally dangerous activity follows, first, from a finding that the activity generates a high risk of harm to others even when conducted with reasonable care. This is true, for example, of holding a tiger in your backyard. No matter how careful you are in penning the tiger in, there is always a risk that it will break free and harm someone. The second set of conditions examined in strict liability cases consists of questions concerning the reciprocity of risk among activities, the degree to which the risk has been assumed, and the social value of the defendant's activity relative to its external harms.

In comparison to *Rylands* strict liability, liability for defamation does not appear at first glance to be based on the nature of the activity. Publishing an article in which you call someone a liar is a discrete act, like a punch in the nose, rather than an activity, such as blasting or holding a lion in your backyard.

In addition, the underlying activity that gives rise to a defamation claim, expression, is quite different from the activity that gives rise to a *Rylands* strict liability claim. *Rylands* strict liability is based on the holding of some agent that is both capable and likely to do enormous damage if it escapes. Unless the activity is of great value to the community, its mere presence is a source of worry and distress to neighbors. Expression, in contrast, is an activity that benefits society. Newspapers and journals disseminate information that enriches our lives every day. Indeed, the law has shown a special solicitude for torts that are closely connected to expression, such as the tort of intentional infliction of emotional distress (Chapter 2). For such torts, the law requires proof of specific intent (intent to harm), which is a more difficult standard to meet than the general intent (intent to execute the act) standard applied to most torts.

Thus, while society has an interest in using strict liability to suppress and discourage potentially harmful activities such as keeping dangerous animals, society has no interest in suppressing the activity of expression. Why defamation would be treated by the law as a strict liability tort, and precisely how it differs in function from other strict liability torts, is, at least on first impression, a puzzle.

To provide a brief preview of what lies ahead in this chapter, defamation law restricts the types of harm eligible for compensation by allowing recovery only in cases where a foreseeable injury to esteem is likely. In other words, communication unlikely to disgrace the plaintiff in the eyes of the average member of the community is not defamatory, no matter how hurtful the words are from the perspective of the plaintiff. In addition, the defenses for defamation have a form remarkably similar to the justificatory theories established under *Rylands*. Recall that if an activity has a substantial residual risk even when the actor takes reasonable care, *Rylands* requires the court to inquire into the degree to which the activity's risk is reciprocated by the risks of other activities, the degree to which the risk has been assumed, and the value of the activity to the community in which the activity takes place. Defamation defenses are based on a similar structure. Reciprocity: If the defendant's speech is simply giving back what's been given to him in an environment in which ill-tempered speech is normal, there is little likelihood of liability. Assumption of risk: If the subject of the defamatory publication has consented to it, or if consent can be implied from the subject's course of conduct, the defendant will not be found liable. Social value: If the defamatory publication is true, or if it protects a substantial interest of the message recipient, a third party, or the defaming party, liability may not be found.

In the parts below I elaborate on these defenses. However, before addressing defenses, I will first lay out the prima facie tort, which is established by proof of foreseeable reputational harm.

II. HARM REQUIREMENT

Although defamation is described as a form of strict liability, it can be described more accurately as a presumption of liability for any *publication* (the technical legal term referring to printed or spoken words) that causes a foreseeable injury to reputation. The foreseeability requirement is a proximate cause limitation, similar to the foreseeability test embedded in the strict liability doctrine for abnormally dangerous activities. In explaining the foreseeable harm requirement here, I will employ the analogy to abnormally dangerous activities.

When a defendant is held strictly liable for an injury caused by his dangerous activity, there are several steps in the chain establishing liability. First, the defendant must have been working with some agent capable of severely harming others, such as explosives. Second, the defendant must have been able to foresee that the dangerous agent might escape, even if the probability of escape is small. Third, the defendant must have been aware that the dangerous agent could severely harm others, and the harm asserted by the plaintiff must have been within the set of injuries associated with the dangerousness of the defendant's activity.

These three steps translate over to defamation. First, the agent, which consists of words, must be of the sort capable of harming reputation. Second, the release, or defamatory effect, of the words must be foreseeable. Third, the potential harm to reputation must be foreseeable, and the plaintiff's actual loss must be of a foreseeable sort.

Words (Dangerous Agent)

The sorts of words that can defame have been divided into the categories of defamatory per se and defamatory per quod. Per se defamatory words would be understood as harmful to reputation within any community, without a need to resort to extrinsic facts to discern the harmful effect. *Per quod* defamation requires resort to extrinsic facts to determine the harmful effect.

Per se defamatory publications consist of (1) *statements that the plaintiff has committed a crime of moral turpitude;* (2) *statements that so denigrate the fitness of the plaintiff as a personal associate as to cause others to ostracize, distrust, or disassociate themselves from the plaintiff; and* (3) *statements that tend to injure the business or professional activities of the plaintiff.* In the first category fall statements such as "the plaintiff is a thief." In the second category fall statements such as that the plaintiff suffers from leprosy or a sexually transmitted disease.[6] In the third fall statements such as the plaintiff has filed for bankruptcy or cheats his customers.

Per quod defamation plaintiffs encounter a higher burden, because they have to prove facts that must be known by the recipient of the communication to discern its harmful effect, and that the publication is likely to have the harmful effect in the eyes of the recipients aware of those facts. Borrowing an example from Prosser,[7] the defamatory effect of referring to a kosher meat seller as a seller of bacon would require the recipient of the communication to know what a kosher meat seller sells and that anyone who sells bacon could not be a kosher meat seller.

The distinction between per se and *per quod* defamation is similar to that between per se and *per accidens* nuisances discussed briefly in Chapter 15. The difference is that per se nuisances are statutorily prohibited activities, while per se defamation is not prohibited by statute. However, the more general distinction between invasions that are considered harmful at all times and all places, and invasions whose harmfulness depends on the circumstances applies to both nuisance and defamation.

The law further distinguishes defamation by written words, *libel*, and defamation by verbal expression, *slander*. A plaintiff in a libel action can recover damages, provided the words are harmful to reputation and the defendant cannot demonstrate that his words are either true or privileged, even if the plaintiff cannot prove the precise amount of the loss he has suffered. A plaintiff in a slander lawsuit, by contrast, can recover for per se defamatory words to the same extent as a libel plaintiff, but

---

[6] Taylor v. Perkins, Cro. Jac, 144 [1607] (thou art a leprous knave).
[7] Prosser, *supra* note 3, at 741; Braun v. Armour & Co., 173 N.E. 845 (1930).

he can recover for *per quod* defamatory words only if he proves an actual injury resulting from the defamation.

Effect (Release)

Continuing with the *Rylands* analogy, given the existence of a dangerous agent, such as explosives, courts still must consider the foreseeability of its release in a manner that may harm others.[8] For example, in *Cambridge Water Co. v. Eastern Counties Leather PLC*,[9] where the defendant's tannery released toxic chemicals that seeped into an aquifer and then to the plaintiff's well more than one mile away, the court held that a reasonable person would not have foreseen the harm to the plaintiff.

Likewise, the mere presence of potentially defamatory words is not enough for liability if their dissemination in a manner that can harm a person's reputation is not foreseeable. For the potentially defamatory words to have any harmful effect on the plaintiff's reputation, they must be communicated to a third person. This proximate cause limitation implies that the reputation-harming statement must be foreseeably *published*, as in being received by a third person. If the plaintiff alone receives the statement, it has not been published.[10]

If the defendant was not aware of or was unable to foresee the publication, he is not liable for defamation. In *Bottomley v. F. W. Woolworth*,[11] the defendant retailer sold a magazine that defamed the plaintiff, without knowing of the defamatory statements in the magazine. The court held that the defendant was not liable because it was not aware of the defamatory statements.

As long as the expression refers to a specific name, the defamatory effect is foreseeable even if the defendant does not know a person with that name, or indeed that such a person exists. The words by themselves provide notice to the publisher that they are likely to harm the reputation of anyone bearing the name they refer to. In this sense, again, liability for defamation is similar to strict liability for blasting, because the law of abnormally dangerous activities does not require the blaster to know the specific victim of a projectile or whether there will be a victim. As long as the blaster knows that the rocks and other projectiles are likely to harm someone if launched from his property into the surrounding area, the foreseeability requirement is satisfied.

This point is illustrated by *E. Hulton & Co. v. Jones*.[12] The defendant, a newspaper in England, published a fictional story, though presented as if true, about an Artemus Jones, a married man who had been observed about town with his mistress. It

---

[8] Rylands v. Fletcher, L.R. 1 Ex. 265 (1866), *aff'd*, L.R. 3 H.L. 330 (1868).

[9] [1994] 2 A.C. 264 (H.L.).

[10] *See, e.g.*, Beck v. Tribert, 711 A.2d 951, 959 (N.J. Super. 1998) (plaintiff sends associates to employer to ascertain employer's opinion of plaintiff, and the friends receive a negative review; not a publication).

[11] [1932] 48 TLR 530.

[12] [1910] A.C. 20.

happened that there was a real Artemus Jones in England, who promptly filed a defamation claim. The defendant's argument that it was not aware of anyone named Artemus Jones was unsuccessful. It was sufficient for defamation that the defendant could have foreseen that the article would injure the reputation of any married man named Artemus Jones.

The *Rylands* analogy appears to break down when we consider the many ways in which a person can defame someone without appearing to do so. He may offer his statement as an opinion ("I believe I saw Artemus Jones with his mistress"), or as a question ("Was that Artemus Jones with a mistress?"), or may refer to a fictional character that message recipients will understand as a representation of the plaintiff. But there are still analogies that can be drawn to *Rylands*. These cases would be similar to the defendant, in the blasting scenario, putting a sign on the rocks that says they were not intended to harm, or that they were intended to hit someone other than the victim.

It should be clear that if a blaster did such a thing, he would not be absolutely immune from strict liability. He understood that the rocks could harm someone. If he claimed that the rocks were not intended to harm anyone, or that they were intended to harm someone other than the victim, a court could still find the foreseeable harm requirement satisfied, provided the facts warranted such a holding.

Similarly, the fact that the defendant frames his statement as opinion, or as a question, does not render harm to reputation unforeseeable. The foreseeable harm requirement is satisfied as long as the statement of opinion implies a defamatory allegation of fact as the basis for the opinion.[13]

In the same vein, even if the publication does not refer to the plaintiff, it may still be defamatory if it is likely to be understood to refer to the plaintiff. In *Bindrim v. Mitchell*,[14] the defendant, Mitchell, registered for nude psychotherapy sessions conducted by the plaintiff, Bindrim, agreeing not to disclose to anyone what happened in the sessions. Mitchell later wrote a novel, with lurid details of the sessions. The plaintiff argued that he had been defamed by the depiction of the fictional character who conducted the sessions. The court concluded that a reasonable person, reading the book, would understand that the fictional character was indeed a representation of the plaintiff.

Similar to the concept of a relevant market in antitrust law, which requires the plaintiff to prove that the defendant's efforts to monopolize affected a market of

---

[13] Dunlap v. Wayne, 716 P.2d 842 (1986); Lewis v. Time Inc., 710 F.2d 549 (9th Cir. 1983); Milkovich v. Lorain Journal Co., 497 U.S. 1, 18–19 (1990); Fitzgerald v. Tucker, 737 So.2d 706, 717 (La. 1999) ("Of course, if a statement of opinion is accompanied by an express statement of fact, that express statement of fact may be actionable if it is defamatory, false, and concerns another. Moreover, if a statement of opinion implies that certain facts exist, then such a statement, even though couched in terms of an opinion, could certainly give rise to a defamation action if the implied factual assertions are defamatory and false."); 1 Robert D. Sack, Sack on Defamation § 2:4.8 (4th ed. 2010) (questions).

[14] 92 Cal. App.2d 61, 155 Cal. Rptr. 29 (1979).

sufficient size to justify the expenditure of resources on antitrust enforcement and adjudication, defamation law is concerned with the effects of the defendant's publication within a relevant community. This aspect of the foreseeability requirement is expressed in the rule that to prove actionable defamation, the publication must foreseeably harm the reputation of the plaintiff in some substantial community with which the plaintiff is associated.[15] Moreover, some courts have held that a relevant community for defamation purposes must be in one in which generally prevailing attitudes and norms are observed, rather than a community consisting of individuals with preferences that deviate far from the norm.[16] If the allegedly defamatory publication is unlikely to harm the plaintiff's reputation in a relevant community to which the plaintiff belongs or may belong, the defendant will not be found liable even if the publication is viewed as harmful in the eyes of the plaintiff.[17] It follows that the plaintiff may lose his lawsuit if the community is too small and deviant in outlook relative to the general community, or the relevant community is too remote from the plaintiff.

For example, in *Saunders v. Board of Directors, WHYY-TV*,[18] the plaintiff, a prisoner, sued the television station for broadcasting, falsely, that he was an FBI informant. The plaintiff feared that the broadcast would put his life in danger among his fellow prison inmates. The court held that in spite of risk to the plaintiff, the statement was not defamatory. First, the statement did not accuse the plaintiff of committing a crime of any sort, and assisting law enforcement is generally thought to be a desirable activity among the general public. Second, the label "informant" would not be considered harmful to reputation in the general community; it would be harmful only within a subset of prison inmates, and defamation law does not aim to protect a person's reputation within small, special communities whose preferences and attitudes deviate strongly from those of the general public.

However, the sorts of deviations that results from religious differences are not necessarily viewed as sufficiently divergent from the general community to fall outside of the scope of defamation liability. In *Jews for Jesus, Inc. v. Rapp*,[19] the court said that it was enough for Rapp to be defamed in the eyes of a substantial and respectable minority of the community (specifically, the Jewish minority) for her

---

[15] Peck v. Tribune Co., 214 U.S. 185,190 (1909) (finding for plaintiff, who did not drink and whose picture appeared in an advertisement for whiskey); Grant v. Reader's Digest Ass'n, 151 F.2d 733 (2nd Cir. 1945) (being referred to, falsely, as a member of the Massachusetts Communist Party is defamatory even though it harms reputation only among people opposed to communism).

[16] Saunders v. Board of Directors, WHYY-TV, 382 A.2d 257, 259 (Del. Super. Ct. 1978) (community of prison inmates versus general community).

[17] *Id.* (statement that plaintiff, a prisoner, was an "informant" that was broadcast on television might be harmful to his reputation within the prison community but not within the broader public). Two cases making the same general point are Connelly v. McKay, 28 N.Y.S.2d 327 (1941) and Sanguedolce v. Wolfe, 62 A.3d 810 (N.H. 2013).

[18] 382 A.2d 257, 259 (Del. Super. Ct. 1978).

[19] 997 So.2d 1098 (Fla. 2008).

defamation claim to be valid. The plaintiff, Rapp, sued after an article was published in the organization's newsletter stating that she had accepted Christian beliefs.

Consider the adjective "dead." The plaintiff may perceive an injury to his reputation by seeing himself described in a publication as dead, but the general rule is that the word "dead" has no harmful effect on the reputation of the person so described.[20] On the other hand, if the description of the plaintiff as dead can be shown to have been part of a scheme to injure the plaintiff, say, by driving customers away from his business, a defamation claim would appear to be maintainable on the theory that the defendant's words were motivated by malice and that the defendant intended to injure the plaintiff. However, the courts that have found special circumstances supporting a defamation claim appear to have done so only when the description of the plaintiff as dead is accompanied by other allegations of fact, such as the cause of death, that are likely to injure his reputation.[21]

The proximate cause limitation denying recovery to a plaintiff who cannot show that the publication harmed his reputation in a relevant community is analogous to the ultrasensitivity limitation on damages for nuisances and for abnormally dangerous activities. Recall that under nuisance law, the plaintiff is denied recovery if the activity of the defendant would not interfere with the quiet use and enjoyment of property of the average person in the community. In *Rogers v. Elliott*,[22] discussed in Chapter 15, the court held that the ringing of a church bell, though painful to the plaintiff, was not a nuisance because it did not annoy the average member of the community. Likewise, under defamation law, a publication that hurts the feelings of the plaintiff but would not be seen by a reasonable person in a relevant community as diminishing his esteem or injuring his reputation is not defamatory. In short, just as the law on strict liability denies compensation to ultrasensitive nuisance plaintiffs, defamation law denies compensation to ultrasensitive defamation plaintiffs.

Harm

While the defamatory effect of a publication may not be easily foreseeable, the harms that might occur as the result of defamation are easy to foresee. First, the plaintiff may suffer emotional trauma from the defamation. Second, the plaintiff may lose business. Third, the plaintiff may lose various advantages and benefits from

---

[20] Decker v. Princeton Packet, Inc., 561 A.2d 1122, 1126 (N.J. 1989); Rubenstein v. New York Post Corp., 488 N.Y.S.2d 331, 333 (N.Y. Sup. Ct. 1985).

[21] Prosser, *supra* note 3, at 739. In some cases, the description of the plaintiff as dead may be accompanied by other words that injure reputation, *see* Estill v. Hearst Pub. Co., 186 F.2d 1017, 1022 (7th Cir. 1951) ("Ordinarily it is not actionable per se to misstate the fact of a person's death. However, here defendant not only falsely stated that plaintiff had died, but purported to state the circumstances under which he died, 'a broken man.' By his complaint plaintiff alleged that this was injurious to him personally and in his professional capacity as an attorney, and had done great damage to his earning capacity as such attorney. We cannot agree that he stated no cause of action.").

[22] 15 N.E. 768 (1888).

social networks unrelated to business; for example, he may be ostracized by family or associates, or excluded from clubs.

In a libel case, or a case of slander by words that are defamatory per se, all three types of harm may form the basis of a damages award. Even if the plaintiff cannot prove a certain loss in business, such as the loss of one or more clients, or exclusion from social clubs, he can recover. The jury has discretion to fix an appropriate award in such a case, though not unlimited. The problem of determining an appropriate award here is equivalent to determining an award in a case of assault, or of intentional infliction of emotional distress.

To recover *special damages*, an actual pecuniary loss must be demonstrated to exist and to have derived from the injury to reputation. The actual loss can be demonstrated from proof that the injury to plaintiff's reputation caused such harms as the loss of a job, loss of business, or the breakup of a marriage.[23] However, if the plaintiff suffers severe emotional trauma from hearing of the defendant's statement, but there is no proof that the allegedly defamatory words harmed his reputation, then he cannot recover for the emotional harm and the physical or economic consequences that flowed directly from it.

For example, in *Terwilliger v. Wands*,[24] the plaintiff, Terwilliger, claimed he fell ill after hearing that the defendant had told a third party that Terwilliger was having sex with a married woman. The court recounted the facts as follows:

> the plaintiff proved ... that in June, 1852, the defendant asked the witness what the plaintiff was running to Mrs. Fuller's so much for: that he knew he went there for no good purpose, and Mrs. Fuller was a bad woman; that the plaintiff had a regular beaten path across his land to Fuller's; and the defendant said to him he went there for no other purpose than to have intercourse with Mrs. Fuller; and that once previously, the defendant told the witness that the plaintiff would do all he could to keep the husband of Mrs. Fuller in the penitentiary so that he could have free access there.[25]

But Terwilliger offered no proof that these statements harmed his reputation in a manner that led to a provable pecuniary loss. The court upheld a judgment for the defendant.

Straightforward utilitarian justifications exist for the differences in the availability of damages for libel and slander plaintiffs. One is that libel and slander are likely to

---

[23] Hood v. Dun & Bradstreet, Inc., 486 F.2d 25, 33 (5th Cir. 1973) ("The loss of employment, income or profits is categorized as special damages and is sufficient injury upon which to predicate an action for libel where the defamatory words are not libelous per se."); Gierbolini Rosa v. Banco Popular de P.R., 930 F. Supp. 712, 719 (D.P.R. 1996) (provided a causal link exists between the defamatory statements and divorce, special damages can be assigned); O'Hara v. Storer Communications, 231 Cal. App.3d 1101 (Cal. App. 4th Dist. 1991) (special damages for income loss due to depression and emotional distress after plaintiff was misidentified as a prostitute on television).

[24] 17 N.Y. 54 (1858).

[25] *Id.* at 57.

have different impacts on reputation. A libelous word probably reflects a bit more thought than the same slanderous word. The libel defendant had comparatively more time to think about his words before fixing them on paper. The slander defendant may have uttered his remarks in anger, and his listeners may have appropriately discounted the remarks. It follows from this that the recipient of a defamatory communication is more likely to infer the existence of a rational basis for the defamatory words when written than when spoken. Another justification for the distinction is that the libel can be spread throughout an entire community and can remain for generations in a fixed form. The impact of a slander, however, depends on the size of the audience at the time it is uttered, and how much work the audience does in passing the message on to others. For words that are not obviously defamatory, the audience may have varying interpretations, and the message may be passed on in different forms. These general distinctions probably justify the common law governing the availability of damages for libel and slander plaintiffs.

In spite of these differences between libel and slander, to some degree the requirement of proving an actual loss for *per quod* slander is redundant and largely supports the initial burden on the plaintiff of proving a foreseeable harm. In a case of slander *per quod*, the plaintiff already has the burden of proving a foreseeable harm to reputation, to prove that actionable defamation did occur. In other words, if the plaintiff cannot prove an injury to reputation, he cannot recover even if the defendant has no justifications to offer. The only cases where the proof of actual loss requirement should make a difference, then, are those where the plaintiff proves a foreseeable harm, and therefore has standing to sue for defamation, and yet cannot demonstrate an actual loss. Such cases clearly exist, and the likely rationale for denying recovery is to control the administrative burden on courts due to frivolous claims.[26]

III. DEFENSES

Defenses under defamation law follow the pattern established in strict liability doctrine. Recall that the Second Restatement of Torts, section 520, provides factors for determining whether an activity is abnormally dangerous:

(a) Existence of a high degree of risk of some harm to the person, land or chattels of others
(b) Likelihood that the harm that results from it will be great
(c) Inability to eliminate the risk by the exercise of reasonable care
(d) Extent to which the activity is not a matter of common usage
(e) Inappropriateness of the activity to the place where it is carried on and
(f) Extent to which its value to the community is outweighed by its dangerous attributes.[27]

---

[26] *See* Chapter 13 on proximate cause.
[27] RESTATEMENT (SECOND) OF TORTS §520 (1977).

I noted in Chapter 15 that the factors of section 520 should be interpreted in light of the theory articulated in *Rylands*.[28] Accordingly, the fourth factor, (d), requires an inquiry into the degree to which the harms externalized by the defendant's activity are reciprocated by the activities of others in the community. The fifth factor, (e), requires an inquiry into the degree to which the plaintiff has impliedly assumed the risk by his conduct, which can inferred from the plaintiff's conduct or from the existence of a benefit that the plaintiff accepted in exchange for being exposed the risk of the defendant's activity. The last factor, weighing social value against social risk, requires an inquiry into the balance between externalized harms and benefits.

The last three factors of section 520 suggest a structure for defenses in defamation law. Reciprocal dealing is a defense. Assumption of risk, in various guises, is a defense too. Finally, and related to the assumption of risk defense, defamation law permits some socially valuable expression to escape condemnation in spite of its harmful effect.

Reciprocity

If two people are hurling similar insults at each other in public, it would be strange for a court to allow one of them to recover for defamation against the other. This intuition is borne out in the law: Similar to the reciprocity theory of *Rylands*, defamation law provides some degree of immunity when the defendant's publication was part of a game of give and take.

In *Kevorkian v. American Medical Association*,[29] the plaintiff, Dr. Kevorkian, famed as a proponent of physician-assisted suicide, sued the AMA for letters and statements to the media by its officers asserting that Kevorkian "poses a great threat to the public," had engaged in "criminal practices," and was "a killer." The descriptions of Kevorkian were defamatory per se. Still, the court found the statements privileged because Kevorkian had sought the very attention he had received, and consequently his reputation was already too low to be reduced substantially by the defendants, and, more importantly, the statements had occurred in the course of a heated public debate, perpetuated by the plaintiff himself, and focused on matters at the heart of the debate.

The reciprocity theory includes under its mantle self-defense and some applications of the implied assumption of risk theory. In many cases of reciprocal defamation, the defendant's actions can be justified as an attempt to defend himself from defamatory statements of the other party, for example by calling the other a "liar" in

---

[28] Rylands v. Fletcher, L.R. 1 Ex. 265 (1866), *aff'd*, L.R. 3 H.L. 330 (1868).
[29] 602 N.W.2d 233 (Mich. App. 1999).

response to the other's defamatory statements.[30] Similarly, a person who provokes a defamatory comment through his own defamatory words could be viewed as having assumed the risk.

In *Haycox v. Dunn*,[31] the plaintiff, Dunn, and the defendants controlled competing newspapers, aligned to competing political factions. The plaintiff sued the defendants for publishing an article that accused him of deliberate falsehoods. The plaintiff's own newspaper, however, had run articles that impugned the character and motives of the defendants. The court held that a privilege exists for defamatory statements made in self-defense, to refute the defamatory statements of another.

The reciprocity defense encompasses abusive words spoken in retaliation, in emotional or excited outbursts. This type of low-level abuse occurs commonly and is part of the give-and-take of life. In *Cinquanta v. Burdett*,[32] the defendant shouted to the plaintiff, his employer, "I don't like doing business with crooks. You're a dead beat. You've owed me $155.00 for three or four months. You're crooks." The plaintiff was unable to prove special damages, and the court rejected his defamation per se claim because the defendant's words did not accuse the plaintiff of having committed a crime of moral turpitude. The court noted, in addition, that the defendant's words had to be interpreted in light of the circumstances, in which the parties were in a heated dispute over money.

The self-defense justification also applies to more limited instances in which the defamatory statement was uttered in an attempt to avoid a greater harm to the speaker or to a third party. Warning others of the conduct of the plaintiff, or trying to prevent theft or to recover stolen property, or to apprehend a thief, are privileged if reasonable under the circumstances.[33] Probably no court would hold a speaker liable for defamation when his statement may have been necessary to prevent death or serious physical injury.

---

[30] Haycox v. Dunn, 104 S.E.2d 800 (Va. 1958); Phifer v. Foe, 443 P.2d 870, 871 (Wyo. 1968) ("After an attack on a defendant by a plaintiff, defendant has a right to defend himself against plaintiff's charges, even if he defames the plaintiff in so doing.").

[31] 104 S.E.2d 800 (Va. 1958).

[32] 388 P.2d 779 (Colo. 1963).

[33] Faber v. Byrle, 229 P.2d 718, 722 (Kan. 1951) ("Touching the question involved in the first cause of action, namely, defendant's statement to an officer, we have held a communication to an officer of the law charging a person with a crime, made in an honest effort to recover stolen property and for the purpose of detecting and punishing the criminal, is privileged"); Flanagan v. McLane, 88 A. 96, 97 (Conn. 1913) ("[S]ince the defendant had an interest in the recovery of the money, and the person to whom she made the communication had a duty to discharge respecting this she had, so long as she did not act with express malice, the right to communicate to the peace officer the circumstances attending the loss of her money, together with her suspicions and belief and every circumstance relevant to the detection of the theft. She must not make such a charge recklessly or wantonly, or without circumstances reasonably arousing suspicion."); Tierney v. Ruppert, 150 A.D. 863 (N.Y. App. Div. 1912) (warning customers of unfair prices, based on reasonable belief, not defamatory); Prosser, *supra* note 3, at 786–787.

Some courts have placed limits on the reciprocity theory. If *A* responds to *B*'s defamatory words not by trying to refute the words, but by making up entirely new and unrelated defamatory charges against *B*, then *A* has gone beyond the boundary of the privilege.[34] Even in this case, provocation by the plaintiff can serve as a reason for reducing damages.[35]

Assumption of Risk

Assumption of risk is equivalent to consent, which is a defense to a tort action (Chapter 2). This rule applies to defamation claims too, and there are many ways in which a defamation plaintiff can assume the risk. Some courts say that public figures assume the risk of defamation, unless the harmful words are attended by malice, by involving themselves prominently in public affairs and debates.[36] But most cases whose outcomes could be explained by the assumption of risk theory do not use the term "assumption of risk"; they are typically decided on the ground that a qualified privilege applies or that there was no publication. Still, the fundamental rationale for many of these cases seems to be assumption of risk.

The most obvious instance is where the plaintiff asks for the defendant's opinion in public, and the opinion given is unflattering. Alternatively, the plaintiff may have asked for a letter of reference or statement to be communicated to a third party, taking the risk that the communication might contain a statement that injures the plaintiff's reputation.[37] Some of these cases are decided against the plaintiff on the

---

[34] Borley v. Allison, 63 N.E. 260, 261 (Mass. 1902) ("One attacked by a slander or libel has a right to defend himself, but he has no right to turn his defense into a slanderous or libelous attack, unless it clearly appears that such attack was necessary for his justification."); Chaffin v. Lynch, 1 S.E. 803, 810 (Va. 1887).

[35] Buck v. Savage, 323 S.W.2d. 363, 372 (Tex. App. 1959) ("There are authorities, however, to the effect that under certain circumstances hearsay testimony of provocation is admissible in libel and slander cases in mitigation of damages. One essential to the application of the rule is that it must be shown that the plaintiff provoked the defamation."); Gressman v. Morning Journal Ass'n, 90 N.E. 1131 (N.Y. 1910).

[36] Gertz v. Robert Welch, Inc., 418 U.S. 323, 345 (1974) (noting that a public figure voluntarily exposes himself to increased risk of reputation injury); Waldbaum v. Fairchild Publications, Inc., 627 F.2d 1287, 1294 (D.C. Cir. 1980) (noting that famous people assume risk that public exposure may lead to misstatements about them).

[37] Garvey v. Dickinson College, 763 F.Supp. 796, 798 (D.C.M.D. Pa. 1991) ("Allan's letter was written to a prospective employer of Peck. Allan could reasonably have believed that the employer had right to a full and fair account of Peck's performance while at Dickinson, including an account of circumstances which caused Peck some difficulty and perhaps detracted from his job performance. His remarks were, therefore, clearly conditionally privileged."); Talens v. Bernhard, 669 F.Supp. 251, 257 (D.C.E.D. Wis. 1987) ("The Court has no doubts that a conditional privilege should apply to the letters sent by Dr. Bernhard. Just as public policy should encourage a free flow of information between former employers and prospective employers, so should it encourage a free flow of information between educators and prospective employers."); PROSSER, *supra* note 3, at 784.

ground that there was no publication,[38] but, again, the fundamental rationale is assumption of risk.

Suppose the plaintiff, after hearing the defamatory words directly from the defendant, immediately relays them to a third person.[39] Courts have described this as a case where there is no publication,[40] but the better view is that it is one of assumption or risk. The publication does occur, but it is entirely due to the plaintiff's conduct.

Assumption of risk can be expanded to cover a very large set of the cases that fall under the doctrine of privilege (discussed in a separate part of this chapter below). Return to the letter of reference example. Even if the plaintiff has not asked for the letter to be sent to a third party, if the plaintiff voluntarily entered into a setting in which such letters may be sent out by his supervisors, he impliedly consented to the risk of defamation, so long as the letters are within the scope of anticipated commentary.[41] Even more broadly, letters of reference, within the scope of anticipated commentary, could be deemed privileged on the theory that the benefits to employees and job applicants of open sharing of opinion by supervisors far outweigh the risks of the occasional defamatory remark. The case law limiting the scope of the *Rylands* strict liability doctrine on the ground that the plaintiffs had impliedly assumed the risk, such as *Rickards v. Lothian*,[42] and *Carstairs v. Taylor* (Chapter 5),[43] would support such a view of privilege under defamation law.

Social Value: Absolute Privilege

The last factor identified in the Second Restatement's formulation of the *Rylands* strict liability test is the question whether the value of the defendant's activity exceeds its dangerous attributes. Analogous reasoning has generated a set of defamation defenses falling under the label *privilege*. The main privileges are for truth, for communication within certain relationships or networks, and for instances where the social value of the communication is greater than its likely harms.

---

[38] Shinglemeyer v. Wright, 82 N.W. 887 (Mich. 1900) (plaintiff asked police officer to ask defendant to repeat allegation that she was a thief; not a publication); Howland v. Blake Manufacturing Co., 31 N.E. 656 (Mass. 1892) (plaintiff sends representative to read letter, in an attempt to meet publication requirement); Haynes v. Leland, 29 Me. 233 (1848) (asking for letter for friend, and letter contains criticism, which plaintiff (friend of friend) reads; not a publication); Beck v. Tribert, 711 A.2d 951, 959 (N.J. Super. 1998) (plaintiff sends associates to employer to ascertain employer's opinion of plaintiff, and the friends receive a negative review; not a publication).

[39] Sylvis v. Miller, 33 S.W. 921 (Tenn. 1896) (plaintiff receives letter with libelous statement and reads it to others).

[40] *Ibid.*

[41] High v. A.J. Harwi Hardware Co., 223 P. 264, 269 (Kan. 1924); Beck v. Tribert, 711 A.2d 951, 959 (N.J. Super. 1998).

[42] [1913] A.C. 263.

[43] [1871] L.R. 6 Exch. 217.

1. Truth as Absolute Privilege

The most important privilege justified on the basis of social value is that for *truth*. If the defendant's harmful comments about the plaintiff are true, or substantially so, the law regards them as nondefamatory. Although the defense of truth has been distinguished by some writers from that of privilege by calling it a "justification,"[44] simple labels convey little useful information about the rationale for the defense. I consider rationales in somewhat more detail later, but the short argument for recognizing truth as a defense is that a right of action for injuries to reputation caused by truthful expression would encourage individuals to hide or obscure the truth whenever disclosing it might generate a defamation claim, and a society in which truthful expression is the norm is preferable to one in which dissembling is the norm.

We are encouraged to soften the impact of our words by using euphemisms and elliptical phrases, but that is often a disservice to both expression and thought. Such language is likely to be confused and misunderstood, and it tends to exhaust the listener who wants to uncover its meaning. A common strategy of presentation, for some speakers, is to go on and on, to the point of wearing listeners down, until they are left too exhausted in the end to question even the silliest ideas and proposals put forth by the speaker. The same is often true of speech that swaddles frank expression in layers of insulation and indirection. Thus, a legal privilege for telling the truth may be desirable not because it takes away an incentive that would otherwise be provided by the law to lie, but because it protects and encourages direct and frank communication, which is essential in the process of distinguishing true from false concepts. Lies are often exposed by immediate observation, as when a speaker refers to a fat person as skinny. But indirect, hazy, or elliptical speech can easily fill the space where lies would be easily exposed.

The burden of proving truth is on the defendant. This means that the defendant must offer evidence that shows that it is more likely than not that his words are true – that is, he must meet the preponderance of the evidence test. This is a sensible allocation of the burden, given that it is the defendant who is the source of the harmful words. For individuals in the publishing business, putting the burden on them to prove truth (under the preponderance standard) gives them an incentive to research the validity of a story that could harm someone's reputation before publishing it. If the plaintiff had the burden of proving falsity, newspapers could run stories and effectively force those who were thereby injured in reputation to come to court and reveal details about their public and private lives to win their defamation lawsuits. The fear of having to put one's life on public display would discourage many victims from ever filing suit, even against injurers who knowingly publish false stories, and consequently shield such injurers from the law.

---

[44] Prosser, *supra* note 3, at 796.

Truth is an *absolute privilege*, in the sense that the defendant escapes liability for defamation even if his publication is motivated by malice. The defendant's publication does not have to be 100 percent true to gain protection from the privilege. Substantial truth is sufficient.[45] On a deeper level, courts appear to be applying a balancing test that seeks to determine whether the difference between the reputational harm of the words chosen and a completely accurate statement is slight, and the burden of achieving greater accuracy comparatively great. It is only through this perspective that one can make sense of the seemingly conflicting holdings.

In *Kilian v. Doubleday & Co., Inc.*,[46] the defendant had written a first-person account of abusive treatment of U.S. soldiers in an army camp during World War II. The account left no doubt that the abusive treatment was directed by Colonel Kilian, the commanding officer at the camp. But the defendant had never been in the camp and had only heard the various versions of the stories from other soldiers. Colonel Kilian had been tried before a military court and acquitted of knowingly permitting the abuses; he was convicted of negligence only. The court reversed a verdict for the defendant on the ground that the evidence did not show that his account was substantially true.

In *Smith v. Byrd*,[47] the plaintiff, Sheriff Byrd, sued a newspaper for defamation when he was described in an article as having shot a man who had run away after being assaulted by the sheriff. The sheriff said the article was false because he was not the shooter, it was his deputy Gillespie. The news reporter said that she had tried several times to speak to the sheriff and his deputy to get their versions of the facts, but neither returned phone calls. Since the facts were in dispute (witnesses said the sheriff did the shooting) and both the sheriff and his deputy had acted in concert, the court held that the story was substantially true.

Comparing *Kilian* and *Smith*, both cases of incompletely true publications, the differences appear both in the burden of avoiding the reputational harm and the degree of departure from truth. The burden of reducing or perhaps avoiding the reputational harm in *Kilian* was slight – indeed, the defendant had expended effort in revising his story to make it seem like a first-hand account when it was not. And although the truth of what occurred in Kilian's camp may have been close to the defendant's story, there was little evidence to support it, and a military trial had failed to uncover evidence of intentional abuse. In *Smith*, by contrast, it would have been quite difficult for the news reporter to determine who really shot the victim. In addition, the difference between the truth and the newspaper's account, if there were any difference at all, would have been slight, and even slighter in its

---

[45] Emde v. San Joaquin County Central Labor Council, 143 P.2d 20, 28 (Cal. 1943); Reilly v. Associated Press, 797 N.E.2d 1204, 1211 (Mass. App. Ct. 2003); Stern v. Cosby, 645 F.Supp.2d 258, 276 (S.D.N.Y. 2009).

[46] 79 A.2d 657 (Pa. 1951).

[47] 83 So.2d 172 (Miss. 1955).

implications for the sheriff's reputation, since the sheriff was legally responsible for the deputy's actions as his principal.

2. Relationship-Based Absolute Privilege

Other absolute privileges are based on the nature of the relationship or network in which the harmful words are shared. If a husband and wife share between themselves harmful words about the plaintiff, the plaintiff has no cause of action for defamation. One could say that there has been no publication in this case,[48] because the husband and wife have been viewed as one person in the law.[49] However, the better justification is the simple policy that the marriage relationship is one in which sincere and direct (even if false) expression should be encouraged, and to hold the husband liable for false comments made about a third party to his wife would obstruct the sort of communication that society should prefer to see, and that will inevitably occur, within such a relationship.

Communication within a corporation or partnership about matters that are related to the business are treated as absolutely privileged by some courts, often under the theory that an intracorporate communication on a business matter is not a publication.[50] Thus, if a manager of one division of a company writes to the manager of another division to complain about the work habits of an employee seeking to be transferred between the two divisions, the words are not actionable. However, if the statements are not related to the business, such as merely personal gossip, or if the statements are shared among employees who have no reasonable interest in the matter, there is no absolute privilege.[51]

Some courts provide weaker protection for intracorporate communication, under the doctrine of qualified privilege, a topic addressed below. The differences between the absolute privilege approach and the qualified privilege approach to intracorporate communication is not great as a general matter, but there are cases where the distinction is important. For courts that apply the absolute privilege doctrine, the key question is whether the publication was sufficiently related to the business of the firm. If a sufficient relationship is found, the publication is absolutely privileged; if not, the publication enjoys only a qualified privilege. For courts that apply the qualified privilege doctrine, these issues are more or less conflated under a balancing test.

---

[48] Dyer v. MacDougall, 93 F.Supp. 484, 486 (E.D.N.Y. 1950) ("A communication from husband to wife in the absence of a third person is not publication, and is not actionable as slander, whatever the motive may be, and though the statement may be false."); Conrad v. Roberts, 147 P. 795, 798 (Kan. 1915) ("there is in law no publication where the words merely pass between husband and wife"); Springer v. Swift, 239 N.W. 171, 174 (S.D. 1931) ("Husband and wife are generally to be considered one person in actions of tort as well as contract; so that confidential communication of defamatory matter by the author to his wife is not a publication.").

[49] Springer v. Swift, 239 N.W. 171, 174 (S.D. 1931).

[50] Mims v. Metropolitan Life Ins. Co., 200 F.2d 800 (5th Cir. 1952).

[51] Arison Shipping Co. v. Smith, 311 So.2d 739, 741 (Fla. Dist. Ct. App. 3d Dist. 1975), General Motors Corp. v. Piskor, 352 A.2d 810, 816 (Md. 1976).

A publication on an important business matter is highly likely to meet the qualified privilege test; the greater the distance from business relevance, the less likely is the privilege. The important difference between these approaches is observed when the publication is motivated by malice. Under the absolute privilege doctrine, intracorporate communications on important business matters, among parties with a direct interest in the matters, remain privileged even if motivated by malice. Under the qualified privilege doctrine, intracorporate communications on important business matters may not be privileged if motivated by malice.[52]

As in the marriage example, the rationale often provided for the privilege of intracorporate communication is that such communication does not amount to publication. But this theory is unavailing where courts apply the qualified privilege doctrine. The better justification is the same as in the marriage example: A law discouraging honest expression within the corporation would be an obstruction to business. Managers do not have time to get all of the facts before recommending, say, whether a person should be hired or fired. Requiring them to do so would reduce the risk of defamation, but the cost would exceed the benefit in most cases.

Judges and legislators are part of a network shielded from defamation claims by the absolute privilege rule. This immunity is especially broad in its protection for judges in their official business,[53] and the policy justification is obvious. A judge could not carry on his work if he had to worry about a defamation claim every time he held that a defendant had broken the law. The same can be said of a prosecutor.[54] Similarly, lawyers enjoy an absolute privilege for publications within the litigation process,[55] though the lawyer's privilege does not extend to statements made outside of the litigation process.[56]

---

[52] Gambardella v. Apple Health Care, Inc., 969 A.2d 736 (Conn. 2009).

[53] Irwin v. Ashurst, 74 P.2d 1127, 1130 (Or. 1938) ("It is well settled in England and in this country, on the ground of public policy, that a judge has absolute immunity from liability in an action for defamatory words published in the course of judicial proceedings."); Stump v. Sparkman, 435 U.S. 349 (1978) (judge absolutely immune from suits for damages for judicial acts).

[54] Office of State Attorney, Fourth Judicial Circuit of Florida v. Parrotino, 628 So.2d 1097, 1098–1099 (Fla. 1993) ("American law has long recognized that prosecutorial immunity from suit rests on the same footing as the immunity conferred upon judges and grand juries. . . . Both judges and prosecutors alike should be free from the threat of suit for their official actions, because permitting suit in this situation could deter a full and unfettered exercise of judicial or quasi-judicial authority.").

[55] Irwin v. Ashurst, 74 P.2d 1127, 1130–1131 (Or. 1938) ("A communication made by an attorney in a judicial proceeding is absolutely privileged if it is pertinent and relevant to the issues, although it may be false and malicious. . . . If the communications be irrelevant, they do not necessarily become actionable. They must be malicious, as well as irrelevant. Because they were uttered in the course of judicial proceedings, the law does not draw the inference of malice from their injurious character, but requires from the complainant party proof of actual malice."); Binder v. Triangle Publications, Inc., 275 A.2d 53, 56 (Penn. 1971) ("All communications pertinent to any stage of a judicial proceeding are accorded an absolute privilege which cannot be destroyed by abuse . . . [t]hus, statements by a party, a witness, counsel, or a judge cannot be the basis of a defamation action whether they occur in the pleadings or in open court.").

[56] Kennedy v. Cannon 182 A.2d 54, 58 (Md. 1962) ("The scope of the privilege is restricted to communications such as those made between an attorney and his client, or in the examination of witnesses by counsel, or in statements made by counsel to the court or jury.") The lawyer (Cannon) for a man

3. Social Value: Qualified Privilege

Qualified privileges are virtually always accompanied by an inquiry into the scope of the privilege and whether the defendant's actions were within the scope. In addition, a finding of malice (that is, intent to harm) destroys the privilege. The case of reciprocity discussed above falls under the qualified privilege category, because the privilege will be found only when the defendant's communication is reasonable in light of the plaintiff's communication, or communication within the special community in which both defendant and plaintiff belong. Closely related to the reciprocity defense is that for self-defense or self-protection. A false statement that has a harmful effect on the reputation of another may still qualify for a limited privilege if the purpose is to protect the speaker from an imminent harm.

Qualified privilege applies also where the defendant's comments are made for the protection or benefit of third parties. The standard example is the letter of reference. Of course, if the reference letter goes beyond matters within the anticipated exchange, the privilege may be lost, depending on the importance of the interest at stake. A letter of reference from a law professor for a student applying for a judicial clerkship is likely to discuss the applicant's qualities as a student. Discussion of personal matters may not be privileged, unless the personal matters affect that student's ability to serve as a clerk. Thus, a purely personal matter that may have nothing do with the student's quality as a writer and researcher may still be privileged because it conveys important information about the student's suitability as a clerk, with whom the judge must work closely. If the professor notes in his letter that the student tends to be irascible, such a communication would be privileged, even though it says nothing about the student's ability to write and research on legal matters.

Another category of qualified privilege consists of communications that are of joint interest between communicator and recipient. The classic example, mentioned earlier, is the communication within a firm, for example, one manager telling another manager within the same firm of a certain employee's work and personal habits. Earlier I noted that some courts apply the doctrine of absolute immunity to intracorporate communication on important business matters. Other courts apply the doctrine of qualified immunity to such communication. Under the qualified immunity doctrine, intracorporate communication on important business matters may still be actionable if the communication includes harmful words motivated by malice.

Courts typically find malice where the communicating party knows that the publication is false and harmful to the person defamed. In *Gambardella v. Apple Health Care, Inc.*,[57] a woman brought her aunt to the defendant health care facility, a nursing home. The aunt died and the woman told the employee who admitted the aunt, Gambardella, that she could take the aunt's property and dispose of it as she wished.

---

accused of raping Kennedy asserted to a reporter that she had consented. The court found that the lawyer's statement was not within the scope of the privilege.

[57] 969 A.2d 736 (Conn. 2009).

The woman also wrote a letter to the facility expressing the same message. A manager of the facility discovered that Gambardella had taken some of the deceased aunt's furniture. After inquiring into the matter, the manager learned that Gambardella had been given permission to dispose of the property as she saw fit. In spite of this, the manager fired Gambardella, publicly accusing of her of stealing the property of a nursing home resident (the deceased aunt). The court, in a state (Connecticut) that applies the qualified immunity doctrine to intracorporate communication, held that the privilege did not apply because the publication evinced malice on the part of the manager. Had the same facts occurred in a state that applies the absolute immunity doctrine, the publication probably would not have been actionable.

The common law created a zone of qualified privilege for commentary on public matters (including public figures), public proceedings, and public officials.[58] This privilege is easy to justify on social welfare grounds. The work of public officials, for example, affects many citizens. If their work is not subjected to robust and unfettered public discussion and criticism, they will have weak incentives to take the public's interests into account in carrying out their work, rather than indulge their own interests. An official might mistreat or punish an individual, say, by denying the individual access to public services, and escape any societal scrutiny if citizens are not free to openly discuss his work without fearing defamation liability.

Like the privilege for criticism of public officials, the privilege for criticism of individuals who gain public notice (public figures) can be defended because of its benefits to society. In *Carr v. Hood*,[59] the plaintiff, author of several popular travel books, sued the defendant for writing a book satirizing the plaintiff's writing style. The court held that the defendant's ridicule was not actionable defamation, and added that

> every man who published a book laid himself before the public, and became a fair subject of criticism. If his book was penned in a pompous and empty stile [sic], ridicule might fairly be used to strip folly of its self-importance.... [I]t was of the highest importance, that criticism should be free, for, without it there could be no improvement in taste, in politics, or in science. Every branch of learning was indebted for its advancement on the severe strictures, which succeeding writers had passed upon the works of each other, and the only question was, whether this author had done more than expose, according to his best judgment, what he conceived to be a vitiated stile of writing.

IV. THE CONSTITUTION AND DEFAMATION LAW

In America today, constitutional law has taken over the areas of qualified privilege for commentary on public matters and public officials in media outlets (books,

---

[58] *See, e.g.,* FRANCIS BURDICK, THE LAW OF TORTS: A CONCISE TREATISE ON THE CIVIL LIABILITY AT COMMON LAW AND UNDER MODERN STATUTES FOR ACTIONABLE WRONGS TO PERSON AND PROPERTY 331–332 (1905).

[59] 170 Eng. Rep. 981 (K.B. 1808).

newspapers, magazines, radio, television). In *New York Times Co. v. Sullivan*,[60] the Supreme Court held that criticism in the press of the official conduct of public officials is not actionable in the absence of proof of malice. This is consistent with the common law, though somewhat broader as a privilege because the plaintiff must prove malice, whereas under the common law the defendant had the burden of proving that his publication was protected by the doctrine of qualified privilege. And burdens of proof matter, especially in defamation law. A plaintiff who has to prove malice must go to court prepared to reveal facts that may not put him in the best light. Many potential plaintiffs might choose to forgo the option of suing for defamation when facing the burden of, and additional scrutiny invited by, trying to proving malice.

The change in the law brought about by *New York Times* was in response to the efforts of one official in Alabama, L. B. Sullivan, to obtain a defamation judgment against the *New York Times* for running an advertisement, taken out by civil rights organizations, criticizing the conduct of Alabama public officials. The statements in the advertisement were false in the hypertechnical sense of not getting every detail right, but largely true in substance. Because of the relatively minor factual errors in the advertisement, Sullivan was able to persuade the Alabama courts to award him a judgment of $500,000. Sullivan's judgment was just one of many defamation awards obtained by officials in southern states against newspapers that published articles critical of their conduct during the American civil rights movement.[61] The defamation judgments against newspapers had the intended effect of muting their criticism of official conduct.

One paradox of *New York Times* – with instructional value for the law – is that Alabama was the first jurisdiction to recognize a common law privilege for criticism of public officials,[62] even before England recognized the privilege.[63] In other words, a state that had once been on the forefront of providing legal protection against defamation claims from public officials later became a symbol of the oppressive potential of defamation lawsuits in the hands of public officials. When a faction with a specific interest in an issue gains control of the public offices and courts of a state, the public officials can join with state court judges to use defamation litigation to stifle opponents. This appears to explain, in short order, the path Alabama law had followed from its earliest years up to *New York Times*. Over time, courts and public officials in Alabama had distorted defamation law to permit it to be used as a tool to suppress political opposition, at least on matters of civil rights. C. Vann Woodward's famous thesis on the evolution of views on civil rights in the South,[64] from a liberal

---

[60] 376 U.S. 254 (1964).
[61] Anthony Lewis, Make No Law: The Sullivan Case and the First Amendment 22–36 (Random House 1991).
[62] Hogg v. Dorrah, 2 Port. 212 (Ala. 1835); Burdick, *supra* note 58, at 332.
[63] Burdick, *supra* note 58, at 332.
[64] C. Vann Woodward, The Strange Career of Jim Crow (1955).

stance to an oppositional conservatism becoming clear around 1900, may provide an explanation for the evolution of Alabama's defamation law as well.

Alabama provides a cautionary tale about the mix of local democracy and defamation law. In spite of the elaborate utilitarian basis of defamation doctrine described in this chapter, the common law of defamation proved to be a feeble match against the power of a dominant political faction on a matter that went to the core of local traditions. Defamation law could provide privileges for reporting and criticism of the work of public officials, but as long as those officials controlled the staffing of courts, the privileges were vulnerable.

In *Curtis Publishing Co. v. Butts*,[65] the Supreme Court extended the malice requirement of *New York Times* to defamation claims brought by public figures. Again, this is broadly consistent with the common law's recognition of a qualified privilege for commentary on public matters, but at the same time a significant shift in the burden of proof. Under the malice standard, an individual who is not a public official, but who may be a public figure, is probably even less likely than a public official to take on the burden of filing a defamation claim in response to a false and damaging story. The reason is that the work of the public official is likely to already be part of public discourse to some degree. The work of a private individual is less likely to be a part of public discourse, and consequently the burden of disclosing private business matters is likely to be greater.

The utilitarian case for shielding citizens from defamation lawsuits brought in response to their commentary on public matters is not nearly as strong when the plaintiffs are ordinary public figures as when they are public officials. Public scrutiny and criticism of government officials provides a valuable service to society. It discourages public officials from using their offices, and the control over public resources which those offices confer, to reward friends and punish enemies at their discretion. The most common feature of bad governments everywhere is their tendency to suppress public criticism. In addition, because most citizens rely on public officials for access to public services, few will take the risk of openly criticizing a public official who has opportunities to retaliate against them. Parents of public school students, for example, are reluctant to criticize the work of the local public school superintendent, because of the fear that he may later deny their children access to services, special programs, or awards offered within the school district. The greater the tendency to retaliate exhibited by the official, the more sensitive the official to the sting of criticism, the less likely criticism will be offered. If the citizen fears, in addition to the threat of exclusion from public services, the risk of a defamation lawsuit, open criticism of the official is even less likely to be observed. In the end, a paradox emerges: an inverse relation between the competence or character of the public official and the willingness of the citizens most familiar with the official's work to criticize it.

---

[65] 388 U.S. 130 (1967).

However, since public figures, as a group, generally have less power than public officials to suppress criticism, the case for taking away some of the protection offered by the common law to all public figures is much harder to make. Compare, for example, the principal of a private school to a public school principle. Parents are more likely to criticize the private school principal because many of them can take their children out at any time and enroll them in another private school. Competition and choice tends to diminish the oppressive power of executives in private institutions. They are less likely as a result to retaliate against criticism and will therefore tend to receive more criticism. Along with the additional criticism may come the occasional defamatory statement.

Of course, many public figures are in positions quite similar to public officials. They control the resources of large private corporations and sometimes use those resources with the same evil intent as the most oppressive governments. But this leads to the suggestion that the public figure category should be subdivided into private individuals who happen to end up in the news because of events beyond their control (say, they were hit by lightning), and other private individuals who climb their way into positions that enable them to use the leverage of corporations, as employers or as suppliers, to discourage those most familiar with their work from ever criticizing it in public.

The Supreme Court distinguished types of public figure along roughly these lines in *Gertz v. Robert Welch, Inc.*[66] *Gertz* described public figures as individuals (1) occupying positions of persuasive power and influence, (2) who have thrust themselves to the forefront of particular controversies to influence the resolution of the issues involved, and (3) whose actions have led to their pervasive involvement in the affairs of society. The Court's rationale focused mostly on the latter two categories, stressing the access such individuals have to the media, to rebut defamatory statements made about them, and their assumption of the risk of defamatory statements through their own efforts to gain public attention. However, the stronger argument, briefly mentioned in *Gertz*, is connected to the first category: that some individuals occupy positions that enable them to suppress criticism with nearly the same effectiveness as a public official.

More important than the definition of public figure, *Gertz* changed the burden of proof in defamation lawsuits against media outlets (news publishers and broadcasters) by requiring the plaintiff, whether a public figure or not, to prove *fault* in publication. The common law had adopted a presumption of liability for words that foreseeably injured an individual's reputation, and the burden of proving truth or the protection of privilege rested with the defendant. Under *Gertz*, the plaintiff has the burden of proving that the news outlet did not take reasonable care in the publication process or intended to harm his reputation. Of course, the information necessary to prove

---

[66] 418 U.S. 323 (1974).

lack of reasonable care on the part of the news outlet is entirely in the hands of the outlet.

In *Philadelphia Newspapers, Inc. v. Hepps*,[67] the Supreme Court extended the wall of legal protection for media outlets by shifting the burden of proof on the matter of falsity to the plaintiff. While the common law permits the defendant to prove truth, *Hepps* requires a plaintiff, whether a public figure or not, to prove falsity against a defendant media outlet. In this case, the actual burden of producing evidence is not heavy on the plaintiff; presumably he already knows whether the newspaper's statement is true or false, and precisely why. The problem for the plaintiff, as noted before, is that the burden of having to reveal facts on private affairs, personal or business, to prove falsity may be sufficient to deter many potential defamation plaintiffs from filing claims against media outlets. The facts revealed by the plaintiff would provide more grist for the mill for media outlets, enhancing the reputational injury suffered by the plaintiff.

V. INTENT, NEGLIGENCE, OR STRICT LIABILITY

I return to the question whether defamation is a form of strict liability, similar to the rules applied to blasting and other dangerous activities. The *Rylands* template is useful in examining defamation, but to understand the law one must go behind the template and examine its utilitarian basis. This returns us to the discussion of Chapter 5.

We are all familiar with the saying "sticks and stones may break my bones, but words can never hurt me." Although words cannot inflict a direct physical harm in the same manner as a sword, they can inflict emotional trauma directly, and they can hurt indirectly by affecting one's relationships with others. Defamation law is concerned with the latter type of harm, the external or relational injury. Words can strengthen or sever relationships, and through these effects materially harm a person who is the subject of another person's speech.

The utilitarian basis for *Rylands* begins with identifying activities and the external effects of those activities. The activity of blasting carries external risks for neighbors of the blasting site, who may easily be injured, even if the blasting is conducted with reasonable care. The external risk created by blasting far exceeds that of other, more common activities, such as gardening, which tend to be neutral in their external effects. The strict liability that the law imposes on blasting has the purpose of inducing such operations to reduce their scale or to find locations where they will cause less harm to neighbors.

To identify the external effects of speech, we should first distinguish truthful speech and false speech. Speech, as a general matter, is a neutral activity, like gardening. Truthful speech, however, is probably more beneficial to society than

[67] 475 U.S. 767 (1986).

most neutral activities. Truthful information, although it may sometimes be harmful to a particular person, enables individuals to make decisions that are consistent with their own plans and preferences. Truthful information, in other words, has the value of a compass, or many tiny compasses spread throughout a society. Just as a compass enables the traveler to find his way north or south, truthful information enables an individual to carry out his own wishes.

In addition to the societal value of truthful information, information is a public good, in the sense that it can be shared by many. Public goods, as noted in Chapter 2, tend to be underprovided relative to their benefits to society. National defense, the classic illustration, is hard to fund adequately on a purely voluntary basis because the benefits are so widely disseminated that each beneficiary has an incentive to push the funding off on someone else, since everyone enjoys the benefits whether they contribute to the funding or not.

This argument suggests that the law should encourage the provision of truthful information. Defamation law does this by making truthful expression absolutely privileged. The external or relational value of truthful expression is recognized as so important in the law that even truthful expression motivated by malice is privileged.

Of course, there is a distinction between expression directed to others about a person and expression directed toward a person. In the former, where defamation law controls, the expression is designed to affect the person primarily through its effects on others related to the person. In the latter, where the effect is direct, the victim of harmful words may be able to sue for intentional infliction of emotional distress (Chapter 4). For this, the courts require evidence of malice and outrageousness, and there is no absolute privilege.

Much lying occurs in the effort to hide feelings or thoughts. Everyone has had the experience of saying "the dinner is excellent," when what we are really thinking is that the food is terrible. These are instances where the speaker feels that the relationship is more valuable than any gain he might perceive in the moment from speaking the truth. The benefits and harms are largely internal to the speaker. One might argue that the recipient is harmed by not hearing the truth about his cooking, but that is entirely speculative. More generally, lying to hide inner feelings, thoughts, or plans may be necessary to avoid harming oneself or others where there is no clear gain to anyone in return. If the law were to punish such lying, it would make virtually all social interaction difficult.

In the defamation context, however, false expression is calculated to have a harmful effect on others, by upsetting bonds of trust or prior assumptions and impressions based on limited information. The gain, if any, goes to the speaker, and the harms are borne by society. The immediate harms to the victim are obvious: emotional harm, severance of valuable connections, such as with customers or employers. However, there are wider social losses. If the victim's customers or clients had chosen to deal with him after concluding that he was preferable to alternatives, their decision to leave him as a consequence of defamatory words hurts them too, by inducing them to choose less preferred options. The victim of defamation, seeing his reputation injured by false speech, loses the value of investments made over time in building his reputation, a type of capital asset. In a world in which defamation went unpunished, the incentives to invest in reputation would be weaker, since the value of reputation could be destroyed easily at any time. This is potentially a great loss to society because the private long-term benefit from building a reputation may be a more important motivational spur than momentary compensation.

What gain is there to the speaker? Iago's statement that "he that filches my good name robs me of that which not enriches him, and makes me poor indeed,"[68] is often repeated in books on defamation law. But Iago's statement is patently false. Robbing a man of his good name can be quite profitable. In all sorts of competitive settings – competition for customers, for business associates, for recognition, or for potential marriage partners – defaming one's rivals can be advantageous. The advantage may be fleeting, but even a fleeting advantage can put one far enough ahead of rivals to effectively destroy their ability to compete in the time period that matters. In the long run, truth will out, but in the long run we are all dead too.

In a world of perfect information it would be impossible to defame anyone. Any such effort would immediately reveal the speaker to be a liar. Similarly, in a world in which everyone lies, it would be quite difficult to defame. Any such effort would be discounted immediately as just another lie.

Indeed, one supposed paradox of lying is that its effectiveness depends on other people telling the truth.[69] But that is too broad a claim about the efficacy of lying. Each of us develops an expectation specific to other individuals regarding the probability each of those individuals may lie. We learn about the truth-telling habits of our associates over time, and where such a history is not available, we develop expectations of the likelihood of a lie based on the position the speaker occupies and the incentives someone in that position would have to tell a lie. We accordingly discount the statements of some speakers because we expect them to tell lies, and therefore lies from such speakers do not fool us. But our individually targeted expectations are often based on imperfect information. Inevitably, we will encounter speakers of whom our expectations are ill-formed or incorrect.

The effectiveness and therefore the rationality of defamation depend on the degree to which information is imperfect – information regarding the subject of the communication and information regarding the truth-telling proclivities of the communicator. The better informed we are, the less effective is defamation. But since our information is often imperfect, defamation can be a rational and effective strategy.

Many pejorative descriptions may not be as harmful today as they were in the past. In the violent, caste-based society in which the common law first developed, with property handed down under the primogeniture rule, an assertion that a man was a

---

[68] WILLIAM SHAKESPEARE, OTHELLO act 3, sc. 3.

[69] SISSELA BOK, LYING: MORAL CHOICE IN PUBLIC AND PRIVATE LIFE (Vintage Books 1989).

bastard might have threatened the subject's livelihood and led to a duel.[70] Today, in America, with the rate of out-of-wedlock birth over 40 percent, a similar assertion would not be viewed as a cause for violence or dispossession of any property. The decriminalization of defamation law, that is, the shift from defamation being both a crime and tort to simply being a tort,[71] reflects in part this gradual change in the social consequences of certain harmful words. But reputations remain important and can be harmed with greater ease today through widespread and fast communication. The fact that times have changed does not imply that defamation law is any less useful today as a deterrent to false, reputation-harming speech.

These observations apply with equal force to the torts labeled false light, misappropriation, and public disclosure of private facts – all falling under the general label "invasion of privacy." False light involves portraying a person in a manner that is false and subjectively harmful or offensive to the person.[72] Misappropriation involves profiting from the use of someone's name or likeness without gaining permission.[73] Public disclosure of private facts is often harmful because it involves the disclosure of only a few of the many facts that could be unearthed about a person, taken out of context or put in public display at a time or in a manner likely to generate unwanted attention, harmful repercussions, or reputational harm.[74] In each of these cases there

---

[70] 3 BLACKSTONE, COMMENTARIES *124–126.

[71] Today, defamation is a subject of tort law. At the time of Blackstone, however, some types of slander were criminal, and libel was both a crime and a tort. *See ibid.* at 124 (imprisonment for words spoken in derogation of a peer, judge, or other great officer), 126 (libel subject to indictment and to private suit). Blackstone notes that every libel has a tendency to break the peace or to provoke others to do so. Again, in an era in which duels were not uncommon, the criminalization of defamation probably served an important function in keeping the peace that most of us would find puzzling today.

[72] Howard v. Antilla, 294 F.3d 244, 248 (1st Cir. 2002) ("One who gives publicity to a matter concerning another that places the other before the public in a false light is subject to liability to the other for invasion of his privacy, if (a) the false light in which the other was placed would be highly offensive to a reasonable person, and (b) the actor had knowledge of or acted in reckless disregard as to the falsity of the publicized matter and the false light in which the other would be placed."). In Peoples Bank and Trust Co. of Mountain Home v. Globe Intern. Pub., Inc., 978 F.2d 1065 (8th Cir. 1992), a ninety-seven-year-old plaintiff prevailed in a false light claim against a tabloid that published an article stating she was leaving her job because she was pregnant.

[73] Solano v. Playgirl, Inc., 292 F.3d 1078, 1088 (9th Cir. 2002) ("To prove a claim of common law commercial misappropriation of privacy, a plaintiff must establish the defendant's use of plaintiff's identity, the appropriation of plaintiff's name or likeness to defendant's advantage, commercially or otherwise, a lack of consent and resulting injury."). For example, in Colgate-Palmolive Co. v. Tullos, 219 F.2d 617 (5th Cir. 1955), the plaintiff prevailed in a misappropriation lawsuit against the defendant, who had used a picture of plaintiff, labeled with someone else's name, in an advertisement for a hair-coloring product.

[74] Armstrong v. Thompson, 80 A.3d 177, 189 (D.C. 2013) ("A plaintiff must show that the defendant (1) published private facts (2) in which the public has no legitimate concern and (3) which publication would cause suffering, shame or humiliation to a person of ordinary sensibilities." For example, in Doe v. Mills 536 N.W.2d 824 (Mich. App. 1995), the defendant was held liable for public disclosure of private facts for using the real name of the plaintiff on signs while protesting outside of an abortion clinic.

is an element of opportunistic profit-taking on the part of the publisher at the expense of the subject. The publications in these categories, like those that are defamatory, have the potential to destroy the subject's incentive to build a good reputation – by appropriating the fruits of those efforts (misappropriation), by preventing the subject from escaping the glare from current or past acts, not publicly known, that are of no consequence to anyone (public disclosure), or by presenting a false version of the facts about a person that is likely to distort or injure his reputation in a manner he subjectively finds harmful (false light). The *Rylands* template used in this chapter to explain defamation law applies equally well to these similar torts.

Aside from truth, the other areas of absolute privilege, such as the absolute immunity of judges, are also due to the great social value of the expression within its context, whether truthful or not. The courts could not function if judges worked under the threat of defamation lawsuits for their decisions; judges would be encouraged to write with timidity and to dissemble to avoid litigation.

In contrast to truthful speech, false speech tends to harm society. To return to the compass analogy, false speech is like a compass with the north arrow replaced by one purporting to point south. The compass still works, but it points the user in the direction opposite to the one he desires to travel. Repeated across society, false speech multiplies its harm by disseminating false compasses to everyone. When false statements are made to injure an individual's reputation, the statements damage relationships and discourage the investments of effort that tend to generate a positive reputation. Because of the external harm due to false speech, the law should discourage it as an activity, and the law does this by adopting a presumption of strict liability for false speech that is harmful to reputation.

However, some false speech occurs in settings where the social value of frank communication more than offsets the expected harm. The absolute privilege observed for judges and legislators provides one example. Even if some judges lie in their opinions, or their statements from the bench, the value of frank and direct speech in these offices probably outweighs the risk of the occasional false statement. And if lying were widespread in judicial writing, defamation liability could do little to help improve matters.

Some false speech occurs in settings where the social value of frank communication is high, but not so high, as a general matter, to outweigh the harm from false speech. The qualified privilege recognized in the area of intracorporate speech is an example of such a setting. Although courts treat this as an area of strict defamation liability, the reasoning of courts in these cases is closer to the negligence standard. The decisions require the court to balance the harm caused by the statement against the value of frank and direct speech under the circumstances of a particular case.

Indeed, many qualified privilege analyses by courts appear to be essentially negligence decisions. Take the case of a third party who writes a letter to the wife of *A* telling her of A's various affairs while traveling on business.[75] There is no bright line rule governing the scope of privilege for such a letter. The courts, on a case-by-case basis, weigh the foreseeable losses avoided by the disclosure against the foreseeable harm created by the disclosure.[76]

Similarly, consider the false statement made to avoid revealing the truth. Joe, walking down the street, holding a large package of bacon, is stopped by Bob, who asks "Where did you buy the bacon?" Joe bought the bacon at Sal's Convenience Store, but does not want to reveal this fact to Bob. Instead, he tells Bob that he bought the bacon at Sam's Store. "But Sam is a kosher meat seller," exclaims Bob, and eventually word travels that Sam, the kosher meat seller, sold bacon to Joe. Sam brings a defamation claim against Joe. Joe is presumptively strictly liable, because liability does not turn on whether he knew that Sam was a kosher meat seller. However, in determining whether Joe is liable, a court would consider Joe's reasons for making the statement to Sam. Suppose Joe did not want to steer Bob to Sal's store, because of a particular danger, which he could not then reveal, that Bob might confront in Sal's store. Again, the court would have to weigh the harm of the statement against the loss avoided in determining whether it was privileged.

The general picture, then, is that defamation liability, rather than being simply a type of strict liability, is an amalgam of strict liability, negligence, and per se legality. The underlying principles that determine the types of claim governed by each legal theory also determine the application of defamation law to each case of harmful speech or writing. The template of *Rylands* helps to explain the law, but only up to a point. The area governed by defamation law is so vast that one must understand, in addition to the parts where strict liability emulates *Rylands*, the parts where liability is out of the question and the parts where liability is determined by a negligence inquiry.

The final question to consider is whether there is any basis for Holmes's suggestion that defamation is a specific intent tort, that is, requiring an intent to harm to hold the defendant liable. Holmes's view can be reconciled with defamation law. First, Holmes began from the view that defamation is a discrete action that harms the plaintiff, like a battery. But unlike battery, defamation law allows for broad justifications, beyond self-defense, defense of others, and defense of property. The justifications have the effect of screening out, from forming a basis for liability, statements that could have served other purposes, or other interests, than simply harming the plaintiff. Consider, for example, the common law qualified privilege

---

[75] Watt v. Longsdon, [1930] 1 K.B. 130 (plaintiff had "orgies" with the dancing girls).

[76] *Id.* at 149–150 ("I have no intention of writing an exhaustive treatise on the circumstances when a stranger or friend should communicate to the husband or wife information he receives as to the conduct of the other party to the marriage. I am clear that it is impossible to say he is always under a moral or social duty to do so; it is equally impossible to say he is never under such a duty. It must depend on the circumstances of each case, the nature of the information, and the relation of speaker and recipient.").

for commentary on public matters, which at the time Holmes wrote would not have been subsumed to any degree within First Amendment law. The qualified privilege had the effect of excluding or screening out, as a basis for liability, commentary on public matters of interest to society. After all of the various screens created by the privileges had been applied, what remained consisted mostly of words that served no other purpose or interest than to harm the plaintiff. An inference of intent to harm was therefore objectively supported by the evidence in the vast majority of cases of liability.

The changes imposed by the Supreme Court on American defamation law do not appear to be dramatic when viewed from this functionalist perspective. Because of the discrete nature of the defamation tort, the requirement that the plaintiff prove fault against media defendants has probably had the same impact as would a rule requiring the plaintiff to prove fault in a battery case. If the plaintiff had to prove fault to prevail in a battery action, the additional burden probably would not alter the plaintiff's prospects much in comparison to the strict liability that has prevailed in the common law of intentional torts. In the vast majority of battery cases, the foreseeability of harm is high, and the ease of avoiding the harm low, which suggests that fault would be found readily. The same is probably true of most defamation cases. The other key change imposed by the Supreme Court, the requirement that the plaintiff prove falsity, is not a substantive change in defamation law, only a shift in the burden of proof. No doubt the requirement has reduced the deterrent effect of defamation litigation on media outlets, by putting an additional obstacle in the way of plaintiffs, but it has not altered the substance of the law.

17

Products Liability

I. EARLY LAW

Early law on products liability, of roughly the mid-1800s, applied the *privity rule*. Under this rule, a seller of a product was responsible in negligence only to the party to whom he sold the product. As a result, consumers of defective products often lost their lawsuits against manufacturers, because they were not in privity of contract. *Winterbottom v. Wright*,[1] a leading case, rejected a suit by a mail deliverer, brought against the supplier of mail coaches to the Postmaster-General, for injury resulting from a latent defect in a coach because the deliverer was not a party to the contract between the supplier and the Postmaster-General.

Almost from the moment the privity rule became established, exceptions began to appear. Judge Cardozo's *MacPherson v. Buick Motor Co.*[2] opinion provides a fascinating description of the growth of exceptions to the privity rule, a growth that culminated in his own decision in *MacPherson* to effectively abolish the rule by giving one of its exceptions an extremely broad interpretation.

The privity rule may appear at first glance to have been a formalist doctrine unrelated to any functional purpose. However, the rule can be understood in functional terms using assumption of risk theory. The simple idea behind it is that in the absence of some warning from the intermediate purchaser about risks to others and an effort to get the original seller to accept responsibility for those risks, the original seller should not be assumed to accept responsibility for harms to third parties that the intermediate purchaser could have foreseen much easier than the original seller. For example, when Wright agreed to supply mail coaches to the Postmaster-General, he may not have known how often the coaches would be used, under what conditions (a defect under some circumstances might not be worrisome, while under others it

---

[1] Winterbottom v. Wright, 152 Eng. Rep. 402 (Ct. Exch. 1842).
[2] MacPherson v. Buick Motor Co., 111 N.E. 1050 (N.Y. 1916).

would be), and by whom. If he were asked to guarantee compensation for injuries suffered by coach drivers, Wright would have inquired into these matters to get a sense of the scope of his liability. Once aware of the scope of liability, he would have priced the product accordingly, perhaps charging an especially high price for coaches that would be used on potholed roads in rural areas and a comparatively low price for coaches that would be used in well-paved cities.

The doctrine of privity was a default rule governing risk allocation. It did not preclude parties from altering the allocation of risk through contract. The intermediate purchaser could write terms into the contract requiring the original seller to accept responsibility for harm to certain third parties (specifically, customers of the intermediate purchaser). However, in the absence of such contract terms, the background understanding under privity doctrine is that the original seller does not implicitly agree to compensate harms to third parties caused by defective conditions in the product. If, in general, the intermediate purchaser has better information than the original seller about those harms, the privity rule would be the efficient default term because it would save the parties the costs of writing special terms into the contract to govern the allocation of liability risk.

As noted, exceptions to the privity rule began to appear early in its life. By roughly 1900, three general exceptions were established in the law. These exceptions permitted a tort plaintiff who was not in privity of contract with the defendant to sue for (1) an act of negligence by a manufacturer or seller that is "imminently dangerous to life or health," committed in the production or sale of an item "intended to preserve, destroy, or affect" life or health; (2) an act of negligence resulting in a defective appliance that injures a business invitee on the owner's premises; and (3) an injury caused by a defective item that the manufacturer or seller sells knowing the item to be "imminently dangerous to life or limb" without giving notice to the buyer of its qualities.[3]

The first exception initially applied to things like explosives and poisons. In *Thomas v. Winchester*,[4] a poison, labeled incorrectly, was sold to a druggist, who later sold it to a consumer. The consumer sued the seller responsible for the false label and won because the defendant's negligence "put human life in imminent danger." The second exception was simply a version of the landowner's duty to an invitee (see Chapter 14). The third exception, for cases of knowingly selling an item with a dangerous defect without providing notice, was grounded in theories of fraud and misrepresentation.[5]

---

[3] Huset v. J. I. Case Threshing Mach. Co., 120 F. 865, 870–872 (8th Cir. 1903).
[4] Thomas v. Winchester, 6 N.Y. 397 (1852).
[5] Kuelling v. Roderick Lean Manufacturing Co., 75 N. E. 1098 (N.Y. 1905) (defendant manufactured a roller made of weak wood, filling the defective part with putty and painting over it; consumer, not in privity, permitted to recover from manufacturer); Lewis v. Terry, 43 P. 398 (Cal. 1896) (seller sold a bed frame, knowing that once weight was put on the frame, it would collapse); Woodward v. Miller & Karwisch, 46 S.E. 847 (Ga. 1904) (seller sold a buggy, knowing that it would collapse).

As Cardozo explained in *MacPherson*, courts following *Thomas v. Winchester* expanded the first exception. One important expansion occurred in *Devlin v. Smith*,[6] where the defendant built a defective scaffold for a painter. The painter's employees were injured when the scaffold collapsed. They successfully sued the defendant because of the first exception to the privity rule. How does a defective scaffold fit within the first exception, initially intended for explosives and poisons? The court in *Devlin* thought there was not a big difference between an explosive and a collapsing scaffold. Both of them put potential victims at risk in a similar way.

Another expansion of the first exception occurred in *Statler v. Ray Manufacturing Co.*[7] The defendant manufactured a large coffee urn with a defect that caused it to explode when heated and sold the urn to a restaurant. The victim recovered against the defendant under the first exception. Again, the court's reasoning was that there was not much of a difference between a real explosive and an exploding coffee urn.

This line of expansions came to its logical endpoint in *MacPherson*. Buick Motor Company sold a car with a defective wheel to a dealer, who sold it to the plaintiff. (The wheel was manufactured by another company and sold to Buick.) The wheel was made of defective wood, which crumbled to pieces while in use. The court allowed the plaintiff to recover from Buick for its negligence in failing to properly inspect the wheel.

Given the scaffold and coffee pot cases, the outcome in *MacPherson* is not surprising. If a scaffold can be threatening to life because it might collapse, and a coffee pot can be similarly threatening because it might explode, it follows that a car wheel can be threatening to life because it might crumble. Cardozo noted that the car was capable of going up to fifty miles per hour. If a car wheel crumbles at that speed, driver and passengers would probably suffer severe injuries.

MacPherson takes the line of cases under the first exception to the privity rule to its logical conclusion, which in the end leaves little of the privity rule. Any defective condition that could cause a serious physical injury could be characterized as putting life at risk. Consider, for example, a Coca-Cola bottle that might explode. The explosion could put out someone's eye or sever an artery. Any defective condition that could cause a serious physical injury could also put life at risk. From this it follows that the first exception to the privity rule looms larger than the rule itself – the exception swallows the rule.

To be sure, Cardozo's expansion does not permit every injured consumer to sue the manufacturer. *MacPherson* requires the existence of a dangerously defective condition, that the condition put someone other than the contracting party at risk (usually consumers of the dealer), and a proximate causation, or foreseeability, link between the original seller's negligence and the plaintiff's injury. The foreseeability requirement excludes claims that result from the plaintiff's negligence, or from

---

6   Devlin v. Smith, 89 N.Y. 470 (1882).
7   Statler v. Ray Mfg. Co., 88 N.E. 1063 (N.Y. 1909).

the unforeseeable intervention of the plaintiff or another party. It also implies that the defendant sold the item without any expectation of it being inspected by an intermediate party before reaching the consumer's hands. And most obvious of all, *MacPherson* requires negligence on the part of the defendant. *MacPherson* does not permit a plaintiff to recover when the defective condition is a purely random occurrence in a reasonably governed production process.

II. *ESCOLA* AND THE POLICY ARGUMENT FOR STRICT PRODUCTS LIABILITY

The next important stage in the development of strict products liability was Justice Traynor's concurring opinion in *Escola v. Coca Cola Bottling Co. of Fresno*.[8] Traynor set forth several policy arguments for strict products liability. I will update Traynor's arguments here to reflect modern scholarship.

The policy arguments for strict products liability can be summarized in three labels: (1) *deterrence*, (2) *risk-spreading*, and (3) *administrative costs*. Consider the deterrence argument first, which encompasses two types of deterrence. The first type concerns the deterrence of negligent practices in the production and marketing process. Product manufacturers are assumed to have an informational advantage over consumers. They know the details surrounding their production decisions, such as the cost of alternative methods of production. A strict liability regime is superior to negligence, one can argue, because it prevents the seller from exploiting his informational advantage with respect to the evidence of his own negligence. Given this informational advantage, a seller can avoid a negligence finding even when he was in fact negligent, because there may be ways the seller was negligent that plaintiffs' lawyers are unable to discover. This implies that sellers sometimes escape liability under the negligence rule when they would not escape it under a perfect, error-free legal system, and this gives them an incentive to forgo care whenever doing so cuts costs. Strict liability prevents this from occurring.

The second type of deterrence concerns the *level of activity*. If consumers are not aware of the risk characteristics of the products they see on the market, strict liability can signal those characteristics to them. How? Because sellers of riskier products will be held liable more often than sellers of safe products, the risky product sellers will have to raise their prices to cover the additional liability. In the resultant market equilibrium, risky products will have higher prices than safe products, and consumers will therefore be discouraged from consuming the risky products. Moreover, since the risk of harm is included within the price of the product, every product's price reflects its true cost to society. Given this, consumers will purchase goods only when their perceived benefits exceed the true cost of the product.

---

[8] Escola v. Coca Cola Bottling Co. of Fresno, 150 P.2d 436 (Cal. 1944) (Traynor, J., concurring in judgment).

The second general argument falls under the label *risk spreading or insurance*. Strict products liability creates an insurance pool among the seller and the consumers of the risky product. Because the product's price will have to cover the liability, every price will consist of two components: one covering the cost of production and sale, and another covering the cost of insurance. The consumer, in effect, buys two products: the item he desires plus an insurance policy that compensates him if he is injured by it. This is thought to be desirable because consumers are risk averse (see Chapter 6) and would therefore prefer to regularly pay a small premium to insure against a large loss that might occur.

The third general argument, under the label *administrative costs*, holds that strict liability is preferable because it avoids complicated doctrinal rules that either serve no useful purpose or take us to the same conclusion that we would reach under strict liability. Traynor, for example, pointed to the frequent reliance on *res ipsa loquitur* doctrine, in lawsuits against sellers of defective products, to argue that we may as well go directly to the final result by adopting strict liability.[9] Calabresi, in his later and more sophisticated argument for strict liability,[10] said that negligence law was unpredictable and involved complicated rules that often diverted liability away from the party who was best able to control the risk of an accident.

Counterarguments can be offered against each one of these arguments. The argument that strict liability leads to superior precaution assumes that the risk of a false acquittal is greater under negligence than under strict liability, which may not be true in every case. The activity-level argument assumes that consumers are unaware of the risk characteristics of products, which may not be true. The insurance argument assumes that it makes sense to structure an insurance market within a product market, even though it will often lead to coverage offered to people (such as risk-seeking consumers) who would be denied coverage in an ordinary insurance market. The administrative cost argument assumes that strict liability is faster and cheaper to administer than negligence, also a claim that should be empirically demonstrated rather than assumed.

Whether strict liability is actually superior to negligence as a general rule is a question that requires empirical examination. As it stands, the empirical evidence is mixed.[11] More importantly, the legal test that has emerged from years of litigation does not deserve the strict liability label. As will become clear shortly, most of the legal theories falling under the strict products liability heading rely on negligence principles. Not much has changed in the law after all.

---

[9] *Id.* at 462–463.

[10] GUIDO CALABRESI, THE COSTS OF ACCIDENTS: A LEGAL AND ECONOMIC ANALYSIS (Yale Univ. Press 1970). For a discussion of Calabresi's theory and insurance in product markets, *see* Kenneth S. Abraham, *Liability Insurance and Accident Prevention: The Evolution of an Idea*, 64 MD. L. REV. 573 (2005).

[11] For an empirical assessment of products liability, with reform proposals, *see* W. KIP VISCUSI, REFORMING PRODUCTS LIABILITY (Harvard Univ. Press 1991).

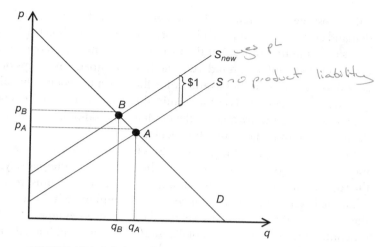

FIGURE 17.1. Market effect of strict liability.

III. ECONOMICS OF PRODUCTS LIABILITY, PART I

Since products liability affects the market, and can be evaluated by considering its effects on the market, one should examine the law within the framework of a market analysis.[12] I use the market framework throughout this chapter as a way of assessing the desirability and scope of products liability. This requires an introduction to *supply and demand analysis,* a subject many students learn in introductory economics courses. It should become clear shortly that we have already introduced market analysis, in Chapter 2, in the course of discussing the incentive effects of strict liability.

Products liability is a mixture of law and policy, with a heavy weight on policy. Many of the court opinions talk about the market effects of liability. Given this, it would be unwise to attempt to evaluate the law of products liability without some framework for understanding the operation of markets.

Figure 17.1 shows the supply and demand curves for a product market. The demand curve, labeled *D*, is downward sloping because as the price of the product

---

[12] The market analysis in this section is set out in more detail in Keith N. Hylton, *The Law and Economics of Products Liability,* 88 NOTRE DAME L. REV. 2457 (2013). For concise and useful discussions of the economics of producer liability, *see* A. MITCHELL POLINSKY, AN INTRODUCTION TO LAW AND ECONOMICS (4th ed. 2011); James M. Buchanan, *In Defense of* Caveat Emptor, 38 U. CHI. L. REV. 64 (1970); Andrew F. Daughety & Jennifer F. Reinganum, *Product Safety: Liability, R&D and Signaling,* 85 AM. ECON. REV. 1187 (1995); A. Mitchall Polinsky & Steven Shavell, *The Uneasy Case for Product Liability,* 123 HARV. L. REV. 1437 (2010); Richard A. Posner & William M. Landes, *A Positive Economic Analysis of Products Liability,* 14 J. LEGAL STUD. 535 (1985). The treatment of products liability in this chapter stresses policy rationales. For extensive discussions of the law, *see* DAVID G. OWEN, PRODUCTS LIABILITY LAW (2d ed. 2008); MARSHALL SHAPO, THE LAW OF PRODUCTS LIABILITY (5th ed. 2010).

falls, consumers generally will purchase more of it. It is helpful to think of the demand curve as a schedule of bids that a consumer is willing to offer as the quantity of his consumption varies. For the first item – say, the first scoop of ice cream – he is willing to submit a high bid. After he has consumed ten scoops of ice cream, he is no longer willing to bid as much for the eleventh scoop. This phenomenon is known among economists as the "diminishing marginal utility" of consumption. As the consumer consumes more of the product, the additional utility that he gets from the additional unit of consumption declines.

Similarly, the supply curve, labeled S, is upward sloping because sellers will bring more of the product to the market as the price rises. Alternatively, one can view the supply curve as representing minimum prices a seller must receive to bring an additional item to the market. Since the minimum price is the level that just covers the cost of production and marketing, the supply curve represents the seller's cost schedule. It shows the incremental cost of bringing an additional unit of output to the market. The supply curve is upward sloping, even in the case of a single supplier, because that supplier will have to squeeze more out of a fixed plant to bring more to the market, and that will inevitably result in an increase in the cost of rolling out an additional unit.

The *market equilibrium*, the price and quantity generated by the market, is represented by the intersection of the supply and demand curves (point A in Figure 17.1). The market equilibrium occurs at the price level that equates the quantity demanded with the quantity supplied. The market price is the point along the vertical axis in Figure 17.1 corresponding to point A, and the market quantity is the point along the horizontal axis corresponding to point A. If Figure 17.1 represents the market in "widgets," then the intersection of the supply and demand curves would provide both the market price of a widget and the quantity of widgets used or consumed.

Each point along the demand schedule represents the incremental benefit from bringing an additional unit of the item to consumers. If there are no externalities (that is, consumption by one person does not benefit or harm a nonconsumer), the demand schedule shows the marginal benefit to society from bringing more units of output to the market. The supply schedule represents the marginal costs from bringing additional units of output to the market. The market equilibrium is best or "socially optimal" because it is the point at which the incremental benefit to society from selling more output is balanced off by the incremental cost. Society cannot enhance its wealth by bringing any more output to the market once it reaches the market equilibrium level.

Suppose the seller markets a product that is defective in a manner that can lead to serious injury to the consumer. Suppose, in addition, that the defective quality is not obvious to the consumer. Let the product be widgets. As the result of random errors or glitches in the production process, one of every 1,000 widgets sold by the manufacturer explodes, injuring the consumer. The errors are not the result of negligence in the manufacturing process. On average, the explosion causes an injury to the consumer with a monetary value of $1,000. Thus, every widget exposes the consumer to an expected monetary loss of $(1/1,000) \times (\$1,000) = \$1$.

Since every widget imposes a cost of $1, above and beyond the production and marketing cost, we can treat the $1 expected loss as part of the cost of marketing widgets. We can introduce the risk cost of $1 into the supply-demand framework by shifting the supply schedule up by $1 to reflect the additional cost, as shown in Figure 17.1. The new supply curve, S_{NEW}, represents all of the costs borne by society in connection to the supply of widgets. Because of this, it is a correct measure of incremental costs.

Now, note that if we use the new supply curve, the intersection between supply and demand occurs at point B. At the new intersection, the price of the widget is higher and the total quantity supplied lower than at point A. The price is higher because it reflects the risk imposed on consumers. The market quantity is lower because consumers purchase less of the item once the true cost, which includes the risk component, is built into the price.

The alternative equilibrium (B) is the optimal outcome. The reason is that it reflects all of the costs and benefits of bringing widgets to the market. The alternative equilibrium occurs where incremental benefits are balanced off by incremental costs.

Even though the alternative equilibrium at point B is optimal, the market will generate point A as the equilibrium. That is because consumers are, by hypothesis, unaware of the explosion risk when they buy a widget. And, in the absence of liability, the explosion risk is not borne by the seller, so the schedule of minimum prices he must receive to supply the market will be determined by the original supply schedule S, not the alternative supply schedule S_{NEW}.

Products liability changes this outcome. If the seller is strictly liable for consumer losses, he will include those losses in his assessment of his own costs. That means the seller will use the alternative supply schedule S_{NEW} as a basis for determining the minimum prices he will accept to provide widgets to the market. The resultant market equilibrium will occur at a price level that equates the total quantity demanded with the total quantity supplied, according to the S_{NEW} supply schedule. This is shown in Figure 17.1 by point B, the optimal outcome.

This supply-demand analysis shows that liability leads to a reduction in the total quantity of risky products and to higher prices for those products, as the risk gets embedded into the product price. Strict products liability therefore leads to a reduction in the consumption of risky products as consumers shift their purchases toward relatively safe products. Strict liability leads to an outcome in which prices reflect risks that consumers cannot discern easily.

This consumption effect is not observed under negligence. If the seller is subjected to negligence liability, then he will take reasonable care. After adopting the reasonable care level, the seller will not be held liable. Any residual risk that makes the product dangerous will be borne entirely by the consumer. The negligence system, unlike strict liability, does not lead to a shift in the market away from risky products and toward relatively safe products. Because of this difference, strict liability is potentially superior to negligence in the product safety context.

IV. RESTATEMENT OF TORTS AND PRODUCTS LIABILITY

Section 402A of the *Restatement (Second) of Torts,* published in 1965, is the first effort toward a general codification of products liability law. Section 402A declares that a seller of "any product in a defective condition unreasonably dangerous" to the consumer is strictly liable for harm caused to the consumer or to his property. An unreasonably dangerous product, as defined by 402A, is one that is "dangerous to an extent beyond that which would be contemplated by the ordinary consumer."[13] This is now known as the *consumer expectations test* for liability: The seller is strictly liable if the product failed to conform to the safety expectations of the average consumer.

Although the Second Restatement provides only one test for liability, the consumer expectations test, the law soon developed into a complicated set of doctrines emanating from three broad products liability theories.[14] One such theory is based on the existence of a *manufacturing defect,* a glitch that occurs in the course of making a product. The typical manufacturing defect case involves a product that deviates from the manufacturer's design and from other units of the same product made by the manufacturer. Consider the manufacture of widgets. One widget in every 1,000 deviates from the norm in a way that is potentially harmful to the widget consumer. A consumer who is injured by such a widget can bring a lawsuit on a theory of strict liability against the manufacturer or seller. The plaintiff is not required to prove fault or unreasonable conduct of any sort. If the plaintiff can present enough evidence to support the inference that his injury is due to the defective widget, and that the defect was present when the product left the seller's hands, he prevails. Thus, the plaintiff is required only to produce evidence that the defect exists, and that excludes the possibility that the defect is due to his own mishandling or the conduct of some third party.

A second theory of products liability governs the *design defect.* The design defect claim asserts that the manufacturer's design is itself unreasonably dangerous. There are two tests courts have applied under this theory: the *consumer expectations* test and the *risk-utility* test. Recall that under the consumer expectations test, the plaintiff is required to show that the product failed to conform to the safety expectations of the average consumer. Under the risk-utility test, the plaintiff is required to show that the product is unreasonably dangerous in the sense that the incremental risk associated with the defendant's chosen design far exceeds the incremental utility when compared to an alternative safer design.

---

[13] RESTATEMENT (SECOND) OF TORTS § 402A cmt. i (1965).
[14] *See* RESTATEMENT (THIRD) OF TORTS: PROD. LIAB. (1998).

The third products liability theory is *failure to warn*. This theory asserts that the seller was aware of the defective condition of the product and failed to adequately warn the consumer. It is governed by negligence principles. If a warning could have been given easily, and the warning probably would have been effective, then the defendant will be held liable if the plaintiff suffered a serious injury because of his lack of information about the condition.

There are comments in the Second Restatement that are still important for today's law. Comment *f* notes that the rule of strict liability "applies to any person engaged in the business of selling products for use in consumption."[15] It goes on to note that it applies to "the owner of a motion picture theatre who sells popcorn or ice cream, either for consumption on the premises or in packages to be taken home."[16] The rule does not apply, however, to someone who sells his own used car, because such a seller is not in the business of selling.

In light of comment *f*, strict products liability can be especially harsh on retailers. Suppose a manufacturer produces a defective power saw, boxes it up, and sells it to Wal-Mart. Suppose, in addition, Wal-Mart handles the power saw with reasonable care. The consumer who purchases the defective power saw and is injured gets to sue Wal-Mart even though Wal-Mart did nothing other than put the item on its shelves for purchase. Some states have modified the law to reduce this burden on retailers.[17]

One of the most important instructions is given in comment *k* of the Second Restatement, which notes that there "are some products which, in the present state of human knowledge, are quite incapable of being made safe for their intended and ordinary use."[18] It points to vaccines and experimental drugs as examples. If a product falls under the comment *k* exception, strict liability does not apply. In other words, as long as the seller takes proper care in the production and marketing of the product, and reasonably warns of the product's dangers, the seller is exempt from strict products liability. Of course, this implies that the seller of such a product can be held liable for failing to provide a reasonable warning, or for negligence in the production and marketing of the product.

Modern case law on comment *k* has focused on whether the defense it provides applies in manufacturing defect cases, design defect cases, and failure to warn cases. As a general matter, courts hold that comment *k* is inapplicable to manufacturing

---

[15] Restatement (Second) of Torts § 402A cmt. f (1965).

[16] *Id.*

[17] Nebraska, for example, bars strict liability claims against all nonmanufacturers of a defective product. *See* Neb. Rev. Stat. Ann. § 25–21, 181 (2011). Roughly half of the states have enacted limited statutory exceptions (requiring, for example, knowledge of defect) for retailers. For a survey of state restrictions on retailer liability for product defects, *see* Robert A. Sachs, *Product Liability Reform and Seller Liability: A Proposal for Change*, 55 Baylor L. Rev. 1031, 1121 (2003).

[18] Restatement (Second) of Torts § 402A cmt. k (1965).

defect claims.[19] Comment *k* is limited by its terms to "properly prepared" products, and courts have read this language to preclude the comment *k* defense in manufacturing defect cases. In design defect cases, the state courts have taken different paths, though all of the paths can be grouped under one of two categories. Some states, following the California Supreme Court decision in *Brown v. Superior Court*,[20] hold that comment *k* bars design defect claims with respect to *all* prescription drugs.[21] Other states apply comment *k* on a case-by-case basis to prescription drugs.[22] In failure to warn cases, courts have held that comment *k* does not provide a defense,[23] which is, of course, consistent with its language.

If the comment *k* exception is to have any grounding in the common law of torts, it can and should be viewed as falling under the theory of strict liability in *Rylands v. Fletcher* (Chapter 5). A vaccine merits an exception to strict products liability on the same grounds that courts have created exceptions to strict *Rylands*-based liability for the provision of public resources, such as natural gas (*Strawbridge v. City of Philadelphia*, Chapter 15). The vaccine offers widely dispersed public benefits. It reduces the rate of disease transmission, which helps even those who do not take the vaccine. Because of these external benefits, there is a strong case for an exception to strict liability. The same may be said of experimental drugs. Whether this argument should, as a normative matter, apply to drugs in general is a more difficult question.[24]

---

19 *See, e.g.,* Toner v. Lederle Laboratories, a Div. of Am. Cyanamid Co., 732 P.2d 297, 305 (Idaho 1987) ("By its terms, comment *k* excepts unavoidably unsafe products from strict liability only where the plaintiff alleges a design defect, and not where the plaintiff alleges a manufacturing flaw or an inadequate warning. . . . [I]f such products are mismanufactured or unaccompanied by adequate warnings, then the seller may be liable even if the plaintiff cannot establish the seller's negligence. Courts and commentators universally agree to this limitation on comment *k*'s grant of immunity from strict liability.") (citations omitted); Savina v. Sterling Drug, Inc., 795 P.2d 915, 924 (Kan. 1990) ("[Comment *k*] cannot apply to products that contain a manufacturing flaw or an inadequate warning but, instead, applies only where the plaintiff alleges a design defect."); Castrignano v. E.R. Squibb & Sons, Inc., 546 A.2d 775, 780 (R.I. 1988) ("We conclude that [comment *k*'s] exemption applies only to allegations of a defective design.") (citing Toner, 732 P.2d at 305; Feldman v. Lederle Laboratories, 479 A.2d 374, 383–84 (N.J. 1984)); Grundberg v. Upjohn Co., 813 P.2d 89, 92 (Utah 1991) ("By its terms, comment *k* excepts unavoidably unsafe products from strict liability only to the extent that the plaintiff alleges a design defect; comment *k*'s immunity from strict liability does not extend to strict liability claims based on a manufacturing flaw or an inadequate warning. . . . This limitation on the scope of comment *k* immunity is universally recognized.") (citing Toner, 732 P.2d at 305).

20 Brown v. Superior Court, 751 P.2d 470 (Cal. 1988).

21 This set of states includes California, Connecticut, Iowa, Louisiana, New York, North Carolina (by statute), Ohio (by statute, reversing Ohio's previous reliance on a case-by-case approach), South Carolina, Texas, Utah, Washington, and Wyoming. Several other states may fall in this category, but the law is insufficiently clear at the time of this writing. For an excellent survey, *see* Jim Beck, *Comment* k, *Some of the Way, Drug and Device Law,* http://druganddevicelaw.blogspot.com/2011/04/comment-k-some-of-way.html.

22 Arkansas, Colorado, Hawaii, Idaho, Illinois, Kansas, Mississippi, Missouri, Nebraska, Oklahoma, and Rhode Island. Other states may fall in this category at some point.

23 *Supra* note 19.

24 *See, e.g.,* Brown v. Superior Court, 751 P.2d 470, 475 (Cal. 1988).

Comment *k* was applied to reverse a lower court decision imposing strict liability in *Brody v. Overlook Hospital*.[25] The plaintiff contracted hepatitis from a blood transfusion. It was known at the time that hepatitis could be transmitted through a transfusion, but no test existed for detecting contaminated blood. *Brody* can be defended on the ground that the availability of blood transfusions provided widely dispersed public health benefits. Holding the supplier strictly liable for the defective condition, on the basis of the consumer expectations test, would tax the supplier for the risks while providing no offset for the widely dispersed public benefits, thus reducing consumption below the socially ideal level.

Brody may seem, at first glance, inconsistent with the general policy of courts to disallow the comment *k* defense in the area of manufacturing defects. But that inconsistency appears only if one interprets *Brody* as a manufacturing defect case. If, on the other hand, one interprets *Brody* as a design defect case, which seems appropriate given that the defective condition was characteristic of the product rather than a particular aberrant sample, then the decision is entirely consistent with the law on comment *k*.

Comment *n* of the Second Restatement explains that contributory negligence is not a defense "when such negligence consists merely in a failure to discover the defect in the product, or to guard against the possibility of its existence."[26] However, contributory negligence in the sense of "voluntarily and unreasonably proceeding to encounter a known danger"[27] is a defense.

The extent to which contributory negligence and assumption of risk are defenses are both complicated issues in products liability law. As a general matter, contributory negligence is a valid defense when the plaintiff's own unreasonably careless conduct is a factor that causes the injury. For example, the plaintiff may have been intoxicated when driving and the door lock defectively designed; an accident occurs and plaintiff is badly injured both as a result of his driving while drunk and the defective condition of the door lock.[28] Another example: the plaintiff is injured when using a product in a manner that violates clear warnings – for example, choosing the wrong tire size for a car in spite of clear specifications.[29] In each of these examples, the contributory negligence defense may be available to the defendant.

As for assumption of risk, comment *n* implies that the version known as *secondary assumption of risk* (see Chapter 10) is a defense to a products liability claim. Secondary assumption of risk consists of voluntarily and unreasonably encountering a known danger and is also a type of contributory negligence. Secondary assumption

---

[25] Brody v. Overlook Hosp., 317 A.2d 3923 (N.J. Super. Ct. App. Div. 1974).
[26] RESTATEMENT (SECOND) OF TORTS § 402A cmt. n (1965).
[27] *Id.*
[28] *See* Daly v. General Motors Corp., 575 P.2d 1162 (Cal. 1978).
[29] McDevitt v. Standard Oil, 391 F.2d 364 (5th Cir. 1968) (product misuse equivalent to contributory negligence); Hood v. Ryobi, 181 F.3d 608, 611 (4th Cir. 1999) (product misuse not foreseeable).

of risk is equivalent to the type of contributory negligence explicitly recognized as a defense under comment *n*.

Primary assumption of risk, which consists of consenting to the risk created by the defendant, is a defense in products liability only under special circumstances, and even then it is generally described using terms other than assumption of risk. The usefulness of the primary assumption of risk defense, to sellers, depends on the type of liability claim – that is, whether it is a manufacturing defect claim, a design defect claim, or a failure to warn claim. In manufacturing defect litigation, primary assumption of risk is almost never a defense, because these are cases in which a particular unit or batch of a product deviates from the norm. For most modern products, with extremely low rates of manufacturing defect, the consumer would predict the risk of a dangerous manufacturing defect to be roughly zero. Since the consumer almost never anticipates a dangerous manufacturing defect, the primary assumption of risk defense is of little use in the manufacturing defect setting. In design defect and in failure to warn litigation, primary assumption of risk is a theory on which a defense can be based, but the theory is incorporated in the consumer expectations doctrine. Under the consumer expectations doctrine, a consumer can lose his design defect or failure to warn case because he was fully aware of the risk characteristics of the product he voluntarily purchased.[30]

V. GENERAL DEFENSES IN PRODUCTS LIABILITY

The most general defenses available to a seller in a products liability case are the rules limiting the type of harm that can be brought within the strict liability rule and the type of defendant that can be sued. These defenses apply to all products liability claims, whether manufacturing defect, design defect, or failure to warn.

Economic Loss Rule

The key rule limiting the type of harm that can be compensated under products liability is the *economic loss rule*, which holds that *a consumer cannot recover if the loss he has suffered is merely a defeated economic expectation*. Products liability law permits *recovery only when the harm occurs to a person or to other property*. When the product destroys only itself, the courts will not permit a tort claim to be brought against the seller.

For example, if a component of a television malfunctions and permanently damages the whole television, the consumer is barred from a tort suit by the economic loss rule. If the consumer were to sue the component manufacturer for the value of the destroyed television, his lawsuit would be dismissed under the rule.

---

[30] Linegar v. Armour of America, 909 F.2d 1150 (8th Cir. 1990) (design); Rix v. Reeves, 532 P.2d 185 (Ariz. App. 1975) (warning).

Obviously, this leads to the question whether the component is destroying other property by destroying the television. In general, courts say that if the malfunctioning component is *integral to the whole product*, then the harm falls under the economic loss rule.

The fundamental reason behind the economic loss rule is to leave some room for the market to work. Product reliability is a matter generally left, by the common law, to the market. You can pay a high price for a television that is extremely unlikely to malfunction, or pay a low price and take your chances. The law permits you to assume the risk with respect to reliability characteristics of products. However, the law does not allow you to assume the risk with respect to latent defects that might cause physical injury or destroy other property. The law implicitly assumes that the market is sufficient to generate socially preferable outcomes with respect to product reliability and performance issues, but insufficient with respect to dangerous attributes.[31]

Indeed, suppose products liability law permitted the consumer to recover for purely economic losses. The market for widgets, say, has high-quality and low-quality widgets. The consumer who purchases a low-quality widget could then sue for the economic loss suffered when the low-quality widget fails to perform in the same manner as the high-quality widget. But then the price of the low-quality widget would have to rise to match that of the high-quality widget, and the market for low-quality widgets would collapse – after all, who would buy a low-quality version of a product for the same price as the high-quality version? Perhaps this is not an immediately troubling outcome in the fictional world of widgets, but in the real world, this translates into the collapse of substantial markets, such as those for inexpensive home appliances.

The economic loss doctrine is sometimes stated broadly as a rule denying the existence of a duty on the part of the potential tortfeasor to take care to avoid causing economic losses to victims. The rule is concerned with economic losses caused by negligence, unaccompanied by physical harm or impact. If a victim is injured physically, he can recover the damages, including economic losses, associated with his physical injury.

An important statement of the economic loss rule, in the broader context of negligent and intentional torts, appears in *Robins Dry Dock & Repair Co. v. Flint*,[32] a Holmes opinion. A stylized version of the facts can be described in a model. Suppose X makes a contract with a dry dock company to repair a boat that will be rented to Z after the repair. The dry dock company negligently damages the boat,

---

[31] This assumption is probably due to the generally high level of product safety in the markets of advanced economies. When the general level of safety is high, consumers have little reason to investigate the dangerous attributes of products – because the vast majority of such investigations will reveal no substantial risk of injury. I have referred to this earlier, in the proximate causation context, as a paradox of safety (Chapter 13).

[32] Robins Dry Dock & Repair Co. v. Flint, 275 U.S. 303 (1927).

delaying its readiness for Z. As a result, Z loses money, and X loses the money it would have earned from renting the boat to Z. Under the economic loss rule, the dry dock company does not have a duty to take care to protect these economic losses – specifically, the profits X and Z would have earned from the boat being ready on time. This rule makes sense for the same reason that a breach of contract lawsuit from X against the dry dock company would not permit X to collect damages for the profits he would have earned from renting to Z, unless X contracted with the dry dock company for such a responsibility or at least notified the dry dock company of the potential loss. In the absence of such notice, contract law does not allow the promisee to recover unforeseeable consequential damages for the breach of a contract.[33] If the law did provide for such damages, contractual promisors would have to adjust the terms of their contracts to protect themselves against the risk of claims for consequential losses, and since they would have no information on the potential size of the losses, many would shy away from entering into such contracts and shrink their businesses accordingly.[34]

Improper Defendant: Agency versus Retail and Policy Considerations

The other general defense to a manufacturing defect claim – again one that is available in any products liability lawsuit – is that the plaintiff has sued the wrong defendant. If the defendant is the manufacturer or the seller of the product that injured the plaintiff, this defense will be unavailable. The rule of section 402A applies explicitly to manufacturers and sellers.

The cases where the *improper defendant defense* raises an interesting question under products liability law are those in which the defendant, although the source of the injurious product, is neither a manufacturer nor a seller, and yet the plaintiff asks the court to apply the rule of strict liability to him. The clearest of these cases, in terms of the law, involves the distinction between services and sales. A pharmacist, for example, is considered to be providing a *service* as the agent of the prescribing physician. The pharmacist is not deemed a product seller and is therefore not subject to strict products liability.[35]

Some cases have suggested a test for determining whether a party is a proper defendant under products liability law.[36] The test is based on the factors that indicate whether strict liability should be preferred to negligence: encouraging care, activity

---

[33] Hadley v Baxendale, 9 Exch. 341, 156 Eng. Rep. 145. (Court of Exchequer, 1854).

[34] This is related to the adverse selection problem discussed in Chapter 17. If contractual promisors raised prices to cover risks of unforeseeable losses to promisees, only high-risk promisees would find the contracts profitable, which would start an adverse selection spiral.

[35] Murphy v. E.R. Squibb & Sons, Inc., 710 P.2d 247 (Cal. 1985); Coyle v. Richardson-Merrell, Inc., 584 A.2d 1383, 1387 (Pa. 1991); RESTATEMENT (THIRD) OF TORTS: PROD. LIAB. §6 (1998).

[36] Francioni v. Gibsonia Trucking Corp., 372 A.2d 736 (Pa. 1977); Cafazzo v. Cent. Med. Health Servs., Inc., 668 A.2d 521 (Pa. 1995).

level deterrence, and insurance – the same factors emphasized in *Escola*. Under the "care" prong, the test asks whether strict liability provides greater incentives for the defendant to take care than would the negligence rule. If so, then this factor would suggest that the defendant should be subjected to strict liability. The second factor, activity-level deterrence, leads to an examination of whether holding the defendant strictly liable would result in a reduction in the consumption of the product responsible for the plaintiff's injury. The third factor of the test, insurance, examines whether holding the defendant strictly liable would result in a socially preferable loss-spreading arrangement.

In *Cafazzo v. Central Medical Health Services, Inc.*,[37] the plaintiff brought a design defect claim against a hospital and a physician for the sale of a defective jaw prosthesis that had been surgically implanted. The court held that the lawsuit could not have a desirable effect on incentives for care in the product design process, because the hospital and doctors had nothing to do with the design of the implant. On the activity-level question – that is, whether strict liability would reduce the consumption of a dangerously defective product – the court found that strict liability would not provide better incentives for safety in the distribution process because it would, through the mechanism of insurance pricing, increase the cost of providing medical care in general rather than the cost of a particularly dangerous medical device. On the question of using strict liability as means of insurance, the court rejected this as a sufficient basis for finding liability.

The reasoning of *Cafazzo* has been accepted by other courts in the medical care context.[38] However, its arguments could be applied just as easily to an attempt to hold a retailer liable for selling a manufacturer's product that is defective because of design, manufacture, or warning. The key question in any case involving a product reseller of any sort – whether a retailer or a hospital – is whether strict liability

---

[37] Cafazzo v. Cent. Med. Health Servs., Inc., 668 A.2d 521 (Pa. 1995).

[38] The service versus sale distinction has been applied in this area by many courts. Other courts have relied on policy arguments similar to those in *Cafazzo*. *See, e.g.,* Royer v. Catholic Med. Ctr., 741 A.2d 74, 78 (N.H. 1999) (concluding "[T]he policy rationale underlying strict liability... does not support extension of the doctrine under the facts of this case," which involved a suit against the hospital for a defective prosthetic knee device.); Parker v. St. Vincent Hosp., 919 P.2d 1104, 1110 (N.M. Ct. App. 1996) ("Having analyzed the policies favoring strict products liability in the context of potential hospital liability for defectively designed medical products selected by treating physicians, we conclude that such liability is inappropriate."). For a summary of leading cases analyzing the issue, *see In re* Breast Implant Prod. Liab. Litig., 503 S.E.2d 445, 451 (S.C. 1998) (holding "health care providers may not be held strictly liable... for products used in the course of providing medical treatment."). *See also* 65 A.L.R.5th 357 (1999). Although decided just prior to *Cafazzo*, Ayyash v. Henry Ford Health Sys., 533 N.W.2d 353 (Mich. Ct. App. 1995) also reasoned that the imposition of strict liability on doctors and hospitals would fail to promote greater care to manufacture safer products and would only increase costs to patients. The *Ayyash* Court held, "Because the primary function of physicians and hospitals is to provide care, not to manufacture or distribute products, those economic theories that underlie the imposition of strict liability upon makers and sellers of products do not justify the extension of strict liability to those who provide medical services." *Ayyash*, 533 N.W.2d at 355.

would provide sufficiently precise regulatory signals (encouraging care, activity level deterrence) in the product distribution process.

In the economic analysis of producer liability earlier in this chapter, I assumed that liability to the consumer would become part of the supply cost of the dangerous product. With the product price reflecting its risk, consumers would have an incentive to choose relatively safe products, other things being equal. The inclusion of retailers as potentially liable parties requires an alteration of this analysis.

Suppose, for example, that there are two types of widget: red and blue. Red widgets explode with a frequency of 1/1,000. Blue widgets never explode. Other than the risk of explosion the widgets are of identical quality. They are manufactured by different firms. Widget manufacturers sell to retailers that resell both types of widget. If the retailers, who are subject to strict liability, are aware that red widgets are the only dangerous ones, they will adjust the price of a red widget to reflect the risk of liability. The result will be the same as shown in Figure 17.1 – consumption of risky red widgets is reduced to the socially ideal level. If, however, the retailers do not know that the red widgets are dangerous and the blue widgets are safe, they will adjust the prices of both types of widget upward to reflect the risk of liability. In this scenario, strict products liability does not lead to a shift of consumption from the relatively dangerous product toward the relatively safe product. Indeed, if the price adjustment reduces the profits of the safe widget manufacturer more than the profits of the risky widget manufacturer, it might lead, perversely, to the withdrawal of the safe product from the market.

For retailer liability to lead to an accurate assignment of risk charges among products, retailers must be able to distinguish the dangerous products from the safe ones. This means that the retailers must have incentives to distinguish risk features among products and to charge different prices for them. These incentives will depend on the availability of information on product risks, the degree of competition among brands, the costs and benefits of creating accurate risk subcategories, and the costs and benefits of differentiating price according to risk category.[39] In short, there is no guarantee that retailers will have incentives under strict liability to charge prices that accurately reflect risk.

As it stands, the law on retailer liability for products is muddled. Some states have enacted statutes that bar strict products liability claims against sellers.[40] Many other

[39] The problem is analogous to that facing a liability insurer, who to minimize costs must set a price for insurance coverage that reflect the risk generated by the insured party. Since the costs of creating a separate risk-based price for every individual would be prohibitive, the insurer creates risk categories based on observable features (e.g., age). For an exploration of these issues in the general torts setting, *see* Guido Calabresi, The Costs of Accidents: A Legal and Economic Analysis 47–64 (Yale Univ. Press 1970).

[40] For example, Georgia and Nebraska bar strict liability claims against retailers. *See* Neb. Rev. Stat. Ann. § 25–21, 181 (2011); Ga. Code Ann. § 51–1–11.1 (West 2012). The protection provided to retailers is quite broad because the statutes bar design defect, manufacturing defect, and failure to warn claims, unless the retailer participated in the manufacture or design.

states, roughly half, have enacted statutes that require knowledge of the defect, or some type of negligence, on the part of the retailer to hold the retailer liable for a product defect.[41] Some states have enacted statutes that explicitly permit lawsuits against all product sellers (manufacturers or retailers).[42] In addition, some states have enacted laws providing a cause of action for sellers to seek indemnification from manufacturers.[43]

To avoid the perverse result in which products liability leads retailers to mark up all prices by a uniform risk premium, whether or not a particular product is dangerously defective, the knowledge requirement adopted in many state statutes would appear to be desirable. Holding retailers strictly liable for manufacturing or design defects of which they are unaware could have perverse effects on the distribution of safe products, perhaps resulting in a more dangerous product mix, and would discourage retailers from expanding their businesses, restricting the sale of safe and dangerous products equally.

The danger of unintended and perverse consequences is especially important with regard to manufacturing defects. For claims that require proof of negligence in warning, or in design under risk-utility principles, most retailers would be exempt from liability because of the plaintiff's inability to prove fault. If the retailer simply resells a product in a sealed package, the basis for a negligent failure to warn claim is generally lacking – unless the retailer has knowledge of the danger. Similarly, the retailer who merely resells a product in a sealed package could hardly be blamed for a design that is unreasonable under risk-utility analysis.

VI. MANUFACTURING DEFECTS

The typical manufacturing defect claim involves a glitch that occurs infrequently in the production process that makes the particular unit consumed or used by the plaintiff dangerous. Suppose, for example, one of every 1,000 widgets produced at the manufacturer's widget plant is defective, in a way that might easily injure a consumer. If that defective widget causes an injury to a consumer or bystander, the seller is strictly liable.

This is one of the few examples in the law of true strict liability. The traditional areas of strict liability in tort law involve animals, nuisances, and abnormally

---

[41] For a survey, *see* Robert A. Sachs, *Product Liability Reform and Seller Liability: A Proposal for Change*, 55 BAYLOR L. REV. 1031, 1121 (2003).

[42] Maine and South Carolina, for example, have statutorily enacted the language of Restatement (Second) § 402A. *See* ME. REV. STAT. tit. 14, § 221 (2011); S.C. CODE ANN. § 15–73–10 (2011). Both states have adopted the risk-utility test (St. Germain v. Husqvarna Corp., 544 A.2d 1283, 1285 (Me. 1988); Branham v. Ford Motor Co., 701 S.E.2d 5, 14–15 (S.C. 2010), *reh'g denied* (Nov. 17, 2010)), which implies that retailers in these states may be effectively exempt from defective design lawsuits.

[43] For example, Arizona, Arkansas, and Oklahoma. *See* ARIZ. REV. STAT. ANN. § 12–684 (2012); ARK. CODE ANN. § 16–116–107 (West 2012); OKLA. STAT. ANN. tit. 12, § 832.1 (West 2012).

dangerous activities. However, in each one of these areas there are important exceptions and defenses, most with their roots in the theory of *Rylands v. Fletcher* (Chapter 5). For example, in the case of wild animals, we have seen (Chapter 15) that attacks that occur in zoos are not subject to strict liability.[44] The policy justification for this is that zoos provide educational and recreational benefits to the public. These benefits offset the extraordinary risks introduced to the public by keeping wild animals.

With respect to manufacturing defects, there is no equivalent to the exceptions and safe harbors implied by the *Rylands* doctrine. If a manufacturing defect causes an injury to a person or to other property, the seller is liable, as a general rule, irrespective of any educational, recreational, or other public benefits that might be associated with the product's distribution or consumption.

One might think that an exception to strict liability for manufacturing defects, grounded in the theory of *Rylands*, could be based on comment *k* of Second Restatement section 402A. Recall that under comment *k*, a seller of an unavoidably unsafe product, usually a drug, is not subject to strict liability. However, comment *k* is inapplicable to manufacturing defects.

Of course, a reason not to recognize such an exception to strict liability can be found in the informational differences between plaintiffs and defendants in manufacturing defect cases. Proving negligence would be difficult, and plaintiffs would inevitably attempt to rely on res ipsa loquitur doctrine. Strict liability may simply get us to the same result with less expense.

VII. DESIGN DEFECTS

Design defect claims assert that the design of a product is defective in a way that is unreasonably dangerous to consumers. Unlike the manufacturing defect claim, which singles out one defective product in a large batch, the design defect claim asserts that *every* product meeting the design specification of the one that caused the plaintiff's injury is defective.

Two legal tests have been recognized by courts in design defect cases. The traditional test is the *consumer expectations test*, described in section 402A of the Second Restatement. Under the consumer expectations test, a product is defective if it is "dangerous to an extent beyond that which would be contemplated by the ordinary consumer who purchases it, with the ordinary knowledge common to the community as to its characteristics."[45] In short, the product is defective if there is an unobservable and dangerous feature in the product. The consumer expectations test

---

[44] Spring Co. v. Edgar, 99 U.S. 645, 649 (1878); Jackson v. Baker, 24 App. Cas. D.C. 100 (1904); Marquet v. La Duke, 55 N.W. 1006 (Mich. 1893); City and County of Denver v. Kennedy, 476 P.2d (Colo. App. 1970).

[45] RESTATEMENT (SECOND) OF TORTS § 402A cmt. i (1965); *see also* Jackson v. Gen. Motors Corp., 60 S.W.3d 800, 804 (Tenn. 2001); McCathern v. Toyota Motor Corp., 23 P.3d 320, 331 (Or. 2001); Potter v. Chicago Pneumatic Tool Co., 694 A.2d 1319, 1330 (Conn. 1997).

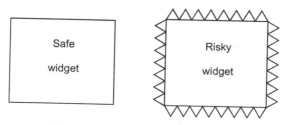

FIGURE 17.2. Safe and risky widgets.

also implies a shield or safe harbor for the seller: if the product's dangerous features are open and obvious, then the product conforms to expectations, and the seller is not liable for injuries caused by the obvious (and dangerous) feature.

For example, suppose the product under consideration is a lawn mower with its blade exposed from the side.[46] There is an obvious risk that the user's foot will be chopped off by the blade when the lawn mower is in operation. The consumer expectations test immunizes the seller from liability for the dangerous condition.

The other legal test applied in design defect cases is the *risk-utility test*, which deems a product defective in design if the additional risks imposed by the design, compared to a safer alternative,[47] are not reasonable in light of the additional utility of the challenged design. The risk-utility test envisions a comparison between the challenged design and some comparatively safe alternative. The court, applying the test, compares the incremental risk characteristics of the challenged design to those of the safer alternative. The court also compares the incremental utility characteristics of the challenged design to those of the alternative. Suppose the incremental utility characteristics sum to U, and the incremental risk characteristics sum to an overall risk charge R. The product is unreasonably defective if $R > U$.

Consider, for example, the widget. One widget, the safe alternative A, has a rectangular shape. The risky widget, B, has the same shape, but with jagged teeth exposed on the sides, as shown in Figure 17.2.

Risk-utility analysis involves comparing the incremental risk characteristics of B, in comparison with A, with the incremental utility of B (again in comparison with A). The exposed teeth clearly make widget B a more hazardous product than A, since the teeth could easily injure anyone who handles the widget. However, the exposed teeth may enhance the utility of the widget, say, by making it easier to adhere to some surface. If the court finds that the additional benefits of having a widget with jagged teeth are greater than the costs associated with the additional risk, the court will deem widget B's design reasonable under the risk-utility test.

---

[46] *See, e.g.*, Bowen v. Western Auto Supply Company, 273 So.2d 546 (La. App. 1st Cir. 1973).
[47] For a discussion emphasizing the role of the safer alternative, *see* James A. Henderson & Aaron D. Twerski, *Achieving Consensus on Defective Product Design*, 83 Cornell L. Rev. 867 (1998).

Return to the lawn mower example. Suppose it would be easy and inexpensive for the manufacturer to cover the exposed blade without reducing the function of the lawn mower. Even though the dangerous feature is obvious to the consumer, the manufacturer would still be liable under the risk-utility test. The reason is that there is a safer alternative – the same lawn mower with a cover over the exposed blade – that functions just as well as the risky product.

John W. Wade proposed a seven-factor test for deciding the risk versus utility question. The Wade factors are as follows:

(1) The usefulness and desirability of the product – its utility to the user and to the public as a whole; (2) The safety aspects of the product – the likelihood that it will cause injury, and the probable seriousness of the injury; (3) The availability of a substitute product which would meet the same need and not be as unsafe; (4) The manufacturer's ability to eliminate the unsafe character of the product without impairing its usefulness or making it too expensive to maintain its utility; (5) The user's ability to avoid danger by the exercise of care in the use of the product; (6) The user's anticipated awareness of the dangers inherent in the product and their avoidability, because of general public knowledge of the obvious condition of the product, or of the existence of suitable warnings or instruction; and (7) The feasibility, on the part of the manufacturer, of spreading the loss by setting the price of the product or carrying liability insurance.[48]

The first five of Wade's factors should be considered part of the risk-utility analysis. Factor (5) appears, at first glance, to be a contributory negligence defense available to the seller, but it can also be viewed as a basic component of an overall assessment of the risk attributes of a product. If a risk is obvious and easy to avoid, such as the sharp edge of a knife, then its obviousness and ease of avoidance should be taken into account in an assessment of its risk attributes. The product is unlikely to cause harm if its dangerous feature is obvious and easy to avoid. However, factors (6) and (7) should not be part of the risk-utility analysis. Factor (6) is concerned with the consumer's expectations. For this reason, it should be considered part of a separate inquiry, specifically the consumer expectations test. Factor (7) is an expression of the insurance rationale for strict liability. However, the insurance rationale should not play a role in determining the balance of risk and utility characteristics of a specific product. It is a distinct inquiry, and one that some courts have explicitly rejected as a basis for producer liability.[49]

The change in price when we move from the risky product to the safe alternative is part of the risk-utility analysis. Why? Price affects utility. If the safe alternative has to be priced at a factor of 100 times that of the risky product to be profitably produced,

[48] John W. Wade, *On the Nature of Strict Tort Liability for Products*, 44 Miss. L. J. 825, 837–838 (1973).
[49] *See, e.g.*, Cafazzo v. Cent. Med. Health Servs., Inc., 668 A.2d 521 (Pa. 1995).

then it will be available to few consumers. The dramatic reduction in availability reduces the overall utility from the product.[50] Indeed, if the safe alternative would be unaffordable to the vast majority of consumers, then it may not be a real alternative. Consumers may be better off using the risky product, since that may be better for them than going without the product at all.

Aesthetic characteristics should be part of the risk-utility test too.[51] The relatively risky design may be desirable to consumers because it appeals to identifiable consumer preferences. A convertible car is a risky design relative to an enclosed car, but some consumers have a taste for the experience of driving a convertible. A sports car that rides low on the ground may be risky in comparison to a sport utility vehicle, but some consumers prefer the look and feel of the sports car. The premium that some consumers are willing to pay for a sports car reflects the utility they perceive in using the product, and should therefore be incorporated in risk-utility analysis.

Consider a simple application of the Wade factors to a generic unsafe design – say, a lawn mower with rotary blades exposed on the side. The lawn mower is clearly useful and desirable under factor (1). However, under factor (2), the exposed rotary blades create a high likelihood that a serious injury will occur to a user of the product. The blades could easily cut into the foot of a user. A safer substitute, a lawn mower with a cover over the exposed blades, is likely to be available on the market, and can easily be produced at a modest surcharge over the unsafe design (factors (3) and (4)). Moreover, the safer design, with a cover on the side, would not interfere with the function of the rotary blade lawn mower. The additional cost of manufacturing and selling the safer design is unlikely to be so high that it would substantially reduce the affordability of the product (factor (4)). Moreover, it is unlikely that the safer design would induce so much unsafe conduct on the part of the user that it would cancel the additional safety benefit. Finally, factor (5), although a user could avoid the danger of the exposed rotary blades, it would be difficult to do so in the course of ordinary use of the product. A person who uses a lawn mower generally walks while pushing it. To avoid coming into contact with the exposed blade, the user would have to consistently maintain a safe distance from the unit housing the blade. Inevitably, some users would fail to maintain a safe distance. The exposed-blade design presents a great risk to users, relative to the safer alternative design, while offering no additional utility.

---

[50] *See, e.g.*, Linegar v. Armour of America, Inc., 909 F.2d 1150, 1155 (8th Cir. 1990) (noting that if the price of the bulletproof vest goes too high, law enforcement agencies will be unable to afford it, which reduces safety).

[51] Calles v. Scripto-Tokai Corp., 864 N.E.2d 249, 265 (Ill. 2007) (noting "appearance and attractiveness" of product as a factor in utility); Bell v. Bayerische Motoren Werke Aktiengesellschaft, 181 Cal. App.4th 1108, 1131 (Cal. App. 2010) (noting that jury may consider "aesthetics" in balancing utility against risk).

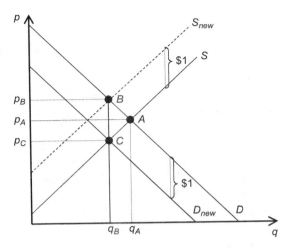

FIGURE 17.3. Market effect of strict liability when consumer is informed.

VIII. ECONOMICS OF PRODUCTS LIABILITY, PART II

Economics of Consumer Expectations Test

Here I return to the economic analysis of products liability. In a previous example, I assumed that because of random errors or glitches in the production process, one in every 1,000 widgets sold by the manufacturer explodes, injuring the consumer. This time I will assume that the explosions occur as the result of a flaw in the design of the widget, resulting in the same probability of injury. On average, the explosion causes an injury of $1,000 to the consumer. Thus, every widget exposes the consumer to an expected loss of $(1/1,000) \times (\$1,000) = \$1$.

Return to Figure 17.1. Suppose the dangerously designed feature of the widget is perfectly obvious to the consumer, so obvious that he can estimate the likelihood of injury. In this event, the amount the consumer is willing to pay for a widget, given that he is aware of the danger, falls by the amount of the expected loss, $1. If he did not know that the widget was dangerous, he would be willing to bid an amount given by the points along the demand schedule in Figure 17.1. If he discovers that each widget will in effect impose a "risk cost" of $1 on him, the consumer will lower his bid by that amount.

To show the effect of risk knowledge in the market analysis, all we need to do is shift the original demand schedule down to D_{NEW}, which is the same as the original demand schedule but shifted down by $1 at each quantity, as shown in Figure 17.3. The market equilibrium when consumers know the product's risk is given by point C in Figure 17.3.

Notice that the new market equilibrium quantity, when the consumer is fully informed about product risk, is at the same amount that would be observed if the consumer were uninformed about the risk and the seller strictly liable (point *B*, Figure 17.1). Recall that I concluded that the amount consumed under strict liability was the socially ideal (or optimal) quantity. That is also true of the amount consumed when consumers are fully aware of the risk characteristics of the product, because it is the same as the amount consumed under strict liability.

The conclusion that follows is that if consumers are fully aware of the risk characteristics of the product, the market equilibrium is the optimal consumption level from society's perspective. In other words, *there is no need to employ strict liability as a means of correcting consumption levels in a market in which consumers are fully aware of product risks.*

The consumer expectations test can be understood better in this framework. The consumer expectations test holds the seller strictly liable when the product's dangerous feature is unobservable, and it immunizes the seller when the dangerous feature is obvious. The market analysis shown in Figure 17.3 indicates that the consumer expectations test generates a consumption level that is optimal. When consumers are uninformed of product risks, the consumer expectations test imposes strict liability, which leads to the ideal consumption level (a market equilibrium at point *B* in Figure 17.3). When consumers are informed of product risks, the consumer expectations immunizes the seller from liability, which also leads to the ideal consumption level (a market equilibrium at point *C* in Figure 17.3). Under the consumer expectations test, the only difference between the market outcome when consumers are informed and the market outcome when consumers are uninformed is the price level, which incorporates an implicit liability premium.

What if the seller is held strictly liable even though the consumer is fully aware of the risk associated with the product? The market analysis becomes a bit more tedious then, but still straightforward. The consumer is fully aware of the product's risk, so he knows that in the absence of any compensation, the widget will impose an expected loss on him of \$1. In the absence of any promise of compensation, the consumer will reduce his bid for the widget by \$1 (see D_{new} in Figure 17.3). Assume, however, that the consumer knows that he will be compensated. Full compensation (although fanciful) means that the consumer will suffer no net harm from the product. Thus, the consumer's demand schedule, assuming full compensation, will stay at the level that assumes complete safety (*D* curve in Figure 17.3), because the consumer will not perceive any loss from the product. The supply curve, however, will shift upward to reflect the cost of liability (S_{new}). The market equilibrium will now occur at the consumption level associated with strict liability (*B* in Figure 17.3), which is (once again) the socially ideal quantity. The lesson that follows is that *when consumers are fully aware of the product's risk, the market equilibrium consumption level will be optimal, whether the seller is held strictly liable or not. Moreover, the only function of strict liability in this case is to force the seller to compensate the consumer. In other words, strict liability, in a setting where the consumer is fully aware of the product's risk, is equivalent to mandatory insurance for the consumer.*

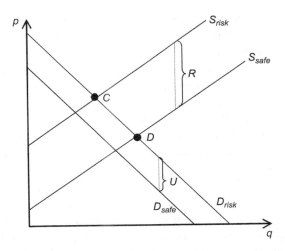

FIGURE 17.4. Market effect of risk-utility test (risk exceeds utility) $R > U$.

Strict liability forces the seller to sell two tied products to the consumer: the product and an insurance policy covering loss from injury. When consumers are unaware of product risk, this forced insurance sale corrects consumption levels by providing an accurate price signal of the product's true cost. However, when consumers are fully aware of the risk, there is no need to correct the price signal to reflect the product's true cost, because consumers already know the true cost.

It would be premature to conclude that the forced tie-in sale of insurance is either neutral or desirable when consumers are aware of the product's risk features. The insurance provided by the law is far more expensive than that provided by the market. Moreover, privately provided insurance policies include provisions that encourage the insured to minimize his own losses. These provisions reduce the total amount of loss by controlling the incentives of insured actors. If the law fails to provide the same provisions, strict products liability will generate greater losses in the aggregate than a system without such a forced tie-in sale of insurance.

Economics of Risk-Utility Test

Now let's consider the risk-utility test, which compares the dangerously defective product to a feasible safer alternative. The demand and supply curves for the safe alternative are represented by D_{safe} and S_{safe} in Figure 17.4. The relatively dangerous product offers both greater utility and greater risk. This is represented by upward shifts in both the demand (shift up by the additional utility U) and supply curves (shift up by the additional risk R). Assuming incremental risk exceeds incremental utility ($R > U$), the relatively risky product can be represented by demand schedule D_{risk} and supply schedule S_{risk} in Figure 17.4. Since incremental risk exceeds incremental utility, the seller of the risky product will be held strictly liable under the risk-utility test.

Recall from the previous discussion that when consumers are fully aware of the product's risk and utility features, imposing strict liability does not alter the consumption level from that of the market equilibrium in the absence of strict liability. The only effect of strict liability, in this case, is to raise the price to reflect the forced sale of an insurance policy. Given this, we should consider the effect of the risk-utility test when the consumer cannot observe dangerous features – that is, where the additional utility is obvious, but the additional risk is hidden.

Assume, then, that the consumer is not aware of the dangerous features of the risky product. Suppose, first, that the seller is exempted from liability. Since the seller is not liable, its overall costs will not include the expense of compensating injured consumers, R. Thus, the supply curve for the risky product seller, which reflects its costs, will be the same as the safe supply curve (S_{safe} in Figure 17.4). Since consumers are assumed to observe the additional utility of the risky product, but not the additional risk, their demand for the risky (and higher utility) product will be reflected by D_{risk} in Figure 17.4. The market equilibrium will be determined by the intersection of the safe supply curve and the demand curve for the risky and higher utility product, which occurs at point D in Figure 17.4.

Suppose liability is determined under the risk-utility test. The seller of the risky product will be held liable because incremental risk exceeds incremental utility. Given this, the supply curve of the risky product seller will incorporate the risk charge, R. The resulting market equilibrium is the consumption level associated with the intersection of the risky supply and risky demand schedules in Figure 17.4 (point C), which is the optimal level of consumption. Thus, *when incremental risk exceeds incremental utility, liability imposed under the risk-utility test achieves the goal of reducing consumption of the risky product to the optimal level.*

Now assume that the incremental risk of the product is less than its incremental utility – that is, $R < U$, as shown in Figure 17.5. In this case, the seller will not be held liable under the risk-utility test. Since the seller is exempted from liability under the risk-utility, the seller's supply schedule is the same as if it produced a safe product (S_{safe} in Figure 17.5). Continuing with the assumption that the consumer is not aware of the product's dangerous features, the consumer's demand schedule is represented D_{risk}. Thus, the market equilibrium occurs at the intersection of the safe supply schedule (S_{safe}) and the risky product demand schedule (D_{risk}), generating the consumption level associated with point B in Figure 17.5. The optimal outcome, however, is at the lower level of consumption associated with the intersection of the risky supply schedule and the risky demand schedule, shown by point C. Thus, *by exempting the seller from liability, the risk-utility test results in overconsumption of the risky product when incremental utility exceeds incremental risk.*

In light of the overconsumption result, what argument could there be for preferring the risk-utility test to the consumer expectations test? Two arguments can be offered.

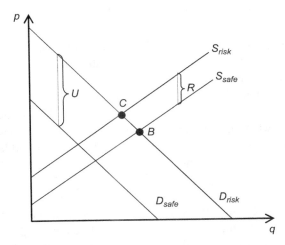

FIGURE 17.5. Market effect of risk-utility test (utility exceeds risk) $R < U$.

First, the risk-utility test is preferable to the consumer expectations test because inherent unobservable risk is a common feature in modern complex products. Consider a complex product, such as the automobile. If courts were to apply the consumer expectations test, then such products would generate an almost limitless set of strict liability claims. In complex products, the number of hidden features that could cause injury to consumers is quite large. Given the number and variety of potential strict liability claims generated by the consumer expectations test, it would be impossible for the manufacturer to eliminate hidden risks through design changes in an efficient manner. Moreover, the signals disseminated by courts would depend as much on the unpredictable outcomes of the litigation process as on the actual statistical frequency of injuries attributable to design features.

One example should be sufficient to demonstrate this point. A familiar problem in the products liability cases is the "X frame automobile," examined in *Dawson v. Chrysler Corp.*[52] The X frame permits the car to crumple inward if struck on the side in a collision. The alternative box frame design would prevent the car from crumpling inward. Which design is safer? The X frame absorbs some of the force of the collision. On the other hand, a driver whose body is located near the crumple zone may be injured by the part of the car that crumples inward. The alternative box frame protects the driver from being injured by the car body crumpling inward. However, a side collision against the sturdy box frame would transmit the force of the blow to the entire frame, causing the objects inside to shift violently. A driver inside of the box frame could be injured as a result of being thrown against the windshield or the other side of the car.

---

[52] Dawson v. Chrysler Corp., 630 F.2d 950 (3d Cir. 1980).

Under the consumer expectations test, the car manufacturer will be subject to liability under both the X frame and the box frame. In both cases, the plaintiff could argue that the design generates a risk of injury that is not immediately observable to the driver. Indeed, most drivers do not know or inquire into whether they are purchasing a car with a box-frame or an X frame. Given the lack of knowledge, the consumer cannot take the specific risks of the frame design into account in determining the amount he is willing to pay for a car. The same structure is evident for many other design features of the car.

The logical endpoint of the consumer expectations test is that the car manufacturer becomes strictly liable for all injuries attributable to unobservable features of the car design. Because there are so many such features, the car manufacturer would become, in effect, the insurer of the driver.

Since drivers are aware that cars are not risk-free products, a consumer expectations rule would force the purchase of a type of insurance that likely exceeds the value that the consumer would put on it. The insurance component would be priced according to the risk of the average driver, when, in fact, drivers vary considerably in the care with which they maintain and operate their vehicles. Careful drivers would be overcharged, and careless drivers undercharged, resulting in a shift toward less care on the roads, which would lead to more accidents and higher insurance prices. In addition, insurance provided by car manufacturers would be more expensive than that provided in the insurance market because it would include the expected cost of litigation (since each claim presents itself in the litigation process instead of the insurance claims process).

In short, the consumer expectations test, given the numerous unobservable features in complex products that can be deemed causally responsible for the victim's injury, creates an expensive and inefficient form of mandatory insurance, with perverse incentives for both consumption and precaution.

The second argument for preferring the risk-utility test to the consumer expectations test is that the risk-utility test provides powerful incentives to design products for which incremental utility exceeds incremental risk. The reason is that strict liability applies, under the risk-utility test, when incremental risk exceeds incremental utility, and there is no liability in the opposite case. The risk-utility test therefore spreads the difference between the payoffs for good and bad designs. As some courts have noted, the test encourages innovation toward safer designs.[53]

The consumer expectations test, by contrast, may not encourage innovation toward safer designs in the short run – and the short run is all that matters for markets in technologically complex products. Return to the X frame versus box frame question of *Dawson*. Under strict liability based on consumer expectations, both frames would lead to liability for the manufacturer. The design that would be preferred by the manufacturer is the one that generates the least liability in the long run. But it may

---

[53] Prentis v. Yale Mfg. Co., 365 N.W.2d 176, 185 (Mich. 1984).

take years, long after the car's design has become obsolete or gone out of fashion, before the manufacturer can distinguish the respective long-run magnitudes of different sources of harm among many design features. If 100 lawsuits based on the X frame design enter the courts one year, and 75 lawsuits based on the box frame design enter in the same year, how can the manufacturer be sure that the numbers will not be reversed in the next year?

Total liability, serving alone as the guide to the manufacturer, may sometimes mislead. Suppose, as an illustration, the box frame leads to ten injuries per year of $100,000 each, and the X frame generates six injuries per year of $200,000 each. The box frame seems preferable, then, because it generates an aggregate harm of $1 million, while the X frame generates an aggregate harm of $1.2 million. If litigation costs borne by the manufacturer amount to $60,000 per case, the X frame would generate a total liability for the manufacturer of $1,560,000, while the box frame would generate a total liability of $1,600,000. The manufacturer would be led by strict liability (under the consumer expectations test) to prefer the X frame even though it is the more harmful choice from the perspective of the consumer.

IX. IMPLEMENTATION OF TESTS

Given the existence of two legal tests for design defect cases, risk-utility and consumer expectations, and fifty states in the United States in which courts are free to decide which test to apply and how the tests should be applied, the products liability doctrine governing design defects is difficult to state concisely. Still, a concise summary can be provided, if one paints with a broad brush.

Three approaches appear to dominate design defect liability law. One relies on the risk-utility theory alone. A second approach is a hybrid of the consumer expectations and risk-utility tests. The third allows plaintiffs to assert both consumer expectations and risk-utility as alternative theories of liability.

The first approach, direct application of the risk-utility test, usually follows the algorithm of Wade. An excellent discussion and defense of the test appears in *Prentis v. Yale Manufacturing Co.*,[54] a Michigan decision adopting the risk-utility test for design defect cases. *Prentis* justifies the risk-utility test on the ground that it provides a dynamic incentive for safer designs.[55]

Surace v. Caterpillar, Inc.,[56] a Pennsylvania decision, applies the risk-utility test using the Wade factors. The court examined whether the defendant's road profiler should have been equipped with a lockout device that would permit ground workers near the machine to disable the profiler, to prevent accidental injuries to the ground workers. Because the defendant's profiler did not have such a device, the plaintiff's foot was mangled by the treads of the machine. The court concluded that the

---

[54] 365 N.W.2d. at 176.
[55] *Id.* at 185.
[56] 111 F.3d 1039 (3d Cir. 1997).

machine may have been defectively designed because a lockout device would not have obstructed its function but would have prevented the accident.

The second approach, reflected in the decisions of several courts, superimposes the consumer expectations test on the risk-utility analysis as an additional defense for the product seller. The resultant test is a hybrid of the risk-utility and consumer expectations tests. The value of the consumer expectations defense in these cases is that it provides an especially clear message on the law with respect to a product. If the product is deemed defective under the risk-utility test, the seller loses. If the product is deemed reasonably safe under the risk-utility test, and the dangers are open and obvious, courts following the third approach often hold that the consumer loses because the product meets consumer expectations.

The second approach is suggested by the Maryland case law on products liability, starting with *Volkswagen of America v. Young*[57] and *Phipps v. General Motors Corp.*[58] In *Volkswagen* the driver was killed when his car seat separated from the floor upon impact, which caused him to fly into the rear portion of the car. The court held that traditional negligence principles apply to the design defect question, unless the defective condition is open and obvious, in which case the plaintiff cannot recover. *Phipps* adopts the risk-utility factors set out by Wade as the method for determining negligence in design – that is, design defect liability – in Maryland.

Another example of the hybrid approach is *Linegar v. Armour of America, Inc.*[59] State trooper Jimmy Linegar was killed at a routine traffic stop when bullets fired by his assailant struck parts of his body not protected by his bulletproof vest. A lawsuit was brought against the manufacturer of the vest, Armour of America, on the theory that its design was defective because it left parts of the wearer's body exposed. The vest consisted of front and back panels that were connected by Velcro straps under the arms. The panels did not meet in the spaces under the arms, leaving exposed areas for bullets to reach. The court, applying Missouri law, held that under the consumer expectations test the plaintiff's design defect claim could not survive because the shortcomings of the vest's design were open and obvious.

Linegar also examined risk-utility arguments in justifying its decision. In comparison to a safer vest design that covered the torso completely, the court noted that the Armour vest obviously exposed the wearer to additional risk. On the other hand, the vest had some functional advantages. It was easier to put on and take off than the proposed safer alternative. It was more likely to be worn because it allowed the wearer to move about easily and trapped less heat. It was also cheaper than the proposed alternative, and this implied another advantage: A more expensive vest would be purchased in lower quantities, providing less overall protection to a budget-constrained police force.

---

[57] 321 A.2d 737 (Md. 1974).
[58] 363 A.2d 955 (Md. 1976).
[59] 909 F.2d 1150 (8th Cir. 1990).

TABLE 17.1. *Outcomes under* Barker

	Risk nonobvious	Risk obvious
Risk greater than utility	Risk greater than utility, defect nonobvious E.g., *Surace, Volkswagen*	Risk greater than utility, defect obvious E.g., lawn mower with exposed rotary blades
Risk less than utility	Risk less than utility, defect nonobvious E.g., design safe for the vast majority of consumers, but hazardous to small minority	Risk less than utility, defect obvious E.g., *Linegar*, exposed airplane propeller, convertible car

Although the court held that the Armour vest satisfied the consumer expectations test, its analysis indicates an acceptance of risk-utility as the fundamental test of liability. The consumer expectations language used by the court served mainly to provide a clear message on the scope of liability for sellers of vests similar to the challenged design.

The third approach, applying both tests, was articulated as the law of California in *Barker v. Lull Engineering Co. Inc.*[60] *Barker* held that "a product is defective in design either (1) if the product has failed to perform as safely as an ordinary consumer would expect when used in an intended or reasonably foreseeable manner, or (2) if, . . . , the benefits of the challenged design do not outweigh the risk of danger inherent in such design."[61] In other words, plaintiffs can assert both the consumer expectations and risk-utility theories. If the plaintiff fails to establish that the product was defective on consumer expectations grounds, he can pursue his risk-utility theory. The plaintiff, in effect, gets two bites at the apple under California law.[62]

The *Barker* doctrine's adoption of both the risk-utility and consumer expectation tests generates four outcomes: (1) incremental risk greater than incremental utility and product meets consumer expectations (risk open and obvious), (2) incremental risk greater than incremental utility and products fails consumer expectations, (3) incremental risk less than incremental utility and product meets consumer expectations, and (4) incremental risk less than incremental utility and product meets consumer expectations. The possible outcomes are shown in Table 17.1, along with

---

[60] 573 P.2d 443 (Cal. 1978).

[61] *Id.* at 446.

[62] Aaron Twerski and James Henderson note that California has restricted the scope of the consumer expectations test since *Barker*. In California, the consumer expectations test now serves to establish liability only when a product fails to meet minimal expectations with respect to safety. *See* Aaron D. Twerski & James A. Henderson, Jr., *Manufacturer's Liability for Defective Product Designs: The Triumph of Risk Utility*, 74 Brook. L. Rev. 106, 1101–1102 (2009). Twerski and Henderson suggest that California limits the consumer expectations test to cases where the evidence indicates that the risk-utility standard is highly unlikely to be satisfied by the seller's product.

examples under each outcome. *Barker* appears to generate a decision that differs from the risk-utility test applied alone in only one of the four outcome categories: when risk is less than utility (passes risk-utility test) and the risk is nonobvious (fails consumer expectations test), which is shown in the lower left cell of Table 17.1.[63] This case of possible inconsistency between *Barker* and the risk-utility test was rendered less likely to occur by a later California decision, *Soule v. General Motors Corp.*[64] In *Soule*, the California Supreme Court indicated that the consumer expectations test is reserved for products that fail to meet minimum safety expectations.

The Restatement (Third) of Torts: Products Liability presents only the risk-utility test.[65] Since the Third Restatement reflects an effort to discern the general pattern in the case law of products liability, this is strong evidence that the risk-utility test dominates the design defect case law. As a means of predicting the outcomes in design defect cases, the risk-utility test performs well.[66] However, some courts continue to use language from the consumer expectations test, probably because it provides greater clarity to defendants on the scope of liability.

Indeed, the fact that the risk-utility test has become the dominant legal standard for defective design cases suggests that the consumer expectations test remains in the case law for two reasons, both having to do with marginal cases. One, favoring plaintiffs, is to serve as a "per se unreasonable" finding when the facts indicate that the risk so far outweighs the utility for the challenged design that there is no plausible defense under risk-utility analysis. Using the language of the *Soule* decision, the product fails to meet minimum safety standards. The other reason one still sees courts referring to the consumer expectations test, this time favoring defendants, is that it serves as a clarifying gloss when the facts indicate that the risk-utility tradeoff so strongly favors the challenged design that the design should be deemed reasonable as a matter of law.

Making Sense of Products Liability Law: Three Case Types

From a functional perspective, the design defect cases can be sorted into three categories. One involves dangerous features that are *obvious and essential (or inherent) to the product's function*. Consider, for example, a convertible automobile. Plaintiffs have sued sellers of convertibles on the theory that they were defectively designed

---

[63] In Tran v. Toyota Motor Corp., 420 F.3d 1310 (11th. Cir. 2005), the plaintiff, less than 5 feet 4 inches tall, sued Toyota on the theory that the seat belt system of her car was defectively designed because the shoulder belt rested against her neck. The plaintiff lost at the trial level under the risk-utility test, but the appeals court reversed because the jury had not been instructed on the consumer expectations test under Florida law, which followed *Barker*. The appeals court's decision suggests *Tran* as an example of a case in which the *Barker* doctrine, as applied in Florida, generates a different result than the risk-utility test.

[64] 882 P.2d 298 (Cal. 1994).

[65] RESTATEMENT (THIRD) OF TORTS: PRODS. LIAB. § 2(b) (1998).

[66] Twerski & Henderson, *supra* note 62.

because they did not protect the occupant in a roll-over accident.[67] While it is certainly true that a convertible fails to protect occupants in a roll-over, a convertible would not be a convertible if it did. The dangerous feature of the convertible is inherent to its design.

Another example of a risk inherent to product design is the bulletproof vest in *Linegar*. The vest exposed its wearer to the risk of taking a bullet in the exposed areas. However, a vest that covered the entire torso would cease to have important functional advantages of the challenged design. The dangerous features of the challenged vest were inherent to its function.

A third example of risk inherent to function is the exposed propeller on an airplane or a boat.[68] One could cover the propeller to minimize the risk that an individual would be injured, but doing so would obstruct the function of the machine.

A second category of cases involves risks that are *obvious but not inherent to the function of the product*, or capable of being reduced substantially without harming functionality. Consider, for example, an onion-topping machine with exposed moving parts,[69] or a carrot-topping machine with exposed blades.[70] Alternatively, consider a printing press that does not contain a guard to keep the employee's hands out of the machine when running,[71] or a lawn mower with an exposed blade that could be covered without reducing functionality.[72]

One popular product that might belong in this category is the sport utility vehicle. Because they are elevated above sedans, they do not allow the driver to see small objects behind or in front of the vehicle. As a result, many sport utility vehicle drivers, about fifty each year at present, run over children, including their own. The risk generated by not being able to see small things in front of or behind the vehicle is obvious and inherent in the design of the product. However, it is also a risk that can be reduced substantially without altering the vehicle's function. A seller can reduce the risk by installing a camera or other device that warns the driver when there are small objects directly in front of or behind the vehicle.

A third category of cases involves risks that are not obvious. One example is the 1963 Corvair, examined in *Larsen v. General Motors Corporation*.[73] The car was designed so that the solid steering shaft extended from almost 3 inches beyond the front tires to the steering wheel directly in front of the driver, exposing the driver

---

[67] *See, e.g.*, Delvaux v. Ford Motor Co., 764 F.2d 469 (7th Cir. 1985). A roughly similar claim, against a motorcycle seller, is that the product's design fails to protect the body of the rider; *see* Toney v. Kawasaki Heavy Indus., Ltd., 975 F.2d 162 (5th Cir. 1992).

[68] Elliott v. Brunswick Corp., 903 F.2d 1505 (11th Cir. 1990) (exposed boat propeller meets consumer expectations and is not unreasonable under the risk-utility test).

[69] Campo v. Scofield, 95 N.E.2d 802 (N.Y. 1951).

[70] 2 Fowler Harper & Fleming James, Jr., THE LAW OF TORTS §28.5 (1956) (rejecting the argument that no liability should lie when warning is obvious and arguing for design change if warning is not sufficient).

[71] Micallef v. Miehle Co., 348 N.E.2d 571 (N.Y. 1976).

[72] Bowen v. Western Auto Supply Company, 273 So.2d 546 (La. App. 1st Cir. 1973).

[73] Larsen v. General Motors Corp., 391 F.2d 495 (8th Cir. 1968).

"to an unreasonable risk of injury from the rearward displacement of that shaft in the event of a left-of-center head-on collision."[74] In other words, a head-on collision would cause the steering wheel shaft to thrust back, transferring the force of a collision directly to the head of the driver.

The risk created by the design of the 1963 Corvair steering shaft was nonobvious and not essential to the design of the product. Buyers of the Corvair could not tell by examining the car in a dealer's showroom that it might cause an injury from the rearward displacement of the steering wheel. Moreover, the car could easily have been designed to function without exposing the driver to this risk.

There is a pattern in the case law across these three case types. The first category, involving dangerous features that are obvious and essential to the product's function, holds strong cases for defendants.[75] For example, design defect suits against convertible sellers claiming that the design failed to protect occupants in a roll-over fall in this category.[76]

Cases in the first category are sometimes decided in favor of the seller on the basis of the consumer expectations test,[77] but the cases would have the same outcome under risk-utility analysis. In other words, these are cases involving products that would pass both the consumer expectations and risk-utility tests. Whenever the risky feature is inherent in the product's design, and the product serves an important function or satisfies a substantial set of consumer preferences, the incremental risks imposed by the design generally will be outweighed by the incremental utility. Consider, again, the exposed propeller of an airplane. It is open and obvious, and because of this a plaintiff would likely lose a design defect claim evaluated on consumer expectations grounds. However, if a court were to apply the risk-utility test, it likely would hold that the exposed propeller was a reasonable design.

---

[74] *Id.* at 497 n.2.

[75] *See, e.g.*, Maneely v. Gen. Motors Corp., 108 F.3d 1176, 1181 (9th Cir. 1997) (a pickup truck is not defectively designed when the cargo bed contains no seatbelts. "This alternative design would transform the cargo-hauling pickup truck into just another passenger-carrying vehicle and would eliminate its utility in carrying cargo.... [T]he gravity and the likelihood of the danger posed by the current design is minimal, because the danger is generally known to the public and can be avoided by proper use of the cargo bed."); Linegar v. Armour of Am., Inc., 909 F.2d 1150, 1154 (8th Cir. 1990) (the bulletproof protective vest the trooper was wearing when he was fatally shot was not defective because "there obviously were trade-offs to be made," and "[a]n otherwise completely effective protective vest cannot be regarded as dangerous, much less unreasonably so, simply because it leaves some parts of the body obviously exposed"); Delvaux v. Ford Motor Co., 764 F.2d 469, 474–75 (7th Cir. 1985) ("[T]he duty of a manufacturer of products with a special design is only to consider alternatives compatible with the special design. A manufacturer is not negligent for not providing his convertibles with steel roofs, because a convertible is designed as a roofless car." (internal citations omitted)); Clark v. Brass Eagle, Inc., 866 So.2d 456, 462 (Miss. 2004) (the paintball gun was not defective and defendant not liable for plaintiff's injuries because "the Brass Eagle paintball gun did not malfunction and operated to their expectations").

[76] Delvaux v. Ford Motor Co., 764 F.2d 469 (7th Cir. 1985).

[77] *See, e.g.*, Linegar v. Armour of Am., Inc., 909 F.2d 1150 (8th Cir. 1990).

The second category, involving dangerous features that are obvious and not essential to the product's function, tends to be examined under the risk-utility test.[78] In other words, although these are products that pass the consumer expectations test, their performance under the risk-utility test has increasingly determined the outcome of the lawsuit. An example is *Micallef v. Miehle Co.*[79] The plaintiff injured his hand when he tried to remove an object from a high-speed printing press. His finger caught in the machine, the plaintiff tried to reach the shut-down button, but it was beyond his reach. The court held that the design was defective because there were safer alternatives – with guards that would have prevented the plaintiff's injury – that would have been equally functional.

The third category of cases, involving risks that are not obvious,[80] tend to be examined under the risk-utility test.[81] The consumer expectations test cannot be applied in a discriminating manner to products with hidden risks. The consumer expectations test would penalize a manufacturer for injuries connected to all hidden risks, without distinguishing product features that enhance the consumer's utility net of risks from product features that do not. Thus, a product like the 1963 Corvair is evaluated, in most courts today, by comparing the incremental risks and utilities of the product's design to some feasible safer alternative design.

Since the risk-utility test appears to explain the outcomes generally in products liability cases today, why do some courts still rely on the consumer expectations test for open and obvious design defects? The answer probably has more to do with the management of litigation than with any quest for logical cohesion in the law. The consumer expectations test, applied in the cases of obvious dangerous features that are inherent to functionality, serves as a predictable standard for litigants. It avoids requiring courts to engage in a balancing test every time a plaintiff brings a design defect claim, and it permits claims to be dismissed early rather than dragged through several stages of litigation. It is equivalent to stating a decision in a case of negligence in terms of an analysis of duty rather than in terms of an analysis of breach.[82]

Convergence of Risk-Utility Test and Negligence Principles

Recall that a negligence action involves four components: duty, breach, causation, and damages. Over time, products liability law has generated analogous components. After adopting the principle of strict liability at the outset (section 402A), products liability has converged in structure with negligence doctrine.

---

[78] *See generally* Twerski & Henderson, *supra* note 62.

[79] 348 N.E.2d 571 (1976).

[80] To be clear, this category encompasses all nonobvious risk-generating features, including those for which risk exceeds utility and those for which risk is less than utility. Risk inherent to function is especially strong case in which the risk exceeds the utility.

[81] Twerski & Henderson, *supra* note 62.

[82] *See* discussion of Palsgraf v. Long Island Railroad Co., 162 N.E. 99 (N.Y. 1928), Chapter 13.

For products liability, the breach question is typically examined under the risk-utility test, a legal standard that has been described as analogous to negligence by courts.[83] The negligence test compares the incremental risk from failing to take care with the burden, or utility forgone, from taking care (Chapter 6). The risk-utility analysis compares the incremental risk from the challenged design to the incremental utility forgone by opting for the safer design. However, a determination that a product fails the risk-utility test does not necessarily put an end to litigation over a challenged design.

Causation in negligence law involves an inquiry into factual and proximate causation. In products liability law, just as in negligence law generally, a finding of factual causation is necessary for liability. If the victim's injury would have happened even if the seller had met the risk-utility standard, then the seller will not be held liable.[84]

Courts examine proximate causation in products liability cases under the heading of *product misuse*. A court may find that a product fails the risk-utility test, and yet hold that the defendant escapes liability because the product was misused by the plaintiff. Viewed in terms of traditional proximate causation analysis, misuse is a type of intervention by the victim (or a third party). Product misuse involves an inquiry into whether the plaintiff's misuse (or third party's misuse) of the product was, or should have been, foreseen by the seller.[85]

---

[83] Prentis v. Yale Mfg. Co., 365 N.W.2d 176, 184 (Mich. 1984) ("The risk-utility balancing test is merely a detailed version of Judge Learned Hand's negligence calculus." (citing United States v. Carroll Towing Co., 159 F.2d 169, 173 (2d Cir. 1947))); Estate of Hunter v. Gen. Motors Corp., 729 So.2d 1264, 1278 (Miss. 1999) ("An examination of the riskutility [*sic*] test establishes that the test is essentially a negligence test"); Banks v. ICI Americas, Inc., 450 S.E.2d 671, 673 (Ga. 1994).

[84] Berry v. E-Z Trench Mfg., Inc., 772 F. Supp.2d 757, 760 (S.D. Miss. 2011) (finding plaintiff's design defect claim defeated given plaintiff's testimony "that he would have attempted to restrain the groundsaw's movement with the same bungee cord even if the wheels had been locked.... In light of these admissions, Berry is unable to prove that 'but for the defendant's negligence, the injury would not have occurred.'" (quoting Glover ex rel Glover v. Jackson State University, 968 So.2d 1267, 1277 (Miss. 2007))); Ogletree v. Navistar Int'l Transp. Corp., 535 S.E.2d 545, 550 (Ga. Ct. App. 2000) ("[T]he jury could not find that but for Navistar's failure to install an alarm, Ogletree's death would have been prevented..."); Baughn v. Honda Motor Co., Ltd., 727 P.2d 655, 666 (Wash. 1986) (manufacturers of a mini-trail bike were not liable because plaintiffs could not say that the accident would not have occurred but for the alleged design defects).

[85] Horn v. Fadal Machining Centers, LLC, 972 So.2d 63, 79 (Ala. 2007) ("[W]hen asserting misuse as a defense ... the defendant must establish that the plaintiff used the product in some manner different from that intended by the manufacturer. Stated differently, the plaintiff's misuse of the product must not have been 'reasonably foreseeable by the seller or manufacturer.'" (quoting Sears, Roebuck & Co. v. Harris, 630 So.2d 1018, 1028 (Ala. 1993))); Halliday v. Sturm, Ruger & Co., Inc., 770 A.2d 1072, 1092 (Md. Ct. Spec. App. 2001) *aff'd*, 792 A.2d 1145 (Md. 2002) ("[E]ven were we to conclude that appellee's failure to include a child safety device on the handgun was a design defect, appellee would still be entitled to summary judgment because of his misuse of the gun.... Misuse therefore negates a design defect claim and it occurs when the product in question is used in a manner not reasonably foreseeable to the seller." (citing Ellsworth v. Sherne Lingerie, Inc., 495 A.2d 348 (Md. 1985))); Simpson v. Standard Container Co., 527 A.2d 1337 (Md. Ct. Spec. App. 1987)); Johansen v. Makita U.S.A., Inc., 607 A.2d 637, 642 (N.J. 1992) ("Under the risk-utility analysis, manufacturers cannot escape liability on the grounds of plaintiff's misuse or abnormal use if the actual use proximate

Even if the seller provides a warning, there remains the question whether misuse should have been foreseen in spite of the warning. In *Hood v. Ryobi America Corp.*,[86] the seller provided a very clear warning not to remove the blade guards from a power saw. What the seller did not do was warn the buyer that removing the blade guards might result in the circular blade detaching and spinning through the air like a whirling miniature buzz saw. The court held that in view of the warning, the buyer's removal of the blade guards was not an event that the seller had a duty to foresee.

As a defense, product misuse is more powerful than the contributory negligence defense, just as proximate cause is a more powerful defense, in ordinary negligence actions, than contributory negligence. A seller who can successfully argue a product misuse defense does not have to meet the demanding proof standard for contributory negligence in products liability cases.[87]

Lastly, what about duty? Under ordinary negligence law, the defendant cannot be held liable for negligence unless he has a duty to the plaintiff. The closest analogue in products liability law is the consumer expectations test, when asserted as a defense. One role that the consumer expectations test plays is to provide a clear statement on the seller's scope of liability. Similarly, in a negligence case, a finding of "no duty," based on a legal principle tied to a particular fact, says that the defendant is not guilty of negligence given the facts of the case, and that under most variations of the facts containing the particular fact that evokes the legal principle, the defendant would not be guilty of negligence. When a court uses consumer expectations language to justify a pro-defendant decision that is equally justifiable under the risk-utility test, it is in effect saying that the defendant did not violate the risk-utility test given the facts and would not violate the test under most readily conceivable variations of the facts.

X. DUTY TO WARN

Duty-to-warn lawsuits are governed by the negligence standard.[88] This means that every duty-to-warn claim requires the plaintiff to argue that there were harms foreseeable to the product seller that could have been avoided with a warning, or with a more detailed warning, and that the burden of warning is less than the foreseeable

---

to the injury was objectively foreseeable."); Thornton v. E.I. Du Pont De Nemours & Co., Inc., 22 F.3d 284, 288 (11th Cir. 1994) ("A manufacturer is not liable for injuries resulting from abnormal use of the product." (citing Union Carbide Corp. v. Holton, 222 S.E.2d 105, 109 (Ga. Ct. App.1975))); Barnes v. Harley-Davidson Motor Co., 357 S.E.2d 127, 130 (Ga. Ct. App. 1987).

[86] 181 F.3d 608 (4th Cir. 1999).

[87] On the proof standard for contributory negligence in product cases, *see* RESTATEMENT (SECOND) OF TORTS § 402A cmt. n (1965).

[88] *See, e.g.,* McCullock v. H.B. Fuller Co., 981 F.2d 656, 658 (2nd Cir. 1992) (under Vermont law, in failure to warn cases "a strict liability claim and a negligence claim are essentially the same"); Enright by Enright v. Eli Lilly & Co., 570 N.E.2d 198, 203 (N.Y. 1991) ("[A] failure to warn of dangers of which the manufacturers knew or with adequate testing should have known . . . though it may be couched in terms of strict liability, is indistinguishable from a negligence claim.").

harms. Thus, in the case of a consumer injured by a product with a dangerous feature, the question before a court would be whether a warning, or a more detailed warning, would have made a significant difference in the likelihood of the injury occurring, and whether such a warning would have been reasonable under the circumstances.

Providing an inadequate warning can be just as bad as failing to provide any warning at all. Products that are used in the home around infants, such as furniture polish,[89] or baby oil,[90] pose a special danger. An inadequate warning, such as one that says the product "may be harmful if swallowed,"[91] might lead parents to assume that the product is safer than it is. If the product is potentially deadly if swallowed, warning only that it is "potentially harmful" may cause the reader to lower his guard. A reasonable warning will signal to the potential victim, or to those taking care of the potential victim, the level of care that is appropriate in light of the seriousness of the risk.

Since a warning is just a statement of information, it would appear at first glance that most plaintiffs should have plausible duty-to-warn theories. After all, if the plaintiff suffers a severe injury that could have been avoided by the defendant issuing a warning, failure to do so would appear to be a straightforward instance of negligence. However, the burden of issuing warnings is not always slight.

What are the burdens of warning? After an injury occurs, the precise warning that should have been given is obvious. However, before the injury occurs, the warning that could have prevented it may not be obvious at all. There may be many ways in which a potentially dangerous product can interact with a consumer to generate an injury. In some instances, the precise interaction that generated an injury may not have been foreseeable. Perhaps all the manufacturer can do is to warn generally against actions that may increase the risk of injury without attempting to specify the precise path leading to the injury.

In addition to the difficulty of foreseeing the path that leads to injury, the product seller should be concerned that a large number of specific warnings might be discounted by the consumer.[92] A consumer confronted with warnings that cover forty different consumer-product interaction paths leading to injury might find the information overwhelming and pay little attention to any of the warnings. How many consumers, for example, would take the time to read a twenty-page warnings pamphlet? Alternatively, a consumer who took the time to read and carefully consider forty different warnings might then injure himself by embarking on the forty-first path to injury. The consumer may think that an explicit, detailed warning covers all

---

[89] Spruill v. Boyle-Midway, 308 F.2d 79 (4th Cir. 1962) (death of infant, from hydrocarbon pneumonia, after ingesting furniture polish).

[90] Ayers v. Johnson & Johnson Co., 818 P.2d 1337 (Wash. 1991) (infant ingests baby oil, which coated his lungs, resulting in severe brain damage).

[91] Spruill v. Boyle-Midway, 308 F.2d 79, 82 (4th Cir. 1962).

[92] Mark Geistfeld, *Inadequate Product Warnings and Causation*, 30 U. MICH. L. J. REFORM 309 (1997).

of the possible interaction paths that might lead to injury. A detailed set of warnings might induce a lack of wariness on the part of the consumer with respect to any hazard that is not specifically mentioned in the list. For all of these reasons, the burden associated with issuing an effective warning may be substantial.[93]

In addition to the burden-benefit test applied to any negligence claim, there is also the question of factual causation. In failure to warn cases there are two factual causation issues. One is a question present in every product liability action: Did the product cause the injury? In many product liability actions involving drugs, this type of causation will not be clear at all (see Chapter 12). Suppose a consumer who takes a medicine to reduce inflammation has a heart attack. Was the heart attack caused by the anti-inflammatory pill, or was it caused by background factors such as lifestyle?

The other major causation issue in failure to warn cases is whether a warning would have altered the interaction path leading to injury. The plaintiff's claim incorporates the theory that a warning would have altered his conduct – that is, the warning would have been heeded. The same theory is incorporated in the plaintiff's claim even when there was a warning, but it lacked sufficient specificity. The defendant is entitled to question whether a warning would have changed the plaintiff's conduct.

For the most part, courts have adopted a *heeding presumption* in failure to warn litigation.[94] This means that courts shift the burden to the defendant to come forward with evidence indicating that the plaintiff would not have heeded the warning if a reasonable one had been provided.

Since warning cases are negligence cases, the plaintiff's contributory negligence is potentially an issue. Suppose the seller issues a warning and the plaintiff is injured by doing something in contradiction of the warning. For example, take the case of a power saw with numerous emphatic warnings in the manual not to remove the blade guard.[95] The plaintiff removes the blade guard, is injured as a result, and sues the seller on the theory that the warning lacked sufficient specification of the risk.

Even if the warning to the consumer lacked sufficient specificity, there exist independent questions whether (a) the plaintiff's conduct constituted unforeseeable misuse of the product in light of the warning (proximate cause), and (b) the plaintiff's conduct was reasonable under the circumstances (contributory negligence). Comment *n* of section 402A, it should be recalled, imposes a high burden on the

---

[93] *See, e.g.,* Cotton v. Buckeye Gas Products, 840 F.2d 935, 937–938 (D.C. Cir. 1988) (noting costs of information clutter in warnings); Hood v. Ryobi, 181 F.3d 608, 611 (4th Cir. 1999) (same); Robinsons v. McNeil Consumer Healthcare, 615 F.2d 861, 869 (7th Cir. 2010) (same).

[94] *See, e.g.,* Coffman v. Keene Corp., 628 A.2d 710, 720 (N.J. 1993); Moore v. Ford Motor Co., 332 S.W.3d 749, 762 (Mo. 2011); Magro v. Ragsdale Bros., Inc., 721 S.W.2d 832, 834 (Tex. 1986); House v. Armour of America, Inc., 929 P.2d 340, 347 (Utah 1996); Town of Bridport v. Sterling Clark Lurton Corp., 693 A.2d 701, 704 (Vt. 1997).

[95] Hood v. Ryobi Am. Corp., 181 F.3d 608, 612 (4th Cir. 1999) (removal of blade guards unforeseeable product misuse).

defendant who alleges contributory negligence by requiring evidence that the consumer, more than merely failing to guard against the possible existence of a defect,[96] "voluntarily and unreasonably" proceeded to encounter a known danger.[97]

The growing acceptance of the risk-utility test in defective design litigation has affected warnings cases. Some courts have permitted plaintiffs to pursue a defective design theory even when the seller has provided a warning.[98] This is not surprising, given the relative trends of the risk-utility and consumer expectations tests in defective design litigation. The dominance of the risk-utility test implies that the mere satisfaction of consumer expectations is insufficient to immunize a product seller from liability based on a defective design theory. This, in turn, implies that a warning that fully apprises the consumer of the risks attached to the seller's product should also be insufficient, as a general matter, to immunize the seller from liability. Thus, in a case in which the dangerous feature of the product is not inherent to its function or its aesthetic appeal, a court may find that a defective design claim can survive even though an adequate warning has been provided.[99]

In addition to questions of specificity or clarity, warnings cases raise questions of behavioral psychology.[100] Even the most careful people have momentary lapses of advertence. A warning that requires the recipient never to have a momentary lapse in judgment or observance has a built-in rate of ineffectiveness. The most efficient way to reduce the likelihood of an injury may be to adopt a safer design.

XI. PREEMPTION

Many products sold today in the United States are regulated by some agency of the federal government. The Consumer Product Safety Commission, the Food and Drug Administration, and the Department of Transportation regulate a large number of the products that the average consumer purchases, from toys to medicines to cars. As one might imagine, this has implications for the operation of the tort system, especially products liability lawsuits.

---

[96] RESTATEMENT (SECOND) OF TORTS § 402A cmt. n (1965).

[97] *Id.*

[98] Uniroyal Goodrich Tire Co. v. Martinez, 977 S.W.2d 328 (Tex. 1998); *see also* Richetta v. Stanley Fastening Sys., L.P., 661 F. Supp.2d 500, 510 (E.D. Pa. 2009) ("[W]hile the warnings accompanying the nail gun (to the extent they are admissible) may be persuasive to a jury in an analysis of [design defect] factors, such warnings are not dispositive."); Hansen v. Sunnyside Products, Inc., 65 Cal. Rptr.2d 266, 277 (1997) ("Whereas an adequate warning will avoid liability on a failure to warn theory, it is but one factor to be weighed in the balance in a design defect case."); Delaney v. Deere & Co., 999 P.2d 930, 942 (Kan. 2000) ("[J]ust because there is a warning on a piece of equipment, the warning does not prevent the equipment from being dangerous.").

[99] *See, e.g.,* Uniroyal Goodrich Tire Co. v. Martinez, 977 S.W.2d 328 (Tex. 1998).

[100] Howard Latin, *"Good" Warnings, Bad Products and Cognitive Limitations,* 41 UCLA L. REV. 1193 (1994); Douglas A. Kysar, *The Expectations of Consumers,* 103 COLUM. L. REV. 1700 (2003); James A. Henderson, Jr., & Jeffrey J. Rachlinski, *Product-Related Risk and Cognitive Biases: The Shortcomings of Enterprise Liability,* 6 ROGER WILLIAMS U. L. REV. 213 (2000).

The most important issue federal regulation introduces into products liability law is that of preemption. A defendant whose product is regulated by the federal government may argue, once a products liability lawsuit has been filed, that the suit should be dismissed – that is, the suit is *preempted* – because the product is regulated by a federal agency, and that the federal regulatory regime bars the state from imposing additional or conflicting regulations. Sometimes defendants win on this argument, sometimes they lose.

The law on preemption is hazy and still in development. It has been in existence for a relatively short period of time; probably the first products liability lawsuit to seriously explore preemption was *Wood v. General Motors Corp.* in 1988.[101] Given this, I will adhere to functionalist principles, in an effort to find the best approach to preemption, and then see if the law appears to be reasonably close to the suggested ideal.

There are two general types of preemption. *Express preemption* refers to the case where a federal statute expressly preempts tort suits grounded in state law. *Implied preemption* refers to the case where the federal statute does not expressly preempt state law tort suits, but a reasonable person would infer that preemption was the intended effect of the statute. Within the category of implied preemption, there are subcategories. Commentators have identified a subcategory called *field preemption*, when the federal statute takes control over the whole field in a way that leaves little for states to regulate.[102] Another category is *conflict preemption*,[103] which occurs when a state tort suit would actually conflict with the goals of the federal statute, requiring the state law to yield under the U.S. Constitution's Supremacy Clause.

Instead of working top-down from these definitions, let's start at the bottom by considering the regulatory problem directly. Why should a tort lawsuit ever be preempted? The most plausible argument is that there is nothing to be gained, in terms of society's welfare, from allowing the lawsuit to proceed. Why might this be the case? Suppose the federal regulatory standard is optimal, in the sense that it establishes a standard of reasonable care for the regulated parties that is best for society's welfare. A tort suit, based on state law, against a defendant who complied with the federal regulatory standard could only be a source of mischief. If the lawsuit fails, then it serves only to harass the defendant who has complied with the federal standard by dragging him into court to defend a standard that is optimal, and with

---

101 Wood v. General Motors Corp., 865 F.2d 395 (1st Cir. 1988).
102 *Id.* at 401 (quoting Schneidewind v. ANR Pipeline Co., 485 U.S. 293, 108 (1988)).
103 *Id.* In Wyeth v. Levine, 555 U.S. 55 (2009), the defendant argued that the plaintiff's theory of warning liability would *obstruct* federal drug labeling regulation. The use of the word "obstruct" rather than "conflict" was apparently for the purpose of conveying a broader sense of conflict. Whether one refers to the tension between federal and state law as "obstruction," "conflict," or to the creation of "obstacles," the essential claim appears to be the same: that allowing the plaintiff to prevail in his state law tort claim would substantially interfere with the goals of the associated federal regulatory program.

which he has complied. If the lawsuit is successful, then not only does it harass the defendant who complied with the federal standard, it also harasses all other potential defendants who have complied with the standard by threatening them with liability for compliance, all for the ultimate payoff of destroying an optimal regulatory standard. Of course, if the defendant did not comply with the regulatory standard, then the lawsuit does not necessarily present a risk of having harmful effects. A lawsuit for failure to comply would serve to help enforce the regulation.

In light of the foregoing, an optimal federal regulation presents an ideal scenario for preempting a tort lawsuit that challenges the regulation. To be clear, by challenging the regulation, I mean a tort lawsuit that seeks to hold the defendant liable even though he complied with the regulation. An optimal regulation, I will assume, is defensible on the basis of the reasonable person standard or the risk-utility test, and anticipates all of the risks to a victim that would form the basis of a tort lawsuit.

Not all regulations are optimal in this sense. However, the key question is whether the regulatory agency has considered the issues that a plaintiff would want the court to consider, and whether the agency has likely done a better job in evaluating those issues than could be expected of a jury or of a judge. If these conditions are satisfied, it would make sense to bar the tort suit by holding that federal regulation preempts such lawsuits.[104]

Consider an example. Suppose the manufacturer makes a medical device that has undergone extensive testing and safety analysis by the FDA. The plaintiff sues on the theory that the design of the device is defective because it fails the risk-utility test. In addition, the regulatory agency has considered precisely the same risk-utility questions that the plaintiff raises in his lawsuit. This would appear to be an ideal case for preemption. Unless new information has appeared that would lead the agency to reverse its earlier approval of the product, there is no reason to believe that a judge or jury would do a better job of examining the risk-utility tradeoffs than the expert agency.

New information suggests itself as one reason to deny the defendant's preemption defense. If new information on risk has emerged that had not been available to the FDA, then the regulatory standard may be suboptimal – that is, may not be reasonable – in light of the new information. Given this, a court might appropriately find that the risk-utility analysis requires the defendant to modify its product or its warning.[105] A finding of preemption would be inappropriate in the case of new information, of which the seller is aware, and which the seller has had ample time to use to lessen the dangerousness of the product or to warn consumers.

---

[104] Steven Shavell, *Liability for Harm versus Regulation of Safety*, 13 J. LEGAL STUD. 357 (1984); Keith N. Hylton, *Preemption and Products Liability: A Positive Theory*, 16 SUP. CT. ECON. REV. 205 (2008); Catherine M. Sharkey, *Products Liability Preemption: An Institutional Approach*, 76 GEO. W. L. REV. 449 (2008).

[105] *See* Wyeth v. Levine, 555 U.S. 555 (2009) (plaintiff's claim is not preempted because new information on risk of drug injection should have been incorporated into warnings).

Another case in which preemption would be inappropriate is where the regulatory agency is not more likely to be accurate in its assessment of the risk-utility tradeoffs than a typical jury or judge. This might occur if the federal agency is staffed with uncredentialed political appointees rather than independent analysts or scientists. If, for example, the FDA review process were one in which friends of important senators, with no training in science, determined which medical devices would be approved, then preemption would be inappropriate. The simple reason is that there would be no basis for believing that a review by an independent court would not provide a more objective and accurate assessment of the risk-utility properties of the product.

The foregoing functional approach to preemption suggests that a finding of preemption would be appropriate, for a regulated product challenged on a defective design theory, when the *regulatory regime has provided a scientifically rigorous review of the product under a process that takes into account the issues and information that would be examined in the plaintiff's lawsuit.*[106] Under these conditions, a reexamination of the product's design, by a court applying the risk-utility standard, is unlikely to provide a more accurate assessment of the risk-utility tradeoffs. To have taken into account the important questions that would be examined in the lawsuit, the regulatory regime would have to have had access to the same information that the court obtained. Thus, if substantial new information bearing on risk is presented to the court, which was not available to the agency when it reviewed the product, preemption would not be appropriate.

The case law is consistent with this straightforward functional theory of preemption. Two sets consisting of cases that appear to conflict support this assertion. The first set of seemingly conflicting cases are *Medtronic, Inc. v. Lohr,*[107] and *Riegel v. Medtronic, Inc.*[108]

In *Lohr,* the Supreme Court found that defective design claims brought against the maker of a medical device were not preempted, even though the relevant federal statute contained a provision that could be read as expressly preempting state tort law. The medical device in *Lohr,* a pacemaker, had been approved by the FDA under the "substantial equivalence test," which permitted the marketing of devices that were equivalent to a device that had been on the market before 1976. However, the substantial equivalence test is not the same as the risk-utility test applied by courts in defective design lawsuits. The risk-utility test requires a careful examination of the risk-utility tradeoffs associated with a challenged design. The FDA's approval of the pacemaker in *Lohr* did not involve an assessment of the same issues. Since the tort law standard was not equivalent to the regulatory standard, preemption would not have been appropriate under the functional approach offered here.

---

[106] Hylton, *supra* note 104.
[107] 518 U.S. 470 (1996).
[108] 552 U.S. 312 (2008).

Compare *Lohr* to *Riegel*, in which the plaintiff challenged the design of a balloon catheter approved by the FDA. The Supreme Court held that the plaintiff's design defect claim was preempted. Unlike the medical device at issue in *Lohr*, the device challenged in *Riegel* had been approved under the "premarket approval process," in which the FDA thoroughly examines risk-utility tradeoffs associated with a proposed medical device. The finding of preemption was appropriate here because the FDA had considered, in a lengthy and rigorous review process, the same issues that would be examined in a product design lawsuit. A decision not to preempt the plaintiff's claim in *Riegel* would have permitted a relatively uninformed jury to contradict the risk-utility assessment of experts.[109]

The second set of seemingly conflicting cases consists of two involving automobile safety standards. In *Geier v. American Honda Motor Co.*,[110] the plaintiff brought a defective design claim based on Honda's failure to install an airbag system. The relevant federal regulatory order was Federal Motor Vehicle Safety Standard 208, which provided several compliance options to car manufacturers.[111] The Court found that the plaintiff's claim was preempted by the federal standard.

In formulating the regulatory standard, the federal agency (Department of Transportation) had taken into consideration the factors that would be examined by a court applying the risk-utility standard. The agency had considered the tradeoffs between the benefits and costs of additional safety, as well as the likelihood that consumers would actually accept, through market purchases or through general compliance, more burdensome safety requirements.[112] Moreover, the agency conducted its analysis with a higher level of expertise than could be expected of a court. There was no evidence of new information that had developed between the time of the agency's standard and the plaintiff's claim that would have led an objective observer to question the agency's analysis. Under these circumstances, the defective design claim required the application of a test that was equivalent to that applied by the federal agency. Since permitting the tort lawsuit to proceed would result in an inexpert jury reexamining risk-utility tradeoffs made by experts, the plaintiff's claim in *Geier* should have been preempted, as it was.

Williamson v. Mazda Motor of America, Inc.,[113] another case involving automobile safety standards but this time finding no preemption, seems at first glance inconsistent with *Geier*. However, the two decisions can be reconciled.

---

[109] If a jury took over the decision process of a group of experts, the likelihood of error associated with the decision process would be greater. In the justification set out here, it is important that the FDA's decision process is rigorous and not obviously under the control of a political faction. If the FDA's decision process were under the control of a political pressure group, a court would have a rational basis for refusing to find preemption.

[110] 529 U.S. 861 (2000).

[111] *Id.* at 875.

[112] *Id.* at 877–881.

[113] 131 S. Ct. 1131 (2011).

In *Williamson*, the Court considered a later version of Federal Motor Vehicle Safety Standard 208, which gave car manufacturers a choice to install either lap belts or lap-and-shoulder belts in rear inner seats (e.g., middle seats or seats next to a minivan's aisle).[114] Mazda had installed only a lap belt in the rear aisle seat of the minivan the plaintiffs were driving when it was struck head-on by another car. One family member sitting in the rear aisle seat, and wearing the lap belt, was killed in the accident; the other family members, wearing lap-and-shoulder belts, survived. The Court held that the regulation did not preempt the plaintiff's product design lawsuit against Mazda.

Although it seems at first that the plaintiffs' suit in *Williamson* should have been preempted under *Geier*, the cases are distinguishable. The Court found that the Department of Transportation had not conducted an analysis of the choice between lap-only and lap-and-shoulder belts at the level of depth as the safety analysis in *Geier*. The agency appeared to have given the manufacturers a choice between lap-only and lap-and-shoulder belts because it had no definite position on the safety question and, in the absence of such a position, had chosen not to impose a significant cost burden on manufacturers.[115] Put another way, the Court found in *Geier* that the agency had considered the risk-utility issues, in addition to questions of compliance well beyond the scope of most judicial analyses of product design disputes; whereas in *Williamson*, the agency's record indicated that it had not conducted a thorough risk-utility assessment – and, moreover, did not even base its regulatory decision on the incomplete assessment of risk that it had conducted.

Although preemption doctrine is still in development, it has become a part of tort law that winds up in the Supreme Court rather frequently. With the occasional shifts in the composition of the Court, and the political pressures associated with questions concerning the balance of state and federal power, there is a high degree of uncertainty surrounding every preemption dispute that comes before the Court. In spite of this, it appears that a doctrine consistent with sound product safety regulation is gradually emerging from the preemption cases in products liability.

---

[114] *Id.* at 1134.
[115] *Id.* at 1138–1139.

18

Damages

Damages traditionally have been classified under two categories: *compensatory* and *punitive*. Compensatory damages are awarded to compensate plaintiffs for losses suffered as the result of some tort. Punitive damages are awarded to plaintiffs to punish and deter tortfeasors.

I. COMPENSATORY DAMAGES

Compensatory damages can be subdivided into *pecuniary* and *nonpecuniary* awards. Pecuniary damages compensate plaintiffs for provable objective losses, such as lost wages and medical expenses. Nonpecuniary damages compensate plaintiffs for emotional injuries, often described as pain and suffering.

Some courts have said that compensatory damages serve the purpose of *restoration*, that is, to restore the plaintiff, as much as possible, to the level of utility he had obtained before the tort occurred.[1] Since individual utility is impossible to measure, the restoration goal has been a persistent source of controversy in the calculation of compensatory damages.

Pecuniary Damages

For the most part, there is relatively little controversy surrounding pecuniary damages. If a plaintiff comes to court with proof that he suffered $10,000 in medical

---

[1] Flannery v. United States, 718 F.2d 108, 111 (4th Cir. 1983) (damages award was not compensatory because the award provided no direct benefit or utility to the plaintiff); Cerretti v. Flint Hills Rural Elec. Co-op. Ass'n, 837 P.2d 330, 341 (Kan. 1992) ("The purpose of awarding [compensatory] damages is to make a party whole by restoring that party to the position he or she was in prior to the injury."); Beaty v. McGraw, 15 S.W.3d 819, 829 (Tenn. Ct. App. 1998) ("The goal [of compensatory damages] is to restore the wronged party, as nearly as possible, to the position the party would have been in had the wrongful conduct not occurred."); McDougald v. Garber, 536 N.E.2d 372, 374 (N.Y. 1989).

expenses as a result of the defendant's tort, the defendant will be held liable for those expenses. Questions regarding adequacy of proof may arise, but these are issues of evidence and not of tort law.

Probably the most important exception in the law governing compensatory damages is that for *economic harms*. Economic harms, such as the loss of a profitable opportunity, can be objectively determined in most cases. In spite of this, the general rule is that *damages for purely economic harms caused by negligence are not recoverable in the absence of a physical impact or physical injury.*[2] To the extent that this rule is grounded in theories of proximate causation, it is not applicable to intentional torts (*Vosburg v. Putney*, Chapter 4). For example, an economic loss resulting from a false imprisonment, with no physical impact, is recoverable.[3]

Nonpecuniary Damages

In comparison to pecuniary damages, nonpecuniary damages are controversial because of the absence of an objective measure of harm. If a tort victim is left a quadriplegic as the result of an accident, how should a court measure the emotional harm suffered by the victim?

In addition to the controversy over measurement, there is a broad exclusion from recovery for pure emotional injury caused by negligence, similar to the general denial of recovery for pure economic losses caused by negligence. *As a general matter, tort plaintiffs cannot recover for emotional harms caused by negligence in the absence of a physical impact or physical injury.*[4] Since emotional harms due to negligence, where there is no resulting physical injury, will always be nonpecuniary in nature, the default rule barring recovery for negligently induced emotional harm is a restriction on the scope of nonpecuniary damages. Also similar to the law on compensation for economic harms, this exclusion rule does not apply to intentional torts.

One could take the position that nonpecuniary damages should always be set at zero, because it is impossible to measure emotional injury. Such an extreme position would elevate administrative ease over all other considerations. However, if administrative ease were viewed as the predominant concern in awarding damages, then not only would nonpecuniary awards be set at zero, but some pecuniary awards would have to be set at zero as well because of the difficulty of precise determination. Consider, for example, a medical malpractice victim who sues a doctor for a negligent

---

[2] *See, e.g.*, People Exp. Airlines, Inc. v. Consolidated Rail, 495 A.2d 107 (N.J. 1985).

[3] *See, e.g.*, Normius v. Eckerd Corp. 813 So.2d 985, 987 (Fla. Dist. Ct. App. 2002) ("We first note that damages recoverable in an action for false imprisonment include bodily injury, physical suffering, physical inconvenience and discomfort, loss of time, losses in the plaintiff's business or employment, and expenses incurred due to the imprisonment.").

[4] People Exp. Airlines, Inc. v. Consolidated Rail, 495 A.2d 107 (N.J. 1985); *see also* discussion of *Dillon v. Legg*, Chapter 13.

misdiagnosis that led to a reduction in the victim's chance of survival from 60 percent to only 30 percent. Damages would be difficult to measure precisely. Medical breakthroughs happen all the time. Someone with a 30 percent chance of survival today might discover that his chance is dramatically greater tomorrow.

A related concern is that awarding nonpecuniary damages opens the door to fraudulent claims. If the defendant's tort has left the plaintiff a quadriplegic, how can a court rigorously evaluate the plaintiff's claim for a given quantity of nonpecuniary damages? Since there is no objective metric, what prevents a plaintiff from choosing the highest number within the limit of the defendant's wealth or insurance policy? However, the view that nonpecuniary awards should be set at zero because of the risk of fraud is another example of putting ease of administration ahead of other concerns. If the desire for fraud-free administration were the key factor determining the availability of damages, then even some pecuniary awards would be impermissible because of the risk of encouraging fraudulent claims.

It goes against human experience to argue that emotional harm does not exist or that it is due entirely to peculiar sensitivities. David Gelernter, severely injured by a mail bomb sent to his Yale University office by the infamous Unabomber,[5] offers the following framing sketch:

> My dreams are bad news, and the dark birds of pain gather as I sleep. They shadow me like vultures all day and settle at night, grabbing hold of the branches.[6]

The difficulty, and perhaps impossibility, of objectively measuring emotional harm has sent courts on a quest for standards to review nonpecuniary awards. Defendants challenge the awards, and appellate courts must therefore establish legal rules that justify them. However, to form a useful opinion on what courts have done in this area, we should first examine the function of compensatory awards.

II. ACCIDENT AND UTILITY

To explore the function of compensatory damages, consider the following model accident. Suppose at time period 0 the victim is in perfect health as he sets off for an errand. His utility level is shown in Figure 18.1 at level U_4.

In time period 1, the victim suffers an accident, which drives his utility down to U_1, as he experiences the pain of the injury. The immediate pain of the accident moment subsides eventually. By time period 2, the immediate pain has subsided, but the victim remains with injuries from the accident, as well as the pain and emotional harm from those injuries. The utility level associated with this state is U_2.

---

[5] Theodore Kaczynski, who killed three and wounded twenty-three from 1978 to 1995 by sending exploding packages through the mail.

[6] DAVID GELERNTER, DRAWING LIFE 41 (1997).

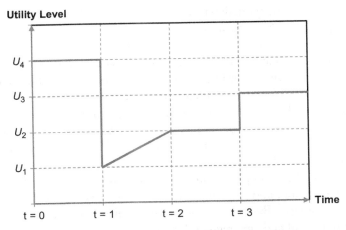

FIGURE 18.1. Utility, injury, and compensation.

The function of a compensatory award is to raise the victim's post-accident level of utility (U_2) up to the pre-accident level (U_4). The pecuniary award accomplishes this task, partly, by covering objective losses, such as medical bills and wage losses. After receiving pecuniary damages, the victim's level of utility rises to U_3. The remaining difference between the pre-accident utility level (U_4) and the post-pecuniary-compensation utility level (U_3) is due to emotional harm. The aim of nonpecuniary damages is to restore the victim's utility level to the pre-accident level, though it is impossible to determine whether that purpose has been accomplished.

Suppose a court were able to issue a nonpecuniary award that managed, perfectly, to move the victim's utility level from the post-pecuniary-compensation level (U_3) to the pre-accident level (U_4). This would be a rather amazing event, because the court would have to determine precisely how much money was necessary to make the victim just as happy as he was before the accident.

Even if the court were to determine a nonpecuniary award that restored the victim to his pre-accident utility level, the award might still fall short of the amount required to compensate him for his entire emotional harm. Recall that on the day of the accident, the victim experienced a sharp drop in utility (from U_4 to U_1). A nonpecuniary award for the current emotional harm that the victim is suffering after the accident might not include compensation for the intense and fleeting pain he suffered at the time of the accident.

What this example illustrates is that a system of compensatory damages that attempts to return the injured victim to his pre-accident level of utility might still fail to compensate for some important losses suffered by the victim. The larger question in the background is precisely what sorts of losses compensatory damages should aim to cover. From an ex post perspective (backward looking), the goal of compensation should be to *restore* the victim, as close as possible, to the same level of utility he enjoyed before the accident. If this goal were accomplished, the victim would be indifferent, after the accident, between living in his pre-accident state and his post-accident state, because his utility level would be the same in both states. From an ex ante perspective (forward looking), the goal should be to compensate the victim so that he would be indifferent, before the accident, between suffering the accident and not suffering the accident.

These two perspectives, ex post and ex ante, point to different levels of compensatory awards. The ex post perspective ignores fleeting and temporary suffering. It also ignores, importantly, any suffering the victim would be unable to perceive ex post, even if he would consider it undesirable when looking from the ex ante perspective. For example, if the accident leaves the victim in a comatose state, the comatose victim may not be able to perceive many of the forms of deprivation he has suffered. From an ex post perspective, there would appear to be no basis, given the goal of returning the victim to his pre-accident utility level, for awarding damages to such a victim beyond the level that compensates for pecuniary losses and for serious ongoing pain. Additional damages, awarded in the quixotic effort to compensate for pain associated with memories and with deprivation of opportunity, would not enhance the comatose victim's utility. It would be pointless to try to compensate for the disutility associated with memories that do not exist or foreclosed opportunities that cannot be perceived.

The ex ante perspective incorporates all forms of suffering and deprivation as a basis for compensation. From the ex ante perspective, the goal of the damages award is to make the prospective victim indifferent, if he were given the choice, before the accident and fully informed as to the losses that the accident would inflict, between suffering the accident plus receiving the damages award and not suffering the accident. To be sure, this goal may be impossible to reach in many cases, but it remains the goal. Thus, if the accident leaves the victim in a comatose state, the ex ante perspective would require compensation for suffering and deprivation of opportunity even if the victim could not perceive these emotional injuries at the time the damages award is issued. As long as the victim would demand compensation today to suffer tomorrow the deprivations associated with his comatose state, the ex ante perspective would require compensation.

Which is the correct approach to damages, the ex post or the ex ante perspective? To answer this question, we have to consider the function of the operative law and the interests protected by it.

Damages should, as a first principle, compensate victims for the interests that are protected by the law. Whether the ex ante or the ex post perspective is appropriate in evaluating damages depends on what interests are protected by the legal rule violated by the defendant.

In general, we can distinguish between trespass and functionally similar rules, and other tort rules such as strict liability and negligence. Calabresi and Melamed, discussed in Chapter 2, framed the distinction as one between *property rules* and *liability rules.*[7] Property rules (trespass and similar rules) aim to prohibit the nonconsensual invasion of a right, such as the right to possess land exclusively or to bodily integrity. A person threatened with a future trespass of such a right can go to court and get an injunction against the threatened trespass. Liability rules (strict liability and negligence), by contrast, do not aim to prohibit the nonconsensual invasion of a right; they aim merely to guarantee that compensatory damages are paid to the victim after an unreasonable invasion or violation (that is, a violation determined after the fact to have been unreasonable) occurs. A person who fears being injured by a future act of negligence (for example, a negligent auto accident) cannot go to court and enjoin the injurer's activity (driving).

Since trespass aims to prohibit the nonconsensual invasion of a right, the damages associated with trespass law should compensate the victim for the interests violated by the trespass. One interest violated by the trespass is the right to be free of an invasion in the absence of consent. It would seem appropriate, then, for damages to include compensation for the nonconsensual invasion itself in the case of a trespass.[8] The appropriate level of compensation for the invasion is the amount of money that the victim would have demanded to permit the invasion to occur.[9] In other words, in addition to compensation for identifiable injuries, damages for trespass should, to compensate the victim for all of the interests protected by the law, include a component that attempts to replicate the hypothetical bargain that the victim and injurer would have made in a consensual transaction.

Return to the model accident discussed earlier (Figure 18.1). Suppose the tort is an intentional blow. If the tortfeasor were to threaten to deliver the blow on a future date, the prospective victim could get an injunction against the threatened action. If tort law is to protect all of the interests protected by the law of battery, then compensatory damages should include compensation for all of the losses suffered as a result of the battery. This implies compensation for wage losses, medical expenses, and emotional harm perceived in the post-accident state. It also implies compensation for the intense suffering of the victim at the moment of the accident (the drop from U_4 to U_1), and for the disutility associated with harms that cannot be perceived by the victim in later periods.[10]

---

[7] Guido Calabresi & A. Douglas Melamed, *Property Rules, Liability Rules, and Inalienability: One View of the Cathedral*, 85 Harv. L. Rev. 1089 (1972). For an updated restatement in light of modern critiques, *see* Keith N. Hylton, *Property Rules and Liability Rules, Once Again*, 2 Rev. Law & Econ. 137 (2006).

[8] This conclusion is an implication of the Calabresi and Melamed framework and was proposed in Gideon Parchomovsky & Alex Stein, *Reconceptualizing Trespass*, 103 Nw. U. L. Rev. 1823 (2010).

[9] Of course, there are many instances in which the victim would not accept any amount of money for the violation. Still, in these instances the court has to objectively determine a compensation award. The difficulty of objectively determining such an award is no greater than determining compensation for emotional harm.

[10] Alternatively, consider a trespass. Richard Roe, a neighbor, while trespassing on Doe's property, accidentally cuts down the old oak tree on Doe's property. A damages award for the trespass should compensate Doe for the reduction in Doe's property resulting from the tree's cutting and any additional damage done to the property. In addition, however, a damages award that compensates the victim for

Negligence and strict liability (liability rules) do not aim to prevent or prohibit nonconsensual invasions of rights, as trespass law aims to do. Negligence and strict liability aim merely to compensate for invasions that are determined after the fact to have violated the relevant legal standards. Negligence and strict liability both have a deterrent effect, to be sure, but there is a difference between the *complete deterrence* sought by trespass law and the *deterrence of unreasonable invasions* sought by negligence and strict liability law. Specifically, since negligence and strict liability do not aim to prohibit or deter all nonconsensual invasions, the compensation provided under these areas of the law should not give the victim a right to seek compensation based on the breach of a hypothetical bargain in which the victim grants permission to invade his rights. Thus, for the torts governed by negligence and strict liability, the correct approach to damages is the ex post perspective. As I hope to show in the next section, this argument has implications for the law on nonpecuniary damages.

III. PAIN AND SUFFERING AND LOSS OF ENJOYMENT OF LIFE

Courts divide nonpecuniary losses into two types: (1) *pain and suffering*, and (2) *loss of enjoyment of life* (or hedonic losses). The first type, pain and suffering, is easy to comprehend – all of us have experienced pain at some point in our lives. The second type, loss of enjoyment of life, refers to the victim's loss of the ability to enjoy activities basic to experiencing life, such as the ability to take part in physical activities, to communicate with others, or to experience pleasure through the senses.[11]

Awareness of Suffering and Deprivation

Two controversial questions regarding nonpecuniary damages are whether the victim has to be cognitively aware of pain and suffering, and whether the victim has to be cognitively aware of deprivations falling under the category of loss of enjoyment of life. The rule in all courts is that *a victim must be conscious of pain to receive an award for pain and suffering*.[12] With respect to cognitive awareness of loss of enjoyment

---

violations of interests protected by the law should attempt to compensate for the subjective value of the tree to Doe. The subjective value is the amount that Doe would pay to retain the tree.

[11] McGee v. A C & S, Inc., 933 So.2d 770, 775–776 (La. 2006) ("Loss of enjoyment of life . . . refers to detrimental alterations of the person's life or lifestyle or the person's inability to participate in the activities or pleasures of life that were formerly enjoyed prior to the injury."); Kansas City S. Ry. Co., Inc. v. Johnson, 798 So.2d 374, 381 (Miss. 2001) ("[Loss of enjoyment of life] damages relates to daily life activities that are common to most people.... [These include] going on a first date, reading, debating politics, the sense of taste, recreational activities, and family activities." (citations omitted)).

[12] *See, e.g.*, McDougald v. Garber, 536 N.E.2d 372, 375 (N.Y. 1989) (requiring "some level of awareness" for recovery of pain and suffering damages); Nichols v. Marshall, 486 F.2d 791, 793 (10th Cir. 1973) ("It appears very clearly that pain and suffering are conscious experiences and do not exist in an unconscious state."); Stone v. Sinclair Refining Co., 200 N.W. 948 (Mich. 1924) (reversible error when jury could have inferred the instructions authorized damages for unconscious pain and suffering); Vanderlippe v. Midwest Studios, Inc., 289 N.W. 341, 349 (Neb. 1939) ("Allowance can

of life, the courts are split. Some do not require the victim to be cognitively aware of the deprivations associated with loss of enjoyment of life.[13] Others hold that the victim cannot receive compensation for loss of enjoyment of life if he is not cognitively aware of the loss.[14] The level of cognitive awareness necessary to justify pain and suffering damages – awareness of pain – is presumably lower than the level of cognitive awareness necessary to recover for loss of enjoyment of life.

As courts and commentators have noted, if the victim cannot receive damages for pain and suffering in the absence of cognitive awareness, then the law gives tortfeasors an incentive to inflict the most severe harm on their victims.[15] In other words, if you run into a pedestrian on the street, you should back up and run him over again to reduce the likelihood that he will be cognitively aware of his later suffering. The cognitive awareness requirement implies that by inflicting more severe injury a tortfeasor can reduce the damages he will be required to pay.

The foregoing discussion of ex post versus ex ante assessments of compensation has implications for the cognitive awareness question. From the ex post perspective, some level of cognitive awareness would appear to be a necessary condition for an award of compensatory damages for emotional harm, whether pain and suffering or loss of enjoyment of life. The sole purpose of the damages award, under the ex post perspective, is to increase the victim's post-accident utility level. If the victim is unaware of the pain, or of being deprived of enjoyment of life, then a compensatory award cannot enhance the victim's post-accident utility.

Worryingly, this argument undermines the basis for awarding pecuniary damages in the absence of cognitive awareness. If the victim is not aware of his surroundings,

only be made for pain and suffering of which the injured person is conscious."); Flory v. N.Y. Cent., 163 N.E.2d 902 (Ohio 1959) (sufficient evidence supported jury finding that decedent was conscious to permit damages for pain and suffering); 2 Jacob A. Stein, Stein on Personal Injury Damages Treatise § 8:6 (3d ed. 2012).

[13] Flannery v. United States, 297 S.E.2d 433, 439 (W.Va., 1982) (a plaintiff can recover loss of enjoyment of life damages, under West Virginia common law, "even though he may not be able to sense his loss of enjoyment of life."); Holston v. Sisters of the Third Order of St. Francis, 618 N.E.2d 334 (Ill. App. Ct. 1993) (damages may be awarded for the loss of enjoyment of life to a disabled person even if victim was unaware of her loss due to deprivation of consciousness); Eyoma v. Falco, 589 A.2d 653, 662 (N.J. Super. 1991) (a victim can receive loss of enjoyment of life damages even in a comatose or vegetative state).

[14] Flannery v. United States, 718 F.2d 108, 111 (4th Cir. 1983) (restricted to Federal Tort Claims Act); Pitman v. Thorndike, 762 F.Supp. 870, 873 (D. Nev. 1991); McDougald v. Garber, 536 N.E.2d 372, 375 (N.Y. 1989); Keene v. Brigham & Women's Hosp., Inc., 775 N.E.2d 725, 739 (Mass. App. Ct. 2002), *rev'd in part on other grounds*, 786 N.E.2d 824 (2003); Ramos v. Kuzas, 600 N.E.2d 241, 243 (Ohio 1992).

[15] McDougald v. Garber, 536 N.E.2d 372, 375 (N.Y. 1989) (noting that requiring awareness could result "in the paradoxical situation that the greater the degree of brain injury inflicted by a negligent defendant, the smaller the award the plaintiff can recover in general damages"). *See also Recent Case, Damages – Loss of Enjoyment of Life – New York Court of Appeals Denies Loss-of-Enjoyment Damages to Comatose Plaintiffs – McDougald v. Garber*, 103 Harv. L. Rev. 811, 816 (1990); Thomas O. Depperschmidt, *Unintended Consequences and Perverse Effects in Forensic Economic Award Calculations*, 4 J. Legal Econ. 65, 67 (Summer 1994).

how can his utility be enhanced or restored by compensating him for pecuniary losses? This is a fair question, but no one expresses such doubt about the validity of pecuniary damages, perhaps because a refusal to compensate for pecuniary losses would weaken deterrence too much or would result in financial losses to others who support the victim.

From the ex ante perspective, cognitive awareness should not be required on the part of the victim to receive a nonpecuniary award. Why? The key question under the ex ante perspective is what level of compensation, objectively determined, would tend to make the victim, fully informed as to the impending losses, indifferent as between the pre-accident and post-accident states – assuming this question is posed to the victim in the pre-accident state. Clearly, the victim would choose to be compensated for pain and suffering, and for loss of enjoyment of life, even if he knows that he would not be aware of these elements of suffering in the post-accident state. In other words, he would not voluntarily put himself in the post-accident state without a promise of compensation for such losses, even though he would not be fully aware of the losses when he is in the post-accident state.

Which perspective on nonpecuniary damages is appropriate, then, the ex ante perspective or the ex post perspective? Based on the argument of the preceding part of this chapter, the answer depends on the type of legal rule violated by the defendant. If the defendant has committed a trespass or similar intentional tort – for example, a battery – then nonpecuniary damages should be awarded in accordance with the ex ante perspective. The reason is that trespass law aims to protect the victim from the nonconsensual invasion itself, in addition to the injuries caused by the invasion. If damages for trespass are to compensate the victim for the legal interests that have been violated, the level of compensation for the violation should be determined by the amount of money that the victim, fully informed as to the harms that would result from the invasion, would have demanded to consent to the invasion. On the other hand, if the defendant has committed a negligent act or omission, or a nuisance, then damages should be awarded in accordance with the ex post perspective. The reason is that damages for instances of negligence or nuisance provide compensation for the violation of a more limited set of interests than protected by trespass law – specifically not including the interest in being free from any nonconsensual invasion. Negligence and nuisance law seek to protect individuals from injuries caused by unreasonable invasions of a protected right rather than the mere nonconsensual invasion of a protected right.

Under the policy offered here the requirement of cognitive awareness should be implied by the purpose of the damages award, which in turn is implied by the legal category to which it is attached. Trespass and similar rules that seek to prohibit nonconsensual invasions should therefore compensate plaintiffs for all of the interests violated by a breach of the rule, whether the victim, after the accident, is cognitively aware of the resulting deprivation or not. Negligence and strict liability, which seek to deter injuries due to unreasonable invasions, should provide compensation to the extent that the invasion has reduced the victim's post-accident utility, which implies a requirement of cognitive awareness.

This prescription differs from the law. The law prohibits an award of damages for pain and suffering when the victim is unaware of the pain,[16] and some courts prohibit damages for loss of enjoyment of life when the victim is unaware of the deprivation.[17] The proposal here, by contrast, is to award compensation for pain and suffering, and for loss of enjoyment of life, whenever the tort is in the nature of a trespass, regardless of the victim's level of cognitive awareness. Reducing damages based on the level of awareness of suffering should be restricted to cases in which the defendant is guilty of a nontrespass tort, such as negligence or nuisance. This approach ensures that damages provide compensation for violations of the interests protected by the law.

An important benefit of compensating for the legal interests violated is that it would eliminate the tortfeasor's existing incentive to inflict the most severe harm possible on his victim, or to be indifferent about inflicting such harm. Take the case of the tortfeasor who negligently runs into a victim with his car. If the tortfeasor backs up and drives over his victim again, then he has committed an intentional tort. Instead of reducing the compensatory damages award to the victim by inflicting more severe harm, which is the perverse incentive created by existing law, he would magnify the compensatory damages award under the prescription offered here.

Disaggregation of Components of Nonpecuniary Awards

Another controversy in damages law is whether courts should issue separate awards for pain and suffering and for loss of enjoyment of life. The concern expressed by some courts is that since neither of these components can be measured precisely, awarding damages for each component separately merely compounds the problem of imprecise measurement. Accordingly, some jurisdictions hold it impermissible for trial courts to issue separate awards for the two components.[18]

The leading case on the disaggregation question is *McDougald v. Garber*,[19] which held that (a) *cognitive awareness is a requirement for recovery of loss of enjoyment of life damages*, and (b) *pain and suffering damages and loss of enjoyment of life damages cannot be issued as separate awards*. The two conclusions are in tension, because disaggregating awards should make it easier for an appellate court to determine whether loss of enjoyment of life damages were awarded appropriately by the trial

---

[16] *See supra* note 12.

[17] *See supra* note 13.

[18] McDougald v. Garber, 536 N.E.2d 372, 376–377 (N.Y. 1989); Huff v. Tracy, 57 Cal. App.3d 939, 943 (Cal. App.3d 1976); Poyzer v. McGraw, 360 N.W.2d 748, 753 (Iowa 1985); Canfield v. Sandock, 563 N.E.2d 1279, 1281–1282 (Ind. 1990); Adams v. Miller, 908 S.W.2d 112, 116 (Ky. 1995) (abrogated on other grounds); Anderson v. Neb. Dep't of Soc. Servs., 538 N.W.2d 732, 740–741 (Neb. 1995).

[19] 536 N.E.2d 372 (N.Y. 1989).

court. If the levels of cognitive awareness required to recover for pain and suffering and for loss of enjoyment of life differ, as seems plausible, then it should be easier for an appellate court to review the appropriateness of both types of award if they are issued separately.

The disaggregation problem is also generated by the *per diem* argument used by some lawyers in their arguments to juries. The *per diem* argument asks juries to consider the pain and suffering experienced by the victim on a daily basis, and to sum up the appropriate per-diem compensatory awards. Some courts have expressed concern that the argument compounds errors in the assessment of nonpecuniary damages.[20]

Nonpecuniary damages are monetary sums assigned by courts to compensate for emotional harms suffered by plaintiffs. Errors in assessment do not result from the choice of measurement, but from variation in the perceptions and attitudes of juries and judges. Thus, the core issue in the controversy over disaggregating components of emotional harm is whether disaggregation enhances variation among court awards for nonpecuniary losses or reduces variation. This is an empirical question that has not been answered.[21]

Because of the important role played by the subjective impressions of judges and juries, variation in court awards for the nonpecuniary losses associated with nearly identical injuries is not necessarily evidence of error in assessment. One person's view of the appropriate monetary award for a particular emotional injury has no greater claim to validity than another person's view. However, variation in awards is a problem for two reasons: (1) variation makes it difficult for potential defendants to predict the damages that might be imposed on them, and (2) variation makes it difficult for appellate courts to review the decisions of trial courts.

The first problem, unpredictability to potential defendants, is a serious one in many settings where the negligence rule applies.[22] Consider, for example, medical

---

[20] *See, e.g.,* Duguay v. Gelinas, 182 A.2d 451, 454–455 (N.H. 1962); Botta v. Brunner, 138 A.2d 713 (N.J. 1958); Henman v. Klinger, 409 P.2d 631, 634 (Wyo. 1966).

[21] One experimental study found that a mock jury gave larger awards when allowed to disaggregate damages. Susan Poser, Brian H. Bornstein & E. Kiernan McGorty, *Measuring Damages for Lost Enjoyment of Life: The View from the Bench and the Jury Box,* 27 Law & Hum. Behav. 53, 58–62 (2003). However, a finding that juries give larger awards under disaggregation does not imply that disaggregation results in greater variation among jury awards. A consistent method of disaggregation might lead to consistently high damages awards, with less variation. The study's findings indicate that there is a framing issue – that is, damages awarded by a jury respond to the manner in which the injury is framed. This implies variation in damages awards based on the method of framing the injury.

[22] One solution offered to the problem of uncertain nonpecuniary damages is to design a schedule for damages awards; *see* Randall R. Bovbjerg, Frank A. Sloan, & James F. Blumstein, *Valuing Life and Limb in Tort: Scheduling "Pain and Suffering,"* 83 Nw. U. L. Rev. 908 (1989); Ronen Avraham, *Putting a Price on Pain-and-Suffering Damages: A Critique of the Current Approaches and a Preliminary Proposal for Change,* 100 Nw. U. L. Rev. 87 (2006). Damages caps – monetary limits on the size of nonpecuniary awards – have been adopted in many states in the area of medical malpractice. On the effects of damages caps, *see* John J. Donohue III & Daniel E. Ho, *The Impact of Damage Caps on*

malpractice. With highly variable pain and suffering awards, physicians and their insurers cannot predict the level of damages associated with a given injury. This uncertainty, in turn, may make it difficult for physicians to find and afford medical malpractice insurance.[23] Thus, uncertainty in damages awards, if it goes too far, can reduce participation in socially desirable activities, such as providing medical care.

The second problem, inability of appellate courts to review trial court judgments, is also a serious one for the reliability of courts. Corruption is not believed to be rampant in American courts.[24] One reason is that appellate courts have been on hand to review the decisions of trial courts. If a judge awards an enormous compensatory award solely to reward a particular plaintiff, or to gratuitously punish a particular defendant, appellate courts stand ready to review the judgment and determine whether it is in accord with existing law. But if the variation in nonpecuniary awards is permitted to grow without bound, appellate courts will increasingly find it difficult to serve this policing function. The absence of such a monitor would give politically influential litigants incentives to press for the staffing of friendly agents in the trial courts.

For these reasons, appellate courts have developed standards for reviewing the damages awards issued by trial courts. In general, appellate courts review compensatory damages awards issued by trial courts under the *abuse of discretion standard*.[25]

Malpractice Claims: Randomization Inference with Difference-in-Differences, 4 J. Emp. Legal Stud. 69 (2007); Jonathan Klick & Thomas Stratmann, *Medical Malpractice Reform and Physicians in High-Risk Specialties*, 36 J. Legal Stud. S121 (2007).

[23] For an empirically informed discussion of the issues, *see* Kathryn Zeiler, *Medical Malpractice Liability Crisis or Patient Compensation Crisis?*, 59 DePaul L. Rev. 675 (2010).

[24] Transparency International's reports on countries in which judicial corruption is widespread do not include the United States. *See generally* Transparency International: The Global Coalition Against Corruption, Global Corruption Report 2007: Corruption in Judicial Systems (Diana Rodriguez & Linda Ehrichs eds., 2007).

[25] Gasperini v. Ctr. for Humanities, Inc., 518 U.S. 415, 418 (1996) (noting the standard of review applied by the Circuit Courts for inadequacy or excessiveness of compensatory damages is abuse of discretion); Saunders v. Firtel, 978 A.2d 487, 495 (Conn. 2009); Anderson v. Welding Testing Lab., Inc., 304 So.2d 351 (La. 1974); Lilly v. Boswell, 242 S.W.2d 73, 78 (Mo. 1951); Kadmiri v. Claassen, 10 P.3d 1076, 1078 (Wash. Ct. App. 2000). Some states employ variations on the abuse of discretion standard in which the appellate court will only disturb the verdict if it "shocks the conscience," Dagget v. Atchison, Topeka & Santa Fe Ry. Co., 313 P.d2 557, 564 (Cal. 1957)), or is the result of "passion or prejudice," Stein v. Spainhour, 521 N.E.2d 641, 644 (Ill. App. Ct. 1988); Morrison v. Bradley, 655 P.2d 385, 388 (Colo. 1982); Minarik v. Nagy, 193 N.E.2d 280, 282 (Ohio Ct. App. 1963); Maxwell v. Aetna Life Ins. Co., 693 P.2d 348, 360 (Ariz. Ct. App. 1984). By statute, New York's standard for appellate review of a new trial due to excessive or inadequate damages is whether the award "deviates materially" from what would be reasonable compensation. Harvey v. Mazal Am. Partners, 590 N.E.2d 224, 228 (N.Y. 1992). Some courts refer to more than one of the aforementioned standards. *See* Gilbertson v. Gross, 45 N.W.2d 547, 549 (Minn. 1951) ("The trial court had the opportunity of observing plaintiff and the other witnesses and of reviewing their testimony, and we must conclude that the record does not establish an abuse of discretion on its part in denying defendants' motion for a new trial on the grounds of passion or prejudice."); Ritter v. Stanton, 745 N.E.2d 828, 844 (Ind. Ct. App. 2001); Advocat, Inc. v. Sauer, 111 S.W.3d 346, 353 (Ark. 2003); Kelly v. Iowa State Educ. Ass'n, 372 N.W.2d 288, 300 (Iowa Ct. App. 1985).

Under this standard, appellate courts seek to determine if the damages award is one that *a reasonable trier of fact* could award for the injuries proven by the victim.[26]

For pecuniary damages, the abuse of discretion standard is relatively easy for an appellate court to apply: examine the evidence, in the light most favorable to the prevailing plaintiff, to see if it supports the award.[27] If the plaintiff has produced credible evidence of medical expenses totaling $10,000, then a pecuniary award of $10,000 will satisfy the standard.

For nonpecuniary damages, the review process is more difficult because there is no factual basis developed in a trial that by itself would enable an appellate court to determine the reasonableness of a nonpecuniary award. As a practical solution to this problem, many appellate courts compare the award issued to the victim to the awards issued previously to victims who have suffered similar injuries.[28] However, some courts have expressed reluctance to put much weight on awards in cases with similar injuries.[29]

Comparing a nonpecuniary award to previous awards is far from ideal. If the first court to assign nonpecuniary damages for a specific injury was stingy, then all future courts will be stingy too. Moreover, the approach requires courts to take into

---

[26] Youn v. Maritime Overseas Corp., 623 So.2d 1257, 1261 (La. 1993); Hawkins v. Walker, 238 S.W.3d 517, 531–532 (Tex. App. 2007); Kadmiri v. Claassen, 10 P.3d 1076, 1078 (Wash. Ct. App. 2000).

[27] Cerretti v. Flint Hills Rural Elec. Co-op. Ass'n, 837 P.2d 330, 343–344 (Kan. 1992) ("If the evidence, with all reasonable inferences to be drawn therefrom, when considered in the light most favorable to the prevailing party, supports the verdict, it will not be disturbed on appeal." (citing Wisker v. Hart, 766 P.2d 168, 170 (Kan. 1988))); Boyle v. Larzelere, 13 N.W.2d 528, 529 (Wis. 1944) ("[A] verdict by the jury upon the amount of pecuniary loss . . . must be sustained if there is credible evidence to sustain it."); Christus Health v. Dorriety, 345 S.W.3d 104, 113 (Tex. App. 2011) (holding sufficient evidence supports the jury's award of pecuniary damages); Morrison v. Bradley, 655 P.2d 385, 389 (Colo. 1982) (holding evidence supported the jury's pecuniary damages award).

[28] *See, e.g.*, Duncan v. Kansas City S. Ry. Co., 773 So.2d 670, 683 (La. 2001) (reducing the general damages award after finding the trial court abused its discretion and upon review of cases involving similar injuries); Gilmore v. Cent. Maine Power Co., 665 A.2d 666, 671 (Me. 1995) (finding the trial court did not abuse its discretion and noting the awarded damages were comparable with damages awarded in cases involving similar injuries).

[29] Many courts acknowledge that awards from other cases should not be a determining factor as to whether the award in a particular case is unreasonable. *See, e.g.*, Dagget v. Atchison, Topeka & Santa Fe Ry. Co., 313 P.d2 557, 564 (Cal. 1957) (holding the court may consider awards from previous cases but case-by-case analysis is required, and it cannot be held as a matter of law that the amount is excessive because it is larger than what is allowed in similar cases) (citations omitted); Miller v. Thomas, 246 So.2d 16, 19 (La. 1971) ("The awards in other cases serve only as an aid in determining whether there has been an abuse of discretion and rivet no steel frame of uniformity."). Some courts find little value in making comparisons or decline to make comparisons to awards from previous cases. *See, e.g.*, Collins v. Hinton, 937 S.W.2d 164, 171 (Ark. 1997) ("[P]recedents are of little value in appeals of this kind, with the understanding that a jury has much discretion in awarding damages in personal injury cases.") (citing Builder's Transp., Inc. v. Wilson, 914 S.W.2d 742 (1996)); Richardson v. Chapman, 676 N.E.2d 621 (Ill. 1997) (declining to make comparisons in determining whether a particular award is excessive); Omlid v. Lee, 391 N.W.2d 62, 64 (Minn. App. 1986) ("[A] verdict generally should not be justified or attacked by comparing it with verdicts from other cases." (citations omitted)).

account the effects of inflation on the comparability of awards over time. However, the alternative is to forgo any objective tool for reviewing nonpecuniary awards, which is potentially costly given its adverse implications for the reliability of the courts.

IV. DEATH AND DAMAGES

A wrongful death action is a lawsuit brought by a surviving relative, typically the spouse, of a person who was killed as the result of a negligent or intentional tort. Obviously, the lawsuit is brought against the person or entity charged with commission of the tort. Such lawsuits were disallowed under the common law, but they are now permitted by statute in every common law jurisdiction.

The persons who may bring a wrongful death action are prescribed by the wrongful death statute of the jurisdiction. In every jurisdiction the surviving spouse and children are permitted to sue, though restrictions may arise in the case of a marital separation or where the children are self-supporting. The extent to which other relatives may be permitted to sue depends on the jurisdiction's statute and its interpretation by courts of the jurisdiction.[30]

Compensatory damages for wrongful death encompass the loss of financial support, loss of companionship, and medical and burial expenses of the deceased. Punitive damages may be sought if the tort meets the standard for such an award (willful, wanton, or malicious).

Consider the typical wrongful death lawsuit: The surviving spouse sues a defendant whose negligence resulted in the death of the other spouse. The key damages component in such a lawsuit is likely to be the loss of financial support. The deceased spouse may have provided a stream of income to the surviving spouse, and that stream will have to be translated to a lump sum amount – that is, from a flow to a stock – to serve as the basis for a damages award. To calculate the value of the loss of support, one will have to employ the concept of *present value*.

To understand present value, consider a promise to receive $1 next year (untaxed). How much is the promise worth today? If the interest rate is 5 percent, the promisor could put a sum of money into a bank account today to be guaranteed a total of $1 in the account next year. That sum of money is the present value of the promise to

---

[30] State wrongful death statutes vary with regard to who can be a beneficiary and the situations that allow certain classes of beneficiaries to recover from a wrongful death action. Many state statutes include "heirs" or "next of kin" as potential beneficiaries, so a particular beneficiary may depend on how the court construes those terms (some limit to lineal descendants whereas others allow collateral relatives). That said, the following relatives (in addition to spouses and children) may be able to bring wrongful death actions depending on the jurisdiction and construction of the applicable statute: parents, grandparents, grandchildren, brothers and sisters, and in some cases aunts and uncles. *See generally* 1 STUART M. SPEISER & JAMES E. ROOKS, JR., RECOVERY FOR WRONGFUL DEATH § 3 (4th ed.); 3 JACOB A. STEIN, STEIN ON PERSONAL INJURY DAMAGES TREATISE § 22:10 (3d ed.).

receive $1 next year. Under the assumption that the interest rate is 5 percent, the promisor would have to put 96 cents in the bank account today to be guaranteed a total of $1 next year. The reason is that if he puts a certain sum in the account today, he will receive the original sum plus 5 percent of that sum next year. Since the amount he receives in the next year is 1.05 times the original sum, the amount necessary to guarantee $1 can be found by dividing $1 by 1.05. It follows that if the interest rate is 5 percent, the *present value* of a promise to receive $1 next year is $1/(1.05), which is slightly more than 95 cents. It also follows that a promise to receive $1 two years from now has a present value of $1/1.05^2, which is roughly 91 cents.

Now consider a stream of income providing $1 per year. If the stream of income lasts forever – that is, it is a *perpetuity* – then it is equivalent to having a permanent bank account that provides $1 in interest income every year. If the interest rate on the account is 5 percent, then the amount of money in the account multiplied by 5 percent must yield $1 per year. This means that the amount of money in the account would have to be equal to $1 divided by the interest rate of 5 percent ($1/0.05), which is $20.[31] Thus, if there is a permanent account paying an interest rate of 5 percent every year, to be guaranteed a stream of interest income equal to $1 per year, beginning next year and going on forever, I will have to put $20 in the bank account today. It follows that if the interest rate is 5 percent, the present value of a stream of income of $1 per year, going on forever, is $20.

Suppose the perpetuity is to become available in 10 years from now. In other words, ten years from today, I will have a permanent account holding $20, with an interest rate of 5 percent, that will start paying $1 in the eleventh year and in each of the following years without end. If the current interest rate is (also) 5 percent, how much money should I save today to have $20 in the permanent account in year ten?

Since the money in the account will have grown by a factor of 1.05^{10} in ten years, I will need to put in $20/1.05^{10}$ in the bank today, which is roughly $12.28. Recall that $20 is equal $1/0.05, the present value of a perpetuity paying $1 every year. It follows, then, that the present value of a perpetuity paying $1 per year that starts eleven years from now is $(\$1/0.05) \times (1/1.05^{10})$. The final step in this lesson is to notice that the present value of an *annuity* that pays $1 per year for ten years, starting next year, is equal to the difference between a perpetuity that starts paying next year and another perpetuity that starts paying in year eleven. Thus, the value of such an annuity is the difference $\$1/0.05 - (\$1/0.05) \times (1.05^{10}) = \$7.72$

So far I have introduced the concept of present value in an intuitive manner by referring to a bank account and using numerical examples. Another way of

---

[31] If the annual rate of interest, r, multiplied by the amount of money in the account, A, is equal to $1 per year, then $r \times A = \$1$. This implies that the amount that must be in the account, given the interest rate, is given by $\$1/r$. Thus, if the annual interest rate is 5 percent, the account must have $20 in it to generate interest income of $1 per year.

understanding present value is to use the standard present value formula. If the interest rate is r, and you are promised to receive $1, n years from today, the present value of that promise is

$$PV = \frac{\$1}{(1+r)^n}$$

A stream of income providing $1 per year for n years (i.e., an annuity) has a present value of

$$PV = \frac{\$1}{(1+r)} + \frac{\$1}{(1+r)^2} + \cdots + \frac{\$1}{(1+r)^n},$$

which is equivalent to

$$PV = \left(\frac{\$1}{r}\right)\left(1 - \left(\frac{1}{1+r}\right)^n\right).$$

Note that as the number of years approaches infinity, $[1/(1+r)]^n$ approaches zero, so the present value of the stream approaches that of the perpetuity, $\$1/r$.

Now we are ready to calculate the damages award for loss of financial support in the wrongful death action example introduced above, that is, where the surviving spouse sues for the death of the other spouse. Suppose the deceased spouse earned $100,000 per year, and that the deceased spouse's life ended this year at age forty. To simplify, assume that the deceased spouse has already contributed $100,000 to the household this year (the year of the accident). If the deceased spouse would have worked up to (and including) age seventy, the surviving spouse has lost thirty years of financial support at $100,000 per year. The present value of that financial support is equal to the value of a thirty-year annuity paying $100,000 per year that begins paying next year. The value of such an annuity is $100,000/0.05 − $100,000/0.05 × $(1/1.05^{30})$ = $1,536,000. Thus, the damages award for loss of financial support that the surviving spouse should seek in a wrongful death action is $1,536,000.

Present value is an important concept in the calculation of damages. In wrongful death lawsuits, present value calculations are necessary in evaluating the key component of the damages award, the loss of financial support. But the significance of the present value concept is not limited to wrongful death actions; it is also useful in calculating damages in any setting where the harm suffered by the plaintiff is experienced on an ongoing or continuing basis, such as in nuisance cases.[32]

Geometric progression associated with the value of money over time enables the use of present value formulae for calculating the damages award when an injury imposes a stream of losses on the plaintiff. In the example considered earlier, I did not consider two important issues that might arise in such calculations. One is growth in the harm over time, and the other is the fact that the harm itself may be uncertain.

---

[32] *See* Chapter 15.

For example, in the wrongful death example, the plaintiff's decedent may have been expected to receive annual wage increases over the thirty years that the deceased spouse would have worked if not for the accident. This implies that the harm imposed on the plaintiff increases over the relevant time period because the lost wage support increases. On the other hand, the deceased spouse may not have remained in the workforce over the entire time period. As the decedent approached seventy, his health may have failed, which might have forced him to quit working. How should these factors be incorporated into the calculation of damages for wrongful death?

Annual wage increases should be anticipated in lines of work where productivity increases with experience. Employees in many industries learn how to do their jobs better as time passes and often develop job-related skills. Employees develop "human capital" over time, and this type of capital enables them to become more productive.[33] For example, a law professor becomes a more productive teacher over time as he becomes more familiar with his subject area and the sorts of questions students tend to have about the subject.

Suppose the decedent would have earned annual wage increases of a fixed percentage every year, perhaps 2 percent or 3 percent. If the percentage is given by ρ, and the salary at the year of death is represented by $\$w$, then the present value formula for the decedent's income stream is now

$$PV = \frac{\$w(1+\rho)}{(1+r)} + \frac{\$w(1+\rho)^2}{(1+r)^2} + \cdots + \frac{\$w(1+\rho)^n}{(1+r)^n}.$$

How should we incorporate the probability that the decedent might have dropped out of the workforce before the final year of work n? That is a complicated issue. The probability of workforce attachment probably remains high for a long time and then falls to a low level, perhaps less than 50 percent, as a worker approaches the retirement year. One simplifying approach to this problem is to assume that the probability of workforce attachment follows the same geometric progression as the wage growth and interest rate factors. Suppose the probability that the decedent is in the workforce in any given year is a fixed percentage greater than the probability that the decedent would have been in the workforce in the following year. For example, if the percentage is 1, then if the probability that the decedent would have been in the workforce in his 45th year of life is 90 percent, the probability that he would have been in the workforce in his 44th year of life is 1 percent greater, or 90.9 percent.

Taking the probability of workforce attachment into account requires us to calculate the *expected present value* of the decedent's future income stream. The difference between the present value and the expected present value is that the latter takes into account the probabilities that the future payments would have been realized. Recall, from Chapter 2, that the expected value of an event is equal to the probability that

[33] *See generally* Gary S. Becker, Human Capital: A Theoretical and Empirical Analysis, with Special Reference to Education (Univ. of Chicago Press, 3d ed. 1993).

the event will happen multiplied by the dollar value of the payoff (or loss) from the event (Expected Value = Probability × Value).

Using the assumption that the probability of workforce attachment follows a geometric decline, and letting δ represent the discount percentage, the expected present value (*EPV*) of the decedent's income stream becomes

$$EPV = \frac{\$w(1+\rho)}{(1+r)(1+\delta)} + \frac{\$w(1+\rho)^2}{[(1+r)(1+\delta)]^2} + \cdots + \frac{\$w(1+\rho)^n}{[(1+r)(1+\delta)]^n},$$

which is equivalent to

$$EPV = \left(\frac{\$w(1+\rho)}{(1+r)(1+\delta) - (1+\rho)}\right)\left(1 - \left(\frac{(1+\rho)}{(1+r)(1+\delta)}\right)^n\right).$$

The advantage of geometric progression assumptions here is that it permits us to see some simple relationships between interest rates, wage growth, and workforce attachment in the calculation of wrongful death damages.[34] If the workforce attachment probability discount factor is the same as the wage growth factor (i.e., $\delta = \rho$), then the expected present value formula simplifies to the same present value formula calculated earlier when I ignored the workforce attachment probability and wage growth issues. It follows that if the wage growth and workforce attachment discount factors are very close, not much accuracy will be lost in the calculation of wrongful death damages if these factors are ignored. If, however, the job attachment discount is greater than the wage growth factor (i.e., $\delta > \rho$), the expected present value of lost income is smaller than the present value sum calculated when ignoring these factors. This is intuitively sensible, because each wage increase is offset, in expected present value terms, by an even greater likelihood that the decedent would have quit the workforce. On the other hand, if the wage growth factor exceeds the workforce attachment discount factor (i.e., $\delta < \rho$), then the expected present value of lost income is greater than the present value sum calculated when ignoring workforce attachment and wage growth.

Let us return to the numerical example, in which the decedent's salary is $100,000 in the year of his death, and the interest rate is 5 percent (i.e., $\$w = \$100,000$, $r = 0.05$). Now, to calculate damages we need only determine the relevant wage growth percentage and the discount factor on the probability of workforce attachment. Suppose wage growth would have been 3 percent each year, and the workforce attachment discount 1 percent. This combination of assumptions might be appropriate if the decedent was a productive worker, expected to advance in his line of work, and also maintained a sufficiently healthy lifestyle that he probably would have remained in the workforce until retirement. Under these assumptions, the

---

[34] An alternative and probably more popular approach to measuring the probability of workforce attachment is to use an exponential decay model where the probability of attachment in year n is equal to $(1 - \delta)^n$. However, I found the exponential decay approach slightly more cumbersome and less clear in its implications than the approach used in the text.

expected present value of lost future income support to the wrongful death plaintiff is $1,969,800, which is substantially more than the amount calculated when ignoring wage growth and job attachment ($1,536,000).

I have so far considered the typical wrongful death case, involving a suit by the surviving spouse (and any children) for a damages award that compensates for the loss of the financial support of the decedent. Survival statutes permit the lawsuit that would have been brought personally by the decedent to proceed, overturning the common law rule that abated the action upon the death of the tort victim.[35] When a parent is killed by a tortious act, the wrongful death statute will likely cover the types of injury for which family members would seek compensation, except for pain and suffering experienced by the deceased.[36]

The more troubling questions in this area arise with the death of a child. Most children provide no income to their households. Yet, most of us have the intuition that the death of a child is, in addition to being the most severe nonpecuniary harm to parents, perhaps the most severe pecuniary loss to society that could be caused by a tortfeasor. Disappointingly, tort damages law offers a confusing smorgasbord of state-specific rules governing damages for the death of a child, with some states making virtually no allowance for a monetary award based on the value of child's life apart from expected financial support to parents.[37] Setting the financial value of a child's life at almost zero, as the least generous states do, might generate the sort of perverse incentives discussed earlier in this chapter in connection with the law on damages for pain and suffering.

The more generous states allow for an action for the financial value of the child's life, which is the expected present value of the child's future income stream if he had survived, sometimes reduced by the amount necessary for self-support.[38] But this raises another issue: How should one calculate the value of a child's life?

The theory behind the calculation of damages awards for death caused by tortious conduct is that the value of the decedent's life can be translated into dollars. This is an uncertain process at best, but a relatively straightforward exercise, using the present value method discussed above, when the victim earns an income. When the victim has no earnings history or experience upon which earnings can be projected, as is true of most children, the uncertainties multiply. In addition, if the income of the parents is used to help estimate the expected income of the child, poor children will be disadvantaged in the damages calculation process. Instead of the present value algorithms commonly used in wrongful death cases, options pricing models

---

[35] *See, e.g.*, Porpora v. City of New Haven, 187 At. 668 (Conn. 1936); Rasmussen v. Benson, 275 N.W. 674 (Neb. 1937); Blisard v. Vargo, 286 F.2d 169 (3d Cir. 1961).

[36] For discussion of the law and implications for tort deterrence, *see* David W. Leebron, *Final Moments: Damages for Pain and Suffering Prior to Death*, 64 N.Y.U. L. Rev. 256 (1989).

[37] For a thorough survey, *see* Thomas R. Ireland & John O. Ward, *The Estate of a Minor Child in a Child Death Case*, 10 J. Legal Econ. 23 (2001).

[38] *Id.*

might provide a useful supplement or alternative approach to estimating the value of a child's life.[39] The variability of life options for the child might imply a relatively high estimate for the value of the child's life[40] and at the same time dampen the impact of current family income.

V. CAUSATION AND DAMAGES

Factual causation and damages are two parts of the case that a tort plaintiff must prove. To prove factual causation, the plaintiff must show that, more likely than not, the injury would not have happened if the defendant had taken care (or otherwise avoided committing the tort). To prove damages, the evidence must show, at a minimum, that the entirety of the loss for which the plaintiff seeks compensation would not have occurred if the defendant had taken care. If some identifiable part of the plaintiff's injury would have occurred even if the defendant had taken care, then the plaintiff will not be able to recover for that portion of his injury.

Given all of this, it seems redundant to have both a causation and a damages element in a torts case. Why not jettison the causation element and focus on damages alone? We examined the function of the causation test earlier (see Chapter 12). However, one major difference between the causation and damages elements of a negligence case is that a finding against causation sets damages at zero, while the consideration of causation in the damages phase of a case may result in a variable reduction in the damages award. In other words, a court could find factual causation in a negligence case and also conclude that not all of the damages asserted by the plaintiff are causally attributable to the defendant.

Consider the following hypothetical, involving a doctor who fails to diagnose a deadly disease in a timely manner. When the patient first visited the doctor, the patient had a 70 percent chance of surviving the disease if treated. In the second visit to the doctor, when the disease was finally diagnosed, the patient had a 20 percent chance of survival, and he died soon after. The negligence claim against the doctor would satisfy the factual causation requirement.[41] However, at the damages phase of the case, the defendant's doctors would surely point out that the patient had only a 70 percent chance of survival when he first visited the doctor. The doctor's negligence is responsible for 50 percent (the difference between the initial 70 percent and the later 20 percent survival probability) of the injury to survivors due to the loss of the patient's life. In the surviving spouse's wrongful death lawsuit, damages will be

---

[39] On the theory of options pricing, *see* Fischer Black & Myron Scholes, *The Pricing of Options and Corporate Liabilities*, 81 J. POL. ECON. 637 (1973).

[40] One of the basic results of options pricing theory is that the value of an option increases dramatically as the variance of the value of the underlying asset increases.

[41] Herskovits v. Group Health Cooperative, 664 P.2d 474 (Wash. 1983).

calculated by multiplying the decedent's lost future income by 50 percent, which reflects causal apportionment.[42]

Strict apportionment of damages on causation grounds may seem harsh in light of the difficulty of establishing causal contributions in malpractice cases. Because of this, many courts shift the burden to the defendant according to the following rule:

> Where the malpractice involves treatment of a preexisting disease, the assessment of damages poses a problem because of the practical difficulty in separating that part of the harm caused by the malpractice from the preexisting disease and its normal consequences. Because of this, courts are now taking the view that in a situation where the malpractice or other tortious act aggravates a preexisting disease or condition, the innocent plaintiff should not be required to establish what expenses, pain, suffering, disability or impairment are attributable solely to the malpractice or tortious act, but that the burden of proof should be shifted to the culpable defendant who should be held responsible for all damages unless he can demonstrate that the damages for which he is responsible are capable of some reasonable apportionment and what those damages are.[43]

The burden-shifting approach implies that, as practical matter, in most scenarios where the patient begins with a greater than 50 percent chance of recovery from the disease or injury, the physician found guilty of malpractice in failing to make a timely diagnosis will be held liable for 100 percent of the damages. In other words, since the physician often will be unable to apportion damages according to causal contributions, he will be saddled with the entire amount of damages rather than a causally determined portion of the damages.

This discussion takes us into one of the controversial recent innovations of tort law: *the lost chance doctrine*. Courts apply the lost chance doctrine to the following type of case: The patient, unaware of the disease he has contracted, has a probability of survival that is *less than 50 percent* when he first visits the doctor, and the doctor negligently fails to diagnose the disease (e.g., cancer). In a later visit, the doctor finally provides the correct diagnosis, but by then the patient's chance of survival is much smaller. Under the lost chance doctrine, courts have permitted plaintiffs to sue for the damages attributable to the doctor's negligence.[44] The doctrine overturns an earlier established rule in causation law that would have denied compensation, because the plaintiff was less than 50 percent likely to survive when the negligent

---

[42] *See, e.g.,* Fosgate v. Corona, 66 N.J. 268, 330 A.2d 355 (1974).

[43] *See* Fosgate v. Corona, 66 N.J. 268, 272–273, 330 A.2d 355 (1974). *See also* Matsumoto v. Kaku, 484 P.2d 147 (Sup. Ct. Hawaii 1971); Graham v. Roberts, 142 U.S. App. D.C. 305, 441 F.2d 995 (1970); Hylton v. Wade, 29 Colo. App. 98, 478 P.2d 690 (1970); Blaine v. Byers, 91 Idaho 665, 429 P.2d 397 (1967); Newbury v. Vogel, 151 Colo. 520, 379 P.2d 811 (1963).

[44] Herskovits v. Group Health Cooperative, 664 P.2d 474 (Wash. 1983) (establishing lost chance doctrine).

failure to diagnose occurred.[45] The lost chance doctrine permits the malpractice plaintiff to sue for the loss resulting from the change in the probability of survival (or of recovery from a serious illness or injury) that can be attributed to the doctor's negligence even though the probability of survival (or recovery) would have been less than 50 percent even if the doctor had never intervened.

Under the lost chance doctrine, plaintiffs are permitted to sue for compensation, but the damages award is reduced to reflect causal apportionment. Thus, if the patient had a 40 percent chance of survival initially and a 20 percent chance of survival at the later visit (when the correct diagnosis was provided), the damages that ordinarily would be awarded in a wrongful death action will be multiplied by 20 percent (the survival probability differential) to arrive at the damages for the lost chance action. Suppose, then, that the present value of the patient's earnings from the date of the negligent failure to diagnose is $1 million. The plaintiff in the wrongful death action could be awarded $200,000 in compensatory damages.

The lost chance doctrine has been controversial because it permits a plaintiff to collect damages even though it was more likely than not that he would have suffered the injury for which he sues even if the defendant had never intervened. Under traditional factual causation law of many jurisdictions, the plaintiff would not prevail.[46] On the other hand, under the same traditional rule, the plaintiff would be eligible for damages if his initial probability of survival (or avoiding serious injury) at the time of the negligent misdiagnosis was greater than 50 percent. Some have argued that the lost chance doctrine creates an asymmetric treatment of damages by moving from an "all or nothing" system to an "all or something" system.[47] In theory, this asymmetrical treatment could distort incentives for doctors to take care, in the direction of excessive care.[48] Doctors would face the risk of paying full damages for negligent misdiagnosis when the patient's probability of survival was greater than 50 percent (without discounting to reflect the actual probability of survival) and partial damages when the probability of survival was less than 50 percent. To award damages that on average reflect injury losses, all damages should be discounted to reflect the actual probability of survival. Since discounting occurs only when the probability of survival is below 50 percent, the average damages award would exceed the value of the average injury.

However, the asymmetry created by the lost chance doctrine is mostly superficial. Once one moves beyond factual causation and looks closely at the damages phase

---

[45] Cooper v. Sisters of Charity, Inc., 272 N.E.2d 97 (Ohio 1971).

[46] Cooper v. Sisters of Charity, Inc., 272 N.E.2d 97 (Ohio 1971) (plaintiff loses suit for negligent misdiagnosis if his probability of survival was less than 50 percent).

[47] Fennell v. S. Md. Hosp. Ctr., Inc., 580 A.2d 206, 212–214 (Md. 1990).

[48] Simmons v. West Covina Medical Clinic, 260 Cal. Rptr. 772, 778 (Cal. App. Ct. 2d Div. 1 1989) (finding adoption of the loss chance doctrine would increase physicians' exposure to liability and, therefore, "would unwisely encourage costly and unreasonable overtesting and overtreatment for defensive purposes.").

of negligence litigation, the perceived asymmetry largely disappears. The reason is that in the case where the plaintiff (or plaintiff's decedent) is more than 50 percent likely to survive or recover, damages may still be reduced to reflect the precise amount of the injury that is attributable to the defendant. Admittedly, the damages are unlikely to be reduced, given that the burden of proof on causation probably will be shifted to the physician and given the difficulty the physician faces in establishing causal apportionment. But the possibility of reducing damages exists nevertheless. In simplest terms, rather than moving the law from "all or nothing" to "all or something," as critics have argued, the lost chance doctrine moves the law from "something or nothing" to "something or something," which is a step toward rather than away from symmetry.

VI. DETERRENCE AND DAMAGES

Up to this point I have described tort damages as serving the purpose of restoring the victim to his preaccident level of welfare. This is correct if one is answering the question, "What should a court that aims to *compensate* a tort victim try to do?" But tort damages serve a *deterrence function* in addition to a compensatory function.

In most cases, the compensatory function is all courts need to consider, because the deterrence and compensation goals are not in tension. But there are settings where the two goals are in tension, and in those settings courts tend to put a greater emphasis on the deterrence function. The next part discusses two such settings: the collateral source rule and punitive damages.

Collateral Source Rule

The *collateral source rule* prohibits the admission of evidence that a plaintiff has received or will receive compensation for his injury from some source other than the defendant. The most common collateral source of compensation for injury is an insurer. In practical terms, the rule means that the defendant in a tort action cannot introduce evidence that the plaintiff has received compensation, partial or full, from his insurance company.

The collateral source rule has been part of the common law in the United States at least since the Supreme Court's decision in an 1854 admiralty case, *The Propeller Monticello v. Mollison*,[49] where the Court referred to the collateral source rule as a long-standing common law policy. The rule was applied in the torts setting in *Harding v. Town of Townshend*.[50]

The collateral source rule is controversial because it permits plaintiffs who carry insurance to be compensated twice – once by the insurance company and a second

---

[49] 58 U.S. 152 (1854).
[50] 43 Vt. 536 (1871).

time by the defendant. Because of this double compensation, many states have enacted statutes abrogating the collateral source rule or limiting its scope. These statutory reform efforts reflect an incomplete understanding of the rule's function.

To understand the function of the collateral source rule, consider the deterrence function of damages. Recall that a reasonable person, under the Hand Formula (Chapter 6), will take care whenever the incremental benefit, in terms of injuries avoided, is less than the incremental burden of care. A potential tortfeasor who faces the prospect of paying damages for the full amount of the victim's injury will take the reasonable level of care.

To see this, suppose the likelihood of an injury occurring is 90 percent when the potential tortfeasor does not take care, and 10 percent when he does take care. Suppose also that the cost of taking care is $50. Finally, suppose the injury loss that the victim will suffer from an accident involving the tortfeasor is $100. The incremental benefit from taking care is the injury probability differential, 80 percent, multiplied by the loss from the injury, $100. Since the incremental burden of care, $50, is less than the incremental harm avoided by care, $80, taking care is reasonable (or socially desirable).

To simplify the remaining argument, assume liability is strict, which means that the potential tortfeasor will have to pay damages whenever he injures a victim, regardless of whether he took care. If the potential tortfeasor takes care, he will pay damages with probability 0.1. The expected value of liability is therefore $0.1 \times \$100 = \$10$. Thus, if the potential tortfeasor takes care, he suffers the cost of taking care plus the expected liability, which is $\$50 + \$10 = \$60$. If the potential tortfeasor does not take care, he bears the expected liability, which is $0.9 \times \$100 = \$90$. Given that it is more costly not to take care than to take care, the potential tortfeasor will take care.

Now suppose the victim has full insurance and the court reduces the victim's damages award by the amount of his insurance. This means that the victim receives nothing for damages. If the potential tortfeasor is aware that the victim will not receive a damages award, he will compare the cost of taking care with the cost of not taking care under the assumption that he will not have to pay damages to the victim. Under these conditions, the potential tortfeasor suffers a cost of $50 if he takes care, and a cost of $0 if he does not take care. Clearly, the potential tortfeasor will choose not to take care. Thus, if the court *does not* apply the collateral source rule (that is, reduces the victim's damages award to zero), the potential tortfeasor will not have an incentive to take care, even though taking care is the decision a reasonable person would adopt. But if the court applies the collateral source rule, the potential tortfeasor will take care.

One might argue that it does not matter that the tortfeasor decides not to take care in the foregoing example. The victim is not really injured in the event of an accident, because he has full insurance. But this view is mistaken.

Imagine a world in which all tort victims have full insurance. The fact that the victims are insured does not mean that injuries are costless. Insurance does not eliminate injury costs. In a competitive insurance market, the charge to the customer for insuring against a specific loss will be equal to the expected payout of the insurer.[51] Rather than eliminating losses, insurance spreads losses over time and across individuals.

Given that insurance spreads losses without eliminating them, the socially optimal outcome – that is, the outcome that reduces the overall accident losses and avoidance costs borne by society to the lowest level – is for potential tortfeasors to exercise a reasonable level of care, and for insurance to be used to spread the residual risks that remain.[52] This optimal outcome can be achieved under the collateral source rule. It cannot be achieved under a rule that permits courts to deduct the insurance payouts from damages awards.

This analysis suggests that abolishing the collateral source rule leads to undesirable outcomes with respect to not only the level of care, but also the level of insurance coverage. In the absence of a threat to pay compensatory damages, potential tortfeasors will not take care. The decision not to take care increases the risk of injury to potential victims,[53] which in turn increases the price of insurance coverage. With insurance more expensive, fewer people will be able to afford it, and those who are unable to afford it may impose greater costs on government aid programs.

Punitive Damages

The purpose of punitive damages is to punish and deter. To gain a deeper understanding of punitive damages, we should first examine why compensatory damages are not sufficient for this purpose.

The case law and commentary have offered numerous justifications for punitive damages: to provide full compensation when compensatory damages are inadequate, to ensure deterrence when compensatory damages are unlikely to deter harmful conduct (because the probability of detection is low, or because compensation falls short of the actual injury), to encourage people to channel transactions through the market by eliminating the gains from expropriation of property or other personal entitlements, to express the community's abhorrence at the defendant's conduct, to

---

[51] *See, e.g.,* Steven Shavell, *On Moral Hazard and Insurance,* 93 Q. J. ECON. 541, 545 (1979).

[52] Steven Shavell, *On Liability and Insurance,* 13 BELL J. ECON. 120 (1982).

[53] Is there any evidence that statutes abolishing or modifying the collateral source rule have led to inferior outcomes? A study of accidental deaths finds that collateral source reform is positively associated with higher rates of accidental death in the United States. Paul Rubin & Joanna Shepherd, *Tort Reform and Accidental Deaths,* 50 J. LAW & ECON. 221 (2007). A study of medical malpractice finds that collateral source reform is associated with a greater frequency of medical errors, Toshiaki Iizuka, *Does Higher Medical Malpractice Pressure Deter Medical Errors?,* 36 J. LAW & ECON. 161 (2013).

discourage violent self-help, and to relieve pressure on the criminal justice system by giving victims an option to use tort law to punish wrongdoers.[54]

However, if we focus on deterrence, which is the fundamental purpose, two justifications span the plausible arguments for punitive damages. One is the *loss-internalization rationale*: Punitive damages may be necessary for deterrence purposes because a compensatory award may fail to internalize to the offender the full costs to society of his conduct. The other is the *gain-elimination rationale*: Punitive damages may be necessary for deterrence purposes to eliminate the prospect of gain to the offender from his tortious conduct.

The loss-internalization rationale is typically offered to support the imposition of punitive damages when the offender's tortious conduct is unlikely to be detected.[55] Suppose, for example, that the offender engages in a fraudulent practice that permits him to steal $100 from one person every day. Since $100 is not enough money to motivate many people to bring suit, especially when lawyers' fees are often an order of magnitude higher, only a fraction of the offender's victims will take the time to sue him in court. Suppose only one out of every ten of his victims files a lawsuit against him. To internalize to the offender the full cost to society of his conduct, the offender should be required to pay a judgment, in every case that comes to court, that is ten times the size of the compensatory award of $100. The total award would then amount to $1,000, which consists of a compensatory award of $100 and a punitive award of $900.

The loss-internalization rationale implies that a multiplier equal to the reciprocal of the probability of liability should be applied to compensatory damages. The punitive award is derived by simply subtracting the compensatory award from the total damages award.

The gain-internalization rationale is based on the notion that *complete deterrence* — the removal of any incentive to engage in the tortious conduct of the offender — requires a penalty that ensures that the offender cannot profit from his conduct.[56] Suppose, for example, that the offender gains $200 in a fraudulent transaction that imposes a loss on the victim of only $100. To offer a specific example, the offender fraudulently acquires an item (e.g., a rare coin) resulting in a loss of $100 to the victim, and then sells the item for $200. Under the gain-elimination theory, the total

---

[54] This list of justifications was offered by Judge Posner in Kemezy v. Peters, 79 F.3d 33, 34–36 (7th Cir. 1996). For an examination of the history of punitive damages with an emphasis on purpose, *see* Anthony J. Sebok, *What Did Punitive Damages Do? Why Misunderstanding the History of Punitive Damages Matters Today*, 78 Chi.-Kent L. Rev. 163 (2003).

[55] *See* A. Mitchell Polinsky & Steven Shavell, *Punitive Damages: An Economic Analysis*, 111 Harv. L. Rev. 870 (1998). An implication of the loss-internalization approach is that punitive damages become equivalent to societal damages; *see* Catherine M. Sharkey, *Punitive Damages as Societal Damages*, 113 Yale L. J. 347 (2003). On optimal damages multipliers generally, *see* Keith N. Hylton & Thomas J. Miceli, *Should Tort Damages Be Multiplied?*, 21 J. Law, Econ. & Organ. 388 (2005).

[56] Keith N. Hylton, *Punitive Damages and the Economic Theory of Penalties*, 87 Geo. L. J. 421, 423 (1998).

damages award would have to be set at a level of at least $200 to ensure that the offender gets no profit out of his conduct. If the total damages award is set at $200, this would imply a compensatory award of $100 (the victim's loss) and a punitive award of (at least) $100.

In the case of the offender who steals $100 from one new victim every day, the gain-elimination and loss-internalization theories would imply the same damages award. If the offender steals $100 from someone every day, he both imposes a loss of $100 and receives a gain of $100. If only one of every ten of the victims sues, then a multiplier of ten would be necessary both to eliminate the gain to the offender and to internalize the loss to society. The only important difference between the gain-elimination and loss-internalization theories as applied in this example is that the loss-internalization theory implies a precise value for the punitive damages award, $900, while the gain-elimination theory implies that $900 is the *minimum* punitive award appropriate for the case.

Jacque v. Steenberg Homes[57] illustrates the different implications of the loss-internalization and gain-elimination approaches to punitive damages. Steenberg Homes had to deliver a mobile home to a customer. They had a choice: use a narrow winding road that was covered with up to seven feet of snow in some parts, or drive across Jacque's property. After being denied permission by Jacque to use his property, the Steenberg Homes employees cleared a path on Jacque's property and then drove their trucks across the property anyway. Jacque brought a trespass claim against Steenberg Homes and was awarded $1 in compensatory damages and $100,000 in punitive damages. The compensatory portion of the award was only $1 because the trespass did not harm Jacque's property.

Could the punitive judgment in *Jacque* be justified under the gain-elimination or loss-internalization approaches to determining punitive damages? Consider the gain-elimination approach first. Under gain elimination, a court would have to assess the gain the defendant received through his tortious conduct. In *Jacque*, Steenberg Homes gained by avoiding the cost of delivering the mobile home by way of the narrow road that was covered in snow. Suppose the cost of using the road, and therefore the gain to Steenberg Homes from trespassing over Jacque's property instead of using the road, was as high as $5,000 – taking into account the man-hours and machinery necessary to clear the road. Suppose, also, that only one of every twenty victims of similar trespasses brings suit. Under these assumptions, the size of the damages award necessary to eliminate any gain on the part of the defendants would be a minimum of $100,000.

To see this, notice that to ensure that Steenberg Homes cannot profit from its trespass, the *expected damages award* would have to be greater than the $5,000 Steenberg Homes would gain by trespassing. The expected damages award is equal to the actual damages award multiplied by the probability of its imposition. If only

[57] 563 N.W.2d 154 (Wis. 1997).

one of twenty victims brings suit for trespass, Steenberg Homes would calculate its expected damages award by multiplying the actual damages award that they anticipate by 5 percent. Since $100,000 multiplied by 5 percent is equal to $5,000, the damages award necessary to eliminate the gain from trespassing to Steenberg Homes is an amount no less than $100,000. Thus, if the actual damages award is at least $100,000, the expected damages award to Steenberg Homes will be at least $5,000, which would strip any foreseeable gains from trespassing.

This analysis implies that the punitive award in *Jacque* is defensible as an application of the gain-elimination approach. The foregoing example suggests that under plausible assumptions, the punitive award may have been the minimum amount necessary to strip the gain from the defendant's trespass.

Now consider the loss-internalization approach applied to *Jacque*. Under loss internalization, a court would multiply the compensatory award by the reciprocal of the probability of liability. Thus, a court would have to focus on the probability that Steenberg Homes would be held liable for a typical trespass. To justify a $100,000 punitive award under the loss-internalization approach, the rate at which victims sue Steenberg Homes would have to be precisely one out of every 100,000 trespass victims. This seems unlikely, and it is moreover doubtful that a court would be able to determine if it were true.

So far, I have focused on approaches to calculating punitive awards. But the two approaches reflect different philosophies toward punishment. The loss-internalization approach aims to make the tortfeasor pay the full social costs of his offensive conduct. If the tortfeasor's gain from his conduct exceeds the full costs, he will not be deterred by the threat of a punitive damages award determined by the loss-internalization method. In contrast, the gain-elimination approach aims to eliminate the prospect of gain to the tortfeasor from his offensive conduct, and thereby to completely deter the offensive conduct by making it unprofitable.

The loss-internalization approach is analogous to setting out a tollbooth requiring the driver to pay a fee to continue on the road. The tollbooth is not there to prevent drivers from using the road; it merely forces them to determine whether paying the fee is worthwhile. By contrast, the gain-elimination approach is analogous, in its effect, to a road block or barrier that seeks to prohibit the driver from going forward, regardless of how much he would be willing to pay to continue on the road.

Let's return to the distinction between property rules (for example, trespass) and liability rules (negligence and strict liability), discussed earlier in this chapter, and in more detail in Chapter 2. Recall, from Chapter 2, that property rules are appropriate in two settings. One is where both the allocation of rights is unambiguous and the cost of gaining consent for the transfer of any of those rights is low. Battery and trespass law provide the obvious examples; in both areas rights are clear, and it is easy for a potential tortfeasor to seek permission before invading the rights of the victim. The second setting in which the property rule is appropriate is where the tortfeasor's conduct should be completely deterred because society gains nothing by allowing it to continue. The standard examples are reckless acts, such as playing with a loaded gun in a crowded area or intentionally driving in the wrong direction on a highway. Liability rules are appropriate in the remaining settings not encompassed within the two just described.

The gain-elimination approach is consistent with property rules, because gain elimination aims to completely deter tortious conduct – just as the injunctive remedies associated with trespass law aim to completely deter threatened trespasses. The loss-internalization approach is consistent with liability rules because it seeks to shift the losses suffered by victims from the tortfeasor's conduct back to the tortfeasor, without completely deterring his conduct.

The gain-elimination approach is most consistent with both the law and the actual outcomes of punitive damages cases. All courts hold that *punitive damages can be awarded only in cases where the defendant's conduct is intentional, malicious, or reckless.* This is the sort of conduct society should seek to completely deter.

Beyond the basic *limitation* to willful or reckless conduct, courts have been flexible in their descriptions of the *purposes* of punitive damages. Some courts have provided a list of factors that can be used to determine the appropriateness of a punitive award.[58] Although not exclusive, such factors include (1) the *reprehensibility of the defendant's conduct*, (2) the *harm likely to result from the defendant's conduct* or the *harm that actually occurred*, (3) the *defendant's awareness*, (4) the *profit derived by the defendant from his conduct*, (5) the *wealth of the defendant*,[59] (6) the *degree of concealment*, (7) the *existence and frequency of similar past conduct*, and (8) the *costs of litigation*.[60]

The one class of punitive damages cases in which the loss-internalization principle may be appropriate consists of those involving the vicarious liability of an employer. Take, for example an employee who commits fraud against customers of the employer, where the employer has not adopted a policy of fraud. Courts have assessed punitive damages awards against employers in such cases.[61] However, the employer's conduct, if innocent, is not the malicious or reckless sort that society wishes to completely deter. On the other hand, a failure to require the employer to pay the full social costs of his agent's tort would leave employers with inadequate

---

[58] *See* Green Oil Co. v. Hornsby, 539 So.2d 218, 223–224 (Ala. 1989) (quoting Aetna Life Ins. Co. v. Lavoie, 505 So.2d 1050, 1062 (Ala. 1987) (Houston, J., concurring specially)). The U.S. Supreme Court subsequently approved of these factors in Pacific Mutual Life Ins. v. Haslip, 499 U.S. 1 (1991). *See also* Garnes v. Fleming Landfill, Inc., 413 S.E.2d 897, 909 (W.Va. 1991) (establishing punitive damages factors for jury instruction and trial court review based on principles inferred from *Green Oil* and *Haslip*); Farmers Insurance Exchange v. Shirley, 958 P.2d 1040, 1053 (Wyo. 1998) (holding the jury should be instructed on the *Green Oil* factors with regard to punitive damages). Other courts have implemented similar but not identical factors as those listed in *Green Oil. See, e.g.*, Alamo Nat'l Bank v. Kraus, 616 S.W.2d 908, 910 (Tex. 1981).

[59] On the importance of wealth in determining damages, *see* Jennifer H. Arlen, *Should Defendants' Wealth Matter?*, 21 J. LEGAL STUD. 413 (1992); Keith N. Hylton, *A Theory of Wealth and Punitive Damages*, 17 WIDENER L. J. 927 (2008).

[60] Green Oil Co., 539 So.2d at 223–224.

[61] *Haslip*, 499 U.S. at 1.

incentives to monitor their employees. The loss-internalization approach is appropriate as a means of requiring employers to take into account the full costs to society of the torts their employees commit.

VII. THE CONSTITUTION AND PUNITIVE DAMAGES

The Fourteenth Amendment of the U.S. Constitution provides that "No State shall... deprive any person of life, liberty, or property without due process of law." The U.S. Supreme Court has in recent years begun to apply this provision, called the Due Process Clause, to review punitive damages judgments. The Supreme Court's case law in this area is still in a developmental stage, and some members of the Court have questioned the entire project of subjecting punitive awards to constitutional review.[62] Nevertheless, the Court has developed guidelines designed to constrain the discretion of lower courts in issuing punitive damages. However, the high level of controversy surrounding the constitutional review of punitive awards, within the Court and among lower courts, suggests that the guidelines are likely to be revised over time or may be jettisoned in the end.

Because of this controversy, I find it preferable to discuss the Court's decisions in light of the deterrence theories presented in the previous part of this chapter. The Court may eventually find itself back at the starting point in this area of the law, and given this it would be more helpful to the student to examine the implications of deterrence theory for the Court's decisions rather than focus exclusively on the particular arguments, varying greatly in persuasiveness, used by the Court.

Should one interpret the Due Process Clause to constrain the discretion of state courts in issuing punitive damages awards? If the Due Process Clause constrains the discretion of courts under any circumstances, then it should be applicable to the awarding of punitive damages as well. Suppose, for example, that a court determined punitive awards by throwing a dart, blindfolded, at a board with various numbers on it. Most observers would view this as a highly defective process, violating the norm of due process. The same could be said of a process in which courts determine guilt by flipping a coin. Thus, as a general matter, the Due Process Clause should be applicable to punitive damages verdicts, just as it should be applicable to any other type of legislative or judicial decision.

There is a big difference, however, between an arbitrary process and a process whose outcomes appear to be difficult to predict with precision.[63] The Supreme

---

[62] BMW of N. Am., Inc. v. Gore, 517 U.S. 559, 598 (1996) (Scalia, J., joined by Thomas, J., dissenting) ("Since the Constitution does not make [the size of punitive damages awards] any of our business, the Court's activities in this area are an unjustified incursion into the province of state governments.").

[63] On the question of predictability, the evidence suggests that punitive awards tend to have a predictable relationship to compensatory awards. *See* Theodore Eisenberg, John Goerdt, Brian Ostrom, David Rottman, & Martin T. Wells, *The Predictability of Punitive Damages*, 26 J. LEGAL STUD. 623 (1997). For a skeptical view of the predictability problem in punitive damages, *see* Michael L. Rustad, *Unraveling Punitive Damages: Current Data and Further Inquiry*, 1998 WIS. L. REV. 15 (1998).

Court has leaned in favor of the predictability concern in reviewing punitive damages verdicts.

In *BMW v. Gore*,[64] the Court held that a punitive damages verdict must satisfy three requirements: (1) it must be reasonable in view of the reprehensibility of the defendant's conduct, (2) it must be reasonable in view of the level of compensatory damages, and (3) it must be reasonable in view of the level of civil penalties that would be imposed under the state's law for the same conduct. Applying these guidelines, the Court struck down the punitive award issued in *Gore*, $2 million, as unconstitutionally excessive.

Gore involved BMW's policy of applying touch-up paint jobs to cars that had suffered minor damage in transport from one of their production plants to the car dealer. BMW did not disclose the touch-ups to customers. Testimony suggested that touched-up cars were worth 10 percent less than new cars that had not been damaged. Since the BMW model that the plaintiff bought was valued at $40,000, the compensatory damages claim was $4,000. The trial court determined that only one out of 1,000 customers who had purchased touched-up cars had brought suit, and on this basis calculated a punitive judgment of $4 million. The punitive judgment was later reduced by the Alabama Supreme Court to $2 million.

The trial court's approach can be examined under the loss-internalization and gain-elimination theories discussed previously. Under the loss-internalization approach, a court should aim to internalize to BMW the full social costs of its conduct. Here BMW transferred $4,000 from the customer to itself by refusing to disclose that the car had received a paint touch-up. If the rate at which BMW was held liable for this conduct was only one out of a thousand instances, then the appropriate internalization penalty would be $4 million (that is $4,000 × 1,000). The internalization approach requires application of a multiplier to the compensatory award, where the multiplier is equal to the reciprocal of the probability of liability. This approach would require the court to issue a compensatory award of $4,000 and a punitive award of $3,996,000. The court's award exceeded the appropriate amount by $4,000, but the difference is not great relative to the total.

Note that the loss-internalization approach requires precision. If the Alabama trial court was incorrect in determining the rate at which BMW would be held liable for its conduct, then its damages award would either overdeter or underdeter. Some commentators criticized the award on the ground that the court had used the wrong multiplier, one that was far too high from the loss-internalization perspective.[65]

Under the gain-elimination approach, a court should aim to ensure that BMW could not gain, prospectively, by its conduct. Since the diminution of the car's value reflected a dollar-for-dollar transfer from the customer to BMW, the defendant's gain was equal to the customer's $4,000 loss. If only one out of one thousand victims

[64]   517 U.S. 559 (1996).

[65]   Polinsky & Shavell, *supra* note 55.

brought suit, the minimum gain-stripping penalty would be $4 million, the same amount as the damages suggested by the loss-internalization approach. However, there is an important difference. Under the gain-elimination approach, the punitive award must be sufficient to eliminate the prospect of gain, which means that once the minimum gain-eliminating award is determined, a court could go above its level without violating the complete deterrence policy. The reason for this difference is that gain elimination is appropriate in instances where the tortfeasor's conduct serves no socially beneficial purpose. Loss internalization is the appropriate policy when the conduct is, as a general matter, socially beneficial.

The conduct at issue in *Gore* was a form of theft, if we take the findings of the trial court as valid. Theft serves no socially beneficial purpose; it is nothing more than a transfer of property from one person to another. It does not add to society's resources; it subtracts by using up resources to transfer wealth. This perspective suggests that the appropriate punishment policy to apply in *Gore* is gain elimination. And if gain elimination is the appropriate policy in *Gore*, the $4 million award would be defensible on deterrence grounds.

The key objection to this line of reasoning is that the facts of *Gore* are a bit more complicated than this argument suggests. Cars will inevitably be damaged in the course of transport. If every little repair of a scratch or nick had to be disclosed, car sellers might not be able to sell many of their cars, because customers would demand an unscratched vehicle. This suggests that there should be a threshold below which disclosures would not be required. If BMW reasonably believed that the touch-up on the car it sold to the plaintiff in *Gore* fell below the threshold for disclosure, then a finding of reprehensible misrepresentation would have been improper.[66] The defensibility of the large punitive judgment in *Gore* hinges almost entirely on the reprehensibility of BMW's conduct.

Gore was the Supreme Court's first opinion to strike down a punitive damages judgment on the ground that it was excessive under the Due Process Clause.[67] Its three-part test – asking whether the award is reasonable in light of reprehensibility, reasonable in relation to compensatory damages, and reasonable in relationship to civil penalties – appears unobjectionable as a set of principles. However, in application the *Gore* test has resulted in a significant change from the approach the Court adopted earlier in *Pacific Mutual Life Insurance Co. v. Haslip*,[68] where it held that the key question in any constitutional due process review of punitive damages is whether the judgment is reasonable in light of deterrence interests. The *Haslip* doctrine required a court of constitutional review to ensure that lower courts

---

[66] BMW's evidence that its disclosure policy was consistent with the laws of 25 states provided substantial evidence that it conduct was not reprehensible; *see* BMW v. Gore, 517 U.S., at 565.

[67] In an earlier case, Honda Motor Co., Ltd., v. Oberg, 512 U.S. 415 (1994), the Supreme Court struck down a punitive damages award on the ground that the *procedure* of appellate review was constitutionally defective under the Due Process Clause.

[68] 499 U.S. 1 (1991).

establish procedures that effectively ensure reasonableness in this sense. This would require some assessment of the deterrence interest. The *Gore* doctrine, by contrast, shifts the focus away from deterrence, and toward the burdensomeness of the award on the defendant.

The first *Gore* factor, reprehensibility of the defendant's conduct, is obviously relevant to an analysis of deterrence. However, a reviewing court should tread with care over this terrain. The attribution of a particular mental state to a guilty defendant (malice versus negligence) is at the core of the responsibilities of a trial court. An appellate court that invades this area of responsibility does so without direct access to the evidence used to make such a judgment. A reviewing court could require a high proof standard – such as "clear and convincing" rather than "preponderance of the evidence."[69] But a decision by an appellate court to effectively overrule a trial court's assessment of mental state, or of the proper punishment that should be associated with a particular mental state, is a step beyond its traditional area of authority and comparative expertise.

The second factor, the amount of the compensatory award in relation to the punitive judgment, is of marginal relevance to an analysis that focuses on deterrence, the primary purpose of a punitive judgment. As the *Jacque* case shows, a compensatory award of $1 could be accompanied by a substantial punitive award ($100,000), and yet this might be reasonable in light of the deterrence interests at stake.

The third factor, the relationship between the punitive judgment and the civil penalties that a state would impose for the same conduct, is of unclear relevance to a deterrence analysis. The rules on penalty imposition may be so vague that it is impossible to determine whether the civil penalties are reasonably related to the punitive judgment. If the state's legislature or regulatory offices have entered into a cozy relationship with the defendant, the civil penalties may not be at a level necessary to deter tortious conduct by the defendant.

In *State Farm v. Campbell*,[70] the plaintiffs, the Campbells, had executed a reckless driving maneuver, forcing oncoming cars off the road, and causing the death of one driver and severe injury of another. State Farm, their insurer, refused to settle the lawsuit against the plaintiffs for the traffic accident even though settlement offers within the policy limit were tendered. After a Utah trial court issued a judgment exceeding the plaintiffs' policy limit, State Farm informed the plaintiffs that they were responsible for the judgment and suggested they put their house up for sale. Eventually, State Farm paid the entire judgment. The plaintiffs brought a lawsuit accusing State Farm of bad faith in the insurance settlement process, a species of fraud. The trial court, in the bad faith lawsuit, gave the plaintiffs a compensatory award of $1 million and a punitive award of $145 million.

---

[69] Owens-Corning Fiberglass Corp. v. Garrett, 682 A.2d 1143 (Md. 1996) (requiring clear and convincing evidence of reprehensible conduct).

[70] 538 U.S. 408 (2003).

The Supreme Court held that the punitive award was unconstitutionally excessive. The main reason was that the evidence did not, in the Court's view, support the Utah courts' conclusion that State Farm's degree of reprehensibility justified such a large punitive damages award. But the Court did not suggest any procedural safeguards, such as a clear and convincing evidence standard,[71] that would minimize the risk that a future court would issue a finding of reprehensibility on weak evidence. Rather than establishing constitutionally based procedural rules to govern the finding of reprehensibility, the Court took the more drastic step of overruling the trial court on the basis of the first *Gore* factor, the lack of a reasonable relationship between the punitive award and the degree of the defendant's reprehensibility.

Applying the second *Gore* factor, the ratio of the punitive to the compensatory award, the Court suggested, for the first time, that a single digit ratio is generally required by the Due Process Clause. The requirement was hedged with so many qualifications that it could be violated in a particular case – for example, a case with a small compensatory award – without requiring a finding of unconstitutionality. But the announcement signaled to lower courts that ratios exceeding a single digit would attract greater scrutiny on appeal. The ratio in Gore, 145 to 1, was deemed excessive under the Court's newly announced ratio test.

Applying the third Gore factor, the ratio of the punitive award to state penalties, the Court held that the punitive award was excessive in light of civil and criminal penalties Utah applied to similar conduct – such as Utah's $10,000 penalty for an act of fraud. Other potential penalties, such as the loss of a business license, were considered too remote to factor significantly into the analysis.

In finding that the evidence of reprehensibility did not support the large punitive award, the Court noted that some of the evidence used by the trial court involved "dissimilar acts." The particular dissimilar act identified by the Court that had been cited most prominently by the trial court was evidence of bad faith conduct in the processing of first-party insurance claims – which the Court viewed as dissimilar to the third-party (liability) insurance claim at issue in *State Farm*. The Court's decision on this matter could be interpreted as scrutinizing or regulating evidence interpretation at the trial court level, an activity appellate courts avoid because of their remoteness from the fact finding process. Trial courts have an unquestioned comparative advantage in the interpretation of facts. Moreover, if a trial court is trying to determine whether a certain act reflects bad faith, evidence on analogous and arguably dissimilar acts by the same defendant might be useful in the process of inferring intent.

The Court's single digit ratio announcement, based on the second *Gore* factor, appears to have been conjured out of thin air and may be inconsistent in many cases with the deterrence purpose of punitive damages. Suppose, for example, the tortfeasor gains $1,200 from his malicious act and at the same time imposes a loss of only $100 on the victim – for example, the tortfeasor steals a rare coin with a market

---

[71] Owens-Corning Fiberglass Corp. v. Garrett, 682 A.2d 1143 (Md. 1996).

value of $100 and sells it to a person who is willing to pay $1,200. If the trial court tries to issue an award that eliminates the tortfeasor's gain, it will have to set the punitive award at a level at least as great as $1,100, coupled with a compensatory award of $100. But this would generate a punitive to compensatory ratio of 11, violating the single digit ratio rule. If, instead, the trial court complies with the single digit ratio rule and imposes a punitive award no greater than $900, the tortfeasor will still profit from his theft and will learn to factor in the single digit multiplier as just a cost of doing business. Instead of deterring the tortfeasor, the single-digit-constrained punitive award may function as a tax that spurs him on to yet more spectacular violations to earn a suitable profit.

In *Philip Morris v. Williams*,[72] the Oregon Supreme Court upheld a $79.5 million dollar punitive damages judgment against Philip Morris for fraudulent practices in the sale of cigarettes. This time, the court did not rely on the *Gore* analysis – which has been called a *substantive due process* analysis because it focuses on the size of the award rather than the procedure by which the award is determined. The Court struck down the punitive judgment on the theory that the Oregon courts had issued and upheld the award to punish the defendant for the injuries suffered by Oregon victims similar to the plaintiff. The Court issued a new procedural safeguard: *Injuries to nonlitigant victims can be considered in the course of determining the defendant's degree of reprehensibility, but the punitive award cannot be designed expressly to punish the defendant for those injuries to nonlitigants.*

The new procedural safeguard of *Philip Morris* does not clearly impose any substantive constraint on the decisions of lower courts. It instructs lower courts not to justify a punitive award by referring to harms to victims other than the plaintiff. However, lower courts are free, under the rule, to refer to such harms in assessing the defendant's degree of reprehensibility, and the defendant's reprehensibility degree can be used to justify a larger punitive award.

In its post-*Gore* decisions, the Supreme Court has been reluctant to consider the implications of deterrence theory and at the same time keen to invade the traditional territory of trial courts. The punitive awards in *State Farm* and in *Philip Morris*, like the award in *Gore*, can be defended on the basis of deterrence policy. The Court made little effort to examine the deterrence function of punitive damages in these opinions, a surprising occurrence in view of the Court's rather sophisticated treatment of the deterrence policy in *Haslip*. The decision to invade an area of trial court specialty – specifically, the grading of fault or reprehensibility – was premature, given the procedural options available, such as a clear and convincing evidence requirement.

The development of constitutional analysis of punitive damages is far from over, given the discordant opinions by members of the Supreme Court. The Court could enhance the predictability of its punitive damages decisions by considering the

---

[72] 549 U.S. 346 (2007). For a discussion of the retribution and deterrence arguments in the case, *see* Mark A. Geistfeld, *Punitive Damages, Retribution, and Due Process*, 81 S. Cal. L. Rev. 263 (2008).

implications of deterrence policy in its review of punitive awards. Another way the Court could enhance predictability is by retreating to the less interventionist doctrine of *Haslip*, which gives lower courts discretion to determine appropriate awards on deterrence grounds.

VIII. DAMAGES AND OPERATION OF THE TORT SYSTEM

To describe tort damages as serving a compensatory function and a deterrence function does not quite do service to the full role played by damages in the tort system. Damages awards determine the operational scope of the tort system.[73] They determine whether a tort victim will file a suit, and, if he files, whether he will settle or pursue the case to a final verdict, or indeed whether a tort victim effectively will have a right of action at all.

Filing a Tort Suit

Suppose a victim suffers a loss of $1,000 as a result of a tort committed by an injurer. For example, suppose the victim is a driver injured in an accident due to the negligence of another driver.

We have assumed in much of the previous discussion that the victim will file a tort suit against the injurer, that the court will evaluate the injurer's conduct to determine whether he was negligent, and that the court eventually will issue a verdict for the plaintiff or for the defendant.

But there is no guarantee that the victim will file a tort suit, even if the injurer's negligence is obvious. Why? The victim's incentive to file a suit depends on the amount of his expected damages in relation to the cost of litigation.

The payoff that a victim gets from filing suit is equal to his damages award. But the damages award is not certain; the court may find that the injurer is not guilty of negligence. Thus, in determining the value of a legal claim, the victim must consider the probability of winning the lawsuit as well as the damages award.

To simplify this presentation, I will assume that the damages award compensates the victim for the entire value of his loss. I will assume also that the plaintiff is rationally motivated to sue, in the sense that he is solely interested in the monetary value of his lawsuit; he is not suing in part to harass the defendant.

I introduced the concept of *expected value* in Chapter 2. Recall that the expected value of an event is equal to the probability that the event will happen multiplied by

---

[73] Operational effect can be distinguished from doctrinal coherence in torts, as well as other areas of the law, as stressed by Guido Calabresi in his book THE COST OF ACCIDENTS: A LEGAL AND ECONOMIC ANALYSIS (Yale Univ. Press 1970). One scholar, developing this point, suggested that tort law should be abolished because it is too costly relative to its benefits. *See* Stephen D. Sugarman, *Doing Away with Tort Law*, 73 CAL. L. REV. 555 (1985).

the dollar value of the payoff (or loss) from the event (Expected Value = Probability × Value). The concept of expected value is crucial to understanding the role played by damages in the operation of the tort system.

The victim (plaintiff) will bring a tort suit only if the expected value of the damages award is greater than his cost of litigation. The expected value of the damages award, to the plaintiff, is equal to the plaintiff's estimate of the probability of winning the lawsuit multiplied by the damages award. Thus, the plaintiff will file suit only if the probability of winning multiplied by the damages award is greater than the plaintiff's cost of litigation. Let W_p represent the plaintiff's estimate of the probability that he will win the lawsuit, L represent the plaintiff's loss, which is also the damages award, and C the cost of prosecuting a lawsuit. The victim will file a lawsuit if his *expected net payoff* from litigation, $W_p \times L - C$, is positive.

Even in instances where the injurer's negligence is obvious, the victim may not file a tort suit. To see this, suppose the plaintiff's estimate of the probability that he will win his lawsuit is 95 percent. Suppose that the loss he has suffered is $1,000. The victim's expected damages award is $0.95 \times \$1,000 = \$950$. If the victim's litigation cost is $100, the expected net payoff to the victim from suing is $950 − $100 = $850, and the victim will sue. However, if the victim's litigation cost is $960, the victim will have no incentive to sue because the expected net payoff is −$10.

It follows that one should observe a link between the cost of litigation and the size of damages awards. If litigation is very expensive, only victims who have suffered large losses will have an incentive to sue. Large damages awards in a particular area of tort litigation, such as medical malpractice, may be evidence that litigation is costly, and therefore only victims who have suffered large losses have incentives to sue, rather than evidence that juries are inclined toward giving generous awards.

Litigation costs also affect the tort system's potential to deter tortious conduct.[74] If high litigation costs make lawsuits prohibitively expensive for many victims, then injurers will not be forced to bear the full costs of their conduct. Suppose, for example, that an injurer's negligent conduct exposes each of four people to a 60 percent chance of being injured. Two of the people will suffer a loss of $1,000 and the other two will suffer a loss of $2,000. The expected value of the loss that the injurer imposes on society is therefore $3,600 ($0.60 \times \$1,000 + 0.60 \times \$1,000 + 0.60 \times \$2,000 + 0.60 \times \$2,000$). To induce the injurer to take the reasonable level of care (as determined by the Hand Formula), the injurer must be presented with an expected liability equal to the expected value of the loss he imposes on society, $3,600. Suppose the probability that a victim will prevail in a lawsuit against the injurer is 100 percent and the cost of bringing a lawsuit is $1,000. Under these

---

[74] Keith N. Hylton, *The Influence of Litigation Costs on Deterrence under Strict Liability and under Negligence*, 10 INT'L REV. L. & ECON. 161 (1990); Janusz A. Ordover, *Costly Litigation in the Model of Single Activity Accidents*, 7 J. LEGAL STUD. 243 (1978).

conditions, only the two victims who suffered a $2,000 loss will have an incentive to sue. This implies that the expected liability of the injurer is only $2,400 (0.60 × $2,000 + 0.60 × $2,000), which is too low to induce the injurer to take reasonable care. The injurer will have an incentive to take reasonable care only if, in addition to the expected liability of $2,400, the injurer's cost of litigation is equal to $1,200. However, there is obviously no guarantee that the injurer's cost of litigation will be sufficiently high to make up the shortfall in deterrence created by the litigation cost barrier to victims.

Filing Suit: Class Actions

Now let's consider the case of numerous victims. Suppose there are one hundred victims, each having suffered a loss of only $10 as the result of a tort committed by the same injurer. The cost of litigation for each victim is $100. No victim will have an incentive to bring suit. Even if the likelihood of winning is 100 percent, no victim will be able to gain a positive net payoff from a lawsuit (because the plaintiff would receive $10 in damages and pay $100 in litigation expenses). The result is that no victim presents a credible threat to sue, and, as a result, the injurer sees no reason to cease his tortious conduct.

One solution to this problem is the *class action*. Under the class action, the victims pursue their damages claims jointly and pool the litigation expenses. In the simple case where the only expense is proving the injurer's fault, and that is the same for every victim, the litigation cost for the entire class is the same as that for one victim, $100.

The class action device permits the tort system to serve its deterrence function in scenarios where numerous victims suffer small harms from some common tort committed by the injurer. For example, suppose 1,000 bank customers suffer a loss of $10 each as a result of some fraudulent practice by the bank. Without the class action device, the bank would see no need to worry about private litigation resulting from its practice.

Return the first example: One hundred victims suffer a loss of $10, and the cost of litigation is $100. The class action will be brought because the total class award $1,000 (100 × $10) is greater than the cost of class litigation ($100). However, note that the viability of a class action depends on several variables: class size, amount of loss, cost of litigation. For example, if the number of victims is only nine, then the total class award would be only $90, which is less than the cost of class litigation. Indeed, the class viability threshold in this example is ten. As long as the number of victims is greater than ten, the class action threat is credible, and the tort system can provide adequate deterrence.

It follows that for a credible threat to bring class litigation to exist, the number of victims in the class must exceed the class viability threshold, which is the ratio of the cost of class litigation to the per victim amount of damages.[75] Of course, I have simplified matters greatly by assuming in my example that the cost of class litigation is independent of the size of the class. In more complicated cases, the cost of class litigation would also include the average of idiosyncratic litigation expenditures that will be made on behalf of individual plaintiffs.

Filing Suit: American Rule versus British Rule

The foregoing discussion assumes that each party bears its own litigation costs, an arrangement known as the *American rule*. In most procedural systems in developed countries, courts have adopted the *British rule*, under which the losing party pays the reasonable litigation expenses of the prevailing party. The biggest component of litigation expenses is the lawyer's fee.

The incentive to sue under the British rule differs from the incentive to sue under the American rule.[76] The victim expects to pay his litigation expenses only if he loses under the British rule. Moreover, if he loses he pays not only his own litigation expenses but those of the defendant too. If the litigation expenses of the defendant are the same as those of the plaintiff, the expected value of bringing suit under the British rule is $W_p \times L - (1 - W_p) \times 2 \times C$. It follows that *if the plaintiff thinks he has a high chance of winning, he is more likely to bring suit under the British rule than under the American rule*. To see this, suppose that the plaintiff believes that his likelihood of winning is 0.95. If the loss is $1,000, and the cost of litigation for each party is $100, the plaintiff's expected net payoff from litigation under the British rule is $0.95 \times \$1,000 - 0.05 \times \$200 = \$950 - \$10 = \$940$. Recall that under the American the expected net payoff under the same conditions is only $850. If the cost of litigation (for each party) is $960, the plaintiff's expected net payoff under the British rule is $950 - \$96 = \$854$. This is far greater than the expected net payoff under the American rule, which under the same assumptions is negative.

Suppose the plaintiff thinks he has a low chance of winning – say, with a probability of only 0.15. Under the American rule, the plaintiff's expected net payoff from

---

[75] Keith N. Hylton, *The Economics of Class Actions and Class Action Waivers*, 23 Sup. Ct. Econ. Rev. (2016). For more general discussions of incentives to sue and class actions, *see* George Priest, *The Economics of Class Actions*, 9 Kan. J. L. Pub. & Pol'y 481 (2000); Thomas Ulen, *An Introduction to the Law and Economics of Class Action Litigation*, 32 Eur. J. L. & Econ. 185 (2011); Samuel Issacharoff, *Assembling Class Actions*, 90 Wash. U. L. Rev. 699 (2013).

[76] Steven Shavell, *Suit, Settlement, and Trial: A Theoretical Analysis under Alternative Methods for the Allocation of Legal Costs*, 11 J. Legal Stud. 55 (1982). In addition to affecting incentives to sue, litigation cost allocation rules may alter expectations regarding trial outcomes and even incentives to take care, see Keith N. Hylton, *Litigation Cost Allocation Rules and Compliance with the Negligence Standard*, 22 J. Legal Stud. 457 (1993); Herbert M. Kritzer, *Fee Regimes and the Cost of Civil Justice*, 28 Civ. Just. Q. 344 (2009).

litigation is $0.15 \times \$1,000 - \$100 = \$150 - \$100 = \$50$. Under the British rule his expected net payoff from litigation is $0.15 \times \$1,000 - 0.85 \times \$200 = \$150 - \$170 = -\$20$. It follows that *if the plaintiff thinks he has a low chance of winning, he is less likely to bring suit under the British rule than under the American rule.*

The upshot of this brief examination of litigation cost allocation rules is that the British rule tends to promote high-quality lawsuits and to discourage low-quality lawsuits, in comparison to the American rule. But this is just a partial conclusion. Some lawsuits appear to be unlikely to win because they involve novel expansions of the law. Taking this into account, the British rule will tend to discourage the pursuit of novel legal theories of recovery, in comparison to the American rule.[77]

Settling a Tort Suit

Even if the victim decides to file a tort suit, he may not pursue the claim all the way to a final judgment in court. The reason is that the victim and the injurer may choose to settle the dispute before it reaches a final judgment – or perhaps before the dispute even gets to court. They may even settle on the steps leading to the courthouse door.

Why would the plaintiff choose to settle his claim? If the plaintiff can receive a payment from the defendant that is at least as large as the expected net payoff from his lawsuit, he will prefer to settle his lawsuit in exchange for the payment from the defendant. Recall that the plaintiff's expected net payoff from a lawsuit is equal to his expected damages award less the cost of litigation, $W_p \times L - C$. If the plaintiff receives a settlement offer from the defendant that is greater than this amount, he will settle.[78]

Will the defendant be willing to pay the plaintiff the amount that the plaintiff demands to settle? The defendant will consider his expected total cost from the lawsuit. The expected total cost of the lawsuit to the defendant is equal to his estimate of the expected damages award plus the defendant's cost of litigation. The defendant's expected damages award is equal to his estimate of the probability that

[77] J. Robert S. Prichard, *A Systematic Approach to Comparative Law: The Effect of Cost, Fee, and Financing. Rules on the Development of the Substantive Law*, 17 J. Legal Stud. 451 (1988); Keith N. Hylton, *Fee Shifting and Predictability of Law*, 71 Chi.-Kent L. Rev. 427 (1995). If the litigating parties are in a contractual relationship, the choice between British and American rules may not affect incentives because the parties can contract around the rule, *see* John Donohue, *Opting for the British Rule: Or, If Posner and Shavell Can't Remember the Coase Theorem, Who Will?* 104 Harv. L. Rev. 1093 (1991).

[78] I assume here, as in the previous part, that the plaintiff is solely interested in the monetary value of his lawsuit. He is not suing, for example, to harass the defendant. It should be clear that if the plaintiff sues in part to harass the defendant, he may not settle in exchange for a payment equal to the expected value of the lawsuit. For analysis of settlement incentives among parties who are rationally motivated, *see* Steven Shavell, *Suit, Settlement, and Trial: A Theoretical Analysis under Alternative Methods for the Allocation of Legal Costs*, 11 J. Legal Stud. 55 (1982).

the plaintiff will win multiplied by the damages award. The defendant will offer a settlement amount that is no greater than the expected total cost of the lawsuit to him. If W_d represents the defendant's estimate of the probability that the plaintiff will win, and C the cost of litigation to the defendant (same as the cost to the plaintiff), the expected total cost of the lawsuit to the defendant is $W_d \times L + C$.

As long as the expected cost of the lawsuit to the defendant is greater than the expected net payoff from the lawsuit to the plaintiff, the parties will be able to settle the lawsuit – in other words, there is a range of possible agreements, or a *settlement range*. The existence of a settlement range does not mean that the parties definitely will settle the lawsuit; it only means that a settlement is feasible. Even if the settlement is feasible, the parties may fail to settle because of strategic behavior in negotiations. The plaintiff may push the defendant to make an offer at the high end of the settlement range, and likewise the defendant may push the plaintiff to settle at the low end of the range. The final outcome from such gamesmanship in bargaining may be a failure to settle.

I will simplify matters by assuming that strategic gamesmanship does not prevent a settlement from occurring. In other words, I assume that the parties will settle the dispute for any payment within the settlement range – that is, any amount less than the defendant's expected cost of the lawsuit and greater than the plaintiff's expected net payoff.

For example, suppose the plaintiff's probability of winning is 95 percent and the loss is \$1,000. Suppose the defendant's estimate of the probability that the plaintiff will win is 90 percent. Suppose the cost of litigation for both plaintiff and defendant is \$100. Under these assumptions, the expected net payoff for the plaintiff is $0.95 \times \$1,000 - \$100 = \$850$. The plaintiff is therefore willing to settle for any payment from the defendant greater than \$850. The expected cost of the lawsuit to the defendant is $0.90 \times \$1,000 + \$100 = \$1,000$. The defendant is willing to settle for any amount less than \$1,000. Thus, if the plaintiff asks for \$900, the parties will settle.

Recall that a settlement range exists as long as the defendant's expected total lawsuit cost is greater than the plaintiff's expected net payoff. This is equivalent to saying that the difference between the plaintiff's expected award and the defendant's expected payout for the award is less than the joint cost of litigation.[79] Thus, if the parties have widely divergent views of the likelihood that the plaintiff will win, the likelihood of a settlement will be relatively low. In addition, the greater the cost of litigation, other things being equal, the greater the likelihood of settlement. The decision to litigate, like the decision to go to war, depends on the total costs of the activity and the divergence between the parties' expected outcomes.

---

[79] $W_p \times L - C < W_d \times L + C$ is equivalent to $W_p \times L - W_d \times L < 2 \times C$. The left-hand side is the difference in the parties' predictions of the expected award, the right-hand side is the total (or joint) litigation cost for the two parties.

Given that settlement will occur when the difference in expected awards is less than the total cost of litigation for the two parties, it follows that if the parties have the same prediction of the likelihood that the plaintiff will win, they will likely choose to settle rather than litigate. This is because the difference in expected awards is zero, which is definitely less than the joint expenditure on litigation. Thus, for the parties to litigate a dispute over monetary damages all the way to a final judgment, the parties must persistently disagree about the likelihood of a verdict for the plaintiff.

If the cost of litigation goes to infinity, litigation will disappear because all disputes will settle. Many have noted the phenomenon of the "vanishing trial" in recent years.[80] The vanishing trial is the result of two factors: convergence in views on the likely outcome of a dispute as the articulation of legal rules develops, and, more importantly, the dramatic rise in the cost of litigation as courts have moved into broader and more costly types of discovery.

The same general implications hold under the British rule for allocating litigation expenses, though with different degrees of intensity. Recall that under the British rule, the losing party pays the winning party's legal fees. The plaintiff will settle only if the amount he receives in settlement is at least as great as his expected net payoff from litigation: $W_p \times L - (1 - W_p) \times 2 \times C$. The defendant will settle only if the amount he pays in settlement is no greater than the amount he expects to pay in litigation: $W_d \times L + W_d \times 2 \times C$. It follows that if both parties agree on the plaintiff's probability of winning, settlement is just as likely to occur under the British rule as under the American rule.[81] The differences between the rules emerge when the parties' trial outcome expectations diverge. If the parties attach different probabilities to the likelihood of a plaintiff victory, and the plaintiff is the more optimistic party, the likelihood of a settlement is lower under the British rule.[82]

This brief comparison of settlement incentives under the American and British rules is limited in its implications because it ignores other channels through which litigation cost allocation rules can influence incentives. If we were to try to answer the question, "Is there more litigation under the British rule than under the American?," we would have to consider the effects of fee-shifting rules on the incentives to file suit, and to comply with the law, in addition to incentives to settle.[83]

---

[80] Marc Galanter, *The Vanishing Trial: An Examination of Trials and Related Matters in Federal and State Courts*, 1 J. EMP. LEG. STUD. 459 (2004); Judith Resnik, *Migrating, Morphing, and Vanishing: The Empirical and Normative Puzzles of Declining Trial Rates in Courts*, 1 J. EMP. LEG. STUD. 783 (2004).

[81] For settlement to occur under the British rule, $W_p \times L - (1 - W_p) \times 2 \times C < W_d \times L + W_d \times 2 \times C$. If W_p and W_d are equal, this relationship will hold, just as it would under the American rule.

[82] Based on the foregoing argument and assumptions, settlement occurs under the American rule if $W_p \times L - W_d \times L < 2 \times C$. Settlement occurs under the British rule if $W_p \times L - W_d \times L < (1 - (W_p - W_d)) \times 2 \times C$. Since $W_p > W_d$ when the plaintiff is the more optimistic party, it follows that settlement is less likely under the British rule.

[83] Keith N. Hylton, *Litigation Cost Allocation Rules and Compliance with the Negligence Standard*, 22 J. LEGAL STUD. 457 (1993); Keith N. Hylton, *An Asymmetric-Information Model of Litigation*, 22 INT'L. REV. LAW & ECON. 153 (2002).

Settlement and Trial Outcomes

That settlement tends to occur when the expected awards differential is less than the joint cost of litigation has implications for how one should interpret trial outcome statistics. The disputes that continue in court all the way to a final judgment are those for which the expected award differential remains relatively large, all the way through the litigation process. These are the disputes whose outcomes are most uncertain. If, by contrast, the likely outcome is clear to both sides of the dispute, the expected awards differential will be relatively small and the dispute will settle.

It follows that as a general matter the cases likely to be litigated to final judgment are those where the outcome is most like a coin toss. If the defendant's conduct was clearly negligent, the case is likely to settle early – and similarly if the defendant's conduct was clearly nonnegligent. The cases that are unlikely to settle are those in which the defendant's conduct is neither clearly negligent nor clearly nonnegligent under existing legal precedents. The rate at which such plaintiffs win their cases should therefore tend toward 50 percent, the same as a coin toss.[84] General data on plaintiff win rates seem to be consistent with this prediction.[85]

The 50 percent tendency does not indicate that juries are flipping coins to determine the outcome. In other words, one would be mistaken to read the trial outcome statistics and conclude that juries were making random decisions. The 50 percent tendency is purely the result of a winnowing (or "trial selection") process that operates through settlement decisions.

However, there are specific pockets of litigation where plaintiff win rates deviate consistently from 50 percent. These obviously cannot be explained by the 50 percent hypothesis. For example, plaintiff win rates in medical malpractice cases consistently fall below the 50 percent level.[86] Should one conclude that these cases reflect a bias on the part of juries in favor physicians? No, the likely explanation is a similar winnowing-through-settlement process, though operating in a special way that reflects informational asymmetry.[87]

If the defendant knows whether or not he complied with the legal standard and the plaintiff does not know, then defendants who are guilty will tend to settle, while defendants who are innocent will tend to litigate. Why? Because the plaintiff, who does not know with certainty whether the defendant was innocent or guilty, will assume the likelihood of defendant guilt is the average among observable similar actors, say, 50 percent. The defendant, on the other hand, knows whether his

---

[84] George Priest & Benjamin Klein, *The Selection of Disputes for Litigation*, 13 J. LEGAL STUD. 1 (1984). For an economic model disputing the 50 percent prediction of Priest and Klein, *see* Steven Shavell, *Any Frequency of Plaintiff Victory at Trial Is Possible*, 25 J. LEGAL STUD. 493 (1995).

[85] Priest & Klein, *supra* note 84.

[86] Theodore Eisenberg, *Testing the Selection Effect: A New Theoretical Framework with Empirical Tests*, 19 J. LEGAL STUD. 337 (1990).

[87] Keith N. Hylton, *Asymmetric Information and the Selection of Disputes for Litigation*, 22 J. LEGAL STUD. 187 (1993).

likelihood of guilt is zero or 100 percent. The defendants who are guilty will take
the settlement, because it is cheaper for them to pay a damages estimate discounted
by 50 percent than to pay full damages at the end of a trial. The defendants who
are innocent will reject the settlement because it is more expensive for them to pay
a damages estimate discounted by 50 percent than to pay zero at end of a trial in
which they are exonerated. Hence, the guilty will tend to settle, and the innocent
will tend to litigate. Plaintiffs will generally lose, resulting in a plaintiff win rate well
below 50 percent. This is the winnowing process that most likely occurs in medical
malpractice litigation, where plaintiff win rates are consistently below 50 percent.[88]

Thus, informational asymmetry appears to explain the relatively low plaintiff win
rates observed in areas such as medical malpractice.[89] The informed guilty tend to
settle, leaving the pool of defendants consisting mostly of the innocent. The results
may lead an observer to believe that courts are favoring defendants, but they are not.

Waiving Tort Rights

Suppose, long before the accident, the prospective injurer approaches the prospective victim and asks the victim to waive his right to bring a tort suit against the injurer.
We have observed that courts may choose not to enforce such a waiver agreement
(see Chapter 9). The common law has long held it unconscionable per se to waive
all potential legal claims against another person. But a more limited waiver might
be enforced. Moreover, enforceable or not, parties may choose to enter into a waiver
agreement in the expectation that the waiving party will honor his promise.

How much will the victim demand in compensation for waiving (equivalently,
selling) his tort claim? The victim will demand an amount sufficient to compensate
him for any increase in the expected harm that might result from selling his tort right
to the injurer. The expected harm to the victim is the probability that the injurer will
harm him, multiplied by the loss from the injury. If the victim sells his right to sue
the injurer, the injurer will no longer need to take care to avoid liability and so will
stop taking care. The victim, on the other hand, knows that once he has waived his
right, he will face a greater risk of being harmed by the injurer. What is important
to the victim in this case, however, is the incremental harm due to the injurer's
decision not to take care – that is, the extent to which the risk of harm increases as a
result of the waiver agreement.

To simplify the remainder, I will assume that liability is strict. This implies that
the victim will be compensated for the harm he suffers, when he retains his right
to sue, whether or not the injurer takes care. Thus, if the victim retains his right to
sue, his expected harm will be zero, because he will be compensated. If the victim
waives his right to sue, his expected harm will be equal to the probability that the

---

[88] *Id.*
[89] *Id.*

injurer will harm him (given the injurer's decision to stop taking care), multiplied by the loss from injury.[90]

The victim does gain a benefit, however, from waiving his right to sue: Having waived his right to sue, he will not have to suffer the cost of bringing suit. This may seem relatively unimportant, but it is a benefit nonetheless.

Putting together the costs and benefits of a waiver, the victim will need to be compensated for the expected injury due to the injurer's lack of care less the cost of suing to collect damages. Thus, if P represents the probability of injury when the injurer does not take care and Q the probability of injury when the injurer does take care, the victim will sell his right to sue in tort for any payment greater than $P \times L - Q \times C$. Suppose, for example, the probability of injury when the injurer does not take care is 0.75, and the probability that the injurer will harm the victim when he does take care is 0.25. Assuming, still, that the victim's loss is $1,000 and the litigation cost is $100, the minimum payment that the victim will require to waive his right to sue the injurer is $0.75 \times \$1,000 - 0.25 \times \$100 = \$725$.

What will the injurer be willing to pay for a waiver from the victim? In the absence of such a waiver, the injurer bears the cost of potential liability (including litigation expenses) and the cost of taking care. In other words, the expected cost to the injurer of the plaintiff's tort right is equal to the sum of the expected liability when he takes care, the expected cost of litigation when he takes care, and the cost of taking care. The injurer will purchase the plaintiff's tort right for any sum of money that is less than the expected cost to the injurer of the plaintiff's tort right. If B represents the cost of taking care, then the expected cost of the plaintiff's tort right to the injurer can be represented by $B + Q \times L + Q \times C$. Continuing with the assumption of the example in the previous paragraph (specifically, that the probability of injury to the victim is 0.25 when the injurer takes care), if the cost of taking care is $700, the expected cost to the injurer of the plaintiff's tort right is $\$700 + 0.25 \times \$1,000 + 0.25 \times \$100 = \$975$.

Waiver agreements are financially feasible when the price the victim demands to sell his right to sue in tort is less than the amount the injurer will pay to purchase the plaintiff's tort right. Once again, saying that an agreement is financially feasible does not mean that it will occur: Strategic gamesmanship in bargaining may prevent the parties from reaching an agreement. However, to simplify matters I will assume that an agreement will occur whenever it is financially feasible. This means that the tort right of the victim will be transferred whenever the price demanded by the victim is less than the amount the injurer is willing to pay for the right. Using the terms introduced above, the right will be transferred from victim to injurer when

---

[90] If we assume, instead, that the negligence rule applies, the victim will not be compensated for the harm that he suffers when the injurer takes care. Thus, the expected incremental harm to the victim is equal to the difference between the probabilities of injury when the injurer takes care and when he does not, multiplied by the loss from the injury.

$P \times L - Q \times C$ is less than $B + Q \times L + Q \times C$. Under the previous numerical assumptions, the parties will enter into a waiver agreement because the defendant will pay up to \$975 for the victim's tort right and the victim will sell it for any amount greater than \$725.

This discussion suggests that the incentive to waive tort rights will be relatively strong when (a) the victim's likely loss, or the probability of injury to the victim, is relatively small, and (b) the cost of taking care, or the cost of litigation, is relatively large. If potential future litigants are in a setting where waiver agreements are easy to make (e.g., they are already in a contractual relationship), we should expect such agreements to be formed.

Waiver agreements can eliminate tort litigation in settings where such litigation reduces society's welfare. The benefit from tort litigation to society is equal to the injuries avoided, as a result of the deterrent threat of litigation, less the cost of avoiding injuries. The cost of tort litigation is the total amount spent on litigation. The waiver conditions discussed above imply that waiver agreements are formed when, and only when, the social benefit from tort litigation is less than its social cost.[91]

The foregoing discussion assumes a relatively high degree of sophistication on the part of the victim. If this assumption is relaxed, one can find circumstances in which a waiver agreement may not be beneficial for society. For example, the victim may not be able to estimate the correct price for a waiver. If the victim cannot set a proper price for the waiver, he may sell his tort right under conditions that are harmful to society – for example, because the waiver results in a drop-off in deterrence in a setting where deterrence is desirable. Lack of sophistication on the part of prospective victims may provide a justification for prohibiting tort waivers.

As discussed in Chapter 9, the common law puts several restrictions on the enforceability of waiver agreements. Waivers may not be enforced because of public policy considerations, or because of special contract law doctrines such as unconscionability, or because the facts suggest a failure of basic offer and acceptance requirements.

This analysis of waiver agreements extends easily to arbitration agreements. Suppose the arbitration forum is a kangaroo court that always sides with the injurer. Under these conditions, signing an arbitration agreement is equivalent to signing a waiver agreement. All of the arguments considered above in relation to waiver agreements would then apply directly to the special case of kangaroo-court arbitration.

---

[91] If the price the prospective victim would ask for a waiver is less than the amount the prospective injurer would pay for it, then $P \times L - Q \times C < B + Q \times L + Q \times C$. Rearranging terms, this is equivalent to $P \times L - Q \times L - B < Q \times C + Q \times C$. The left-hand side is the social benefit from tort litigation, and the right-hand side is the overall cost of tort litigation. For a general discussion *see* Keith N. Hylton, *Agreements to Waive or to Arbitrate Legal Claims: An Economic Analysis*, 8 Sup. Ct. Econ. Rev. 209 (2000). On the social welfare effects of litigation, *see* Steven Shavell, *The Social versus the Private Incentive to Bring Suit in a Costly Legal System*, 11 J. Legal Stud. 333 (1982); Keith N. Hylton, *The Influence of Litigation Costs on Deterrence under Strict Liability and under Negligence*, 10 Int'l Rev. L. & Econ. 161 (1990).

If the arbitration forum is a genuine one rather than a kangaroo court, the arguments developed above continue to apply to some extent. The price that a prospective victim would charge for a predispute arbitration agreement would reflect the incremental probability of harm resulting from any slack in deterrence and the plaintiff's cost savings from arbitration. The amount that a prospective injurer would pay for such an agreement would reflect the savings, in the cost of taking care, resulting from the slack in deterrence, and the savings in anticipated liability and litigation expenses. When the incremental loss in deterrence minus the reduction in harm-avoidance costs is less than the incremental savings in litigation costs, a commitment to arbitration would make the parties jointly better off. Of course, this proposition assumes a high level of sophistication for both victim and injurer, which may not be valid.

Class actions introduce some special considerations in the analysis of waivers. Recall that a class action presents a credible threat of litigation only if the number of victims in the class exceeds the class viability threshold – that is, the number of victims necessary to make the class action economical. If potential victims waive their class action rights, the number of nonwaiving potential victims could fall below the viability threshold. Thus, the decision to waive is extremely important when the number of potential victims is close to the viability threshold. An individual potential victim may fail to take into account the effects of his waiver on the entire class of victims. A waiver by a potential victim at the viability threshold would eliminate the litigation rights of remaining victims and the associated deterrent function of tort law.[92]

Subrogation

In a subrogation agreement, a party that compensates the victim for his loss gains the right to pursue the injurer for the amount that the party has paid to the victim in compensation. In the typical agreement of this sort, a medical insurer that has agreed to pay for the medical expenses of the insured gains the right to sue the injurer for those expenses.

As in the waiver agreement studied earlier, the prospective victim sells his right to sue in tort, as part of the subrogation agreement. However, the difference between the subrogation agreement and the waiver agreement is that the subrogation agreement involves a sale to a party who generally will enforce the tort right,[93] while the waiver agreement involves the extinguishment of the tort right.

Because of this difference, the prospective victim will sell his tort right to the subrogating entity for a different price – in fact, a much lower price – than he would

---

[92] Keith N. Hylton, *The Economics of Class Actions and Class Action Waivers*, 23 SUP. CT. ECON. REV. 420 (2016).

[93] To be sure, the promise to enforce the tort right is not open ended. If the value of the tort claim is less than the expense of litigating, the subrogating entity may choose not to litigate, just as the victim himself might choose not to litigate a small claim.

sell under a waiver agreement. The reason he would sell for a lower price is because he is not waiving protection under tort law and thus incurring a greater risk of injury.

To simplify matters, assume for the moment that the subrogation agreement covers all of the losses that the prospective victim will suffer from a tortious injury. For example, this assumption would be valid in a case where the subrogating entity insures medical expenses, and the victim suffers only medical expenses as the result of a tortious injury.

What does the victim get out of a subrogation agreement? He avoids the burden of having to pay to litigate. On the other hand, the victim transfers his claim to damages to the subrogating entity. Since the subrogating entity maintains the threat to sue in tort, the injurer will continue to take care. Thus, the victim will sell his right to sue to the subrogating entity for an amount equal to the expected injury he would suffer (given that the injurer takes care) less the expected cost of litigation – that is, $Q \times L - Q \times C$.

Why would the subrogating entity purchase the right to sue? If the subrogating entity can litigate less expensively than the victim can, then both the victim and the subrogating entity may benefit from the transfer of the victim's tort right to the subrogating entity. The subrogating entity may be able to litigate less expensively than the victim can because it is a "repeat player" in litigation, while the prospective victim has never been to court. If the subrogating entity is the typical large medical insurance company, it has ready access to a staff of lawyers and has had repeated interactions with courts.

Indeed, in the case where the cost of bringing suit is prohibitive to the victim, the subrogation option enables tort law to maintain its capacity to deter tortious conduct. In the absence of the subrogation option, the victim would not have a credible threat to sue, and the injurer would therefore not have an incentive to take care.[94]

Consider the following example. Again, to simplify the presentation I will assume that liability is strict. Suppose the probability that the injurer will injure the victim is 0.25 when the injurer is taking care. The value of the potential lawsuit to the prospective victim is therefore $0.25 \times \$1,000 - 0.25 \times \$100 = \$225$. If the cost of litigation for the subrogating entity is only \$10, the value of the victim's potential lawsuit in the hands of the subrogating entity is $0.25 \times \$1,000 - 0.25 \times \$10 = \$247.50$, which implies that the subrogating entity will be willing to pay the prospective victim an amount of money greater than the value of the tort right to the victim

---

[94] Through subrogation, insurers can maintain the deterrent threat of tort law. Of course, tort victims often sue because the defendant is insured. The insurance defendants maintain may often work to enhance their incentives to take care, as insurers monitor precautionary effort, *see* Omri Ben-Shahar & Kyle D. Logue, *Outsourcing Regulation: How Insurance Reduces Moral Hazard*, 111 MICH. L. REV. 197 (2012). On other ways in which insurance affects the tort system, *see* Tom Baker, *Liability Insurance as Tort Regulation: Six Ways That Liability Insurance Shapes Tort Law in Action*, 12 CONN. INS. L. J. 1 (2005).

to gain ownership of that right. The medical insurer might offer a discount on insurance coverage to share part of the economic value of the subrogation right with the prospective victim.

I have assumed, to simplify the discussion, that the subrogation contract covers the entire loss that will be suffered by the prospective victim. It is more realistic to assume that the contract will not cover the entire loss. A medical insurer's subrogation agreement will cover only medical expenses attributable to a tort, excluding nonmedical harms such as lost wages. In this more realistic scenario, the subrogation agreement transfers only part of the victim's loss (e.g., only medical expenses) to the subrogating entity, leaving the rest in the victim's hands. In this case, the victim and subrogating entity may both pursue the injurer separately for their respective claims, or join forces to sue the injurer for the combined value of their claims.

Although traditionally subrogation has occurred through contractual agreements, courts have applied an equitable subrogation doctrine in settings where the insurer has not expressly contracted for the insured party's tort right. Thus, if the insurer has compensated the victim, courts will permit the insurer under equitable subrogation to seek compensation from the injurer.

Subrogation and Insurance

Since subrogation is often a part of the insurance relationship, this is a good place to elaborate on the connections between the tort system and the insurance market. Why do people buy insurance? Why do companies sell insurance?

Risk aversion leads people to buy insurance. A risk-averse person will pay more than $1 to avoid a situation where they will lose $2 with probability 50 percent and $0 with probability 50 percent. A risk-neutral individual will pay no more than $1 to avoid such a risk. A risk-loving individual will pay strictly less than $1 to avoid such a risk.

Another way of looking at risk aversion is to consider the *expected value* of a risk. Suppose the risk is one of losing $2 with probability 50 percent or losing $0 with probability 50 percent. The expected value of this risk is equal to the sum of the losses multiplied by their respective probabilities: $0.5 \times \$2 + 0.5 \times \$0 = \$1$. A risk-averse person will pay more than the expected value of a risk to avoid it. A risk-neutral person will pay no more than the expected value of the risk to avoid it. A risk-loving person will pay strictly less than the expected value of the risk to avoid it.

The reason a market for insurance exists is because risk-averse people will pay more than the expected value of a risk, while a risk-neutral insurance company can profit by charging a price that is greater than the expected value of the risk. If the insurance firm pools risks in a manner that enables it to predict that its costs will approximate the average level of risk, the firm will earn a profit by selling insurance policies priced above the sum of the firm's per-customer average level of risk and administrative cost.

Return to the example considered earlier, where liability is assumed to be strict. Since the injurer is incentivized to take care by the threat of tort liability, the probability that the injurer will injure the victim is 0.25. The victim's loss if injured will be $1,000. Thus, the victim faces a gamble in which he will lose $1,000 with probability 25 percent and $0 with probability 75 percent. The expected value (actually, loss) of this gamble is $0.25 \times \$1,000 + 0.75 \times \$0 = \$250$. Since the victim is risk-averse, however, he will be willing to pay more than $250 to be insured against this risk. Suppose the victim is willing to pay $280 for insurance. Given this, the insurance company, which is risk-neutral, can earn a profit by selling insurance to the victim as long as its per-customer administrative cost is less than $30. If, in addition to selling insurance, the insurance company forms a subrogation agreement with the victim, the insurance company can enhance its profits further. The cost of litigation for the subrogating entity is only $10, which implies that the value of the victim's potential lawsuit in the hands of the subrogating entity is $0.25 \times \$1,000 - 0.25 \times \$10 = \$247.50$.

All of this assumes the insurance firm and the victim have the same information on the victims' losses and the relevant probabilities. Suppose, however, there are two victims; one will suffer a loss of $500, the other will suffer a loss of $1,500. The insurance company thinks that the loss of each victim will be $1,000. Because of risk aversion, the victim who will suffer a loss of $1,500 will be willing to pay more than $375 for insurance (the expected loss for such a victim is $0.25 \times \$1,500 = \$375$) – suppose he is willing to pay $390. The victim who will suffer a loss of $500 will be willing to pay more than $125 for insurance – suppose he is willing to pay $150. If the insurance company offers a price of $280 for insurance, reflecting its assumption that each victim will suffer a loss of $1,000, the only victim who will purchase the policy is the high-loss victim, who will suffer a loss of $1,500. As a result, the insurance company will lose money on the policy. If the insurance company cannot make a profit selling only to the high-loss victim, it will exit the market.

This is an example of *adverse selection in the insurance market*. If victims have more information on their potential losses and likelihood of suffering losses than the insurance firm has, an adverse selection spiral may occur, in which only the most risky victims purchase insurance. As the pool of insured shrinks, the insurance firm finds itself less able to make a profit from the dwindling pool of high-risk customers and eventually shuts down. Several rules in tort law appear to be designed to avoid the creation of adverse selection spirals in insurance markets (see *Ryan*, Chapter 13; *Moch*, Chapter 14).

Selling Tort Rights to Third Parties

In the previous two parts, we considered the sale of tort rights to the prospective defendant (waiver) and to an insurer (subrogation). These rights transfers are permitted by the law, though with heavy restrictions in the case of waivers.

Settlement is also a type of market transfer. The plaintiff who settles his tort lawsuit essentially sells his right to sue, after it has materialized in the form of a claim to be compensated for an injury, to the defendant. It follows, then, that settlement is also a type of "legal right transfer" permitted under the law.

Can you sell tort rights to anyone?[95] For example, rather than settle with the defendant, can the plaintiff sell his claim to damages to a third party, who then can choose whether to pursue the judgment in court or settle with the defendant? Alternatively, can a person sell his tort right to a third party even before a claim to damages has materialized (i.e., before any injury has occurred)?

These questions are not merely of theoretical interest. Take the case of a tort victim with an existing claim for $10,000 in damages. Suppose a third party offers to pay the victim $6,000 and in exchange gain ownership of the tort judgment? Equivalently, suppose a third party offers a nonrecourse loan to the victim of $6,000 in exchange for the right to take the entire judgment awarded by the court? These exchanges are equivalent; the loan is equivalent to a purchase of the tort right. Moreover, the market for lawsuit financing has expanded greatly in recent years. Many small businesses offer "lawsuit loans" to tort victims – these are loans offered to tort victims with existing claims in exchange for the right to all or part of the judgment. More recently, deep-pocketed firms have started to finance large-scale lawsuits (for example, multi-million-dollar class actions) in exchange for a portion of the judgment.

Since a lawsuit loan is equivalent to the sale of the right to a judgment to a third party (the lender), and since a settlement is equivalent to the sale of the right to a judgment to the defendant, it seems that any objection one might raise to the lawsuit loan must also apply to the settlement. The lawsuit loan is just a different type of settlement, where the plaintiff first sells (or settles) with the third party, and the third party then settles with or litigates against the defendant.[96]

What about selling a tort right to a third party before it has materialized? If the law permits waivers, it would appear reasonable for it to also permit sale to third parties, since a waiver implies all of the risks that might arise from the sale to a third party. In spite of this reasoning, sales of unmaterialized tort rights raise some issues not observed in the case of materialized (i.e., existing claims to compensation) rights.[97]

First, if you try to sell your unmaterialized tort rights to a third party, you had better choose the buyer carefully. Recall that the prices that the prospective victim would

---

[95] *See generally* Michael Abramowicz, *On the Alienability of Legal Claims*, 114 YALE L. J. 697 (2005); Robert Cooter, *Towards a Market in Unmatured Tort Claims*, 75 VA. L. REV. 383 (1989); Marc J. Shukaitis, *A Market in Personal Injury Tort Claims*, 16 J. LEGAL STUD. 329 (1987); Keith N. Hylton, *The Economics of Third-Party Financed Litigation*, 8 J.L. ECON. & POL'Y 701 (2012).

[96] On the case for third-party funding of lawsuits, *see* Jonathan T. Molot, *A Market in Litigation Risk*, 76 U. CHI. L. REV. 367 (2009); Hylton, *supra* note 95.

[97] Keith N. Hylton, *Toward a Regulatory Framework for Third-Party Funding of Litigation*, 63 DEPAUL L. REV. 527 (2014).

charge for his tort right are quite different in the waiver and subrogation context. Specifically, the prospective victim would charge a much higher price in the waiver context, because in the waiver setting the victim is incurring the additional risk of injury that arises because of the loss of the deterrent threat of litigation. In the subrogation setting, the deterrent threat remains and is probably stronger.

This suggests that the sale of tort rights to a third party might introduce risks that are not present in the waiver case. The main risk is the inability of the seller to tell who the buyer is. You might sell your tort right to a third person, thinking that he will behave just as the insurance company does in the subrogation setting, but he may in fact transfer the right to the prospective injurer (waiver). Once again, the risks of injury resulting from an indirect sale to the injurer are no greater than the risks resulting from a direct sale to the injurer. But the key difference between the two cases is that an indirect sale is more likely to involve a seller who does not know the identity of the final purchaser. This lack of information could justify additional restraints on the sale of tort rights to third persons.

As it happens, the law on the sale of tort rights to third persons is in a state of muddle today.[98] The common law generally prohibited sale of tort rights under the doctrines of maintenance, champerty, and barratry.

Maintenance is providing financial or other support to a lawsuit. *Champerty* is a special type of maintenance in which the third party collects a portion of the judgment. *Barratry* is the practice of stirring up litigation and has been described as "a continuing practice of maintenance or champerty."[99] Maintenance, champerty, and barratry are related, in the sense that maintenance is analogous to a single act polluting the litigation environment, champerty to pollution for profit, and barratry to a nuisance-like process of continuing offenses. Each of these practices was considered harmful to society under the early common law. Blackstone, referring to the practices, said that

> These pests of civil society, that are perpetually endeavoring to disturb the repose of their neighbours, and officiously interfering in other men's quarrels . . . the Roman law . . . punished by the forfeiture of a third part of their goods, and perpetual infamy.[100]

Today, the law governing maintenance, champerty, and barratry is unclear. Some states (Massachusetts, New Jersey, South Carolina) have abolished the doctrines.[101] Other states have modified them significantly. The prohibitions that exist do not appear to be enforced; there is a brisk and open business, almost everywhere, in the provision of money in exchange for a share of the proceeds of tort suits.

---

[98] *See generally* Anthony J. Sebok, *The Inauthentic Claim*, 64 VAND. L. REV. 61 (2011).

[99] *In re Primus*, 436 U.S. 412, 424 n.15 (1978).

[100] 4 WILLIAM BLACKSTONE, COMMENTARIES *134–135.

[101] Saladini v. Righellis, 687 N.E.2d 1224, 1224 (Mass. 1997); Schomp v. Schenck, 40 N.J.L. 195, 203–04 (N.J. 1878); Osprey, Inc. v. Cabana Ltd. P'ship, 532 S.E.2d 269, 277 (S.C. 2000).

IX. INJUNCTIONS

Some tort plaintiffs are not seeking money; they are seeking to enjoin the defendant's conduct. Suppose, for example, the potential injurer threatens to destroy a tree on the potential victim's property. The victim can go to court to enjoin the threatened trespass.

However, the victim has the option in this hypothetical not to seek an injunction, and to sue for damages after the invasion. What is the advantage of seeking an injunction when you can sue for damages instead?

Injunctions versus Damages

Let's look more closely at this hypothetical. Suppose the loss suffered by the victim, if the injurer cuts down the tree, is $1,000. This amount is the sum of the costs to the victim of (a) removing the tree, (b) damage to the land or other property of the victim, and (c) diminution in the value of the victim's property resulting from the loss of the tree (because prospective purchasers of the property would pay more if the tree were there). If the victim brings a lawsuit for damages, he will collect no more than $1,000. The damages award compensates the property owner for the *objective losses* that he suffers as a result of the tree being cut down.

If the victim is awarded an injunction, he would avoid all of the objective losses that he would incur if the injurer cut down the tree (because the injurer would be enjoined from acting), and he would also avoid losing any *subjective value* he puts on the tree. The victim may have become accustomed to the tree being on his property for a long time, or may simply like to look at the tree and might be willing to pay money just to keep it there. The additional loss avoided, beyond the objective losses, is the loss in subjective value. For simplicity, assume this additional loss is also $1,000.

It follows that the main difference between an injunction and an award for damages is that the award for damages compensates for objective losses, while the injunction prevents the loss of both objective and subjective elements of value. Thus, if the plaintiff sues for an injunction, the value of the award to him will be $2,000 (the sum of objective and subjective losses avoided). If the victim sues for damages, the value of the award to him will be only $1,000.

The greater protective scope of the injunction implies that plaintiffs generally will prefer the injunction to the damages award. To be sure, this is not true in every case. Suppose the property owner does not like the tree and would prefer to see it removed. In this case, the subjective valuation of the owner is negative. He would prefer the damages award to the injunction.

In most cases, though, the injunction will be preferable to the damages award, in the eyes of the plaintiff. Consider, for example, a nuisance. Suppose the injurer's business regularly sends thick clouds of smoke over to the victim's property. A court could award the plaintiff an injunction (in addition to damages for existing harm) or give the plaintiff a damages award for the total harm from the nuisance.[102] Since the nuisance is a continuing one, the choice between remedies requires a decomposition of the plaintiff's injuries. The plaintiff's injuries would consist of some that he has suffered already (existing harm) and others that he will suffer in the future (future harm). If the court awards an injunction, the injunction will prevent future harm, but will do nothing to remedy existing harm. To remedy both types of harm, the court will have to award an injunction plus a damages award for existing harm. If the court awards damages only, it will have to compensate for existing harm and for future harm, and compensating for future harm is a complicated matter. The court could give a lump sum award that compensates the plaintiff for existing harm and for expected future harm (permanent damages). But such an award might encourage the defendant to ramp up the nuisance after paying the judgment – on the reasoning that having bought the cow, he may as well squeeze every last drop of milk out of it. Alternatively, the court could give periodic damages awards in the future, which would require the parties to return to court at specified intervals. It should be clear that the injunction will often be preferable to the plaintiff and to the court. The injunction provides greater protection to the victim, avoids perverse incentives that might lead the nuisance source to ramp up the interference, and avoids the administrative burden of calculating damages that would compensate for the total harm.

For the reasons just given, courts have generally favored injunctions in nuisance disputes, but the injunction is by no means guaranteed. In nuisance disputes, courts balance the equities associated with the award of an injunction (see Chapter 15), which means they consider the total costs and benefits to the community from shutting down the nuisance.[103] If it is clear that shutting down the nuisance will not harm the community significantly, an injunction is the preferred remedy because of the aforementioned administrative and incentive problems associated with issuing damages awards for nuisances. If shutting down the nuisance will harm the community (by shuttering a business that employs most of the residents), an award of damages will be preferred under the equity balancing test.

In cases of trespass, such as encroachments on property, the general approach is to award the injunction if the trespass was a knowing and intentional one, rather than one resulting from an innocent mistake.[104] If the trespass results from an innocent

---

[102] For a discussion of the choice, *see* Boomer v. Atlantic Cement Co., 257 N.E.2d 870 (N.Y. 1970). *Boomer* is discussed in Chapter 15.

[103] Under principles of equity, a plaintiff seeking a permanent injunction must demonstrate (1) that it has suffered an irreparable injury; (2) that remedies available at law, such as monetary damages, are inadequate to compensate for that injury; (3) that, considering the balance of hardships between the plaintiff and defendant, a remedy in equity is warranted; and (4) that the public interest would not be disserved by a permanent injunction. eBay Inc. v. MercExchange, 547 U.S. 388, 391 (2006).

[104] Warsaw v. Chi. Metallic Ceilings, Inc., 676 P.2d 584, 590 (Cal. 1984); Mid-America Pipeline Co. v. Wietharn, 787 P.2d 716 (Kan. 1990); Swaggerty v. Petersen, 572 P.2d 1309, 1315–1316 (Or. 1977);

mistake, courts balance the equities.[105] Thus, a court may deny an injunction for an encroachment and limit the plaintiff to monetary damages, if the unlawful encroachment was innocent and the cost of removal by the defendant would be greatly disproportionate to the injury to the plaintiff from its continuation.[106]

The default rule of awarding an injunction for intentional encroachments has implications for the remedy issue in nuisance disputes. If the nuisance is so severe that it amounts to a dispossession, then the nuisance is equivalent to a taking of property. A thick cloud of black smoke that envelopes the plaintiff's property is likely to be viewed as the same, from the plaintiff's eyes, as an opaque awning built over his land. Thus, injunctions in nuisance disputes can be justified, quite apart from the administrative and incentive issues discussed above, on the straightforward theory that a nuisance that is equivalent to a taking should be enjoined, just as an encroachment that amounts to a taking would be enjoined. The administrative and incentive issues discussed above justify an even broader scope for injunctions in nuisance disputes than this takings theory implies.

Now let's return to the tree hypothetical. Since the victim is seeking an injunction only, how will he know if he is going to be better off by getting an injunction? The benefit of the injunction to the victim is $2,000 – which reflects $1,000 in objective losses avoided and another $1,000 in subjective loss avoided. Suppose, in addition, that the likelihood that the victim will be awarded an injunction is 85 percent, and let the cost of litigation be $100. Using the concepts introduced earlier in this chapter, the expected net payoff to the victim from seeking an injunction is 0.85 × $2,000 − $100 = $1,600. Since the expected net payoff to the victim is positive, he will go to court to seek an injunction. This example suggests that the incentive to file for an injunction is similar to the incentive to file a suit for damages.

The total cost to the injurer (defendant) of the suit to enjoin depends on the monetary value the injurer would put on his wish to destroy the tree. If the defendant is willing to pay $1,500 to destroy the tree, and the defendant's cost of litigation is $100, the expected cost to the defendant of the plaintiff's suit to enjoin is 0.85 × $1,500 + $100 = $1,375.

Injunctions and Settlement

What about incentives to settle a suit for an injunction? The injunction scenario is more complicated than that of the lawsuit for damages. In the lawsuit for damages, a settlement means that the defendant pays the plaintiff some amount of money to get the plaintiff to drop his lawsuit. Once the lawsuit is dropped, the parties remain

---

[105] *see generally* Douglas Laycock, *The Neglected Defense of Undue Hardship (and the Doctrinal Train Wreck in* Boomer v. Atlantic Cement), 4 J. TORT L. 1 (2012). Swaggerty v. Petersen, 572 P.2d 1309 (Or. 1977); Peters v. Archambault, 278 N.E.2d 729 (Mass. 1972).

[106] Peters v. Archambault, 278 N.E.2d 729 (Mass. 1972).

in the status quo. In the injunction scenario, the parties must decide whether to opt for a settlement that permits the injurer to continue with his activity (or threatened activity) or a settlement that discontinues his activity. An *injunctive settlement* is an agreement that would implement the terms of the injunction that the plaintiff seeks in court, discontinuing the defendant's activity.

In the injunctive settlement, the plaintiff either receives from or pays money to the defendant, and in return the defendant agrees to discontinue the activity that the plaintiff seeks to enjoin. Returning to the tree example, since the victim values the tree at $2,000, a settlement agreement would entail the victim getting something worth $2,000 with certainty (the tree) and either receiving from or paying money to the injurer. The injunctive settlement would be preferable, in the victim's eyes, to the injunction lawsuit as long as the total sum the victim receives from the settlement is greater in value than the expected gain from the injunctive lawsuit, $1,600. For the injurer, an injunctive settlement would entail forgoing $1,500 with certainty and receiving from or paying some money to the victim. This would be preferable to bearing the cost of the injunctive lawsuit if the total sum the injurer loses in the injunctive settlement is less than $1,375.

Notice that there is something strange in this example. The defendant, to agree to an injunctive settlement, must receive a payment from the plaintiff! The defendant will lose $1,500 for sure in the injunctive settlement, and the expected value to the defendant of the total cost of the injunctive lawsuit is only $1,375. Thus, for the defendant to accept the injunctive settlement, he will have to receive money from the plaintiff. The plaintiff, on the other hand, is willing to pay to settle the suit because he receives a sure gain of $2,000 in the injunctive settlement, while forfeiting an expected gain from the suit of only $1,600.

The settlement payment from the plaintiff to the defendant is known as a *reverse payment settlement*, and, as this example suggests, such settlements can easily be observed in connection with injunctive litigation.[107] They are more likely to be observed as the plaintiff's gain from the injunction increases relative to the defendant's loss. In the example just considered, the plaintiff's gain from the injunction, $2,000, exceeds the defendant's loss, $1,500, so the conditions are opportune for a reverse payment settlement. Reverse payment settlements are also more likely as the defendant's prediction of the plaintiff's likelihood of obtaining the injunction declines relative to the plaintiff's. However, in the example here both parties have the same predictions.

The reasoning that would lead disputing parties toward a reverse payment settlement agreement might also lead a court to award a reverse payment remedy, as occurred in *Spur Industries v. Del E. Webb Development Co.*[108] The court awarded

---

[107] Keith N. Hylton & Sungjoon Cho, *The Economics of Injunctive and Reverse Settlements*, 12 Am. L. & Econ. Rev. 181 (2010).

[108] 494 P.2d 700 (Ariz. 1972).

an injunction in favor of the plaintiff developer, Webb, but required the plaintiff to compensate the defendant cattle feedlot for the cost of moving. The court noted that the developer would reap a financial windfall, in the form of a greatly increased property value, as a result of the injunction, and thus considered it fair to require the developer to compensate the feedlot owner.

Reverse payment settlements have become a topic of controversy in patent infringement litigation, because of the suspicion that a payment from a patent holder (plaintiff) to an alleged infringer (defendant) should be taken as evidence of a plan to reduce competition.[109] This discussion shows that the factors motivating reverse payment settlements are quite general and may be observed in settings where the litigating parties are not in competition in the market.

Many of the topics considered in the foregoing material, such as injunctions, settlements, waiver agreements, may seem a bit far afield for a chapter on damages. However, the anticipated damages award and its relation to the injury suffered by the tort plaintiff explain many features of the tort system in operation. By understanding the factors that motivate individuals to file tort suits, to settle them, to seek nonpecuniary damages, to seek punitive damages, to seek an injunction, or to waive their tort rights, the student of tort law can gain a better understanding of the rules governing the tort system's operation.

---

[109] FTC v. Actavis, Inc., 570 U.S. 756 (2013).

Index